Business Ethics in Canada

Third Edition

Business Ethics in Canada

Third Edition

EDITED BY

Deborah C. Poff
University of Northern British Columbia

Wilfrid J. Waluchow
McMaster University

Prentice Hall Allyn and Bacon Canada
Scarborough, Ontario

Canadian Cataloguing in Publication Data

Main entry under title:
Business ethics in Canada
3rd ed.
ISBN 0-13-079602-6

1. Business ethics. 2. Business ethics — Canada — case studies. I. Poff, Deborah C. (Deborah Charmaine), 1950- . II. Waluchow, Wilfrid J., 1953- .
HF5387.B88 1999   174'.4'0971   C98-931484-7

  © 1999 Prentice-Hall Canada Inc., Scarborough, Ontario

Prentice-Hall, Inc., Upper Saddle River, New Jersey
Prentice-Hall International (UK) Limited, London
Prentice-Hall of Australia, Pty. Limited, Sydney
Prentice-Hall Hispanoamericana, S.A., Mexico City
Prentice-Hall of India Private Limited, New Delhi
Prentice-Hall of Japan, Inc., Tokyo
Simon & Schuster Asia Private Limited, Singapore
Editora Prentice-Hall do Brasil, Ltda., Rio de Janeiro

ISBN 0-13-079602-6

Vice President, Editorial Director: Laura Pearson
Acquisitions Editor: Dawn Lee
Developmental Editor: Sharon Loeb
Production Editor: Matthew Christian
Copy Editor: Allyson Latta
Marketing Manager: Christine Cozens
Production Coordinator: Peggy Brown
Cover Design: Sarah Battersby
Page Layout: Janette Thompson (Jansom)

1 2 3 4 5 WEB 03 02 01 00 99

Printed and bound in Canada.

Visit the Prentice Hall Canada Web site! Send us your comments, browse our catalogues, and more. **www.phcanada.com** Or reach us through e-mail at **phabinfo_pubcanada@prenhall.com**

To Alex and Donna,
with love and appreciation

Contents

vii

Preface

This third edition of *Business Ethics in Canada* takes what is best from the previous editions and adds to the strength of the book in a number of ways. First, there are seven new Canadian Cases exploring a range of ethical issues, such as freedom of expression in advertising versus the rights of individuals to have their health protected; age discrimination; rights based on religious practices; the duty to warn; and an interesting case of fraud by employees doctoring their expense claims.

The organization of this text is designed to provide, first, a new and improved general Introduction to ethical theories for students who may have little or no background in philosophy or ethics. It is a clear and readable introduction to the general topic. Each Part provides some articles that raise general principles of ethics and morality as well as topical and timely issues students will face as they enter their professions as business people and professionals. The use of real moral and legal cases, rather than hypothetical, primarily from a Canadian context, allows students to struggle with actual problems, and assess and evaluate what their response might have been in similar situations.

The topics for the nine parts of this text lead the reader from general issues of ethical decision-making to current issues faced in the marketplace today. Teachers using this text may choose particular sections of current controversy, or use the entirety of the readings as a broadly based treatment of the world of business ethics in Canada.

As well, this edition of *Business Ethics in Canada* informs the reader specifically about trends in Canada in the evolution of ethical behaviour in corporations. The text tracks the changing climate in affirmative action, and readers will undoubtedly find interest in the "Save the Males" article on backlash. This updated edition also brings new material to the ever-changing international global marketplace. The articles by Poff, Singh, and Carasco explore issues of environmental protection and economic development in the global context.

In short, *Business Ethics in Canada* provides the reader with timely, up-to-date, theoretical, empirical, and legal materials on issues of relevance to ethicists in Canada today. The format is clear, accessible, and user-friendly for both teachers and students.

Acknowledgments

The editors would like to acknowledge the contribution of the following reviewers: Chris Tucker, University of Waterloo; Philip MacEwen, York University, Atkinson College; and Albert Wingell, University of Toronto, St. Michael's College.

INTRODUCTION
Ethical Theory
in Business

Wilfrid J. Waluchow

MORAL PHILOSOPHY

Contrary to a popular slogan, the phrase "business ethics" is not a contradiction in terms. Decision-making in business has and always will have a moral dimension, just as it does in medicine, government, the professions, and life in general. It is possible to conduct business in an ethical manner, and so questions concerning the ethics of business—i.e., business ethics—are significant. The interests of business people and moral philosophers do converge.

If the interests of business people and moral philosophers or "ethicists" converge, then what are their respective roles? Moral philosophers are not moral experts, capable of providing ready-made answers when difficult or intransigent moral conflicts arise in business. Rather, they perform more modest tasks: clarifying the terms of moral debate; scrutinizing distinctions to see if they stand up to rational examination; assessing the validity and cogency of arguments; and examining the fit between moral principles and moral practice.

Moral philosophers also will defend their own moral theories and convictions, particulary when they detect unwarranted, dogmatic beliefs in business practice or the theories proposed by other moral philosophers. But a student unaccustomed to the ways of the moral philosopher might find his arguments a trifle strange. The moral philosopher often will seek to defend or justify the obvious—e.g., that it is morally wrong to deceive a client intentionally about the dangerous defects hidden in one's product, or that it is wrong knowingly to dump deadly toxins into a community's water supply. At other times, the moral philosopher will offer arguments which question the obvious. He might even try to defend a position that seems patently false to many or most people—e.g., that it is morally questionable to use one's good looks to attract customers, or that wining and dining clients is morally wrong.

1

The moral philosopher's chief motivation for defending *or* questioning the obvious is expressed in a maxim propounded by the ancient Greek philosopher Socrates: *the unexamined life is not worth living*. Socrates and other moral philosophers want to know why we should believe the things we do—even those things we firmly and passionately believe to be true. Many of our moral beliefs just *seem* right to us. We've never had occasion to question them or to ask ourselves why we hold them. If pushed to articulate the grounds or bases of our moral beliefs, we often are unable to provide them, and if we do manage to come up with something, we often find that our grounds do not stand up well to scrutiny.

For example, it may seem obvious that sales people should not intentionally withhold information that is relevant to a customer's decision to buy a product. We might offer this general principle, *P*, as an obvious grounding for certain of our moral judgments, e.g., that it is wrong to deceive customers intentionally about the dangerous defects in one's product. If I know that the chemicals I am about to sell, while otherwise safe, are highly unstable and liable to explode under normal conditions of transport, then I do my customer, and perhaps other innocent bystanders, a serious injustice if I conceal this information.

But now ask whether principle *P* stands up to rational scrutiny. A relevant piece of information in almost any sales situation is the availability of less expensive alternatives offered by the competition—information customers obviously would like to know, and that sales people are often in a position to provide. If we accept principle *P* and require that sales people divulge any and all information relevant to their customers' decisions, we thereby require that sales people tell their customers about the lower prices offered down the road, do we not? Doesn't the unacceptability of this requirement show that principle *P* must be rejected or at least modified in some way? If so, what might the alternative be? It is here that the moral philosopher might be of some help. Moral philosophers should be viewed as partners with people in business in worrying through troublesome moral questions that arise in the practice of business.

The family of activities pursued by the moral philosopher is prompted largely by a desire for clarity of thought and integrity of action. But moral philosophy is not the moral conscience of business and the related professions. Moral philosophers are not out to criticize for moral failure—except perhaps when blind dogma rules moral practice, where the lives we lead remain largely unexamined. To raise or consider moral questions surrounding business practice is not to imply that there is something inherently immoral or unethical about business—although some will defend this view—nor is it to question the integrity of people in business. It is merely to seek the clarity and understanding which philosophical reflection often brings. The student of moral philosophy must be prepared to approach the subject with a willingness to challenge the obvious, and to consider seriously both the questionable and the strange.

Morality versus Ethics

Moral persons are equally distributed throughout all walks of life, including business. Morality is always of relevance in business. Business people agonize over the right thing to do in difficult cases, whether the issue is insider trading or padding an expense account. Those who disagree with others, or are generally perplexed, do not necessarily have any less moral integrity. No one can claim to be a moral expert. Ethics or ethical theory, however, is another matter. Ethics, as opposed to morality, is the systematic, critical study of the basic underlying principles and concepts utilized in thinking about moral life. Ethics, so understood, is something the average person concerns herself with infrequently, if ever. But this is not true of moral philosophers or "ethicists." They are primarily concerned with ethical theory, and as a result have acquired a certain level of argument that can be of use to non-philosophers in finding their way through the tangled moral issues to which the practice of business often gives rise. In later sections, we will consider the ethical theories of some of the most influential moral philosophers of Western civilization, but first we should look at the nature and role of ethical theories in general.

LEVELS OF MORAL RESPONSE

Put to an opponent of bribery in international business the question "Why do you think it's wrong to bribe a foreign official to secure a contract for your company?," and it can trigger one of three different types of responses.

The Expressive Level

At the most basic level, the answer to this question is likely to be "Because bribery is repugnant" or "I hate that kind of under-handedness." These responses are un-analysed expressions or feelings which, in themselves, do not constitute any kind of justification or reason for the position taken. This is not to deny that feelings are relevant to morality or that moral convictions are often accompanied by strong emotions. It is simply to say that the mere fact that one feels a certain way about an action or practice is not an adequate justification for a moral pronouncement on that practice.

The Pre-Reflective Level

At the next level of response, justification is offered by reference to values, rules, and principles—i.e., norms—accepted uncriti-cally, most often in the form of what we will call a "conventional" norm. Such a standard may be expressed in a legal injunction, in one of society's conventionally accepted values, in a church pronouncement, or in a professional or corporate code of ethics. It is a defining feature of this level of response that such conventional norms are uncriti-cally accepted and acted upon. We don't stop to think *why* we should act or base our judgments upon the conventional norms or why they are good standards to adopt. While any behaviour ensuing from conventional norms may be classified as conventionally moral or ethical, it is a species of externally directed behaviour—the blind following of standards set by somebody else. Assuming the norms are good ones, this is not neces-sarily bad. Sometimes conventional norms are capable of reasoned defence; they can be fully justified morally. Sometimes there is good moral reason to follow conventional rules because they *are* accepted conven-tionally, since conventional norms can help to foster common understandings, and serve to ground others' expectations concerning how we will conduct ourselves. Sometimes it is crucial to know that other people will be playing by the same rules that we are. Imagine, for example, what it would be like if there were no conventionally accepted rules governing the making of promises. We would never be certain whether a promise had been made, or whether its author con-sidered it at all binding.

It is a serious mistake, however, to think that morality is exhausted by conventional norms or that moral justification ends with the invocation of a conventional rule. The norms must always be subject to critical moral scrutiny. Perhaps there are much bet-ter rules that we should try to persuade oth-ers to adopt, or perhaps existing conventions are morally objectionable. That *X* is gener-ally accepted as morally right, never in it-self proves that *X is* morally right. Slavery was at one time widely accepted as morally correct. Slavery nonetheless was, and always will be, morally wrong.

The Reflective Level

At this level of response, our moral judgments are not based entirely on conventional norms blindly accepted, but on principles, rules, and values to which we ourselves consciously subscribe and with regard to which we, as rational moral agents, are prepared to offer reasoned moral defence. It is possible, of course, that the norms to which we subscribe at the reflective level are also norms conventionally accepted. They might, for instance, be norms that have found their way into a professional code by which one is expected to abide. But at the reflective level of moral response, we are prepared to consider for ourselves whether they are justified, or whether other, perhaps wholly novel, norms are those by which people should lead their lives.

At the reflective level, one's opposition to bribery might take the following form: "I oppose bribing foreign officials because it provides the company offering the bribe an unfair advantage over its competitors." Here a *reason* is given—a *basis* or *ground* for the moral judgment is provided. The complexity and sophistication of a response at this level invites competing judgments with plausible bases. One can imagine, as a reply to the above, the following retort: "Bribery may be wrong in theory. But if everyone is doing it, and it's the only way to do business in countries with corrupt officials, then the company deciding not to offer a bribe suffers an unfair *dis*advantage. On top of all that, a manager who, on principle, declines to offer a bribe and thereby loses a lucrative contract, violates the fiduciary responsibility she has to earn the highest profits she can for her shareholders." As this example illustrates, ethics at the reflective level admits to few easy answers!

Of the three levels considered, the reflective level is the one at which most of the discussion in this book takes place, despite grounds for misgivings about the possibilities for full resolution of moral controversies at this level. Reflection does not guarantee agreement. As will be evident throughout this book, moral reflection often yields "a" defensible position, but not "the only" defensible position. People not only feel differently at the expressive level, and favour different conventional rules at the pre-reflective level, but also reach different conclusions at the reflective level. It is important to stress, once again, that there are no moral experts, and that at each level, including the reflective one, we often are met with genuine dilemmas and competing bases for moral belief. Arriving at unassailable moral judgments is difficult, and some think impossible, not only because there are different levels of approach to morality but also because people approach moral questions from very different perspectives.

A VARIETY OF APPROACHES

The different approaches moral agents take to moral questions may be illustrated by distinguishing among three ways in which the term "know" can be used.

Sometimes the claim to "know" amounts to nothing more than a claim to *feel* sure or certain—a subjective, psychological criterion. While emotionally reassuring, a feeling of certainty is not a reliable mark of *bona fide* moral judgment. Others with different, even opposing, moral views may feel just as strongly that they are right. One who claims to know, and tries to add as a warrant that he feels certain about what he believes, offers no warrants at all. His certainty is no more a warrant than is the certainty with which many people at one time believed slavery to be morally justified.

Second, the claim to "know" may be a claim that the position held is the one for which the best reasoned justification seems possible. The requirement of reasoned defence is acknowledged here, as is the possibility that the position held may not be the only defensible one. Such a claim recognizes that rational people of good will and integrity may reasonably disagree about moral matters, and that no one can declare, with absolute certainty, that he has the one right answer.

The third use of "know" is much stronger than the second, and, according to many moral philosophers, is quite unwarranted. It is equivalent to the following: "I know my view is the right one, and anyone who disagrees with me suffers from moral blindness or misunderstanding." Leaving aside the question whether in moral life there are ever uniquely correct solutions to moral issues, the degree of self-assurance underlying the above claim amounts to audacity and arrogance. Even a commitment to the notion that there is a "final truth" in ethics should be accompanied by the acknowledgment that in practice we must operate in humility, with only partial knowledge and approximations to the truth.

Misgivings about the ethical enterprise may go even deeper than the foregoing comments suggest. There are profound philosophical disputes about the status of ethics itself—about whether moral judgments are in the end capable of full justification. Three of the more extreme difficulties are as follows.

The issue of verification The problem of verification in the context of moral judgments may be illustrated by reference to the following scenario.

Apple Mary is sitting in the downtown Hamilton market selling her produce. Suddenly, a suspicious-looking character furtively slips in behind her and clubs her. As she falls to the ground, her assailant scoops up her purse and vanishes.

Imagine two witnesses commenting as follows:

A. Did you see that?

B. I did.

A. What a dreadful thing to happen in downtown Hamilton.

B. I agree.

A. What that man did was terribly wrong.

B. I didn't see anything wrong.

A. How can you possibly say that?

B. Easily. Let's go over what happened carefully.

A. Let's do that.

B. I saw Apple Mary sitting at her stall. I saw a man creep up behind her. I saw him lift a club and bring it down on her head. I saw Mary slump to the ground and her assailant take off with her purse. I didn't see any wrong.

The clue to the dispute between A and B is to be found in the ambiguity of the word "see." Of course, B is correct if by "see" we mean *physical seeing*. We do not see the wrong in the way we see arms raised, clubs wielded, and purses snatched. *Moral seeing* is more like "seeing that" (making a judgment) than seeing with our eyes. We see that assault is wrong. We see that stealing is wrong. Moral insights are expressed in the form of judgments that are not verifiable empirically in the way observational statements are. Rather, they are substantiated by reference to principle, rules, or values that serve as their grounds or warrants. According to the first ethical theory we will examine—as well as one version of the second—we justify our actions in terms of the following schemata:

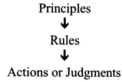

Principles
↓
Rules
↓
Actions or Judgments

The contemplated action, or a moral judgment concerning it, falls under a rule, and the rule, in turn, conforms to a higher-order principle. By contrast, the third theory we will consider involves identifying principles specifying *"prima facie* duties," and in situations of conflicting *prima facie* duties, determining which takes precedence. But more on this later. The point to be stressed at this stage is that we do not *see* moral properties in the way we see the club hit Apple Mary. Moral judgments are not open to empirical verification—indeed they cannot be substantiated by way of a universally agreed-upon routine or procedure. There are numerous competing theories on how our moral judgments are to be substantiated. Most, but not all, may be mapped onto the above schemata.

A plurality of ethical systems The plurality of the approaches to the justification of moral judgments may be a cause for dismay. It is one thing to be made aware that the morality of our actions is not open to empirical verification; it is quite another to learn that different ethical theories prescribe quite different routines to be utilized in moral reasoning. It would certainly be simpler if there were only one theory and one routine. The only problems then remaining would be problems of casuistry (i.e., application of rules or principles to particular cases). But we have yet to discover an ethical theory upon which all reasonable people agree, and, as we have already seen, there are those who believe that no such theory will ever be found. As the understanding we have of ourselves and the world around us increases, we should expect our ethical theories to change and progress. The best we can do at present is to engage in the pursuit of a defensible ethical theory, and to try to learn as much as we can from those who have done so in the past. There is much to be learned from the theorists whose views will be outlined below.

The limits of justification If one were to adopt, for example, a Kantian or rule-utilitarian position, the prescribed routine for justifying moral judgments would be more or less clear. It might be difficult to tell precisely what the theory requires of us in a particular case, but how to go about trying to answer that question would be reasonably clear. For Kant, as we shall see, an action is morally obligatory if it conforms to a rule, and the rule, in turn, conforms to a principle Kant calls the categorical imperative. For a rule-utilitarian, there is an analogous procedure. Our actions must conform to a rule, and the rule must conform not to Kant's categorical imperative but to the "principle of utility." For fully committed utilitarians or Kantians, justification is limited to judgments made within the prescribed framework. They enquire, "Does the action in question conform to the rule, and the rule to the (appropriate) principle?" If the answer is affirmative, the morality of the action is settled, and they know what the theory prescribes as the right thing to do.

It is possible, of course, for a rule-utilitarian to raise questions about Kant's categorical imperative, or for a Kantian to challenge the principle of utility. This would involve raising questions concerning the validity of the frameworks themselves. In such cases, what we have is a *philosophical* dispute—the kind of dispute that is a primary concern of ethical theorists. Utilitarians and Kantians will each marshal philosophical arguments that challenge the validity of the other's ethical theory. They will do so even when it is clear what the opposing frameworks require of us in particular cases, and even when the different frameworks prescribe exactly the same actions. The two theorists may agree on what we should do, but disagree about why we should do it, since the philosopher is concerned with understanding *why* we should do certain things and refrain from others.

External philosophical questions concerning the validity of ethical frameworks are best dealt with in books devoted exclusively to ethical theory. This is not such a book. In what follows, we will outline five competing frameworks, and only briefly mention some of the many external, philosophical questions that have been raised about them. Some students will probably feel a strong affinity for one of the five theories discussed in a later section, but most will find something of value in each one. This is not surprising. Four of the theories to be examined reflect currents of thought that have dominated Western culture in recent centuries and the fifth is expressive of a powerful contemporary movement. For those strongly inclined to think that one of the theories represents the truth of the matter, the old adage should be borne in mind: "Those who live in glass houses should not throw stones." External challenges to other systems should be seasoned with a measure of caution and humility, and with the recognition that questions of morality and ethics are ones upon which reasonable people of good will and integrity often reasonably disagree.

Given these profound difficulties with the ethical enterprise, the student may wonder why we should bother at all with an introduction to ethical theory. Why not just get on with an analysis of the various specific moral issues arising in the practice of business—issues such as affirmative action or manipulative advertising? One response is that we are not warranted in dropping ethical theory altogether simply because it has difficulties. Quantum physics is fraught with theoretical difficulties too, but it would be silly to give it up entirely because of this. Another response is that there are valuable lessons to be learned from the way in which some of the greatest thinkers within our cultural history have seriously and systematically approached ethical issues. These are thinkers whose formulations have been extremely influential, and whose theories provide the frameworks within which current ethical disputes are argued. One cannot get too far in modern moral debate without encountering some appeal to the concept of utility, or to the value of individual autonomy. These two concepts are the cornerstones of the theories of Mill and Kant, respectively.

SOME BASIC CONCEPTS

Before examining the theories of Kant and Mill, and Ross, Aristotle and the feminists, we should look at some basic terminology employed by ethical theorists. This terminology will be introduced by way of noting several distinctions.

First, we should distinguish between *judgments of obligation* and *judgments of value*. Judgments of obligation concern what we ought to do. In expressing such judgments, we use sentences such as the following: "You *ought* to have told the truth to your client"; "Your *duty* was to protect the financial interests of your shareholders"; "You were under an *obligation* to honour your contract"; "It wasn't *right* to run that kind of advertisement"; "He had a *right* to that property." All of these judgments have to do directly with our conduct, with how we should behave.

Judgments of value, by contrast, are not directly related to action. These are judgments not about the right thing to do but about what is good or has value. For instance, the judgment that freedom is a good thing for human beings to enjoy, or that pleasure is the only thing of intrinsic worth, are judgments of value. They don't tell us what it is right to do, as do judgments of obligation.

According to some ethical theories, a judgment of obligation is dependent on, and follows directly from, a judgment of value. If an ethical theory does hold that judgments of obligation are dependent in this way, then it is what philosophers call a teleological or consequentialist theory of obligation. A teleological theory of obligation posits one—and only one—fundamental obligation, and that is to maximize the good consequences and minimize the bad consequences of our actions. Insofar as we need to know, on such theories, which consequences are good—in order to maximize them—and which are bad—in order to minimize them—it is easy to see why a teleological theory of obligation presupposes a theory of value. Such a theory will provide us with the basis for justifying our judgments of value and, ultimately, our judgments of obligation.

The duty to maximize the good and minimize the bad consequences of our actions is the only fundamental duty on a teleological theory of obligation. On such a theory, then, any other obligations, such as the obligation to honour our contracts or to tell the truth, are secondary, and derivable from this one primary obligation. Mill's utilitarianism, as we shall see, is a teleological theory of obligation. In his view, all questions concerning what we ought to do should be decided ultimately on the principle of utility, which requires that we maximize what is intrinsically good, namely, happiness or pleasure, and minimize what is intrinsically bad, namely, unhappiness or pain.

In contrast to teleological theories of obligation are non-teleological or *deontological theories of obligation*. Deontological theories of obligation essentially deny what teleological theories assert. They deny that we have one and only one fundamental duty to maximize the good and minimize the bad consequences of our actions. Basically, this denial can take two forms. First, a theory may suggest that the good and bad consequences of our actions have no bearing whatsoever on whether they are morally right or wrong. Such a strong deontological theory of obligation can operate independently of any theory of value. We needn't know, as we do with teleological theories of obligation, what the good is, if we are to know what we ought to do; our obligation does not in any way involve the maximization of good consequences, and so we needn't have a theory of value to tell us what that is. Kant, as we shall see, appears to have held a strong deontological theory. Kant is notorious for suggesting that the rightness or wrongness of our actions is totally independent of whether they maximize good consequences. According to Kant, a judgment of obliga

tion—such as the judgment that vendors must tell their customers the truth about dangers inherent to the product they sell—is in no way justified in terms of consequences. It is justified if, and only if, it meets the categorical imperative test, which ignores consequences altogether.

A deontological theory of obligation need not, however, follow Kant's lead and claim that the consequences of our actions are completely irrelevant to their rightness or wrongness. There is a second kind of deontological theory that makes the weaker, negative claim that good and bad consequences are not always the only factors of moral importance, and that we have other basic obligations in addition to our duty to maximize the good and minimize the bad consequences of our actions. According to Ross, for example, the principle of *beneficence,* which requires promoting the good of others in our actions, is only one of a number of basic principles defining our moral obligations. Others include the obligation to be grateful for benefits given, and the duty to be fair to other people. In Ross's view, we sometimes have a duty to be grateful even when neglecting this duty would on that occasion lead to the best consequences overall. There are some actions, e.g., displays of gratitude, which are right, regardless of their consequences. There are other actions, e.g., instances of unfairness, which are sometimes wrong, even when they lead to good consequences.

Unlike Kant and Mill, then, Ross suggests that we have many fundamental obligations. The duty to be grateful and the duty to be fair are not based on any ultimate principle of obligation. This clearly separates Ross from Kant and Mill. We frequently have a duty to be fair, Mill would urge, but this is because being fair normally maximizes the balance of good over bad consequences. Ross will have none of this. For him, the duty to be fair is as important as the duty to maximize good consequences, and our many basic obligations cannot be reduced to any of the others. Ross's theory of obligation, insofar as it is not based on a single, fundamental principle defining a single, fundamental obligation, is a *pluralist theory of obligation*. A pluralist theory of obligation, put simply, is one that does not posit a single, fundamental obligation upon which all other obligations are based. A *monistic theory of obligation*, by contrast, does posit one such obligation. A utilitarian will be happy to talk of obligations to tell the truth or to be fair to others in our dealings with them. She will simply add that we have these obligations because fairness and truth-telling usually lead, in the end, and all things considered, to the best consequences. Hence her theory is monistic. So too is Kant's.

To recapitulate, teleological theories of obligation are all logically dependent on theories of value. Some deontological theories of obligation are also dependent on a theory of value, while others are not. Strong deontological theories such as Kant's exclude as irrelevant questions about good or bad consequences of our actions (i.e., the value or disvalue to be realized in them). They therefore have no need of a theory of value. But most deontological theories do have such a need, since most deontological theories are pluralistic, like Ross's, and include principles that direct us— but not exclusively—to the good and bad consequences of our actions.

Turning to theories of value, we find that these too may be categorized as either monistic or pluralistic. A *monistic theory of value*, as one might expect, posits one and only one thing, or characteristic of things, as being of value for its own sake. In other words, it posits only one thing or characteristic as *intrinsically valuable*. Hedonism is one influential type of monistic theory of value. On this view, pleasure is the only thing that is valuable for its own sake. Anything else we value, say money or friendship, is valuable only *instrumentally*,

as a means to the pleasure it brings. Classical utilitarianism of the form espoused by Mill and his teacher Jeremy Bentham is hedonistic. But classical utilitarianism needn't be hedonistic. Utilitarians who agree on a theory of obligation may divide on their theories of value. G.E. Moore, for instance, was, like Mill, a utilitarian. But unlike Mill, Moore espoused a pluralistic theory of value, which saw pleasure as only one of many things of intrinsic value; knowledge and aesthetic experience were other things worthy of pursuit for their own sakes.[1]

If a person holds a pluralistic theory of value, then he is faced with a difficulty similar to one with which defenders of pluralistic theories of obligation must grapple: what to do in situations where two or more values conflict or cannot be pursued together. If both freedom from manipulation and pleasure are intrinsically valuable, then we may have to choose somehow between allowing advertisers to manipulate us with their entertaining ads, and prohibiting such activities entirely. But is it possible to compare these very different values? Is comparing freedom from manipulation with pleasure, so as to see which has the greater value or importance in the circumstances, something that can be done rationally? Is an attempt to compare the two things a bit like trying to compare apples with oranges? If, on the other hand, we adopt a monistic theory of value, we may seem to rid ourselves of such problems. We only have to compare, say, one pleasure with the next. But there are serious difficulties even here. How does one compare one person's pleasure with that of another person, especially if those persons are as different as U.S. president Bill Clinton and Pope John Paul II? Monistic theories of value face another difficulty of some importance. According to many people, there are numerous things in the world that are ultimately, irreducibly valuable. Friendship, for example, seems to be compromised if its value is reduced to the pleasure it brings. As will be seen, the attempt to place "value" on human lives and welfare—an integral part of cost-benefit analysis—is fraught with such difficulties. Some of these difficulties will be explored later in discussions of worker health and safety, and the impact of business activities on the environment.

FIVE ETHICAL THEORIES

There follows now a brief survey of five major types of ethical theory. The main reason for including the theories of Kant and Mill is that their contributions have dominated Western moral thought since the scientific revolution. Kant strove to establish ethics as a purely *rational* enterprise. Mill believed that an objective standard of right and wrong could be discovered using the methods of the empirical sciences. If the rightness of our actions depends on the pleasure and pain they produce, we ought to be able to estimate their rightness by empirical observation, measurements, and induction. Mill's utilitarianism is an ancestor of modern theories of cost-benefit analysis. Between them, Kant and Mill uncover the respective roles of intention and consequences in shaping our moral responses. One cannot get very far in a discussion of ethics without paying deference to the Kantian notions of autonomy and universalizability—or the injunction to treat human beings as ends in themselves and not merely as means, or without paying deference to Mill's emphasis on protecting and promoting human happiness or well-being.

W.D. Ross's reaction to Kant and Mill is an invaluable contribution to ethics. In certain crucial respects, it seems to reflect more accurately the ordinary thinking and practice of moral agents rather than the more systematic reflections of professional moral philosophers. This quality is particularly evident in Ross's opposition to Kant's and Mill's reductionism in moral theory. While acknowledging the powerful contributions of Kant and Mill to ethical theory, Ross was unwilling to subscribe to a monistic theory of obligation, and resisted elevating either the categorical imperative or the principle of utility to the status of a foundational first principle from which all other moral principles, rules, and judgments follow. In coming to grips with the moral issues considered in this text, it will be difficult to escape making reference to Ross's notion of *prima facie* duty.

Contemporary ethical theorists have experienced a renewed interest in the ethical writings of the ancient Greek philosopher, Aristotle. Among Aristotle's many contributions to the history of ethical thought is his doctrine of the mean. As we will see below, Aristotle attempts to isolate a number of virtues that we can more or less express or display in our lives when we aim for the golden mean between undesirable extremes. For example, we display the virtue of courage when, in conducting our lives, we successfully steer clear of the extremes of cowardliness and foolhardiness. Courage is the mean between these two vices, and a courageous person is one whose character and (developed) dispositions lead him to act in neither a foolhardy nor a cowardly manner.

Those who are even more impressed than Ross with the immense complexity of moral life, and with the difficulties encountered when we try to articulate rules and principles to cover all cases, may find enormous potential in the Aristotelian approach. It is a consequence of Aristotle's conception of the moral life that there are no hard-and-fast rules or principles to tell us whether, and to what extent, our conduct approximates the relevant mean and is therefore virtuous. There are also no hard-and-fast rules to tell us what to do when our situation involves more than one virtue, as when our beneficence inclines us towards deliberately misleading someone who would be "better off not knowing," but our wish to be an honest person leads us in the other direction. In addressing moral questions we are not asking for rules that tell us what to do on some particular occasion. Rather, we are asking ourselves what kind of person we would be, what kinds of virtues we would display, were we to conduct our lives in a particular manner. And to these types of question, there are almost never uniquely correct answers. Perhaps in this respect Aristotle's theory more accurately reflects our moral experience, and the humility of which we speak above.

Finally, we have included a section on "feminist ethics." Feminist writings in ethics are characterized more by the approach taken to ethical theory than by any distinctive set of principles, rules, or values. Feminist ethics is marked by a heightened concern for the personal and social contexts in which ethical decisions are made, and by the ways in which traditional ethical theory, with its attempt to discover universal, and therefore necessarily abstract, moral norms, ignores the context in which decisions are made. Of particular concern to feminists is the perceived failure of mainstream ethical theory to appreciate the context of oppressed individuals, such as women and the socially vulnerable, and the various ways in which their legitimate concerns and interests are ignored, undervalued, or suppressed. Insofar as business practice has traditionally been dominated by men, and insofar as it involves, by its very nature, relationships with potentially vulnerable individuals—e.g., consumers, employees, and the chronically unemployed—there is especially good reason to consider the lessons of feminist ethicists for business practice.

Utilitarianism

Utilitarianism is a monistic, teleological theory of obligation which, owing to its teleological nature, rests on a theory of value. A utilitarian's theory of value can, of course, be either monistic or pluralistic. We shall largely ignore the different theories of value espoused by utilitarians, and concentrate instead on their theories of obligation.

Essentially, there are two different kinds of utilitarianism: *act* and *rule*. Act utilitarianism (AU) defines the rightness or wrongness of individual actions in terms of the good or bad consequences realized by those actions. In other words, AU defines the rightness or wrongness of an action in terms of its "utility" and "disutility." The term utility stands for whatever it is that is intrinsically valuable on the utilitarian's theory of value; disutility, for whatever is intrinsically bad. According to John Stuart Mill, actions are right in proportion as they tend to promote happiness; wrong as they tend to produce the reverse of happiness."[2] For him, "utility" means happiness, and "disutility," unhappiness. Mill went on to identify happiness with pleasure and unhappiness with pain. Hence, Mill may be characterized as a *hedonistic* utilitarian, one on whose theory of value, pleasure is the only thing of intrinsic worth. But a utilitarian needn't make this identification, nor need he define utility in terms of happiness. Some utilitarians think it best to define utility in terms of the satisfaction of our actual preferences, while others would have us look to satisfy preferences we would have were we fully informed and rational. Regardless of the theory of value with which it is associated, however, AU always makes the following claim:

> AU: An act is right if, and only if, there is no other action I could have done instead which either (a) would have produced a greater balance of utility over disutility; or (b) would have produced a smaller balance of disutility over utility.

We must add (b) to account for those unfortunate situations in which, whatever we do, we seem to cause more disutility than utility—where we're damned if we do and damned if we don't. In short, AU tells us to act always so as to bring about the best consequences we can, and sometimes that means trying to make the best of a bad situation.

AU was made famous in the modern era by Mill and Bentham, at a time when many people thought that some individuals simply counted more than others, that members of the aristocracy, the Church, or a particular race were in some sense more worthy or superior than others, and were therefore deserving of special consideration or privilege. The utilitarians were part of a social revolution that would have none of this. In the famous words of Bentham, "each is to count for one, none to count for more than one." In other words, according to utilitarians, *all* those affected by my actions should count *equally* in my deliberations concerning my moral obligations. The equal happiness of the King is to count equally with the equal happiness of the milk man. Mill put this important point this way:

> I must again repeat what the assailants of utilitarianism seldom have the justice to acknowledge, that the happiness which forms the utilitarian standard of what is right in conduct is *not* the agent's own happiness but that of all concerned. As between others, utilitarianism requires him to be as *strictly impartial as a disinterested benevolent spectator*.[3]

Thus, built into AU is a commitment to equality and impartiality. We are to be concerned equally and impartially with the happiness or welfare, i.e., utility, of all those, including ourselves, who might be affected by our actions. On these grounds alone, AU is a very appealing theory. What could be better than to be sure that I always maximize, not only my own happiness or that of my friends, but the happiness of all those people affected by my actions, whoever they might be? What more could morality require?

Despite its inherently desirable features, many philosophers have come to find serious difficulties with AU, leading some utilitarians to opt for an alternative form of the theory. One of the more serious difficulties revolves around special duties and special relationships. These include duties of loyalty, of fidelity, and of familial obligations, resting in part on the special relationships that arise out of family ties and require some degree of partiality and special concern towards family members. It would be wrong, some think, to be impartial between friends and family, on the one hand, and perfect strangers on the other. The same might be said when instead of family, we speak of our special relationships with the company, our employees, or our own country.

Let's centre on promises as an illustration of the difficulties facing AU. Suppose I am the executive director of a non-profit association such as the Heart Foundation. I have made a firm agreement with the booking agent at the Holiday Inn to hold the foundation's yearly convention at his hotel. The agent is an old business acquaintance with whom the foundation has dealt for years and who has always treated me fairly, courteously, and efficiently. He has even given the foundation the odd special break now and then. Several months later, however, I discover that the recently opened Walnut Inn is willing to give me a much better deal than my friend at the Holiday Inn. The foundation will be way ahead even after we pay the standard cancellation fees to the Holiday Inn. It is also clear that Holiday Inn will lose big if we pull out. The cancellation fees will not be nearly enough to compensate for the arrangements they have made and the bookings they have lost because they were holding their facilities for us. Despite this, I add up the utilities and disutilities involved for all affected, and correctly conclude that overall utility would be maximized if my friend and the Holiday Inn were left holding the bag, despite the special relationship we have developed over the years and despite the commitment I have made. Indeed, as a "good-act" utilitarian, I consider it my moral obligation to maximize utility, even at the expense of harming some individuals and violating the trust that has been placed in me.

Many think examples such as this one show that AU takes promises, commitments, special relationships of trust, and so on, far too lightly. Indeed, some think AU makes such factors totally irrelevant, since AU is a monistic theory of obligation that posits one and only one obligation—to maximize utility. Future consequences are all that count. Past commitments are irrelevant. A defender of AU, on the other hand, will probably reply that the critic has simply failed to consider all the relevant consequences. Of crucial importance here is not simply the fact that a much better deal can be arranged with the Walnut Inn but also the fact that going with the new hotel will destroy a valuable relationship which, in the long run, would add significantly to the future utility I can bring about in my role as executive director. Who knows whether Walnut Inn will give me the same deal in the future? Probably they won't. Who knows whether the Holiday Inn will be willing to make the same concessions they have made in the past if I desert them now? Surely they will not. All of these long-range, indirect consequences of breaking the agreement, when put into the balance, tip the scales in favour of keeping the initial agreement with Holiday Inn. Those who think, say its defenders, that AU takes special relationships and commitments far too lightly have simply ignored all the long-range, indirect effects of doing so.

So the defender of AU has a fairly forceful reply to such counter-examples to this theory of obligation. We should always be sure to ask the following when a critic provides such an example: Have all the relevant consequences, long-range and indirect, as well as immediate and direct, been accounted for? More often than not they haven't been, whether we're talking about breaking hotel bookings, lying to a close friend about her prospects for promotion, or padding an expense account.

Philosophers are fairly industrious when it comes to thinking up counter-examples to ethical theories. Having met with replies such as the one outlined above, they alter counter-examples to get rid of those convenient indirect, long-range effects upon which the defence is based. Some have dreamt up the Desert Island Promise Case, a version of which follows.

> Suppose you and a friend are alone on a deserted island. Your friend is dying and asks you to see to it when you are rescued that the elder of his two sons receives the huge sum of money your friend has secretly stashed away. You now are the only other person who knows of its existence. You solemnly promise to fulfil your friend's last request, and he passes away secure in the knowledge that his last wish is in good hands. Upon rescue, you are faced with a dilemma. The elder son turns out to be a lazy playboy who squanders to no good end—and with no pleasure—whatever money he has. Even when he has lots of money to spend, he still ends up being miserable and causing misery to other people. Your friend's younger son, however, is an aspiring researcher in dermatology. He is on the brink of uncovering a solution to the heartache of psoriasis, but will fail unless he receives financial backing. All his grants have been denied unjustly, and he has been left in desperation. As a good act utilitarian, you reason that utility would obviously be maximized if your solemn word to your dying friend were broken and you gave the money to the younger son. Think of all the utility that would be realized, all the suffering that would be alleviated! Compare this with the very little utility and considerable disutility that would result were you to give the money to the elder son.

Notice that in this case all the indirect, long-range consequences to which appeal was made in the hotel-booking case are absent. No one will know that the promise is being broken, and there are no valuable, utility-enhancing relationships in jeopardy. Your friend is dead. There seems little doubt in this case that the promise should be broken according to AU, as a moral obligation. But surely, the opponent will argue, this cannot be so. Solemn promises to dying friends, regardless of the good consequences that might be realized by breaking them, *must* be kept, except perhaps where impending disaster would result from keeping them. That AU seems to give no weight at all to such promises shows that it is a faulty theory of obligation. Solemn promises should weigh heavily—and independently of good consequences. Hence AU cannot be an adequate theory.

So promises and other special commitments pose difficulties for AU. Free riders do, too. Suppose there is a temporary but serious energy shortage in your community. All private homes and businesses have been requested to conserve electricity and gas. Private homes are to keep their thermostats no higher than 15 degrees Celsius, and all businesses are temporarily to cut production by one half. Everyone's chipping in this way will avoid a serious overload that would prove disastrous. Being a good-act utilitarian, and knowing the tendencies of your neighbours, you reason as follows: "I know that everyone else will pay scrupulous attention to the government's request, so the potential disaster will be averted regardless of what I do. It will make no difference whatsoever if I run my production lines at two-thirds capacity. The little bit of extra electricity we use will have no negative effect at all. Of course, if everyone ran at two-thirds, then disaster would result. But I know this isn't going to happen, and so the point is irrelevant. As for my employees, they will see a reduction, and assume that the cut was to one half, so no one will know but me. Using two-thirds, then, will in no way prove harmful, but it will make a considerable amount of difference to my balance sheet! The extra production will enable the company to show a much higher profit this year. All things considered, then, it is morally permissible—indeed, my moral obligation—

to run at two-thirds. This is what AU tells me I should do."

Imagine the moral outrage that would result were your acting on this line of reasoning to become common knowledge. You would be labelled a "free rider," one who rides freely while others shoulder the burdens necessary for all to prosper. Your actions would be thought most unfair to all those who had willingly sacrificed their best interests for the good of everyone concerned; all this despite your efforts to maximize the utility of your actions.

In response to these (and similar) sorts of objection, some utilitarians have developed an alternative to AU. Consider further what would be said if your free riding came to light. The probable response would be the following: "Sure, no one is harmed if you use the extra electricity. But imagine what would happen if everyone did what you are doing. Imagine if that became the norm. Disaster would result!" The request "Imagine what would happen if everybody did that" has great probative force for many people. Unless *everyone* could do what I propose to do without serious harm resulting, then many are prepared to say that it would be wrong for *anyone* to do it, and hence wrong for me to do it. In response to the force of this intuition, some utilitarians have developed a very different variety of theory called *rule utilitarianism (RU)*. On this version, the rightness or wrongness of an action is not to be judged by its consequences, but rather by the consequences of everyone's adopting a general rule under which the action falls.

As an introduction to RU, consider a case outlined by John Rawls in his paper "Two Concepts of Rules."[4] Rawls asks you to imagine that you are a sheriff in the U.S. deep south. A white woman has been raped, and although the identity of the rapist is unknown, it is clear that the offender was black. The predominantly white and racially bigoted community is extremely agitated over the incident and great social unrest is threatening. Riots are about to break out, and many people will be killed. If you were able to identify and arrest the rapist, the unrest undoubtedly would subside; but unfortunately you have no leads, other than the fact that the rapist was black. It occurs to you that you don't really need the actual culprit to calm things down. Why not simply concoct a case against some black man or other who has no alibi, and have him arrested? The crowd will be placated, and although one man—possibly or even probably innocent—will suffer, many innocent lives will be saved.

Rawls uses this example to illustrate an apparent weakness in AU, and how RU allows one to overcome it. The consequences of framing the (possibly) innocent black are far better (or less bad) in terms of utility than allowing the riot to occur. Hence AU seems to require the frame—an action which is clearly unjust. (Of course, the defender of AU has several tricks up her sleeve at this point. She can once again appeal to the possible indirect effects of the frame. Suppose the lie came to light. Terrible social paranoia and unrest would result; people would no longer trust the judicial system and would wonder constantly whether they might be the next person to be framed. Indirect consequences such as these, the defender of AU will argue, clearly outweigh any short-term, direct benefits.) But Rawls suggests that we consider a different question from the one AU would have us ask. We are to consider whether a general rule that permits the framing of innocent persons could possibly figure in a moral code, general acceptance of which would result in the maximization of utility. If it could not, which is surely the case, then the proposed frame is impermissible. Since no such general rule could find its way into an acceptable moral code, largely for the reasons mentioned above, an action in accordance with that rule would be morally wrong. Hence, it would be morally wrong on RU to frame the pos-

sibly (probably) innocent black, even if the consequences of that particular action would be better that those of the alternatives.

We are morally required, on RU, not to perform actions that individually would maximize utility. Rather, we are to perform actions that accord with a set of rules, general observance of which by everyone would maximize utility. Actions are judged according to whether they conform with acceptable rules; only the rules themselves are judged in terms of utility.

> RU: An act is morally right if it conforms with a set of rules, general observance of which by everybody would maximize utility.

One extremely important difference between RU and AU is worth stressing. It is quite possible, on RU, to be required to perform an action which does not, on that particular occasion, maximize utility. Observance of the best set of general rules does not always, on each individual occasion, lead to the best consequences; it *generally* does, but there are exceptions. The defender of RU seems willing to live with this for the sake of overall, long-term utility gains, and the ability to deal with desert-island promises, free riders, and so on.

RU is not without its difficulties, of course. For example, some utilitarians claim that RU really does violate the spirit of utilitarianism, and amounts to "rule worship."[5] If the ideal behind utilitarianism is the maximization of utility, then should we not be able to deviate from the generally acceptable rules when doing so will serve to maximize utility? If the defender of RU allows exceptions to be made in such cases, then he runs the risk of collapsing his RU into AU. The rules would no longer hold any special weight or authority in our moral decisions. We would end up following the rules when it is best to do so, and departing from them when that seems best.[6] In each case we seem led to do what AU requires, namely, maximize the utility of our individual actions. If, on the other hand, the defender of RU holds fast and says we must never deviate from rules that generally advance utility but sometimes do not, then the charge of "rule worship" comes back to plague the utilitarian.

A second problem facing RU can be summed up in a example. Suppose it were true that the best set of rules for the circumstances of our society would place an obligation on first-born children to provide for their elderly parents. I, the younger of two daughters, reason that I therefore have no obligations whatsoever to provide for my elderly parents, even though I know that my elder sister is unwilling to provide more than the 50 percent she thinks we each ought to provide. My parents end up living a life of abject poverty on only 50 percent of what they need to sustain themselves. Something seems clearly wrong here. Our obligations, it would seem, cannot be entirely a function of an ideal code that may never in fact be followed by anyone except me. We seem to require, in an acceptable moral theory, some recognition of how other people in fact are behaving, what rules they in fact are following. The rules they are following may be perfectly acceptable but not ideal, in which case I should perhaps follow them, too. This precept is as true in the business world as elsewhere. Financial ruin would be the result were an idealistic business person to act according to an ideal code, general observance of which would maximize utility, when no one else was prepared to do so. Perhaps here the excuse "But no one else is willing to do it" has some purchase.

There are significant differences between AU and RU, and neither theory is free from difficulty. AU requires that we always seek, on each particular occasion, to maximize utility. It has difficulties with, among other things, free riders, desert-island promises, and sheriffs tempted by good consequences to commit injustice. RU tells us to perform actions that conform to a set of rules, general

observance of which would lead to the best consequences overall. This theory seems to provide solutions to many of the problems plaguing AU, but it does so only at the expense of introducing new puzzles of its own. It must somehow provide a bridge between the best ideal code and the actual beliefs, practices, and accepted rules of one's society, all the while steering a course between rule worship and a straightforward reduction to AU.

Deontological Ethics—Immanuel Kant

Kant, like Mill, proposes a monistic theory of obligation. Unlike Mill's theory, however, Kant's theory is thoroughly non-consequentialist. It denies that the consequences of our actions are what determine their rightness or wrongness:

> An action done from duty has its moral worth, *not in the purpose* [the consequences] to be attained by it, but in the maxim in accordance with which it is decided upon; it depends, therefore, not on the realization of the object of the action, but solely on the *principle of wisdom* [the maxim] in accordance with which, irrespective of all objects of the faculty of desire [i.e., pleasure, happiness, preferences] the action has been performed.[7]

In this remark, we see that Kant's ethical theory includes a deontological theory of obligation. The morality of an action is determined not by its consequences, but by the maxim—the general principle—to which it conforms. Its moral worth lies not in the happiness or pleasure it produces, but in the *kind* of action it is. Let's try to see a bit more clearly what all this means.

A key notion in Kant's theory is that of a *maxim*. By maxim, Kant means a general rule or principle that specifies what it is one conceives of oneself as doing and the reason for doing it. For example, suppose I decide to tell a lie in order to avoid serious financial loss. The maxim of my action could be expressed in the following way: "Whenever I am able to avoid serious financial loss by lying, I shall do so." This maxim makes plain that I conceive of myself as lying, and that my reason is the avoidance of financial loss. It makes plain that I consider the avoidance of such a loss a *sufficient reason* to lie. Were I to act on my maxim, in effect I would be expressing my commitment to the general rule whose scope extends beyond the particular situation in which I find myself. In supposing that the avoidance of serious financial loss is a sufficient reason in this situation to lie, I seem to commit myself to holding that in any other similar situation— i.e., any other case in which a lie would serve to avoid a serious financial loss—I should tell a lie. This *generalizability of reasons* and maxims can be illustrated through an example involving a non-moral judgment.

Suppose you and I are baseball fans.

Me: "The Toronto Blue Jays are a good baseball team because their team batting average is about .260 and the average ERA among their starting pitchers is under 3.50."
You: "What is your opinion of the Montreal Expos?"
Me: "They're a lousy team."
You: "But their team batting average is also about .260 and the average ERA among their starters is 3.40."

I am stuck here in a logical inconsistency. I must either modify my earlier assessment of the Blue Jays—say that they too are a lousy team—or admit that the Expos are also a good team. By citing my reasons for judging the Blue Jays a good ball team, I commit myself to a general maxim that *any* baseball team with a team batting average of over .260 and whose starting rotation has an ERA of below 3.50 is a good baseball team. If I don't like the implications of that general maxim, i.e., I still

think the Expos are a bad ball team, then I must either reject or modify the maxim. Perhaps I'll add that in addition to a team batting average of over .260 and an ERA among starting pitchers of under 3.50, a good baseball team must have several "clutch" players. I would add this if I thought that the absence of clutch players explains why the Expos, unlike the Blue Jays, are not a good team. Of course, I could make this alteration only if I thought the Blue Jays did have at least a few clutch players.

So, my maxim—that whenever I can avoid serious financial loss by lying, I will— insofar as it expresses a general reason, applies to other situations similar to the one in which I initially act upon it. But this isn't the full extent of my commitment. If avoiding serious financial loss is a sufficient reason for my telling a lie, then it must also be a sufficient reason for anyone else who finds himself in a situation just like mine. According to Kant, and virtually all moral philosophers, acting upon a maxim commits me, as a rational moral agent, to a *universal* moral rule governing all persons in situations just like mine (in the relevant respects). I must be prepared to accept that a sufficient reason for me is a sufficient reason for anyone else in precisely my situation. If I think some other person in a position to avoid serious financial loss by lying should *not* tell the lie, then I must either retract my earlier maxim or specify some relevant difference between our situations, as I did when I tried to show that the Expos are a bad baseball team despite their strong team batting average and pitching staff.

Acting for reasons, that is, acting rationally (which, according to Kant, is required if we are to be moral), commits me to universal rules or maxims that I must be prepared to accept. Kant expresses this point in terms of my capacity to will that my personal maxim should become a universal law. According to the first formulation of the categorical imperative, the fundamental principle of obligation in Kant's monistic system, "I ought never to act except in such a way that I can also will that my maxim should become a universal law."[8] Later he writes, "Act as if the maxim of your action were to become through your will a universal law of nature."[9] Immoral maxims and the immoral actions based upon them can never, under any conceivable circumstances, pass Kant's categorical imperative test—not because the consequences of general observance of an immoral maxim would be undesirable in terms of utility, but because the state of affairs in which the maxim is observed as a universal law is logically impossible or inconceivable.

Some states of affairs simply cannot exist, in the strongest sense of "cannot." The state of affairs in which I am, at one and the same time, Robbie's father *and* Robbie's son is logically impossible. It cannot exist. Were I for some strange reason to will that this state of affairs exist, my will, Kant would say, *would contradict itself.* It would be willing inconsistent, contradictory things—that I am Robbie's father and son at one and the same time. Now consider a case actually discussed by Kant, and of obvious relevance to business, where promises play an essential role. Suppose that a man

> finds himself driven to borrow money because of need. He well knows that he will not be able to pay it back; but he sees too that he will get no loan unless he gives a firm promise to pay it back within a fixed time. He is inclined to make such a promise; but he has still enough conscience to ask, "Is it not unlawful and contrary to duty to get out of difficulties in this way?" Suppose, however, that he did resolve to do so, the maxim of his action would run thus: "Whenever I believe myself short of money, I will borrow money and promise to pay it back, though I know that this will never be done." Now this principle of self-love or personal advantage is perhaps quite compatible with

my own entire future welfare; only there remains the question "Is it right?" I therefore transform the demand of self-love into a universal law and frame my question thus: "How would things stand if my maxim became a universal law?" I then see straight away that this maxim can never rank as a universal law of nature and be self-consistent, but must necessarily contradict itself. For the universality of a law that everyone believing himself to be in need can make any promise he pleases with the intention not to keep it would make promising, and the very purpose of promising, itself impossible, since no one would believe he was being promised anything, but would laugh at utterances of this kind as empty shams.[10]

It is important to be clear about what exactly Kant is saying in this passage. He is not objecting to insincere promises on the grounds that they will cause others to lose confidence in us and thereby jeopardize the good consequences of future promises, nor is he arguing that false promises contribute to a general mistrust of promises and the eventual collapse of a valuable social practice. These *consequentialist* considerations to deontologist Kant are totally irrelevant to questions of moral obligation. Kant's point is a very different one. He is suggesting that a state of affairs in which everyone in need makes false promises is incoherent. There is a contradiction because, on the one hand, everyone in need *would* borrow on false promises. They would be following the maxim "as a law of nature," with the same regularity as the planets observe Kepler's laws of planetary motion. Yet, on the other hand, in this very same state of affairs, no one *could* borrow on a false promise, because if such promises were always insincere, no one would be stupid enough to lend any money. Promising requires trust on the part of the promisee, but in the state of affairs contemplated, there just couldn't be any, and so promises of the sort in question would simply be impossible. Hence any attempt to will, as a universal law of nature, the maxim "Whenever I believe myself short of money, I will borrow money and promise to pay it back, though I know that this will never be done," lands us in contradiction. "I . . . see straight away that this maxim can never rank as a universal law of nature and be self-consistent, but must necessarily contradict itself."[11]

With Kant, then, we have a moral test of our actions that does not lie in an assessment of their consequences; nor does the test lie in weighing the consequences of adopting a general rule that licenses those actions. Rather, the test considers the logical coherence of the universalized maxim upon which I personally propose to act. Whether this test successfully accounts for all our moral obligations is questionable. Is there anything incoherent in the state of affairs in which everyone kills her neighbour if he persists in playing his stereo at ear-piercing levels? Such a state of affairs might be highly undesirable, but it seems perfectly possible or conceivable. Yet killing off annoying neighbours hardly seems the right thing to do.

Kant provided two further formulations of his categorical imperative. The additional formulations bring to light two important principles that most people find highly appealing and which may prove helpful in dealing with many of the problems discussed in this text.

According to Kant, if I act only on maxims that could serve as universal laws, I will never treat people as *mere means to my ends*. The categorical imperative requires that I "Act in such a way that [I] always treat humanity, whether in [my] own person or in the person of any other, never simply as a means, but always at the same time as an end."[12] In more colloquial terms, we should never just *use* people. The emphasis here is on the *intrinsic worth* and *dignity* of rational creatures: I treat rational beings as ends in themselves if I respect in them the same value I discover in myself, namely, my freedom to determine myself to action and to act for reasons that I judge for myself. As Kant observes, there can be nothing more dreadful to a rational creature than that his actions should be subject to the will of another. I treat others as mere things rather than as persons, subject them to my will in the way I do a tool, if I fail to respect their dignity. This principle has an important role to play in assessing, for example, manipulative advertising, employment equity, or a worker's "right" to choose safe or hazardous working conditions.

Kant's third formulation of the categorical imperative seems closely tied to the second. In effect, it spells out what gives rational agents their dignity and worth. It requires that we treat others as *autonomous* agents, capable of self-directed, rational action. The capacity to rise above the compelling forces of desire, self-interest, and physical necessity, to act freely on the basis of *reasons*, is what gives rational beings their dignity and worth. To treat a person as an end in herself, then, is to respect her autonomy and freedom. As noted, it rules out various kinds of manipulative practices and paternalistic behaviours. In a case involving asbestos poisoning (discussed later in Part 3), company doctors neglected to tell workers the alarming results of their medical tests. This action was rationalized on the grounds that nothing could be done to curb the disease anyway, and so the workers were better off not knowing. Such paternalistic conduct clearly violates Kant's categorical imperative. It fails to respect the autonomy and dignity of the asbestos workers. This conduct might have been fully justified by AU, although whether in the long run such deceptions serve to maximize utility is certainly an arguable point.

Kant provides a clear alternative to the monistic, teleological theory of obligation propounded by the act and rule utilitarians. Kant's theory is clearly deontological and, at the very least, monistic in its intent, since he attempts to ground all our obligations on one fundamental principle: the categorical imperative. Kant puts forward three formulations of this principle, although it is difficult to see how they are exactly equivalent. In any event, we may view Kant as requiring that we ask the following three questions:

1. Would I be unable to consistently will, as a universal law, the personal maxim upon which I propose to act?

2. Would my action treat some rational agent (including possibly myself, in which case I would be guilty of self-degradation) as a mere means?

3. Would my action violate the autonomy of some rational agent, possibly myself?

Should any of these three questions be answered in the affirmative then Kant would hold that my moral obligation is to refrain from acting on my personal maxim.

Pluralism—W.D. Ross

Ross's theory of obligation arose mainly out of his dissatisfaction with utilitarian theories. While Ross's main target was G.E. Moore, his criticisms are relevant to utilitarianism in general, particulary AU. According to Ross, utilitarianism in all of its guises grossly oversimplifies the moral relationships in which we stand to other people. Utilitarianism is, in the end, concerned exclusively with the overall consequences of our actions (the maximization of utility), or the rules under which we perform our actions. In Ross's view, morality does indeed require this kind of concern, but not exclusively. Ross believes utilitarians err in thinking that consequences are all that matter, in thinking that "the only morally significant relationship in which my neighbours stand to me is that of being possible beneficiaries [or victims] of my action."[13] In other words, utilitarianism errs in being a monistic, teleological theory of oblig-

ation. Ross proposes instead a pluralistic theory of obligation that recognizes several irreducible moral relationships and principles. In addition to their role as possible beneficiaries of my actions, my fellow human beings "may also stand to me in the relation of promisee to promiser, creditor to debtor, or wife to husband, of child to parent, of friend to friend, of fellow countryman to fellow countryman, and the like."[14] "The like" no doubt includes the relation of sales person to customer, employer to employee, and manufacturer to consumer, relationships that are integral to business life, and which are ignored at the cost of moral confusion.

In Ross's view, utilitarianism not only oversimplifies the moral relationships in which we stand to others, but also distorts the whole basis of morality by being thoroughly teleological in orientation. On utilitarian theories, we must always be *forward-looking* to the future consequences of our actions or rules. But sometimes, Ross proposes, morality requires that we look *backwards* to what has occurred in the past. There is significance, for example, in the sheer fact that a promise has been made, a promise that has moral force independently of any future good consequences there might be in its being kept. This moral force explains why we should normally keep promises made by dying friends even if utility would be maximized were we to break them. A promise itself, by virtue of the kind of action it is, has a moral force that is totally independent of its consequences. Teleological theories, because they ignore such features and are entirely forward-looking, distort morality. Promises, contracts, agreements, loyalty, friendship, and so on, all have moral force; all can give rise to obligations independently of good or bad consequences.

Ross provides us, then, with a pluralistic, deontological theory of obligation. In this theory, we find a number of fundamental principles, only some of which are consequentialist in orientation. According to Ross, each of these principles specifies a *prima facie* duty or obligation. These are duties we must fulfil *unless* we are also, in the circumstances, subject to another, competing *prima facie* duty of greater weight. We have a *prima facie* duty to tell the truth, which means that we must always tell the truth unless a more stringent duty applies to us and requires a falsehood. An example from Kant illustrates this feature nicely.

Kant is notorious for arguing that the categorical imperative establishes an unconditional duty always to tell the truth. He has us consider a case in which a murderer comes to our door asking for the whereabouts of his intended victim. Should we tell him the truth—that the victim is seeking refuge in our house—the latter will be murdered. Both AU and RU would undoubtedly license a lie under such extraordinary circumstances, but, according to Kant, the categorical imperative does not. The duty to tell the truth is unconditional, despite the consequences of its observance. "To be truthful (honest) in all declarations . . . is a sacred and absolutely commanding decree of reason, limited by no expediency."[15] According to Ross's theory, though, Kant's case is clearly one in which our *prima facie* duty to be truthful is overridden or outweighed by more stringent duties to our friend.

Ross's list of *prima facie* duties provides a helpful classification of the various duties and morally significant relationships recognized in our everyday moral thinking. There are the following:

1. Duties resting on previous actions of our own. These include:

    (a) duties of *fidelity* arising from explicit or implicit promises;

    (b) duties of *reparation*, resting on previous wrongful acts of ours and requiring that we compensate, as best we can, the victims of our wrongful conduct.

2. Duties resting on the services of others; duties of *gratitude* that require that we return favour for favour.

3. Duties involving the *fair* distribution of goods; duties of *justice* that require fair sharing of goods to be distributed.

4. Duties to improve the condition of others; duties of *beneficence* (which in part forms the basis of utilitarian theories of obligation).

5. Duties to improve our own condition; duties of *self-improvement.*

6. Duties not to injure others; duties of *non-maleficence.*[16]

Ross's list of duties may not be exhaustive, and, no doubt, many would quarrel with some of the duties he has included. For instance, it might be questioned whether duties of self-improvement belong on a list of *moral* duties. It is plausible to suppose that moral duties arise only in our relationships with other people, that the demands of morality govern *interpersonal* relationships only. Allowing one's talents to lie unused or allowing one's health to deteriorate may be imprudent or foolish, but is it immoral? Perhaps it is if others, say our children, are depending on us. But in this case, it's not a moral duty of self-improvement that is violated but rather duties such as the duties of beneficence and non-maleficence. Another questionable candidate is the duty to be grateful. If someone does me a favour, is it true that I am *required*, as a matter of *duty*, to be grateful? Is gratitude something that can be subject to duty, or, rather, is it something that must be freely given, given not out of a sense of duty but out of genuine, heartfelt gratitude? If a favour is done with the sense that something is owing as a result, then perhaps it is not really a favour at all, but an investment.

In any case, the intention here is not to take issue with Ross's list—only to suggest that its contents are perhaps open to question. This leads to a point of some significance. According to Ross, that we have the *prima facie* duties he mentions is simply *self-evident* to any rational human being who thinks seriously about the requirements of morality. The existence of these duties, and the validity of the principles that describe them, are known through moral intuition. To say that a principle is self-evident and known through intuition is to say that its truth is evident to an attentive mind, that it neither needs supporting evidence nor needs to be deduced from other propositions, but stands alone as something obviously true. In this instance, it stands alone as something whose truth is known directly through moral intuition.

This feature of Ross's theory is very controversial among philosophers, who are generally suspicious of "self-evident principles" and "intuition." In the case of morality, the apparent obviousness of some principles, and the certainty with which many believe them, seem better explained by things such as uniform moral upbringing and common experiences. And then there is the problem of disagreement. If a principle truly is self-evident, then shouldn't *everyone* agree on its validity? Yet this is seldom, if ever, the case with moral principles, including those on Ross's list. One who asserts that her claims are self-evident has little to say to us if we wish to disagree with her. She can ask that we think again, but she cannot undertake to prove her claims to us. If her claims truly are self-evident and known through intuition, they are in need of no proof—and more importantly, none can be given. So if, after careful reflection, you continue to disagree with some of the principles of Ross's list, he has little recourse but to accuse you of moral blindness. He must view you as equivalent to a person who cannot see the difference between red and blue; your moral blindness is on a par with his colour blindness. One might ask whether this is a satisfactory response to serious moral disagree-

ments among reasonable people of good will and integrity.

Ross believes that his self-evident principles articulate *prima facie* moral obligations. These obligations hold unless overridden in individual cases by a more stringent or weightier duty. As for how we are to determine which of two or more *prima facie* duties has greater weight in a given case, Ross provides no answer except to say that we must use our best judgment, and fails to tell us the considerations upon which our judgments are to be based. Ross is fully aware that in most cases of conflicting obligations it is far from clear which duty is more stringent. Reasonable people of moral integrity will disagree. We therefore seem left with a serious gap in the theory, and must either accept that in cases of conflict there just is no one right thing to do— that the best we can do is fulfil one of our conflicting duties and violate the other; or we must continue to look for a criterion in terms of which conflicts can be resolved.

It is at this point that the utilitarian will be more than happy to offer assistance. In his view, Ross has isolated the basis for a set of rules that are indeed important in everyday moral thinking. According to the defender of AU, these Rossian rules are useful *guidelines* or *rules of thumb* that we are well-advised in most cases to follow. If we follow them regularly, our actions will in the long run end up maximizing utility. The act of promising usually does maximize utility, as does a display of gratitude. But in cases in which a conflict between the rules arises, or where an applicable rule seems inappropriate for good utilitarian reasons, we must resort directly to the AU criterion and decide which action will maximize utility. As for the proponent of RU, she will likely claim that Ross's rules will almost certainly figure in the set of rules, the general observance of which, within a modern society, will maximize utility. The proponent of RU is also likely to claim that in cases in which the rules conflict, direct recourse must be made to the principle of utility, and the rule which, in the circumstances, will lead to the maximization of utility. Of course, Ross must reject the utilitarian's offer of rescue. Were he to follow the utilitarian's lead, he would in effect be adopting the principle of utility as defining a single, ultimate obligation, and this would be to deny Ross's central claim that each of his *prima facie* duties is equally important and irreducible. However, without a means of adjudicating among conflicting *prima facie* duties, Ross leaves us short, just where we need guidance the most.

Virtue Ethics—Aristotle

What Should We Be? versus What Ought We to Do?

Despite their many differences, the theories of Kant, Ross, and the utilitarians had at least one thing in common: they were all designed to answer directly the question "What ought I to do?" In other words, these theories were designed to help us determine what action(s) we should perform in particular circumstances. The concern, in short, was with the rightness of actions, with determining wherein our duty lies. According to Kant, the question "What ought I to do?" is answered by determining whether the maxim of one's action can be universalized. For rule utilitarians, the answer lies in whether the rule(s) under which one acts maximize(s) overall utility. Although act utilitarians believe that rules have no role in our moral reasoning, except as rules of thumb, the question remains: "What is the right thing for me to do in these circumstances?" According to act utilitarians, we answer this question by determining which of the actions open to us would maximize utility. Ross, too, was concerned to help us determine what we should do in particular

circumstances, with determining the course of (right) action wherein our moral duty lies. Modern theories sometimes transform the questions of Mill, Ross, and Kant into questions about our rights, but still the emphasis is on the evaluation of actions, on determining what we have a right to do.

Much earlier in the history of moral philosophy, the Greek philosopher Aristotle sought to cast ethics in an entirely different mould. This is a mould that some contemporary moral philosophers find highly appealing, partly because it allows us to avoid many of the difficulties encountered by the traditional deontological and utilitarian theories, but also because it is thought to provide a much better understanding of our moral lives, what it is we strive to be in pursuing the moral life, and why the moral life is important to us. The fundamental ethical question for Aristotle is not "What ought I to *do*?" but "What should I *be*?" As one similarly minded theorist put it,

> . . . morality is internal. The moral law . . . has to be expressed in the form, "be this," not in the form "do this." . . . the true moral law says "hate not," instead of "kill not." . . . the only mode of stating the moral law must be as a rule of character.[17]

For Aristotle, moral behaviour expresses *virtues* or qualities of character. There is a much greater emphasis on "character traits" and "types of persons," than on rules, obligations, duties, and rights. Aristotle is interested in questions such as these: Should we *be* niggardly or generous? Hateful or benevolent? Cowardly or courageous? Overindulgent or temperate? In what do these traits consist? How are they cultivated? And how do they figure in a life well lived? In discussing these questions about the character traits integral to moral life, Aristotle offered exemplars of virtue to emulate and vices to avoid, rather than rules or principles to be obeyed or disobeyed. In short, for

Aristotle, morality is *character oriented* rather than *rule driven*. Aristotle would no doubt have frowned on modern ethical theories that divorce actions and questions about them from the character of moral (or immoral) agents who perform them. Aristotle was not interested in the mere doing of actions, but also with the character of the doer from whom actions flow. Praiseworthy and blameworthy actions are not those that match up to a particular template of rules or principles, but rather ones that flow from and reveal a certain type of character. Moral agency is not merely a matter of which rules to follow, but a whole way of life that requires a unity of thought and feeling characteristic of what Aristotle called "virtue."

Theoretical and Practical Reason

Aristotle divided knowledge into the theoretical and the practical. *Episteme* is concerned with speculative or theoretical inquiries, and its object is knowledge of the truth. This was contrasted with *phronesis* or practical knowledge, which focuses on what is *"doable"* rather than on what is *knowable* for its own sake. Without *phronesis*, particular virtues of character (e.g., courage, moderation, and generosity) would not be achievable by human beings, and the conduct that flows from and expresses these virtues would not be probable. It is central to Aristotle's view of human knowledge and moral excellence that whereas the intellectual virtues associated with *episteme* can be acquired through teaching, the virtues of character achievable via phronesis require practice until they become "second nature." Moral virtue cannot just be taught, it requires "training" and "habituation," the doing of virtuous actions. In order to be a virtuous person, one must develop the disposition to be virtuous; and this requires training and the doing of virtuous actions until this becomes a settled disposition.

Human Good

Aristotle's ethical theory is teleological. "Every art and every inquiry, every action and choice, seems to aim at some good; whence the good has rightly been defined as that at which all things aim."[18] There are different goods corresponding to the various arts and modes of inquiry. Seamanship aims at safe voyages, the musical arts at the creation of beautiful music, and the medical arts aim at health. Presumably the "commercial arts" aim at things such as the satisfaction of material needs and wants. Is there, Aristotle asks, a good for human beings as such? If so, then perhaps we can begin to understand what we might call the "art of living well" by considering what is necessary to the achievement of that end. Just as we can understand proper commercial practice in relation to the good that business strives to achieve, perhaps we can also understand moral life in relation to the good for humans that moral life strives to achieve. So Aristotle is interested in action insofar as it contributes to the good for human beings. The right thing to do is best understood in relation to what is conducive to the good for human beings, just as a "proper prescription" is best understood in relation to what is conducive to the patient's health, or a good manufacturing design is best understood in relation to efficient production.

In his classic work, *Nicomachean Ethics*, Aristotle confines his discussion of the good— that at which all things aim—to human good. The good aimed at by human beings is *eudaemonia*, usually translated as "happiness" or "well-being."[19] Some people identify human good with such things as wealth, pleasure, and honour, but Aristotle quickly shows that these people cannot be right. Wealth, for example, is at best a (very unreliable) means to happiness, not happiness itself. Pleasure is not the good for human beings even though it is true, as Aristotle's teacher Plato argued, that the good person takes pleasure in virtuous activity. Pleasure is not itself the good, but only an external sign of the presence of goodness. One will experience pleasure when one does things well, but doing well does not consist in the achievement of pleasure. In Aristotle's sense of the term, happiness or well-being is something enjoyed over a lifetime in the exercise of virtues such as courage, moderation, and generosity of spirit. In one sense the exercise of the virtues is a means to the achievement of happiness or well-being. In a deeper sense, it is not. The exercise of virtue is integral to the achievement of happiness, constitutive of it, not merely a prepayment of dues to insure happiness. In short, the virtuous life is not a means to the end of well-being; it *is* the life of well-being.

Virtue

Central to the Aristotelian conception of ethics and the good life is, as we have seen, the notion of "virtue." Aristotle's definition of this key notion is as follows: Virtue is "a state of character concerned with choice, lying in a mean, i.e., the mean relative to us, this being determined by rational principle, that principle by which the man of practical wisdom would determine it . . ."[20] The key notions in this definition need to be clarified.

A central element in Aristotle's conception of virtue is "disposition." Virtue, as we will see, is a kind of disposition. William Frankena summarizes the nature of dispositions as follows:

> . . . dispositions or traits . . . are not wholly innate; they must all be acquired, at least in part, by teaching and practice, or, perhaps by grace. They are also traits of "character," rather than traits of "personality" like charm or shyness, and they all involve a tendency to do certain kinds of action in certain kinds of situations, not just to think or feel in certain ways.

They are not just abilities or skills, like intelligence or carpentry, which one may have without using.[21]

Linguistically, terms describing dispositions are often contrasted with "occurrence" terms. A dispositional term like "timid" tells us a good deal more about a person than the occurrence word "frightened." The former tells us something about the character of the individual, whereas the latter may tell us nothing more than that the person was in a particular state on some occasion or other. It is possible that the state we might call "Tom's being frightened" occurred on some occasion even though Tom has no disposition to be frightened. Very little future behaviour can be predicted from being told that someone is frightened or angry, even if we know the reasons why he is frightened or angry. On the other hand, if we are told that Jack is timid or irascible, then we can predict that he will tend to get frightened or angry in circumstances that would not frighten or anger other people with a more courageous or gentler disposition. Having such dispositions does not, of course, rule out the possibility of sometimes acting "out of character." There are some provocations that would try even the patience of Job, some tasks so dangerous as to deter the most courageous and resolute persons, and some offers that even the most conscientious person cannot refuse. Dispositions, as tendencies, have an elasticity about them.

Aristotle's definition of virtue begins with virtue as a disposition, but it does not end there. Virtue is a disposition to *choose well*. Commenting on the etymology of the Greek word for choice, *prohairesis*, Aristotle writes, "the very term *prohairesis* . . . denotes something chosen before other things."[22] Choosing something before other things requires (a) the presence of alternatives. Without alternatives there can be no choice. It also requires (b) deliberation about the relative merits of the alternatives open to the agent. Virtuous actions are principled and thoughtful. They are responses rather than reactions. Deliberation about the alternatives open to the agent requires (c) ranking of those alternatives. One alternative is preferred to another and chosen. Finally, *prohairesis* presupposes (d) voluntarism. Virtue requires that we are responsible for our own actions. We are the begetters or efficient causes of our own actions, agents not patients. Our actions must be "self-caused," i.e. "in our power and voluntary."[23]

Aristotle emphasizes that primarily choice is restricted to means and not ends. The ultimate and remote end of our choosing, *eudaemonia* or happiness, is fixed by human nature. Just as all things within the universe have an essential nature (understood by Aristotle in terms of a unique function the thing serves) in relation to which their "good" can be understood, human nature provides a natural basis for understanding the good for human beings. This particular feature of Aristotle's view allows him to avoid arbitrariness in his ethics; ethics is not based on variable social norms or customs, or on the personal predilections of individuals or groups of individuals. Ethics is not "culturally relative" or "subjective," on this account; it is grounded in nature and to that extent "objective." Although the "objectivity" of the Aristotelian schema allows Aristotle to avoid relativism, it is a serious source of concern for some. Many critics see danger in the idea that there is a largely fixed, essential human nature in terms of which the moral life, and the requirements it places upon us, are to be understood. Some followers of Aristotle have argued that procreation is "natural" to human beings (as it is to all organisms) and that so-called "artificial" means of reproduction are therefore inherently suspicious, and perhaps even immoral. Others take a similar line of argument in supporting the view that homosexuality is immoral. Whether such views follow from the Aristotelian system, and

whether Aristotle would himself accept the views attributed to his conception, are highly questionable. But there is, nevertheless, cause to be concerned about a theory that seeks to define the moral in terms of what is "natural" for human beings. All too often what is thought to be "natural" is really only the conventional, as those engaged in the practice of international business become all too aware. And as feminists and other social critics point out, the conventional is often the result of bias, misunderstanding, and oppression.

If the ultimate end of our choosing is fixed by human nature, and the alternatives open to us when we seek to be virtuous are alternative ways of promoting this end, i.e., alternative ways of promoting *eudaemonia*, then the following question arises. Is Aristotle in fact advocating what we might call the *principle of eudaemonia*, as opposed to the principle of utility? And is this not a principle that can be applied, either directly or indirectly, to our actions in such a way that we have a means of determining morally right actions? For example, particular virtues such as truth-telling, promise-keeping, and their ilk could be viewed as means toward achieving the ultimate end of *eudaemonia* or happiness. If this is so, then in actual fact there may be little to distinguish Aristotle's so-called "virtue ethics" from the action-centred "duty ethics" of Kant, Mill, and Ross.

Although there is some truth in this assessment of Aristotle's ethics, it would be a mistake to exaggerate it. And this is because, for Aristotle, virtuous action is not action that accords with a principle, but rather action that springs from a disposition to choose a way that lies between two extremes—the one an excess and the other a deficiency. Virtuous action lies in choosing the mean between extremes of behaviour, one of which is a vice through excess, the other of which is a vice through deficiency. And Aristotle is clear that there is no arithmetical formula which allows us to determine with precision what lies at the mean in a particular set of circumstances. This is one reason why he says that the mean must be determined "relatively to us," and determined not by a rule universally applicable and established in advance, but by a rule "by which a practically wise man would determine it." On Aristotle's account, there is a kind of indeterminacy in moral judgments when it comes to deciding on particular courses of action. The variable contexts of moral life prevent us from fashioning hard-and-fast rules or procedures for settling what we ought to do. The best we can do is rely on *phronesis*, our virtuous dispositions, and the examples set by paragons of virtue. We must, in other words, try under the circumstances to act as "the man of practical reason would act." This is the best that we can do. Whether this is a weakness in Aristotle's account of moral life is a good question. Perhaps the best answer is to point out that this inherent indeterminacy better reflects moral reality and the perplexing dilemmas with which we are often faced, than do theories or professional codes of conduct, which purport to provide ready-made answers that fail to emerge when we seek to apply the theories to concrete circumstances. Is it any more helpful to be told that one must maximize utility, or seek to treat humanity as an end in itself, than it is to be told that one must seek a mean between deficiency and excess? In explicitly acknowledging that moral theory can provide only a limited amount of help, Aristotle's theory may in fact be the more honest one.

Virtue lies at the mean between the vices of excess and deficiency. Two virtues, courage and moderation (or temperance), are chosen by Aristotle to elucidate his doctrine of the mean. The accounts are perhaps dated, but they nevertheless serve to illustrate the main lines of Aristotle's thought. For Aristotle, courage is primarily a virtue of soldiers, and his examples are culled entirely from the battlefield. Courage is located between the defect of fear and the excess of overspiritedness or brashness. When the occasion arises, a courageous soldier can be counted on to subdue fear and enter bravely into the fray, even in the face of death. Cowardice is the vice (defect) associated with fear. In more modern parlance, we may link it with the instinct of "flight" in the face of danger. But rashness is also a vice, in this case an excess associated with spiritedness. This vice we may link with the instinct of "fight" in the face of danger. But one can be too spirited. Soldiers emboldened by anger may rush impulsively into the fray, "blind to the dangers that await them."[24] "Right reason" moderates fear, and courage emerges as fear tempered by spirit.

Aristotle's assignation of courage to the battlefield is far too restrictive for our purposes in this book. We shall be looking for displays of courage in the more familiar domains of business practice. These domains are also "battlefields" of sorts, in which individuals face, for example, insensitive employers, unsafe working conditions, manipulative advertisers, and the conflicting demands of loyalty to the firm and loyalty to the wider community. They are also domains in which business people face difficult decisions profoundly impacting upon the well-being of others. A CEO may be forced to decide whether to shut down an inefficient plant upon which an entire community depends. An employee may have to decide whether to "blow the whistle" on the harmful activities of the company, thereby preventing serious harm to the community but seriously threatening his own interests and those of a company to which he has some loyalty. Aristotle's ethics-of-virtue may prove helpful in such circumstances. While it may prove impossible to determine a hard-and-fast rule to answer our moral questions in such instances, it may be possible to answer this question: "What kind of people do we wish to be when we are faced with such circumstances?" Do we wish, for example, to be cowardly, fearful of reprisal should we inform the authorities that our company is dumping dangerous toxins into the local river? Suppose we decide against blowing the whistle. Is this how "the man of practical wisdom would act," lacking in regard for others, insensitive to the fact that great harm will befall other innocent parties if we look after our own interests first? Or do we want to be courageous, moderating our fear of reprisal as much as it lies within us to do so? In another context the relevant question might be as follows: What kind of people do we want to *be* in the face of opportunities to exploit impoverished workers in developing countries? To these questions we may find reasonable answers, even if there are no rules by which they can be determined, and even if we must in the end still choose for ourselves that course of action which best exemplifies the virtuous mean.

The second virtue upon which Aristotle focuses is temperance, which moderates our appetites for food, drink, and sex. One can eat too little or too much food. Aristotle designates health as the goal of eating. Gluttons are guilty of excess. They live to eat rather than eat to live. They dig their graves with their teeth. They imperil rather than preserve their health by overeating. This is a vice of excess. The vice of defect or deficiency involves eating insufficient food in circumstances in which there is enough to go around. In time of scarcity and famine, failure to eat sufficient food is not morally blameworthy. Strictly speaking, in such circumstances eating insufficient food does not qualify as a voluntary activity. Although Aristotle does not mention it, malnutrition can be caused by eating the wrong foods, not just by failing to eat enough food. One can be malnourished on a diet of soda pop and chips, or with fad diets motivated by an inordinate preoccupation with slimness. In such cases, Aristotle would attribute malnutrition to vice, rather than misfortune or famine.

To be clear on Aristotle's ordering of values in this context, it must be borne in mind that while health is an immediate end of eating, it is not good in itself. Rather, it is a means to happiness or well-being, i.e., *eudaemonia*, and is properly conceived only in this way. Relative to moderation in partaking of food and drink, health is a proximate end, but relative to the final end—happiness—it is usually a necessary means. This last point must be kept clearly in mind in commercial contexts where there is sometimes a tendency to confuse means with ends. Life, health, and the satisfaction of consumer preferences are important ends of human action, including commercially motivated action, but only if and to the extent that they contribute to what really counts: *eudaemonia*. When they do not, the person of practical reason and virtue will no longer see them as worthy of pursuit. Life, health, and the satisfaction of consumer preferences are goods that confer rightness on the means for their achievement, but only when these contribute to *eudaemonia*.

Feminist Ethics

Many contemporary women find all the approaches to ethics outlined above to be in many respects unsatisfactory and alienating. These theories were all developed by men who, the feminists claim, inadvertently brought to bear upon their theoretical positions a number of biases and ways of viewing the world that skew the results of their analyses. The resultant theories do little justice to the moral concerns and experiences of women. Indeed, in the view of most feminist ethicists, the traditional theories "do not constitute the objective, impartial theories that they are claimed to be; rather, most theories reflect and support explicitly gender-biased and often blatantly misogynist values."[25] It would be impossible to provide a complete and fully accurate account of the important, multifaceted themes pur sued by feminist ethicists. Instead, we will attempt, in what follows, to sketch two of the most common concerns of feminists regarding traditional ethical theories.

Let us begin with some important respects in which there is a natural affinity between modern feminist ethics on the one hand, and the ethics of business on the other. First, there is the issue of power relationships. Built right into many commercial contexts is a power imbalance. For example, there is the typical power imbalance between vulnerable employees in need of employment, and employers whose resources and power of dismissal often place them in a superior position. There is also the typical power imbalance between, on the one hand, wealthy corporations and the advertising skills and resources at their disposal and, on the other, consumers, whose relative lack of knowledge and resources places them at a severe disadvantage in responding to manipulative advertising. As a consequence of such inherent power imbalance, many business ethicists follow Kant's lead in stressing the crucial role of autonomy and control in respecting the inherent dignity of persons. It is on such a basis, for example, that they argue for strong employee and consumer rights.

Feminists share a concern with power imbalances, principally between men and women, but also between other advantaged and oppressed groups such as adults and children, the able and the disabled, and the rich and the poor. Many feminists would point out that both the commercial professions and the field of ethical theory have historically been dominated by men whose perspectives may have been biased against women. Some traditional ethicists, e.g., Kant and Aristotle, thought that women have a decidedly different character from men, and are, to a much greater extent than men, moved by emotion as opposed to reason. In the view of these theorists, this tendency towards the emotional serves as a barrier to the level of abstract reasoning required for

satisfactory moral thought. Feminist ethicists are concerned about undermining these stereotypes and asserting the equal ability of women to engage in moral thought.

Another similarity shared by feminist and business ethicists is their focus on the importance of *context* in making moral decisions. Whereas traditional ethical theory tends to the abstract and general, *applied ethics*, of which business and medical ethics are primary examples, tend towards the concrete and the particular. Business ethics, for example, focuses on the concrete situations in which decisions affecting the welfare of investors, employees, consumers, and the wider community must be made. As a result, advocates of feminist ethics quite often invoke examples and issues that arise within concrete, everyday contexts, and point to these as illustrative of the need to depart from abstract theorizing and to focus on individual cases in all their particularity.

This leads to one of the most serious complaints made against traditional ethical theory by feminist ethicists. Most feminists are opposed to the search for abstract, universalizable principles and rules (or even virtues) with which to answer everyone's moral questions. The theories of Kant and Mill are often cited as illustrative of the vacuousness, indeed the perniciousness, of traditional ethical theory. In the view of many feminist critics, Kant's theory rejects the emotional, personal component of moral life in favour of the rational universalizability of individual maxims. In seeking rationally to universalize our maxims, we are inescapably led to ignore or submerge our concern for all those complex factors that *individuate* our situations and the relationships in which we find ourselves. Most importantly, perhaps, in seeking such abstractions, we are led to ignore or abstract away all that makes us individual persons enmeshed in interpersonal relationships involving caring and trust. Among the factors so eliminated are the emotional bonds between people and the special concerns they have for one another, as parents, friends, siblings, colleagues, and employers. In seeking to universalize, we are, it is claimed, led to forget that most of the time we approach one another—and believe ourselves right in doing so—not as strangers subject to the same set of universalized maxims or rights, but as unique individuals in highly personal, context-specific relationships in which we have much invested emotionally. These are relationships which, by their very nature, cannot be reduced to universalized rules and principles. According to one leading feminist bioethicist,

> Because women are usually charged with the responsibility of caring for children, the elderly, and the ill, as well as the responsibility of physically and emotionally nurturing men, both at work and at home, most women experience the world as a complex web of interdependent relationships, where responsible caring for others is implicit in their moral lives. The abstract reasoning of morality that centres on the rights [and duties] of independent agents is inadequate for the moral reality in which they live. Most women find that a different model for ethics is necessary; the traditional ones are not persuasive.[26]

The feminist concern for the importance of context leads in another direction as well. Feminist ethicists argue not only for the importance of appreciating the factors that individuate one case from the other, and tie us to one another in a variety of personal ways, but also stress the importance of appreciating the wider context of decision-making. This is a context which, more often than not, profoundly influences the options available, or the options thought to be available, to us. Feminists look beyond the individual situations in which decisions are made, and question the social and political institutions, practices, and beliefs that create those situations and define the available options. Consider, for example, the case of equity hir-

ing. Here a plethora of ethical questions arise. Is it morally right to hire a less qualified minority candidate, thereby depriving a "more qualified" applicant of a position? Is this reverse discrimination? And if so, is reverse discrimination any less wrong than discriminating against members of minority groups? As another example, consider what some refer to as "sexist" advertising, but which others view as just plain good advertising, tailored to what consumers want and will respond to positively. Is it right to prevent companies from employing such advertising strategies, or would this be to restrict, without good cause, their freedom to advertise and sell their wares? These questions, and many others like them, are ones which everyone in business ethics will wish to address. But feminist ethicists want to dig much deeper than some. They want to uncover for discussion the variety of social, political, and environmental factors that give rise to such questions and possibly frame the available answers. They wish to expose, for example, certain dangerous social factors which, it is argued, lead consumers to respond to sexist ads. These include, for example, stereotypes of femininity, which are arguably harmful to women. If women are portrayed as "sex objects," will they be taken seriously in the boardroom? Will they even make it to the boardroom? More generally, does the perpetuation of stereotypes in advertising lead to discriminatory practices? According to feminists, important questions such as these tend to be ignored by mainstream ethical theories. This is partly because such theories ignore the wider social and political contexts in which these important questions arise.

To sum up, feminist ethics is marked by its rejection of traditional ethical theory as far too abstract and concerned with universalized rules and principles. As such, traditional ethical theory misses out on two fronts. First, it renders irrelevant a host of individuating factors that inform our moral lives, and which most of us, women in particular, consider integral to moral assessment. These include the importance of personal relationships and the emotional bonds that exist between individuals who care for one another. Second, traditional ethical theory often ignores the wider social, political, and environmental contexts in which moral questions are shaped and the available options are defined.

THE LANGUAGE OF RIGHTS

An introduction to the basic theories and concepts of ethics would be radically incomplete without some mention of "rights." At one time, it was quite natural to express moral requirements using concepts such as "ought," "duty," and "obligation." The three ethical theories just discussed were presented by their authors using these terms and concepts. Today, however, our moral vocabulary is dominated by the notion of rights. Instead of saying "You *ought* not to have done that," a modern person is more apt to remark, "You had no *right* to do that." But rights come in a variety of forms. In order to facilitate discussion of the moral issues raised in this book, a brief analysis of these differences follows. The conceptual map sketched is largely derived from the theory proposed early in this century by the American legal scholar Wesley Hohfeld, and from the more recent account developed by the contemporary moral philosopher Joel Feinberg.[27]

Hohfeld attempted to explicate the various normative relationships expressible in the vocabulary of rights by arranging certain basic concepts in pairs of opposites and correlatives. He thought that the best way to explain a group of related concepts is to outline the logical relationships that hold among them: pairs of correlatives must always exist together, and opposites cannot exist in the same person in relation to the same subject matter. For example, duty and privilege are opposites, so if I have a duty to help you, I cannot also have the privilege

of not helping you. Hohfeld formally defined the notions "correlative" and "opposite" as follows:

> *A* and *B* are *correlative* if and only if the presence of the one in an individual X implies the existence of at least one other person Y in which the other is present.

> *A* and *B* are *opposites* if and only if the presence of the one in an individual X implies the absence in himself, X, of the other.

> The correlatives are right/duty and privilege/no right. The opposites are right/no right and privilege/duty.

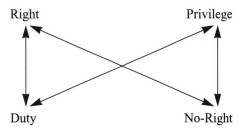

In the above diagram, the correlatives are connected by vertical arrows, the opposites by diagonal arrows.

Claim-rights

Strictly speaking, Hohfeld thought, a right is an *enforceable claim* to someone else's action or non-action. If one has a right to something, then one can demand it as one's due, as that to which one is entitled. The other person, or group of persons, has a correlative duty or obligation to respect your claim. For instance, I have a right not to be assaulted by you. This entails that you are under an obligation of non-action—a duty not to assault me. This kind of right, a claim against other people, is what Hohfeld calls a *claim-right*. A claim-right is always paired with a corresponding duty or obligation, which applies to at least one other person. Violation of my claim-right is always the violation by someone else of her duty towards me.

Claim-rights come in a variety of different forms. Joel Feinberg distinguishes among

(a) *in personam* and *in rem* rights;

(b) positive and negative rights; and

(c) passive and active rights.

In personam rights are said to hold against one or more determinate, specifiable persons. These are determinate persons who are under the corresponding or correlative obligations. For example, if Miriam owes Beth a weekend at The Royal York Hotel, then there is a specific person, Miriam, against whom Beth enjoys her claim-right. Other examples are rights under contract, rights of landlords to rent payments from their tenants, the right against one's employer to a safe and healthy working environment, the right to equitable compensation for one's services, and so on. Many of the duties on Ross's list of *prima facie* duties could easily be expressed in terms of the correlative claim-rights. Paired with a Rossian duty of fidelity, for example, would be a claim-right against a person with whom one has made a contract to the honouring of the agreement. That person has a duty to perform his end of the deal; you have a correlative claim-right to his performance.

In rem rights, on the other hand, are said to hold not against some specifiable, nameable person or group of persons, but against "the world at large." For instance, my right not to be assaulted holds not against any particular person or group of persons, but against anyone and everyone who might be in a position to commit such an offence against me. All other such persons have a correlative duty not to assault me. This latter, correlative duty, would no doubt fall under Ross's duties of non-maleficence.

A positive right is a right to someone else's positive action. A negative right, on the other hand, is a right to another person's non-action or forbearance. If I have a positive right to something, then this means that there is at least one other person who has an obligation to *do* something, usually something for my benefit. By contrast, I have a negative right when there is at least one other person who has a duty to refrain from doing something that affects me in some, usually undesirable, way. Depending on what it is that the other person(s) must refrain from doing, my negative right can be either passive or active.

Active rights are negative rights to go about one's own business, free from the interference of others. Paired with active claim-rights are duties of non-interference. Business people who complain that government should "get off their backs" are usually asserting active claim-rights not to be interfered with or hindered in their commercial ventures. Corresponding to such rights, they argue, is a duty on the part of government to allow business people a certain degree of freedom and autonomy. As we shall see in Part 1 of this text, the free-market libertarianism of Milton Friedman is fundamentally based on the assertion of negative, active rights to non-interference.

Passive negative rights are rights not to have certain things done to us. We might, for convenience, call them "security rights." Obvious examples are the right not to be killed and the right not to be assaulted. We might add here the right not to be inflicted with disease and injury by negligent or reckless employers. Those who assert a right against hostile corporate takeovers presumably have in mind a negative, passive right not to be adversely affected by the activities of corporate raiders. Passive rights are not rights against interference with one's own activities; they are not rights to do things without interference. Rather, they are rights not to have certain unwanted or harmful things done to us.

It is worth noting that, typically, active rights of non-interference can be protected only at the expense of other people's passive security rights. The active right of a manufacturer to pursue a livelihood within the capitalist system often competes with the passive, *in personam*, security rights of workers. It also competes with the passive, *in rem* rights of the community, or world at large, not to have its environment fouled by industrial activities. In general, a key problem of moral, legal, and political philosophy is how to balance active freedom rights against passive security rights. Different theories will place differing emphases on the competing rights. The same is true in the area of business ethics. A free-market capitalist like Friedman will place greater weight on active freedom rights, while environmentalists, workers' rights activists, and critics of the capitalist system, typically will place far greater weight on passive security rights. Sometimes they will go so far as to assert positive rights to assistance from employers and government. The resolution of such conflicts is as difficult as is the resolution of conflicts among Ross's *prima facie* duties.

To recapitulate, claim rights can be either *in personam* or *in rem*, positive or negative, and if they are negative, they can be either passive or active. Always correlated with any one of these rights is a duty or obligation on the part of at least one other individual. Such rights are claims against others who are under duty to respect them.

Liberties or Privileges

According to Hohfeld, some of the situations in which people assert rights do not involve claims against others who are under correlative obligations. Rather, they involve what Hohfeld calls "privileges" or "liberties." My having a privilege does not entail others being under obligation to me. Rather, it entails only the *absence of duty* on my part. Hence, the opposite of privilege is duty. If I enjoy the privilege of doing something, then I am free or at liberty to do it (or not do it), and do no wrong should I exercise my privilege. In short, a privilege is "freedom from duty." An example from law

might help to clarify the nature of privileges.

In most legal systems, there is a standing duty to provide the court with whatever information it requests. However, most jurisdictions also recognize a right—a privilege—against self-incrimination. In this special area—i.e., evidence which may implicate them in a crime—citizens are at liberty to decline the court's request. Here they enjoy an absence of duty. But if I have no *claim-right* against self-incrimination, only a privilege, then a sharp lawyer who somehow gets me to incriminate myself has in no way violated my rights. Were my right a claim-right against her, then the lawyer would be under a corresponding duty or obligation to respect a claim that I would have against her. But with privileges, there are no such corresponding duties—only the absence of duty on my part. I have a freedom to act (or not to act), but it is not a freedom that enjoys the protection afforded by corresponding duties on the part of other people to respect my freedom. There is no requirement on their part that they refrain from interfering with my actions.

Examples in business in which the notion of a privilege or liberty arises are not perhaps as obvious as in law, but can be found, however, in situations in which some people are exempt from duties to which they would otherwise be held. Employees, for instance, are granted the privilege of entering the employer's premises. Some are also privileged with respect to confidential information. Access to private premises or confidential information is something from which the public is barred. The public is under duty to respect the confidentiality of private company records. They have no right to these privileged items. Those who are privileged, however, enjoy a freedom from this duty. They are exempt from the general duty to keep away or to mind their own business, which applies to the public generally.

The correlative of a privilege is what Hohfeld, finding no better term available, calls "no-right": If X has the privilege of doing A, there is no other person who has a right against him that he do or not do A. If my employer grants me the privilege of examining confidential documents for purposes of an audit, then he has no right against me that I not examine those documents. He does not enjoy against me the right he enjoys against everyone else to whom he has not granted this special privilege. These others, because of the claim-right—the enforceable claim my employer has against them—are of course under duty to "mind their own business."

It is worth stressing once again that privileges are unprotected freedoms. Contrast a situation in which you are granted the privilege of examining confidential company documents with that of a court-appointed auditor. If the auditor is granted a claim-right to examine the files, then my employer must respect that right. He has a duty to turn them over and does wrong if he fails to do so. If, by contrast, my employer, upon granting me the privilege of examining the documents, forgets to give them to me, he has in no way violated my rights. I enjoy a mere privilege, not a claim-right with which is paired a corresponding duty.

Further Reflections on Rights

One should be alert when encountering talk of "rights." It is important to ask whether the right being asserted is a claim-right or a privilege. These are different conceptually and have very different implications. If the right is a claim-right, then one should ask whether it is *in rem* or *in personam*. It may be particularly crucial to determine whether the right is negative or positive. Does it require only that others refrain from doing something, or does it require a positive action? This important difference figures prominently in many public debates. One famous case in which the difference proved crucial was the United States Supreme Court's decision in

Roe v. Wade. The Court ruled that every woman has a right to abort a fetus within specified limits. This decision was interpreted by some to mean that the court had recognized a positive right to abortion, which entailed aid and financial assistance from the state. A 1977 ruling, however, made it clear that while it was unconstitutional to prevent a woman from having an elective abortion within the prescribed limits, women did not have a right to aid or financial assistance. In other words, *Roe v. Wade* had granted only a *negative*, not a *positive* right to an abortion.

The difference between positive and negative rights is as vital in ethical and political theory as it is in the law. Some theories emphasize negative rights and liberties (almost) to the exclusion of positive rights. Friedman and other libertarians, such as Robert Nozick and Jan Narveson, stress the liberty or privilege to pursue one's own interests free from any positive duties to provide for others.[28] They also give great weight to the protections afforded by negative, active claim-rights to non-interference. The free market demands such enforceable claims and is corrupted by misguided state intervention in the name of positive rights. Theories of this sort find appeal in the notion of the individual's unconstrained (but protected) freedom to pursue her own interests and projects as she sees fit and as she defines them. The fundamental purpose of morality and law, on this view, is simply the protection and enhancement of individual liberty.

Some theories are willing to assert positive rights to assistance from others. Utilitarians who wish to employ the vocabulary of rights will be prepared to affirm positive rights when their observance generally serves to maximize utility. On such a theory, we are not merely to leave people alone, but are to concern ourselves with their welfare and be willing, at least sometimes, to sacrifice our own interests for theirs. As we saw earlier, the same is true on Ross's theory. In addition to the duty of non-maleficence, to which corresponds a negative right against the duty holder, Ross includes a duty of beneficence, with which will be paired a positive right to beneficent actions on the part of others.

CONCLUDING THOUGHTS

As the above discussion clearly illustrates, there are numerous moral theories and different vocabularies with which to express them. The following question naturally arises: How should someone interested in applying the insights of ethical theory to actual practice respond to this somewhat perplexing situation? The strategies one could adopt in linking moral theory to practice are numerous and varied. Nevertheless, it is possible to isolate three basic patterns of response.

(a) Make decisions on an *ad hoc*, case-by-case basis, ignoring ethical theories altogether.

Despite the undeniable importance of individual context, this is neither a promising nor an inviting option. Although there is some measure of truth in the adage that "no two cases are ever alike," it would be a mistake to exaggerate it. Any two cases will necessarily be unlike one another in many respects, but it fails to follow that they will be unlike one another *in the relevant respects*. No two murders are completely similar, but they are alike in what is often the only relevant respect: an innocent human being has been killed. If cases can be classified as being similar to one another in a limited number of relevant respects, and these cases are familiar and recurring ones, then the possibility arises of discovering moral rules and principles to govern them. We are able to fashion workable legal rules governing murder because there are a limited number of recurring, relevant aspects of murder cases that can be dealt with according to simple, general rules. The same is often true with moral rules and principles. So while we must be sensitive to the importance of varying contexts, to what individu-

ates us in our personal relationships with others, and to the dangers inherent in Aristotle's attempt to ground morality on a fixed human nature, we should also be sensitive to the importance of similarities. My relationship with my daughter is unique and special to me. It may also be very different from the relationship shared by fathers and daughters in other, more patriarchal cultures. But the relationship I share with my daughter may yet be in many ways relevantly similar to the unique, special relationships many fathers have with their daughters.

If the possibility of moral norms, and ethical theories to support and explain them, exists, then it would be counterproductive to ignore them entirely. We would have to "start from scratch" every time we had to make a difficult moral decision. This would be inefficient, to say the least, and would be a hindrance to moral understanding. Understanding the world involves recognizing similarities and differences among situations and people. Without moral rules, principles, values and virtues, and theories to generate them, we make it difficult, if not impossible, to gain moral understanding. So long as we do not claim too much for it, working with an admittedly limited theory is better than working with no theory at all.

(b) Make a firm and irrevocable commitment to a particular *ethical theory*.

While this option promotes single-mindedness, and simplifies our moral deliberations, it has the serious disadvantage of creating a blind spot to the possible insights of other ethical theories and approaches. It compels one to resolve all moral quandaries within the boundaries of the theory chosen, and this smacks of artificiality and arbitrariness. This will be so unless one is convinced that one "knows the truth" with absolute certainty, an unlikely possibility for someone willing to ascend to the reflective level of moral thinking. Blindly committing oneself to an ethical theory or approach is no better than blindly committing oneself to a conventional rule or a rule found in a professional code of ethics. It is to descend to the pre-reflective level, where blind acceptance replaces critical reflection and the possibility of moral progress.

(c) Allow for both fixity and flexibility.

This is clearly the preferred option. The fixity is provided by acknowledging that moral conflicts need not, and perhaps should not, be resolved within a moral vacuum, and that the application of an ethical theory with which one is not entirely happy can nevertheless shed light on the issues in dispute. It may at the very least bring some of the important considerations into relief, where they may be more easily examined and reasonably discussed. Flexibility arises in acknowledging that competing theories and approaches may well offer insight as well, and that one's own favoured theory is always open to improvement or, at some point, rejection. Reasonable flexibility may even lead us judiciously to extract rules, principles, or values from competing systems as determined by their apparent relevance to the case in question. It may be true that sometimes Mill provides a better answer than does Kant—and that the tables are reversed at other times. It may also be true that sometimes the feminists are right in stressing the individuating features of a moral situation, features which might in some instance render the relevant issue incapable of resolution by way of a universalizable moral principle. This is not necessarily a cause for dismay, as Ross seemed to appreciate.

Consider an analogous case in physics. Sometimes the wave theory provides a better account of the properties and behaviour of light than does the particle theory. At other times the reverse is true. A single, unified theory would no doubt be preferable. But until such time as one becomes available, it would be imprudent to ignore the existing theories altogether, or to subscribe to one and forget about the other(s). The same is true in moral philosophy. We must not let our failures to achieve completeness, or our failures to appreciate in all cases the full range of factors at play in particular contexts, blind us to the incremental gains in knowledge that have been made. Perhaps we would do well, in the end, to heed Aristotle's caution that "precision is not to be sought alike in all discussions. We must be content, in speaking of such subjects [as ethics and politics], to indicate the truth roughly and in outline."[29]

ENDNOTES

1. See G.E. Moore, *Principia Ethica* (London: Cambridge University Press, 1903).

2. John Stuart Mill, *Utilitarianism* (New York: Bobbs Merrill, 1957), p. 10.

3. *Utilitarianism*, p. 22.

4. John Rawls, "Two Concepts of Rules," *The Philosophical Review*, Jan. 1955.

5. See J.J.C. Smart and Bernard Williams, *Utilitarianism: For and Against* (London: Cambridge University Press, 1973), p. 10.

6. See David Lyons, *The Forms and Limits of Utilitarianism* (Oxford: Oxford University Press, 1965), where it is argued that any version of RU faithful to the utilitarian credo collapses logically into AU.

7. Immanuel Kant, *Groundwork of the Metaphysics of Morals*, trans. H.J. Paton (New York: Harper & Row, 1964), pp. 67–68.

8. Ibid., p. 70.

9. Ibid., p. 89.

10. Ibid., pp. 89–90.

11. Ibid., p. 90.

12. Ibid., p. 96.

13. W.D. Ross, *The Right and the Good* (Oxford: Clarendon Press, 1930), p. 21.

14. Ibid., p. 13.

15. Immanuel Kant, "On a Supposed Right to Lie From Altruistic Motives" in Lewis White Beck, ed. and trans., *Critique of Practical Reason and Other Writings in Moral Philosophy* (Chicago: The University of Chicago Press, 1949), pp. 346–350.

16. *The Right and the Good*, p. 21.

17. Leslie Stephen, *The Science of Ethics* (New York: G.P. Putnam's Sons, 1882), pp. 155, 158.

18. Aristotle, *Nicomachean Ethics*, translated by J.L. Ackrill (New York: Humanities Press, 1973), 1094 a1-3.

19. *NE*, 1095 a16-20.

20. *NE*, 1106 b36-1107 a2.

21. William Frankena, *Ethics* 2nd ed. (Englewood Cliffs: Prentice-Hall, 1973), 63.

22. *NE*, 1112a 16-17.

23. *NE*, 1113b 20.

24. *NE*, 1116 b37.

25. Susan Sherwin, "Ethics, 'Feminine Ethics', and Feminist Ethics," in Debra Shogan ed., *A Reader in Feminist Ethics* (Toronto: Canadian Scholars' Press, 1993), p. 10.

26. Ibid, p. 14.

27. See W. Hohfeld, *Fundamental Legal Conceptions* (New Haven: Yale University Press, 1919) and Joel Feinberg, "Duties, Rights and Claims" in *Rights, Justice and the Bounds of Liberty* (Princeton: Princeton University Press, 1980).

28. Nozick's provocative political theory is developed in his *Anarchy, State and Utopia* (Oxford: Blackwell's, 1974). For Narveson's view, see "Have We a Right to Non-Discrimination?" p. 279 ff., this text, and *The Libertarian Idea* (Philadelphia: Temple University Press, 1989).

29. *NE*, 1094 b12, 18.

WHAT BUSINESS DOES ETHICS HAVE IN BUSINESS?

INTRODUCTION

In this section, we begin with the most basic of all questions regarding business ethics, a question that must be addressed before we can begin to consider the various issues discussed in subsequent parts. The question: What business does ethics have in business? Is it the case that business is business and ethics is ethics, and never the twain shall meet? Or does ethics in fact play a vital part in the everyday practice of business? If so, what kind of role does it play? Is there perhaps a special ethics governing the role of business person, as distinct from the ethics of people in everyday life, or is all daily conduct governed by the same standards?

These are the questions discussed by the authors in Part 1. The section opens with a famous and influential essay by the economist Milton Friedman. According to Friedman, the role of ethics in business is rather limited, or at least it would be if business people were clear-headed about the roles

they should play in society. Friedman is concerned to combat what he takes to be a pernicious doctrine: the social responsibility thesis. According to this thesis, at least as Friedman sees it, business people are not to be concerned exclusively with financial profit, but must take a central, perhaps leading, role in protecting and improving society and the environment; their concern should lie with their fellow humans, not with profit. Friedman will have none of this. In his view, "there is one and only one social responsibility of business—to use its resources and engage in activities designed to increase its profits so long as it stays within the rules of the game, which is to say, engages in open and free competition without deception or fraud." The "rules of the game" of which Friedman speaks are those found in law, and in the requirement that all business activities be conducted without outright deception or fraud. This latter requirement is based on Friedman's belief that fully informed, free exchanges of goods are the most efficient and politically desirable means of rationally distributing goods within society. Within these constraints, essential for the proper working of the free market, a responsible business manager will simply pursue profits.

Friedman's view has basically three grounds. First, managers have a fiduciary obligation (a Rossian duty of fidelity) to advance and protect the interest of those whom they serve. The "key point is that, in his capacity as a corporate executive, the manager is the agent of the individuals who own the corporation . . . and his primary responsibility is to them." This is the "Loyal Agent's Argument," which serves as the primary focus of Part 4 of this text. Friedman is stressing the importance of the special relationship existing between the business manager and the owners (usually the stockholders) of the company he helps to manage. According to Friedman, it would be a violation of duty were the manager to strive, out of some misguided sense of social responsibility, to advance the welfare or utility of society as a whole. It would be as wrong for a business manager to ignore the special duty he owes to the owners (who enjoy correlative claim-rights against him) as it would be for parents to ignore the special duties they owe to their children. Recall W.D. Ross's claim that, in addition to their role as possible beneficiaries of my actions, fellow human beings "may also stand to me in the relation of promisee to promisor, creditor or debtor, or wife to husband, of child to parent, of friend to friend . . . and the like." "The like," Friedman would add, includes the relation of manager to company owner(s). This special relation founds special duties of fidelity.

Friedman's second ground lies in his belief that productive organizations must aim directly at the maximization of profits if society is to achieve an acceptable level of consumer satisfaction. Society is in the long run better off in terms of social utility if business people take, as their primary goal, the pursuit of personal and corporate profit, says Friedman. We're all better off if companies

try to make money for themselves by producing the best products for the least money. The invisible hand of the free market will ensure that such selfishly motivated competitive behaviour results in the overall maximization of social utility. Were business people to aim directly at social utility instead, the free market would be corrupted. Prices would rise along with inefficiency, and production would drop off. The well-intentioned, but seriously misguided, efforts of business people would prove futile, and we would all be worse off. Note the distinctly utilitarian flavour of this argument. Its structure is quite similar to arguments fashioned by act and rule utilitarians to show how utility is maximized by such activities as keeping promises, honouring commitments, and paying one's own way. In all these cases, the argument goes, utility is maximized in the long run if we refrain from applying the principle of utility directly, and instead follow practices and rules of thumb that indirectly lead to the best consequences overall.

Friedman's third ground lies in his political libertarianism, a theory that celebrates the liberty of individuals to pursue their own interests, projects, and welfare according to their own individual rights. It is a theory that stresses the value of Hohfeldian liberties and negative claim-rights and looks with suspicion upon positive rights and government efforts to protect them. Libertarianism essentially views human beings as autonomous individuals whose liberty to acquire, trade, dispose of, or otherwise use their own private property for their own purposes must be respected so long as the individual in question respects the similar liberty of others. All exchanges of private property should be made freely, openly, and honestly. In this way, no one's property will be forcefully and unjustly appropriated by others who have no right to it. Society, on this model, is a collection of individuals and the voluntary associations into which they enter for mutual gain. The notion that people should be forced to help one another is anathema to libertarians.

Friedman's political libertarianism clearly underlies his views on the proper role of government, which is to protect property and ensure that all exchanges are unforced and voluntary, that is, freely and knowledgeably undertaken; hence the desirability of legal regulation requiring no more than that transactions be open and free from deception and fraud. Were government—or moralists—to require anything more of business people, instead of autonomous individuals freely, openly, and efficiently engaging in exchange for mutual advantage, we would have the unjust and inefficient appropriation of private property. We would have, to use Friedman's own words, "pure and unadulterated socialism," where the scope of government extends "to every human activity," and liberty is threatened.

So Friedman would be opposed, on grounds of political principle and utility, to laws and doctrines of social responsibility requiring such things as affirmative action in employment or employment equity. Forcing companies to spend money to aid underprivileged groups would be unjustly restricting a company's right to use its private capital to its own best advantage. It would also be playing havoc with the free market in which labour, as much as wood, steel, and computer programs, is a commodity with a certain value for which an appropriate price must be paid. This price must be determined by the free market. Analogous objections would be made to other "socially responsible" initiatives, such as efforts to avoid pollution or reduce inflation.

In summary, Friedman proposes a theory that sees a threat to individual liberty, autonomy, and utility in doctrine requiring business people to assume, in their roles as business people, responsibilities other than maximization of profits within "the rules of the game."

None of the other authors whose work is represented in Part 1 sees a danger in such doctrines. Mulligan objects to Friedman's platform on a number of grounds. He questions the paradigm upon which Friedman's critique of the social responsibility thesis is based. Mulligan sees that efforts to be "socially responsible" are not always the product of a "Lone Ranger" executive, deciding to pursue social objectives without the consent of other stakeholders. As Mulligan explains, socially responsible actions are often the result of decisions taken in accordance with corporate policy. "Founders, board members, major stock-holders, and senior executives may all participate in defining a mission and in setting objectives based on that mission. In so doing, these people serve as "legislators" for the company." It is worth noting, perhaps, that the fundamental obligation of managers on Friedman's account is not, strictly speaking, to maximize *profits*, but to advance the *desires* of the owners. Friedman's view is that the desires of owners *usually* lie in profit maximization. Yet it is quite possible, and if Mulligan is correct, quite normal, for the owners' desires to extend beyond the bottom line. If so, then socially responsible business activities may be required by Friedman's very own premises!

Mulligan also questions, along with Michalos, Friedman's suggestion that business people are ill-equipped to predict and assess the future consequences of "socially responsible" actions and policies. Citing the ability of successful business people to make difficult decisions under less than optimal conditions of knowledge, Mulligan suggests that a business person is perhaps better off than many others in trying to evaluate the social consequences of business decisions. He "has even less cause than most moral agents to abstain from social responsibility out of a sense of the futility of knowing consequences, since he is more practiced than most in the techniques for making action decisions in the absence of certainty."

In sharp contrast to Friedman, Michalos defends the claim that business people cannot isolate themselves from their *general* moral responsibilities as moral agents. There is no special morality for business people as distinct from the morality of all persons as moral agents. On the contrary, Michalos suggests, "There can be only one kind of morality, and it is universal. Businesspeople, like everyone else, must be judged morally responsible or irresponsible in terms of this morality. There is no third option." But what does it mean to be morally responsible in business? According to Michalos, human action, and thus the action of people in business, is morally responsible "insofar as it is reasonably intended to impartially maximize human well-being"—not, it should be stressed, the well-being of owners alone. Michalos is quite clearly advocating a utilitarian theory of some kind, a monistic theory of obligation that views our sole fundamental obligation to lie in the maximization of utility (or welfare). Michalos's utilitarian theory requires that a business person consider impartially the possible impact of her activities upon all those whose utility might in some way be affected by those activities. It rejects Friedman's notion of special fiduciary relationships existing between managers and owners as grounds for the right, and indeed the duty, of managers to concern themselves (almost) exclusively with the commercial interests of owners. It is therefore a much wider, and potentially much more demanding conception of morally responsible action than is advocated by Friedman. In defence of his wider conception, Michalos answers 14 different arguments which have at one time or other been advanced against the sort of conception he favours. Some of these objections are clearly Friedman's, or at least derivative of Friedman's main theses. It will be worthwhile to consider how Friedman might respond to Michalos's challenge, and whether there are other viable conceptions of morally responsible business activity in addition to the ones these two writers defend. For instance, should an acceptable theory of moral responsibility in business recognize the importance of the fiduciary duties

upon which Friedman lays so much stress, but insist, along with W.D. Ross, that those duties are *prima facie only*? If they are only *prima facie*, then the possibility arises of competing duties, say of non-maleficence and possibly even beneficence, which compete with and sometimes override the fiduciary duties. For those inclined, along with Michalos, towards a monistic, utilitarian conception, perhaps room must be made for Friedman's "ground rules" within the utilitarian framework, along the same lines as utilitarian accounts of the binding quality of promises and other special commitments.

Leonard J. Brooks offers an article that deals with specific Canadian directions in business ethics. He examines the factors and the key individuals that have shaped business ethics in Canadian corporations. It is Brooks's position that the absence of national institutional frameworks, such as those which exist in the United States, has resulted in the evolution of Canadian business ethics in response to broader socio-political and economic forces.

Brooks's article is followed by a thoughtful piece by Sir Adrian Cadbury, chairperson of Cadbury Schweppes PLC. Sir Adrian's comments are especially pertinent given their source. Some think that pious talk of ethics is simply out of place in the real business world where managers have neither the time, nor the ability, nor the inclination to take ethics seriously. Yet as Cadbury makes plain, "Business is part of the social system and [business people] cannot isolate the economic elements of major decisions from their social consequences." If Cadbury is right, those who take this advice to heart will profit for having done so, both in terms of moral integrity *and* the bottom line.

Our last article provides a theoretical framework based upon empirical evidence on the status of ethical behaviour in Canadian companies. This study provides an interesting examination of the status of explicit mechanisms to instill ethical behaviours in 171 Canadian companies.

THE SOCIAL RESPONSIBILITY OF BUSINESS IS TO INCREASE ITS PROFITS

Milton Friedman

When I hear businessmen speak eloquently about the "social responsibilities of business in a free-enterprise system," I am reminded of the wonderful line about the Frenchman who discovered at the age of 70 that he had been speaking prose all his life. The businessmen believe that they are defending free enterprise when they declaim that business is not concerned "merely" with profit but also with promoting desirable "social" ends; that business has a "social conscience" and takes seriously its responsibilities for providing employment, eliminating discrimination, avoiding pollution and whatever else may be the catchwords of the contemporary crop of reformers. In fact they are—or would be if they or anyone else took them seriously—preaching pure and unadulterated socialism. Businessmen who talk this way are unwitting puppets of the intellectual forces that have been undermining the basis of a free society these past decades.

The discussions of the "social responsibilities of business" are notable for their analytical looseness and lack of rigor. What does it mean to say that "business" has responsibilities? Only people can have responsibilities. A corporation is an artificial person and in this sense may have artificial responsibilities, but "business" as a whole cannot be said to have responsibilities, even in this vague sense. The first step toward clarity in examining the doctrine of the social responsibility of business is to ask precisely what it implies for whom.

Presumably, the individuals who are to be responsible are businessmen, which means individual proprietors or corporate executives. Most of the discussion of social responsibility is directed at corporations, so in what follows I shall mostly neglect the individual proprietor and speak of corporate executives.

In a free-enterprise, private-property system a corporate executive is an employee of the owners of the business. He has direct responsibility to his employers. That responsibility is to conduct the business in accordance with their desires, which generally will be to make as much money as possible while conforming to the basic rules of the society, both those embodied in law and those embodied in ethical custom. Of course, in some cases his employers may have a different objective. A group of persons might establish a corporation for an eleemosynary purpose—for example, a hospital or school. The manager of such a corporation will not have money profit as his objective, but the rendering of certain services.

In either case, the key point is that, in his capacity as a corporate executive, the manager is the agent of the individuals who own the corporation or establish the eleemosynary institution, and his primary responsibility is to them.

Needless to say, this does not mean that it is easy to judge how well he is performing his task. But at least the criterion of performance is straightforward, and the persons among whom a voluntary contractual arrangement exists are clearly defined.

Of course, the corporate executive is also a person in his own right. As a person, he may have many other responsibilities that he recognizes or assumes voluntarily—to his family, his conscience, his feelings of charity, his church, his clubs, his city, his country. He may feel impelled by these responsibilities to devote part of his income to causes he regards as worthy, to refuse to work for particular corporations, and even to leave his job, for example, to join his country's armed forces. If we wish, we may refer to some of these responsibilities as "social responsibilities." But in these respects he is acting as a principal, not an agent; he is spending his own money or time or energy, not the money of his employers or the time or energy he has contracted to devote to their purposes. If these are "social responsibilities," they are the social responsibilities of individuals, not of business.

What does it mean to say that the corporate executive has a "social responsibility" in his capacity as businessman? If this statement is not pure rhetoric, it must mean that he is to act in some way that is not in the interest of his employers. For example, that he is to refrain from increasing the price of the product in order to contribute to the social objective of preventing inflation, even though a price increase would be in the best interests of the corporation. Or that he is to make expenditures on reducing pollution beyond the amount that is in the best interests of the corporation or that is required by law in order to contribute to the social objective of improving the environment. Or that, at the expense of corporate profits, he is to hire "hard-core" unemployed instead of better-qualified available workmen to contribute to the social objective of reducing poverty.

In each of these cases, the corporate executive would be spending someone else's money for a general social interest. Insofar as his actions in accord with his "social responsibility" reduce returns of stockholders, he is spending their money. Insofar as his actions raise the price to customers, he is spending the customers' money. Insofar as his actions lower the wages of some employees, he is spending their money.

The stockholders or the customers or the employees could separately spend their own money on the particular action if they wished to do so. The executive is exercising a distinct "social responsibility," rather than serving as an agent of the stockholders or the customers or the employees, only if he spends the money in a different way than they would have spent it.

But if he does this, he is in effect imposing taxes, on the one hand, and deciding how the tax proceeds shall be spent, on the other.

This process raises political questions on two levels: principle and consequences. On the level of political principle, the imposition of taxes and the expenditure of tax proceeds are governmental functions. We have established elaborate constitutional, parliamentary and judicial provisions to control these functions, to assure that taxes are imposed so far as possible in accordance with the preferences and desires of the public—after all, "taxation without representation" was one of the battle cries of the American Revolution. We have a system of checks and balances to separate the legislative function of imposing taxes and enacting expenditures from the executive function of collecting taxes and administering expenditure programs and from the judicial function of mediating disputes and interpreting the law.

Here the businessman—self-selected or appointed directly or indirectly by stockholders—is to be simultaneously legislator, executive and jurist. He is to decide whom to tax by how much and for what purpose, and he is to spend the proceeds—all this guided only by general exhortations from on high to restrain inflation, improve the environment, fight poverty and so on and on.

The whole justification for permitting the corporate executive to be selected by the stockholders is that the executive is an agent serving the interests of his principal. This justification disappears when the corporate executive imposes taxes and spends the proceeds for "social" purposes. He becomes in effect a public employee, a civil servant, even though he remains in name an employee of a private enterprise. On grounds of political principle, it is intolerable that such civil servants—insofar as their actions in the name of social responsibility are real and not just window-dressing—should be selected as they are now. If they are to be civil servants, then they must be selected through a political process. If they are to impose taxes and make expenditures to foster "social" objectives, then political machinery must be set up to guide the assessment of taxes and to determine through a political process the objectives to be served.

This is the basic reason why the doctrine of "social responsibility" involves the ac-

ceptance of the socialist view that political mechanisms, not market mechanisms, are the appropriate way to determine the allocation of scarce resources to alternative uses.

On the grounds of consequences, can the corporate executive in fact discharge his alleged "social responsibilities"? On the one hand, suppose he could get away with spending the stockholders' or customers' or employees' money. How is he to know how to spent it? He is told that he must contribute to fighting inflation. How is he to know what action of his will contribute to that end? He is presumably an expert in running his company—in producing a product or selling it or financing it. But nothing about his selection makes him an expert on inflation. Will his holding down the price of his product reduce inflationary pressure? Or, by leaving more spending power in the hands of his customers, simply divert it elsewhere? Or, by forcing him to produce less because of the lower price, will it simply contribute to shortages? Even if he could answer these questions, how much cost is he justified in imposing on his stockholders, customers and employees for this social purpose? What is his appropriate share of others'?

And, whether he wants to or not, can he get away with spending his stockholders', customers' or employees' money? Will not the stockholders fire him? (Either the present one or those who take over when his actions in the name of social responsibility have reduced the corporation's profits and the price of its stock.) His customers and his employees can desert him for other products and employers less scrupulous in exercising their social responsibilities.

This facet of "social responsibility" doctrine is brought into sharp relief when the doctrine is used to justify wage restraint by trade unions. The conflict of interest is naked and clear when union officials are asked to subordinate the interest of their members to some more general social purpose. If the union officials try to enforce wage restraint, the consequence is likely to be wildcat strikes, rank-and-file revolts and the emergence of strong competitors for their jobs. We thus have the ironic phenomenon that union leaders—at least in the U.S.—have objected to Government interference with the market far more consistently and courageously than have business leaders.

The difficulty of exercising "social responsibility" illustrates, of course, the great virtue of private competitive enterprise—it forces people to be responsible for their own actions and makes it difficult for them to "exploit" other people for either selfish or unselfish purposes. They can do good—but only at their own expense.

Many a reader who has followed the argument this far may be tempted to remonstrate that it is all well and good to speak of [G]overnment's having the responsibility to impose taxes and determine expenditures for such "social" purposes as controlling pollution or training the hard-core unemployed, but that the problems are too urgent to wait on the slow course of political processes, that the exercise of social responsibility by businessmen is a quicker and surer way to solve pressing current problems.

Aside from the question of fact—I share Adam Smith's skepticism about the benefits that can be expected from "those who affected to trade for the public good"—this argument must be rejected on grounds of principle. What it amounts to is an assertion that those who favor the taxes and expenditures in question have failed to persuade a majority of their fellow citizens to be of like mind and that they are seeking to attain by undemocratic procedures what they cannot attain by democratic procedures. In a free society, it is hard for "good" people to do "good," but that is a small price to pay for making it hard for "evil" people to do "evil," especially since one man's good is another's evil.

I have, for simplicity, concentrated on the special case of the corporate executive, except for the brief digression on trade unions. But precisely the same argument applies to the newer phenomenon of calling upon stockholders to require corporations to exercise social responsibility (the recent G.M. crusade, for example). In most of these cases, what is in effect involved is some stockholders trying to get another stockholder (or customers or employees) to contribute against their will to "social" causes favored by the activists. Insofar as they succeed, they are again imposing taxes and spending the proceeds.

The situation of the individual proprietor is somewhat different. If he acts to reduce returns of his enterprise in order to exercise his "social responsibility," he is spending his own money, not someone else's. If he wishes to spend his money on such purposes, that is his right, and I cannot see that there is any objection to his doing so. In the process, he, too, may impose costs on employers and customers. However, because is far less likely than a large corporation or union to have monopolistic power, any such side effects will tend to be minor.

Of course, in practice the doctrine of social responsibility is frequently a cloak for actions that are justified on other grounds rather than a reason for those actions.

To illustrate, it may well be in the long-run interest of a corporation that is a major employer in a small community to devote resources to providing amenities to that community or to improving its government. That may make it easier to attract desirable employees, it may reduce the wage bill or lessen losses from pilferage and sabotage or have other worthwhile effects. Or it may be that, given the laws about the deductibility of corporate charitable contributions, the stockholders can contribute more to charities they favor by having the corporation make the gift than by doing it themselves, since they can in that way contribute an amount that would otherwise have been paid as corporate taxes.

In each of these—and many similar—cases, there is a strong temptation to rationalize these actions as an exercise of "social responsibility." In the present climate of opinion, with its widespread aversion to "capitalism," "profits," "the soulless corporation" and so on, this is one way for a corporation to generate goodwill as a by-product of expenditures that are entirely justified in its own self-interest.

It would be inconsistent of me to call on corporate executives to refrain from this hypocritical window-dressing because it harms the foundations of a free society. That would be to call on them to exercise a "social responsibility"! If our institutions, and the attitudes of the public make it in their self-interest to cloak their actions in this way, I cannot summon much indignation to denounce them. At the same time, I can express admiration for those individual proprietors or owners of closely held corporations who disdain such tactics as approaching fraud.

Whether blameworthy or not, the use of the cloak of social responsibility, and the nonsense spoken in its name by influential and prestigious businessmen, does clearly harm the foundations of a free society. I have been impressed time and again by the schizophrenic character of many businessmen. They are capable of being extremely far-sighted and clear-headed in matters that are internal to their businesses. They are incredibly short-sighted and muddle-headed in matters that are outside their businesses but affect the possible survival of business in general. This short-sightedness is strikingly exemplified in the calls from many businessmen for wage and price guidelines or controls on income policies. There is nothing that could do more in a brief period to destroy a market system and replace it by a centrally controlled system than effective governmental control of prices and wages.

The short-sightedness is also exemplified in speeches by businessmen on social responsibility. This may gain them kudos in the short run. But it helps to strengthen the already too prevalent view that the pursuit of profits is wicked and immoral and must be curbed and controlled by external forces.

Once this view is adopted, the external forces that curb the market will not be the social consciences, however highly developed, of the pontificating executives; it will be the iron fist of Government bureaucrats. Here, as with price and wage controls, businessmen seem to me to reveal a suicidal impulse.

The political principle that underlies the market mechanism is unanimity. In an ideal free market resting on private property, no individual can coerce any other, all cooperation is voluntary, all parties to such cooperation benefit or they need not participate. There are no "social" values, no "social" responsibilities in any sense other than the shared values and responsibilities of individuals. Society is a collection of individuals and of the various groups they voluntarily form.

The political principle that underlies the political mechanism is conformity. The individual must serve a more general social interest—whether that be determined by a church or a dictator or a majority. The individual may have a vote and a say in what is to be done, but if he is overruled, he must conform. It is appropriate for some to require others to contribute to a general social purpose whether they wish to or not.

Unfortunately, unanimity is not always feasible. There are some respects in which conformity appears unavoidable, so I do not see how one can avoid the use of the political mechanism altogether.

But the doctrine of "social responsibility" taken seriously would extend the scope of the political mechanism to every human activity. It does not differ in philosophy from the most explicitly collectivist means. That is why, in my book *Capitalism and Freedom*, I have called it a "fundamentally subversive doctrine" in a free society, and have said that in such a society, "there is one and only one social responsibility of business—to use its resources and engage in activities designed to increase its profits so long as it stays within the rules of the game, which is to say, engages in open and free competition without deception or fraud."

A CRITIQUE OF MILTON FRIEDMAN'S ESSAY "THE SOCIAL RESPONSIBILITY OF BUSINESS IS TO INCREASE ITS PROFITS"

Thomas Mulligan

In his famous essay, Milton Friedman argues that people responsible for decisions and action in business should not exercise social responsibility in their capacity as company executives. Instead, they should concentrate on increasing the profits of their companies.[1]

In the course of the essay, he also argues that the doctrine of social responsibility is a socialist doctrine.

The purpose of this paper is to assess the merit of Friedman's arguments. I shall summarize his main arguments, examine some of his premises and lines of inference, and propose a counter-argument.

FRIEDMAN'S ARGUMENT: CORPORATE EXECUTIVES SHOULD NOT EXERCISE SOCIAL RESPONSIBILITY

Friedman argues that the exercise of social responsibility by a corporate executive is:

(a) unfair, because it constitutes taxation without representation;

(b) undemocratic, because it invests governmental power in a person who has no general mandate to govern;

(c) unwise, because there are no checks and balances in the broad range of governmental power thereby turned over to his discretion;

(d) a violation of trust, because the executive is employed by the owners "as an agent serving the interests of his principal";

(e) futile, both because the executive is unlikely to be able to anticipate the social consequences of his actions and because, as he imposes costs on his stockholders, customers, or employees, he is likely to lose their support and thereby lose his power.

These conclusions are related.

Points (b) and (c) depend on (a), on the ground that "the imposition of taxes and the

From *Journal of Business Ethics* 5 (1986) 265–269. © 1986 by D. Reidel Publishing Company. Reprinted by permission expenditure of tax proceeds are governmental functions." Point (d) also depends on (a), because it is precisely in imposing a tax on his principal that this executive fails to serve the interests of that principal. Point (e) depends, in part, on (d), since it is the executive's failure to serve the interests of his principal which results in the withdrawal of that principal's support.

Point (a) is thus at the foundation of the argument. If (a) is false, then Friedman's demonstration of the subsequent conclusions almost completely collapses.

Is it true, then, that the executive who performs socially responsible action "is in effect imposing taxes . . . and deciding how the tax proceeds shall be spent?"

To make this case, Friedman argues by depicting how a company executive would perform such action.

He first introduces examples to illustrate that exercising social responsibility in business typically costs money. He mentions refraining from a price increase to help prevent inflation, reducing pollution "beyond the amount that is in the best interests of the corporation" to help improve the environment, and "at the expense of corporate profits" hiring 'hardcore' unemployed.

To establish that such costs are in effect taxes, he argues:

1. In taking such action, the executive expends "someone else's money"—the stockholders', the customers', or the employees'.

2. The money is spent "for a general social interest."

3. "Rather than serving as an agent for the stockholders or the customers or the employees . . . he spends the money in a different way than they would have spent it."

The first two premises suggest a similarity between this money and tax revenues, with respect to their sources and to the purposes for which they are used. However, an expense is not yet a tax unless it is *imposed* on the contributor, irrespective of his desire to pay. Only Friedman's third premise includes this crucial element of imposition.

This third premise reveals the essential character of the paradigm on which Friedman bases his whole case.

FRIEDMAN'S PARADIGM

In the above examples of socially responsible action and throughout his essay, Friedman depicts the corporate executive who performs such action as a sort of Lone Ranger, deciding entirely by himself what good deeds to do, when to act, how much to spend:

> Here, the businessman—self-selected or appointed directly or indirectly by the stockholders—is to be simultaneously legislator, executive and jurist. He is to decide whom to tax by how much and for what purpose.

On this paradigm, the corporate executive does not act with the counsel and participation of the other stakeholders in the business. This is the basis of Friedman's claim that the executive is *imposing* something on those other stakeholders—unfairly, undemocratically, unwisely, and in violation of a trust.

But does Friedman's paradigm accurately depict the socially responsible executive? Does it capture the essential nature of socially responsible action in business? Or has he drawn a caricature, wrongly construed it as accurate, and used it to discredit the doctrine it purportedly illustrates?

A COUNTER-PARADIGM

Friedman's paradigm is valid in the sense that it is certainly possible for a corporate executive to try to exercise social responsibility without the counsel or participation of the other stakeholders in the business.

Friedman is also correct in characterizing such conduct as unfair and as likely to result in the withdrawal of the support of those other stakeholders.

Yet Friedman insists, at least with respect to the executive's employers, that the socially responsible executive "must" do it alone, must act in opposition to the interests of the other stakeholders:

> What does it mean to say that the corporate executive has a "social responsibility" in his capacity as a businessman? If this statement is not pure rhetoric, it must mean that he is to act in some way that is not in the interest of his employers.

There is no good reason why this remarkable claim must be true. The exercise of social responsibility in business suffers no diminishment in meaning or merit if the executive and his employers both understand their mutual interest to include a proactive social role and cooperate in undertaking that role.

I propose a different paradigm for the exercise of social responsibility in business—one very much in keeping with sound management practice.

A business normally defines its course and commits itself to action by conceiving a mission, then proceeding to a set of objectives, then determining quantified and time-bound goals, and then developing a full strategic plan which is implemented by appropriate top-level staffing, operating procedures, budgeted expenditures, and daily management control.

Many stakeholders in the business participate in this far-reaching process.

Founders, board members, major stockholders, and senior executives may all participate in defining a mission and in setting objectives based on that mission. In so doing, these people serve as "legislators" for the company.

Top management's translation of these broad directions into goals, strategic plans, operating procedures, budgets, and daily work direction brings middle management, first-line management and, in some companies, employee representatives into the process. This is the "executive branch" of the business.

When the time comes to judge progress and success, the board members and stockholders serve as "jurists" at the highest level, and when necessary can take decisive, sometimes dramatic, corrective measures. However, the grass-roots judgment of the court of employee opinion can also be a powerful force. More than one company has failed or faltered because it did not keep a course which inspired and held its talented people.

In sum, a business is a collaborative enterprise among the stakeholders, with some checks and balances. In general, this system allows to any one stakeholder a degree of participation commensurate with the size of his or her stake.

For a business to define a socially responsible course and commit to socially responsible action, it needs to follow no other process than the familiar one described in the preceding paragraphs.

On this paradigm, if socially responsible action is on the corporate executive's agenda, then it is there because the company's mission, objectives, and goals—developed collaboratively by the major stakeholders—gave him license to put it there and provide parameters for his program. Lone Ranger executives are no more necessary and no more welcome in socially responsible business than in one devoted exclusively to the maximization of profit.

This paradigm conforms more accurately than Friedman's to the reality of how action programs—socially responsible ones or otherwise—are conceived and enacted in a strategically managed business. The corporate executive in this process, in contradistinction to Friedman's corporate executive, does not impose unauthorized costs, or "taxes," on anyone. On this account, he usurps no governmental function, violates no trust, and runs no special risk of losing the support of the other stakeholders.

THE PROBLEM OF KNOWING FUTURE CONSEQUENCES

The preceding argument addresses most of Friedman's objections to a corporate executive's attempts to exercise social responsibility.

Friedman, however, provides one objection which does not rest on his paradigm of the Lone Ranger executive. This is the objection that it is futile to attempt socially responsible action because the future social consequences of today's actions are very difficult to know.

Suppose, he writes, that the executive decides to fight inflation:

> How is he to know what action of his will contribute to that end? He is presumably an expert in running his company—in producing a product or selling it or financing it. But nothing about his selection makes him an expert on inflation. Will holding down the price of his product reduce inflationary pressure? Or, by leaving more spending power in the hands of his customers, simply divert it elsewhere? Or by forcing him to produce less because of the lower price, will it simply contribute to shortages?

The difficulty of determining the future consequences of one's intended good acts has received attention in the literature of philosophical ethics. G.E. Moore in his early twentieth century classic *Principia Ethica*, writes of "the hopeless task of finding duties"[2] since, to act with perfect certainty, we would need to know "all the events which will be in any way affected by our action throughout an infinite future."[3]

Human life, however, requires action in the absence of certainty, and business people in particular have a bias toward action. They do not wait for perfect foreknowledge of consequences, but instead set a decision date, gather the best information available, contemplate alternatives, assess risks, and then decide what to do.

Decisions about socially responsible actions, no less than decisions about new products or marketing campaigns, can be made using this "business-like" approach. The business person, therefore, has even less cause than most moral agents to abstain from social responsibility out of a sense of the futility of knowing consequences, since he is more practiced than most in the techniques for making action decisions in the absence of certainty.

SOCIAL RESPONSIBILITY AND SOCIALISM

Some of Friedman's most emphatic language is devoted to his position that the advocates of social responsibility in a free-enterprise system are "preaching pure and unadulterated socialism."

He asserts this view in the first and last paragraph of the essay, and concludes:

> The doctrine of "social responsibility" . . . does not differ in philosophy from the most explicitly collectivist doctrine.

Friedman's argument for this conclusion is located roughly midway through this essay, and it too rests on his paradigm of the socially responsible executive "imposing taxes" on others and thereby assuming governmental functions:

> He becomes in effect a public employee, a civil servant. . . . It is intolerable that such civil servants . . . should be selected as they are now. If they are to be civil servants, then they must be elected through a political process. If they are to impose taxes and make expenditures to foster "social" objectives, then political machinery must be set up to make the assessment of taxes and to determine through a political process the objectives to be served.

This is the basic reason why the doctrine of "social responsibility" involves the acceptance of the socialist view that political mechanisms, not market mechanisms, are the appropriate way to determine the allocation of scarce resources or alternative uses.

I shall raise three objections to this line of reasoning.

First, this argument rests on the paradigm which has already been called into question. If we accept the counter-paradigm proposed above as truer to the nature of a socially responsible corporate executive, then there is no basis for saying that such an individual "imposes taxes," becoming "in effect" a civil servant.

Second, it is not apparent how the propositions that, under the doctrine of social responsibility, a corporate executive is "in effect" imposing taxes and "in effect" a civil servant logically imply that this doctrine upholds the view that political mechanisms should determine the allocation of scarce resources.

To the contrary, as Friedman points out, his paradigmatic executive is not a true political entity, since he is not elected and since his program of "taxation" and social expenditure is not implemented through a political process. Paradoxically, it is Friedman who finds it "intolerable" that this agent who allocates scarce resources is not part of a political mechanism. Nowhere, however, does he show that acceptance of such a political mechanism is intrinsic to the view of his opponent, the advocate of social responsibility.

Third, in order to show that the doctrine of social responsibility is a socialist doctrine, Friedman must invoke a criterion for what constitutes socialism. As we have seen, his criterion is "acceptance of the . . . view that political mechanisms, not market mechanisms, are the appropriate way to determine the allocation of scarce resources to alternative uses."

The doctrine of social responsibility, he holds, does accept this view. Therefore the doctrine is a socialist doctrine.[4]

However, this criterion is hardly definitive of socialism. The criterion is so broad that it holds for virtually any politically totalitarian or authoritarian system—including feudal monarchies and dictatorships of the political right.

Further, depending on the nature of a resource and the degree of its scarcity, the political leadership in any system, including American democracy, is liable to assert its right to determine the allocation of that resource. Who doubts that it is appropriate for our political institutions, rather than market mechanisms, to ensure the equitable availability of breathable air and drinkable water or to allocate food and fuel in times of war and critical shortages?

Therefore, Friedman has not provided a necessary element for his argument—a definitive criterion for what constitutes socialism.

In summary, Friedman's argument is unsound: first, because it rests on an arbitrary and suspect paradigm; second, because certain of his premises do not imply their stated conclusion; and, third, because a crucial premise, his criterion for what constitutes socialism, is not true.

Although he complains of the "analytical looseness" and "lack of rigor" of his opponents, Friedman's argument has on close examination betrayed its own instances of looseness and lack of rigor.

CONCLUSION

I have considered Friedman's principal objections to socially responsible action in business and argued that at the bottom of most of his objections is an inaccurate paradigm. In response, I have given an account of a more appropriate paradigm to show how business can exercise social responsibility.

Friedman is right in pointing out that exercising social responsibility costs money. If nothing else, a company incurs expense when it invests the manhours needed to contemplate the possible social consequences of alternative actions and to consider the merit or demerit of each set of consequences.

But Friedman is wrong in holding that such costs must be imposed by one business stakeholder on the others, outside of the whole collaborative process of strategic and operational business management. He presumes too much in intimating through his imagined examples that the business person who pursues a socially responsible course inevitably acts without due attention to return on investment, budgetary limitations, reasonable employee remuneration, or competitive pricing.

My purpose has been to provide a critique of the major lines of argument presented in a famous and influential essay. The thrust has been to show that Friedman misrepresents the nature of socially responsibility in business and that business people *can* pursue a social[ly] responsible course without the objectionable results claimed by Friedman. It would be another step to produce positive arguments to demonstrate why business people *should* pursue such a course. That is an undertaking for another occasion.

For now, I shall only observe that Friedman's own concluding statement contains a moral exhortation to business people. Business, he says, should engage in "open and free competition without deception or fraud." If Friedman does not recognize that even these restrained words lay open a broad range of moral obligation and social responsibility for business, which is after all one of the largest areas of human interaction in our society, then the oversight is his.

ENDNOTES

1. Milton Friedman, "The Social Responsibility of Business Is to Increase Its Profits," *New York Times Magazine*, 13 September 1970, p. 32 ff. Unless otherwise noted, all quotations are from this essay. (See this text, p. 43.)

2. G.E. Moore, *Principia Ethica* (London: Cambridge University Press, 1971), p. 150.

3. *Ibid.*, p. 149.

4. In the concluding paragraph of his essay, Friedman states, "The doctrine of 'social responsibility' taken seriously would extend the scope of the political mechanism to every human activity." "Every human activity" certainly seems at least one extra step beyond the set of activities involved in "the allocation of scarce resources to alternative uses." Unfortunately, Friedman's essay contains no explication of the reasoning he used to make the transition from the language of his argument midway through the essay to the grander claim of this concluding paragraph.

MORAL RESPONSIBILITY IN BUSINESS,

OR FOURTEEN UNSUCCESSFUL WAYS TO PASS THE BUCK

Alex C. Michalos

INTRODUCTION

In the Middle Ages, philosophic essays had a standard form. An author would begin by stating a thesis to be proved. Then arguments opposed to that thesis would be presented and systematically demolished. Following the demolition, the author would present arguments in favour of the thesis. If all went according to plan, nothing further could be done. There would be no good reasons left supporting the other side, and only good reasons left supporting the author's thesis. It's a tedious process to be sure, but effective. By the time one reaches the end, one is pretty sure of one's conclusion.

This is not the Middle Ages, so I am not going to provide that sort of analysis. Instead, I am going to undertake the first half only. My thesis is that businesspeople should be morally responsible agents *as* businesspeople. In other words, my thesis is that businesspeople ought to be morally responsible agents not merely in their role as

citizens of a moral community, but in their role as people engaged in competitive enterprise. My strategy of defence will be to present apparently plausible arguments opposed to my thesis, and to show that these arguments are defective. If I am successful, you will be persuaded that, so far as we know, there are no good reasons to deny or reject my thesis. I leave it to another occasion to persuade you that there are, in addition, good reasons to accept it.

Before I get to those defective arguments, however, let me clarify some terminology.

Complementary versus Contrary Terms

The words "moral" and "ethical" in English are ambiguous insofar as they may be used merely to designate classifications or to designate evaluations. So it will be useful to eliminate this ambiguity. First, it is necessary to distinguish complementary from contrary terms. *Complementary terms* are used to divide the world, the whole world, into two mutually exclusive and exhaustive classes. For example, everything in the world is a competitor or a non-competitor, a horse or a non-horse, a banana or a non-banana. Quite generally, take any word at all and then put a "non" in front of it, and you have a pair of complementary terms. Thus, whatever "moral" and "ethical" mean, one may divide the whole world into things that are moral and nonmoral, or ethical and nonethical. To say that actions are moral or nonmoral, when these words are used as complementary terms, is not necessarily to make a moral appraisal of those actions; it is, or may be, merely to classify the actions prior to a moral evaluation. To perform the latter task, one would make use of contrary terms.

Contrary terms are used to divide only a part of the world into mutually exclusive and exhaustive classes. For example, within the subset of the world known as competitors, there are winners and losers. All competitors are winners or losers. Similarly, within the subset of actions appraised from a moral point of view, there are morally good and morally bad (evil) actions. Unfortunately, in English one may use the words "moral" and "ethical" alone as abbreviations of "morally good" and "ethically good," respectively. In such cases, the words are used as contrary terms and their opposites are "morally bad" and "ethically bad," respectively, or simply "bad." Thus, in the next section when social are distinguished from moral responsibilities, it is the complementary or classificatory sense of the word "moral" that is intended. The distinction is not between morally good and bad responsibilities, but between moral responsibilities and nonmoral responsibilities.

Social versus Moral Responsibilities

In most of the literature on business ethics, people refer to social responsibilities and

contrast them with other kinds of responsibilities. In virtually all cases, the phrase "social responsibilities" is used to designate what are really "moral responsibilities," roughly as these will be defined shortly. The issues typically discussed under the rubric of "social responsibilities" are usually not merely matters of good manners or etiquette, but of something much more serious. So, it will be useful to clarify this distinction.

Roughly speaking, one may say that human action is socially responsible insofar as it does not violate any rules of etiquette, good manners, good taste or generally accepted social practice. Examples of socially responsible behaviour include such things as thanking people for gifts received, arriving at and leaving parties at suitable times, answering letters or other messages requesting acknowledgement, and so on. Socially responsible action is necessary for human community, and in one way or another appropriate criteria of evaluation and sanctions for irresponsible action are routinely developed in all societies.

There are at least two ways to identify morally responsible action, a narrow way and a broad way. Narrowly speaking, one may say that human action is morally responsible, or simply moral, insofar as it does not violate any generally accepted moral maxims. Examples of moral maxims include such things as "One should not steal," "One should always tell the truth," and "One should avoid harming innocent people." Broadly speaking, one may say that human action is morally responsible or moral insofar as it is reasonably intended to impartially maximize human well-being. Since the actual consequences of action often involve unexpected, unintended and uncontrollable elements, one cannot require the actual maximization of well-being with every action of every agent every moment of every day. Instead, one requires a reasonable amount of attention to the likely consequences of one's action, a reasonable amount of care with one's performance and a relatively clear intention to act so as to produce a fairly specific sort of result. In particular, one should intend and try to act so that everyone affected by one's actions is affected in an even-handed, unbiased, impartial or a similar way unless there are good reasons for affecting some people in different ways.

Perhaps the easiest and most morally neutral way to understand the terms "impartial," "even-handed" and "unbiased" in the preceding sentence is probabilistically. That is, these terms should be understood as indicating that one is intending and trying to act such that every person affected by one's action has the same probability or chance of being affected in roughly the same way. More precisely, one is trying to give every affected person both an equal probability and as high a probability as possible (consistent with the former) to maximize their well-being. Since there is a generally accepted formal principle of justice that demands that similar people and similar actions should be treated in similar ways unless there are good reasons for treating them in different ways, the broad criterion of morally responsible action includes a condition of justice. Thus, on this broad account of moral action, one who acts morally must also act justly to some extent. It is not clear (to me at least) that morality and justice are entirely coextensive domains, but there is some overlap.

Clearly, what I have called the narrow and broad ways to identify morally responsible action might not define exactly the same set of actions. What's more, this might not be merely the result of a semantic disagreement or the fact that people have just never gotten around to articulating all the moral maxims they implicitly accept. On the contrary, the narrow and broad ways to identify morally responsible action might be based on significantly different views of what is required for such action. In particular, some people might believe that no one is ever morally required to try to maximize

anyone's well-being. They might say that morality is essentially concerned with trying to prevent certain kinds of harm from certain kinds of people, and that while universal beneficence is praiseworthy, it cannot be morally required. In short, they might say such beneficence is appropriate for saints or those who aspire to sainthood, but it has no essential role to play in the morality of ordinary people.

There is no rule book to consult now in order to decide whether a reasonable and morally good person should adopt the narrow or broad way to identify morally responsible action. In fact, I prefer the broad way because I think a world populated by people holding such a view would be a better place to live in than a world populated by people holding the other view, all things considered. In other words, I think a world populated by people motivated by universal beneficence would be better than one motivated merely by a desire to prevent certain harms. Moreover, since morality is to some extent always a matter of aspiration rather than achievement and the latter may easily be constrained by limitations in the former, I think wisdom is on the side of taking a broad view of morally responsible action.

Moral Maxims versus Moral Theories

It will be worthwhile to draw one other fundamental distinction before proceeding to the main part of my story. I have already referred to moral maxims such as "One should tell the truth," "One should not steal," and so on. In all countries around the world maxims of this kind are recommended. Students are sometimes shocked by this assertion, for they often have the mistaken belief that in some far-off places radically different maxims are accepted. Of course there are *some* contradictory moral maxims recommended in different countries, e.g., that women should or should not have to cover their faces, or that men should or should not be allowed to have more than one wife. However, that is entirely consistent with my claim that there are some universally accepted maxims. To take the simplest example just to prove my point: around the world it is universally accepted that it is morally wrong to kill innocent babies for pleasure. Such actions, including the particular motive mentioned, are always condemned. Furthermore, there are no societies in which a contradictory maxim would be recommended. That is, there are no societies (and I would be willing to bet there never have been any) in which the following maxim is part of their moral codes: "It is morally right to kill innocent babies for pleasure" or, briefly, "One ought to kill innocent babies for pleasure."

Although there is universal agreement about some moral maxims, there is no such agreement about the justification, reason or warrant for accepting these maxims. Much of moral philosophy is concerned with questions of justification. We want to explain why it is reasonable to accept some maxims and not others. As rational beings, we want to have good reasons, warrants, or justifications for accepting some maxims and rejecting others. In other words, we want our moral judgements to be well-grounded or well-supported rather than capricious, unprincipled or *ad hoc*. In short, we want to have our moral maxims derivable from moral theories. Just as any scientist wants to have generally acceptable theories to account for observable facts and law-like regularities, moral philosophers want to have generally acceptable moral theories to account for moral claims and maxims.

Moreover, just as all scientific theories are fallible and limited, so are all moral theories. In truth, there are few, if any, scientific theories that can claim the longevity of some moral theories, which also surprises some people. In particular, for better or worse, no scientific theory has lasted as long as the theory that moral maxims ought to be accepted because they are legislated by God. But longevity is beside the point here. The main point is that while there is some universal agreement about some moral maxims, there is no universal agreement about moral theories. Thus, it is obvious that whenever one is engaged in any moral controversy, it is a wise strategy to try to resolve issues at the level of moral maxims. If that is impossible and one must resort to higher-level moral theories, one is bound to encounter more problems. Again, as rational beings, we must have theories, and occasionally theoretical agreement is precisely what is required to solve some lower-level problems. But, to paraphrase a remark made by Martin Luther King Jr. concerning violence, when you resort to theories, the main issues tend to be theoretical, and practical questions of right and wrong may be swept aside.

Let's now examine in detail the 14 arguments already alluded to.

ARGUMENTS AND REPLIES

1. Adam Smith's Argument

Whether or not the 18th century economist endorsed exactly the following argument, it is often attributed to him and is generally consistent with his views. Simply stated, the argument is that if each person would pursue his or her own interests in a fairly enlightened way, then in the long run social well-being or welfare would be maximized. Moreover, people do seem to be naturally inclined to pursue their own interests rather than anyone else's. Therefore, it is pointless for businesspeople or anyone else to concern themselves with morally responsible action. In short, if people would do what comes naturally instead of trying to perform the relatively unnatural actions recommended by moralists, the very results that the latter desire would be achieved. Clearly then, the recommendations of the moralists are at best redundant.

Reply

The trouble with this argument is that its premises are empirically incorrect. If it is true that people are naturally inclined to pursue their own interests and it is also true that such activity will naturally maximize social well-being, then why has the latter not occurred? Presumably, a world that has recessions and depressions, unemployment, poverty and inefficiencies resulting from near-monopolies is not a world in which social well-being is being maximized. Moreover, it cannot plausibly be argued that we have not waited long enough to obtain the benefits of unbridled, universal, self-interested action, because virtually all of the restraints and remedial activities introduced into allegedly free markets have only been introduced when the destructiveness of unbridled self-interested action was obvious to everyone. For example, since self-interested monopolists would try to exploit everyone else (as long as that was perceived to be in their own interests), practically everyone has been willing to introduce anti-monopoly laws *a priori* into allegedly free-enterprise systems. What's more, empirical research has repeatedly shown that the closer one comes to monopolistic domination of a market (in food, cars, fuel, etc.), the more consumers are robbed through gross inefficiencies in production and inflated prices. Again, unemployment insurance was introduced only after it became clear that the unbridled avarice of some people would keep many other people without any adequate means of support. Similarly, social insurance systems were initiated only after it became clear that many old people, single-parent mothers and children would live and die in poverty unless the state intervened for them.

Instead of arguing that we have not waited long enough to obtain the benefits of unbridled self-interested action, one might argue, following Plato nearly four hundred years before Christ, that people don't always know what is really in their own interests. Whatever their natural inclinations might be, people tend to misperceive, misrepresent and generally make mistakes when they try to look out for themselves. In fact, one might add a heavy dose of stupidity to human avarice to account for the fact that things haven't turned out as Smith predicted. That, I suppose, is a bit extravagant. It's bad enough to have a theory that leads to false predictions. To suggest that one's theory leads to false predictions because most people are too stupid to make the most of their avarice really adds insult to injury. It would be simpler and wiser to just abandon the theory altogether.

2. Agnosticism Regarding Ends

A second argument that might be used to argue that businesspeople should not be concerned with morally responsible action involves agnosticism regarding the appropriate ends of such action. According to this view, no one knows exactly what goals, objectives, aims or ideal ends are really desirable for all the people in any society. Therefore, it is pointless at best and possibly dangerous, at worst, to try to get businesspeople (or anyone else, for that matter) to pursue such allegedly desirable ends.

Reply

Given the great variety of human interests, abilities and resources, as well as what the economist Frank Knight called the "perversity of folks," it is indeed unlikely that there are many ideal ends that are desirable for every person in every society. Fortunately, however, it is also irrelevant. Just as it would be silly to abandon rules of the road because some people can't tell their right hand from their left, it would be silly to abandon the pursuit of all ideals because some people can't benefit from their pursuit or realization. There are plenty of identifiable goals whose realization *would* be desirable for the vast majority of people in any society, i.e., there are plenty of socially and morally desirable goals. For example, most people would benefit from full employment, an equitable distribution of wealth and incomes, safety from environmental pollutants, the elimination of dangerous food additives and unsafe consumer durables (cars, toys, household appliances, etc.), universal and adequate health care and education, good housing and transportation, and equitable access to political power.

3. Agnosticism Regarding Means

Supposing it is granted that there are clearly identifiable socially and morally desirable ends to pursue, it might be argued that it is pointless and perhaps even dangerous to urge businesspeople to pursue them because no one knows exactly what any particular person, in particular circumstances, must do to achieve such ends. The road to hell is certainly paved with good intentions. Among those who believe that full employment is a desirable goal, for example, some seem to think the most efficient means of achieving this would involve government regulation only to prevent monopolies or obviously harmful activities; others think some government planning can be useful in the allocation of private resources and public resources; and some think total government control of all means of production is the best strategy. Again, according to some people, children are most likely to get an adequate education if schools are controlled by local communities, while others believe that because of the great disparities in local com-

munity resources, the best strategy involves some national intervention and contribution. Thus, in view of such controversies over the appropriate means to obtain recognized desirable ends, agnosticism is justifiable, for businesspeople as well as everyone else.

Reply

This argument proceeds from relatively reasonable premises to an unreasonable conclusion. From the facts of controversies and difficulties regarding the identification of optimal strategies to be used to pursue shared ends, it is concluded that total agnosticism is warranted. But if such agnosticism means the denial of any knowledge regarding appropriate means to obtain shared desirable ends, then the argument involves a *non sequitur*. It is plainly false that we know of no appropriate strategies to follow to try to realize our goals. In the case of the pursuit of full employment, for example, we know that it is useful in the first place for governments to obtain reliable and valid labour force statistics, including numbers of available workers by geographic region, age, sex, education, skill training and employment status. It is useful to have a thorough understanding of a nation's resource production and consumption, past, present and estimated future supplies and demands. In the third place it is useful to set relatively realistic employment targets and finally to experiment with a variety of tactics for hitting those targets. Of course, there will be controversies and difficulties in the pursuit of shared goals since all knowledge is fallible, all activities have some unintended consequences and very often the intended consequences of social engineering will not equally satisfy every affected person. Still, to grant all this is to grant nothing sufficient to warrant total agnosticism and abandonment of attempts to find optimally desirable means to obtain similar ends.

4. Absence of right

Roughly speaking, we may say that one has a right to something insofar as one has a special entitlement or claim to it which everyone else has a duty or obligation to recognize. Rights may be described as positive or negative, depending on whether people have a duty to provide things in someone else's interests, or merely to avoid doing some things or to prevent some things that would harm someone else from being done. For example, in Canada, children are supposed to have a positive right to at least a primary school education, which means that adults have an obligation to provide it. All people are supposed to have a negative right to life, which means, at a minimum, that all of us have a duty to avoid wantonly destroying other people's lives, or at a maximum, that all of us have a duty to prevent the wanton destruction of people's lives. Hence, in the interests of insuring that Canadians have these rights protected, we are taxed to pay for the operation of educational institutions, our systems of criminal justice punish people legally for intentionally taking people's lives, and in some instances we morally condemn people for failing to prevent such destruction.

A fourth argument leading to the conclusion that businesspeople should not be concerned with morally responsible action *as* businesspeople is based on the simple premise that businesspeople do not have a right to engage in such action. According to this view, there is nothing in the special role, expertise or character of such people that would give them such a right, and in any case few people outside the class would recognize any obligation to provide or prevent anything in the interest of protecting the alleged right.

The idea behind this argument is that businesspeople have certain roles to play and a certain kind of expertise which are relatively limited. To suppose or demand that an obligation to perform morally responsible action can or should be included in the definition of those roles, or in every sort of expertise is a mistake. Thus, for example, the business of selling shoes, insurance or cars can and should be defined without any appeal to moral responsibilities, and one may be a good shoe salesperson, insurance agent or car dealer without having anything to do with such responsibilities. On the contrary, one's responsibilities would include, say, knowledge of the different qualities of shoes, the requirements of different people for different shoe styles, the appropriate prices to pay to suppliers and to charge to consumers, and so on. These sorts of things, it would be said, cannot reasonably be expected to create rights to making moral decisions.

Reply

In response to this argument, it may be insisted that businesspeople *as* businesspeople certainly have a right to act rationally. This may be regarded as a positive right insofar as some education, training and socialization is a necessary condition of rational action, and initially someone (without specifying the particular agent) has to provide it. Indeed, it may be said that education, training and socialization must be provided precisely in the interest of protecting people's right to act rationally. Without some of the former, most human babies would not even survive to adulthood, since rational action is typically necessary for survival.

If it is granted that businesspeople have a right to act rationally, then it must be granted that they have a right to estimate all the consequences of their actions, as far as that is possible in different circumstances. Without such estimates, people could not assess the ratio of benefits achieved to costs expended. In other words, without such estimates, people couldn't determine if their actions were self-constructive or self-destructive, i.e., they couldn't assess the survival value of their actions. That ignorance, of course, should be resisted. Thus, it must be insisted that people have a right to estimate all the consequences of their actions, and that must include all the moral and immoral consequences of their actions too. Insofar as businesspeople are interested in performing rational actions, they must also have a right to perform them. Moreover, this implies a right to consider and perform morally responsible actions, since these also produce benefits and costs.

5. Level of Competence

Supposing it is granted that businesspeople have a right to perform morally responsible actions *as* businesspeople, it might still be argued that since they will have such low levels of competence regarding moral actions, they should not be encouraged to perform them. Given a society in which most people are relatively free to choose their occupations, it is likely that people who choose the world of business or competitive enterprise probably are more interested in engaging in the activities characteristic of this world than in those of its alternatives. Similarly, those who choose careers in government service, social work or, broadly speaking, in any of the "helping professions" (such as the ministry or priesthood, teaching, lawyers working in legal aid and public health personnel) probably are more interested in engaging in the activities characteristic of these occupations than in those of business. Clearly, the career interests of those in the helping professions are more compatible with those of moralists than the career interests of businesspeople. Moreover, it is likely that interest is usually a necessary condition of competence, since people are not likely to be or become good at doing things that they are not interested in doing. Thus, in fact the most competent people regarding morally responsible actions will probably be outside the world of business

and, therefore, these are the people who should be urged to perform such actions rather than businesspeople. The latter will almost certainly botch the job.

Reply

Those who use the preceding argument incorrectly assume that competence in performing morally responsible actions is an exclusive trait which people develop at the expense of other traits. On this view, becoming a morally responsible person is analogous to developing a special skill or becoming a specialist in a particular area of knowledge. Becoming a morally responsible person, on this view, is like becoming a good dentist or historian. It is simply another kind of specialization. On this view, if, for example, *Maclean's* or *Time* wanted to include reports of morally responsible actions, they would merely add another section. Besides their traditional sections on business, sports, books, international affairs, and so on, there would be a section on morality. Presumably, it would be a section reporting on who did what morally good or bad thing to whom, for what and with what interesting consequences.

If one adopts what I earlier called the narrow way to identify morally responsible actions, there is a strong tendency to think of morality in precisely this way, that is, as a specialized field with special interests, principles and practitioners. Then one is hardpressed to find good reasons for most people, who typically would not think of themselves as specialists in moral matters, to be interested in such matters. Short of striving to become some sort of new renaissance person or the local champion at *Trivial Pursuits* [sic] there would appear to be little motivation for most people to try to keep up with the news in yet another area of specialization. Might as well leave it to those who go in for that sort of thing.

As you might have expected, the unhappy scenario just described provided one of the motivating factors for my adoption of what I called the broad way of identifying morally responsible actions. With this view of such actions, there would be no special section of *Maclean's* devoted to morality because there is no such specialization. On this view, *any* action has moral significance insofar as it is appraised from a moral point of view. In other words, *any* action has moral significance insofar as it is assessed from the point of view of its being reasonably intended to impartially maximize human well-being. Thus, if, to continue my illustration, the editors of *Maclean's* wanted to include reports of morally responsible actions, they would not add any new reports or any new sections. Instead, they would merely appraise the actions routinely reported in their specialized sections from a moral point of view. Competence in making such appraisals is not, therefore, an exclusive trait of moral specialists. On the contrary, since such appraisals involve the most comprehensive review of any and every human action, urging people to adopt a moral point of view is tantamount to urging them to develop a uniquely inclusive trait. It is a habit of mind, a mental set or disposition to think of all actions from the point of view of their moral impact, which is thoroughly inclusive rather than exclusive.

6. Reduced Economic Efficiency

In the interest of trying to impartially maximize human well-being, one might fail to maximize profits. In that case, one would also fail to be economically maximally efficient. Insofar as one fails to be economically maximally efficient, one is being wasteful, since inefficiency simply means there is less output per unit of input than there could be. Thus, since wastefulness is inexcusable, it should not be allowed to occur for the sake of achieving other goals.

Reply

This objection represents the tip of an iceberg involving a variety of more or less controversial arguments concerning an alleged trade-off between the aims of economic efficiency and morality. In the fifth volume of my *North American Social Report* (D. Reidel, 1982), I presented nearly two dozen arguments that have been used by proponents of one side or the other. For present purposes, it is enough to report two main conclusions of that analysis. First, it is of course possible to imagine situations arising in which one would be faced with a choice between economic efficiency and morality. Second, given the distribution of wealth and income in Canada (and even more in the United States), it is highly probable that such choices do not arise. Since the richest 20 percent of Canadians own around 70 percent of the wealth, the other 80 percent of the population has to get along on the remaining 30 percent. Under these circumstances, it is virtually impossible for the wealthy fifth to actually use much of their wealth. In the simplest terms, one can only consume so much lobster and champagne, take so many trips, wear so many suits and dresses, live in so many houses, and even enjoy the natural beauty of one's own land, to a certain point of saturation.

Moreover, except for the very needy, few people make the maximum use of things they own. So one would expect that those who can accumulate goods at the relatively lowest personal cost would also be the most wasteful. They would have more things lying around idle and they would be least concerned with apparent waste. In short, given the current distribution of wealth and the likely uses to which that wealth can be and is put, it is highly probable that *any* activity that would tend to redistribute wealth in the direction of greater equality (in the interest of morality) would reduce waste and would, therefore, be economically efficient.

Put more bluntly, I think that the current distribution of wealth in Canada creates such gross economic inefficiency that it is practically impossible to make adjustments toward greater equality in the interest of morality that would not create greater economic efficiency.

7. Increased Government Control

Ignoring my first reply to the argument concerning reduced economic efficiency, further developments in that scenario may be elucidated. In particular, the "nonmoralists" may argue that the immediate result of excessive wastefulness will be shortages, and that excessive shortages will lead directly to increased demands for government intervention. When the government finally intervenes, it will probably be in the form of regulating production and prices, and rationing consumption. The latter combination of activities, then, will probably lead directly to so-called black markets, that is, to illegal transactions in which the unscrupulous few rip off those who may or may not be able to afford to be ripped off. Increased illegal activities, of course, tend to generate increased demands for greater law enforcement, meaning additional government bureaucracy to manage additional taxation, to pay for more salaries of more law enforcement personnel (police officers, clerks, court officials, correctional officers and institutions), and to pay for more buildings and the sophisticated technological hardware characteristic of our modern enforcement agencies. Thus, since no one in his or her right mind wants to live through this scenario, everyone should be reluctant to suffer economic inefficiency even if it requires ignoring alleged moral responsibilities. Indeed, faced with the spectre of such an outrageous scenario, many people would be inclined to describe their perceived oblig-

ations in fairly moralistic terms. That is, they would be inclined to insist that in the interests of humanity, civilization or a free society such a scenario should be resisted.

Reply

Naturally, I would welcome the move from the talk about economic efficiency to talk about humanity or, more particularly, morality. It is always helpful to have agreement about relatively ultimate aims, or about that for the sake of which relatively immediate actions are being performed or recommended. However, for present purposes, it will be wise to concentrate on those who might not.

Since, for the sake of argument (i.e., Argument #6), I have allowed the other side to assume that actions performed in the interest of morality would lead to reduced economic efficiency, it is worthwhile to remember that standard practices allegedly leading to increased efficiency are notoriously inefficient. In order to avoid any misunderstanding or confusion about apparent paradoxes, one must never forget that all measures of efficiency are ratios of benefits to costs, and that there is no standard rule book to tell people exactly *how* to measure *which* benefits and costs to *whom* in *what* time period. Thus, it is easy for an employer to replace relatively expensive human labour (people, that is) with relatively cheap machines, and to increase efficiency defined as a greater benefit to cost ratio *for the employer*. On the other hand, since the very same replacement (by hypothesis) puts some people out of work, it is easy for these employees to show a decrease in efficiency defined as a smaller benefit to cost ratio *for the employee*. Hence, the fact that efficiency measures are essentially ratios with controversial numerators and denominators largely explains the apparent paradoxes involved when certain actions are claimed to be both efficient and inefficient. Without first getting some agreement about how to measure which benefits, etc., it is logically impossible to obtain generally recognized definitive answers.

In the absence of the required agreement about how to measure whose benefits, I would merely remind those who use this seventh argument that widespread poverty and unemployment are two extremely wasteful by-products of the sort of economic efficiency they are recommending. As the economists of the "small is beautiful" or "appropriate technology" view have argued, it cannot be rational to try to continually replace labour with capital when there is relatively plenty of the former and little of the latter. In more human terms, it cannot be reasonable to insist on capital accumulation for a few in the interest of a kind of "efficiency" that makes relative paupers of many others.

Consideration of waste aside, the main reply I would offer to the argument before us is that the alleged choice between a free society and a society highly controlled by government is a false dichotomy. All highly industrialized societies are characterized by high levels of functional interdependence. In such societies almost everyone is more or less dependent on many other people to maintain his or her lifestyle. Although it is possible for people to raise their own sheep, spin the wool, weave cloth, manufacture needles, design clothes, carve buttons, make clothes, etc., few people have the inclination to engage in such activities. The vast majority of people prefer a style that makes them more dependent on the productive activities of others. In highly industrialized societies, this preference has the unfortunate by-product that most people are probably even more dependent on others than they would like to be or should be for their own best interests. Indeed, the whole field of business ethics is largely a response to the realization that a system of production, distribution and consumption of goods and services is almost synonymous with a way of life.

Such a system necessarily socializes, conditions and, finally, even controls people in fundamental ways. Thus, if one were going to insist on any dichotomy, I would suggest at the risk of oversimplification, that between control by elected officials in the public interest, and control by private industrial officials in their own interests. Given the fact that people will certainly become socialized with certain kinds of expectations, aspirations and ideas about a good life, the real issue is how such a life should be defined and what strategies should be used to achieve it. It is a raw red herring to suggest that it is possible to just let everyone do whatever turns them on. That never happens. Moreover, as argued earlier, it is highly unlikely that the result of such unconditioned activity would benefit most people. Finally, granted that in fact elected officials do not always act in the interests of society as a whole and that private industrial officials do not always act in their own interests narrowly defined, this sort of dichotomized thinking is probably not particularly helpful in the long run.

8. Loyal Agent's Argument

Elsewhere I have examined this argument in considerable detail. I will summarize that discussion here. [See this text, p. 196 ff.] The argument runs as follows. (1) As a loyal agent of some principal (i.e., employer), I ought to serve his or her interest as he or she would serve them if the latter had my expertise. (2) Such a principal would serve his or her own interests in a thoroughly egoistic way. Therefore, (3) as a loyal agent of such a principal, I ought to operate in a thoroughly egoistic way in the interests of that principal. In other words, loyal agency seems not only to permit but to require that people should be selfish in the interests of their employers.

Reply

One may be regarded as operating in a thoroughly egoistic way if all one's actions are designed to optimize one's own interests and one has no inclination at all to identify the interests of anyone else with one's own. One may very well be a self-confident, self-starting, self-sustaining and self-controlled individual. These are all commendable personal characteristics. But one must be selfish, self-centred and/or self-serving. In conflict situations when there are not enough benefits to satisfy everyone, an egoist will try to see that his or her own needs are satisfied whatever happens to the needs of others. One is more interested in being first than in being nice, and one assumes that everyone else is too. One may even believe that if everyone behaved this way, the world's resources would be used in a maximally efficient way and everyone would be materially better off. But that is a secondary consideration. One's first consideration—the only prudent one—is to look out for Numero Uno, oneself.

The trouble with the loyal agent's argument is that both premises are problematic. The second premise assumes that all people are egoists; but people who try to defend their actions are *not* egoistic. Their basic assumption is that they are loyal agents motivated by a desire to serve the best interests of their employers. However, if it is possible for them to have such nonegoistic motives, then it must be possible for other people to have such motives too. Hence, the very assumption required to make the argument look plausible in the first place makes the second premise look implausible. So the argument is self-defeating.

The first premise—that an employee's responsibility is to the employer alone—looks as innocuous as motherhood and apple pie, and in a way it is. Its only weakness is that its limitations are not built into it. In this respect it is like most moral principles and rules of law. Short of turning every principle and rule into a self-contained treatise, it is impossible to indicate every possible exception. For example, no one should kill anyone, except *maybe* in self-defence, war, capital punishment, euthanasia or suicide. Similarly, a loyal agent ought to pursue the interests of his or her employer except. . . . In the famous Nuremburg trials, the Charter of the International Military Tribunal recognized, for instance,

> . . . that one who has committed criminal acts may not take refuge in superior orders nor in the doctrine that his crimes were acts of states. These twin principles working together have heretofore resulted in immunity for practically everyone concerned in the really great crimes against peace and mankind. Those in lower ranks are protected against liability by the orders of their superiors. The superiors were protected because their orders were called acts of the state. Under the Charter, no defence based on either of these doctrines can be entertained.

Canadian and American laws relating to loyal agency do not sanction any illegal or unethical actions. Thus, there is no doubt at all that the first premise of the loyal agent's argument cannot be regarded as a licence to break laws. No respectable court would permit it. In fact, although the courts have no special jurisdiction over moral law, they have shown no reluctance to condemn immoral acts allegedly performed in the interests of fulfilling fiduciary obligations.

9. Materialist Orientation

In the fifth argument above it was indicated that people whose primary interests are in business would probably have low levels of competence in performing morally responsible actions. I replied that the flaw in this argument was the assumption that competence in performing morally responsible actions was an exclusive trait or skill, and that the broad way of understanding morality which I have adopted is more inclusive than exclusive. One might still argue that, given the materialistic orientation of businesspeople, when they try to make a broad benefit-cost analysis in the interest of morality, they are bound to spoil it. As Aristotle said a long time ago, as a person's character is, so is the world seen. People who spend most of their time evaluating things from a materialistic point of view will tend to make moral evaluations from the same point of view. So, when they try to do things in the interests of everyone impartially, they will probably not be doing the sorts of things moralists would like them to be doing. For example, from the point of view of Canadian businesspeople, the support of economic research designed to show that Adam Smith's argument (Argument #1) was basically sound might be regarded as impartially benefiting everyone. Quite generally, then, such people might regard anything that reinforces their view of the world as impartially benefiting everyone. Thus, urging these people to be universally beneficent might lead to universal materialism, which most moralists would find unacceptable.

Reply

As suggested earlier, it is almost certainly an oversimplification to say that businesspeople usually have a materialistic orientation. Given the variety of businesses that people can enter, the variety and ambiguity of human motivations, and the variety of personal philosophies of life and lifestyles, it is unlikely that people in business, broadly construed, are uniformly materialistic. If there is any reliable and valid research indicating such bias, I haven't seen it. Secondly, it would be a mistake to think that all materialism is dangerous and objectionable. Some material goods do make positive contributions to the quality of life, e.g., reliable consumer durables such as cars, household appliances, dwelling units and communications hardware (telephones, radio, television). Finally, Aristotle's remark

is obviously not the whole truth. As much as people's interests influence what they perceive and believe, what they perceive and believe also influences their interests. Indeed, my reading of the evidence accumulated so far indicates that perception and belief contribute more to interest than the reverse. But the literature on this subject is diverse, complicated and controversial.

10. Need for Pluralism

In a pluralistic society like Canada, there are many perspectives from which controversial issues may be viewed. There are many important issues about which various people have unsettled opinions, and there are others about which there are solid and contradictory opinions. To expect business people to have uniform and settled opinions, and to urge them to see that these are predominant is unwarranted and unwise. It is unwarranted because there is no good reason to expect businesspeople as such to be intellectually more tidy or clearheaded than the rest of the population and, therefore, it is unwise to urge these people to strive to make their views predominant over all others. Given the enormous overt and covert power of businesspeople, they might go even farther than they already have to create a one-dimensional society. The only reasonable course to follow is a pluralistic one.

Reply

This argument, too, is a red herring. To urge businesspeople to engage in morally responsible action is to urge *only* businesspeople to engage in such action. Of course pluralism will and ought to continue, if that means that there should be a variety of perspectives from which important issues may be viewed. No one in his or her right mind would insist on silencing all voices but one, or on excluding all points of view but one. It would be as bad to have only businesspeople steering the ship of state as it would be to have only philosophers, moralists or gymnasts doing so.

The other problem with this argument is that it is self-defeating. If it is true that businesspeople are so powerful that they represent a threat to the rest of society, then morally irresponsible businesspeople would represent an even greater threat. Hence, if this argument has any value at all, it is only to reinforce the view that urges businesspeople to be morally responsible.

11. Overload

The world of competitive enterprise is notoriously complicated already. Compared to those in other occupations, business executives have a relatively high incidence of heart attacks and strokes. To insist that such overloaded people should take on yet another responsibility and, indeed, such a controversial and inherently complex one as moral decision-making, is to risk complete systemic failure. Quite apart from the arguable facts that the engagement of businesspeople as such in morally responsible action would be redundant and incompetent, there is no good reason to risk destroying currently reasonable business practices by overloading decision-makers.

Reply

If this argument proves anything, it proves too much. Life, after all, is complicated. So, if complexity were sufficient to eliminate the burden of attending to moral responsibilities, then all of us could take a permanent moral holiday. Clearly, however, a society in which no one attended to any moral responsibilities would have virtually nothing to recommend it as a human and humane community. In such a society, if it could ever be called that, life would be "nasty, brutish and short," as the 17th century British philosopher Thomas Hobbes

said. Secondly, the argument still seems to presuppose that morality is some kind of specialization which people can get into or not, as they choose. As I have indicated above, this is a mistake. The moral point of view is not another specialized perspective, but is inherent in all major decisions.

12. Inconsistency

Perhaps one of the most frequently heard arguments against businesspeople engaging in morally responsible action is that such action is logically inconsistent with competitive enterprise. To engage in competition in an open market is essentially to try to do better than others. The rough rule is to buy cheap and sell dear. To engage in morally responsible action is essentially to try *not* to have some come out better than others. The rule then is to buy and sell at no monetary gain. Thus, those who recommend that businesspeople as such should be morally responsible are talking literal nonsense and recommending that businesspeople should perform actions that are aimed both to make someone and no one come out better, which is absurd.

Reply

I believe the unsoundness of this argument may be demonstrated by consideration of competitive games of fair play. For example, there is apparently nothing immoral about such competitive games as chess, tennis, golf and track-and-field events, to name only a few. Rules are designed to insure that, in principle, all competitors have an equal probability of winning. Each chess player gets the same number of pieces, uses the same board, has the same time constraints and so on. Moreover, each player is free to play, or not, depending on the relative benefits and costs of playing. Hence, since chess games are thoroughly competitive and morally unobjectionable, it is logically possible for something to be so. Thus, those who think there is some logical absurdity involved in recommending that business-people should be moral and competitive are plainly wrong. If there is any inconsistency involved, it is certainly not a matter of logic or conceptualization.

13. The Godfather's Argument

The Godfather's argument in that excellent book and series of movies was simply that as long as a business provides goods and services demanded by some consumers and a substantial family income for producers, few people should ask anything more of it. After all, business is business, and businesspeople are not saints any more than the rest of us. Life, as the great British-American philosopher Alfred North Whitehead said, is robbery. All living things draw their sustenance from other living things. So, a Godfather-type disciple might have concluded, we are doomed to be predators. The most we can hope for is to make a reasonable living for ourselves and our families, granting always that there is an unattractive aspect to our business activities.

Reply

Dazzling—and pragmatic—as the rhetoric may sound, it's still nonsense. Granting that all living things live by consuming the corpses of other living things, it does not follow that we are all robbers, thieves or murderers. Poetic licence is not a licence to commit logical fallacies. There are important differences between, for example, chopping up vegetables for a Caesar salad and chopping up Caesar. The facts that some people may be willing to pay to have someone murdered and that some other people are willing to perform the murder are not sufficient to justify the transaction. The person whose life is being negotiated also has an interest that ought to be protected, as do the rest of us whose lives would be at risk if such business transactions were legal.

14. Particular Morality

Finally, one might argue that the basic presupposition of this essay is a red herring, because few if any businesspeople have to be persuaded to be morally responsible. How many people in business have you ever heard saying that they should be morally irresponsible, immoral, morally bad or evil? Not many, probably. No one is born a businessperson. Most people in business were taught roughly the same moral maxims at home and in school, and most of these maxims had roughly the same origins in the Judeo-Christian religions. So most people have been socialized to be morally responsible. Businesspeople generally intend to act and are expected to act the same as everyone else. Thus, to assume that businesspeople are in need of special remedial training, encouragement or admonitions to be nice is simply to make a false assumption.

On the other hand, it is true that the moral maxims to which virtually everyone is exposed are not necessarily predominant in the world of competitive enterprise. Just as chess players and golfers agree to accept particular rules of behaviour for the sake of their games, businesspeople also adopt special rules for the sake of their work. Like chess players, then, businesspeople may be said to have particular codes of ethics in addition to and occasionally in opposition to ordinary or universal ethics. Many actions that would appear to have questionable moral status, judged by the maxims of universal morality, may be morally good judged by the maxims of the particular morality of the world of business. Therefore, instead of condemning businesspeople for acting immorally, one ought at least to appreciate their particular ethical positions and perhaps praise them for steadfastly adhering to the rules of their own game.

Reply

This apparently tolerant approach to the identification and appraisal of morally responsible action is yet another self-defeating argument. Insofar as the argument has any strength at all, it tends to undermine *all* morality. One of the basic aims and functions of morality or codes of ethics is the resolution of disputes involving conflicting interests. Moral maxims and, more importantly, the ideal of universal beneficence are designed to provide rules for settling disputes without resorting to legislated civil or criminal laws. The recognition of a supreme moral principle of action, namely, the intention to impartially maximize human well-being, is a necessary condition of morality achieving its basic aims. Without such a tie-breaking principle, a principle to adjudicate between conflicting interests or lower level maxims, appeals to morality are useless.

Thus, the concept of particular moralities is logically incoherent, for it entails maxims of action which both include and exclude a supreme principle. In other words, it posits a set of maxims which are relatively equal in status but also not relatively equal to one supreme principle. Unless the maxims of any so-called particular morality are roughly equal to those of other particular moralities, one cannot use them to claim special privileges for one's behaviour. However, granting them such equal status implies eliminating the possibility of appealing to them to resolve conflicts. If, for example, businesspeople, bandits and baseball players all have equally important ethical codes to live by, then, when there are conflicts between people in different groups, each can retreat to his or her own special code, with the result that no resolution of the conflict is possible. If one would take the additional step that some people seem to recommend, namely, that everyone should have his or her own moral code, then morality would be radically relativized and absolutely useless. Clearly, the way out of this logical and moral morass is simply to abandon the idea of particular morality. There can be only one kind of morality, and it is universal. Businesspeople, like everyone else, must be judged morally responsible or irresponsible in terms of this morality. There is no third option.

This essay first appeared in the first edition of this text; an earlier version was presented at the 17th World Congress of Philosophy in Montreal, Quebec, August 1983. Most of the 14 arguments presented here were suggested in T. Beauchamp and N. Bowie's *Ethical Theory and Business* (Prentice-Hall, 1983). The author of this essay would like to express his thanks to the editors and authors of that volume.

4

BUSINESS ETHICS IN CANADA:
Distinctiveness and Directions

Leonard J. Brooks

Motivated by different concerns from those in the United States and Europe, Canadian business ethics applications, research and learning experiences are distinctive. Future developments post 1995, while responsive to global concerns and concerns common to all of North America, are also likely to follow somewhat independent directions in the future.

Business ethics in Canada have been shaped by pressure from several quarters: Canadian society in general, active share ownership from churches and other responsible institutional or ethical investors, self-interest of executives including proactive behavior based on developments in the US. In addition, business ethics developments in Canada have been facilitated by the emergence of a group of consultants, the interest of academic researchers, and the interest of the Canadian accounting profession. These pressures will be discussed in turn to provide an understanding of the past and an inkling of the future.

PRESSURES FROM SOCIETY IN GENERAL

Business ethics in Canada have been shaped by concerns on the part of society in general for health, conscience, the environment, and for good corporate governance. These concerns, while different from those experienced in the US, have been influenced somewhat by US developments.

For example, concerns for the prevention of fraud and unethical business practices have been dominant in the US, whereas these issues have only recently joined the front rank in Canada. Canada does not have, for example, the equivalent to a *Foreign Corrupt Practices Act* or a *Whistleblower Protection Act*. Similarly, our significant dependence on global markets and the large

Journal of Business Ethics 16: 591–604, 1997 © Kluwer Academic Publishers. Printed in the Netherlands.

component of foreign ownership of our industry have produced different stimuli than in the United States. Our greater dependence on global markets has caused many organizations to focus on becoming leaner, and ethics observers to coin the phrase "corporate anorexia" for repeated downsizing. Downsizing has also followed the takeover of many of our companies by foreign (including American) companies, that have gone on to redistribute Canadian production facilities on a globally optimal basis.

The result of these economic pressures has been to contribute to a heightened public awareness of and sensitivity to the ethics of our workplaces. Heightened public awareness and sensitivity to stakeholder needs is also evident in the public funding of medical care in Canada. Hence it is not surprising that Canadian rules and regulations cover such issues as the health of our workers, sexual and other harassment, the employment of women and visible minorities, and the protection of workers' rights to form unions and in regard to civil liberties. Legislation, regulation and oversight of these areas is ongoing at the federal, provincial and municipal levels. The City of Toronto and other municipalities, for instance, passed no smoking by-laws covering public buildings and workplaces in the late 1980s, and have restricted bidders on government contracts to those companies that are prepared to disclose their equal gender and diversity of employment policies and performance.

In the area of protection for the environment and our flora and fauna, much of Canada has been aware that our resources, though vast, are finite. Since the 1950s central Canada has experienced air and water pollution largely originating in the Ohio Valley which through acid rain has neutered our lakes and killed or weakened our deciduous forests. Sulfur from our smokestacks has, in turn, been polluting the north-eastern US. Locally there have been cases of water pollution from pulp mills and mining or re-

fining operations that have led to the poisoning of humans, fish and game, and which have rendered rivers useless. Environmental concerns came to a head in 1988 when the Government of Canada passed the *Canadian Environmental Protection Act* which provides a framework subsequently used as a model by most of the Provinces. In the years since, the enforcement and related penalties have been growing tougher, to the point that companies can suffer a fine of up to $1 million per day, and directors and officers of an offending company can be forced to pay fines personally and/or to go to jail (Bata Shoe, 1992). As in the United States where the November 1, 1991 introduction of the *US Sentencing Guidelines* triggered interest in reducing fines, having in place a "due diligence" process can reduce these legal risks substantially, and executives of high-risk enterprises have become keenly aware of the attractiveness of proactively avoiding environmental malfeasance. The Canadian public have clearly taken the view that corporations can and should take action to protect the environment for current and future generations, and both politicians and companies have responded. In fact, in some areas such as gold mining, the combination of environmental and health and safety regulations have apparently made it more attractive to develop mines in the US rather than inside Canada (*Corporate Ethics Monitor*, 1994, 50).

Based on this limited portrayal, it is evident that in 1995 the Canadian public has a highly developed sense of conscience, and of concern for health and the environment. Politicians have shown a willingness to respond. Executives and directors, particularly of larger companies, now generally recognize at least their legal responsibilities in these areas; and some go beyond legal minima and are recognizing the need to be more responsive to the over-riding need for good governance processes to ensure good performance in these areas as well as others. Some companies have gone even further to position themselves as having an ethical competitive edge. It should be noted that progress to this stage has not been without concerns by executives over the impact of new regulations on their corporations' global competitive positions, and by politicians over the possibility of the flight of investment to less aggressive regulatory jurisdictions. These concerns may forestall Canadian commitments already made to proceed toward sustainable development.

PRESSURES FROM ETHICAL AND OTHER RESPONSIBLE INVESTORS

Pressure for a good ethical governance process has not just been from the public in general. Investors wishing to reflect their values as they invest have created a market for ethical investment funds that screen portfolios on particular criteria. Investors, including many pension and endowment funds, who recognize that ownership carries responsibility for the behavior of investee corporations, have assumed an activist role and have put their views forward to companies whose shares they own. This has lead to a transition from a governance model focusing on short-term returns to shareholders, to longer term profitability with accountability to stakeholders and sensitivity to their needs. The most significant groups interested in ethical investing are discussed below in the chronological sequence of their impact.

Social Audits by the United Church of Canada

In the late 1960s, the United Church of Canada stepped up its program of corporate responsibility by engaging in the first social audits in Canada. Church audit teams interviewed corporate directors and executives, and surveyed employees, to assess the prac-

tices of companies in which the Church's pension and general funds were invested. This process was instrumental in raising the awareness of executives to ethical problems and, in many cases, started Canadian corporations toward the development of ethical codes of conduct. This social audit process was described in articles in the *CA Magazine* (Brooks and Davis, 1977) and in *Accounting Organizations & Society* (Brooks, 1980).

Task Force on the Churches and Corporate Responsibility (TCCR)

TCCR is an ecumenical coalition of Canadian churches including The United Church of Canada, the Anglican Church of Canada, the Evangelical Lutheran Church in Canada, the Presbyterian Church in Canada, the Roman Catholic Church represented by the Canadian Conference of Catholic Bishops and individual orders and communities, and the Society of Friends (Quakers). TCCR was established in Toronto in 1975 to enable the churches to exercise corporate responsibility both as shareholders and as organizations, and it has proven effective as a vehicle through which the churches can address issues of concern with corporate management and other shareholders.

Beginning with a focus on apartheid in South Africa, TCCR has put many issues before corporate management and other investors, such as: human rights, military exports, international lending and third world debt, corporate disclosure, aboriginal issues and treatment of indigenous peoples abroad, environmental protection in both developing countries and at home, corporate governance, and responsible investment. As the organization celebrates its twentieth anniversary with a growing membership, current activity includes ecological concerns particularly in forestry, climate change and environmental reporting; corporate accountability and global impacts; aboriginal land rights; corporate governance, e.g., board diversity, confidential reporting; human rights; and banking services to the entire community including the poor.

Individuals and institutions subscribing to TCCR's bi-monthly receive position papers, submissions to various regulatory bodies and articles on related matters as well as a detailed annual report on TCCR's activities. Executives interested in formulating a strategy for responsible performance should obtain a copy of "Principles for Global Corporate Responsibility: Bench Marks for Measuring Business Performance" published in 1995 by TCCR in company with The Ecumenical Committee for Corporate Responsibility (ECCR—churches in Britain and Ireland) and The Interfaith Center on Corporate Responsibility (ICCR—churches in the USA).

Allenvest and Fairvest Securities Corporation

During the 1980s and early 1990s, the most outspoken investment adviser on ethical/governance issues was William Allen of Toronto. He, with TCCR, led a high profile fight against such governance problems as: poison pill arrangements that were too generous to executives and unfair to minority shareholders, inordinately short notification and voting periods, etc. With Mr. Allen's death in October 1991, the organization changed its name from Allenvest to Fairvest, and continues to be active in speaking out on governance issues and in advising its investor clients. Specifically, Fairvest provides a clearing house for information on shareholder issues as they arise, helps institutional investors react effectively to proxy proposals within the mandatory 21-day response window by providing a proxy analysis service, and publishes a bi-monthly newsletter, the *Corporate Governance Review*.

Ethical Mutual Funds and Other Large Responsible Investors

Similar to developments in the US, socially responsible investment objectives have been pursued by large pension funds such as the Ontario Municipal Employees Retirement System (OMERS) and the Ontario Secondary School Teachers Federation (OSSTF), a large financial institution (the Caisse Populaire in Quebec), a set of ethical mutual funds (see Table I) begun by the Van City Credit Union of Vancouver in 1987 and a growing number of private investors. Some of these do their own research while others use consultants to provide screens of investee company operations. Their concerns include corporate governance issues, such as: confidential voting, board diversity, poison pills and their effect on shareholders' rights, independence of directors, the separation of CEO and Chairman, and reasonable executive compensation, as well as the treatment of: women and minorities, shareholder rights and responsibilities, the environment, the record of health and safety, production of military or harmful products, and, to a lesser extent, the other aspects reviewed in the *Corporate Ethics Monitor* list cited below. In addition to stimulating interest among executives in these topics, ethical investors have helped to sensitize corporate management in Canada to ethical problems in general. Perhaps more importantly, the performance of these ethically invested funds has demonstrated to Canadian executives that observing ethical principles does not mean that profits will suffer. Ethical investors, like some large corporations, have provided examples that other Canadian executives are willing to emulate.

Social Investment Organization (SIO)

In 1989, a group of individuals decided to develop a not-for-profit organization similar to that of the same name in the US. Under the leadership of Executive Director Marc de Sousa-Shields, conferences on ethical investing have been sponsored, and newsletters as well as analyses have been published on such issues as: workforce diversity, employee relations, the environment, corporate citizenship, community economics and international investment. SIO has made a special multi-volume study of the social and environmental impacts of Canadian industrial activity beginning with the Canadian forest products industry. From its Toronto offices, the SIO provides members with timely updates on business ethics issues such as the Body Shop controversy, and overviews of the nature and performance of Canadian ethical mutual funds (see Table I, p.76).

PRESSURES FROM DIRECTORS, EXECUTIVES AND EMPLOYEES

Directors and executives have, of course, felt the need to protect themselves and their companies from exposure to fines, jail and loss of reputation from ethical malfeasance, particularly in the area of environmental management and protection. To this end, they have introduced and revised codes or ethics/conduct and some have embarked on setting up an ethical corporate culture to guide their employees. In the areas of environmental performance as well as health and safety, employees have often been very receptive and supportive of the initiatives of senior officers, and have been pushing for initiatives where none have been suggested.

Tragedy has also played a part in influencing executives to take a proactive stand on ethical issues. In 1979 a freight train carrying chlorine gas was de-railed in the center of Mississauga, the city of 400 000 which is immediately upwind of Toronto. Much of Mississauga was evacuated within hours and remained quarantined for most of a week in what has been recognized as a model of emergency disaster management.

Needless to say the public in central Canada was sensitized to the problems of toxic chemical products. Shortly thereafter a large dark blob was discovered on the bed of the St. Clair River which runs between Detroit and Windsor and from which the drinking water for each city is taken. The blob was subsequently attributed to repeated toxic spills from the refineries, including Dow Chemical's, located along the shore in Sarnia, Ontario. In December 1984, the tragedy in Bhopal, India, took place, and the senior executive in Canada, Norman Kissick, found, to his chagrin, that there was nothing he could do after the event in the short run to protect his company or improve the situation of those in India. Shortly after, however, Norman and David Buzzelli, then the President of Dow Chemical Canada, initiated the development of the Responsible Care Program, a voluntary self- and peer-review program designed to safeguard employees, the environment and the public, from poor manufacturing, storage and shipping practices in the member firms of the Canadian Chemical Producers Association as well as their suppliers and customers (*Corporate Ethics Monitor*, 1991, pp. 37, 38). From its beginning in 1990, the success of this proactive program has grown to the point that it has been replicated in over thirty countries around the world. Under David Buzzelli, Dow Chemical Canada was one of the first Canadian companies to report publicly on environmental performance and to embrace sustainable development.

Concern for the potential consequences of environmental malfeasance was responsible for the inclusion of one of the world's first environmental responsibility clauses in any loan agreement. In its early financing in the late 1980s of the Canary Wharf rebuilding project in London, England, the Royal Bank of Canada included a clause that made the entire loan due and callable if any environmental regulation were to be broken.

Such clauses are commonplace in major financings today both inside and outside of Canada.

It is also true that some directors and executives have been motivated by altruism in their choice of corporate programs, particularly those that interface with host communities or employees. Intention, of course, is difficult to discover and verify, but cases of anonymous donations and participation in community support programs do exist.

Most interestingly, some directors and executives have taken the view that ethical practices should be undertaken because they will generate profits. This is the reason given by senior management at the Bank of Montreal for their ground-breaking gender-equity studies and programs (*Bank of Montreal, Report to Employees*, 1991). They have argued that women are as smart and capable as men, so that to continue voluntary or involuntary practices that present barriers to employing a full 50% share of women at all levels within the Bank would restrict the profitability of the Bank. By approaching this issue as a business problem rather than a gender problem, they have been very successful in convincing many of their employees and others that reducing barriers to gender-equity is worth supporting. Their changes have been so successful that many women have transferred their banking business to the Bank. Moreover, many women from other Canadian banks have applied to become employees of the Bank of Montreal.

CONSULTANTS, RESEARCHERS, CENTRES AND OTHER FACILITATORS

EthicScan and *The Corporate Ethics Monitor*

Although in 1995 there are upwards of 15 ethics consultants and academic consultants practicing in Canada, one of the earliest to be established and certainly the largest is EthicScan Canada in Toronto. Founded in 1987 by David Nitkin, the operation employs up to six and provides the following services:

- 1500-company database of corporate social performance indicators;
- publishes the bimonthly *The Corporate Ethics Monitor*;
- information for investment funds, corporations and personal investors;
- bench-marking practices and codes;
- authorship of the *Ethical Shoppers Guide to Canadian Supermarket Prices* (1992) and of *Shopping With a Conscience: the Informed Shoppers Guide to Retailers, Suppliers, and Service Providers in Canada* (forthcoming in 1996);
- training programs, videos;
- ethical assurance: ethics audits, sniff tests, etc.

The Corporate Ethics Monitor, which I edit, provides ethical performance comparisons of two Canadian industries in each issue, plus feature columns covering such areas as media content analyses and commentary, and important governance and ethical management matters. In an Open Forum Section, edited by Vincent Di Norcia, book reviews, cases and informed commentary are made available. The comparisons of corporate ethical performance are based on interviews and external audit procedures on almost 80 aspects of corporate activity under the following headings: code of ethics, direct job creation, employment of women, hiring and promotion programs, charitable donations, community relations, progressive staff policies, employee gain-sharing opportunities, labour relations/health and safety, environmental management, environmental performance, international relations, business practice issues, Canadian sourcing, and candor quotient which represents the degree to which the corporation being assessed co-operated with the assessment. Data from *Monitor* corporate social

TABLE 1   Canadian ethical mutual funds: A performance update as at November 16, 1995

Performance Update

Type of Fund	RRSP eligible	Assets ($ millions)	6 Mth.	1 Year	2 Years	3 Years	5 Years	10 Years
Environmental funds								
Clean Environment								
Balanced	Balanced	Y	16.7	1.5	8.2	0.2	14.1	
Equity	Canadian Equity	Y	31.0	5.8	13.2	0.0	15.1	
Income	Canadian Bond	Y	3.0	1.0	4.7			
International	International Equity	N	3.3	0.7	3.2			
Fonds Desjardins Environment	Canadian Equity	Y	11.8	2.4	5.9	4.9	9.3	6.3
Dynamic Global Green	International Equity	N	2.6	5.1	0.8	-9.0	6.3	1.2
Total Environmental Funds Assets			**68.4**					
Social Funds								
Ethical Funds								
Ethical Balanced	Balanced	Y	105.0	8.7	14.2	5.8	9.4	8.5
Ethical Global Bond Fund	International Bond	Y	6.5	4.3				
Ethical Growth	Canadian Equity	Y	175.7	4.6	10.4	4.6	11.5	8.7
Ethical Income	Canadian Bond	Y	58.0	8.4	18.3	6.0	8.3	8.9	8.8
Ethical North American Equity	N.A. Equity	N	18.4	19.4	23.8	11.8	15.8	13.6	8.7
Ethical Money Market	Money Market	Y	30.3	3.0	5.8	4.8	4.9	6.1	8.0
Ethical Pacific Rim Fund	Asia/Pacific Rim	N	4.0	3.9				
Ethical Special Equity Fund	Canadian Small Equity	Y	3.4	5.5				
Investors Summa	Canadian Equity	Y	105.9	5.0	8.0	3.4	9.1	11.4
Crocus Fund	Labour Sponsored	Y						
First Ontario	Labour Sponsored	Y						
Working Opportunities	Labour Sponsored	Y	82.7	2.1	3.3	2.3	2.1	
Working Ventures	Labour Sponsored	Y	506.3	3.1	5.7	3.7	3.6	4.3
Total Social Fund Assets			**1096.2**					

Fund averages

Canadian Environment Equity	42.8	4.1	9.6	2.5	12.2	3.2	0.0
Canadian Social Equity	281.6	4.8	9.2	4.0	10.3	10.1	0.0
Canadian Social & Environmental Equity	324.4	4.5	9.4	3.2	11.3	6.6	0.0
Labour Sponsored Equity	589.0	1.3	2.3	1.5	1.4	1.1	0.0
International Social & Environmental Equity	9.9	3.2	1.3	-3.0	2.1	0.4	0.0
Social & Environmental Balanced	121.7	12.7	7.9	7.0	4.8	11.3	0.0
Canadian Bond	61.0	4.7	11.5	3.0	4.2	4.5	4.4
Total Assets	**1164.6**						

Performance comparisons

Benchmarks

Consumer Price Index	0.5	2.5	1.2	1.4	2.0	3.3
TSE 300	5.4	6.4	4.8	13.0	10.9	8.6
Five Year GIC Rates	3.6	8.0			10.4	10.3

Fund Averages

Money Market	3.1	6.0	5.1	5.0	6.3	7.9
International Equity	3.5	1.1	4.2	12.9	11.9	9.8
North American Equity	10.7	16.6	8.6	12.5	16.2	11.1
Canadian Equity	3.7	4.5	3.0	11.5	10.3	8.1
Balanced	4.9	8.6	4.2	9.3	10.4	8.4
Canadian Bond	7.0	14.4	4.9	7.2	10.7	10.1
Small Capital	4.7	7.7	1.3	18.9	15.1	9.0
Asia Pacific Rim	0.1	-10.7	-1.0	12.9	9.1	10.1
International Bond Fund	0.9	-5.9	-2.9	4.4	7.5	10.1
Labour Sponsored Funds	-11.8	-20.4	2.3	2.1	4.3	

Source: Social Investment Organization *Forum*, December 1995, article by Eugene Ellmen: "What to Look For in the Canadian Equity-Based Ethical Mutual Funds," Table originally from SIO and the *Globe & Mail*, November 16, 1995.

performance analyses undertaken in 1993, 1994 and 1995 is summarized in Table II to provide a status report on the activities of large Canadian companies.

Canadian Centre for Ethics & Corporate Policy (CCECP)

Established in 1988 in Toronto, under the leadership of Graham Tucker, the CCECP has provided forums for discussion of ethical issues of concern to business leaders by means of a luncheon speakers series, occasional conferences and related proceedings, a library, a source of speakers and seminar leaders, and continually updated ethics resource kit entitled: *Developing and maintaining an ethical corporate culture* (Brooks and Smith, 1995). Introduced as a means of assisting executives with the successful implementation of ethical management practices, the resource kit includes text, seminal readings, references and speeches covering: the need for an ethical corporate culture, how to communicate values through mission statements and codes, management leadership and support, developing an understanding of ethical expectations, reinforcement and compliance, measuring monitoring and reporting ethical performance, and how to handle key ethical issues.

The Canadian Centre, which was begun as a Canadian version of the Chicago-based Center for Ethics & Corporate Policy, has itself been a model for the development of similar forum-providing units in Vancouver and Calgary. The Canadian Centre is financed through the donations of its corporate and individual members.

The Centre for Corporate Social Performance and Ethics (CCSPE)/Clarkson Centre for Business Ethics

Professor Max Clarkson, one of the founding directors of the CCECP, decided that there was a need in Canada for a university-based centre which would undertake both academic research and consulting to business. In 1988 he established the CCSPE at the Faculty of Management of the University of Toronto to fill this need. In addition to the collection and computerization of data on corporate codes, the provision of consulting services to corporations on the creation/revision of ethics codes, the development of training programs, and the analysis of corporate governance systems, the Centre has organized invited conferences on "Stake-holder Theory and The Management of Ethics in the Workplace," and has either published the related proceedings or has facilitated their publication in *Business & Society* (1994, pp. 82–131). In 1996, the CCSPE became the Clarkson Centre for Business Ethics.

The Centre for Applied Ethics (CAE)

Michael McDonald, then a Professor at the University of Waterloo, was asked in 1988 by the Social Sciences and Humanities Research Council of Canada (SSHRCC) to review how applied ethics research was being done in Canada, who was doing it and how such research could be stimulated. His comprehensive report (1989) on the subject was very well received. In it he proposed the creation of an "Applied Ethics" stream in a "Strategic Grant" system that would provide grants to refereed proposals. In order to stimulate applied ethics research, he suggested the establishment of an e-mail network (the Canadian Business and Professional Ethics Network, CBPENET) which, together with a host Centre (the CAE), was launched at the University of British Columbia (UBC) in 1992. This network enabled the creation of a "virtual" critical mass of ethics researchers in Canada before other similar research networks were even thought of. The discussions using this network have greatly aided the researchers and corporations involved. A subsidiary network of accounting ethics researchers has subsequently been created. [For further details please refer to the accompanying article by Michael McDonald.] In his position as the Maurice Young Professor of Applied Ethics at UBC, Michael has provided stimulation to both the research and applied business ethics community across Canada.

Journal of Business Ethics (*JBE*) and Researchers

It is difficult to identify the precise nature of the influence on business ethics in Canada resulting from the senior editors, Alex Michalos and Deborah Poff, of *JBE* resident in Canada. It is clear that they have become known to researchers and to business executives, such that the ideas in *JBE* are studied by both groups, and have been for the past 14 years. While it is beyond the scope of this article to provide a list of Canadian researchers and their interests, anyone with an interest in doing so could make a reasonable start on it by reviewing the bibliography in this and the other articles in this series on business ethics in Canada.

The Accounting Profession

The interest of the Canadian accounting professions in business and professional ethics has been continuing with articles appearing in the *CA Magazine*, *Cost & Management*, and the *CGA Magazine* from time to time, but with growing regularity in the early 1990s. There have been several monographs published by the professional accounting bodies which bear upon business and professional ethics, including:

- Canadian Corporate Social Performance (Brooks, 1986)
- The Ethical Foundations of Public Accounting (Gaa, 1994)
- Ethical Reasoning in Accounting and Auditing (Ponemon and Gabhart, 1993)
- Macdonald Report (1988)

Quite recently there has been an interest in developing a method of accounting for the environmental expenditures and impacts of corporations (see for example: Rubenstein, 1989 and 1994). Similarly, interest has been stimulated in the management of companies to facilitate sustainable development. To assist in raising awareness of these issues and to encourage better practices, the Canadian Institute of Chartered Accountants (CICA) and two other Toronto-based organizations, the *Financial Post*, and TCCR, have joined to co-sponsor annual awards for the best environmental disclosure reporting.

One of the most interesting new services to be made available through the accounting firms or their consulting operations has been the launching of a "Diagnostic Model for Corporate Governance" by Ernst & Young in Toronto. This is a service which appeals to senior executives who wish to avoid serious fines and/or even jail for environmental and other ethical malfeasance. They simply cannot afford to overlook opportunities to strengthen due diligence procedures and develop governance processes that are credible and responsible.

The understanding that an ethical corporate culture is essential for proper corporate behavior lies behind the development of a new research and standard-setting thrust at the CICA under the rubric of "Criteria for Control." Several monographs have been published under the CICA's "Control and Governance Series" (CICA, 1995). It is evident, with legal costs and settlements against auditors soaring, that unless a proper control system is in place, the audit risk associated with a client may be too great to assume. Similarly, without a proper system of ethics-based control, there is an enhanced risk to investors of illegal or unethical transactions which, in turn, place their investment at significant risk.

Recognizing that the ethics of their clients is important to their well-being, as are proper judgments by their personnel, the accounting community have funded a Centre for Accounting Ethics at the University of Waterloo. To date there has been a conference and several publications, including:

- *Annotated, Bibliography of Accounting Ethics*, by John McCutcheon, 1994.

- *Ethics and Positive Accounting Theory*, by Gordon Richardson and Patricia O'Malley, 1995.

- *Foundations of Business Ethics*, by Jan Narveson and Carl Hahn, 1995.

The Society of Management Accountants of Canada (SMAC), headquartered in Hamilton, Ontario, has also been active in both the sponsorship of a research monograph, and of an awards process for corporate social responsibility reporting excellence in annual reports of Canadian companies. The research monograph is entitled *Canadian Corporate Social Performance* (Brooks, 1986), and the awards process is overseen by Prof. Leo-Paul Lauzan of the Université du Quebec à Montreal. The SMAC has introduced a required, standalone ethics module for its students.

The Certified General Accountants Association of Canada (CGAAC), the third professional accounting organization in Canada, has made a significant contribution by funding research studies by Gaa (1994) and Ponemon and Gabhart (1993) through its Research Foundation in Vancouver. In addition, the CGAAC has mounted a major effort to publish an *Ethics Readings Handbook* authored by Michael McDonald (1994) and to build ethics into its curriculum on a course-by-course basis.

Both the SMAC and the CICA have published either an ethics case forum or an ethics column on an on-going basis in their professional journals, *Cost & Management*

and *CA Magazine*. All three professional bodies have published numerous articles on business and professional ethics outside of these on-going features.

Ethics Practitioners Association of Canada/Consultants

During 1995, a group of Canadian ethics consultants met and decided to form an association located in Toronto that would include ethics officers, academics and consultants. Just underway, the Ethics Practitioners' Association of Canada (EPAC) intends, among other issues, to promote the development of corporate social responsibility awareness and standards for Canadian corporations, as well as maintaining and improving the qualifications and standards of the ethics practitioners profession.

At this stage not all ethics consultants have joined EPAC. Notable among those are two from Toronto: Richard Findlay who has been offering strategic ethical advice for over a decade; and Michael Jantzi Research Associates whose computerized Canadian Social Investment Database offers information on the environmental, labour and social performance of major Canadian private and public companies. While it is impossible to know everyone who considers themselves to be an ethics consultant at any point in time, seeking lists from EPAC, SIO, CAE and CCECP would probably identify most of the non-academic ethics consultants in Canada.

DEVELOPMENTS IN EDUCATION

Learning about ethics in Canada can be divided into learning by business executives and managers, and learning at the university level. During the last five years business ethics has become a stand-alone and even compulsory course in about 30% of our university business programs, and is also covered as part of topics presented in the basic courses in accounting, marketing, and strategic management (see for example Singh, 1989). As an instructor, the reception that I have found given to these offerings has been increasingly warmer to the extent that the majority of students look forward to discussing the cases, problems and principles that we examine. Business executives and managers, on the other hand, are not well equipped to deal with ethical dilemmas, and relatively few companies have begun training programs to illuminate their codes of conduct (some of which are in their fourth edition) or provide ready references for making ethical decisions. Business executives and managers in Canada, like those in the United States, continue to learn mainly from disaster and example.

Fortunately, universities are taking a more proactive approach to the development of business ethics programs, and have provided funded chairs and PhD programs, notably at the University of British Columbia and at York University in Toronto, with another one in prospect at the University of Toronto. PhD students are now in programs at York University, where Wesley Cragg is the George R. Gardiner Professor of Business Ethics, at the universities of British Columbia, Alberta, Western Ontario and at McGill; and should make a significant contribution when they emerge.

Canadian professors have published books, texts and chapters on business and professional ethics, in several areas. Examples of this would include: *Boardroom Renaissance* (Gillies, 1992); *Good Management: Business Ethics in Action* (Bird and Gandz, 1991); *Engineering Ethics: Practices and Principles* (Stevenson, 1991); *Professional Ethics for Accountants* (Brooks, 1995); chapters in *Accounting* and *Auditing* (Lemon et al., 1993 and 1996).

In addition, although providing a research overview is the province of other pa-

pers, it is worth noting that professional participation by Canadians is active in such as: editorial boards of the *Journal of Business Ethics* and *Business Ethics Quarterly*; academic discussion on the CBPENET, and the publication of many articles.

STATUS REPORT ON CORPORATE SOCIAL PERFORMANCE IN CANADA

The status and trends of business ethics in Canada can be seen to a considerable degree by examining the extent of corporate social performance on the 80 indicators identified in industry analyses published 12 per year in the *Corporate Ethics Monitor*. The performance of the 36 industries (273 companies) reviewed in 1993, 1994, and 1995 is summarized in Table II.

Most of the trends revealed in Table II are reflective of increasing corporate concern for ethical behaviour, for example: more ethics training, more women in management, and more attention to environmental impact management. However, variances do exist among industries analysed (see Table III) depending on their exposure to environmental and other risks, and to public or interest group pressures.

SUMMARY

Canada has never had a national regulatory body such as the Securities and Exchange Commission in the US, nor has it had a *Foreign Corrupt Practices Act*. Lacking this institutional structure, business ethics in Canada have developed in relation to broad and changing socio-political pressures from stakeholders and emerging global economic realities.

It would be fair to say that the two Centres, the CCECP and the CCSPE, as well as EthicScan, TCCR and Allen/Fairvest have provided the dominant practical influences

TABLE II **Status of Canadian corporate social performance for large companies based on 1993-1995 industry analyses published in the *Corporate Ethics Monitor***

Social performance dimension	Status/benchmarks	Average incidence from 36 industry analyses		
		1995 n = 105	1994 n = 93	1993 n = 75
Code of ethics for guidance	Over 60% have a code	63.8	62.7	52.0
Reinforcement: training	25–30% of companies	33.8	18.4	18.7
Reinforcement: annual sign-off	25–30%	29.0	22.7	25.3
Employment of women as:				
Directors	Under 10%, growing slowly	10.6	3.3	4.5
Senior Management	Over 10%, depending on industry	13.5	5.3	N/A
Management	Over 20%, depending on industry	26.3	16.6	N/A
Workforce as a whole	Over 40%, range 1–92.5%	44.2	40.4	N/A
Hiring & promotion programs				
Employment equity	40–60%	53.4	40.1	60.1
Affirmative action	20–25%	22.8	19.4	24.0
Charitable donations				
Pledged of 1% of pre-tax profits	25% pledged to Imagine Campaign	24.8	20.4	26.7
Community relations				
Scholarships for employees	22%	20.9	22.5	9.4
Scholarships for employees' children	25–30%	31.6	24.8	12.2
Matching gift program	25–30%	31.4	25.8	20.0
Progressive staff policies				
Sponsored daycare	20%	23.9	15.1	18.7
Extended maternity leave	Up to 45%	44.9	29.2	45.4
Employee assistance programs	More than 2/company, 50% co.'s	2.8	54.9	42.8
Health promotion plan	2 approx. per company	1.9	2.1	N/A
Retirement counselling	44–55%, growing	57.1	45.4	30.7
Employee gainsharing opportunities				
Share ownership plan—employee contributions	40–50%	49.5	38.9	53.4
Stock option plan	65–75%	62.8	76.6	66.7
Profit sharing plan	40–50%	40.3	50.9	22.7
Labour relations, health & safety				
% with unionized workforce	35–65%	34.0	48.8	64.4
Union decertification cases (last 10 years)	1.3	1.3	1.4	N/A
Strkes/lockouts (in last 10 years (Average))	1.3	1.3	2.0	N/A
Environmental management				
Formal environmental code	60%, growing	60.1	53.8	40.1
Environmental audit program	50–60%, growing	59.1	47.5	26.8
Frequency of environmental audits	1.5–1.9 years	1.9	1.5	N/A
Senior position with environment resp.	45%, growing	44.9	39.9	34.9
Internal staff environmental committee	10–29%	10.5	29.0	N/A
Environmental committee of the board	10–20%	10.5	17.3	8.0
Environmental reports to the board	2+ to 4+ per year	4.15	2.6	N/A
Internal recycling programs	4+ to 6+ per company	6.0	4.6	N/A
Issue public environment report	22–30%	22.9	28.0	N/A
Other	Request from author			
Candor quotient	65% of questions answered	65.0	63.7	69.9

TABLE III	Industries included in corporate social performance analyses	
1995 Analyses	**1994 Analyses**	**1993 Analyses**
Power utilities	Forest companies (Part 2)	Phone utilities
Chemical producers	Funeral services	Trading & distribution
Telephone utilities	Iron & steel	Information technology
Entertainment	Pharmacy	Broadcast cable/communications
Retain chains (Part 1)	Environmental	Natural gas
Pipelines	Groceries	Fabrication & engineering
Industrial products (Part 1)	Gold mining	Insurance
Retail chains (Part 2)	Hotel	Business communications
Car rental companies	Automobiles	Banks
Hardware chains	Metal mining	Transport
Financial	Accounting & management	Forest (Part 1)
Industrial products (Part 2)	Construction & engineering	Courier

on the largest corporations in Canada that have been seeking to improve their ethical performance. The CBPENET and recommendations for research funding which were established by Michael McDonald have provided a similar dominant steering effect on business ethics research in Canada. In view of the fact that members of the accounting professions in Canada occupy a key role in the development in [sic] corporate systems of control, it is apparent that thrusts by the accounting professions to encourage greater awareness of ethical problems, and what to do about them, will become dominant influences on applied business ethics in the future.

[The year] 1996 may bring a national regulator, and pressure is growing for statutes proscribing corruption. Until these developments transpire, bringing with them pressures for businesses to develop specific anti-corruption mechanisms in their codes of conduct and in other ways, the preoccupation with broader ethical issues will continue, perhaps providing a model for other nations, including the US, to learn from.

REFERENCES

Bank of Montreal, *Report to Employees*, The Task Force on the Advancement of Women, The Bank of Montreal, Toronto, Canada, November 1991, 26. See also the *Milestones Report* that followed.

Bata Shoe, see *R v. Bata Industries Limited* (1992), 90R (3d) 329 (Ont. Prov. Ct.).

Bird, F. and J. Gandz: 1991, *Good Management: Business Ethics in Action* (Prentice-Hall, Scarborough, Canada), p. 460.

Brooks, L.J.: 1980, "An Attitude Survey Approach to the Social Audit," *Accounting, Organizations & Society* 5(3), 341–355.

Brooks, L.J.: 1986, *Canadian Corporate Social Performance* (Society of Management Accountants of Canada, Hamilton, Canada), p. 267.

Brooks, L. J.: 1995, *Professional Ethics for Accountants* (West Publishing Company, St. Paul), p. 315.

Brooks, L.J. and W.R. Davis: 1977, "Some Approaches to the Corporate Social Audit," *CAMagazine* 110(3), March, 34–45.

Brooks, L.J. and S. Smith, eds.: 1995, *Developing and Maintaining and Ethical Corporate Culture* (Canadian Centre for Ethics & Corporate Policy, Toronto, Canada).

Centre for Accounting Ethics Publications, University of Waterloo, Waterloo, Canada: *Annotated, Bibliography of Accounting Ethics*, by John McCutcheon, 1994; *Ethics and Positive Accounting Theory*, by Gordon Richardson and Patricia O'Malley, 1995.

Clarkson, M.B.E., "Proceedings of a Workshop on the Stakeholder Theory of the Firm and the Management of Ethics in the Workplace," May 20–21, 1993, Centre for Corporate Social Performance & Ethics, Faculty of Management, University of Toronto, Toronto, Canada, 1993, and "The Toronto Conference: Reflections on Stakeholder Theory," Business & Society 33(1), April 1994, 82–131.

Corporate Ethics Monitor (CEM): 1994, ed. Leonard J. Brooks, published bi-monthly by EthicScan Canada Limited, Toronto, Canada, ISSN 0841-1956. See: "Ethical Performance Comparison: Selected Gold Mining Companies," Issue 6(4), 50–55.

CICA Control and Governance Series, CICA, Toronto, Canada: Guidance on Control, 1995; Guidance for Directors—Governance Process for Control, 1995.

Gaa, J.C.: 1994, *The Ethical Foundations of Public Accounting* (CGA—Canada Research Foundation, Vancouver), p. 162.

Gillies, J.M.: 1992, *Boardroom Renaissance* (McGraw-Hill Ryerson, Toronto, Canada), p. 264.

Lemon, M., W.T. Harrison and C.T. Horngren: 1996, *Accounting* (Prentice-Hall, Scarborough, Ontario), Canadian 3rd edn.

Lemon, M., AA. Arens and J.K. Loebbecke: 1993, *Auditing: an Integrated Approach* (Prentice-Hall, Scarborough, Ontario, Canadian 5th ed.), p. 857.

Macdonald, W.A. et al.: 1988, *Report of the Commission to Study the Public's Expectations of Audits* (Canadian Institute of Chartered Accountants, Toronto, Canada), June, p. 167.

McDonald, M.: 1989, *Towards a Canadian Research Strategy for Applied Ethics* (Canadian Federation of the Humanities, Ottawa), 343 pps.

McDonald, M.: 1994, *Ethics Readings Handbook* (Certified General Accountants Association of Canada, Vancouver, Canada), expandable.

Narveson, J. and C. Hahn: 1995, Foundations of Business Ethics, CGA—Canada Research Foundation, Vancouver, 57.

Ponemon, L.A. and D.R.L. Gabhart: 1993, *Ethical Reasoning in Accounting and Auditing* (CGA—Canada Research Foundation, Vancouver), 148 pps.

Principles for Global Corporate Responsibility: Bench Marks for Measuring Business Performance, The Task Force on the Churches and Corporate Responsibility (TCCR), Toronto, Canada, 1995, 10 pages plus appendices.

Rubenstein, D.: 1989, "Black Oil, Red Ink," *CAMagazine* (Canadian Institute of Chartered Accountants, Toronto, Canada), p. 29.

Rubenstein, D.: 1994, "Beyond the Clear-cut," *CAMagazine* (Canadian Institute of Chartered Accounts, Toronto, Canada), pp. 22–29.

Singh, J.B.: 1989, "The Teaching of Ethics in Canadian Schools of Management and Administrative Studies," *Journal of Business Ethics*, 51–56.

Stevenson, J.T.: 1990, *Engineering Ethics: Practices and Principles* (Canadian Scholars' Press, Toronto, Canada), 2nd ed.

ETHICAL MANAGERS MAKE THEIR OWN RULES

Sir Adrian Cadbury

In 1900 Queen Victoria sent a decorative tin with a bar of chocolate inside to all of her soldiers who were serving in South Africa. These tins still turn up today, often complete with their contents, a tribute to the collecting instinct. At the time, the order faced my grandfather with an ethical dilemma. He owned and ran the second-largest chocolate company in Britain, so he was trying harder and the order meant additional work for the factory. Yet he was deeply and publicly opposed to the Anglo-Boer War. He resolved the dilemma by accepting the order, but carrying it out at cost. He therefore made no profit out of what he saw as an unjust war, his employees benefited from the additional work, the soldiers received their royal present, and I am still sent the tins.

My grandfather was able to resolve the conflict between the decision best for his business and his personal code of ethics be-cause he and his family owned the firm which bore their name. Certainly his dilemma would have been more acute if he had had to take into account the interests of outside shareholders, many of whom would no doubt have been in favor both of war and of profiting from it. But even so, not all my grandfather's ethical dilemmas could be as straightforwardly resolved.

So strongly did my grandfather feel about the South African War that he acquired and financed the only British newspaper which opposed it. He was also against gambling, however, and so he tried to run the paper without any references to horse racing. He decided, in the end, that it was more important that the paper's voice be heard as widely as possible than that gambling should thereby receive some mild encouragement. The decision was doubtless a relief to those working on the paper and to its readers.

The way my grandfather settled these two clashes of principle brings out some practical points about ethics and business decisions. In the first place, the possibility that ethical and commercial considerations will conflict has always faced those who run companies. It is not a new problem. The difference now is that a more widespread and critical interest is being taken in our decisions and in the ethical judgments which lie behind them.

Secondly, as the newspaper example demonstrates, ethical signposts do not always point in the same direction. My grandfather had to choose between opposing a war and condoning gambling. The rule that it is best to tell the truth often runs up against the rule that we should not hurt people's feelings unnecessarily. There is no simple, universal formula for solving ethical problems. We have to choose from our own codes of conduct whichever rules are appropriate to the case in hand; the outcome of those choices makes up who we are.

Lastly, while it is hard enough to resolve dilemmas when our personal rules of conduct conflict, the real difficulties arise when we have to make decisions which affect the interests of others. We can work out what weighting to give to our own rules through trial and error. But business decisions require us to do the same for others by allocating weights to all the conflicting interests which may be involved. Frequently, for example, we must balance the interests of employees against those of shareholders. But even that sounds more straightforward than it really is, because there may well be differing views among the shareholders, and the interests of past, present, and future employees are unlikely to be identical.

Eliminating ethical considerations from business decisions would simplify the management task, and Milton Friedman has urged something of the kind in arguing that the interaction between business and society should be left to the political process. "Few trends could so thoroughly undermine the very foundation of our free society," he writes in *Capitalism and Freedom,* "as the acceptance by corporate officials of a social responsibility other than to make as much money for their shareholders as possible."

But the simplicity of this approach is deceptive. Business is part of the social system and we cannot isolate the economic elements of major decisions from their social consequences. So there are no simple rules. Those who make business decisions have to assess the economic and social consequences of their actions as best they can and come to their conclusions on limited information and in a limited time.

As will already be apparent, I use the word ethics to mean the guidelines or roles of conduct by which we aim to live. It is, of course, foolhardy to write about ethics at all, because you lay yourself open to the charge of taking up a position of moral superiority, of failing to practice what you preach, or both. I am not in a position to preach nor am I promoting a specific code of conduct. I believe, however, that it is useful to all of us who are responsible for business decisions to acknowledge the part which ethics plays in those decisions and to encourage discussion of how best to combine commercial and ethical judgments. Most business decisions involve some degree of ethical judgment; few can be taken solely on the basis of arithmetic.

While we refer to a company as having a set of standards, that is a convenient shorthand. The people who make up the company are responsible for its conduct and it is their collective actions which determine the company's standards. The ethical standards of a company are judged by its actions, not by pious statements of intent put out in its name. This does not mean that those who head companies should not set down what they believe their companies stand for—hard though that is to do. The character of a company is a matter of importance to those in it, to those who do business with it, and to those who are considering joining it.

What matters most, however, is where we stand as individual managers and how we behave when faced with decisions which require us to combine ethical and commercial judgments. In approaching such decisions, I believe it is helpful to go through two steps. The first is to determine, as precisely as we can, what our personal rules of conduct are. This does not mean drawing up a list of virtuous notions, which will probably end up a watered-down version of the Scriptures without their literary merit. It does mean looking back at decisions we have made and working out from there what our rules actually are. The aim is to avoid confusing ourselves and everyone else by declaring one set of principles and acting on another. Our ethics are expressed in our actions, which is why they are usually clearer to others than to ourselves.

Once we know where we stand personally we can move on to the second step, which is to think through who else will be affected by the decision and how we should weight their interest in it. Some interests will be represented by well-organized groups; others will have no one to put their case. If a factory manager is negotiating a wage claim with employee representatives, their remit is to look after the interests of those who are already employed. Yet the effect of the wage settlement on the factory's costs may well determine whether new employees are likely to be taken on. So the manager cannot ignore the interest of potential employees in the outcome of the negotiation, even though that interest is not represented at the bargaining table.

The rise of organized interest groups makes it doubly important that managers consider the arguments of everyone with a legitimate interest in a decision's outcome. Interest groups seek publicity to promote their causes and they have the advantage of being single-minded: they are against building an airport on a certain site, for example, but take no responsibility for finding a better alternative. This narrow focus gives pressure groups a debating advantage against managements, which cannot evade the responsibility for making decisions in the same way.

In *The Hard Problems of Management*, Mark Pastin has perceptively referred to this phenomenon as the ethical superiority of the uninvolved, and there is a good deal of it about. Pressure groups are skilled at seizing the high moral ground and arguing that our judgment as managers is at best biased and at worst influenced solely by private gain because we have a direct commercial interest in the outcome of our decisions. But as managers we are also responsible for arriving at business decisions which take account of all the interests concerned; the uninvolved are not.

At times the campaign to persuade companies to divest themselves of their South African subsidiaries has exemplified this kind of ethical high-handedness. Apartheid is abhorrent politically, socially, and morally. Those who argue that they can exert some influence on the direction of change by staying put believe this as sincerely as those who favor divestment. Yet many anti-apartheid campaigners reject the proposition that both sides have the same end in view. From their perspective it is self-evident that the only ethical course of action is for companies to wash their hands of the problems of South Africa by selling out.

Managers cannot be so self-assured. In deciding what weight to give to the arguments for and against divestment, we must consider who has what at stake in the outcome of the decision. The employees of a South African subsidiary have the most direct stake, as the decision affects their future; they are also the group whose voice is least likely to be heard outside South Africa. The shareholders have at stake any loss on divestment, against which must be balanced any gain in the value of their shares through severing the South African connection. The divestment lobby is the one group for whom the decision is costless either way.

What is clear from this limited analysis is that there is no general answer to the question of whether companies should sell their South African subsidiaries or not. Pressure to reduce complicated issues to straightforward alternatives, one of which is right and the other wrong, is a regrettable sign of the times. But boards are rarely presented with two clearly opposed alternatives. Companies faced with the same issues will therefore properly come to different conclusions and their decisions may alter over time.

A less contentious divestment decision faced my own company when we decided to sell our foods division. Because the division was mainly a U.K. business with regional brands, it did not fit the company's strategy, which called for concentrating resources behind our confectionery and soft drinks brands internationally. But it was an attractive business in its own right and the decision to sell prompted both a management bid and external offers.

Employees working in the division strongly supported the management bid and made their views felt. In this instance, they were the best organized interest group and they had more information available to them to back their case than any of the other parties involved. What they had at stake was also very clear.

From the shareholders' point of view, the premium over asset value offered by the various bidders was a key aspect of the decision. They also had an interest in seeing the deal completed without regulatory delays and without diverting too much management attention from the ongoing business. In addition, the way in which the successful bidder would guard the brand name had to be considered, since the division would take with it products carrying the parent company's name.

In weighing the advantages and disadvantages of the various offers, the board considered all the groups, consumers among them, who would be affected by the sale. But our main task was to reconcile the interests of the employees and of the shareholders. (The more, of course, we can encourage employees to become shareholders, the closer together the interests of these two stakeholders will be brought.) The division's management upped its bid in the face of outside competition, and after due deliberation we decided to sell to the management team, believing that this choice best balanced the diverse interests at stake.

Companies whose activities are international face an additional complication in taking their decisions. They aim to work to the same standards of business conduct wherever they are and to behave as good corporate citizens of the countries in which they trade. But the two aims are not always compatible: promotion on merit may be the rule of the company and promotion by seniority the custom of the country. In addition, while the financial arithmetic on which companies base their decisions is generally accepted, what is considered ethical varies among cultures.

If what would be considered corruption in the company's home territory is an accepted business practice elsewhere, how are local managers expected to act? Companies could do business only in countries in which they feel ethically at home, provided always that their shareholders take the same view. But this approach could prove unduly restrictive, and there is always a certain arrogance in dismissing foreign codes of conduct without considering why they may be different. If companies find, for example, that they have to pay customs officers in another country just to do their job, it may be that the state is simply transferring its responsibilities to the private sector as an alternative to using taxation less efficiently to the same end.

Nevertheless, this example brings us to one of the most common ethical issues companies face—how far to go in buying business. What payments are legitimate for companies to make to win orders and, the reverse side of that coin, when do gifts to employees become bribes? I use two rules of thumb to test whether a payment is acceptable from the company's point of view: Is the payment on the face of the invoice? Would it embarrass the recipient to have the gift mentioned in the company newspaper?

The first test ensures that all payments, however unusual they may seem, are recorded and go through the books. The second is aimed at distinguishing bribes from gifts, a definition which depends on the size of the gift and the influence it is likely to have on the recipient. The value of a case of whiskey to me would be limited, because I only take it as medicine. We know ourselves whether a gift is acceptable or not and we know that others will know if they are aware of the nature of the gift.

As for payment on the face of the invoice, I have found it a useful general rule precisely because codes of conduct do vary round the world. It has legitimized some otherwise unlikely company payments, to the police in one country, for example, and to the official planning authorities in another, but all went through the books and were audited. Listing a payment on the face of the invoice may not be a sufficient ethical test, but it is a necessary one; payments outside the company's system are corrupt and corrupting.

The logic behind these rules of thumb is that openness and ethics go together and that actions are unethical if they will not stand scrutiny. Openness in arriving at decisions reflects the same logic. It gives those with an interest in a particular decision the chance to make their views known and opens to argument the basis on which the decision is finally taken. This in turn enables the decision makers to learn from experience and to improve their powers of judgment.

Openness is also, I believe, the best way to disarm outside suspicion of companies'

motives and actions. Disclosure is not a panacea for improving the relations between business and society, but the willingness to operate an open system is the foundation of those relations. Business needs to be open to the views of society and open in return about its own activities; this is essential for the establishment of trust.

For the same reasons, as managers we need to be candid when making decisions about other people. Dr. Johnson reminds us that when it comes to lapidary inscriptions, "no man is upon oath." But what should be disclosed in references, in fairness to those looking for work and to those who are considering employing them?

The simplest rule would seem to be that we should write the kind of reference we would wish to read. Yet "do as you would be done by" says nothing about ethics. The actions which result from applying it could be ethical or unethical, depending on the standards of the initiator. The rule could be adapted to help managers determine their ethical standards, however, by reframing it as a question: If you did business with yourself, how ethical would you think you were?

Anonymous letters accusing an employee of doing something discreditable create another context in which candor is the wisest course. Such letters cannot by definition be answered, but they convey a message to those who receive them, however warped or unfair the message may be. I normally destroy these letters, but tell the person concerned what has been said. This conveys the disregard I attach to nameless allegation, but preserves the rule of openness. From a practical point of view, it serves as a warning if there is anything in the allegations; from an ethical point of view, the degree to which my judgment of the person may now be prejudiced is known between us.

The last aspect of ethics in business decisions I want to discuss concerns our responsibility for the level of employment; what can or should companies do about the provision of jobs? This issue is of immediate concern to European managers because unemployment is higher in Europe than it is in the United States and the net number of new jobs created has been much lower. It comes to the fore whenever companies face decisions which require a trade-off between increasing efficiency and reducing numbers employed.

If you believe, as I do, that the primary purpose of a company is to satisfy the needs of its customers and to do so profitably, the creation of jobs cannot be the company's goal as well. Satisfying customers requires companies to compete in the marketplace, and so we cannot opt out of introducing new technology, for example, to preserve jobs. To do so would be to deny consumers the benefits of progress, to shortchange the shareholders, and in the longer run to put the jobs of everyone in the company at risk. What destroys jobs certainly and permanently is the failure to be competitive.

Experience says that the introduction of new technology creates more jobs than it eliminates, in ways which cannot be forecast. It may do so, however, only after a time lag, and those displaced may not, through lack of skills, be able to take advantage of the new opportunities when they arise. Nevertheless, the company's prime responsibility to everyone who has a stake in it is to retain its competitive edge, even if this means a loss of jobs in the short run.

Where companies do have a social responsibility, however, is in how we manage the situation, how we smooth the path of technological change. Companies are responsible for the timing of such changes and we are in a position to involve those who will be affected by the way in which those changes are introduced. We also have a vital resource in our capacity to provide training, so that continuing employees can take advantage of change and those who may lose their jobs can more readily find new ones.

In the United Kingdom, an organization called Business in the Community has been established to encourage the formation of new enterprises. Companies have backed it with cash and with secondments. The secondment of able managers to worthwhile institutions is a particularly effective expression of concern, because the ability to manage is such a scarce resource. Through Business in the Community we can create jobs collectively, even if we cannot do so individually, and it is clearly in our interest to improve the economic and social climate in this way.

Throughout, I have been writing about the responsibilities of those who head companies and my emphasis has been on taking decisions, because that is what directors and managers are appointed to do. What concerns me is that too often the public pressures which are put on companies in the name of ethics encourage their boards to put off decisions or to wash their hands of problems. There may well be commercial reasons for those choices, but there are rarely ethical ones. The ethical bases on which decisions are arrived at will vary among companies, but shelving those decisions is likely to be the least ethical course.

The company which takes drastic action in order to survive is more likely to be criticized publicly than the one which fails to grasp the nettle and gradually but inexorably declines. There is always a temptation to postpone difficult decisions, but it is not in society's interests that hard choices should be evaded because of public clamor or the possibility of legal action. Companies need to be encouraged to take the decisions which face them; the responsibility for providing that encouragement rests with society as a whole.

Society sets the ethical framework within which those who run companies have to work out their own codes of conduct. Responsibility for decisions, therefore, runs both ways. Business has to take account of its responsibilities to society in coming to its decisions, but society has to accept its responsibilities for setting the standards against which those decisions are made.

INSTILLING ETHICAL BEHAVIOR IN ORGANIZATIONS: A Survey of Canadian Companies

R. Murray Lindsay

Linda M. Lindsay

V. Bruce Irvine

With the growing realization that North America is experiencing an ethical crisis in business, public interest in ethics is at an all time high (Grier, 1991). Almost every day one can pick up a newspaper or watch television and be presented with yet another calamity caused, at least in part, by unethical behavior, with consequences reaching far beyond company walls. The *Wall Street Journal* and the *Financial Post* print over 200 such stories each month (Beauchamp and Bowie, 1988). Specific examples in Canada are the Hagersville tire fire, the disputed takeover of Dome Petroleum, the fall of Campeau, demonstrations opposing clearcut logging, the feud in Canadian Tire, and the collapse of Principal Trust. In all likelihood, such publicized incidents represent only a fraction of the cases that go untold.

Yet, one can also observe that many executives are going to some length to counter this negative image of business by publicizing examples of their companies' ethical behavior in the press, financial reports, and in their public speeches. Indeed, there is a growing recognition among business leaders that "good ethics is good business" (Kelly, 1989). For example, the CEO of Dupont voluntarily stopped production of chlorofluorocarbons—a $750 million a year business for the company—when he learned that they just *may* be harmful to the Earth's ozone layer (Kirkpatrick, 1990).

With such examples of both ethical and unethical corporate behavior, it becomes of interest to know why some organizations behave ethically while others do not. Jackall (1988) argues that unethical actions of managers do not result from individual moral deficiencies alone, but are encouraged by the bureaucratic structure of modern corporations. Individuals in such organizations

Journal of Business Ethics 15: 393–407, 1996. © 1996 Kluwer Academic Publishers. Printed in the Netherlands.

often have to compromise their personal ethics in order to advance (cf. Grosman, 1988; Shultz, 1989). Indeed, Frederick, based on data from 10 studies, concluded that "even the most upright people are apt to become dishonest . . . when placed in a typical corporate environment" (as cited in Shultz, 1989, p. 57).

The perspective adopted in this study is that an organization's management control system can play an important role in directing and influencing employees to pursue ethical behavior (see Murphy, 1988). Specifically, by reconstructing procedures, processes and systems to foster an ethical dimension, employees are provided with an overall context of corporate values within which to pursue profits. To this end, the paper develops a theoretical framework of control for instilling ethical behavior by linking various ethics related control mechanisms identified in the literature to the primary components of management control systems. In addition, the results of a survey investigating the control mechanisms that Canadian companies are using to formally instill ethical behavior in employee decision making are reported. This survey represents a replication and extension of the Center for Business Ethics's (1986) survey of *Fortune*'s 1000 industrial and service corporations in the United States and, to a lesser extent, Sweeney and Siers' (1990) survey of controllers employed in *Fortune* 500 U.S. companies which examined ethical codes of conduct.

MANAGEMENT CONTROL SYSTEMS AND ETHICAL BEHAVIOR

A firm's management control system (MCS) is designed to motivate employees to perform activities that will further the organization's goals (Merchant, 1985). A MCS consists of three components (Otley and Berry, 1980; Emmanuel et al., 1990).

(1) specifying and communicating objectives;

(2) monitoring performance through measurement (feedback/control); and

(3) motivating employees to accomplish objectives by linking the reward system to objective achievement.

All three components are necessary. The setting and communicating of objectives—statements of purpose or desired achievements—is essential because without aim or purpose control has no meaning (Otley and Berry, 1980). The second component provides feedback on the performance of those being measured, allowing management to monitor the implementation of plans designed to achieve the firm's objectives and to take corrective action as needed (Euske, 1984; Anthony, 1988). The final component serves to motivate and encourage employees to perform in a goal congruent manner (Merchant, 1985; Anthony, 1988). A key point is that the absence of any one of these components seriously impairs the effectiveness of the others.

With respect to controlling for ethical behavior, seven specific mechanisms have been identified in the literature:

Code of ethics A document that provides employees in an organization with the company's ethical policies and a common foundation for administering these policies (Center for Business Ethics [CBE], 1986; Sweeney and Siers, 1990);

Whistleblowing system Formal processes and means which enable employees to report unethical activities to parties who may be able to take action (Greenberger et al., 1987; Neilsen, 1987);

Ethics focused reward system A formal reward system which directly promotes, measures, and rewards the ethical behavior of employees (Wilson, 1983; Velasquez, 1990);

Ethics committee A formally specified group of employees responsible for developing, updating, and enforcing the code of ethics (CBE, 1986; Murphy, 1988);

Judiciary board An independent group which acts as the enforcement mechanism for discovering or reacting to ethical problems (Aram, 1986; Murphy, 1988; Neilsen, 1989; Shultz, 1989);

Employee training in ethics A formal program of seminars, guest speakers, workshops, and training programs developed for the purpose of exposing and educating employees in ethics and ethics related issues (CBE, 1986; Murphy, 1988); and

Ethics focused corporate governance A decision making process which includes representatives from as many constituencies of the organization as possible (e.g. labor, civic, environmental, and consumer groups) in order to allow corporate leadership to fully assess, consider, and balance the various competing interests of the organization and its constituents (Aram, 1986; CBE, 1986);

Figure 1 lists these mechanisms and links them to one of the three components of a management control system. While each mechanism (except the ethics committee) has been categorized within only one of the three MCS components based on its primary role, it should be recognized that the boundaries are fuzzy and some overlap exists for some mechanisms.

To elaborate on Figure 1, a code of ethics is used to specify objectives, while meetings and training sessions are used to communicate and explain these objectives to organizational members. An organization's ethics committee can play a major role in establishing the code. Also, ethics focused corporate governance can be used to define objectives by involving various constituents in decision making. However, following from control theory, the specification of objectives alone will not necessarily motivate employees to undertake goal congruent behavior. Controlling for ethical behavior also requires that performance be monitored or measured with respect to the ethical objectives. Whistleblowing channels are a form of monitoring because they provide a source of feedback on company activities. Feedback is also provided from the monitoring of ethical behavior undertaken by a firm's judiciary board or ethics committee. Finally, reward systems belong in the final phase of the control process in that what gets measured and rewarded gets done.

RESEARCH DESIGN

The researchers significantly modified the instrument developed by the Center for Business Ethics (1986). The original instrument was considered to be too long and repetitive. While including all seven mechanisms, the questionnaire focused on codes of ethics, whistleblowing channels, and ethics

FIGURE 1	Ethics related control mechanisms linked to management control system components
Components of a MCS	**Ethics related control mechanisms**
• Specifying and communicating objectives	• Code of ethics • Employee training ethics • Ethics focused corporate governance • Ethics committee
• Monitoring performance (feedback/control)	• Whistleblowing channels • Judiciary board • Ethics committee
• Motivation by linking rewards to performance	• Ethics focused reward system

focused reward systems in order to achieve a reasonably acceptable length and to encompass each MCS component. Previous research indicates that the use of the other four mechanisms is minimal. The instrument was pre-tested by controllers of 10 firms and this resulted in several changes being made to improve the clarity of the questionnaire.

Controllers were selected to respond to the questionnaire. Controllers play a key role in designing and implementing a MCS, as well as providing the feedback information that helps make the system work (Pipkin, 1989). In addition, controllers are often responsible for helping to enforce company policies and are entrusted with special fiduciary responsibility when it comes to business ethics (Schlank, 1985a). As Schlank (1985b, p. 6) put it: controllers are the "keepers of the corporate conscience." Thus there is good reason to consider controllers as knowledgeable when seeking information on the use of ethics related control mechanisms.

Three hundred questionnaire packages were sent to controllers employed by companies in Canada. The companies were selected using a stratified, random sample from a population of non-Quebec registered companies identified in the *Financial Post*'s Top 1000 industrial and service corporations list.[1] A stratified sample was used to ensure that the sample mirrored the population with respect to size (as measured by sales).

The data collection procedure began with a telephone call to the controllers in the sample in order to obtain their names so that a personalized letter could be used, as well as to ask for their participation. Only six of the 300 controllers stated outright that they would not participate. A package containing the questionnaire, instructions, a postage-paid return envelope and a postcard was then mailed to the sample of controllers. The instructions indicated that the postcard was to be returned to the researchers separately from the questionnaire. This allowed the researchers to identify non-respondents, while

guaranteeing the anonymity of respondents. Three weeks after the initial mailing, a follow-up letter was sent to non-respondents reminding them of the questionnaire and the importance of their responses.

Of the 300 questionnaires distributed, 171 were returned by the cut-off date, providing an overall response rate of 57 percent. Confidence intervals were calculated to test the representativeness of respondents with respect to the population on four key variables: size (as measured by sales), controlling interest of the company (foreign parent, Canadian parent, government), nature of ownership if no controlling interest (publicly owned, publicly owned with significant government interest, privately owned, and cooperative), and industry. These tests indicated that the respondent companies were generally representative of the population in terms of size and industry. However, two out of the seven comparisons produced statistically significant differences with respect to the controlling interest (government) and nature of ownership (publicly owned) strata. The respondent companies were distributed in approximately equal proportions among the following four sales categories : (1) smaller than $104 million (41 firms); (2) $104 to $227 million (48 firms); (3) $228 to $589 million (41 firms); and (4) $590 million or more (41 firms).

RESULTS

The results of the survey are reported in two parts. The first provides a general overview of the organizational practices being used to instil ethical behavior in employees. Summary frequency statistics are reported for the seven mechanisms of interest. The second part of the analysis examines responses to the more detailed questions relating to the three primary mechanisms under investigation (code of ethics, whistleblowing, and ethics focused reward system). Differences in proportions among the various subpopulations were examined using *t*-tests and are reported for statistically significant comparisons.[2] No significant differences were found in the second part of the analysis.

An Overview of Companies' Practices with Respect to Instilling Ethical Behavior

(i) Are ethical concepts included in corporate mission statements?

Of the 164 respondents who answered this question, 72 (43.9%) indicated that ethical concepts and philosophies are included, 80 (48.7%) said that they are not, and 12 (7.3%) did not know.

In examining the results by organizational size, 62 percent of the large firms (i.e. sales greater than $590 million, representing the top one-quarter of the sample) included ethical concepts in their mission statements as compared to only 28 percent for small companies (i.e. sales smaller than $104 million, representing the bottom one-quarter of the sample) [$p < 0.005$]. This result suggests that large organizations are reacting—at least superficially—more quickly than small companies in responding to the need and the increasing public demand for greater social responsibility (CBE, 1986; Sweeney and Siers, 1990).

The data was also categorized by the nature of the controlling interest of the firm. Nearly 64 percent of the foreign controlled companies indicated that their mission statement included ethical issues as compared to only 45 percent for Canadian controlled companies ($p < 0.11$). No further statistical differences were detected when investigating the remaining strata.

(ii) Are companies taking steps to instil ethical behavior?

The results of a question asking controllers whether their company was taking any steps to instil ethical behavior are presented in Table I. Of the 171 responding companies, 84 (49%) indicated that they use or were in the process of implementing at least one of the seven ethics related control mechanisms under investigation in this study. Thirty-three organizations use only one mechanism, 30 use two, 11 use three, four companies use four, four use five, and two companies use six control mechanisms. No company uses all seven mechanisms.

Eighty-seven respondents (51%) indicated that they did not use any of the seven mechanisms. Of these, 42 state their company has taken some other explicit action to instil ethical behavior. Five main categories of actions were reported.[3] One consisted of firing individuals who act unethically or using written or verbal warnings with respect to borderline cases (five firms). Second, ten respondents stated that the strength of their organizations' corporate culture is a viable mechanism for instilling ethical behavior. Third, six companies use internal and external audits to detect illegal behavior. Fourth, 19 respondents indicated that an informal code of ethics is present in their organizations. Finally, eight controllers indicated that their company's concern for the environment is instilled through the use of board and special meetings.

Further analysis indicated that 70.7 percent of the large companies employ at least one of the seven mechanisms as compared to only 29.3 percent for small companies ($p < 0.001$). Companies in which the controlling interest is held by a foreign parent (47 firms) utilize one or more of the seven mechanisms more often than those in which the controlling interest is held by a Canadian parent (33 firms) [93.6% and 54.5% respectively; $p < 0.001$]. Seven of the eight companies whose controlling interest is held by the government (i.e., local, provincial, or federal) reported that they use one or more of the seven mechanisms.

In summary, approximately 74 percent (126 of 171) of the companies were taking some specific action to instil ethical behavior in employee decision making. This finding is reasonably comparable to the Center for Business Ethics's (1986) result of 80 percent.[4]

(iii) To what extent are the seven mechanisms used?

The results reported below are based on answers from the 84 respondents who reported that their company uses or is in the process of implementing at least one of the seven mechanisms. Table II reports the number of companies who are using, implementing, and not using each mechanism.

Seventy-four (88%) of the 84 companies use a code of ethics. This percentage increases to 93 percent when the four firms in the process of implementing a code are included. Forty-three percent of the firms employ and an additional 3.6 percent are in the process of implementing some form of whistleblowing system. The third most popular mechanism was employee training in ethics, with 26 percent of the respondents indicating that it is used and 4 percent are in the process of implementation. Each of

the remaining four mechanisms (ethics focused reward system, ethics committee, judiciary committee, judiciary board, and ethics focused corporate governance) are used in less that 17 percent of the firms.

The studies by the Center for Business Ethics (1986) and Sweeney and Siers (1990) surveying U.S. companies found that codes of ethics are more prevalent in larger organizations. An analysis was performed to determine if companies in Canada follow a similar pattern. The results indicate that they do. The 20 largest companies (sales over $1.3 million) all use a code of ethics, as compared to only 67 percent for the 19 smallest companies (sales under $68 million) [$p < 0.02$]. No further statistically significant differences were detected for the remaining subpopulation strata.

(iv) Who plays an important role in the design and implementation of ethics related control mechanisms?

Table III lists the percentages for the position/function of the person considered by respondents to play an important role in designing and/or implementing a particular ethics related control mechanism. To use

TABLE I	Are companies taking any actions to instil ethical behavior?	Number of companies	% of responses
Companies using, or in the process of implementing, any of the seven ethics control mechanisms		84	49.1%
Companies which do not use any of the seven mechanisms but which are taking other explicit actions to instil ethical behavior		42	24.6%
Total number of companies taking some specific action		126	73.7%
Companies which were taking no actions to instil ethical behavior		26	15.2%
Companies for which respondents did not know whether or not specific actions were being taken		19	11.1%
Total number of companies taking no action or in which any action being taken was not known by respondents		45	26.3%
Total number of respondents		171	100.0%

TABLE II	The extent to which the mechanisms are used*					
Ethics related control mechanisms	**Have mechanism**		**Implementing mechanism**		**Do not have mechanism**	
	n =	%	*n =*	%	*n =*	%
Code of ethics	74	88.1	4	5	6	6.9
Whistleblowing channels	36	42.9	3	3.6	45	53.5
Ethics focused reward system	10	11.9	0	0	74	88.1
Ethics committee	12	14.3	0	0	72	85.7
Judiciary board	4	4.8	0	0	80	95.2
Employee training in ethics	22	26.2	3	3.6	59	70.2
Ethics focused corporate governance	13	15.5	1	1.2	70	83.3

* For those companies indicating that they used or are implementing one or more of the seven mechanisms (n = 84).

the code of ethics as an example, senior or executive officers were reported to be important in 66 companies (73.3%), middle managers in 12 companies (13.3%), the controller's department in 9 firms (10%), and an outside person in 3 companies (3.4%). As Table III indicates, senior or executive officers dominate in four of the seven mechanisms. Middle management, in conjunction with senior management, play an important role for designing and implementing employee training in ethics. Finally, department personnel, in conjunction with senior management, play an important role in the implementation of judiciary boards. By and large, few firms are seeking outside assistance in designing and implementing the various mechanisms.

TABLE III	Position of person playing an important role in the design and/or implementation of control mechanisms							
Control mechanism		**A**	**B**	**C**	**D**	**E**	**F**	**G**
	(n =)	%	%	%	%	%	%	%
Code of ethics	90*	73.3	13.3	10	0	0	3.4	0
Whistleblowing channels	39	59	17.9	17.9	2.6	0	2.6	0
Ethics focused reward system	1	0	100	0	0	0	0	0
Ethics committee	12	58.3	33.3	0	0	0	8.4	0
Judiciary board	9	44.4	11.1	0	44.4	0	0	0
Employee training in ethics	24	37.5	41.7	8.3	12.5	0	0	0
Corporate governance	10	60	10	10	10	0	0	10

* The total n for each mechanism may exceed the totals reported in Table II because more than one function was selected by some respondents.
A　Senior or executive officers
B　Middle managers
C　Controller
D　Department personnel
E　Hourly employees
F　Persons from outside the organization
G　Other

The findings with respect to the importance of senior management in implementing mechanisms was not unanticipated. Their commitment is critical if ethical considerations are to be incorporated in decision making. (National Institute of Business Management, 1987; Murphy, 1988). Nonetheless, it should be noted that everyone needs to be included in the implementation effort; it is not just a management concern (National Institute of Business Management, 1987). For example, employee involvement and approval is vital during the development of a code of ethics because it is during this phase that all viewpoints must be recognized and where commitment to the resulting code originates (Brooks, 1989).

Detailed Analysis

1. Code of Ethics

The questionnaire solicited a variety of information regarding the use of ethical codes of conduct by asking respondents to answer a series of questions. Summary results to these questions are presented in Table IV. The total number of responses for each question are not always the same because one of the respondents chose not to answer two of the questions.

Fifty-two (68%) of the 76 respondents indicated that every employee in the organization receives a written copy of the code. These results are similar to those of Sweeney and Siers (1990) where 57 percent of the respondents indicated that all employees received a copy of the code. Further information was obtained from the 24 respondents replying negatively to the question. In these companies, 100 percent of senior management and 92 percent of middle management were provided with a copy. Employees in staff positions were given a copy in 75 percent of the companies. These results are also similar to those obtained by

Sweeney and Siers (1990), where senior and middle management and staff personnel were given a copy of the code in 100, 99 and 75 percent of the companies respectively.

The second question asked whether the company had a formal program to educate employees regarding the nature, provisions, and requirements of the code. Forty-one percent replied that they did. This result was similar to Sweeney and Siers' (1990) finding of 43 percent. The most frequently used programs are (1) special indoctrination seminars, conferences, and workshops for new employees (12 out of 31 firms); (2) publications issued occasionally (11 out of 31 firms); and (3) seminars, conferences and workshops for middle and/or senior management personnel (7 out of 31 firms).

The third question examined whether there was a general understanding of the code among all employees. Of the 76 respondents, 67 percent replied that there was, 17 percent indicated that such an understanding did not exist, and 16 percent stated that they did not know.

The fourth question asked respondents whether every employee had an obligation under the code to report actual or potential personal conflicts with the code. Seventy-eight percent of the 76 controllers reported that every employee had such an obligation. A related question was also asked regarding employees' obligation for reporting actual or potential conflicts of their peers, superiors, or subordinates with provisions of the code. Fifty-seven percent reported that such a requirement existed.

Effective codes need to be revised periodically in order to reflect current ethical problems brought about by changes in societal expectations, as well as industry and organizational practices (Murphy, 1988). The fifth question therefore examined whether there was an on-going review and revision of the code. Forty-nine percent of the 75 respondents stated that there was a mechanism in place for the on-going review

TABLE IV	Company practices regarding codes of ethics								
Question	Yes		No		Do not know		Total	
	n =	%	*n =*	%	*n =*	%	*n =*	%
Does every employee in the company receive the code?	52	68.4	24	31.6	0	0	76	100
Does your company have a formal program to educate employees regarding the nature, provisions, and requirements of the code?	31	41.3	43	57.3	1	1.4	75	100
Do you believe there is a general understanding of the code among all employees?	51	67.1	13	17.1	12	15.8	76	100
Does every employee have an obligation under the code to report actual/potential conflicts with the code?	59	77.6	14	18.4	3	4	75	100
Does every employee have an obligation under the code to report actual/potential conflicts of peers, superiors, or subordinates?	43	56.6	29	38.2	4	5.2	76	100
Is a mechanism in place for the on-going review and/or revision of the code?	37	49.3	24	32	14	18.7	75	100
Does the code specify disciplinary measures for failure to comply with it?	39	51.3	34	44.7	3	4	76	100

and/or revision of the code. Thirty-two percent reported that no such mechanism existed, while 19 percent indicated that they did not know.

The final question reported in Table IV examined whether the code specified disciplinary measures for failure to comply with its provisions. This was the case in 51 percent of the companies.

In addition, information regarding how companies determine whether employees are complying with the provisions of the code was obtained. Sixty-two (82%) of the 76 respondents indicated that their company monitored compliance with the code in some way. Of these, 40 (64%) use a periodic sign-off procedure, whereby employees are requested to sign to the effect that they are in compliance with the code. Eleven companies (18%) include compliance with the code in performance evaluations. Finally, 11 respondents (18%) chose the "other" category; however, they did not provide any information regarding the specific procedures used.

2. Whistleblowing Systems

As the environments in which corporations operate become increasingly complex and risk bearing, and in an era of rapidly changing regulatory standards, determining what constitutes ethical behavior becomes increasingly difficult. This places a premium on instituting processes for encouraging frank discussion and good conflict resolution (National Institute of Business Management, 1987, p. 75). A good whistleblowing system can play an important part in such a process.

As shown in Table II (see p. 97), 39 (46%) of the 84 organizations using formal ethics related control mechanisms employed or were in the process of implementing some form of whistleblowing system, making it the second most popular mechanism. Further information regarding this system was obtained. The reader should note that not all of the 39 controllers responded to this part of the questionnaire.

The literature on whistleblowing systems indicates that two main issues are involved in their design: (1) whether whistleblowing should be encouraged inside or outside the organization; and (2) whether the whistleblower's identity should be kept confidential (Neilsen, 1987; 1989). In this regard, all 28 respondents reported that their companies encourage whistleblowing inside rather than outside of the organization. In addition, 24 (86%) of the 28 respondents stated their company keeps the whistleblower's identity confidential.

The study by the Center of Business Ethics (1986) indicated that the use of an ombudsperson is one type of whistleblowing system used by organizations in the United States. Information was collected on whether Canadian companies use ombudspersons. Twenty-seven (73%) of the 37 companies using whistleblowing channels did not employ an ombudsperson, five companies (14%) did, and 5 respondents (14%) indicated that they did not know. When choosing an ombudsperson the five companies all reported that the three most important qualifications considered are training in ethics or business ethics, management experience, and personal integrity. In four of the five companies respondents indicated that a person is appointed to the position rather than being elected or volunteering.

3. *Ethics Focused Reward Systems*

As reported in Table II (see p. 97), only 10 (12%) of the 84 companies adopting at least one of the seven mechanisms use an ethics focused reward system. The analysis for this mechanism is based on the responses to three questions.

The first question sought to determine whether ethics compliance was part of the performance review of employees. Only one of the 10 respondents reported positively to this question.[5] With respect to the second question, no company formally rewarded employees for exhibiting ethical behavior. The final question sought to determine whether those identified as having exhibited unethical behavior were penalized by the organization. This was the policy for 8 of the 10 companies.

The fact that 88 percent of the 84 companies attempting to instil ethical behavior did not have an ethics focused reward system raises important questions regarding the motivation that organizations are providing their employees to behave ethically. For those 10 companies employing this mechanism, the results indicate that management relies almost exclusively on negative rather than positive reinforcement as the means to achieve the organization's ethical goals. While negative reinforcement policies are no doubt appropriate in certain situations of ethical misconduct (e.g., taking a bribe), firms are failing to benefit from the significant motivational benefits of positive reinforcement (see Herzberg, 1987).

Positive reinforcement can be expected to be beneficial when it is based on an employee's display of good judgment and/or moral fortitude in a difficult situation (as opposed to situations where employees simply follow the dictates of the code of conduct, e.g., not taking a bribe). A specific example might be reporting "bad news" early to one's superior as opposed to attempting to hide the problem or, worse yet, attempting to mask the problem by undertaking behavior which is actually dysfunctional to the organization.[6] Divesting of an important business area when there is knowledge that environmental concerns might arise in the future is another example. Regardless of whether rewards are directly linked to such behavior, if these employees get promoted then the message becomes clear: behaving ethically is the right thing to do. Such is a platform on which strong ethical cultures are built.

DISCUSSION AND FURTHER ANALYSIS OF RESULTS

One hundred and twenty-six (74%) of the 171 respondent companies were taking some specific step to instil ethical behavior in decision making. Within this group, 84 companies were utilizing at least one of the seven mechanisms of interest to this study. While this overall result is fairly encouraging, indicating that ethical elements are receiving consideration in a good number of organizations operating in Canada, particularly in the larger ones, the following analysis suggests that much improvement remains to be accomplished.

The most frequently used mechanism is the code of ethics, with 46 percent of this study's respondents reporting using or in the process of implementing the mechanism. This result is considerably lower than the 75 percent result obtained by the Center for Business Ethics study. For the subgroup of firms using one or more of the seven mechanisms under examination, this percentage increases to 93%, indicating that the use of a code is the dominant plank in any firm's attempt to instil ethics into organizational decision making. The prominent use of a code of ethics was not unexpected. A code clarifies what is meant by ethical conduct and, in so doing, establishes standards for employees to gauge their behavior. However, while the use of a code is very important in instilling ethical behavior, it must be recognized that it constitutes only a first step (National Institute of Business Management, 1987, p. 80).

Conflicting results were obtained with respect to the enforcement of the code. Sixty-two (82%) of the 76 companies reported that their company monitored compliance with the code in some way, typically through self-reporting, e.g., sign-off procedures. On the other hand, and similar to the CBE study, only 14 percent have an ethics committee and only 5 percent of firms have a judiciary

board—mechanisms which many consider to be an integral part of the enforcement of an organization's code (Brown, 1987; Cottell, 1987; Brooks, 1989; Shultz, 1989). More encouraging is the result that 46 percent of the firms have a whistleblowing system.

These results are difficult to interpret. For example, does the scarcity of ethics committees and judicial boards indicate firms are not serious and that the compliance procedures adopted are merely window dressing? Gellerman (1986) argues that the most effective deterrent is to "heighten the perceived probability of being caught." It is difficult to envision how this probability can be very high if firms do not possess ethics committees or judiciary boards. Without meaningful feedback, management is not in a position to ascertain whether organizational behavior is consistent with the code.

That many companies may only be paying lip service to the idea of promoting ethical behavior is further suggested by the results that communication of the code, as well as education about it, are poor. Only 68 percent of the companies provide a copy of the code to every employee, while only 41 percent have a formal program to educate employees about it. Moreover, only 30 percent of the firms adopting one or more of the mechanisms provide their employees with training in ethics (see Table II, p. 97). Finally, 50 percent of the firms have no mechanism in place to review and revise the code, hardly the situation providing for a living document that can be used to guide one's behavior. In this regard, Thompson's (1992) comments in an essay entitled "Rhetoric and Reality" are particularly pertinent:

> "It's the right thing to do," the oatmeal commercial likes to say. . . . No doubt these efforts [adopting codes of conduct] are largely sincere and directed by people of integrity and goodwill. But consider what happens after the code of conduct is published and delivered to employees. Does an intensive effort

begin to ensure the code is understood by all employees? Is it positioned as a part of everyday working life, visible in all the decisions and actions of the employees individually and the company itself? Or, does management heave a collective sigh of relief saying, "Well, we got that out of the way, let's get back to the real business of the business"? All too often, I suggest, the sigh of relief wins. The rhetoric, the fine words and phrases crafted by corporate speech writers for top management are often not backed up by communication and training for all levels of employees, or any effective form of support (pp. 54–55).

Further evidence for this contention is provided by the result that only 10 of the 84 companies adopting one of the seven mechanisms utilize an ethics focused reward mechanism. A related result is that only 51 percent of the companies specified disciplinary measures in the code for failures to comply with it (see Table IV, p. 99). As the study by the National Institute of Business Management (1987) explains, a good ethical program cannot be patchwork in nature. It needs to be woven into the entire fabric of corporate life. Failure to seriously monitor, measure and reward (punish) the performance of individuals on the ethical plane will leave codes of conduct operating in a vacuum, of little use in actually promoting ethical behavior.

In interpreting this analysis through the framework presented in Figure 1 (see p. 93), one summary conclusion is clear. For those firms taking specific steps to instil ethics into organizational decision making, the overwhelming majority are focusing only on the first component—specifying and communicating objectives—and even here the efforts are incomplete with respect to the communication aspect. They are doing very little with respect to the other two components, i.e., monitoring ethical performance/behavior and motivating ethical behavior by linking rewards/punishments

to performance. Based on control theory, the absence of these latter two components can be expected to impair a firm's formal efforts at instilling ethical behavior among employees.

A second major finding is the apparent confidence that management has in the judgment of individual employees in leaving it up to them to determine what does and does not constitute ethical behavior. One hundred and forty-two (84%) of the 171 controllers reported that consensus among employees exists as to what constitutes appropriate ethical behavior within their organization. One would think that acquiring consensus on such a multi-faceted issue would at least require a code of conduct defining ethical behavior, as well as employee training in ethics. However, only 78 companies possess a code of ethics and, as previously reported, only 52 firms give a copy of the code to everyone. Furthermore, only 25 firms provide training to their employees on ethics. Given such a state, how can consensus be reached as to the appropriate standards of conduct? Without standards, employees will use widely varying criteria in assessing the acceptability of various practices (Bruns and Merchant, 1990). In this connection, Bruns and Merchant's (1990, p. 22) conclusion based on a study examining managers' attitudes towards short-term earnings management is alarming. They write: "It seems many managers are convinced that if a practice is not explicitly prohibited or is only a slight deviation from rules, it is an ethical practice regardless of who might be affected. . . ."

Finally, the Center of Business Ethics (CBE) study's results for U.S. companies provide a relevant benchmark to compare the practices of Canadian companies. Five of the seven control mechanisms included in this study were examined by the CBE (1986). Table V compares the absolute utilization percentages obtained in this study with those of the CBE study for each mech-

TABLE V	A comparison of absolute utilization percentages of mechansims with those reported by the Center for Business Ethics (1986) study		

Mechanism	Percentage of respondents utilizing mechanism	
	CBE+	Current study*
Code of ethics	74.6	45.6
Ethics committee	14.3	7.0
Judiciary board	1.0	2.3
Employee training in ethics	35.5	14.6
Ethics focused corporate governance	16.5	8.2

+ The CBE percentages were calculated by taking the number of firms reporting using the mechanism (Table III, p. 97) divided by 279 (the total number of respondents in the study).
* Includes those firms in the process of implementing the mechanism. Total number (N) of respondents for the current study is 171.

anism. As can be seen from examining Table V, companies operating in the United States are adopting four out of the five mechanisms to a greater extent than their Canadian counterparts. Nevertheless, an interesting observation to note is that the rankings of the most frequently used mechanisms are the same in both countries. However, readers should interpret Table V cautiously as the results could be significantly distorted by non-response bias, particularly in the CBE study where the response rate was only 28%. The specific concern is that organizations taking formal steps to instil ethical behavior might be more likely to respond than organizations possessing no mechanisms, thus vitiating the comparison.

In an attempt to reduce the effects of any potential non-response bias, Table VI compares the utilization frequencies for only those companies taking steps to instil ethical behavior in their companies (in the current study, any company implementing one or more of the seven mechanisms). The last

TABLE VI	A comparison of mechanism utilization percentages with those reported by the Center for Business Ethics (1986) study (for only those companies taking steps to instil ethical behavior)		

Ethics related control mechanism	CBE research+ %	Current research* %	95% confidence interval %
Code of ethics	93.3	92.9	87.7–98.5
Whistleblowing system	n/a#	46.4	35.5–57.2
Ethics focused reward system	n/a	11.9	5.0–18.8
Ethics committee	17.9	14.3	6.8–21.8
Judiciary board	1.3	4.8	0.2–9.4
Employee training in ethics	44.4	29.8	20.0–39.6
Ethics focused corporate governance	20.6	16.7	8.7–24.7

+ N equals 223.
* N equals 84.
# The CBE study did not investigate this mechanism.

column of Table VI provides the 95 percent confidence interval for the results obtained in the current study. If the CBE result is contained within the confidence interval, the results of the two studies can be considered to be reasonably equivalent. As can be seen, these results vary drastically from those reported in Table V, suggesting that the concern for non-response bias may be justified. The differences in percentages regarding the use of a code of ethics, ethics committee, judiciary board, and ethics focused corporate governance are all relatively small (less than 4%). The only real discrepancy, where the CBE results are outside of the confidence interval for the current study, relates to employee training in ethics, where U.S. companies utilize more employee training than Canadian firms.

In conclusion, the situation existing in Canada in 1991 appears reasonably comparable to the one existing in the United States in 1984/1985 when the CBE study was conducted. This time lag might suggest that American companies are further along in their efforts at instilling ethical decision making among their employees than Canadian companies. The previously reported finding that companies with foreign parents (primarily those located in the U.S.) have more ethics related control mechanisms than companies with Canadian parents is also suggestive that Canadian firms might be lagging behind their American counterparts. One reason which may explain this situation is that management of Canadian organizations may perceive there is less need for *formal* control mechanisms because there have been fewer instances of unethical behavior in Canada and, consequently, less public pressure to respond. Nonetheless, any conclusions in this area are beyond the scope of this study. Surveying firms in both countries simultaneously along with undertaking a systematic inquiry focused at discovering why the lag exists would be necessary.

CONCLUSION

This paper has developed a theoretical framework of control for instilling ethical decision making by linking the various ethics related control mechanisms identified in the literature to the primary components of a management control system. In addition, and while much more research needs to be undertaken in this area, the findings of this study provide considerable insight into the ethics focused control mechanisms that are being utilized by Canadian companies. These findings should serve to provide important baseline information for future studies.

Like all studies, this study has limitations which should be considered in interpreting the findings. The characteristic problems with mail surveys apply to this study, although every effort was taken to minimize them. The study obtained a 57 percent response rate which can be considered to be very good. Moreover, population checks with sample data suggest that the sample is reasonably representative on key attributes. Nonetheless, a non-response bias may still exist. Readers are therefore cautioned against making sweeping generalizations. In addition, the use of the *Financial Post*'s list of companies, along with the omission of companies operating in Quebec, provide a population which is unrepresentative of all companies in Canada. As well, the demographics provided by the *Financial Post* were sometimes difficult to interpret in terms of placing a company in a particular subpopulation category. Lastly, due to the importance of minimizing respondents' time in completing the questionnaire, the study could not examine all the variables which might be expected to play an important role in influencing ethical decision making, e.g., corporate culture, leadership.

Finally, this study was based on the premise that an organization's management control system can play an important role in directing and influencing employees to pursue ethical behavior. Clearly, the use of a MCS (in terms of the mechanisms discussed in this paper) in itself is not sufficient for instilling ethical behavior in employee decision making. For example, one can envision a situation where short term earnings are being stressed by management resulting in employees feeling the need to compromise their ethics—despite any formal ethical codes of conduct to the contrary. In this situation, the wider control system, i.e., management's emphasis/communications, would be providing ambiguous or conflicting messages.[7] Nonetheless, this premise needs to be examined empirically with respect to a number of issues. Specific questions might include: how important is the formal management control system (MCS) in instilling ethical behavior? Also, does the formal MCS play a secondary role to more important factors, e.g., leadership and culture, or is its role complementary, i.e., both are needed? Answers to these types of questions can be expected to shed much needed light on the development of effective control systems for instilling ethical behavior in organizations.

ENDNOTES

1. Quebec companies were excluded because of translation difficulties.

2. All tests are two-tailed.

3. Some firms are in more than one category.

4. The 95 percent confidence interval for the present study was 67.1 to 80.3 percent.

5. This result would seem to be at odds with the finding reported above which indicated that 11 firms incorporated compliance with the code during performance evaluations. This inconsistency might suggest that the questionnaire did not ac-

curately capture respondents' situations with respect to the use of ethics focused reward systems, at least in the sense intended by the researchers.

6. The management accounting literature is replete with examples of subordinates undertaking dysfunctional behavior in order to perform well on performance criteria (see Hopwood, 1976; Emmanuel et al., 1990). However, for a contrary example related to this discussion, see Simons (1987, p. 351).

7. See Rotch (1993) for a broader view of management control systems and the importance of recognizing the interdependence of the components of control.

REFERENCES

Anthony, R.: 1988, *The Management Control Function* (Harvard University Press, Cambridge, Mass).

Aram, J: "The Art of Preventing Moral Dilemmas," *Business and Society Review* (Fall), 35–39.

Beauchamp, T. and N. Bowie: 1988, *Ethical Theory and Business* (third edition) (Prentice Hall, Englewood Cliffs, New Jersey).

Brooks, L.: 1989, "Ethical Codes of Conduct: Deficient in Guidance for the Canadian Accounting Profession," *Journal of Business Ethics* 8, 325–335.

Brown, A: 1987, "Is Ethics Good Business?", *Personnel Administrator* (Feb.), 67–71.

Bruns, W.J. and K. Merchant: 1990, "The Dangerous Morality of Managing Earnings," *Management Accountant* (Aug.), 22–25.

Centre for Business Ethics: 1986, "Are Companies Institutionalizing Ethics?" *Journal of Business Ethics* 5, 85–91.

Cottell, P.: 1987, "Ethical Grounding Among Managerial Accountants," *Akron Business and Economic Review* (Summer), 31–39.

Emmanuel, C., D.T. Otley and K. Merchant:

1985, *Accounting for Management Control* (2nd edition), (Chapman and Hall, London).

Euske, K.: 1984, *Management Control: Planning, Control, Measurement and Evaluation* (Addison-Wesley Publishing Company, Reading, Massachusetts).

Gellerman, S.W.: 1986, "Why 'Good' Managers Make Bad Ethical Choices," *Harvard Business Review* (July–Aug.) 85–90.

Greenberger, D., M. Miceli, and D. Cohen: 1987, "Oppositions and Group Norms: The Reciprocal Influence of Whistle-blowers and Co-workers," *Journal of Business Ethics* 6, 527–542.

Grier, D.: 1991, "It's The Detail That Counts," *CA Magazine* (Aug.), 45–48.

Grosman, B.: 1988, *Corporate Loyalty: A Trust Betrayed* (Viking Press, Penguin Books, Toronto).

Herzberg, F.: 1987, "One More Time: How Do You Motivate Employees?" *Harvard Business Review* (Sept./Oct.), 109–120.

Hopwood, A.: 1976, *Accounting and Human Behaviour* (Prentice Hall: Englewood Cliffs, New Jersey).

Kelly, D.: 1989, "Business Ethics: The Case Against Benign Neglect," *Management Accounting* (April), 18–19.

Kirkpatrick, D.: 1990, "Environmentalism: The New Crusade," *Fortune* (Feb.), 44–50.

Jackall, R.: 1988, *Moral Mazes: The World of the Corporate Manager* (Oxford University Press, Oxford).

Merchant, K.: 1985, *Control in Business Organizations* (Pitman Press, Boston, Mass).

Murphy, P.: 1988, "Implementing Business Ethics," *Journal of Business Ethics* 7, 907–915.

National Institute of Business Management: 1987, *What You Should Know About Business Ethics* (National Institute of Business Management Inc., New York).

Neilsen, R.: 1987, "What Can Managers Do About Unethical Management?" *Journal of Business Ethics* 6, 309–320.

Neilsen, R.: 1989, "Changing Unethical Organizational Behavior," *The Academy of Management Executive* III, 123–130.

Otley, D.T. and A.J. Berry: 1980, "Control, Organization, and Accounting," *Accounting Organizations, and Society* 5, 231-246.

Pipkin, A.: 1989, "The Controller's Role En Route to the 21st Century," *CMA Magazine* (April), 10–18.

Rotch, W.: 1993, "Management Control Systems: One View of Components and Their Interdependence," *British Journal of Management* 4, 191–203.

Schlank, R.: 1985a, "The Business Ethics of the Eighties," *Controllers Quarterly* 1, 14–18.

Schlank, R.: 1985b, "The Most Difficult Ethical Dilemmas of the Eighties," *Controllers Quarterly* 1, 6–10.

Shultz, C.: 1989, "Playing Fair," *CA Magazine* (Aug.), 57–59.

Simons, R.: 1987, "Planning Control and Uncertainty: A Process View," in W.J. Bruns and R.S. Kaplan (eds.), *Accounting & Management* (Harvard Business School Press), pp. 339–362.

Sweeney, R. and H. Siers: 1990, "Survey: Ethics in Corporate American," *Management Accounting* (June), 34–40.

Thompson, T.: 1992, "Rhetoric and Reality," *CA Magazine* (Aug.), 54–56.

Velasquez, M.: 1990, "Corporate Ethics: Losing it, Having it, Getting it," in P. Madsen and J.M. Shafritz (eds.), *Essentials of Business Ethics* (New York, Penguin Books).

Wilson, G.: 1983, "Solving Ethical Problems and Saving Your Career," *Business Horizons* (Nov./Dec.), 16–20.

SUGGESTED READINGS

Carson, T. "Friedman's Theory of Corporate Social Responsibility." *Business and Professional Ethics Journal*, Vol. 12, No. 1 (1993), pp. 3–32.

Donaldson, J. and P. Davis. "Business Ethics? Yes, but What Can It Do for the Bottom Line." *Management Decision*, Vol. 28, No.6 (1990), pp. 29–33.

Donaldson, Thomas. "Constructing a Social Contract for Business." In *Corporations and Morality*. Englewood Cliffs, NJ: Prentice-Hall, 1982.

Flew, Anthony. "The Profit Motive." *Ethics*, 86 (1976).

Friedman, Milton. *Capitalism and Freedom*. Chicago: The University Of Chicago Press, 1962.

Goldman, Alan. "Business Ethics: Profits, Utilities, and Moral Rights." *Philosophy and Public Affairs*, Vol. 9, No. 3, 1980.

Hodges, Luther, and Friedman, Milton. "Does Business Have a Social Responsibility?" *Magazine of Bank Administration*, 47 (April 1971).

Laufer, W. and Diana C. Robertson. "Corporate Ethics Initiatives as Social Control." *Journal of Business Ethics*, Vol. 16, No. 10 (July 1997), pp. 1029–1048.

Levitt, Theodore. "The Dangers of Social Responsibility." *Harvard Business Review* (Sept/Oct 1958).

Litzinger, William and Thomas Schaefer. "Business Ethics Bogeyman: The Perpetual Paradox." *Business Horizons* (March/April 1987).

Makover, J. and Business for Social Responsibility. *Beyond the Bottom Line, Putting Social Responsibility to Work for Your Business and the World*. Simon and Schuster, 1994.

Narveson, Jan. "Justice and the Business Society," In T. Beauchamp and N. Bowie (eds.), *Ethical Theory and Business*. Englewood Cliffs, NJ: Prentice-Hall Inc., 1983.

Nunan, Richard. "The Libertarian Conception of Corporate Property: A Critique of Milton Friedman's Views on the Social Responsibility of Business." *Journal of Business Ethics*, 7, 1988.

Pastin, Mark. "Ethics and Excellence." *New Management* (Spring, 1987).

Pattantyus, John. "Profits and Ethics." In James Wilber (ed.), *Economic Analysis*, Proceedings of the Twelfth Conference on Value Enquiry.

Patten, John. "The Business Ethics and the Ethics of Business." *Journal of Business Ethics, 3*, 1984.

Pava, Moses and Joshua Krausz, "Criteria for Evaluating the Legitimacy of Corporate Social Responsibility." *Journal of Business Ethics*, Vol. 16, No. 3 (February 1997), pp. 337–347.

Seldon, Richard, (ed.). *Capitalism and Freedom: Problems and Prospects: Proceedings of a Conference in Honor of Milton Friedman*. Charlottesville: University Press of Virginia, 1975.

Shaw, B., and F.R. Post. "A Moral Basis for Corporate Philanthropy." *Journal of Business Ethics*, 122, 1994, pp. 745–751.

Sorenson, Ralph. "Can Ethics and Profits Live Under the Same Corporate Roof?" *Financial Executive* (March/April 1988).

Stroup, Margaret et al. "Doing Good, Doing Better: Two Views of Social Responsibility." *Business Horizons* (March/April, 1987).

Trundle, Robert. "Is There Any Ethics in Business Ethics?" *Journal of Business Ethics* 8, 1989.

CORPORATIONS, MORAL AGENCY, AND LIABILITY

INTRODUCTION

What precisely is a corporation? Is it merely an aggregate or collection of individual shareholders, managers, and employees? Or is it something distinct unto itself? If corporations are distinct, then does it make any sense at all to conceive of them as non-human "persons" to whom one can ascribe intentions, aims, goals, responsibilities, and perhaps even rights?

These are difficult conceptual questions with which the law has grappled for many years. In a famous Canadian case, *Rex v. Fane Robinson Ltd.*, the question arose as to whether a corporation can be guilty of a criminal offence, which typically requires what lawyers call *mens rea*. That is, to commit a criminal offence, a person must not only perform an action (*actus reus*) but must (normally) do so knowingly, intentionally, or recklessly, with a "guilty mind." It is highly problematic to decide whether a corporation is the kind of thing logically capable of

acting—let alone the kind of thing that can possess a guilty mind. There is no doubt that the various people within corporations perform actions and sometimes have guilty minds, but it is questionable whether the same thing can be said about the corporation itself. There is something very common-sensical and appealing in the view, expressed by Viscount Haldane in *Lennard's Carrying Co. v. Asiatic Petroleum Co.*, that "A corporation is an abstraction [a legal fiction]. It has no mind of its own any more than it has a body of its own. . . ." This had been the view of the presiding judge in *Fane Robinson*. Judge Tweedie had dismissed criminal charges laid against Fane Robinson Ltd. on the ground that "there is no power in a corporation to commit criminal acts in which *mens rea* is a material element, even with the authorization of the shareholders or the directors." The shareholders and directors might be liable, but not the company itself, and the charge had been laid against the latter. The Alberta Court of Appeal thought otherwise. It overturned Tweedie's verdict, claiming that George Robinson and Emile Fielhaber "were the acting and directing will of Fane Robinson Ltd. . . . their culpable intention (*mens rea*) and their illegal act (*actus rea*) were the intention and the act of the company. . . ."

In *Regina v. Andrews Weatherfoil Ltd.*, similar issues arose. The principal question before the English Court of Appeal was whether the trial judge had properly instructed the jury concerning the law of corporate liability. It is not sufficient, in establishing liability on the part of the corporation itself, to show that criminal acts were undertaken by a "responsible agent" or "high executive" or "manager." It must be shown, the Court said, that a "natural person" is in a "sufficiently responsible" position. Presumably that person must, as the court noted in *Fane Robinson*, be the "acting and directing will" of the company. If he is not, then he alone, not the company itself, is criminally liable. Nevertheless, in both *Andrews Weatherfoil* and *Fane Robinson*, there is clear acceptance of the proposition that corporations can be entities unto themselves and that these entities are capable of possessing a "guilty mind."

In a more recent case, *Regina v. Safety-Kleen Canada Inc.*, an employee knowingly gave false information to a provincial officer and knowingly falsified a manifest in transporting waste. In determining whether the company for which the individual worked could also be considered liable for the employee's actions, the court addressed the question of due diligence on the part of the employer. "The availability of the defence to a corporation will depend on whether such due diligence was taken by those who are the directing mind and will of the corporation, whose acts are therefore in law the acts of the corporation itself."

Legally speaking, a good deal can hinge on whether criminal actions are properly attributable to companies or only natural persons. If the company must pay the fine, then the money is likely to come from company resources. But the company's pockets will likely be much deeper than those of individual directors. If so, then directors may not be nearly so motivated to avoid illegal activities as they would be were they, not the company, the ones held accountable.

Philosophers have recently begun to ask whether moral personhood and responsibility can sensibly be ascribed to corporations. Here the question is whether a corporation is a "moral agent" capable of performing intentional actions for which moral praise and blame are appropriate. Some argue that corporations do have moral standing in much the same way as they have legal standing. Others argue that this is sheer nonsense. To speak of corporations as moral agents is to indulge in a moral fiction, just as speaking of corporations as legal persons is, for some, to subscribe to a legal fiction. Referring to a corporation as though it were itself an agent, over and above the people who labour within the corporate structure, is just a shorthand way of referring to a complex group of natural persons. To say that Pacific Western Airlines acquired Wardair is merely a shorthand way of saying that certain human beings within the corporate structure of PWA acted in such a way that they (and perhaps others, e.g., shareholders) assumed a controlling interest in Wardair. The corporation didn't act—only those responsible people did. On this account, it makes no sense, literally speaking, to ascribe actions, responsibilities, and rights to PWA itself, as though these were distinct from the actions, responsibilities, and rights of the human beings who collectively make up the groups we call the shareholders and directors of PWA.

In the first of our selections, Peter French defends the Moral Person Theory against the kind of objections sketched in the preceding paragraph. It is French's belief that moral agency and responsibility can indeed be ascribed, quite literally, to companies who are moral agents. According to French, every corporation has a corporate internal decision structure (a CID structure) that is capable of transforming the actions of natural, biological persons—say, the corporate directors—into the intentional actions of the corporation itself. These are actions of the corporation, performed by the corporation, and for corporate reasons. Such a transformation occurs when (a) conditions specified in the appropriate decision-making procedures are satisfied by the directors' actions, and (b) the decision is consistent with, or is an instance of, established corporate policy. Under these conditions, the decision is "corporate intentional" and thus morally accountable as the actions of a moral person—the corporation.

In assessing French's theory, it might be useful to ask the following questions. How does one determine what is really "corporate policy" and thus the company's reasons for action? What are these "corporate reasons" upon which French places so much emphasis? Do we look to what certain key people within the corporate structure say are the company's aims and ideals? Or do we look, rather, to what these people actually do or bring about? The two are not always identical. And what are we to say when the directors' understanding of company policy is different from that of the shareholders? Indeed, will we often, if ever, find substantial agreement among shareholders concerning the ideals and goals of the company? If not, does this lack of agreement undermine the suggestion that there is something called "corporate policy" and "corporate reasons for action" in terms of which human actions are transformed into the actions of a corporation?

Yet another question worth pondering is whether French has succeeded in showing that corporations are moral agents. It might be true that companies are things over and above the human persons who function within corporate structures, but it does not follow from this alone that they are moral

agents. As a parallel, consider long-standing sports teams, which seem to have an identity over and above their individual members. It makes sense, for example, to talk of the Montreal Canadiens, a team with a certain character and tradition, which at one time included Rocket Richard, at another Guy Lafleur, and now includes Patrick Roy. The team persists through time even though its members constantly change. It would be a mistake to identify the team with any particular group of individuals who at any given moment in time constitute its membership. But it would require a great leap of logic to infer from this that the Montreal Canadiens is a moral agent.

The same may be true of corporations. Massey-Ferguson was a company that had existed for many years and whose identity, character, and traditions persisted even though the human persons who functioned within it had changed dramatically over the years. All this may be true enough and shows the good sense in suggesting that corporations are things over and above their members. But as with sports teams, the following question remains: Are corporations moral agents? The answer to this question must be left to the reader, who should once again bear in mind this point: It fails to follow from the fact that X *is a thing in itself* that X *is a moral agent*.

It is here that Patricia Werhane's critique of the moral personhood thesis takes its lead. According to Werhane, the corporation is not the kind of entity to which one can sensibly ascribe moral agency. It may be a thing unto itself, but it is not a moral agent. As evidence for this thesis, Werhane points out that a corporation is restrained and determined by its formal structures in ways that render it incapable of moral action. She agrees with French that corporate activities are rule-governed, but submits that "these rules, as impersonal operating procedures, preclude rather than imply moral agency. And just as it is silly to ascribe moral responsibility to machines, so too, the organization, structure and goals of a corporation suggest that it does not make sense to ascribe to it moral responsibilities." The important point here is that moral responsibility requires freedom and the ability to entertain and evaluate alternative courses of action—a kind of flexibility and freedom sorely lacking within corporate structures. The very (CID) structures upon which French so heavily relies to effect his corporate transformations in fact undermine the attempt, according to Werhane. Despite all this, Werhane suggests, "a corporation might adopt moral goals . . . or might institutionalize morally appropriate behaviour as a corporate aim so that such a corporation could be labelled socially responsible." But again, this is different from moral agency: ". . . moral agency cannot be ascribed to formal institutions."

John Bishop takes a slightly different tack in his article in examining whether senior executives are responsible for disasters that result from corporate activities in the corporations in which they are employed. In Bishop's examination, he deals with the case of senior executives not knowing the information that could prevent the disaster because of "negative information blockage" within the organization. Bishop concludes that executives are professionally responsi-

ble for creating work environments in which negative information comes forward to be addressed; that is, part of the responsibility for preventing disaster is making sure that negative information does not get blocked from the appropriate decision-makers.

In a second article, "The Hester Prynne Sanction," French assumes that both corporations and the corporate executives with those companies can and should be held accountable for unacceptable events. Having made that assumption, he spends most of this chapter examining the appropriate punishment for the offending corporation and corporate executives. French's suggestion is shame-based punishment (i.e., metaphorically, the Hester Prynne "scarlet letter").

Angelo Corlett's article, which follows, is a direct rebuttal to French's suggestion. Among Corlett's argument is one that guilt-based punishment is more appropriate for an individual than for a corporation, and that a corporation can escape the consequences by "recharter[ing] itself under another name," or passing the financial consequence of any negative sanction on to consumers. Both French's creative Prynne sanction and Corlett's detailed rebuttal stimulate the reader to examine corporate accountability in a new light.

THE CORPORATION
AS A MORAL PERSON

Peter A. French

... I am interested in the sense ascriptions of moral responsibility make when their subjects are corporations. I hope to provide the foundation of a theory that allows treatment of corporations as members of the moral community, of equal standing with the traditionally acknowledged residents: biological human beings, and hence treats responsibility ascriptions as unexceptionable instances of the perfectly proper sort without having to paraphrase them. In short, corporations can be full-fledged moral persons and have whatever privileges, rights and duties as are, in the normal course of affairs, accorded to moral persons. ...

I shall define a moral person as the referent of any proper name or description that can be a non-eliminatable subject of what I shall call (and presently discuss) a responsibility ascription of the second type. The non-eliminatable nature of the subject should be stressed because responsibility and other

moral predicates are neutral as regards person and person-sum predication.[1] Though we might say that The Ox-Bow mob should be held responsible for the death of three men, a mob is an example of what I have elsewhere called an aggregate collectivity with no identity over and above that of the sum of the identities of its component membership, and hence to use "The Ox-Bow mob" as the subject of such ascriptions is to make summary reference to each member of the mob. For that reason mobs do not qualify as metaphysical or moral persons.

There are at least two significantly different types of responsibility ascriptions that should be distinguished in ordinary usage (not counting the laudatory recommendation, "He is a responsible lad.") The first type pins responsibility on someone or something, the who-dun-it or what-dun-it sense. Austin has pointed out that it is usually used when an event or action is thought

Adapted from *American Philosophical Quarterly*, Vol. 16, No. 3 (July 1979). Reprinted by permission.

by the speaker to be untoward. (Perhaps we are more interested in the failures rather than the successes that punctuate our lives.)

The second type of responsibility ascription, parasitic upon the first, involves the notion of accountability. "Having a responsibility" is interwoven with the notion "Having a liability to answer," and having such a liability or obligation seems to imply (as Anscombe has noted[2]) the existence of some sort of authority relationship either between people or between people and a deity or in some weaker versions between people and social norms. . . .

A responsibility ascription of the second type amounts to the assertion of a conjunctive proposition, the first conjunct of which identifies the subject's actions with or as the cause of an event (usually an untoward one) and the second conjunct asserts that the action in question was intended by the subject or that the event was the direct result of an intentional act of the subject. In addition to what it asserts, it implies that the subject is accountable to the speaker . . . because of the subject's relationship to the speaker (who the speaker is or what the speaker is, a member of the "moral community," a surrogate for that aggregate). The primary focus of responsibility ascriptions of the second type is on the subject's intentions rather than, though not to the exclusion of, occasions. Austin wrote: "In considering responsibility, few things are considered more important than to establish whether a man *intended* to do A, or whether he did A intentionally."[3] To be the subject of a responsibility ascription of the second type, to be a party in responsibility relationships, hence to be a moral person, the subject must be at minimum, what I shall call a Davidsonian agent.[4] If corporations are moral persons, they will be non-eliminatable Davidsonian agents.

For a corporation to be treated as a Davidsonian agent it must be the case that some things that happen, some events, are describable in a way that makes certain sentences true, sentences that say that some of the things a corporation does were intended by the corporation itself. That is not accomplished if attributing intentions to a corporation is only a shorthand way of attributing intentions to the biological persons who comprise [sic], for example, its board of directors. If that were to turn out to be the case, then on metaphysical if not logical grounds there would be no way to distinguish between corporations and mobs. I shall argue, however, that *Corporation's Internal Decision Structure* (its CID Structure) is the requisite redescription device that licenses the predication of corporate intentionality.

Intentionality, though a causal notion, is an intentional one and so it does not mark out a class of actions or events. Attributions of intentionality in regard to any event are referentially opaque with respect to other descriptions of that event, or, in other words, the fact that, given one description, an action was intentional does not entail that on every other description of the action it was intentional. A great deal depends upon what aspect of an event is being described. We can correctly say, e.g., "Hamlet intentionally kills the person hiding in Gertrude's room," (one of Davidson's examples), but not "Hamlet intentionally killed Polonius," although "Polonius" and "the person hiding in Gertrude's room" are co-referential. The event may be properly described as "Hamlet killed Polonius" and also as "Hamlet intentionally killed the person hiding in Gertrude's room (behind the arras)," but not as "Hamlet intentionally killed Polonius," for that was not Hamlet's intention. (He, in fact, thought he was killing the King.) The referential opacity of intentionality attributions, I shall presently argue, is congenial to the driving of a wedge between the descriptions of certain events as individual intentional actions and as corporate intentional actions.

Certain . . . actions are describable as simply the bodily movements of human beings, and sometimes those same events are redescribable in terms of their upshots, as bringing about something, e.g., (from Austin[5]) feeding penguins by throwing them peanuts ("by" is the most common way we connect different descriptions of the same event[6]), and sometimes those events can be redescribed as the effects of some prior cause; then they are described as done for reasons, done in order to bring about something, e.g., feeding the penguins peanuts in order to kill them. Usually what we single out as that prior cause is some desire or felt need combined with the belief that the object of the desire will be achieved by the action undertaken. (This, I think is what Aristotle meant when he maintained that acting requires desire.) Saying "Someone (X) did y intentionally" is to describe an event (y) as the upshot of X's having had a reason for doing it which was the cause of his doing it.

It is obvious that a corporation's doing something involves or includes human beings doing things and that the human beings who occupy various positions in a corporation usually can be described as having reasons for *their* behavior. In virtue of those descriptions they may be properly held responsible for their behavior, *ceteris paribus*. What needs to be shown is that there is sense in saying that corporations and not just the people who work in them, have reasons for doing what they do. Typically, we will be told that it is the directors, or the managers, etc., that really have the corporate reasons and desires, etc., and that although corporate actions may not be reducible without remainder, corporate intentions are always reducible to human intentions.

Every corporation has an internal decision structure. CID Structures have two elements of interest to us here: (1) an organizational or responsibility flow chart that delineates stations and levels within the corporate power structure and (2) corporate decision recognition rule(s) (usually embedded in something called "corporation policy"). The CID Structure is the personnel organization for the exercise of the corporation's power with respect to its ventures, and as such its primary function is to draw experience from various levels of the corporation into a decision-making and ratification process. When operative and properly activated, the CID Structure accomplishes a subordination and synthesis of the intentions and acts of various biological persons into a corporate decision. When viewed in another way, as already suggested, the CID Structure licenses the descriptive transformation of events, seen under another aspect as the acts of biological persons (those who occupy various stations on the organizational chart), into corporate acts, by exposing the corporate character of those events. A functioning CID Structure incorporates acts of biological persons. For illustrative purposes, imagine that an event E has at least two aspects, that is, can be described in two non-identical ways. One of those aspects is "Executive X's doing y" and one is "Corporation C's doing z." The corporate act and the individual act may have different properties; indeed they have different causal ancestors though they are causally inseparable. (The causal inseparability of these acts, I hope to show, is a product of the CID Structure: X's doing y is not the cause of C's doing z nor is C's doing z the cause of X's doing y, although if X's doing y causes event F then C's doing z causes F and vice versa.)

Although I doubt he is aware of the metaphysical reading that can be given to this process, J.K. Galbraith rather neatly captures what I have in mind when he writes in his recent popular book on the history of economics: "From [the] interpersonal exercise of power, the interaction . . . of the participants, comes the *personality* of the corporation."[7] I take Galbraith here to be quite literally correct, but it is important to spell out how a CID Structure works this "miracle."

In philosophy in recent years we have grown accustomed to the use of games as models for understanding institutional behavior. We all have some understanding of how rules in games make certain descriptions of events possible that would not be so if those rules were non-existent. The CID Structure of a corporation is a kind of constitutive rule (or rules) analogous to the game rules with which we are familiar. The organization chart of a corporation distinguishes "players" and clarifies their rank and the interwoven lines of responsibility within the corporation. An organizational chart tells us, for example, that anyone holding the title "Executive Vice President for Finance Administration" stands in a certain relationship to anyone holding the title "Director of Internal Audit" and to anyone holding the title "Treasurer," etc. In effect it expresses, or maps, the interdependent and dependent relationships, line and staff, that are involved in determinations of corporate decisions and actions. The organizational chart provides what might be called the grammar of corporate decision-making. What I shall call internal recognition rules provide its logic.

By "recognition rule(s)" I mean what Hart, in another context, calls "conclusive affirmative indication"[8] that a decision on an act has been made or performed for corporate reasons. Recognition rules are of two sorts. Partially embedded in the organizational chart are procedural recognitors: we see that decisions are to be reached collectively at certain levels and that they are to be ratified at higher levels (or at inner circles, if one prefers that Galbraithean model). A corporate decision is recognized internally, however, not only by the procedure of its making, but by the policy it instantiates. Hence every corporation creates an image (not to be confused with its public image) or a general policy, what G.C. Buzby of the Chilton Company has called the "basic belief of the corporation,"[9] that must inform its decisions for them to be properly described as being those of the corporation. "The moment

policy is side-stepped or violated, it is no longer the policy of that company."[10]

Peter Drucker has seen the importance of the basic policy recognitors in the CID Structure (though he treats matters rather differently from the way I am recommending.) Drucker writes:

> Because the corporation is an institution it must have a basic policy. For it must subordinate individual ambitions and decisions to the *needs* of the corporation's welfare and survival. That means that it must have a set of principles and a rule of conduct which limit and direct individual actions and behavior . . .[11]

Suppose, for illustrative purposes, we activate a CID Structure in a corporation, the Gulf Oil Corporation. Imagine that three executives *X, Y* and *Z* have the task of deciding whether or not Gulf Oil will join a world uranium cartel. *X, Y* and *Z* have before them an Everest of papers that have been prepared by lower-echelon executives. Some of the papers will be purely factual reports, some will be contingency plans, some will be formulations of positions developed by various departments, some will outline financial considerations, some will be legal opinions and so on. In so far as these will all have been processed through Gulf's CID Structure system, the personal reasons, if any, individual executives may have had when writing their reports and recommendations in a specific way will have been diluted by the subordination of individual inputs to peer group input even before *X, Y* and *Z* review the matter. *X, Y* and *Z* take a vote. Their taking of a vote is authorized procedure in the Gulf CID Structure, which is to say that under these circumstances the vote of *X, Y* and *Z* can be redescribed as the corporation's making a decision: that is, the event "*XYZ* voting" may be redescribed to expose an aspect otherwise unrevealed, that is quite different from its other aspects, e.g., from *X*'s voting in the affirmative.

Redescriptive exposure of a procedurally corporate aspect of an event, however, is not to be confused with a description of an event that makes true a sentence that says that the corporation did something intentionally. But the CID Structure, as already suggested, also provides the grounds in its other type of recognitor for such an attribution of corporate intentionality. Simply, when the corporation act is consistent with an instantiation or an implementation of established corporate policy, then it is proper to describe it as having been done for corporate reasons, as having been caused by a corporate desire coupled with a corporate belief and so, in other words, as corporate intentional.

An event may, under one of its aspects, be described as the conjunctive act "X did a (or as X intentionally did a) & Y did a (or as Y intentionally did a) & Z did a (or as Z intentionally did a)" (where a = voted in the affirmative on the question of Gulf Oil joining the cartel). Give the Gulf CID Structure, formulated in this instance as the conjunction of rules: when the occupants of position A, B and C on the organizational chart unanimously vote to do something and if doing that something is consistent with an instantiation or an implementation of general corporate policy and *ceteris paribus*, then the corporation has decided to do it for corporate reasons, the event is redescribable as "the Gulf Oil Corporation did j for corporate reasons f," (where j is "decided to join the cartel" and f is any reason (desire + belief) consistent with basic policy of Gulf Oil, e.g., increasing profits) or simply as "Golf Oil Corporation intentionally did j." This is a rather technical way of saying that in these circumstances the executives voting is, given its CID Structure, also the corporation deciding to do something, and that regardless of the personal reasons the executives have for voting as they do and even if their reasons are inconsistent with established corporate policy or even if one of them has no reason at all for voting as he

does, the corporation still has reasons for joining the cartel; that is, joining is consistent with the inviolate corporate general policies as encrusted in the precedent of previous corporate actions and its statements of purpose as recorded in its certificate of incorporation, annual reports, etc.

The corporation's only method of achieving its desires or goals is the activation of the personnel who occupy its various positions. However, if X voted affirmatively purely for reasons of personal monetary gain (suppose he had been bribed to do so) that does not alter the fact that the corporate reason for joining the cartel was to minimize competition and hence pay higher dividends to its shareholders. Corporations have reasons because they have interests in doing those things that are likely to result in realization of their established corporate goals regardless of the transient self-interest of directors, managers, etc. If there is a difference between corporate goals and desires and those of human beings it is probably that the corporate ones are relatively stable and not very wide ranging, but that is only because corporations can do relatively fewer things than human beings, being confined in action predominately to a limited socioeconomic sphere. The attribution of corporate intentionality is opaque with respect to other possible descriptions of the event in question. It is, of course, in a corporation's interest that its component membership view the corporate purposes as instrumental in the achievement of their own goals. (Financial reward is the most common way this is achieved.)

It will be objected that a corporation's policies reflect only the current goals of its directors. But that is certainly not logically necessary nor is it in practice true for most large corporations. Usually, of course, the original incorporators will have organized to further their individual interests and/or to meet goals which they shared. But even in infancy the melding of disparate interests and purposes gives rise to a corporate long-range point of view that is distinct from the intents and purpose of the collection of incorporators viewed individually. Also, corporate basic purposes and policies, as already mentioned, tend to be relatively stable when compared to those of individuals and not couched in the kind of language that would be appropriate to individual purposes. Furthermore, as histories of corporations will show, when policies are amended or altered it is usually only peripheral issues that are involved. Radical policy alteration constitutes a new corporation, a point that is captured in the incorporation laws of such states as Delaware. ("Any power which is not enumerated in the charter and the general law or which cannot be inferred from these two sources is *ultra vires* of the corporation.") Obviously underlying the objection is an uneasiness about the fact that corporate intent is dependent upon policy and purpose that is but an artifact of the socio-psychology of a group of biological persons. Corporate intent seems somehow to be a tarnished illegitimate offspring of human intent. But this objection is another form of the anthropocentric bias. By concentrating on possible descriptions of events and by acknowledging only that the possibility of describing something as an agent depends upon whether or not it can be properly described as having done something (the description of some aspect of an event) for a reason, we avoid the temptation to look for extensional criteria that would necessitate reduction to human referents.

The CID Structure licenses redescriptions of events as corporate and attributions of corporate intentionality while it does not obscure the private acts of executives, directors, etc. Although X voted to support the joining of the cartel because he was bribed to do so, X did not join the cartel, Gulf Oil Corporation joined the cartel. Consequently, we may say that X did something for which he should be held morally responsible, yet whether or not Gulf Oil Corporation should be held morally responsible for joining the cartel is a question that turns on issues that may be unrelated to X's having accepted a bribe.

Of course, Gulf Oil Corporation cannot join the cartel unless X or somebody who occupies position A on the organizational chart votes in the affirmative. What that shows, however, is that corporations are collectives. That should not, however, rule out the possibility of their having metaphysical status, as being Davidsonian agents, and being thereby full-fledged moral [legal] persons.

This much seems to me clear: we can describe many events in terms of certain physical movements of human beings and we also can sometimes describe those events as done for reasons by those human beings, but further we can sometimes describe those events as corporate and still further as done for corporate reasons that are qualitatively different from whatever personal reasons, if any, component members may have for doing what they do.

Corporate agency resides in the possibility of CID Structure licensed redescription of events as corporate intentional. That may still appear to be downright mysterious, although I do not think it is, for human agency as I have suggested, resides in the possibility of description as well.

Although further elaboration is needed. I hope I have said enough to make plausible the view that we have good reasons to acknowledge the non-eliminatable agency of corporations. I have maintained that Davidsonian agency is a necessary and sufficient condition of moral personhood. I cannot further argue that position here (I have done so elsewhere). On the basis of the foregoing analysis, however, I think that grounds have been provided for holding corporations *per se* to account for what they do, for treating them as metaphysical persons *qua* moral persons.[12]

ENDNOTES

1. See Gerald Massey, "Tom, Dick, and Harry, and All The King's Men," *American Philosophical Quarterly*, Vol. 13 (1976), pp. 89–108.

2. G.E.M. Anscombe, "Modern Moral Philosophy," *Philosophy*, Vol. 33 (1958), pp. 1–19.

3. J.L. Austin, "Three Ways of Spilling Ink," in *Philosophical Papers* (Oxford: Oxford University Press, 1970), p. 273.

4. See for example Donald Davidson, "Agency," in *Agent, Action, and Reason*, edited by Binkley, Bronaugh, and Marras (Toronto: University of Toronto Press, 1971).

5. Austin, p. 275.

6. See Joel Feinberg, *Doing and Deserving* (Princeton, NJ: Princeton University Press, 1970), p. 134f.

7. John Kenneth Galbraith, *The Age of Uncertainty* (Boston: Houghton-Mifflin Co., 1971), p. 261.

8. H.L.A. Hart, *The Concept of Law* (Oxford: Clarendon Press, 1961), Ch. VI.

9. G.C. Buzby, "Politics—A Guide to What A Company Stands For," *Management Record*, Vol. 24 (1962), p. 5ff.

10. Ibid.

11. Peter Drucker, *Concept of Corporation* (New York: John Day Co., 1964/1972), pp. 36–37.

12. This paper owes much to discussions and comments made by J.L. Mackie, Donald Davidson and Howard K. Wettstein. An earlier version was read at a conference on "Ethics and Economics" at the University of Delaware. I also acknowledge the funding of the University of Minnesota Graduate School that supports the project of which this is a part.

FORMAL ORGANIZATIONS, ECONOMIC FREEDOM, AND MORAL AGENCY

Patricia H. Werhane

Contemporary societal expectations place an onus of moral responsibility on the activities of economic institutions, specifically on the activities of modern business corporations. However the economist Milton Friedman claims that:

> Few trends could so thoroughly undermine the very foundations of our free society as the acceptance by corporate officials of a social responsibility other than to make as much money for their stockholders as possible.[1]

In this paper I shall make three arguments. First, I shall argue that while society tends to hold corporations morally responsible, and while one might agree that corporations should be morally accountable, corporations, as formal institutions, are so structured that such accountability is philosophically inappropriate. I shall criticize certain recent suggestions offered to make sense

out of corporate moral responsibility because these suggestions either confuse corporations with other kinds of institutions, or they tend to confuse the concept of social responsibility with moral accountability.

Second, I shall claim that my conclusion that corporations are not structured as moral agents does not support Friedman's argument that in a free society the only responsibility of business is to its stockholders. This is because social responsibility and moral accountability are not interchangeable concepts, and because profit maximization and social responsibility are not contradictory corporate functions.

I shall conclude the paper by arguing that Friedman's notion of a free society involves the notion of moral accountability, and that corporate moral agency is a condition for the proper functioning of a private free enterprise system. Thus, if economic freedom and autonomy are important, cor-

From *Journal of Value Inquiry* 14 (1980). Copyright © 1980 Martinus Nijhoff Publishers. Reprinted by permission.

porations might wish to examine what the notion of institutional moral agency entails.

A number of contemporary philosophers have attempted to justify the argument that it is appropriate to hold corporations morally responsible. In a recent paper entitled "The Moral Responsibility of Corporations"[2] David Ozar tries to establish the claim that corporations are single individuals or are sometimes treated as individuals, and thus, like individual human beings, corporations are morally liable. To this end Ozar compares corporations to other kinds of institutions such as clubs and nations. Ozar points out that corporations, like clubs and nations, operate like single individual entities. Corporations have legal status as individuals, and each of these kinds of institutions has rules or by-laws governing their actions considered as individuals. The rule model, Ozar argues, implies agency. And because we hold clubs and nations morally responsible, so too we can hold other rule-governed institutions such as corporations morally responsible.

The issue Ozar's paper raises is not whether we treat corporations as individuals nor whether corporations adopt rule-governed behavior. Rather the issue centers on whether all rule-governed behavior implies moral agency so that it makes sense to say that corporations, like clubs and nations, operate as *morally responsible* individuals. There are important differences in the roles of institutional rules and goals, and differences in the relationships between the institution and its members. These differences, I shall argue, preclude making the analogy that corporations, like clubs and nations, are moral individuals.

The relationship of a club or a nation to its members or citizens is different from the relationship of a corporation to its employees. The well-being of individuals, or groups of individuals, constitutes an essential part of the ends or goals for which a club or nation is constituted. Clubs and nations are, by and large, structured for their members, and many, if not all, of the rules, by-laws, constitutions, etc., of these institutions apply to their members or to the rights and conduct of their members. The modern business corporation however, is an economic institution structured primarily for the achievement of material ends external to the corporation. Corporate goals include customer satisfaction, technological advancement, market penetration, profit maximization, etc. Corporate rules and guidelines are aimed at the efficient maximization of these goals. "Following a rule" in corporate activities usually involves maximizing corporate goal achievement as efficiently and productively as possible. Thus the corporation is a formal organization constituted to achieve impersonal ends external to the organization.

In his paper, "Morality and the Ideal of Rationality in Formal Organizations"[3] John Ladd argues that corporations are formal organizations in another sense. Corporate employees are impersonal members of corporations. Employees are one of the means through which a corporation is a success or failure, but not an end for which the corporation operates. In corporations, clubs and nations, many of the activities of their respective members are regulated by corporate policies, by-laws and constitutions. But while rules and goals of clubs and nations are structurally connected to their members or citizens, corporate aims and company guidelines are not so related to company employees. In a corporation rules function more like operating instructions than moral prescriptions, since in corporate activities disobeying a rule means not performing one's job.

In modern corporations employee rights are defined by institutions external to the corporation, e.g., unions, government agencies, and laws. But seldom are employee rights embodied in the structure of the corporation as an institutional part of its operations. In talking about actions of clubs and nations, however, the rights or absence of rights of its members or citizens is an important issue. Corporate employees' rights are an issue only insofar as these contribute to corporate success. As a club member or a citizen I have, at least in principle, a right to protest rules, goals or actions of my club or country when I think they are unjust or unfit. In a corporation, employees have no such rights. Such protests would be considered inappropriate, the employees would be accused of disrupting economic activities, and the employee likely would be fired.

One might suggest that stockholders, who are the owners of corporations, have a relationship to a corporation somewhat analogous to the relationship of a club member to a club, since one of the aims of a corporation is to maximize earnings for shareholders. However, this is not the case. Because most stockholders are not corporate employees nor sit on boards of directors, most stockholders have little or no responsibility for what happens in a corporation. They are not involved in establishing corporate aims nor in realizing (or criticizing) these aims, and there is some question whether stockholders have *any* decision-making rights. In reality, stockholders are an abstract group of owners who happen to hold stock on the particular day when earnings are paid out.

Clubs and nations are so structured, then, that the club or nation is responsible to each of its members, and its members have certain rights defined by the club. Moreover, members of a club or nation are morally responsible or held responsible for the activities of that club or nation. For example, we tend to hold the German nation as a whole responsible for Nazi activities during World War II, even though many Germans were not Nazis. However it would be illogical to hold assembly-line workers at General Electric responsible for General Electric's alleged price-fixing activities in the 1960s. Thus one might ascribe moral responsibility to a club or nation, and therefore to its members, but such ascription of moral agency to a corporation is questionable in light of the largely abstract and impersonal relationships of the corporation both to its employees and its stockholders.

Thus, as Ladd argues in his paper, corporations are structured very much like machines. Corporate rules and operating procedures, like the design and structure of a machine, are set up to achieve external economic ends rather than designed in relation to, or as a consequence of member employees.[4] Each employee in a corporation, like each part in a machine, plays an important role in achieving corporate ends, but any weak or dissident employee, like any malfunctioning part, could be, and should be, replaced in order to operate at maximum corporate efficiency. Therefore, while corporate activities are rule-governed, these rules, as impersonal operating procedures, preclude rather than imply moral agency. And just as it is silly to ascribe moral responsibilities to machines, so too, the organization, structure and goals of a corporation suggest that it does not make sense to ascribe to it moral responsibilities.

The notion of corporate responsibility might be explained in terms of social responsibility. It is often claimed that corporations have certain kinds of responsibilities to the society in which they operate. It is then claimed that we can ascribe such responsibilities to corporations despite the way in which corporations are structured as formal institutions, and that such responsibility can be defined as "moral accountability."

To make this point Kenneth Goodpaster, in his paper "Morality and Organizations,"[5] suggests that the comparison of corporations to machines is too static and too narrow. Corporations operate more like organisms than machines, because corporations, like other organisms, interact with society through various feedback mechanisms. Just as the environment and societal expectations trigger certain kinds of responses in other organisms, so too corporations often act or react according to the kinds of feedback they receive from society. If this model is descriptive of corporations, Goodpaster argues, then it allows a "space" in which a corporation might be expected to adopt moral goals as a response to community criticism or esteem.

The idea that formal organizations might adopt moral goals is further developed by Thomas Donaldson in his paper, "Moral Change and the Corporation."[6] Donaldson points out that even in the pursuit of economic ends corporations often react to moral restraints imposed on them by society. Moreover, Donaldson argues, it is not impossible, and indeed it is highly plausible to suggest that formal institutions such as corporations could adopt moral goals. These goals could be institutionalized within the structure of the corporation such that they became ends for which a corporation might operate. For example, a corporation could adopt a policy of hiring qualified minorities without giving up its goal of economic gains.

Both Goodpaster and Donaldson have enhanced the concept of corporation and shown that it is not impossible for a formal organization to adopt goals which we would ordinarily label as "moral." I would suggest, however, that they have not succeeded in demonstrating that corporations, like clubs, nations, and human individuals are moral agents. For while a corporation might adopt moral goals in response to societal feedback or might institutionalize morally appropriate behavior as a corporate aim so that such a corporation could be labeled socially responsible, this is different from moral agency, and moral agency cannot be ascribed to formal institutions.

To argue this point, let us consider a mythical example. One might imagine a corporation which was operated solely by robots and computers. Such an organization, let us call it Robotron, would have a charter and legal status. It would operate like other

corporations. It would own property, manufacture products, conduct marketing, correspond with other corporations and with customers, replace obsolete equipment, develop new product lines, write proxy statements, answer SEC inquiries, etc. Robotron would have stockholders and pay out dividends. Only a visitor to corporate "headquarters" would learn that Robotron had no human employees. And such a corporation could be programed to respond to feedback from societal expectations such as requests for anti-pollution devices, safer products, etc. In fact one could imagine that Robotron was an organization such as CARE which institutionalizes valued moral goals as its corporate aims.

This corporation, Robotron, meets all the Donaldson-Goodpaster requirements. It lives up to societal expectations, it conforms to requests of government agencies, it institutionalizes moral goals in its operations, and from an economic point of view it operates efficiently and profitably. But Robotron, I would argue, is not morally responsible. It is not morally responsible because it is not a moral agent. And its lack of moral agency is not merely a result of its lack of human employees. Even if Robotron *did* have human employees, the relation between Robotron and its computers would be much the same as the relation between Robotron and its human employees, because the structure of Robotron as a formal organization would remain unaltered. Decision making by non-human employees would consist of institutional decisions, and non-efficient employees, like obsolete computers, would be replaced. And the role of the human or computer employee in achieving corporate moral goals, such as those of CARE, would be the same as in achieving the production of light bulbs or airplane engines.

This last point needs elaboration. What I am suggesting is that the qualitative value of institutional goals does not necessarily determine whether or not the institution is a moral agent. CARE has highly commendable goals, and most of its employees are not robots. But CARE is a formal organization. The relationships of the institution and institutional goals to its employees are impersonal relationships. This is because the operators of any corporation, whether they are human or robots, are themselves merely operators. They are part of the institution only to achieve ends which are not their own. Their choices are important only when they affect the success of achieving corporate goals. And corporations, such as CARE, exist not for their members but for the successful pursuit of ends which have little or no relation to the employees who realize them.

Therefore one may assign corporations and other formal organizations moral goals, and these institutions may institute moral goals themselves into their corporate structure as part of their operating procedures. Such corporations are socially responsible institutions and society should commend these actions. However, even in these cases I would suggest that one cannot make the further claim that these corporations are morally responsible. Social responsibility does not necessarily imply moral agency. Corporations are not structured such that they operate as moral agents. The relationship of corporate members (employees, robots and stockholders) to corporate rules and goals and the absence of a reciprocal relationship between the corporation and its employees precludes such agency.

It is beyond the scope of this paper to explore what corporate moral agency might entail. I would suggest, however, that if it is the case that a corporation such as Robotron can operate as a socially responsible organization it is obvious that merely to alter the goals of a formal organization does not, in itself, alter the moralness of the institution as an agent. Achieving corporate moral agency would involve, in brief, internal alterations of corporate structure; that is, there would have to be a radical restructuring of the relationship of the corporation, both to its goals and even more importantly to its member employees. And the role of the individual in the organization would have to be such that the Robotron analogy will not hold.

Corporations have been operating as highly successful economic institutions for some years. The fact that they are not structured as morally responsible agents might not be offensive to them. Such institutions never made that claim nor thought that moral agency was necessary for economic success. Why, then, might the question of moral agency be important to a business corporation? In what follows I shall develop the claim that moral agency is necessary for economic freedom and autonomy. Applying this to formal institutions, if corporations wish to operate freely without social or governmental constraints and if this form of operation actually enhances the economic life of the community as some economists suggest, then corporations might wish to take the idea of moral agency seriously.

Milton Friedman argues that economic freedom is a necessary condition for political freedom. By economic freedom Friedman has in mind a society consisting of autonomous privately owned economic enterprises each pursuing its own ends and freely competing with each other in the marketplace. In this society government would have little or no role in economic activities and political power and economic success would be separate. In such a society, Friedman suggests, economic freedom, and thus political freedom prevails.[7] It is this concept of economic freedom that prompts Friedman to claim that profit maximization and social responsibility are incompatible corporate goals. Friedman's picture of ideal free enterprise is incomplete on two grounds. First, as I suggested earlier, social responsibility is not incompatible with the operations of formal organizations. Thus a corporation might be socially responsible, it might adopt moral goals as part of its corporate aims, and be highly profitable as well. Second, Friedman does not consider corporate *moral* responsibility an issue at all, because, I think, Friedman would agree that moral agency does not apply to formal economic institutions. However a difficulty arises because there is an inconsistency in Friedman's concept of a corporation as a *free autonomous* institution to whom the notion of moral agency does not apply. This inconsistency is best illustrated by re-examining the computer corporation, Robotron.

Suppose Robotron began manufacturing toxic substances injurious to the health of anyone who came in contact with the substance. Societal mechanisms would interfere with Robotron's program and alter its manufacturing techniques to prohibit further manufacture of these toxic substances. No one would accuse Robotron of moral irresponsibility; it just happened to manufacture socially unacceptable substances. Nor would we accuse society of interfering with the rights and freedoms of Robotron since, as a formal organization made up of nonhumans, Robotron has no rights or freedoms. Any formal organization which operates impersonally is, in principle, in the same position as Robotron. Because it neither understands the concept of moral responsibility nor acts as a moral agent, such an institution cannot expect to be treated as a free autonomous agent. And society should feel no moral compunction in enforcing its demands on such an institution.

It would appear, then, that if the concept of economic freedom makes sense, and if as Friedman suggests, such freedom is necessary for political freedom, the notion of moral agency as applied to economic institutions is very important. Corporations cannot expect to operate freely *and* non-morally. Freedom and moral agency go together, and it is in-consistent to demand one without accepting the consequences of the other.

I am not arguing that all corporations should restructure themselves as moral agents. Nor am I agreeing (or disagreeing) with Friedman's claim that economic freedom is a condition for political freedom. But I am pointing out that freedom and autonomy imply moral agency, and moral agency does not apply to corporations as formal organizations. Therefore corporations cannot expect to be treated as free autonomous enterprises. Thus if economic freedom is a value, and if corporations wish to operate without societal constraints, then they need to examine what might be involved in reconstituting themselves as morally accountable institutions.

ENDNOTES

1. Milton Friedman, *Capitalism and Freedom* (Chicago: The University of Chicago Press, 1962), p. 133.

2. David Ozar, "The Moral Responsibility of Corporations," in Thomas Donaldson and Patricia H. Werhane, eds. *Ethical Issues in Business: A Philosophical Approach*, (Englewood Cliffs, NJ: Prentice-Hall, Inc., 1979).

3. John Ladd, "Morality and the Ideal of Rationality in Formal Organizations," *Monist*, 54 (1970), pp. 488–516.

4. Ladd, p. 400.

5. Kenneth Goodpaster, "Morality and Organizations," paper originally presented at the Pacific Division Meetings, American Philosophical Association, 1978; Donaldson and Werhane, 1979.

6. Thomas Donaldson, "Moral Change and the Corporation," *Proceedings of the Bentley College Second National Conference on Business Ethics*, 1979.

7. Friedman, pp. 1–6.

THE MORAL RESPONSIBILITY OF CORPORATE EXECUTIVES FOR DISASTERS

John D. Bishop

I. INTRODUCTION

When large corporations are criticized for causing disasters, the senior executives of those corporations usually protest their personal innocence, and deny that they should bear any moral responsibility for the tragedy. They often protest that they were not given information which could have warned them of impending problems even though they made honest efforts to obtain such information. Subsequent investigations have sometimes revealed that others in the corporation (often engineers) knew of safety problems, but that this information failed to reach decision making executives. Examples of this phenomenon include the cargo door problem on the DC-10, and the explosion of the Challenger—both tragedies involving loss of life.

This denial of moral responsibility intuitively conflicts with the high remuneration that CEOs and other executives receive in return for being responsible for corporations. In particular, it conflicts with the bonus remuneration which they receive if the corporation performs well. If they benefit when the corporation flourishes, should they not accept responsibility when things go horribly wrong?

The denial also conflicts with the current trend in our society of holding senior executives more socially responsible (Brooks, 1989). To note a single example, a U.S. District Judge recently insisted that the CEO of Pennwalt Corp. should personally attend his court to enter a plea on a toxic spill charge. Note that the judge was not making a legal point (corporate lawyers could have just as easily entered the plea), but a point about social responsibility (*Globe and Mail,* 1989).

This paper will analyse to what extent we can or should hold executives morally responsible for disasters. In particular, it will

From *Journal of Business Ethics*, 10 (1991), 377–383. Copyright © 1991 Kluwer Academic Publishers. Reprinted by permission of Kluwer Academic Publishers.

examine the case in which knowledge indicating impending problems is available to someone in the corporation, but has failed to reach decision making executives.

To help clarify the issues that the rest of the paper will deal with, the next section will eliminate some cases in which executives clearly are not responsible. Section III will elaborate on the reasons executives give for denying responsibility; in particular this paper concentrates on the case in which executives claim that they did not have and could not be expected to have had information vital to preventing the disaster. The reasons why apparently powerful executives cannot get information from their own corporation needs to be examined carefully (Section IV) before moving on in the final two sections to analysing to what extent we are justified in holding executives morally responsible.

It perhaps should be made clear at the outset that moral responsibility, or the lack of it, does not have direct implications for legal liability. The legal aspects of this problem are complicated, especially when the tragedy is in one country, and the corporate head office is in another. Legal issues are not dealt with in this paper.

II. LIMITS ON EXECUTIVE RESPONSIBILITY

It is commonplace in discussing morality that people should not be held responsible for events over which they have no influence or control. In this section, several types of events over which executives have no influence are eliminated from discussion. Executives cannot be held responsible for acts of God, nor, in their role as executives, for actions which are not performed on behalf of the corporation. Events not excluded in this section are not necessarily the moral responsibility of executives, but they are the actions which will be the basis of discussion in the rest of this article.

It can be accepted that executives are not responsible for obvious "acts of God." This does not mean that they should not be held accountable for the results of a natural event, for they may well be in a position to determine the outcomes even when the event itself is inevitable. For example, suppose an earthquake causes a factory to collapse, killing several workers. Obviously, we cannot hold the executives of the company which owns the factory responsible for the earthquake itself; earthquakes are natural events which are beyond human control. However, we might hold the executives responsible for the factory being built in an earthquake zone, or we might hold them responsible for the use of money saving construction methods which caused the building to collapse. In these cases, we would consider the executives at least partly responsible for the workers' deaths. The fact that a person has no influence or control over an event does not necessarily exempt him or her from responsibility for the consequences of that event. What we hold him or her responsible for are the actions which determined those consequences.

Corporate executives, in their role as executives, should also not be held responsible for events which are not the result of the corporation's activities. The concepts of the "executive's role" and of the "corporation's activities" both need explaining.

Executives, because they are people, have moral responsibilities, as citizens, neighbours, parents, etc. Such responsibilities, while not being denied, will not be discussed in this paper. The purpose of the present discussion is limited to the moral responsibility of executives in their role as executives. However, this should not be taken to mean that the moral principles that apply to persons acting in the role of executives are any different from those which apply in the rest of their lives. Although it is sometimes argued that the morality of professional activities differs from the morality of everyday life (Carr, 1968), that is a position which cannot be applied to executives without the most careful examination (Callahan, 1988-A; Gillespie, 1983; Nagel, 1978). We will not go into this debate here; since this paper does not discuss the actual moral duties of executives as executives, we need not discuss how they differ from their other duties.

The notion of "corporate activities" also needs expanding. It has been argued that corporations are moral entities in their own right, and that corporations can commit actions (French, 1977). This is a position which I reject for the sorts of reasons outlined in Danley (1980). However, in this paper, I will avoid further discussion of this issue because it is not relevant to the current topic. Even if corporations are moral agents and as such are held responsible for corporate activities, this does not exempt the people in the corporation from also being held responsible for their role in those activities. Moral responsibility is not a fixed quantity; its assignment to one moral equity does not necessarily reduce the responsibility of other moral agents. Thus corporate executives can be held morally accountable for the same events for which the corporation is also accountable, though not necessarily to the same degree or for the same reasons. Because of this, we do not have to decide on corporate moral responsibility to discuss the issue of the responsibility of executives for their role in corporate actions.

"Corporate activities" can also refer to the actions of the corporation's employees which are done in their capacity as employees. Presumably, executives are in a position to influence such actions on the part of employees, and it is their responsibility for such actions that the rest of this paper will be concerned with. Executives may, for social reasons, be in a position to influence employee behaviour off the job, but the use of such influence does not concern us here. We will confine our examination to events

which result from the actions of employees while on the job. To hold the executives responsible for such events (if we decide to do so) is to hold them responsible for the actions of others, but it is assumed that executives have some influence or control over the actions of employees. The question we need to discuss is to what extent the executive has such influence and control, and whether it extends only to actions the executive directly instigates, or to all actions and omissions of employees as employees.

Even though we will confine the discussion to executive responsibility for actions employees commit in their capacity as employees, for convenience sake such employee actions will sometimes be referred to as the actions of the corporation. This should not be taken to imply that corporations can actually commit actions; the phrase is used as shorthand. Similarly, by employee actions, we mean only those committed as employees.

III. WHY EXECUTIVES MAY NOT BE MORALLY RESPONSIBLE

When things go horribly wrong, executives sometimes deny responsibility on the grounds that they did not know, and could not be expected to know, the information they needed to prevent the disaster. They maintain this even when some of the corporation's employees knew, or ought to have known, the relevant information.

Consider the case of DC-10 Ship 29, which crashed near Paris on March 3, 1974 when its cargo doors flew off. All 346 people aboard were killed. Subsequent investigations revealed that McDonnell-Douglas, the manufacturer of the aircraft, was aware of the cargo door problem, and that Ship 29 had been returned to the corporation for FAA ordered corrections to the door locking mechanism (French, 1984; Eddy *et al.*, 1976). These corrections were never made, though stamped inspection sheets indicated they had been. John Brizendine, President of the Douglas division of McDonnell-Douglas, denied all knowledge of this failure to fix the doors (French, 1982), though it is clear that at least some people in the company must have known. Since there is no reason to question Brizendine's honesty, we will assume that the information that could have prevented the disaster failed to reach him. (We will also assume that he would have acted on the information if he had received it.)

As a second example, consider the explosion of the Challenger space shuttle, again with loss of life. Engineers at Morton Thiokol, which manufactured the solid rocket booster, had repeatedly expressed concerns, in written memos and verbally, about possible failure of O-ring seals on cold weather launches (Grossman, 1988). These concerns failed to reach decision making management at NASA, who maintain that they would have stopped the launch had they been aware of the engineers' opinion (Callahan, 1988-B). Again, vital information that could have prevented disaster failed to reach executives responsible for the final decision.

I do not want to raise the issue of the honesty of the executives when they claim they did not know. It has transpired in some cases that executives knew more than they were willing to admit—such was the case in the Dalkon shield tragedy (Mintz, 1985), or the knowledge of tobacco executives about early cancer studies (White, 1988). However, it is clear that executives often do not know, and are not told even if others in the corporation have the information. The immorality of lying, and of being able to stop a disaster and not doing so, are beyond doubt; the responsibility (if any) of executives when they actually are not told is more problematic, and is the central topic of this paper. It will be assumed that in the cases cited (the DC-10 cargo door problem and the Challenger disaster), executives were in fact in the dark about impending problems.

IV. NEGATIVE INFORMATION BLOCKAGE

Can executives be taken seriously when they claim that they cannot be expected to know about impending tragedy? After all, they have the authority to demand that information be given to them. And it is their job to know what is going on in their corporation. If someone in the company has or can get the information (which is the most interesting case), then why cannot the executives simply send a memo to all employees saying such information is to be sent directly to their attention? This question needs to be examined carefully if we are to determine whether executives are responsible when disaster strikes, or whether we should accept the claim that they did not know and could not have known the information needed to prevent the tragedy.

The problem with getting information to executives is a well-known phenomenon in corporate and other hierarchical organizations which I will call "negative information blockage." In brief, information regarding the riskiness of a corporation's plans is stifled at source or by intervening management, even when senior executives have demanded that such information be sent on to them. This phenomenon needs to be analysed further.

The notion of negative information requires the distinction between a corporation's objectives and its constraints. The objectives (or goals—I will use the two words interchangeably) of a corporation are what its senior executives are perceived as wanting to achieve. These objectives are, of course, the executives', but it is convenient to refer to them as the corporation's. These goals may or may not be what the executives think they want to achieve, or what they say they want to achieve; corporate mission statements may not be honest or may not be believed. The actual goals of the executives (or the corporation) can only be identified by examining what sorts of behaviour the executives reward, as will be discussed below.

The constraints on a corporation are those facts which affect the pursuit of its goals, and which cannot be changed, at least in the short run. Some constraints are physical, and cannot be violated by anyone in the corporation even if they wanted to. For example, the cabins on jet aircraft need to be pressurized—that need is a fact which no manufacturer can do anything about. Other constraints are moral, legal, or mandated by safety. These constraints can be ignored by a corporation or its employees, and it is these sorts of constraints which interest us.

Objectives and constraints are very different concepts, though sometimes constraints are recognized in statements of a company's objectives. For example, the objective of an aircraft manufacturing corporation might be stated as: "To produce aircraft which can be safely operated." Here safety, which is a constraint, looks like it is part of the objectives, but this appearance does not stand up to analysis. The objective is to produce operable aircraft; safety is actually a constraint on that goal because airplanes cannot be operated if they fall out of the sky. Safety is not a separate or secondary goal, but a condition of achieving the actual goal of making operable aircraft.

Within a corporation, goals and constraints are treated very differently. Rewards are given for employee behaviour which appears to help the company achieve its goals. Observing legal, moral, and safety constraints is seldom rewarded; it tends to be assumed that employees will observe such constraints without reward. Instead, employees in companies which enforce constraints are usually punished when violation of the constraint is discovered; they are not usually rewarded just for observing constraints. Complete failure of a corporation to enforce legal, moral or safety constraints raises obvious moral problems; this discussion will be centred on the more interesting

case in which constraints are enforced by the corporation (i.e., by the executives), but ignored by some of the employees. Why they are ignored, even under the threat of punishment, has to do with the different ways in which executives encourage employees to pursue goals, and discourage them from violating constraints.

In general, employee behaviour which enhances corporate goals is rewarded, observing constraints is not. Hindering objectives is almost always punished. Constraints are constraints on the pursuit of the company's goals, and hence observing them can threaten an employee's rewards. In fact, observing constraints and asking one's management to do so as well may impede the company's goals to the point where the behaviour itself is punished. Surely this encourages violation of constraints.

There are other pressures on employees to put rewards for pursuing goals before the observance of constraints. Violation of constraints is only punished if one is caught; hence there is an element of gamble involved. The time factor also plays a major role; rewards are usually immediate, while discovery of violated constraints may be months or years away, by which time the employee has had his promotion and is safely elsewhere.

To complicate matters further, corporations are hierarchical. If an employee does resist temptation and observes constraints at the risk of losing rewards, his manager, or his manager's manager, may not. If getting a company to observe a constraint requires escalating concerns to the senior executive level (and this is the case we are concerned with in this article), then a single failure to resist temptation may block the concern from reaching the executives. This is the phenomenon of negative information blockage.

Since negative information blockage is inherent in the nature of goals, constraints, rewards and punishments, then to what extent can executives be held responsible for getting information past the blockage? The next section will consider two possible views of this topic.

V. EXECUTIVE RESPONSIBILITY AND NEGATIVE INFORMATION BLOCKAGE

The first of the two views is that executives are responsible for doing whatever they can to prevent negative information blockage. They have a moral duty to structure the corporation to ensure that risks of disaster are discovered and made known to themselves (and then, of course, to act on the information). They have a moral responsibility to do as much as they can to prevent tragedy.

What exactly executives can do I will not discuss in detail; a few examples will suffice. They can offer rewards of information brought to them; they can keep an "open door" policy so junior employees can go around the blockages; they can set a personal example of concern for moral, legal, and safety constraints. These ideas are generally discussed in business ethics literature under the topic of whistleblowing, since whistleblowing is often the result of frustration with negative information blockage. (See, for example, Callahan, 1988-C). Without going into further detail on what executives can do, we can summarize the first view of corporate executive responsibility by suggesting they should do whatever is reasonably possible to prevent knowledge of potential disasters from being blocked before it reaches them.

The second view is that executives, especially CEOs, are responsible for preventing tragedy, excepting only those cases, such as acts of God, which were discussed above in Section II. This view is radically different from the first; just how different can be seen if we consider how executives would be judged in the event of a tragedy. On the first

view, the impartial spectator making moral judgements would inquire what steps the executives had taken prior to the tragedy to make sure information on the impending disaster had been conveyed to them. And, of course, they would ask whether the executives had acted on anything they knew. On the second view, the impartial spectator would hold the executive morally responsible for the failure to acquire sufficient information to prevent the tragedy, regardless of whether or not steps had been taken to circumvent negative information blockage. This view is essentially holding that since the tragedy happened, the steps taken were obviously not sufficient, and hence the executives are morally culpable.

It should be noted that on the second view, we are holding executives morally responsible even though they did not know the disaster might happen, and even though they may have taken some steps to acquire the knowledge. We are holding them morally responsible for the result, not the effort. The first view holds them responsible only for the effort.

There are many cases in life where people are held responsible for results rather than effort: it is one of the painful lessons we learn as children. For example, on examinations, students, especially in such subjects as medicine and engineering, are quite rightly marked on results, not the amount of effort they put into studying. And executives themselves do not hesitate to hold employees responsible for getting results.

Demanding results on the job, not just effort, is acceptable because it is necessary. When an engineer designs a bridge, it is important to society that it does not collapse. It is important to society that doctors are competent, not just that they are doing their best. We are often justified in holding people responsible for doing their job well.

If people fail in their jobs, they may or may not be held legally liable depending on the circumstances, but in any case their careers suffer, and they may lose their jobs. The fact that they are held responsible is reflected in the impact on their professional standing when they succeed or fail. To distinguish this type of responsibility from legal and moral responsibility, I will refer to it as professional responsibility.

The case of professional responsibility that best parallels the situation of executives is that of cabinet ministers in a parliamentary system. When things go wrong in an area of ministerial responsibility, the minister is held accountable and is expected to resign. They are not supposed to argue that they tried, that they have not been negligent, or that they are not legally liable. Thus Lord Carrington resigned when Argentina invaded the Falklands; he did not stay on protesting that it was not his fault (though it probably was not). The questions we must now deal with are: should we apply professional responsibility to executives? And secondly, how does professional responsibility relate to moral responsibility?

VI. PROFESSIONAL RESPONSIBILITY

The concept of professional responsibility applies when the outcome of a professional activity is of great concern to a person or people other than the person doing the activity. It especially applies if the outcome is of concern over and above any contract the professional has with some other person, or if the outcome is of great concern to bystanders. Let me illustrate these points with an example.

When I buy a pair of shoes and find them faulty, I take them back to the shoe store and generally will be satisfied if I am given back my money. The responsibility is limited to reversing the contract. When I go to the doctor for an operation, I am not interested in hearing that he or she will refund me the cost of the operation if it goes wrong, especially if I die. We can say in this case that the doc-

tor has a professional responsibility which goes beyond the "contract." It goes beyond because the consequences of failure go beyond the contract. Similarly, if an engineer designs a bridge that collapses, then refunding the money he or she received for the design hardly helps those who were on the bridge when it collapsed. It helps so little that that course of action is seldom pursued. The engineer, in this case, has a professional responsibility.

Liability laws generally reflect the fact that responsibility can extend far beyond reversing the original contract, but this discussion is not an attempt to define legal liability. The point is that professional responsibility arises when the consequences of failure have effects on other people (customers or by-standers) which exceed the confines of the initial contract.

Clearly, this applies to executives. If they fail to create a corporate culture which overcomes negative information blockage and disaster results, it often involves the death of their customers (or of their customers' customers, as in the case of the DC-10s). It is clear that we are justified in holding executives professionally responsible when tragedy happens. In other words, we hold them professionally responsible for failing to obtain the information needed to prevent the disaster whether or not they tried to.

But is holding executives professionally responsible different from holding them morally responsible? In the cases we have been examining, there is a close connection between the two.

Executives and everyone else have a moral responsibility to ensure that their activities do not result in the deaths of others if that result can be prevented. Executives, therefore, have a moral responsibility to do their best to obtain the information needed to prevent disasters. They have a professional responsibility, as we have seen, not just to do their best, but to actually succeed in preventing avoidable disasters. The latter grows out of the former in the sense that executives have a professional responsibility to succeed in fulfilling their moral responsibilities. (Of course, they also have professional responsibilities with other origins as well.) Thus, although normally a person only has a moral responsibility for trying to avoid immoral results, in this case (and in others) a person has a professional responsibility to succeed in fulfilling the underlying moral responsibility.

This conclusion has a major implication for judging executives; namely, when tragedy happens, we are justified in holding them responsible based on moral values. If they object that they did not have the information necessary to prevent the disaster and that they had made an honest effort to obtain that information, then we can accept that as individuals they have fulfilled their moral obligations. (We are assuming honesty.) But as professional executives, they have failed to fulfil their professional obligation to carry out moral requirements. We are still justified in holding them responsible based on moral considerations.

REFERENCES

Brooks, L.J.: 1989, "Corporate Ethical Performance: Trends, Forecasts, and Outlooks," *Journal of Business Ethics* 8, No. 1, pp. 31–38.

Callahan, J.C.: 1988-A, *Ethical Issues in Professional Life* (Oxford University Press, Oxford), pp. 49–50.

Callahan, J.C.: 1988-B, *Ethical Issues in Professional Life* (Oxford University Press, Oxford), p. 342.

Callahan, J.C.: 1988-C, *Ethical Issues in Professional Life* (Oxford University Press, Oxford), pp. 337–339.

Carr, A.Z.: 1968, "Is Business Bluffing Ethical?," *Ethical Issues in Professional Life*, C. Callahan, ed. (Oxford University Press, Oxford), pp. 69–72.

Danley, J.R.: 1980, "Corporate Moral Agency: The Case for Anthropological Bigotry," *Ethical Issues in Professional Life*, J.C. Callahan, ed. (Oxford University Press, Oxford), pp. 269–274.

French, Peter A.: 1977, "Corporate Moral Agency," *Ethical Issues in Professional Life*, J.C. Callahan, ed. (Oxford University Press, Oxford), pp. 265–269.

Gillespie, Norman Chase: 1983, "The Business of Ethics," *Ethical Issues in Professional Life*, J.C. Callahan, ed. (Oxford University Press, Oxford), pp. 72-76

Globe and Mail: 1989, "Polluting Firm's Chairman Hauled into Court by U.S. Judge," Associated Press, *Globe and Mail*, August 10, 1989, p. B10.

Grosman, Brian A: 1988, *Corporate Loyalty: A Trust Betrayed* (Penguin Books, Markham, Ont.), pp. 177–179.

Mintz, Morton: 1985, *At Any Cost: Corporate Greed, Women, and the Dalkon Shield* (Random House, Inc., New York).

Nagel, Thomas: 1978, "Ruthlessness in Public Life," *Ethical Issues in Professional Life*, J.C. Callahan, ed. (Oxford University Press, Oxford), pp. 76–83.

White, Larry C.: 1988, *Merchants of Death: The American Tobacco Industry* (Beech Tree/ Morrow, New York).

THE HESTER PRYNNE SANCTION

Peter A. French

Perhaps the most quoted line in the long history of the discussion of corporate criminal liability is attributed to Edward, First Baron Thurlow, Lord Chancellor of England. The line is:

> Did you ever expect a corporation to have a conscience, when it has no soul to be damned, and no body to be kicked?[1]

Baron Thurlow was concerned with how effectively to punish a corporation that had committed a serious crime when the corporation cannot be thrown into jail, when large fines can usually be passed on to consumers, and so on. This is a crucial practical issue because the idea of corporate criminality will be an empty theoretical one if the courts have no effective means of punishing a corporation that has been found guilty of criminal violation, and the courts have been busy lately in hearing corporate criminal cases.[2] ("Corporate crimes," as I use the term, are

not to be confused with "white-collar crimes." White-collar crimes are typically perpetrated by managers, accountants, etc., against their own corporations. Corporate crimes are those that involve general corporate policy or decisionmaking, for example, the manufacture of defective, life-threatening products, pollution of the environment, wrongful death in certain airline disasters, antitrust violations, and price fixing.)[3]

Baron Thurlow's dictum is firmly cemented in the foundation of the retributive views that sustain our penal system. The firm hand of retribution, with its biblical "eye for an eye" authority, still commands the high ground of our thinking about the punishment of criminals,[4] and perhaps it should. If a corporation has no body to kick (leaving to God the business of souls and eternal damnation), how can it retribute its felonious behavior? It has no eye to be exchanged for an eye it has blinded by unsafe working conditions. It has

From *Business and Professional Ethics Journal*, 4, no. 2 (1984), 19–32. Reprinted by permission of the author.

no neck to stretch for the wrongful deaths it has caused in product explosions. Or so the story is meant to go.

Retributivism, however, does not have to be understood in strict biblical, in-kind terms. Capital punishment in the case of human murderers, for example, in many jurisdictions has been replaced by life sentences that carry possible parole stipulations, and the old Anglo-Saxon notion of wergeld is frequently utilized in settling wrongful-death suits. The price of a human life may not always come cheap, but it is being set by the courts and paid by corporate offenders or their insurance carriers. In the famous Ford Pinto case in Indiana the company used the insurance industry figure of $200,000, as the value of a human life when it defended its cost-benefit analysis regarding the redesign of the gas tanks on the Pinto. The particulars of how that figure is determined are not important. If I may mention, however, I have had some direct dealings with wergeld that produced a substantially larger sum for the value of human life. In Minnesota a few years ago, I was hired as a consultant to a legal firm to develop the case for a farm family suing a trucking company for the wrongful death of their eleven-year-old son. The firm argued that because the child was the fifth in the family and was not essential to productive operation of the farm, the most it should have to pay was the relatively standard $200,000. To counter that position I presented the view that the family must be adequately compensated for its non-financial losses: the unrequitable affection for the child, the loss of familial association, the value of future tender relationships between parents and siblings and the dead child. The wrongful death of the child induced a vacancy in a family that had not only a financial and emotional investment in the child, but an identity relationship to the child. There were no firm legal precedents for my arguments, but it proved successful and the family received a wergeld

settlement many times greater than the original offer.

The idea that a corporation can pay a court fine or a set sum to the relatives of its victim in a homicide case and thereby expiate its guilt is, however, regarded by many people as a shocking affront to justice.[5] After all, the price of such a punishment can be written off as just another cost of business, and in the normal course of events it may be passed on to the consumers of the corporation's products or services. The penal effect of the punishment is absorbed by the innocent. But what are the alternatives? Certainly a whole corporation cannot, as Baron Thurlow knew, be tossed in jail, and when the crime is a truly corporate one it will strain the concept of justice to punish individual employees or managers or directors if, as is normally the case, such persons can demonstrate that they did not have the relevant intentions nor the required capacities to constitute the *mens rea* required by law for successful criminal prosecution.[6] Vicarious liability or guilt by association in these instances is hardly likely to satisfy the demands of justice. Frankly, very few of these cases are really reducible to matters of individual negligence, let alone intentional recklessness.[7] Most of the existing penal options, such as license or charter revocation, are usually ineffective. Furthermore, fines and forced closings tend to hurt those who are the least closely associated with the relevant corporate decisionmaking: stockholders and low-level employees.

Stockholders, however, need not be of much concern to us. They are protected by SEC regulations and if they suffer from corporate punishment, that is a risk they undertook when entering the market. Often stockholders benefit for a period of time from the undetected crime. I see no reason why they ought not bear some of the burden of its retribution. The stockholders, after all, are free to trade their holdings in the market and never were assured of a clear profit. Also, the stockholders might consider pressing a civil suit against the corporation that cost them a significant value of stock because of its criminal behavior. A class-action suit by stockholders who claim damage under such conditions could even have a second-level retributive result. If the corporation were forced to pay stockholders for losses resulting from corporate crime, some deterrent aims of punishment might also be accomplished.

It is likely, as we know, that corporations will try to recover heavy fines in the form of higher prices. The limit to that kind of practice, thankfully, is set by the marketplace. The only exceptions would be in public utilities or in other monopoly or semimonopolistic enterprises where consumers must deal with the criminal corporation or forego the service. Such corporations are generally regulated by government agencies, and pricing increases to offset penalties could be prevented if those agencies act in the best interests of the community at large.

It should be mentioned with respect to the harming of innocent employees that when a human being is convicted of a felony and punished, his or her family and dependents are frequently cast into dire financial straits. The harm done to them, though they may be totally innocent of any complicity in the crime, may, in fact, far outweigh that done to the incarcerated felon. After all, the convicted criminal receives three meals a day and lodging. His or her family may be reduced to penury and find that meals are only a sometime thing, and then hardly nutritious. In many jurisdictions, little or no official interest is paid to these innocent sufferers. Why should we be concerned with the employees who work for offending corporations?[8]

These problems, then, are not major, but the fining of corporations is just not perceived in the corporate world as punishment comparable to incarceration of the human felon. Because of that fact, many believe that, at least as a practical matter, and regardless of whether punishment is morally justified, corporations should not even be subject to the criminal law.[9] Such a view, however, can lead to a number of socially unacceptable outcomes, perhaps the worst of which is that many offenses will go unpunished because the offense is of a peculiarly corporate nature. An important form of social control of the most powerful institutions in our community will then be relinquished to the reasonable demands of our canons of individual criminal justice. Do we then have no viable theoretical and practical options?

I propose to commend an alternative type of punishment, though I must stress that in isolation from other available sanctions, such as fines and probation orders, the punishment I have in mind will not likely have the full reformative or deterrent effects a concerned citizenry would desire. In some cases it will best be used only to augment other sentences, though in many cases it may be sufficient punishment and have all of the generally desired retributive, and even deterrent, effects.

The moral psychology of our criminal legal system is guilt-based,[10] and guilt is an economic notion. Guilt historically has been viewed as a form of debt, either or both to the specific victim harmed or to the society as a whole. Crime unbalances the books. To expiate guilt, the guilty party must repay, compensate, or restore—hence the fine system and the wergeld practices. Punishment is an institutional vehicle of repayment and restoration. When the debt is retired the original *status quo* is restored. This idea has deep roots. The Latin *debitum* in the Lord's Prayer was rendered in Old English as *gylt*, and, of course, there is that popular expression, "paying one's debt to society."

Guilt is a threshold notion and so depends upon a sense of boundaries and limits, usually as set by rules or laws. Guilt is centrally a transgression, a trespass. Either the defendant is guilty as charged or not guilty. Guilt is a minimum maintenance notion. In short, guilt avoidance involves meeting only basic standards of behavior. As should be expected, guilt-based moralities are statute-dominated. To feel guilty is to feel one has done something that is forbidden or restricted. For the more sophisticated, it may also be to realize or believe that one has done something that falls beneath the minimal behavior requirements of the society.

In contrast to cultures having a guilt-based morality, certain cultures, and in part our own, place primary emphasis on the personal worth and image of the members of society. In such moralities the central notion is shame rather than guilt.[11] Shame, in fact, may be a more primitive moral notion than guilt. There are no natural expressions of guilt as there surely are for shame, for example, blushing. We do say, of course, that someone "looks guilty," meaning that he or she is displaying certain kinds of behavior—for example, shifty eyes and nervousness—but nothing so directly relates to guilt as blushing, hanging one's head, or covering one's face to communicate one's sense of shame.

In a shame-based morality, evaluation of behavior is not primarily made against rules or laws that have established minimal constraints. Moral and personal worth is usually measured against role or identity models. To have shame or to be shameful a person must regard his or her behavior as being below or short of what is expected of or associated with the role, station, or type with which he or she identifies himself or herself. The feeling of shame is the feeling of inadequacy or inferiority.

Shame involves a subjective feeling of self-reference. Experiences of shame are experiences of exposure, characterized by a sense of loss of the identity one thought one had. A crucial element in a shame-based morality is a stress on the individual's self-conception as measured against ideal models that are accepted by the person as appropriate to that individual's way of life. Shame, then, has both a private and a public aspect.

(In fact, the Greeks and the French have two words for these two sides of shame.)

Shame is a visual concept. Its root meaning is to cover one's face or hide. It relates to the way one looks to oneself and to the way one thinks one looks to others. If you are ashamed, you want to cover yourself. You do not want to be seen.

Interestingly, the language indicates that being without shame, being shameless, is not a respectable thing, though being guiltless is. The most dangerous persons are the brazen incorrigibles who in Zephaniah's words "knoweth no shame."[12] To be unaffectable by shame is to be antisocial and, worse than that, to have no concern for self-image. Shame operates in the field of honor and self-respect rather than being associated with following legal and social rules. Shame is also described as the experience of having shattered a trust or of having been implicated in a shattering of trust. Self-respect, honor, personal worth, and trust provide the conceptual structure of a shame-based moral constraint system. They are also central notions of free-enterprise business.

An adept penal system would be one that could induce shame when there has been a notable incongruity with appropriate models, when trust has been shattered, and that could utilize the visual and media capabilities of the society to heighten and focus the awareness of the offender, as well as the community at large, of serious shameful behavior.

But why is shame so valuable a moral emotion in a criminal context? The answer uncovers the penal virtues of shame over guilt. Shame cannot be purged by mere repayment. Shame is not transferable to debt, and wergeld in no way relieves shame. Paying a fine cannot restore the *status quo* disrupted by shameful actions. It cannot reestablish worth or trust. Regaining worth, reclaiming identity, is not a question of purchase. The shameful person must act in positive, creative, possibly even heroic ways so that he or she may again see himself or herself and be seen as worthy. The greater the shame the more extraordinary and prolonged must be the behavior that reestablishes worth. Confession relates to guilt. Guilty-feeling persons seem almost compelled to communicate. Shameful people have no desire to talk of their shame and confession does not dent the shame. Notice the difference between condemnation and contempt. The society condemns the guilty, but it holds the shameful in contempt; it derogates the social status of the shameful person, whereas only a price is extracted from the guilty. There is also something very spontaneous about the social reaction to the shameful person, who is abandoned, exiled, or cast out. The response to the guilty is not extemporaneous. Punishment is contrived as an instrument of restoration through which, by suffering, the guilty's relationship to the rest of society is repaired.

Our current penal system only incidentally, accidentally, induces shame in offenders. There is, however, a sanction that specifically derives its force from the concept of shame, that could be purposefully utilized in this country (as it once was), and that could have especially sanguine effects in corporate criminal cases. For obvious reasons, I shall call it the Hester Prynne Sanction. Recall *The Scarlet Letter*?[13]

> The penalty thereof is death. But in their great mercy and tenderness of heart, they have doomed Mistress Prynne to stand only a space of three hours on the platform of the pillory, and then and thereafter, for the remainder of her natural life, to wear a mark of shame upon her bosom." "A wise sentence!" remarked the stranger gravely bowing his head. "Thus she will be a living sermon against sin.[14]

The Hester Prynne sanction, it should be noticed, is not directly a monetary penalty. Adverse publicity could contribute to the achievement of monetary retributive effects by costing the corporation business. That is not, however, the reason for utilizing the sanction. Primarily, the Hester Prynne

Sanction threatens prestige, image, and social standing. It really works only when the offender comes to regard himself or herself as having acted disgracefully, as having broken a trust, or as having failed to measure up to personal and social standards. The offender should come to view the sanction as a legitimate damaging blot on his or her reputation; as a mark of shortcoming; as an indicator of the disgust of others; as a signal that identity must be rebuilt.

The Hester Prynne Sanction is particulary suited to corporate offenders because image, reputation, and social acceptance are at the very heart of modern corporate life.[15] Little sustained success has even been enjoyed by a company with a bad reputation. Official censure is not an inconsequential matter where corporate achievement depends on communal standing. In fact, the Hester Prynne Sanction could prove far more effective in dealing with corporate offenders than with human criminals. For a corporation to survive, it simply must garner and nurture a good image among the constituents of its marketplace. Furthermore, writing corporate punishments in terms of adverse-publicity orders is more likely to minimize the kinds of unwanted externalities that plague the monetary sanctions now used by the courts against corporate offenders.[16] It is noteworthy that the U.S. National Commission on reform of Federal Criminal Laws in its 1970 draft report supported the use of a tactic that sounds remarkably like the punishment of Hester Prynne:

> When an organization is convicted of an offense, the court may in addition or in lieu of imposing other authorized sanctions, . . . require the organization to give appropriate publicity to the conviction . . . by advertising in designated areas or in designated media. . . .[17]

Sadly, the Commission's *Final Report*[18] lacked this recommendation because of strong corporate lobbying. My argument is directed toward a revival of the basic idea.

Despite the almost universal corporate aversion to a tarnished image, it should be pointed out, "bad press" is hardly penal and can be countered by corporate media campaigns intended "to put a different face on the matter." Quite simply, if the Hester Prynne Sanction is to be retributively penal, the convicted corporation must regard the publicity as not only noxious, but a justified communal revelation of the corporation's disgrace, its shameful actions.

A shame-based sanction functions, as previously noted, only in relation to some sort of model identity against which the offender judges himself and expects to be judged by the institutions of social order and justice. Where do we find such models for corporations? The Scarlet Letter provides only the structural or formal aspects of the matter. Hester was judged unworthy against a model of human fidelity that was deeply embedded in the puritanical society of early Boston. That model was understood and internalized throughout her community. It was not a product of law, though surely many of the old Bostonian laws were derived from the same set of conceptions that engendered the model.

Throughout the centuries we have articulated human ideal models,[19] though we seem less intent on this enterprise in recent decades. These models are a part of our history, legend, education, religion, and literature. There surely are corporate ideal models in our culture as well, though they are of a more recent origin. The content of such models need not here be specified, though we should expect to find such features as profitability, social responsiveness, industriousness, and humaneness in them. In fact, we may now have better pictures of these corporate ideal models than we have for ordinary human beings. In short, we seem to have a number of generally shared basic ideas about what a socially responsible corporation ought to look and act like and, by and large, most corporations embrace these ideals, at least in their documents, codes of employee conduct, and public relations releases. The particulars of our corporate model especially seem to take shape in the forefront of our thinking when we witness things that have gone corporately wrong, as, for example, in the recent disaster in Bhopal, India.

The courts have the authority and the social credibility to force corporations to confront their failures, to live up to the community expectations engendered by their roles and public images. Court-ordered adverse publicity could provide an official revelatory apparatus, the modern substitute for the pillory, where the corporate offender stands contemptible before its community, forced to confront the fact of its inadequacy. Shame is, after all, an identity crisis.

The exciting aspect of the Hester Prynne Sanction, however, is that the suffering of adverse publicity does not restore the offender's social status. It does not relieve the shame. Only positive corrective acts can do that. But look where this gets us: the imposition of the Hester Prynne Sanction on a corporation broadcasts a corporate offender's behavior, thus arousing (1) appropriate social contempt, (2) a recognition of a failure to measure up, and (3) the kind of adjustments to operating procedures, policies, and practices that are required for the corporate offender to regain moral worth in both its own eyes and those of the community. Rehabilitation is thereby served by retribution.

It will surely be noted that the Hester Prynne Sanction, as I have described its potential use in corporate criminal cases, has clear affinities to sanctions that are already commonly used in professional organizations. Most professional societies, in fact, use censure and publicity as their primary penalty against members or associated institutions that violate their codes of professional ethics. The American Society of Civil Engineers, for example, imposes such a penalty and may also require censured members to discuss their offenses in professional public meetings.[20] For years the AAUP has used a censure list devised to shame institutions that have violated academic freedom. The major difference between the Hester Prynne Sanction and these censure techniques is that it is a court-ordered and supervised sanction. It relates to the whole community rather than to a professional body and it is imposed for criminal offenses and not just violations of professional codes.

The Hester Prynne Sanction might have significant retributive and deterrent effects on corporate offenders, but as a primary penal device some legal theorists have thought it prone to fail for a number of practical reasons.

In the first place, as we all know, government is a rather poor propagandist.[21] It is not very persuasive, and very rarely is it pithy. (Have you ever seen a catchy piece of government-written prose that could rival the output of Madison Avenue?) For the adverse-publicity sanction to have the desired effect, for it to have a genuine impact on the offending corporation's established image, the courts will have to employ clever writers and publicists, not the run-of-the-mill bureaucratic scribblers who crank out the government's literature.

Such a concern can be easily addressed. Courts have the power to write their orders in such a way that the cost of the adverse publicity is paid by the criminal corporation from its own advertising budget to a competitive agency (other than ones that carry its accounts), which will then manage a campaign as approved by an officer of the court (perhaps a college professor trained in advertising and marketing). The corporation will have to submit its previous year's advertising budget to be used as a starting line, a percentage of the advertising budget will be set aside for the adverse-publicity campaign, and that percentage will be carried through all annual budgets until the expiration of the order. In this way, even if the corporation increases its advertising budget to attempt to entice sales, it will have to pay

a higher adverse-publicity cost. The court-appointed overseer will instruct the agency to expend all funds in the adverse-publicity budget annually and to do so in outlets roughly equivalent to those used by the usual corporate advertising agencies. For example, the agency will not be allowed to place adverse publicity in obscure small-town newspapers if the corporation does not generally advertise in such ways. The private sector would then be actively engaged in the penal process and a whole new and respectable area of advertising will provide jobs and new paths of expression for the creative imagination to wander.

A frequently voiced second concern is that the level of anticorporate "noise" in our society is so great as to devalue the effect of specific adverse-publicity orders.[22] The newspaper editorialists, the campaigning politicians, the special interest groups, the conservationists, the Naderites, the assorted movie and TV actors and actresses with various causes all contribute to a confusing cacophony of charges that are usually indirect, unsubstantiated, and certainly not properly adjudicated. Can this noise be controlled? Probably not, and it is not a good idea to pursue such a line in a free country. Against this noise, however, a well-developed adverse-publicity campaign, identified clearly as court-ordered, is still likely to draw special attention. The public may never be very discriminating, but generally the fact that a court has ordered a certain publicity campaign as punishment for a particular criminal offense should pierce the shield of apathy behind which the public hides from the onslaught of ordinary corporate criticism.

It will be suggested that corporations can dilute the Hester Prynne Sanction through counterpublicity.[23] There is no denying the power of Madison Avenue agencies to create clever and effective image building, even in the face of severe public or government criticism. But the sanction can be written in such a way, as suggested above, to offset any corporate counterattack.

Furthermore, the court has the power to order the corporation not to engage in any advertising directed specifically toward rebutting or diluting the sentence. If the corporation were to promote its own case after having lost in court and received an adverse-publicity sentence, it would be in contempt of the court and sterner measures would be justified. Oil companies like Mobil, it might be remembered, mounted effective replies to the media charges leveled against them during the energy crisis. Also, corporations after *Central Hudson Gas & Electric Corp. v. Public Service Commission* [447 U.S. 557 (1980)] clearly have First Amendment rights to express opinions on matters of public concern.[24] Corporate rebuttals to adverse-publicity orders, however, would not be protected by Central Hudson, and the Mobil commercials were certainly not attempts to minimize the effectiveness of any court orders. The oil companies had been charged only in the field of public opinion and their response was a totally appropriate defense in that venue.

The Hester Prynne Sanction may prove efficacious in fraud, public safety, and felony cases, but some doubt it can be equally effective in regulatory cases. Gulf Oil, for example, was convicted of illegal campaign contributions in connection with the Watergate scandals.[25] The publicity was profuse, but there is little evidence that it hurt Gulf Oil sales. Two responses seem appropriate. The first is to point out that in the regulatory cases adverse publicity occurred in the ordinary media coverage of the events. It was not court-ordered in lieu of or in addition to some other penal sanction, such as a stiff fine. In effect, it was incidental and as the story faded from the front page or the first fifteen minutes of the telecast, its intensity diminished. But, it just may be the case that the Hester Prynne Sanction does not produce significant desired effects in the case of certain crimes. I make no claim that adverse-publicity orders will always suffice to achieve the retributive ends of the legal

system. A mix of sanctions will undoubtedly be required. I would argue that adverse-publicity orders are more likely than most other sanctions to produce what might be called "rehabilitative outcomes," reformed corporations. Fines certainly are too easily assimilated to business costs.

The Hester Prynne Sanction, however, may produce some of the same externalities as fines.[26] After all, if it is really effective, some say that it should lead to decreased sales and the corporation's employees at the lowest levels could be made to suffer layoffs and other unwanted effects.[27] This should not overly concern us. Such externalities plague penal sanctions of all kinds. More to the point, however, the true question is whether the Hester Prynne Sanction is justifiable over the simple assessment of a fine when both produce basically equivalent externalities. I think that I have offered some firm reasons for the court to prefer, at least with regard to certain crimes, the Hester Prynne Sanction rather than or in addition to fines. It is worth briefly noting that in a recent study of seventeen major corporations that have suffered adverse publicity over an offense or serious incident (though such publicity was not court-ordered) executives at the middle and higher levels of management reported that loss of corporate prestige was regarded as a very major corporate concern.[28] Indeed, the loss of prestige was regarded as far more serious than the payment of a stiff fine. The payment of the fine and the suffering of court-ordered and supervised adverse publicity are simply not equivalent punishments.

The Hester Prynne Sanction is also, for moral reasons, to be preferred over community-service orders. The celebrated case of *United States v. Allied Chemical Company* [(1976) 7 Env. Rep. (BNA) 29; File CR-76-0129-R (U.S. Dist. Ct., Eastern Div. of Va., Richmond Div. 1976)], in which Allied Chemical was fined $13.24 million after a no-contest plea to 940 counts of pollution of the James River and other Virginia waterways, is often cited as an example of creative sentencing leading to the development of an alternative to the traditional sanctions.[29] The Allied Chemical fine was reduced to $5 million when the company agreed to give $8,356,202 to the Virginia Environmental Endowment. Strictly speaking, the court did not order community service, but it did accept the company's establishment of the endowment as mitigatory. In another case, *United States v. Olin Mathieson* [Criminal No. 78-30 (U.S. Dist. Ct., Dist. of Conn. June 1, 1978)], the company pleaded no contest to the charge of conspiracy involving the shipment of rifles to South Africa. The judge imposed a $45,000 fine after Olin Mathieson agreed to set up a $500,000 New Haven Community Betterment Fund. (The maximum penalty could have been $510,000.)

Although neither of these cases really involved the imposition of a community-service sanction (the defendants essentially wrote a check), some legal theorists have recently argued that the lessons learned in them indicate the desirability of providing the court with such a sentencing option.[30] There are certain practical problems with this approach that warrant only brief mention. Perhaps the most serious is that the corporation's costs in buying or performing community service are tax-deductible charity contributions and standard court-imposed fines are, of course, nondeductible. However, legislation could correct this deficiency.

It must also be realized that the performance of community service is a positive, image-enhancing action. It can be expected to elevate the public's opinion of the criminal corporation. In fact, the results of corporate community-service projects and charitable contributions are likely to make a rather favorable impression on the members of society, while the reasons the donor corporation embarked on this apparently altruistic ventures are likely to be forgotten or lost in the outpouring of grateful sentiment. There is, however, an obvious corrective for this difficulty: to invoke the Hester Prynne Sanction

in conjunction with community-service sentencing. Simply, the court can require that the service project be clearly identified as court-ordered as a penalty for a specific criminal offense. Every association drawn by the corporation to its beneficence would have to include an adverse-publicity reference to its criminal conviction as the reason for the service. Although community service does not seem to stand on a par with the Hester Prynne Sanction and the traditional sentencing options, should it be encouraged? I think there are reasons that its use should be very restricted and that it should never be used in isolation from more penal sanctions.

The socially conciliatory aspect of community service, the fact that such endeavors can restore lost prestige and polish tarnished images, makes such civic contributions a major avenue for corporations to regain status and acceptance lost through conviction and broadcast in accord with the imposition of a Hester Prynne sentence. A shamed company, as earlier noted, cannot simply buy its way back to social grace. It needs to perform especially worthy deeds to achieve restoration. Community service is certainly of the type of action it needs to perform to achieve such ends. But for there to be worth in the doing of such deeds, they must be voluntary. If they are performed under a form of duress, they are not actions of the person compelled to perform them. Insofar as none of our principles of responsibility capture them for that person, they do not accrue to the moral credit of that person. They would seem to be extended acts of the judge who decided to whom and how much. The convicted corporation is little more than an instrument of the court's conception of social need. A recent Nebraska sentence is a case in point. A corporation convicted of bid rigging in highway construction contracts was ordered to donate $1.4 million to establish a permanent professional chair in business ethics at the state university.[31]

The community-service sanction, when conjoined to the Hester Prynne Sanction (ideally) or to a fine, can, however, have a certain morally desirable outcome, besides the fact that some good was done (the service was performed or the donation to a worthy cause was made) and regardless of the reasons for its performance. Forced charitable deeds might serve to inculcate a habit of social concern in the corporation. At the very least, the sentenced corporation might come to view a continuance of community involvement as a way of currying future judicial favor. Aristotle maintained that a person is good by doing good deeds, by getting into the habit of doing such things.[32] A community-service sentence could start a corporation on the path to virtue. Hence, there may be a re-habilitative value in the sanction despite the involuntary nature of the service performed by the convicted company.

There is, however a notable amount of uncertainty that such an outcome will ensue from this type of sentencing. It does not seem likely enough to be a justifying reason for use of the sanction. In fact, the best reason for a judge to order community service would be to achieve the charitable ends themselves. The rehabilitation of the offending corporation would seem to be an incidental upshot. Judges, however, are not necessarily in the best position to decide on our social or charitable needs. Furthermore, other than monetary or time loss, the penalty relationship of the sentence to the crime may be remote.

All of these factors militate against the use of community-service orders in corporate criminal cases, unless they are augmented by stiff fines and/or the Hester Prynne Sanction. In comparison with the other discussed sanctions, adverse publicity, with its primary shaming function, would seem to be preferable on both practical and moral grounds. In any event, it is clear that there are effective and morally justifiable sentencing options (though community service is the least preferable) that support the inclusion of corporate entities among those persons who are subject to the criminal law. Baron Thurlow's demurral on the notion of corporate criminal liability

may be set aside. Corporations are not only intentional agents, moral persons, they are proper subjects of the criminal law and all its fury. They can be stigmatized and they can be "kicked" in ways comparable to those visited on human offenders.

ENDNOTES

1. *The Oxford Dictionary of Quotations*, 2d ed. (Oxford: Oxford University Press, 1966), p. 547.

2. See, generally, Marshall B. Clinard and Peter C. Yeager, *Corporate Crime* (New York: Free Press, 1980).

3. See, e.g., Brent Fisse and John Braithwaite, *The Impact of Publicity on Corporate Offenders* (Albany, NY: State University of New York Press, 1983), chaps. 2–18, p. 317.

4. See, e.g., J. Murphy, *Retribution, Justice, and Therapy* (Boston: D. Reidel, 1979); R. Singer, *Just Deserts: Sentencing Based on Equality and Desert* (Cambridge, MA: Ballinger, 1979); A. Von Hirsch, *Doing Justice: The Choice of Punishments* (New York: Hill and Wang, 1976). But see John Braithwaite, "Challenging Just Deserts: Punishing White-Collar Criminals," *Journal of Criminal Law and Criminology* 73 (1982): 723–763.

5. See, generally, Victoria Lynn Swigert and Ronald A. Farrell, "Corporate Homicide: Definitional Processes in the Creation of Deviance," *Law & Society Review* 15 (1980): 161–182; Brent Fisse, "Reconstructing Corporate Criminal Law: Deterrence, Retribution, Fault, and Sanctions," *Southern California Law Review* 56 (1983): 1141–1246.

6. See, further, Peter A. French, *Collective and Corporate Responsibility* (New York: Columbia University Press, 1984), chap. 11.

7. See, e.g., Fisse and Braithwaite, *The Impact of Publicity on Corporate Offenders*, p. 303.

8. See, generally, John C. Coffee, Jr., "'No Soul to Damn: No Body to Kick': An Unscandalized Inquiry into the Problem of Corporate Punishment," *Michigan Law Review* 79 (1981): 386–459, pp. 401-402.

9. See, e.g., Gerhard Mueller, "Mens Rea and the Corporation," *University of Pittsburgh Law Review* 19 (1957): 21–50.

10. See, generally, Walter Kaufmann, *Without Guilt and Justice* (New York: Delta, 1973).

11. See, further, Peter A. French, "It's a Damn Shame," unpublished manuscript (1984). For a psychodynamic analysis of shame, see Helen M. Lynd, *On Shame and the Search for Identity* (London: Routledge & Kegan Paul, 1958).

12. Zephaniah 3:5.

13. Nathaniel Hawthorne, *The Scarlet Letter* (1850; New York: Pocket Books, 1954).

14. Ibid., p. 63.

15. See, e.g., Wally Olins, *The Corporate Personality: An Inquiry into the Nature of Corporate Identity* (New York: Mayflower Books, 1981); Charles Channon, "Corporations and the Politics of Perception," *Advertising Quarterly* 60, 2 (1981): 12–15; Nancy Yashihara, "$1 Billion Spent on Identity: Companies Push Image of Selves, Not Products," *Los Angeles Times*, 10 May 1981, pt. 6, pp. 1, 17.

16. See Fisse and Braithwaite, *The Impact of Publicity on Corporate Offenders*, pp. 308–309.

17. U.S. National Commission on Reform of Federal Criminal Laws, *Study Draft* (Washington, DC: U.S. Government Printing Office, 1970), #405.

18. U.S. National Commission on Reform of Federal Criminal Laws, *Final Report* (Washington, DC: U.S. Government Printing Office, 1971), #3007.

19. See, generally, Kaufmann, *Without Guilt and Justice*; Fred L. Polak, *The Image of the Future: Enlightening the Past, Orienting the Present, Forecasting the Future* 1 and 2 (New York: Oceana Publications, 1961).

20. See Stephen H. Unger, *Controlling Technology* (New York: Holt, Rinehart, and Winston, 1982).

21. See, further, Coffee, "'No Soul to Damn,'" pp. 425–426; Fisse and Braithwaite, *The Impact of Publicity on Corporate Offenders*, pp. 291–292.

22. Coffee, "'No Soul to Damn,'" p. 426. See, further, Fisse and Braithwaite, *The Impact of Publicity on Corporate Offenders*, pp. 291–292.

23. See, further, Coffee, "'No Soul to Damn,'" p. 426; Fisse and Braithwaite, *The Impact of Publicity on Corporate Offenders*, pp. 295–298.

24. See, generally, Herbert Schmertz, *Corporations and the First Amendment* (New York: Amacom, 1978); William Patton and Randall Bartlett, "Corporate 'Persons' and Freedom of Speech: The Political Impact of Legal Mythology," *Wisconsin Law Review* 1981: 494–512.

25. See John J. McCloy, *The Great Oil Spill* (New York: Chelsea House, 1976).

26. Coffee, "'No Soul to Damn,'" pp. 427–428.

27. But see Fisse and Braithwaite, *The Impact of Publicity on Corporate Offenders*, pp. 306–309.

28. Ibid., chap. 19.

29. See, further, Brent Fisse, "Community Service as a Sanction against Corporations," *Wisconsin Law Review* 1981: 970–1017.

30. Fisse, "Community Service as a Sanction against Corporations."

31. *New York Times*, July 29, 1983, p. 1.

32. Aristotle, *Nicomachean Ethics*, trans. M. Ostwald (Indianapolis: Bobbs-Merrill, 1962), p. 33.

FRENCH ON CORPORATE PUNISHMENT: Some Problems

J. Angelo Corlett

In *Corporate and Collective Responsibility* (New York: Columbia University Press, 1984), Peter A. French argues that corporations as well as corporate-individuals can and should be held morally responsible for untoward events of which they are intentional agents. Moreover, he argues, guilty corporations can and ought to be punished for their wrongdoings. The purpose of this paper is to examine his theory of corporate punishment, and to show why it is problematic. One assumption I shall make is that corporations can be guilty of and responsible for wrongdoing.

The punishment of corporations, which I shall refer to as corporate punishment, is a primary stumblingblock to French's collective and corporate responsibility theory. Retribution, he states, need not always be made in kind. The reason why this is so is because the corporation has no eye to ex-

change for an eye that it might have destroyed. Straightaway, then, there is a difficulty in effectively and sufficiently punishing a corporation which is responsible and guilty for causing an untoward event (French, p. 188).

Take the recent Union Carbide toxic chemical leakage in Bhopal, India, where Union Carbide is responsible (I shall assume) for approximately two thousand deaths and several more short- and long-term illnesses of Indian people. The question here is how to administer punishment to Union Carbide so that both parties are treated justly. Thus a main question regarding the punishment of guilty corporations is how to effectively and sufficiently deal with corporations that are found guilty of untoward events.

French explores some proposed methods of corporate punishment and notes why these are problematic. First, he argues that fining a

From *Journal of Business Ethics*, 7 (1988), 205–210. © 1988 by D. Reidel Publishing Company. Reprinted with permission of Kluwer Academic Publishers.

guilty corporation is inadequate because the cost of the fines can be easily absorbed by raising consumer prices. Second, French argues that the revocation of a guilty corporation's charter or license to operate in a given locale is problematic for at least two reasons: (a) The corporation might be able to reconstruct itself under a new charter, management and a new name in that locale or elsewhere in order to resume corporate activities; (b) Innocent employees of the corporation are likely to be adversely affected economically by a charter revocation (French, p. 188). Insofar as the Bhopal incident is concerned, fining Union Carbide or revoking its charter are inadequate penalties for its wrongdoing. For both such punishments are likely to be passed on to the consumer in the form of higher prices for Union Carbide products. What, then, can be done to effectively and sufficiently punish corporations that are found guilty of untoward events?

As a remedy for this puzzle of corporate punishment French suggests what he calls the "Hester Prynne Sanction." The Hester Prynne Sanction consists largely of an institutionalized psychological punishment administered to the corporation that is found guilty of wrongdoing. It takes the form of a court ordered adverse publication of the corporation, the cost of which is paid by the guilty corporation. The aim of the sanction is to create a psychological disposition of shame within the corporation for that of which it is guilty. French thinks that such shame, when the guilt of the corporation is made public, is most fatal to any corporation because public shame damages a corporation's prestige. According to higher-level management, a corporation's loss of prestige is the worst thing that can happen to it (French, p. 200).

There are, however, a number of difficulties which plague the utilization of the Hester Prynne Sanction against guilty corporations. First, the loss of prestige of a corporation may contribute to the financial failure of that corporation. In turn, this will adversely affect the economic condition of that corporation's work force, causing undue immiseration to its workers. (Here I assume that the work force does not play a primary role in that which makes the corporation guilty of wrongdoing.)

To this criticism French replies that the adverse economic effects that the Hester Prynne Sanction might have on a guilty corporation's work force "should not overly concern us" (French, p. 200). But this is a concern unless and until French can provide a successful argument which shows that it ought to be of no concern. Such an argument would at least have to consist in his showing that there is a genuine and significant causal connection between the untoward event and the work force of the corporation that is found guilty of that untoward event. If this is not shown, and if the Hester Prynne Sanction is imposed on a corporation the work force of which is not causally related to an untoward event in question, then the work force is punished unfairly. French himself uses this criticism against the suggestion of charter revocations and fines for corporations that are found guilty of wrongdoing. But he fails to see that this criticism also applies to his suggestion that the adverse economic effects the Hester Prynne Sanction might have on a corporation's work force ought not to overly concern one.

A second problem with the use of the sanction against guilty corporations is that the corporation might escape such financial loss and the immiseration of its workers by passing on the cost of the sanction to consumers in the form of higher prices. French uses this as an argument against the suggestion of fining corporations that are found guilty of wrongdoing. However, he does not see that the adverse effects of the Hester Prynne Sanction may be evaded by a corporation in the same manner. If a corporation is punished by means of French's sanction, then it may raise the prices of its products to the consumers in order to make up for the loss of profit due to the adverse publicity brought on by the sanction. On French's view, there is nothing which ensures against this possibility.

A third problem with the use of the Hester Prynne Sanction against guilty corporations is that the guilty corporation can simply, if it knows that it is economically advantageous for it to do so, recharter itself under another name, management, etc., in order to avoid the shame occasioned by the sanction. That is, the corporation can simply file bankruptcy and reorganize itself in such a way that one would not recognize the new corporation as being (for the most part) the same as the previous corporation, rather than suffer the embarrassment and costliness of the sanction. There are at least two ways that a corporation might recharter itself. First, it can recharter itself under a new name while continuing to do business in the same industry. Second, it can recharter itself under a new name while taking up business in another industry. An example of the first sort of reorganization would be an oil company simply changing its name in order to avoid the social stigma attached to it by the Hester Prynne Sanction. An example of the second sort would be that oil company rechartering and entering into a different field of business altogether, say, computer technology. In this latter case, a corporation could escape the adverse affects of the sanction by making itself unrecognizable to both the media (which is said to be the primary tool used by the court to execute the Hester Prynne Sanction) and to the public. On French's view, there seems to be nothing stopping a guilty corporation from evading the effects of the sanction in this manner. Moreover, French argues against the revocation of charters for guilty corporations on the ground that innocent people related to the corporation are negatively affected. But he fails to realize that this argument also applies to the Hester Prynne Sanction. French provides no

reason why a corporation found guilty of wrongdoing could not recharter itself in order to avoid the humiliation of the sanction. Again, French's arguments are turned against him.

A fourth weakness of the Hester Prynne Sanction against guilty corporations is that it depends too much on the reliability of the media to effectively carry out the sanction insofar as publicity is concerned. This is especially true if the corporation in question has significant ties with the media. Under such conditions the media might be prone to tone down its coverage of the corporations in question out of either a loyalty to the guilty corporation of out of fear that the sanction might spell the demise of that corporation upon which the media is itself financially dependent. Thus any damage to the reputation of the guilty corporation by the sanction might also lead to the demise of the media itself because of its significant economic ties to the guilty corporation. On French's view, there seems to be no doubt about the media's motives or ability to carry out the Hester Prynne Sanction effectively.

A fifth puzzle with the use of the Hester Prynne Sanction against guilty corporations is that its scope is limited. It may indeed work in a situation where a corporation is found guilty of systematically abusing its workers, or where a corporation is found guilty of producing and selling, say, automobiles which malfunction slightly. In these cases the sanction might serve well as a deterrent to the continuation of such unacceptable business procedures. However, the sanction is unable to effectively and sufficiently punish corporations that are found guilty of gross forms of negligence. For example, the effect of the Hester Prynne Sanction on Union Carbide for the Bhopal incident would in no way do justice to the immensity of Union Carbide's responsibility to the families of those who were killed and severely injured by the toxic chemical leakage. The public shame of Union Carbide is at best only a necessary punishment. It is not a sufficient punishment for the incident of which Union Carbide is responsible. Neither the short nor long-term effects of the Hester Prynne Sanction on Union Carbide could begin to render a just punishment for the fatal occurrence at Bhopal.

Furthermore, even if it is a statistical fact that, generally speaking, corporate management thinks that the loss of prestige resulting from the Hester Prynne Sanction (or something akin to it) is the most devastating punishment that a corporation guilty of wrongdoing can receive, this is irrelevant. In the case of Union Carbide it is certainly in the corporation's best interest to be publically shamed because justice actually requires that somehow the corporation ought to recompense for the deaths and illnesses of thousands of Indian people. In such a case Union Carbide would obviously accept public shame over a much more severe punishment, say, the death penalty or long-term imprisonment with no chance of parole for certain constituents of the corporation who are the primary responsible agents of the Bhopal incident. So it is simply a mistake to punish corporations according to a standard with which they agree or find acceptable. The very fact that the management of such corporations considers the publicity of guilty corporations and the shame that ensues to be an acceptable punishment might serve to destroy or severely limit the deterrent force of the Hester Prynne Sanction. Punishing guilty corporations according to a standard which their membership accepts is akin to punishing a criminal according to what that criminal finds to be an acceptable punishment! The Hester Prynne Sanction is only useful in cases of minor corporate offences; it is an ineffective and insufficient punishment for instances of more significant corporate wrongdoing.

To this French might reply that the implementation of more stringent penalties on corporations that are found guilty of gross forms of wrongdoing would tend to render such corporations impotent in the marketplace of trade and competition. Moreover, it might stifle business and technological growth altogether if corporations are to be severely punished for the unfortunate results of what are otherwise quite "natural" business practices. To this reply I simply answer that justice cannot be tailored to the methods of business or technological manifest destiny. This is the sort of morality that leads to corporate wrongdoing in the first place. Rather, corporations must themselves act according to the dictates of what justice requires in given circumstances. The circumstances of justice must determine the practices of corporations, not vice versa.

French states that the Hester Prynne Sanction might be more effective as a punishment for corporate wrongdoing if it is coupled with a planned and enforced community service project the cost of which is covered by the guilty corporation (French, pp. 200-201). An example of this might be punishing an oil company guilty of environmental pollution by having it pay for high-level research in ecological and environmental preservation.

But there are puzzles with French's suggestion. One is that the financial status of such research is directly dependent on the financial stability of the funding corporation. But if the corporation is adversely affected by the sanction, then it might fall on economic hard times, threatening the operation of the environmental research. Moreover, since the corporation funds the research, it can in some way influence and hence bias the reports coming out of the research so that such reports do not further complicate the adverse conditions of the corporation or industry. For example, the corporation might strongly suggest or even dictate that the research be done in areas of environmental studies which reflect a positive outlook toward the corporation rather than a negative one. Even if this is not the case, the researchers might come to the realization that their wages can be threatened if they produce and publicize any environmentally negative studies related to the guilty corporation. And if the public considers these studies, the stock of that corporation could drop to a drastic level, not to mention the fact that the public could boycott the purchase of that corporation's manufactured products enough to force it into dire financial conditions, leaving its research institute and its employees without funding. A further problem with French's position on this matter of a guilty corporation's being punished by having to fund research projects is that such a penalty in no way serves as a recompense for gross forms of corporate wrongdoing. For example, forcing Union Carbide to fund, say, chemical engineering research in no way amounts to a fair punishment for its responsibility and guilt regarding the Bhopal incident. Even if such research is not problematic in the ways I describe, and even if such a punishment is coupled with the Hester Prynne Sanction, a punishment much more severe is needed to effectively and sufficiently penalize Union Carbide for the magnitude of the untoward event of [sic] which it is responsible. Moreover, linking the Hester Prynne Sanction with community service might yield another undesirable consequence. French is concerned with creating an attitude of corporate shame for corporate wrongdoing. But he fails to realize that linking the sanction to community service (whether it be environmental research, support of the arts, or whatever) may serve as a guilty corporation's opportunity to boast—as is often done—of its community service achievements, thereby deceiving the public regarding the actual reason why the corporation is performing such services.

A seventh problem with the Hester Prynne Sanction is that it is to some degree hypocritical. It is the context of corporate competition that creates a problem of hypocrisy for corporate punishment theories like French's. The same system that encourages corporate competition and corporate success is the same one which seeks to punish corporations for pursuing such ideals. The hypocritical nature of the Hester Prynne Sanction, then, consists in the fact that it seeks to punish corporations for doing what they are encouraged to do (i.e., making a profit and bettering the economic achievements of all other corporations) as corporate enterprises.

Since French takes the name of his sanction from Hawthorne's *The Scarlett Letter*, an illustration from that story will suffice to suggest the hypocritical nature of the Hester Prynne Sanction. The reader will recall that in Hawthorne's story Hester Prynne commits adultery with the town cleric. She is "tried" and sentenced to the humiliation of having to wear a scarlet letter in order to publicize her wrongdoing. Now there are several things to note about this story. First, Hawthorne is widely known as a *critic* of the Puritan culture. The point of his story, secondly, is to suggest the hypocritical nature of that culture. The townspersons are not genuinely concerned about the welfare of this woman who is caught in the web of a most complex human relationship. Their concern is punishment. They are unconcerned with the fact that Hester Prynne is a victim of the social situation in which she finds herself. They are unconcerned with the fact that the society is "set up" in such a manner that only certain "crimes" (or "sins") are socially apparent (i.e., adultery in the case of some women) while other "crimes" are not obvious to the public, but are regularly practiced by the very persons who condemn Hester Prynne. Certainly the story of Hester Prynne is a seething indictment of the intolerance and self-righteousness of the Puritan culture. Just as the Puritan culture fosters a way of life which gives rise to various wrongdoing, so does the social order in which corporations operate. And just as it is hypocritical for the Puritans to adversely publicize the "sinful" deed of Hester Prynne, it is also hypocritical for corporations to be adversely publicized for socially unacceptable practices. How can French suggest punishment for guilty corporations when the "free market" system itself forces corporations (if they desire to be successful) to compete under terms which encourage such abuses? Will the corporations which are without sin cast the first stone?

Now I am in no way hinting that French intends to punish corporations guilty of wrongdoing in an intolerant or self-righteous way. However, French does not explain the court's procedural fairness in punishing corporations that are found guilty of causing untoward events. He does not show how the system will operate in a fair manner when punishing such corporations. There seems to be no reason why one should not expect to find the same arbitrary and politically and economically motivated procedures in punishing guilty corporations which exists presently, i.e., where a corporation is punished for wrongdoing, but other corporations which contributed indirectly to the same untoward event are not punished. Certainly equal punishment under the law applies to the corporate realm. Moreover, French's utilization of the term "Hester Prynne Sanction" perhaps betrays an ignorance regarding the fundamental points of Hawthorne's story. Hester Prynne, according to Hawthorne, is treated wrongly for her "offence," suggesting that any mode of punishment akin to that which she receives is equally wrong. Perhaps French ought to rename his suggested method of corporate punishment.

Furthermore, French states that the Hester Prynne Sanction is an effective means of corporate punishment in a shame based society like our own (French, pp. 192–193). It is true that the success of the sanction depends on the guilty corporation's ability to feel shame for what it has done wrong. But what if it has little or no capacity for such a feeling under any circumstance? What if, moreover, the corporation is perfectly willing to delude the courts, media and the public into thinking that it is shameful about doing a wrongful

deed, but it in fact places more emphasis on profit-making than on moral practices in business? What if a guilty corporation is perfectly willing to undergo the Hester Prynne Sanction so long as it does not interfere with significant profit-making? Does not the sanction then lose its sting? Can the Hester Prynne Sanction be of help in punishing such corporations? French seems to have assumed, rather naively, that all corporations will feel shameful regarding their corporate wrongdoing. Moreover, he assumes that in the light of such shame corporations will be deterred from repeat offences by way of the sanction. I believe this is false at least is some cases. The primary reason that some corporations feel shameful for doing something which is deemed unacceptable is because they are caught. This can, however, hardly be seen as shame if by "shame" one means a genuine remorse for one's actions and a genuine effort to change one's ways. I submit, then, that corporations are not automatically shameful of their wrong actions. A case in point is Union Carbide, which (as far as I am aware) offers no more than $2000 to the surviving families of each dead victim of the Bhopal incident, while it offers nothing to the thousands of surviving victims of that disaster. Obviously, a corporation which is clearly responsible for, and feels genuine remorse for, an untoward event of this magnitude would make a much more generous offer to both the families of those who died and to those who survived the chemical leakage. Thus, the Hester Prynne Sanction assumes that guilty corporations will feel shameful about their wrongful acts, but it is by no means clear that corporations will or do exhibit such a feeling. As long as a guilty corporation can find avenues to increase its profits, there seems to be no reason for that corporation not to continue in its wrongful ways, despite the effects on it as a result of the Hester Prynne Sanction. This undercuts the sanction because if there is no guarantee that guilty corporations will feel such shame, then the possibility of corporate rehabilitation is wanting, making the Hester Prynne Sanction an ineffective means of corporate punishment.

In conclusion, nothing on French's view of the use of the Hester Prynne Sanction against guilty corporations ensures against the following: (1) The unjust immiseration of the guilty corporation's work force; (2) The ability of the guilty corporation to escape the financial penalty of the sanction by raising its prices for the consumer; (3) The ability of the guilty corporation to reorganize itself and thereby escape the public shame of the sanction; (4) The possibility of the media's ineffectiveness in carrying out the sanction; (5) The limited scope of the sanction on those corporations guilty of gross forms of wrongdoing; (6) The guilty corporation's ability to control the findings and operations of its court appointed research facility; (7) The hypocritical nature of the sanction; (8) The possibility that some corporations will not feel shameful about their wrongful deeds. These are eight reasons why the utilization of French's Hester Prynne Sanction is problematic as a punishment for corporate wrongdoing.

Although the Hester Prynne Sanction is useful in some cases of minor corporate wrongdoing, it is not useful as a punishment for corporations guilty of gross wrongdoing, such as the Union Carbide incident in Bhopal. What French needs in order to ensure the success of his claims regarding corporate punishment is a general theory of punishment which is capable of giving an effective and sufficient punishment to corporations guilty of gross wrongdoing. What he needs is a theory of corporate punishment which: (1) does not permit a corporation found guilty of wrongdoing to evade the guilt, shame and negative effects of the punishment; (2) does not permit the punishment to adversely affect (in any way) innocent employees or the general public in any significant manner; (3) does not permit the guilty corporation a way by which to benefit financially from the punishment; and (4) has a genuine rehabilitative intent and effect (instead of a crippling one) on the punished corporation. Moreover, such a theory of corporate punishment must be based on an adequate concept of corporate moral personhood. How such a theory might be explicated is the subject of another paper.

I am grateful to Burleigh T. Wilkins, Philosophy Department, University of California, Santa Barbara, and B. Celeste Corlett, Psychology Department, University of California, Santa Barbara, for their comments on earlier drafts of this paper.

CASE 1 Rex v. Fane Robinson Ltd.

Ford J.A. (for the Court): This is an appeal by the Crown from the dismissal by Tweedie J. of two charges preferred against Fane Robinson Ltd., a corporation, of (1) conspiracy to defraud and (2) obtaining money by false pretenses, which that learned Judge dismissed on the ground that, *mens rea* being an essential element of both offenses, a corporation cannot be guilty of either. In the course of his reasons Mr. Justice Tweedie says that "even if the directors or the shareholders themselves had passed any resolution authorizing such act, in my opinion, that could be of no effect as there is no power in a corporation to commit criminal acts in which *mens rea* is a material element, even with the authorization of the shareholders or the directors."

The question is, in my opinion, one which in Canada may be treated as not being settled by any binding authority.

After reading and considering, with many others, the cases cited on the argument I have, not without considerable hesitation, formed the opinion that the gradual process of placing those artificial entities known as corporations in the same position as a natural person as regards amenability to the criminal law has, by reason of the provisions of the *Criminal Code*, reached that stage where it can be said that, if the act complained of can be treated as that of the company, the corporation is criminally responsible for all such acts as it is capable of committing and for which the prescribed punishment is one which it can be made to endure…

… As stated by Viscount Haldane, L.C., in *Lennard's Carrying Co. v. Asiatic Petroleum Co.*, [1915] A.C. 705 at p. 713:

> A corporation is an abstraction. It has no mind of its own any more than it has a body of its own; its active and directing will must consequently be sought in the person of somebody who for some purposes may be called an agent, but who is really the directing mind and will of the corporation…his action must, unless a corporation is not to be liable at all, have been an action which was the action of the company….

… As stated by Lord Blackburn in *Pharmaceutical Soc. v. London & Provincial Supply Ass'n* (1880), 5 App. Cas. 857 at p. 869: "A corporation cannot in one sense commit a crime—a corporation cannot be imprisoned, if imprisonment be the sentence for the crime; a corporation cannot be hanged or put to death if that be the punishment for the crime; and so, in those senses a corporation cannot commit a crime. But a corporation may be fined, and a corporation may pay damages."

… I find it difficult to see why a corporation which can enter into binding agreements with individuals and other corporations cannot be said to entertain *mens rea* when it enters into an agreement which is the gist of conspiracy, and if by its corporate act it can make a false pretence involving it in liability to pay damages for deceit why it cannot be said to have the capacity to make representation involving criminal responsibility.

It is perhaps unnecessary to add that a corporation like any other "person" is entitled to all the safeguards which the law provides before anyone can be found guilty including, of course, that cardinal rule that guilt must be proved beyond a reasonable doubt.

…The facts are that Fane Robinson Ltd. was incorporated in 1935 and has since carried on the business of garaging and repairing automobiles. It took over shortly after its incorporation two businesses one of which was that previously carried on by George Robinson who with Emile Fielhaber were its incorporators and provisional directors. At all material times George Robinson, Emile Fielhaber and Adolph Fielhaber were the directors of the company, George Robinson being its President and Emile Fielhaber its Secretary-Treasurer. Adolph Fielhaber took no active part in the operation of the company. There was only one other shareholder. Since its incorporation the company has held only three meetings of directors, the first that of the provisional directors, held July 13, 1935, the second being the First Meeting of Directors held on the same day and the third on April 2, 1940. Only one meeting of shareholders has been held, being that held on the same day as, and between, the meeting of the provisional directors and the first meeting of directors.

At the first meeting of directors George Robinson was appointed manager of the company's plant and was instructed to take possession as soon as possible and commence operations. He was at all material times the "service manager in charge of repairs" to automobiles and Emile Fielhaber the "bookkeeper in charge of accounts."

In 1937 on the instructions of an adjuster for the Saskatchewan Mutual Fire Ins. Co., a motor truck, which had been damaged in a collision and which that company had insured against collision damage, was taken to the garage of the respondent company and was there repaired on the account of the adjusters. On the books of the respondent company the actual account for labour and material and profit was charged as $339.80.

It was orally agreed by George Robinson, Emile Fielhaber and the representative of the firm of adjusters having charge of the adjustment of the loss that the account of the respondent company for repairs should be increased fictitiously to the sum of $404.80 and the adjuster should represent to the Insurance Company that the sum was the cost of the repairs of the truck and that Fane Robinson Ltd. should pay him the sum of $30.

In pursuance of the oral agreement as above, Fane Robinson Ltd., the respondent, rendered to the firm of adjusters an account for the repairs at the agreed amount of $404.80 and the individual in charge of the adjustment represented in writing to the Insurance Company that that sum was the cost of the repairs by Fane Robinson Ltd. and that the net cost of repairs for which the Insurance Company was liable to the assured was $379.80 after deducting $25 under the terms of the insurance policy.

The Insurance Company in reliance on the report of its firm of adjusters, which was signed by the individual in charge of the adjustment, and in reliance on the bona fides of the account of $404.80 furnished by Fane Robinson Ltd., paid by cheque to Fane Robinson Ltd., the sum of $379.80 and in pursuance of their oral agreement, out of the proceeds

of the cheque for $379.80, George Robinson paid to the individual adjuster $10 and Emile Fielhaber paid him $20. It would appear that the respondent company benefited to the extent of $10 by the fictitious increase in its account for repairs. The first count in the charge is that between October 12th and December 31st Fane Robinson Ltd. did conspire with R. Noel Saunders, who is the individual adjuster above mentioned, and divers other persons unknown, by deceit and falsehood to defraud the Insurance Company by falsely and fraudulently representing that the costs of the repair of an automobile owned by one G.F.W. Otto was $404.80 instead of $339.80, the actual cost of repairs; contrary to the provisions of the *Criminal Code* of Canada and amendments thereto.

The second count is that between the same dates the respondent did by false pretences and with intent to defraud, procure the sum of approximately $40 from the Insurance Company, contrary to the provisions of the *Criminal Code* of Canada and amendments thereto.

The respondent appeared by attorney, pleaded not guilty to both charges and elected for trial by a Judge without the assistance of a jury.

...In my opinion George Robinson and Emile Fielhaber were the acting and directing will of Fane Robinson Ltd. generally and in particular in respect of the subject-matter of the offenses with which it is charged, that their culpable intention (mens rea) and their illegal act (actus reus) were the intention and the act of the company and that conspiracy to defraud and obtaining money by false pretences are offenses which a corporation is capable of committing.

I would allow the appeal and direct a conviction to be entered against Fane Robinson Ltd. on both counts and sentence it to a fine of $150 on each.

Lunney J.A., dissenting, agreed with the trial judge that: "A corporation acts through its directors. There is no evidence whatever disclosed in the minutes of the meetings of the directors or the shareholders which are in evidence, that any authority by resolution was ever given to the directors acting in their official capacity to enter into the conspiracy alleged in the first count, or to procure by false pretences the money alleged in the second count.... *Mens rea* being an essential element of the charge as preferred and there being no expressed statutory provision making the corporation criminally responsible for the acts of its officers or servants in a case in which *mens rea* must be established, both charges against the accused will be dismissed."

Appeal allowed.

Reported in (1941) 76 C.C.C. 196. Alberta Court of Appeal.

CASE 2	Regina v. Andrews Weatherfoil Ltd.

Eveleigh J. (for the Court): On March 23, 1971, at the Central Criminal Court, in a trial which lasted over six weeks, Andrews Weatherfoil Ltd., Sidney Frederick Charles Sporle and Peter George Day were charged with bribery and corruption under the *Public Bodies Corrupt Practices Act* 1889, s. I, in relation to council building contracts of the Battersea Metropolitan Borough Council and the London Borough of Wandsworth Council when Sporle was member and chairman of the housing committee or member of the council. [Only the appeal by Andrews Weatherfoil Ltd. is set out below.]

Andrews Weatherfoil were given leave to appeal against conviction on two grounds of their notice of appeal.

The prosecution's case was the [sic] Sporle used his position on the council to obtain sums of money in return for support in obtaining building contracts from the council. The evidence showed, it was said, a systematic course of conduct to show favour where he had financial expectations and that when he acted in purported discharge of his duties to the council he failed to disclose his interest. In this way it was sought to show that he acted intending to benefit his employers or their nominees without regard to the interest of the council. Once his support for candidates for contracts from the council was shown to be given with improper intentions or motives (it being too much of a coincidence that so often those he supported turned out to be his employers), there was material relevant to the question of the existence of an antecedent agreement to do so in return for benefits to himself which the evidence showed he received.

In this connection the fervour of his support for the cause of his employers was also relied upon. Thus it was said he was so determined to assist Ellis (Kensington) Ltd. that he even threatened Culpin—independent architect appointed to carry out some of the council's plans—with the possible loss of council work unless Ellis (Kensington) Ltd. were given sub-contracts. So too, in relation to Andrews Weatherfoil Ltd., he made a similar threat to Harding. Both of these gentlemen refused to be coerced.

The grounds upon which Andrews Weatherfoil were given leave to appeal were: (1) Failure properly to direct on law as to the criminal responsibility of a limited liability company for the act of a servant. (2) Failure to deal with the correct factors that in law determine the question whether a criminal intention in an employee is also that of the company.

On examination these two grounds overlap, for in the present case the offence was not an absolute statutory offence, but involved criminal conduct and a guilty mind on the part, it was said, of the company's senior employees. The question therefore of the status and authority of the person or persons responsible was of great importance. The prosecution concedes and, in the view of this Court, rightly concedes that the learned judge's direction was not adequate.

There were three people who were alleged by the prosecution to have the status and authority to involve the company itself in criminal liability for corruption in connection with the offer of employment to Sporle as a reward for anticipated favours from him. Those three were Mr. Neuman, the managing director, Mr. Allen, a "technical director," and Mr. Williams, the manager of the or *a* housing division. That these three were concerned in the engagement of Sporle there is no doubt. The actual offer of employment was made by Mr. Neuman in a letter which Allen had some part in drafting. Whether or not it was one, two or all of these three who sought or were party to seeking favours for Andrews Weatherfoil from Sporle as a return for the offer of employment was, as is usually the case, a matter of inference from the evidence. The learned judge directed the jury as follows: "If an act is done by anyone who is in control of a company and who is in authority to perform an important act of that sort, then that act of that person can be the act of the company itself ... if an act is done by a responsible agent of a company, if in the course of that act that agent commits an offence and he does it in the name of the

company, then the company is liable ... if an agent acts corruptly on behalf of the company, the corruption of the agent is the corruption of the company. That is not an absolute rule; it is a principle which depends on the circumstances of the offence." And again: "... if one of these people, Williams or Allen or Neuman or any combination of them acting as a high executive of Andrews Weatherfoil, indulges in the employment of a person to act corruptly to further the interests of the company of which that man is one of the executive directors, the company is responsible and the company is guilty of a criminal offence."

On counsel drawing the judge's attention to the fact that Williams was not a director, he continued: "There is no magic in being a director. If you are the manager of the housing department or in any high executive position in such a way that you can recommend to your managing director that someone should be employed, as it is said Allen [sic] recommended Sporle, in those circumstances the person who recommends it, who is in a high position, if you are satisfied that he did that in the name of the company and it was corrupt, the company can be liable." And finally: "That is a matter for you as to whether or not you are satisfied that that employment by Sporle was done with the approval and knowledge of a high executive of Andrews Weatherfoil acting as an agent of the company for the purpose of his employment to the knowledge of the executive or executives and was corrupt."

It is not every "responsible agent" or "high executive" or "manager of the housing department" or "agent acting on behalf of a company" who can by his actions make the company criminally responsible. It is necessary to establish whether the natural person or persons in question have the status and authority which in law makes their acts in the matter under consideration the acts of the company so that the natural person is to be treated as the company itself. It is often a difficult question to decide whether or not the person concerned is in a sufficiently responsible position to involve the company in liability for the acts in question according to the law as laid down by the authorities. As Lord Reid said in *Tesco Supermarkets Ltd. v. Nattrass*, [1971] 2 W.L.R. 1166 at p. 1176: "it must be a question of law whether, once the facts have been ascertained, a person in doing a particular thing is to be treated as the company or merely as the company's servant or agent. In that case any liability of the company can only be a statutory or vicarious liability." At p. 1179 Lord Reid added: "I think that the true view is that the judge must direct the jury that if they find certain facts proved, then as a matter of law they must find that the criminal act of the officer, servant or agent including his state of mind, intention, knowledge or belief is the act of the company." It follows that it is necessary for the judge to invite the jury to consider whether or not there are established those facts which the judge decides as a matter of law are necessary to identify the person concerned with the company. This was not done in the present case.

The Court was invited to apply the proviso to section 2(1) of the *Criminal Appeal Act* 1968. It is not possible, however, to decide whether or not the jury regarded Mr. Neuman, Mr. Allen or Mr. Williams, or any or what combination of them, as responsible for the criminal act. Mr. Williams' position in the company is not at all clear and the description "housing manager" does not succeed in making it so. To a lesser extent that is true of Mr. Allen. Consequently it is impossible to say that the jury would have arrived at the same verdict if properly directed and it follows that this appeal must succeed.

Appeal allowed.

Reported in (1971), 56 Cr. App. R. 31. Court of Appeal (Criminal Division), England.

CASE 3   Regina v. Safety-Kleen Canada Inc.

Opinion: The judgment of the court was delivered by Doherty, J.A.

I.

The appellant [Safety-Kleen] and Paul Howard, one of its employees, were jointly charged with three offences under the Environmental Protection Act. The first count alleged that they were in possession of waste for which the generator of the waste had not completed a manifest. Count 2 alleged that the appellant and Howard had knowingly given false information in a return made to a provincial officer. Count 3 alleged that they used a truck for transportation of the waste for which a provincial certificate of approval had not been issued. All of the charges arose out of a single incident during which Mr. Howard transferred waste from a disabled truck to one of the appellant's trucks.

The appellant and Howard were convicted on counts 1 and 2 and acquitted on count 3 by a Justice of the Peace. Howard did not appeal. The appellant unsuccessfully appealed both convictions to the Ontario Court (Provincial Division). The appellant then obtained leave to appeal to this court ...

II.

The appellant operates a fleet of waste oil collection trucks and several waste oil transfer stations in Ontario. The waste oil collected by the appellant is eventually taken to its facility in Breslau, Ontario for refining and resale.

The waste disposal industry is heavily regulated. Part of that regulatory scheme requires the preparation of a document, called a manifest, each time waste is moved from the generator of the waste to the ultimate recipient of it. By regulation ... the manifest must have three parts. Part A must be completed by the generator of the waste, Part B by the transporter of the waste, and Part C by the recipient of the waste. Copies of Parts A and C must be forwarded to the Ministry by the generator and recipient, respectively.

On November 12, 1991, Ken Corcoran, a principal of Ken's Vacuum Pumping, an independent contractor, picked up a load of oily waste water at a Petro-Canada station in Perth. Ken's Vacuum Pumping was authorized by the Ministry of the Environment to collect and transfer this waste. Mr. Corcoran intended to transport the waste water to the appellant's waste oil station in Trenton. It was then [to] be transferred to the appellant's truck and taken to Breslau. Petro-Canada filled out Part A of the manifest showing the appellant's transfer station as the intended recipient. Mr. Corcoran filled out Part B of the manifest.

Mr. Corcoran's truck developed mechanical problems and he could not make it to Trenton. He drove his truck to his garage and called Mr. Howard, who was the appellant's representative in the area. Mr. Corcoran had dealt with Mr. Howard on numerous previous occasions. Mr. Howard drove his truck to the appellant's garage. He and Mr. Corcoran decided to transfer the waste water from Mr. Corcoran's disabled truck to Mr. Howard's truck. Both men knew that they needed verbal authorization from the Ministry of the Environment to do so. They also knew that the transfer required a new manifest complete with a new generator number. After one attempt to contact the Ministry proved unsuccessful, Mr. Corcoran and Mr. Howard went ahead without authorization and transferred the waste water into Mr. Howard's truck. Mr. Howard immediately completed Part C of the original manifest showing that the waste water had been received at the appellant's transfer site in Trenton at 2:30 p.m. [T]his was patently false. In fact the waste water [w]as transferred at Mr. Corcoran's garage at about 9:30 a.m.

An investigator with the Ministry of the Environment happened to see Mr. Howard's truck at Mr. Corcoran's garage that morning. He waited until Mr. Howard drove out onto the highway and then directed him to pull over. Mr. Howard immediately acknowledged that he had taken the waste from Mr. Corcoran's truck. The investigator, acting under lawful authority, asked Mr. Howard to produce the manifest. Mr. Howard did so and readily admitted that it was false in that it indicated that the waste had been transferred at the appellant's transfer site in Trenton at 2:30 p.m. This falsehood would, of course, have been obvious to the investigator since the truck had not yet reached Trenton and it was not yet 2:30 p.m.

III.

The appeal concerns the liability of the appellant, a corporate employer, for the misconduct of Mr. Howard, its employee. The appeal from the conviction on count 2 involves a consideration of the scope of corporate responsibility for offences

He was also the appellant's sole representa-

which require proof of a culpable state of mind. The appeal from the conviction on count 1 involves a consideration of the due diligence defence as applied to the employer where the employee's acts are admittedly negligent. I will address the appellant's liability on count 2 first.

IV.

Count 2 alleged that the appellant knowing gave false information in a return to a provincial officer ... Assuming that the manifest was a return, it is clear that the offence was made out against Mr. Howard. The manifest was false and Mr. Howard knew it was false. In determining the appellant's liability it is necessarily to begin by placing the offence ... into one of the three categories identified in *R. v. Sault Ste. Marie (City)* ...The parties agree that this offence falls into the first category (*mens rea* offences) as it is an offence which requires proof of a culpable state of mind. Specifically, the prosecution had to prove that Mr. Howard knew the document was false.

Corporations can be convicted of crimes involving a culpable mental state. Absent a statutory basis for that liability, corporate liability for such crimes is determined by the application of the identification theory set down in *R. v. Canadian Dredge & Dock Co. Ltd.*, [1985] ... and developed in *Rhone v. Peter A.B. Widener* [1993] ... In *Rhone*, Iacobucci J. succinctly summarized the inquiry demanded by the identification theory ...

> ... the focus of [the] inquiry must be whether the impugned individual has been delegated the governing executive authority" of the company within the scope of his or her authority. I interpret this to mean that one must determine whether the discretion conferred on an employee amount[s] to an express or implied delegation of executive authority to design and

supervise the implementation of corporate policy rather than simply to carry out such policy. In other words, the Courts must consider who has been left with the decision-making power in a relevant sphere of corporate activity.

The inquiry described by Iacobucci J. is a fact-driven one which looks beyond titles and job descriptions to the reality of any given situation. Mr. Howard was a truck driver of the appellant. He was also the appellant's sole representative in a very large geographical area. He was responsible for collecting waste, completing necessary documentation, maintaining the appellant's property in the region, billing, and responding to calls from customers and regulators. When Mr. Howard was on holidays, the appellant did not do business in the region. Mr. Howard did not, however, have an[y] managerial or supervisory function. He took no role in shaping any aspect of the appellant's corporate policies ...

There is no doubt that Mr. Howard had many responsibilities and was given wide discretion in the exercise of those responsibilities. It is equally clear that those, like Mr. Corcoran, who dealt with the appellant in the area, equated Mr. Howard with the appellant corporation. Neither of these facts establish the kind of governing executive authority which must exist before the identification theory will impose liability on the corporation. Mr. Howard had authority over matters arising out of the performance of the task he was employed to do. It was his job to collect and transport waste to its eventual destination in Breslau. His authority extended over all matters, like the preparation of necessary documentation, arising out of the performance of those functions. I find no evidence, however, that he had authority to devise or develop corporate policy or make corporate decisions which went beyond those arising out of the transfer and transportation of waste. In my opinion, Mr. Howard's position is much like that of the tugboat captain in *The Rhone* ... Both had extensive responsibilities and discretion, but neither had the power to design and supervise the implementation of corporate policy. The majority of the Supreme Court of Canada concluded that the captain was not a directing mind of his corporate employer. I reach the same conclusion with respect to Mr. Howard ...

In my opinion, there was no basis on which the corporation could be held liable on count 2 of the information. I would quash that conviction and enter an acquittal ...

V.

Count 1 in the information is a strict liability offence. Mr. Howard pleaded guilty to that charge. The appellant could escape liability only if it could show on the balance of probabilities that it exercised due diligence. The words of Dickson J. in *R. v. Sault Ste. Marie* ... aptly describe the meaning of due diligence in this context:

> ...The due diligence which must be established is that of the accused alone. Where an employer is charged in respect of an act committed by an employee acting in the course of employment, the question will be whether the act took place without the accused's direction or approval, thus negating wilful involvement of the accused, and whether the accused exercised all reasonable care by establishing a proper system to prevent commission of the offence and by taking reasonable steps to ensure the effective operation of the system. The availability of the defence to a corporation will depend on whether such

due diligence was taken by those who are the directing mind and will of the corporation, whose acts are therefore in law the acts of the coloration [sic] itself.

As the above passage makes clear, an employer must show that a system was in place to prevent the prohibited act from occurring and that reasonable steps had been taken to ensure the effective operation of that system. The trial judge addressed the question of due diligence in her reasons. She said in part:

> I cannot accept the defence of due diligence on behalf of the company. Certainly the court does not look for perfection, but it is necessary that there appears to be a sense of compliance to the regulations by the company. The company had put their drivers in a position of a self-reporting situation. They had delegated to their drivers a degree of trust to comply with the regulations. Nevertheless, it is still their responsibility to ensure strict compliance. They cannot delegate and then close their eyes to noncompliance. There are not sufficient safety guards within their system to check for this type of irregularity in completion of such an important document ...

The trial judge was also critical of the appellant's training program in so far as it failed to adequately deal with emergency situations like that encountered by Mr. Howard in this case.

The judge of the Provincial Division did not interfere with the trial judge's finding that the appellant failed to exercise due diligence. I see no error in law either in the trial judge's treatment of the evidence or the ultimate conclusion arrived at by her. I would dismiss the appeal on count 1 ...

Ontario Court of Appeal, 114 C.C.C. 3d 214, February 27, 1997. Judges: Doherty, Austin and Charronn JJ.A.

SUGGESTED READINGS

Clement, Wallace. *The Canadian Corporate Elite: An Analysis of Corporate Power.* Toronto: McClelland and Stewart, 1975.

Corlett, J. Angelo. "Corporate Responsibility and Punishment." *Public Affairs Quarterly* 2, 1988.

Donaldson, Thomas. *Corporations and Morality.* Englewood Cliffs, NJ: Prentice-Hall Inc., 1982.

French, P. (1995). *Corporate Ethics.* Fort Worth: Harcourt Brace

French, Peter. *Corporate and Collective Responsibility.* New York: Columbia University Press, 1984.

French, Peter. "Institutional and Moral Obligations." *Journal of Philosophy* 74, 1977.

French, Peter. "The Principle of Responsive Adjustment in Corporate Moral Responsibility: The Crash on Mount Erebus." *Journal of Business Ethics* 3, 1984.

Law Reform Commission of Canada. "Working Paper 16." *Criminal Responsibility for Group Action,* 1976.

May, L. *The Morality of Groups: Collective Responsibility, Group-Based Harm, and Corporate Rights.* South Bend, Indiana: Notre Dame Press, 1987.

Phillips, M. "Corporate Moral Personhood and Three Conceptions of the Corporation," *Business Ethics Quarterly*, 2, 1992, pp. 435–459.

Porter, John. *The Vertical Mosaic.* Toronto: University of Toronto Press, 1965.

R. v. MacNamara, (No. 1) (1981) 56 C.C.C. (2d) 193 (Ont. C.A.)

R. v. N.M. Paterson and Sons Ltd. (1980), 117 D.L.R. (3d) 517 (S.C.C.)

Rafalko, R. "Corporate Punishment: A Proposal." *Journal of Business Ethics*, 8, 1989, pp. 917–928.

Rafalko, R. "Remaking the Corporation: The 1991 US Sentencing Guidelines." *Journal of Business Ethics*, 13, 1994, pp. 625-636.

Ross, Murray. *Canadian Corporate Directors on the Firing Line.* Toronto: McGraw-Hill Ryerson Ltd., 1980.

Schrader, D. *The Corporation as an Anomaly.* Cambridge: Cambridge University Press, 1993.

Smyth, J.E. "The Social Implications of Incorporation." In J.S. Ziegel (ed.), *Canadian Law.* Toronto: Butterworths, 1967.

Werhane, P. *Persons, Rights and Corporations.* Englewood Cliffs, N.J.:Prentice-Hall, 1985.

HEALTH AND SAFETY
IN THE WORKPLACE

INTRODUCTION

Every year workers all over the world die or are permanently disabled as a result of work-related diseases or injuries. In many cases, both workers and employers have long been aware of the relationship between working in an industry and developing a particular disease. In the asbestos industry, for example, there is a well-established, high correlation between working in the industry and developing asbestosis, lung cancer, gastrointestinal cancer, and mesothelioma.

The question is this: Who is responsible for such work-related diseases? If an employee chooses to work in an industry with serious and proven health hazards, can the company be held responsible for any related health problems that the employee subsequently develops? Some labour advocates argue that the most hazardous jobs are those requiring the least education. Consequently, workers in these jobs tend not to have the resources to acquire safe work. If this is the case, employees may believe that they have little choice but to work in dangerous work environments if they are to be employed at all. Should employees be held responsible for their decisions to work in hazardous conditions, or do corporations have a responsibility to minimize the hazards in the workplace?

Apologists for the business-as-usual outlook would argue that the employer has a primary responsibility to maximize profit. To minimize the danger to employees in some industries would be extremely expensive. Consequently, it is argued, the employer has conflicting responsibilities if she is required both to maximize profit and to provide a safe work environment for employees. Besides, some occupations have inherent risks. The following questions arise: How does a corporation, or its executives, balance these conflicting responsibilities? And again, what is an acceptable risk? Who is responsible for risk-taking?

In "The Worker as Victim," Harry Glasbeek argues that as long as risk is assessed in terms of an underlying "pure market" ideology, workers will suffer. Since market ideology panders to the consumer, "profitability over safety" is favoured. Glasbeek argues further that market ideology results in a number of "fictions," the dominant one being that "workers, like consumers, may bargain for more safety." The consequence of this fiction is that it is believed that "whatever conditions prevail must be the result of trade-offs workers make between wages and . . . job security, on the one hand, and safety on the other." This type of victim-blaming will continue as long as the root of the problem remains uncovered. One route to exposing the "inhumanity of profiteering at the expense of human life" is to hold employers personally responsible for harm done to employees. Glasbeek believes that once it is recognized that "the infliction of harm on workers may be classified as criminal," the preconditions for change will be present.

In this regard, it is worth mentioning an Illinois case in which three company officials were each found guilty of murder in the work-related death of their employee, Stefan Golab, a Polish immigrant who died in February 1983, from exposure to hydrogen cyanide fumes. In June 1985, the former president, plant supervisor, and foreman of the now-defunct Film Recovery Systems Inc. were each sentenced to 25 years in prison and fined $10 000 (U.S.). They had argued that Stefan Golab died of a heart attack. The three defendants were also found guilty of 14 counts of reckless conduct related to injuries suffered by other workers at the plant. The trial judge ruled that the conditions under which Golab and his co-workers performed their duties were "totally unsafe" and that the three officials were "totally knowledgeable" of the hazardous situation. During the trial, it was discovered that the plant's workers—most of whom were illegal aliens and spoke little English—were not warned that cyanide was dangerous. Nor did company officials respond to repeated instances of vomiting and nausea among workers. It was further established that a readily available and inexpensive antidote to cyanide poisoning was not kept at the plant.

Do employees have the right not to have certain diseases or harms inflicted upon them? Alan Gewirth begins his article by asserting that they do have such a right, at least with respect to cancer. Gewirth states that "every person has a basic right not to have cancer inflicted on him by the action of other persons." He further states that since it is fairly well established that 80 to 90 percent of all cancers are caused "by the controllable actions of human beings," those human beings who contribute to the causation of cancer, and who do so knowingly, can be held to be both causally and morally responsible for their actions. Gewirth argues that according to what he calls the *informed control criterion*, individuals can be held morally responsible for knowingly inflicting a harm that they could prevent.

But is such a right defensible, and if so, what does it entail? Some would argue that although we have a right to life, that right no more entails protection of the environment to guarantee our health, including the workplace, than it entails an obligation not to choose to self-induce disease (e.g., an obligation not to smoke). Gewirth discusses these and related difficulties, such as whether workers have the right to choose to work in dangerous environments, in "Human Rights and the Prevention of Cancer."

The above-mentioned articles discuss such issues as employer liability, personal responsibility, acceptable levels of risk in the workplace, freedom of choice, and conflicting interests. Keep in mind, while reading these articles, the issues raised in Part 1 and 2; namely, are corporations, as such, moral agents, and if so, what degree and type of responsibility do they have?

In the first case study in this chapter, Lloyd Tataryn brings home poignantly the tragedy of work-related disease and death in the Canadian asbestos industry. For more than 100 years, Quebec's Thetford Mines has been the centre of asbestos production in Canada. Tataryn underlines the long-standing deceit and misinformation that falsely reassured workers that their heath was not seriously threatened by their work. He notes that as early as 1918, insurance companies were fully aware of the health hazards of the asbestos industry. Years later, physicians at Thetford Mines were still knowingly misinforming workers. Tataryn writes, "The evidence continues to mount showing that asbestos companies maintained a policy of not telling workers they were suffering from asbestos-related diseases until the men became physically disabled." Is this one of those cases in which Glasbeek would argue that employers should be held criminally liable for harm to workers? Or are the workers themselves at least partially to blame for the results of their own ignorance?

The last case in this chapter concerns the right to refuse to work in a dangerous working environment. "Antonia Di Palma and Air Canada" involves a flight attendant's refusal to work, and her claim that she should not have to work in what she believed was a dangerous work environment (i.e., an environment where, she claimed, there was not enough air). The case is an interesting one because it involves a thorough examination of the meaning of "danger" under the *Canadian Labour Code* as well as the limitations under that code.

THE WORKER AS VICTIM

Harry J. Glasbeek

The newspapers carried the news. The television cameras whirred. A fusillade of fierce questions was directed at the government at Queen's Park. It had been revealed that asbestos, widely used in the construction industry in Ontario, was now leaking through its encasing materials, entering the atmosphere and endangering the public including, heaven preserve us, schoolchildren! This shocking discovery led to some monitoring, the temporary closing of some public schools and inevitably, to mendacious reassurance by government officials.

Without minimizing the potential danger of asbestos, it seems trivial compared to the risks workers have been exposed to in the workplace for years. Perhaps the most useful aspect of the publicity surrounding the asbestos-in-the-schools issue is that a more hospitable climate for the airing of workers' grievances has been created. Certainly, the newspapers have carried more items recently on occupational health problems, particularly where asbestos has been involved.

There is much to agitate about. Hard figures about carnage in the workplace are difficult to come by, especially as the connection between work environment and debilitating diseases is often disputed or unrecognized. But carnage it is. Dr. Paul Rohan has shown that from 1973 to 1976 one work injury happened every seven seconds, while an accident causing death occurred every 129 to 130 minutes in 1968, 1970, 1971 and 1976—and these were the "best" years in his 10 year study![1] As many as 10,000 workers per annum suffer from job-related cancers, asbestosis, silicosis and others. These figures do not include many diseases not yet acknowledged as work-related, just as various cancers now recognized were once omitted.

Increased public awareness of industrial health could be beneficial depending on what the public is asked to do by reform-

From *The Canadian Forum*, March 1981. Reprinted by permission of the author.

ers. Two demands are repeatedly made: one is for improvement in compensation schemes for disabled workers and their dependents; the second is for a better regulatory scheme to include appropriate safety standards and enforcement. The quest for more stringent administration has been and will be unrewarding if some basic premises are not challenged. Saskatchewan, Manitoba and Ontario, for instance, have well-designed statutory schemes obliging employers to provide an environment satisfying the required standards. The employer must give workers access to information about processes and materials used in the workplace as well as levels of exposures to toxic substances. Workers must be represented on joint employer-employee committees which have investigatory, monitory and recommendatory powers. In addition, government inspectors have inquisitorial, reporting and sanctioning powers. The government agency can also set ideal standards, including the proscription of certain activities, processes, and substances. The schemes, however, will not significantly reduce workplace hazards unless officials publicly recognize that *the assumptions of the capitalist mode of production are challengeable.*

All enterprise, no matter who owns the means of production, creates risk. To declare that a work environment with an acceptable risk level must be created is to beg the question. An acceptable risk depends on the balance achieved when the legitimacy of an enterprise is weighed against physical integrity. As long as the legitimacy of the enterprise is judged by market criteria of the Adam Smith type, that is, accepting the notion that any enterprise which can compete and survive is legitimate, the balance will favour profitability over safety. This is so because profitability is seen as directly related to acceptability by informed consumers of the product or service. It does not take an economic genius to note the many deviations from this model. Yet this pristine approach is used as an unarticulated premise when industrial health and safety standards are regulated. But reliance on the market argument is even more inappropriate here than in other facets of the economy. The dominant fiction is that workers, like consumers, may bargain for more safety, thus, whatever conditions prevail must be the result of trade-offs workers make between wages and say, job security, on the one hand, and safety on the other. The absurdity is obvious. While the state, through its regulatory agencies, provides minimum safeguards—in much the same way as it provides for minimum wage rates—it never withdraws from the precept that the antediluvian, pure market doctrine should be the governing assumption. This rigid ideological perspective can only harm workers.

The assumption that certain enterprises should not be undertaken at all is seen as beyond the realm of options available to the state. Only enterprises acknowledged as immoral, in a very particular sense of that word, will be inhibited: for instance brothel keeping or contract killing. This assumption also greatly inhibits the state's will to require entrepreneurs to obtain permits ensuring that a plant is designed with sufficient ventilation, proper sound systems and other safety measures *before* it operates. One industrial engineer in Quebec said that if design engineers had a legal duty to build in safety systems rather than to save employers money the industrial accident rate could be halved.[2]

There are usually some safety requirements which entrepreneurs must satisfy before they can set up business. But these are trivial, seldom ensuring a safe environment for workers. These entry barriers for manufacturers and miners are very low compared to those which have to be cleared by entrepreneurs whose activities may affect consumers rather than workers. For instance, note the quality and quantity of state control over entry into medicine, law and dentistry, or over the creation of banks. Look at the state's insistence on land developers' compliance with building and zoning regulations. These controls while often benefitting the controlled groups constrain human and other capital which the state is reluctant to fashion merely to protect workers.

The third adverse effect of the market ideology is that the efficiency of any regulatory mechanism will depend on the *nature* of the standards set and their enforcement. Standard-setting takes place in the context of two assumptions: the need to preserve profitability and a preference for letting individuals voluntarily *come to terms*. One of the wondrous by-products of the application of this naive free enterprise model is that there is no such notion as a "reasonable" profit. The market makes the decision about what is acceptable. Hence, regulators are regularly met with the argument that more stringent safety regulations may eliminate profit or reduce it to a level where investment would diminish, market activity would decline and unemployment would be caused. Administrators who accept this line of argument—as is the unsurprising norm, given that the nastier employers occasionally fortify the abstract theory by closing down plants, as Johns Mansville has done in Scarborough, do so without regard for, or a realistic appraisal of, whether the assets and profitability of an industry can weather the storm of new regulations. Anyone who doubts this proposition should simply think of the way environmental agencies act when setting out to control polluters and killers like Inco and Dow Chemical. These economic giants are treated by the regulators as if the slightest imposition would drive them out of business.

In the occupational health and safety sphere the results are there for all to see. Given the context in which these decisions are made, we expect to find standards slow to evolve, inadequate, and that enforcement will leave a lot to be desired. All these ex-

pectations are realized. For instance, the predecessor of the present Ontario Occupational Health and Safety Act, Bill 139, was introduced in 1976 with great governmental flourish. The minister, Bette Stephenson, said that standards for 14 substances known to be toxic and extremely disabling unless controlled (such as asbestos, arsenic and lead), would be set immediately. *To date no such new standards have been promulgated.* Similarly, the debate about standards for particular substances seems to assume as a basic premise that the balance between profitability and safety will always lead to the conclusion that there is a safe level of exposure to all substances. Administrators, not having workers' safety as their own priority, are encouraged in this view by *hired gun* scientists. It is ludicrously easy for entrepreneurs to find apparently respectable experts who will say that it has not been proved beyond all doubt that there is a substantial causal link between a process or material and a particular disease. Faced with such an argument, regulators not ready to confront the issue that there may be unreasonable profit, are loath to impose serious restrictions on the existing *modus operandi* of employers. If safety, however, were the higher priority and profit were not treated as sacrosanct, the burden would shift. Rather than having to be overwhelmingly convinced that there is a causal connection between a toxic substance and a disease, the regulators might set a tough standard, or even prohibit use of a toxic substance altogether, until it were proved truly safe at a particular level of exposure. That capitalists well understand the significance of supporting the idea that the burden to inhibit use should be on workers, is regularly demonstrated by the advertisements run by safety associations (read employers' representatives) in conjunction with the Workers' Compensation Board of Ontario. These ads stress that severe injuries could largely be avoided if only workers used more care. If they wore their helmets, the right boots, put ladders away, safety would be assured! *There has never been an advertisement emphasizing that plant design, speed-up or undermanning causes accidents.*

Finally, enforcement by the government agencies of their own standards leaves much to be desired. Unions tell of instances in which a sudden clean-up of the workplace occurs because the employer has apparently been forewarned of an inspection. But even where the inspectors seek to do their job diligently, enforcement will not be strict. The number of inspections depends in the first place on the number of inspectors available which is determined by the political will of the government. When Sterling Lyon's government took power in Manitoba, it left intact a legislative scheme which looked good, but diminished the inspection force so much that the scheme was left relatively toothless. In the USA inspectors considered 98 percent of all violations non-serious and imposed an average fine of $18.00.[3] This suggests another built-in problem with enforcement. Sociologists have repeatedly found that inspectors see fines as a final resort, one which stigmatizes and blames employers. Inspectors prefer voluntary cooperation.[4] The notion that the workplace relationship is a collaborative one plays a large role in fortifying this attitude. It also accords with the view that, wherever possible, individuals should be given the opportunity to settle their own problems.

This precept of the importance of self-determination is also reflected in the newer and more promising legislative schemes. Much of the monitoring and correcting is now left to joint committees of employers and employees, supported by inspectors and administrative standard-setters. Because this system fails to challenge the right of a capitalist to be enterprising until the governing authorities are satisfied that restraint is needed, substantive progress towards a safer work environment will be exceptionally

slow. Joint committee members have to learn what to look for and, even then, it is unlikely that, in anything but the most egregious circumstances, will a *joint* committee make a recommendation costly to the employer. Secondly, standard-setters will be very cautious about imposing restrictions on entrepreneurs. The battle of expertise, with its skewed burden of proof, ensures such wariness. For instance, it takes the US National Institute of Occupational Health and Safety approximately six years to devise an optimal level of exposure to a toxic substance. The proclamation of this standard is then subjected to political lobbying, dilution and further delay.[5] (It is worth noting that there are thousands of known toxic substances already in use.) Further, the inherent barrier to regulation is heightened by the general reluctance to regulate entrepreneurs in the prevailing conservative climate which opposes governmental intervention. Thus, while new legislative schemes appear better than old, the outlook for workers remains grim. What is to be done?

The welcome publicity given to the dangers inherent in many substances now used in the workplace should be used to direct an attack on the root of the problem, the reverence for profit-making rather than seeking to make current regulations more sophisticated. The revolution of the proletariat is the ideal solution. While waiting for it (but without holding our collective breath), we need to adopt strategies aimed at revealing the class nature of the work relationships and the inevitable results of the dominance by the capitalist class and the destruction of workers.

Under the new pieces of legislation, workers have been given the right to refuse to work in dangerous conditions, but they have to be reasonable in their refusal. They will be represented by an employee safety representative when arguing that their refusal is reasonable. Even if their refusal is deemed unreasonable at this juncture, they are not to be punished for it. How long they can insist on their right to refuse further is still problematic. There are still many legal difficulties, the foremost being the question of what is a reasonable refusal; others include whether an assignment to another task is a penalty and whether a refusing worker is to be paid. To evaluate the advantage bestowed by these kinds of provisions, it is pertinent that the right to refuse to work in unsafe conditions was recognized nearly 100 years ago and was not very helpful to workers then. What is new is the removal of fear of punishment if the worker turns out to have been wrong but reasonable in his assessment of this situation. Unchanged, however, is that the assessment of what is reasonable still depends on considerations which place productivity above safety. The trick is to change this. This might be done if all workers in a plant downed their tools when one or more of them felt that unsafe conditions existed. This would be, on the face of it, flaunting the processes setting up a right to refuse to work. Those processes, however, are ideally suited to cause as little interruption in productivity as possible.

In this light, a recent decision by the Ontario Labour Relations Board to uphold the right of 12 Inco workers to refuse to work because they could reasonably have believed that conditions were unsafe is welcome. But the decision stopped well short of granting permission to all workers in a plant to refuse, in concert, to work until conditions are made safe. The emphasis of the board's rather unexpectedly benign interpretation was still that the refusing workers must have reason to fear for their own safety. Workers are not to be encouraged to support others in their quest for greater safety. It could, after all, lead to a collective questioning of the practice of balancing employer profit against workers' welfare. It is unlikely, given the prevailing ideology of trade unions in Canada, that this interpretation of the law will be challenged. A strategy must be fashioned which will

demonstrate that the root of the health and safety problem is the inhumanity of profiteering at the expense of human life. This can be done by teaching the public that if the cold balancing of monetary advantage against physical well-being occurred outside the work place, it would attract the strongest condemnation which society can bestow: *it would be treated as criminal behaviour*. Today, even when public and politicians accept the need and desirability of enforcing regulatory schemes vigorously, even if it means fining people, they do not think of this in the same way as they do about the enforcement of society's regulations against rape, dope peddling, arson or murder. This instinctive differentiation between "real" crimes and mere breaches of administrative rules is due to the pervasive effect of the ideology which inhibits more stringent controls over employers. It should be attacked.

Charles Reasons has shown that if we chose to categorize injuries at work as assaults upon workers, the chance of injury to a worker because of a work-related assault is twenty-five times higher than his or her chance of being the victim of an offense classified under the *Criminal Code*. Similarly, he found that workers are more than three times as likely to die as a result of working than as a result of acts committed by assailants away from work. He also calculated that death from occupational disease is more than ten times that resulting from homicide. The difference in our treatment of assailants outside the work force and of those in it must, in law, be justified by an argument that conduct, to be adjudged criminal, must be intentional. That is, it must be carried out with the intent to hurt, to maim, and therefore, employers are not to be compared to street offenders because they never actually want to hurt their workers: injury is inflicted incidentally. Ironically this justification is one of the strengths of the suggestion that criminal law proper should be used against employers.

Successful prosecution will alert the public to the fact that failure to provide safeguards for workers' safety is so immoral as to be criminal in the same sense as rapes and murders are criminal.

The technical difficulties which have to be overcome to use the criminal law to this effect are significant, but not insurmountable. While lawyers deem it necessary to talk as if no person could ever be convicted of a crime if his or her conduct did not render him or her personally blameworthy according to society's accepted mores, the courts have given several shades of meaning to the word *intentional*. One result is that it is possible to convict drivers of criminal negligence who injure someone while drunk; that is, at a time when they may not have had a subjective intent to harm or may have been incapable of wilfully disregarding anyone's safety. In effect, they are held culpable in such cases because they should have known, while still sober, that if they drank before driving they might cause grievous injury. The real blameworthiness in such cases lies in deliberately putting oneself in a position where a reasonable standard of care could not be achieved. It is quite possible that certain workplace circumstances can, by analogy, lead to successful criminal convictions. For instance, as a matter of criminal law, there is no *a priori* reason why an employer who ignores recommendations about safety by a joint committee, or by an inspector, or who ignores emissions or noise statutes, should not be held criminally responsible. There are many provisions of the *Criminal Code* which can be interpreted as characterizing such behaviour as criminal; to cite but a few: criminal negligence (section 202), the unlawful endangering of a servant or apprentice by a master (section 201), wilfully breaching a contract (section 380) and criminal conspiracy (section 423).

There are difficulties in making such provisions applicable to work situations, but they are not overwhelming. They have been discussed at length elsewhere. For the moment, it suffices that these well-established heads of acknowledged criminal liability are technically available to be used against employers who harm workers.

The most important of the possible gains to be made by the use of this tactic is that once the public becomes aware that the infliction of harm on workers may be classed as criminal, it will be easier for politicians to accede to workers' demands that the burden of proof be changed. That is, the reasonableness of profitability, even if profit-making is still seen as a good idea, may be differently assessed because it will be understood that the side effects of the garnering of profit may be so immoral as to be criminal. Secondly, there is something very satisfying about using the criminal law, normally used to oppress the working class, against the establishment which created it. (The use of the criminal law against trade unions is well-known, and let it be noted that the majority of people in jail are former unemployed or poorly paid persons.) Furthermore, even if few prosecutions actually lead to convictions, the fear put into the occupants of executive boardrooms will bear useful fruit. Criminal convictions of crimes—other than *normal* business crimes such as bribery and corruption—carry a real stigma in that segment of our class-ridden society: note Ford Motors' violent reaction to the criminal charges laid against it in the Pinto case. There had been many civil actions against Ford over the exploding car before this prosecution, but none caused anything like the eruption of fear and anger which the Indiana criminal charges produced. There was much public rejoicing by Ford spokespersons and financial editorial writers when Ford was acquitted. This raises the spectre that failing criminal prosecutions may legitimate unacceptable employer practices. They may. But take comfort from the fact that since Ford's acquittal in Indiana, several other states' attorneys-general have spoken about initiating their own criminal prosecutions against Ford. They seem to feel that the Indiana case was lost because of the limited resources of the county prosecutorial offices in that case and because of a significant procedural ruling by the trial judge which removed much damaging evidence from the jury's ken. But it may be true that only the spectacular nature of the Pinto case has led to this promising attitude in public officials who sense there may be political mileage in taking on an undoubted villain. Such enthusiasm is not likely to be found in provincial Crown offices in Canada toward criminal charges in occupational health cases. But, again, this is not a negative aspect of the strategem. The very reluctance the powers-that-be are likely to evince when asked to prosecute employers in the same way as garden-variety criminals may well lead to greater public awareness of the class bias of the legal system and its functionaries.

The use of criminal prosecutions will not bring about the millennium. But it may lead to a heightening awareness and then to more beneficial standards being set more quickly and being enforced more effectively, without our having to wait for a change in ownership of the means of production, or the total discrediting of the god profit.

Most importantly, it is action, not reaction.

ENDNOTES

1. Paul Rohan, "The Trend of Work Injuries in Canada," and "Les accidents du travail: la situation au Quebec," *Canadian Family Physician*, Vol. 24 (June 1978).

2. Mr. Claude Lajeunesse as reported in *The Gazette*, Aug. 12, 1975.

3. Per Senator Harrison A. Williams, Jr. (Dem.-N.J.), Chairman of the Senate Committee on Labor and Public Welfare, *Trial Magazine*, Sept./Oct. 1975.

4. E.G. Carson, "Some Sociological Aspects of Strict Liability and the Enforcement of Factory Legislation" *Modern Law Review* 33, p. 396, and "What Collar Crime and the Enforcement of Factory Legislation" (1970), *British Journal of Criminology* 10, p. 383.

5. United States, General Accounting Office, Report to the Senate Committee on Labor and Public Welfare: *Slow Progress Likely in Development of Standards and Harmful Physical Agents Found in Workplaces* (1973), p. 7.

6. Data from Reasons, Patterson & Ross, *Assault on the Worker, Occupational Safety and Health in Canada* (Toronto: Butterworths, 1981).

7. Glasbeek and Rowland, "Are Injuring and Killing at Work Crimes?" (*Osgoode Hall Law Journal*, 17, 1979), pp. 506–594.

HUMAN RIGHTS AND THE PREVENTION OF CANCER

Alan Gewirth

Every person has a basic human right not to have cancer inflicted on him by the action of other persons. I shall call this right the RNIC (the Right to the Non-Infliction of Cancer). Since it is a species of the right not to be killed or severely injured, the RNIC is perhaps too obvious to need any justificatory argument. Nevertheless, it raises questions of interpretation that have an important bearing both on the ascription of responsibility and on the requirements of social policy.

Closely related to the RNIC is a further right, which I shall call the right of informed control. Each person has a right to have informed control over the conditions relevant to the possible infliction of cancer on him or herself. This is also a basic human right not only because of its connection with well-being but also because informed control is a component of freedom, which is a necessary condition of action and of successful action.

To understand the RNIC, we must consider what it is to inflict cancer on other persons, who is responsible for this infliction, and how it can be prevented. Although the RNIC requires that all persons refrain from inflicting cancer on others, as a practical matter it is only some persons who are in a position to do such inflicting and to prevent it, so that they must especially be viewed as the respondents having the correlative duty to forbear and to prevent. The above questions about infliction hence come down to the issue of the causal and moral responsibility for other persons' getting cancer.

According to current estimates, 80% to 90% of all cancers are caused by the controllable actions of human beings. In the case of cigarette smoking the victims may be held to inflict the cancer on themselves. But in very many cases, it is other persons who cause the victims to get cancer, and it is to

From the *American Philosophical Quarterly*, Vol. 17, No. 2 (April 1980). © *American Philosophical Quarterly*, 1980. Reprinted by permission.

such cases that the RNIC directly applies. So far as our present knowledge goes, this causation occurs from an increasingly familiar variety of interrelated policies and situations, stemming in part from the vast explosion of physiochemical technology since World War II, that expose the recipients or victims to carcinogenic dangers: in industrial occupations, through air, water, and land pollution, by food additives and pesticides, and in many other ways. The victims include workers in factories producing asbestos and vinyl chloride, consumers of sodium nitrite and various chemical emissions, and very many other workers and consumers. Bioassays have shown the cancerous effect of various substances on test animals, and epidemiological studies have shown the relative distribution of cancerous effects or symptoms among persons who are exposed to the substances, as contrasted with persons not so exposed. In this way we have learned which substances are correlated with which symptoms—for example, vinyl chloride with cancer of the liver, asbestos with certain forms of lung cancer, and so forth—and we can thereby come considerably closer to establishing causal connections.

Serious effects to prevent these cancers must be determined by the specific principles that underlie the RNIC and the right of informed control. First, if we know which substances are causally related to cancer, then exposure to these substances must be prohibited or carefully regulated. Second, every effort must be made to acquire the relevant knowledge and to publicize the results. Hence a major part of the causal and moral responsibility for inflicting various cancers can be attributed to manufacturers, employers, and sellers of various products who control the situations in which the cancers are caused if these persons are made aware of the causal connections and do nothing to stop the actions and policies, in the industrial processes and in marketing, which lead to the cancerous effects. A secondary

responsibility can also be attributed to government officials, ranging from legislators to administrators charged with enforcing already existing laws, if, while having knowledge of these carcinogenic dangers, they do not take adequate steps to prevent them.

The basis of this responsibility is similar to that which applies to other forms of killing. The general prohibition against killing innocent humans extends not only to murder but also to manslaughter and other kinds of homicide, including those that stem from advertently negligent and other actions whose likely or foreseeable outcome is the death of their recipients. The general point is that if someone knows or has good reasons to believe that actions or policies under his control operate to cause cancer in other persons, then if he continues these actions or policies, he is in the position of inflicting cancer on these other persons, and he violates a basic human right: he is both causally and morally responsible for the resulting deaths and other serious harms. I shall refer to this as the *informed control criterion* for attributing responsibility.

This criterion is distinct from the criterion of intentionality. To be responsible for inflicting lethal harms, a person need not intend or desire to produce such harms, either as an end or as a means. It is sufficient if the harms come about as an unintended but foreseeable and controllable effect of what he does. For since he knows or has good reasons to believe that actions or policies under his control will lead to the harms in question, he can control whether the harms will occur, so that it is within his power to prevent or at least lessen the probability of their occurrence by ceasing to engage in these actions. Thus, just as all persons have a right to informed control, so far as possible, over the conditions relevant to their incurring cancer and other serious harms, so the causal and moral responsibility for inflicting cancer can be attributed to persons who have informed control over other persons' suffering the lethal harms of cancer.

There is a problem about the informed control criterion for attributing responsibility. Consider, for example, the case of automobile manufacturers. They know, on the basis of statistics accumulated over many years, that a certain percentage of the cars they make and sell will be involved in highway deaths and crippling injuries. Hence, since the actions and policies of making automobiles are under the manufacturers' control, why can't we say that they too are causally and morally responsible for inflicting these deaths and injuries on the victims and hence violate their basic human rights? Or consider the case of the civil disobedients during the 1950s and 1960s, who knew or had good reasons to believe that their unauthorized marches, demonstrations, sit-ins, burning of draft cards, and similar activities frequently led or threatened to lead to riots, bloodshed, and other serious harms, including deaths. Since the actions and policies of engaging in such activities were under the control of the civil disobedients, why can't we correctly say that Martin Luther King and the other demonstrators also were causally and morally responsible for inflicting these injuries and deaths on the respective victims and hence violated their human rights?

To answer these questions, I shall refer to a certain principle, [relevant to] the attribution of legal and moral responsibility, which, paraphrasing Hart and Honoré, I shall call the "principle of the intervening action."[1] The point of this principle is that when there is a causal connection between some person A's doing some action X and some other person C's incurring a certain harm Z, this causal connection is "negatived" or removed if, between X and Z, there intervenes some other action Y of some person B who knows the relevant circumstances of his action and who intends to produce Z or who produces Z through recklessness. For example, suppose Ames negligently leaves open an elevator shaft—call this action X—and Carson falls through the shaft and is severely injured—call this harm Z. According to the principle, the causal connection between X and Z is negatived or removed, so far as moral and legal responsibility is concerned, if some other person Bates, who knows the elevator is not there, intentionally or recklessly entices Carson to step into the elevator shaft. Here it is Bates's intervening action Y that is the direct cause of Carson's falling through the elevator shaft and suffering the harm Z, and for purposes of assigning responsibility this action Y removes or "negatives" the causal connection between X and Z, and hence also removes Ames's responsibility for the injuries suffered by Carson. The reason for this removal is that Bates's intervening action Y of enticing Carson to step into the absent elevator is the more direct or proximate cause of his getting hurt, and unlike Ames's negligence, Bates's action is the sufficient condition of the injury as it actually occurred. Even if Bates's does not intentionally bring about the injury, he is still culpable according to the informed control criterion, for he knows that the elevator is not there and he controls the sequence of events whereby Carson is injured.

The principle of the intervening action enables us to see the difference between the case of the producers of carcinogens and the cases of automobile manufacturers and the civil disobedients. In the latter cases, an intervening action Y of other persons occurs between the initial action X and the harms suffered, Z. When the automobile manufacturers turn out cars, this does not itself usually cause or explain the suffering of injuries by the drivers and car occupants. There intervenes the reckless car operation of the drivers—their going too fast, not using seat belts, driving while drunk, and so forth, all of which are under the drivers' own direct and informed control. Similarly, when the civil disobedients staged demonstrations and there ensued riots and injuries, it was their vehement, determined opponents whose intervention directly operated as the sufficient conditions of the riots and injuries. These opponents voluntarily and with relevant knowledge engaged in the violent resistance and counteraction, which were hence under their control; and this counteraction negatived or removed the causal connection between the demonstrations and the injuries. Thus it was not the auto manufacturers and the civil disobedients who can correctly be held to have inflicted the respective injuries, but rather the drivers and the counterdemonstrators, so that, on the informed control criterion, the causal and moral responsibility lies with them.

In the case of the producers of most carcinogens, on the other hand (omitting for now the manufacturers of cigarettes), there is no similar intervening action between their production or marketing activities and the incurring of cancer. The workers, consumers, and other persons affected do not actively and knowingly contribute to their getting cancer in the ways in which the drivers and the rioting opponents actively and knowingly contribute to the ensuing injuries. To be sure, the workers work and the consumers eat and so forth, and these actions are under their respective control. But such actions are part of the normal course of everyday life; they do not involve new intervening actions that go outside the presumed normal cause-effect sequences on the part of persons who are informed about the carcinogenic properties of the substances they use; hence, their actions do not break or "negative" the causal connection between the exposure to carcinogens and the getting of cancer. It is for this reason that these cancers may correctly be said to be other-inflicted, i.e. inflicted on the victims by other persons, the manufacturers or distributors, who hence are guilty of violating the RNIC, as against the self-inflicted cancers that result from such actions as cigarette smoking, or the self-inflicted injuries that result from reckless car-driving.

It may still be contended that part of the causal and moral responsibility for inflicting cancer on workers and consumers rests with the victims themselves, in that they have at least a prudential obligation to use due caution just as motorists do. There is indeed some merit in this connection; but it is important to note its limits. The contention may be viewed as resting in part on the hoary maxim *caveat emptor*. Since workers and consumers are buyers or takers of offers made by employers, distributors, and so forth, the maxim says that it is these buyers who must exercise proper caution in accepting the offers.

While the maxim has much plausibility as a counsel of prudence, it has serious limitations when viewed morally. We can especially see this if we look at a general point about the moral principle which is at the basis of a civilized society. This is a principle of mutual trust, of mutual respect for certain basic rights: that persons will not, in the normal course of life, knowingly inflict physical harm on one another, that they will abstain from such harms insofar as it is in their power to do so, insofar as they can informedly control their relevant conduct. The normal course of life, in a society like ours, includes hiring persons for work and selling substances for use, including consumption of food and other materials. Hence, when workers agree to work for others and when consumers agree to buy various products, they have a right to assume, on the basis of this moral principle, that the work and the products will not be physically harmful to them in ways beyond their normal ability to control, or at least, if there is knowledge or good reason to believe that the products are harmful, as in the case of cigarettes, that full knowledge and publicity will be given to this fact. Failing this knowledge and publicity, the primary responsibility for inflicting cancer on workers and buyers, and thereby violating a basic human right, rests with the employers and producers, since it is they who knowingly offer the conditions of work and the products for sale. What is especially serious about this infliction, by contrast with cases to which the principle of the intervening action applies, is that there is not the same opportunity on the part of the victims to control, with relevant knowledge, the causal factors that proximately impose the cancerous harms on them, so that their own right of informed control is violated.

The most direct requirement that the RNIC lays on the responsible agents is simply that they cease and desist from these lethal policies. This requirement must be enforced by the state because of the pervasiveness and seriousness of the harms in question, especially where the actual or potential victims lack the power and the knowledge to enforce the requirement themselves, and because the voluntary cooperation of the agents in stopping such infliction cannot be assumed. Whether this enforcement takes the form of an outright ban on the use of certain substances or the setting of standards that specify the levels at which various potential carcinogens may be used, in either case there must be appropriate sanctions or penalties for the violators. In addition, sufficient information must be made available so that all persons potentially affected may be able to help to control the conditions that affect them so severely. Thus both the state and the various employers, manufacturers, and distributors are the respondents of the RNIC, and their correlative duties have to an eminent degree the moral seriousness and coercibility that go with all basic human rights.

I have thus far presented the RNIC as an absolute right not to have cancer inflicted on one by the action of other persons. I now want to look more closely at the respect in which it is indeed absolute.

To say that someone has an absolute right to have or do something X means that his having or doing X cannot justifiably be overridden but any other considerations, so that there is a completely exceptionless prohibition on all other persons against interfering with the right-holder's having or doing X. Now there are familiar difficulties with trying to show that any right is absolute, including not only the First Amendment rights to speech, press, and assembly but even the right to life, including the right of innocent persons not to be killed. Without going into these, we must note the more specific difficulties that arise if we try to construe the RNIC as an absolute right.

The difficulties I have in mind are not those that may stem from certain utilitarian consequentialist ways of overriding the RNIC whereby it might be argued that cancer may justifiably be inflicted on some persons in order to maximize utility, if great goods may be attained or great evils avoided thereby. Such arguments may take either the science fiction form, whereby inflicting cancer on one person would somehow lead to eternal bliss for everyone else, or a somewhat more sober form whereby, for example, injecting cancerous cells into someone's bloodstream would somehow help to provide an experimental basis for finding a cure for certain cancers. While the right even of an innocent person to life may not be absolute, the kinds of crisis situations in which this right might be overridden are not applicable to violating any person's right not to have cancer inflicted on him, no matter how many other persons might be benefited thereby.

It must also be noted that the RNIC deals only with the infliction of cancer on some person without his consent or against his will. Thus it does not directly apply to a case where someone may give his informed, unforced consent to have cancer cells injected in him in the context of experimental research toward finding an effective cure or therapy. In such a case the cancer that may result is to be regarded as self-inflicted rather than other-inflicted. I shall deal below with some other aspects of such presumed consent.

There appear, however, to be ways of overriding the RNIC that appeal neither to the kind of utilitarian consequentialism just mentioned nor to presumed consent. These ways may seem to lead to the conclusion that the prohibition against inflicting cancer on other persons should be *prima facie* and probabilistic rather than absolute and apodictic.

We may distinguish two areas of such probabilism. The first bears on the cause-effect relation between exposure to various substances and the incurring of cancer. It will be recalled that in explicating the RNIC I said that if someone "knows or has good reasons to believe" that actions or policies under his control operate to produce cancer in other persons, then he is in the position of inflicting cancer on these other persons. The question now is: when can someone be said to know or to have good reasons to believe that his actions inflict cancer?

The difficulty here is that the causal relation in question seems to be one of degree. Some substances, such as β-napthylamine and asbestos, have a very high ability to induce cancer. But with other substances the ability and the correlative risk, as determined on a statistical frequency basis, are much lower. There is a currently unresolved controversy on this question of degrees. One view holds that there is a threshold of dosage of carcinogens, below which they do not induce cancers; the other view holds that there is no such threshold, in that any amount of carcinogen, no matter how small, may lead to cancerous tumors. This latter view is reflected in the Delaney clause that deals with food additives: "no additive shall be deemed safe if it is found to induce cancer when ingested by man or animal, or if it is found, after tests which are appropriate for the evaluation of the safety of food additives, to induce cancer in man or animal. . . ."[2] Here, then, use of the additives in question is strictly prohibited without regard to the degree of risk to humans at any level of use, and without regard to possible benefits.

The merits of such a blanket prohibition, in the case of other substances as well as food additives, are clear. So long as it is not known

which particular workers in the various potentially lethal occupations will get cancer and which not, and similarly which consumers of the various suspect food additives and other substances, the only completely safe course would seem to be a blanket prohibition of the respective exposures. To the objection that such absolutism would entail prohibiting the use of automobiles and of many other modern conveniences, since these too carry the risk of death, the reply is, as before, that automobiles do not usually become harmful apart from the controllable, variable actions of the persons who use them, so that they do not pose the risk of death from external causes, i.e., causes external to their users, in the way that carcinogens do.

On the alternative view of the threshold controversy, it is maintained that just as automobiles may be made safer by a variety of devices that are within the power of their makers and users, so too the risks of getting cancer from various substances may be reduced by lowering the degree of exposure to them. For example, even in the case of vinyl chloride, an exposure standard of one part per million is thought to render it relatively even if not absolutely safe for the workers who are exposed to it, especially by contrast with the previous unregulated concentration of 200 to 5,000 parts per million.

I have two conclusions on this issue, one firm, the other tentative. The firm conclusion is that, in keeping with the right of informed control, it is necessary to try to reduce further the ignorance reflected in the varying probabilities of the cause-effect relations involved in carcinogenesis. For this purpose, intensive research must be pursued, within the limits of safety to humans, to ascertain the more specific causal variables, so that we understand more fully just which substances, at what levels of exposure, carry what risks of cancer to which persons. And the results of this research must be fully disseminated and used both in manufacturing and marketing operations and in appropriate legislation.

My more tentative conclusion is that, in contrast to construing the RNIC as an absolute right against even the slightest risk of cancer, a sliding scale may be introduced. Whether the use of or exposure to some substance should be prohibited should depend on the degree to which it poses the risk of cancer, as shown by bioassays and epidemiological studies. If the risks are very slight, so that, for example, use of the substance increases the chance of getting cancer from 1 in 10,000 to 2 in 10,000, or if the risk can be made very slight by drastically reducing the level of exposure, as in the case just cited of vinyl chloride, and if no substitutes are available, then use of it may be permitted, subject to stringent safeguards.

Does this conclusion entail that the RNIC is not an absolute right? The answer depends on how the word "inflict" is construed. If "inflict" is viewed solely as causal, with no reference to moral responsibility of the agent, then there is a sense in which the tentative conclusion I have reached would remove the absoluteness of the RNIC. For while the conclusion does not say that there may be exceptions to the prohibition against actually inflicting cancer, it does say that certain minimal risks of inducing cancer may be allowed, or that the risk of cancer may be increased so long as the level attained is still very low in the way just indicated.

The case is otherwise, however, if the RNIC's prohibition against inflicting cancer is viewed in the light of the ascription of moral responsibility. Since the RNIC is a strict right, it entails that persons strictly ought to refrain from inflicting cancer on other persons. Now this "ought," like other moral "oughts" addressed to agents, is limited by the possibility of informed control, and hence of knowing the likelihood of one's actions causing such infliction. For insofar as "ought" implies "can," to say that *A* ought not to do *X* implies that he can refrain from doing *X* and also that he can have the knowledge needed for such refraining.

Thus, the extent of the RNIC's requirement and of the moral responsibility that stems from violating it is likewise limited by this possibility of knowledge.

In this context of moral responsibility, then, the RNIC is to be construed as entailing: Don't inflict cancer on other persons so far as you know or have good reason to believe that any of your actions will constitute or produce such infliction, and don't increase the risk of cancer for other persons beyond the minimal level just indicated. On this construal, the RNIC remains an absolute right even where it allows certain minimal risks of persons' getting cancer as a result of the actions of other persons. For the latter are morally responsible only if they can know or can have good reasons for believing that their action will lead to other persons' getting cancer. Where they do not and cannot have such knowledge, the informed control criterion for ascribing responsibility does not apply, nor, usually, does the intentionality criterion. This point is a quite general one. In the case of every moral precept addressed to actual or prospective agents, there is the limitation of their being able to know whether the actions they perform are or are not instances of what the precept prescribes or prohibits. The degree of such knowledge may vary with different circumstances. But especially in cases where the prohibition is as important as in the case of not inflicting cancer, there also remains the requirement that one must try as fully as possible to ascertain whether one's actions will in fact constitute an infliction of cancer, so that the right of informed control is again of central importance.

Let us now turn to a second area of probabilism that may be invoked to mitigate the absoluteness of the RNIC's prohibition against inflicting cancer, and that has been implicitly present in my preceding discussion. This area bears not on the varying probabilities of the cause-effect relations themselves in the production of cancer, but rather on a weighing of certain values in reaction to those probabilities. The weighing in question is concerned with the relation between the benefits obtained by prohibiting carcinogenic exposures and the costs of such prohibitions; or alternatively with the relation between the benefits obtained by accepting certain risks of cancer and the costs of accepting those risks. It is here a matter of the cost-benefit analysis dearly beloved of economists, which is simply the contemporary version of the pleasure-pain calculus long pursued by utilitarians.

In view of the extreme importance to human well-being of preventing cancer, and the human right to the non-infliction of cancer, how can the avoidance of such infliction be legitimately subjected to a cost-benefit analysis whereby its benefits are weighed against various costs? The better to understand this question, let us compare the problem of preventing cancer with such a situation as where coal miners are trapped in a mine by an explosion. So long as there is any hope of rescuing the miners, all possible means are used to effect a rescue. Except where other human lives are at stake, questions of cost are deemed irrelevant, and so too is the number of miners; less effort would not be made to rescue one miner than to rescue fifty, except insofar as less equipment might be needed to rescue the one. The basis of such unlimited effort to save human lives is that the right of an innocent person to continue to live is normally regarded as absolute, being limited only by the right to life of other persons, and human life is considered to be priceless, in the literal sense of being without price; it is incommensurable with, cannot be measured in terms of, money or any other material goods that might be needed to preserve the life or lives that are endangered.

There are obvious dissimilarities between such a situation and the prevention of cancer. In the former case the lethal danger is actual and immediate, not potential

and remote; it is a danger to determinate individuals, not to some general percentage or statistical frequency out of a much larger, less determinate population; and the life-saving operations that are called for are similarly determinate and immediate. Partly because of these differences and partly for other reasons, economists and others have engaged in the cost-benefit analyses mentioned before. There is, after all, time for calculation, and the calculation bears especially on how much, from among the total values both of the individuals directly concerned and of society at large, it is worth spending in order to avoid the risks of cancer and other lethal harms.

To see how such cost-benefit analyses are even minimally plausible in this context, we may note that many kinds of human decisions involve at least implicit views as to the monetary value of human life. Examples are when someone takes out a life insurance policy, when society takes or fails to take measures to improve automobile safety, and when a court awards money damages to a family, one of whose members has been killed through someone else's fault. Morally repugnant as it may be, then, putting a specific money evaluation on human life seems to be a feature of at least some segments of individual and social decision-making.

Accepting for the present at least the possibility of such a procedure, we may ask how the money value of a human life is to be estimated. Economists have answered this question in different ways, but the way that is most favoured is based on the familiar idea of a Pareto improvement.[3] According to this, one allocation of resources is an improvement over another if it involves at least one person's being made better off while no person is made worse off. The criterion of being made better off consists simply in the preferences of the person concerned, so that if some person prefers allocation X to allocation Y, then he is made better off by X than by Y. And if no person prefers Y to X, then the change from X to Y is a Pareto improvement. Thus if some person A is willing to accept some life-risking situation R on payment to him of a certain sum of money S by another person B who is willing to make this payment, then A's having R and S together is to that extent a Pareto improvement over the situation or allocation where he does not have R and S. On this view, the monetary value of A's life to himself is measured by the minimum sum of money he is willing to accept to compensate for the risk of losing his life in some activity or other.

There is a direct application of this Pareto criterion to the case of cancer, especially as this is incurred by industrial workers in various occupations. According to the criterion, the risk of cancer may be imposed on some worker in some job if he is willing to accept that risk on payment to him of a certain sum of money. Since he prefers a situation where he works at some carcinogenically risky job and hence earns money to a situation where he has no job at all, or since he prefers a carcinogenically riskier job at more pay to a less risky job at less pay, while in each case no one else is made worse off, it follows that the former situation is in each case a Pareto improvement over the latter. Hence, in contrast to the earlier position whereby human life is priceless and the RNIC is an absolute right, according to this new position human life turns out to have a price, and the right to the non-infliction of cancer is now limited not only by unavoidable deficiencies of knowledge but also by the willingness of potential victims to accept financial compensation.

There are, however, serious difficulties with this probabilistic alternative. I shall waive the question of whether the risk of getting cancer can be rationally compensated for by any amount of money or other satisfactions. It might be thought that the RNIC is not affected by such cases, since the risk of cancer is here assumed to be imposed on some person with his consent. But there still

remain the questions of whether this consent is informed and unforced. Is each of the persons who chooses among alternatives able to know the degree of risk of the possibly carcinogenic alternative for which compensation is required? In the case of the industrial workers in factories making asbestos, kepone, vinyl chloride, and other lethal substances, they were surely not aware of the risks during the years that elapsed between their initial exposure and the time when some of them came down with cancer. For them, consequently, the Pareto criterion would not apply insofar as it assumes that persons who express their preferences by their acceptance of compensation for risks are aware of the magnitude of the risks. And even when, as is increasingly the case in recent years, research is pursued into carcinogens and its results are made public, there remains the question of whether complicated statistical calculations can be understood and used by the workers who are most vulnerable to their possibly varying implications. In such circumstances it becomes very difficult to apply the right of informed control.

The Pareto criterion's applicability is also dubious over a wide range of cases because of a difficulty bearing on distributive justice. Since the poorer a person is, the greater is the marginal utility for him of a given sum of money, whereas the opposite is true the richer a person is, the poor are willing to accept much greater risks for considerably less money. Thus, in effect, they and their relative poverty are exploited as a way of getting them to do dangerous work far beyond what others will accept. While this is, of course, a very old story, it casts doubt on the economists' model of citizens' sovereignty where workers "voluntarily" accept compensation for risks and thereby show that they consider themselves to be better off than they would be without the risks and the compensation. For many workers are in effect confronted with a forced choice, since the alternative to their taking the risky job with its slightly added compensation is their not having any job at all. Where workers and others do not have the power to ward off such risks by themselves, it is an indispensable function of government to protect such persons from having to make such forced choices, and hence to protect their right both to the non-infliction of cancer and to the non-imposition of serious risks of cancer. This function can be generalized to the more extensive duty of the supportive state to try to provide opportunities and means of knowledge and well-being so as to reduce the vulnerability of poorer persons to such coercive alternatives. In this and other respects, the prevention of other-inflicted cancers merges into more general issues of the distribution of power and wealth in a society.

A quite central difficulty with this application of cost-benefit analysis is that human life or health is not a commodity to be bought, sold, or bid for on the market. Thus the Pareto criterion is mistaken in principle insofar as it assumes that any great risk of death can be compensated for by any amount of money. There are important differences in this regard between engaging in carcinogenic work risks, on the one hand, and buying life insurance, driving cars, or doing aerial acrobatic stunts, on the other. Even though in buying life insurance one implicitly places a certain monetary value on one's life, this is different from undertaking the risk of carcinogenic work for pay. In buying life insurance one recognizes that death is inevitable for everyone sooner or later, and one does not thereby voluntarily incur the serious risk of death. But to undertake the risk of cancer by one's work is not itself inevitable, so that the compensation involves putting a market price on one's life in the context of a controllable, avoidable choice. In addition, the worker in a carcinogenic industry usually does not have the same kind of control over his degree of risk as does the driver of a car or an aerial acrobat. Hence

the cause for outright prohibition of more than minimal risk in the former case is much stronger than it is with regard to auto driving or aerial acrobatics despite the dangers of death common to these kinds of cases.

A further issue about the economic valuation of human life bears on who does the valuing. It is one thing for a person to put a money value on his own life where he has a relatively unforced choice between alternative ways of life and work. It is another thing for other persons to put this money valuation on his life, as is done when the benefits of making jobs less risky and hence prolonging workers' lives are weighed against alternative uses of public money, such as building new roads or ball parks. In such cases the worker and his life are made economic objects vulnerable to the preference or choices of other persons rather than of himself. The very possibility of making such choices on such grounds represents a drastic lowering of public morality.

A related criticism must be made of the suggestion that the Pareto criterion should be applied to tax firms or manufacturers so as to encourage them to remove or lower the levels at which their workers are exposed to cancer. For a firm may choose or prefer to pay the tax rather than remove the risk, while passing the tax on to its customers and, under conditions of oligopoly, suffering little or no financial drain. Such payment would be small comfort to the workers who continue to be exposed to the lethal dangers. This taxational incentive approach also has the severe difficulty previously noted, that it makes persons' lives and health matters of bargaining or purchase rather than viewing them as basic goods and rights not subject to such cost-benefit calculation.

Thus far I have been dealing with a view of cancer as inflicted on persons against their will by the direct or indirect actions of other persons. It is to these interpersonal transactions that the RNIC directly applies. As against such other-inflicted cancers, let us briefly consider the lung cancer derived from cigarette smoking as a self-inflicted kind of harm. This distinction between other-inflicted and self-inflicted harms may be contested in the case of cigarettes on the ground that the blandishments of advertisers and, for young people, the models set by their peers constitute externally-caused incentives to smoke, so that the resulting lung cancers are here also other-inflicted. There is indeed some truth to this, especially in the case of the cigarette manufacturers. Since the lethal impact of smoking cannot be controlled by individual smokers in anything like the same degree that motorists can control the dangers of auto driving, cigarette manufacturers bear a much heavier responsibility for the resulting deaths than do auto manufacturers. The principle of the intervening action applies in much lesser degree to the former than to the latter because the actions of making cigarettes easily available and attractive have a much closer causal connection to the ensuing lethal harms, despite the intervention of the victims' choices to smoke.

I shall here assume, however, that the final choice to smoke rests with the individual himself, and that he is capable of withstanding the advertisers' blandishments. The fact remains that his smoking may be morally wrong because he may impose serious burdens on others. If he becomes hospitalized, his family suffers and he uses extremely valuable and costly facilities and services for which he may not be able to pay, or even if he can, he still makes extremely stringent demands on others which his knowing, controllable actions might have prevented. He also violates both an important prudential duty to himself and also a moral duty to himself as a rational person who is aware of the moral requirements of not burdening others.[4]

How, then, should the self-inflicted carcinogenesis of cigarette smoking be dealt with? While outright prohibition is a possibility, it would perhaps be too violative of individual freedom and, as with the 18th Amendment [to the U.S. Constitution]*, there would be too many possibilities of abuse and evasion. On the other hand, simply to leave the smoker alone would also be unacceptable because, even if we give up all paternalistic concern for his own well-being, there would still remain the problem of externalities, the costs he imposes on others.

The solution I suggest is that the smoker should be made to bear the full cost of his habit, including its external effects. These could be calculated in terms of the excess medical facilities, support of his dependents, and other costs he imposes on others. This would be an application of the Pareto criterion in that the smoker would have to compensate those who would otherwise bear the cost of his habit. If he chooses to pay this compensation, the outcome is a Pareto improvement, since he prefers his smoking together with paying the extra money for it to going without smoking, while, since other persons are compensated, they are not made worse off.

Why is such a compensation permissible in the smoker's case and not in the case of workers in carcinogenic industries? In each case it is the inflicter of cancer who has to pay. There is, however, a difference between a person paying others in order to inflict cancer on himself and his paying his workers in order to inflict cancer on them. The latter, as we have seen, violates the RNIC while the former does not. There is also a difference between the potential cancer victim's paying others, as in the smoking case, and others' paying him, as in the occupational health case. But there is also a more important difference. The industrial worker who is allowed to take money compensation for working in a high-risk industry is told, in effect, that he must choose between losing his job or livelihood and risking his life to cancer. This is an inadmissible choice. The smoker, on the other

---

*Refers to the prohibition on the "manufacture, sale or transportation of intoxicating liquors . . .".—ED.

hand, is confronted with a choice between saving his life from cancer and saving his money, or, alternatively, between continuing his enjoyment of smoking, thereby risking his own life, and paying a larger sum of money. This choice, whatever its psychological hardship for the smoker, is not of the same order of extreme objective adversity as in the case of the high-risk worker. This initial much greater relative economic vulnerability of the unskilled industrial workers makes a crucial difference.

I conclude, then, that the probabilistic issues of the carcinogenic cause-effect relations and cost-benefit analysis do not materially affect the conclusion drawn earlier. So far as the moral responsibility of agents is concerned, the Right to the Non-Infliction of Cancer is an absolute human right, and it requires the most determined effort both to ascertain when such infliction is likely to occur and to take all possible steps to prevent it, and thereby to make its respondents fulfill their correlative duties.

ENDNOTES

1. See H.L.A. Hart and A.M. Honoré, *Causation in the Law* (Oxford: Oxford University Press, 1959), pp. 128 ff., 195 ff., 292 ff.

2. U.S. Code 21, 348 (c) (3). For this reference and for a valuable discussion of related issues I am indebted to Jerome Cornfield, "Carcinogenic Risk Assessment," *Science*, Vol. 198 (18 November 1977), pp. 693–699.

3. cf. E.J. Mishan, "Evaluation of Life and Limb: A Theoretical Approach," *Journal of Political Economy*, Vol. 79 (1971), pp. 687–705; M.W. Jones-Lee, *The Value of Life: An Economic Analysis* (Chicago: The University of Chicago Press, 1976), Chs. 1–3.

4. See Albert L. Nichols and Richard Zeckhauser, "Government Comes to the Workplace: An Assessment of OSHA," *The Public Interest* no. 49 (Fall 1977), p. 64 ff.

CASE 4	From Dust to Dust

Lloyd Tataryn

Every time a life insurance company shoves another sky-scraper into the air, it acts as a reminder that every year millions of dollars are made from making book on people's lives. But general run-of-the-mill bookies are clearly not in the same league as those who gamble on life expectancy rates. Insurance companies refuse to take the same risks as even the most conservative bookmakers. Skilled actuaries are paid handsome salaries to calculate the odds on who will fully pay their insurance premiums before reaching life's finish line, and who, on the other hand, are bad life risks. Actuaries take the guesswork out of dying. Insurance companies simply refuse to play hunches or to finalize deals when the odds are not in their favour.

Consider workers who make a living in the asbestos industry. As early as 1918, North American insurance companies were declining to insure asbestos workers. The companies had stumbled onto certain facts of death—facts of death which governments and industries were not willing to acknowledge until decades later.

Asbestos workers die at high rates from asbestosis, a disease caused by severe scarring of the lung. They die at excessive rates from lung cancer, gastro-intestinal cancer (cancer of the colon, rectum and oesophagus), and mesothelioma, a cancer of the lining of the chest and abdominal cavities. It is little wonder that back in 1918 asbestos workers were considered bad insurance risks. Unfortunately, as we shall see, the odds against them are little better in the 1970s. In Canada, governments and corporations have casually gambled with the health of asbestos workers. Asbestos workers have had to pay with disease-wracked bodies when the health wager was lost.

The use of asbestos dates back to Greek and Roman times when it was known as the "magic mineral". Asbestos has amazing filtering powers, can withstand the fiercest heat, and is almost immune to the forces of corrosion and decay. Yet asbestos is so pliable that it is the only mineral that can be spun into thread and woven into cloth. In fact, the Emperor Charlemagne amused himself and convinced visiting knights of his magical powers by throwing an asbestos table cloth into a fire and removing it unscathed. But asbestos was a suspected health hazard even in those bygone days. As early as the first century A.D., Pliny the Elder, after a trip through the Roman Provinces, confirmed reports by Strabo, the Greek geographer, that slaves who wove asbestos into cloth were suffering from a sickness which left them short of breath. Years later, the disease was labelled asbestosis.

Asbestos remained a novelty mineral, primarily woven into prized robes for priests and kings or rare cremation garments for deceased monarchs, until 1879, when it was first mined for wide commercial use in Thetford Mines, Quebec. Canada has since become the world's largest producer of chrysotile (white) asbestos, accounting for over 40 percent of world production. In 1973, close to two million tons of asbestos were shipped out of Canada, bringing in over $243 million. Approximately 80 percent of Canada's total asbestos production is mined and milled in Quebec. As in 1879, the town of Thetford Mines is the heart of Quebec's asbestos production.

Given the long association between asbestos and ill health and given the fact that the commercial production of asbestos originated in Thetford Mines, it would be logical to assume that the Canadian and Quebec asbestos industries would have taken every conceivable step to clean up their environments and prevent the development of asbestos-related disease. Not so. According to a 1976 federal report on asbestosis, ". . . ample evidence exists that workers are being subjected to substantial levels of asbestos in the workplace, resulting in increased incidents of asbestos-related disease."[1]

In April, 1976, Judge René Beaudry released an interim report of his investigation into the Quebec asbestos industry. The report was sharply critical of the asbestos industry's attempts to duck its responsibility to improve working conditions. According to Beaudry, asbestos companies "tended to medicalize the problem of air quality in the asbestos industry." The companies' approach to health was "based on medical compensation rather than the protection of workers' health . . .". Beaudry observed that the asbestos entrepreneurs channelled their industrial health efforts into fighting legal battles against compensation claims rather than into cleaning up hazardous work environments. Medical doctors were hired to contest asbestosis claims submitted to the Workmen's Compensation Commission, although "all the necessary data exists to initiate the technical control of asbestos dust." This led Beaudry to conclude:

> The industry seems to think that the number of compensated cases repre-

sents the air quality in the work environment. It seems that the [asbestos industry] wanted to prevent the payment of compensation more than the prevention of asbestosis.[2]

Judge Beaudry was appointed to investigate the Quebec asbestos industry shortly after an embarrassed provincial government was publicly accused of collaborating with the asbestos industry to cover up dangerous working conditions in Thetford's mines and mills. The Quebec asbestos unions based their allegations on asbestos air samples which had been collected illegally and in secret from the work environment. In 1976, the gathering of those samples led to the longest strike in the town's history. . . .

Since the 1949 recognition that "asbestos dust is harmful," the asbestos companies have indeed acted as if no "contractual obligation" exists to eliminate asbestos exposure. Quebec workers have continued to endure death and disease due to asbestos exposure. In the years 1970 to 1974, over two hundred and fifty asbestos cases were compensated in Quebec.[3] In 1974 alone, eighty-five workers were so severely damaged by asbestos fibres that they were awarded lifetime indemnities by the Workmen's Compensation Commission. Many more have succumbed to asbestos-related cancer.

Knowing what we know about the effects of asbestos on the body, it would seem sensible to have at least provided workers with precise information about the asbestos dust levels they worked in. Yet before the 1975 strike, access to government and company dust surveys had been repeatedly denied to Thetford workers—which explains Paul Formby's furtive air-sampling activity in Thetford's asbestos operations and the union militancy which resulted from the secret testing. . . .

The findings convinced the CNTU [Confederation of National Trade Unions] that a clinical survey of Thetford's asbestos workers was essential, and the union grimly urged Mount Sinai's [New York] experts to visit their area. Formby, who agreed to handle the logistical details of the proposed expedition, lobbied on behalf of the CNTU and helped to tip the hospital's decision in favour of a Quebec visit.

In the fall of 1974, a team of seven doctors and a group of technical experts openly travelled to Thetford Mines to examine the area's asbestos workers. Two Canadian doctors assisted the New York team. More than twelve hundred men who had drilled, blasted, and sweated a living in Thetford's mines and mills for twenty or more years were carefully examined.

Dr. Donald Haigh was one of the Canadian doctors who helped examine the workers. His initial evaluation was not comforting. "They were pretty sick people," he says, "and some of them were sick and didn't realize it. I met one fellow who had a symptom in his fingernail beds called clubbing,[4] which is a peripheral sign of lung disease. I said to him 'You have clubbing; you're sick; you have lung disease.'

"He was shocked! He was surprised! Then the man told me, 'I thought my fingers were like this because it was hereditary. You see, my father and all my brothers have clubbing.'

"To this man, being sick was part of his life. Everybody around him was sick. To him sickness was a natural way of life ..."

"These people," says Haigh, "are required to have a yearly examination and a chest X-ray at the industrial clinic, which is a clinic in Thetford supported by the companies. The industrial clinic classifies these men. People who are Class A have no disease and are allowed to work in the dust at their regular jobs. But I know that many of the people who were Class A, or at least Class A a few months before we saw them, were sick. And a lot of them knew they were sick. You would ask somebody if they had shortness of breath, and they'd say sure they had shortness of breath. You'd ask them if they had trouble climbing stairs, and they'd say sure they had trouble climbing stairs. These people weren't normal! How the industrial clinic arrived at their Class A classification I haven't any idea."

Jean-Baptiste Fortin, a former Thetford asbestos worker, insists that doctors at the medical clinic run jointly by the asbestos companies—Asbestos Corporation, Lake Asbestos of Quebec, Carey Canadian Mines, National Asbestos Mines, Bell Asbestos Mines—minimized the workers' health problems in order to protect the companies. Ever since his sixtieth birthday, Fortin has lived with a five-foot-high oxygen tank resting in the corner of his bedroom. Asbestosis has left him continually short of breath. He is forced to replenish his lungs with gulps of oxygen from the tank when his breathing problems intensify. The shortest walks leave him breathless. Even talking can be an effort and, as he relates his experience, beads of sweat glisten on his forehead.

"Every year we went for tests at the companies' clinic," he says, "and I was always Class A. I was always Class A until 1971 when I went to Montreal to get another opinion on asbestosis. There they decided to re-class me. The first time I went to Montreal they declared me 50 per cent incapacitated. In 1972, they declared me 100 per cent incapacitated. That's why I say the clinic was working for the companies, not for us."

On January 12, 1972, Emile St. Laurent received a Class A classification from the Thetford industrial clinic. On August 20, 1974, at the age of fifty-nine, Emile St. Laurent died of asbestosis.

Asbestosis does not creep up on its victims. A person is not free from asbestosis one day and debilitated with the lung disease the next. Mount Sinai doctors say that lung scarring due to asbestos exposure would be readily apparent on one's chest X-rays long before the disease snuffed out one's life.

Emile's widow, Dolores St. Laurent, is extremely bitter. "We never heard about it at all," she says. "He was always fine, classed as 'number one'. But since his last visit to the clinic you could see his health wasn't getting better. He was going from worse to worse. His breathing was really difficult. Most of the time he had trouble. And I'll tell you that most of the time around the house he did nothing …

"I knew that there was dust and that he worked there thirty-eight years, but I still blame the clinic because they gave these regular tests and we learned nothing from them. If only the industrial clinic had said something. They could have mentioned a spot on the lung or something like that. If only they'd said something. But they never did. Every year they never did."

Hervé Boutin is yet another asbestosis victim. His face is the colour of chalk and his conversation is liberally sprinkled with coughing and wheezing. "I went to the industrial clinic and they always told me I didn't have it," he says. "I even asked them once if I had it and they said, 'Oh, only a touch. Nothing worth mentioning.'

"Then I decided to go to Montreal. They told me I had it and classed me as having 25 per cent. The second year I went they classed me at 40 per cent. And the third time I returned, they put me at 60 per cent.

"I never believed them at the clinic and I told them so a few times. They said there's no dust on my lungs, but I knew there was anyway. Even better, I said to one of them, 'It's there but you don't want to tell us.' 'But sir,' he said, 'if we classified you anything other than A, you'd have to change jobs. That's why we classify you as A. But there's not enough dust to harm you.' That's what they told," says Boutin, with a touch of irony. "Not enough to harm you."

Dr. Paul Cartier ran the companies' clinic from 1940 until 1974. When the results of the Mount Sinai study were finally made public, Dr. Cartier openly stated that he hadn't always informed workers suffering from asbestosis of the full extent of their illness on humanitarian grounds: "I figured it was in their best interests to stay at their jobs. Besides, they didn't want to be reported ill and transferred to [a] lower-paying job where they might have earned as much as fifty dollars less a week." Cartier also noted that "even if they had left their work completely and gone on to drive cabs, for instance, it might not have arrested the progressive effects of asbestosis."

The evidence continues to mount showing that asbestos companies maintained a policy of not telling workers they were suffering from asbestos-related diseases until the men became physically disabled. In 1949, Dr. Kenneth Wallace Smith, then the medical officer for Johns-Manville Canada in Asbestos, Quebec, filed a health report with the asbestos company's head offices in the United States. The report indicates that Dr. Smith discussed the potential asbestos danger with Johns-Manville (JM) executives and records their reaction, which, according to Smith, was: "We know that we are producing disease in the employees who

manufacture these products and there is no question in my [our] mind that disease is being produced in non-JM employees who may use certain of these products." Smith noted in his report that asbestosis was "irreversible and permanent" and added "but as long as a man is not disabled it is felt he should not be told of his condition so that he can live and work in peace and the company can benefit by his many years of experience."

Smith's reports to Johns-Manville came to light through a series of recent lawsuits filed against U.S. asbestos companies by American asbestos disease victims. The victims allege that asbestos companies deliberately withheld information on the deadly effects of asbestos exposure from them.

ENDNOTES

1. Canada, Department of National Health and Welfare, *Report of the Asbestos Working Group*, P. Bergeron, L. Guinton, G. Schreiber and J.H. Smith (Ottawa, 1976), p. 5.

2. T. Beaudry, G. Lagrace and L. Jakau, *Rapport Préliminaire: Comité d'étude sur la salubrité dans l'industrie de l'amiante* (Avril, 1976), p. 39.

3. G. Schreiber et al., *Report of the Asbestosis Working Group*, p. 23.

4. Finger clubbing is a thickening of the tissue at the fingertips which often occurs with asbestosis.

| CASE 5 | Antonia Di Palma and Air Canada |

Canadian Labour Relations Board Reports, July 14, 1995. Report by Veronique L. Marleau, Canadian Labour Relations Board

Ms. Di Palma, an employee of Air Canada, has been working as a flight attendant for 24 years. She told the Board that on September 9, 1994, on a Toronto-Montreal flight, the last leg of a four-day cycle, she started to have a headache about 30 minutes before landing. She felt that there was a lack of air in the aircraft and asked Captain Smith, the chief pilot, to increase the airflow. The air pack was at the normal setting. He refused, explaining that the setting of the airflow was determined by the aircraft operating manual. He said that everything was normal (all the instruments showed normal air circulation) and asked her how the other flight attendants were feeling. She replied that she did not know. He asked her if she needed a doctor. No, she said, what she needed was more air. This was at a time when the flight crew were rushing to finish the service. She continued to work and then started to feel a pressure in her chest and to feel light headed. At this point the aircraft had started its descent. She felt dizzy and bent her head. She then told Mr. Roger Marcil, the purser, that she was sick. He gave her oxygen. As she was breathing through the mask, she told Mr. Marcil that she believed that the environment was dangerous to her health and asked him to tell the captain that she was refusing to work for the remainder of the flight. Roger Marcil left and when he came back, she asked him what he had told to the captain. He replied that he had said that she was refusing to work.

Believing that Ms. Di Palma was feeling sick, Captain Smith arranged for medical assistance upon arrival. He did not treat Ms. Di Palma's action as a refusal to work and, as a result, the procedure for work refusals on aircraft that are in operation was not followed and no investigation by the employer ... was undertaken upon arrival.

Mr. Leonard Lafleur, manager-customer services for Air Canada, and Mr. Luc Bergeron, Ms. Di Palma's supervisor and also a manager at Air Canada and co-chairperson of the Occupational Health and Safety Committee ("OH&S Committee") were nevertheless present upon arrival, along with a medical team and an ambulance. As Ms. Di Palma was coming out of the aircraft, she was asked whether she needed an ambulance. She said she did not. She then went to sit with Messrs. Bergeron and Lafleur in a quiet area. They asked her what had happened. She said that the captain had refused to increase the airflow. She had had previous discussions with Mr. Bergeron about this. She completed an injury report, the details of which she provided later. She did not say to either of them that she had exercised her right to refuse to work because, as she told the Board, she took it for granted that they knew. They told her to take her time, offered her a taxi, and Mr. Bergeron accompanied her home in the taxi....

On September 29, 1994, [Air Canada] issued a new technical bulletin which was immediately brought to the pilots' attention via the computer system and incorporated shortly thereafter in the company's aircraft operating manual, thus making it a compulsory procedure. That bulletin was aimed at rectifying the situation that had triggered Ms. Di Palma's refusal to work. It stated that pilots now had to select the HIGH setting any time a crew member requested it. The procedure already in existence since May 12, 1993 but which had been until then left to the pilot's discretion, was now rendered mandatory.

Ms. Di Palma, who in the meantime had resumed her regular duties as flight attendant and continued to work her normal flight cycle, was informed of the implementation of the technical bulletin. She considered this solution unsatisfactory and requested time to think about it. She then decided to continue to refuse to work pursuant to the Code and informed the employer of her decision. In Ms. Di Palma's opinion, the only adequate solution would be to leave the air flow on HIGH at all times, since there should be no need to have to ask the chief pilot for more air ...

The right to refuse to work and the process that must be followed when that right is exercised are set out in ss. 128 and 129 of the Code [R.S.C. 1985, c. 9 (1st Supp.), s. 4], the relevant parts of which provide as follows:

128.(1) Subject to this section, where an employee while at work has reasonable cause to believe that

(a) the use or operation of a machine or thing constitutes a danger to the employee or to another employee, or

(b) a condition exists in any place that constitutes a danger to the employee, the employee may refuse to operate the machine or thing or to work in that place.

(2) An employee may not pursuant to this section refuse to use or operate a machine or thing or to work in a place where

(a) the refusal puts the life, health or safety of another person directly in danger; or

(b) the danger referred to in subsection (1) is inherent in the employee's work or is a normal condition of employment.

(3) Where an employee on a ship or an aircraft that is in operation has reasonable cause to believe that

(a) the use or operation of a machine or thing on the ship or aircraft constitutes a danger to the employee or to another employee, or

(b) the condition exists in a place on the ship or aircraft that constitutes a danger to the employee

the employee shall forthwith notify the person in charge of the ship or aircraft of the circumstances of the danger and the person in charge shall, as soon as practicable thereafter, having regard to the safe operation of the ship or aircraft, decide whether or not the employee may discontinue the use or operation of the machine or thing or to work in that place and shall inform the employee accordingly.

(4) An employee who, pursuant to subsection (3), is informed that he may not discontinue the use or operation of a machine or thing or to work in a place shall not, while the ship or aircraft on which the employee is employed is in operation, refuse pursuant to this section to operate the machine or thing or to work in that place ...

Commenting on the notion of danger in an earlier decision [*LaBarge and Bell Canada*, (1981)] the Board explained the distinction between what constitutes a normal condition of work and what is a dangerous working environment ...

A certain degree of danger exists in most occupations but the risk of injury naturally varies from industry to industry. For example, bank employees are not exposed to the dangers normally faced by miners. A steel erector's normal day's work contains extreme danger as compared with a letter carrier's and we are now well aware of the risk of employment injury an asbestos worker is normally exposed to. Those are the normalities contemplated by subsection (12). It does not include unlawfully dangerous workplaces or work practices regardless of how normal they may have become to employees. In short, normal or standard work practices are a consideration when assessing whether or not a danger is so imminent that it prevents an employee from continuing to perform his duties. A finding that imminent danger does not exist under section 82.1 does not necessarily mean that danger does not actually exist or that remedial action or further inquiry is not required ...

For the purposes of these sections ... the risk cannot be something that is inherent in an employee's work or a normal condition of employment ... For example, a steeplejack could not refuse to work at heights because of a personal fear of heights. Working at heights is inherent in a steeplejack's work and it is also a normal condition of employment. If, however, icy conditions prevailed, the steeplejack could refuse to work in those conditions and would receive the full protection of the Code.

... [I]n order to meet the Code's definition, the danger must be immediate and real: in other words, the risk to the employee must be serious to the point where the work must stop until the situation is rectified, i.e. the source or the cause of danger removed. Evidently, this would not imply replacing one dangerous situation with another ... This also means that the risk must not originate from the employee's personal condition. Furthermore, the danger must be one that Parliament intended to cover ... Accordingly, this would exclude a danger arising from a situation where the risk is inherent in the employee's work or is a normal condition of work.

That interpretation is also in keeping with the spirit and purpose of the right of refusal which is designed as "an emergency measure to deal with dangerous situations which crop up unexpectedly," not as a primary vehicle to attain the objectives of ... the Code or as a "last resort" to bring existing disputes to a head or to settle longstanding disputes ...

Ms. Di Palma's safety concerns during the September 9, 1994 flight pertained to the sufficiency of the airflow on board the aircraft. This is what made her consider the environment dangerous to her health. In her report on the issue, she stated that she felt "a lack of air (HYPOXIA)" and, more particularly, a "lack of oxygen." Ms. Di Palma did not claim or suggest that the air quality *per se* was deficient in the sense that her safety was endangered by exposure to a hazardous substance. In other words, she did not claim that the air was contaminated; what she claimed was that there was not enough air. Thus, although the safety concern under consideration here clearly falls under the overall air quality heading, it is one of air quantity, not one of air quality *per se*.

This was made clear in Ms. Di Palma's November 16, 1994 written confirmation to the company concerning her decision to continue to refuse to work. We will recall that prior to this, the company had taken steps to rectify the situation that had triggered Ms. Di Palma's refusal to work by issuing a new technical bulletin in which the selection of the pack's HIGH setting any time a crew member requested it was rendered mandatory. In support of her decision to continue to refuse to work, Ms. Di Palma stated:

> Mr. Lafleur, I am READY and WILLING to work my flight tomorrow morning but only if I am guaranteed in writing that the airflow will be on maximum at all times, on all air-

crafts [sic], no matter what the load is and without having to ask the pilots for more air once I am already feeling the symptoms of lack of oxygen, because at this point the damage to my body has already been done.

I have repeatedly suffered deprivation of oxygen on my flights and my physical and mental health has [sic] been affected by it. I can no longer continue to do so.

Thus, the issue to be determined here is whether ... the quantity of air available for flight attendants on board the aircraft involved in Ms. Di Palma's work refusal constituted a danger to the employee ...

We must remember that the danger contemplated by the Code must be so immediate and real that all work activity must be interrupted until the situation is corrected. This was clearly not the case here ... The purported danger was not one contemplated by the Code. At best, it was a condition inherent to Ms. Di Palma's work, although one which, as everyone recognizes, is in need of constant monitoring and improvement. At worst, it was a personal condition. It may very well be that Ms. Di Palma is more sensitive to this type of environment than the greater majority of people. However, if this is the case, this is not a relevant factor since the danger contemplated must originate from the environment, not from the person who feels it.

Undoubtedly, the issue of airflow and, more generally, of overall air quality is a very sensitive one for all parties involved and a very emotional one for Ms. Di Palma. This was reflected in the great care everyone took in presenting their case. However, there is no doubt either that the safety issue which is at the source of the purported danger invoked here is an ongoing one. The situation that triggered Ms. Di Palma's work refusal

was no more than the crystallization of a longstanding dispute concerning the procedure governing airflow on board A320 aircraft. The problem is not new, and discussions about airflow and overall air quality have been ongoing for some time between the company and [the Canadian Union of Public Employees] through the OH&S Committee. These problems are not limited to the A320 fleet. Ms. Di Palma does not deny this. In fact, she referred several times to her history of difficulties in this regard during various flights, some of which were not on the A320 aircraft.

The symptoms experienced by flight attendants, such as fatigue, headache, tiredness, nausea and illness are often attributed to cabin air quality. However, that assumption still remains to be confirmed. Other studies suggest that those symptoms are more likely due to an interaction of factors that include cabin altitude, flight duration, jet lag, turbulence, noise, work levels, dehydration, and an individual's health and stress. Given this, it has been recognized that there was a need both for further study and monitoring of the situation as well as for the development of standards adapted to the uniqueness of the cabin environment ...

Even though the situation which triggered Ms. Di Palma's refusal did not constitute a danger within the meaning of the Code, it was certainly one for which remedial action and further inquiry were required. Air Canada responded to the concerns expressed, having since taken steps to correct the situation. Although the changes brought to the procedure governing the use of air packs did not satisfy Ms. Di Palma, this nevertheless represented a significant improvement to the situation that prevailed prior to her refusal. Ms. Di Palma insisted that the airflow setting be left on high at all times, a position which was endorsed by CUPE.

In this regard, we should point out that the evidence adduced indicated rather that such a solution may prove more problematic than the one it is meant to correct. A system built to function at a normal setting cannot be used consistently at maximum capacity without the possibility of creating safety hazards, such as premature deterioration of the aircraft, as well as causing other types of discomfort which, for some people, may prove to be less tolerable than for the ones who are insisting on that solution.

Taking everything into consideration, we agree ... that danger within the meaning of the Code did not exist as far as Ms. Di Palma's work environment was concerned on that September 9, 1994.

SUGGESTED READINGS

Badaracco, Jr. *Loading the Dice: A Five-County Study of Vinyl Chloride Regulation.* Boston: Harvard Business School Press, 1985.

Beattie, Margaret. "Women, Unions, and Social Policy." *Journal of Business Ethics*, Vol. 2, No. 3 (August 1983), pp. 227–231.

Berman, Daniel. *Death on the Job.* New York: Monthly Review Press, 1978.

Curran, Daniel. "Regulating Safety: A Case of Symbolic Action." In J. Desjardins and J. McCall (eds.), *Contemporary Issues in Business Ethics*. Belmont, California: Wadsworth Publishing Company, 1985.

Deutsch, Steven. "Introduction: Theme Issue on Occupational Safety and Health." *Labor Studies Journal*, 6, 1, pp. 3–6.

Dewey, Martin. *Smoke in the Workplace.* Toronto: Non-Smokers' Rights Association Smoking and Health Action Foundation, 1985.

Faden, Ruth R. "The Right to Risk Information and the Right to Refuse Health Hazards in the Workplace." In T. Beauchamp and N. Bowie (eds.), *Ethical Theory and Business*, 2nd ed. Englewood Cliffs, NJ: Prentice-Hall, 1983.

Grcic, J. "Democratic Capitalism: Developing a Conscience for the Corporation." *Journal of Business Ethics*, 5, 2, 1985, pp. 145–150

Hitt, Michael, Amos Orley, Jr., and Larkin Warner. "Social Factors and Company Location Decisions: Technology, Quality of Life and Quality of Work Life Concerns." *Journal of Business Ethics*, Vol. 2, No. 2 (May 1983), pp. 89–99.

Hitt, Michael. "Technology, Organizational Crime and Effectiveness." *Journal of Business Research*, 1976, pp. 378–397.

Jain, Harish C. "Management of Human Resources and Productivity." *Journal of Business Ethics*, Vol. 2, No. 4 (November 1983), pp. 273–289.

Lagrega, M.P. Buckingham and J. Evans. *Hazardous Waste Management.* New York: McGraw-Hill, 1994.

MacCarthy, Mark. "A Review of Some Normative and Conceptual Issues in Occupational Safety." In J. Desjardins and J. McCall (eds.), *Contemporary Issues in Business Ethics*. Belmont, California: Wadsworth Publishing Company, 1985.

Neyman, J. "Public Health Hazards from Electricity-Producing Plants." *Science*, 1977.

Nielsen, Richard P. "Should Executives Be Jailed for Consumer and Employee Health and Safety Violations?" *The Journal of Consumer Affairs*, 13, 1979, pp. 128–134.

Rashke, Richard. *The Killing of Karen Silkwood: The Story Behind the Kerr-McGee Plutonium Case.* Boston: Houghton-Mifflin Co. 1981.

Shaw, W and V. Barry (eds.). *Moral Issues in Business*, 6th edn. Belmont California: Wadsworth, 1995.

Tremblay, Henri. "Organizational Development at Steinberg's Limited: A Case Study." In H. Jain and R. Kanungo (eds.), *Behavioural Issues in Management: the Canadian Context*. Toronto: McGraw-Hill Ryerson, 1977.

EMPLOYEE LOYALTY AND MORAL INDEPENDENCE

INTRODUCTION

In Part 2 of this text, various authors discussed the moral status of corporations. They asked such questions as the following: Can corporations be considered to be moral agents in the same way in which persons are considered to be moral agents? And, who should be held accountable for corporate wrongdoing?

In Part 4, we will discuss these and similar issues from the perspective of the worker. What, for example, are the limitations that a corporation may justifiably impose upon individual decision-making? Does loyalty to a company which is, after all, performing a useful service to the public through its business activity, require the individual to support company policy even when the policy contravenes the individual's personal beliefs? Should there be legal protection for employees who "blow the whistle" on corporate wrongdoing?

You will recall from the introduction to this text, "Ethical Theory in Business," that contemporary moral philosophy, as well as common parlance with regard to morality, stresses the notion of rights. Generally speaking, when individuals refer to rights in the context of expressing personal beliefs or values contrary to those of an employer, they are referring to Hohfeld's concepts of liberties or privileges, as outlined in the introduction. A Toronto police officer who refused to enforce a trespassing law because he did not agree with the law concerning access to abortion argued that his paid occupation did not involve duties to act in ways contrary to his religious belief system. The officer believed that in such a case, he should have a "freedom from duty" or the liberty to follow his own conscience. Conversely, companies have in the past argued that they should not be held responsible for individuals' decision-making on behalf of the company when that decision-making is illegal and/or immoral.

All these questions take on even greater significance in the case of the government employee upon whom the demands of loyalty may pull in more than one direction. One might ask whether civil servants are, for example, employees of the people or of the political party in power. Government employees are, needless to say, often required to enforce laws and carry out policies that have considerable impact on the social and economic conditions of life in Canada. And, of course, political elections often result in new governments with new policies. In the light of these facts, important questions arise. For instance, should government employees be permitted publicly to question government policies with which they disagree? Do they have the right to campaign actively against those policies? If so, do those rights extend as far as do the rights of people who do not work for their government?

Unions and professional groups often demand unconditional loyalty as well. The 1986 Ontario doctor's strike raised serious questions about demands that are sometimes made in the name of group solidarity or loyalty. In this case, physicians were asked to support a province-wide strike and to force the closure of emergency hospital wards, despite the acknowledged risks to patients. Are such demands morally defensible on grounds of loyalty? Should a doctor feel obliged by membership in a collegial association to pursue a course of action he might otherwise find morally objectionable? These are some of the many questions we will explore in this section.

In "The Loyal Agent's Argument," Alex Michalos argues that even in a hypothetically simplified case in which we assume that an individual blindly and unthinkingly attempts to serve her company's interests, the appeal to loyal agency as a defence will not logically make sense.

Deborah Poff extends Michalos's argument in "The Loyal Agent's Argument Revisited," and states that even if we examine complex appeals to loyal agency on the part of more intelligent loyal agents, the appeal will still not work. Poff's contention is that loyal agency arguments are never adequate to absolve individuals from responsibility for knowingly doing what is wrong.

In our next article, Frederick Elliston discusses whether employees are justified in anonymously blowing the whistle on employers who are engaged in immoral or illegal activities. Blowing the whistle on an employer can result in the loss of a job or the possibility of being harassed in the workplace or discriminated against in future employment. This would seem to suggest that employees should be allowed to blow the whistle on company wrongdoing anonymously. However, this leaves the door open for a hostile employee to abuse the employer with false accusations of wrongdoing. If an employee wants to get even with a company (perhaps for overlooking him in job promotion), the employee could falsely accuse the company of wrongdoing. Elliston reviews many of the arguments for and against anonymous whistleblowing, and concludes with a defence of the practice as a means to redress corporate wrongdoing.

Mike Martin examines various positions on the obligation to whistleblow among engineers. The position he takes is that there is a *prima facie* obligation to blow the whistle under conditions in which "one has good reason to believe there is a serious moral problem, has exhausted normal organizational channels . . . has available a reasonable amount of documentation, and has reasonable hope of solving the problem by blowing the whistle." Martin does not believe such obligation is absolute, and provides examples, the context of which would suggest that individuals may reasonably appeal to other obligations as mitigating circumstances.

This part of the text ends with a famous case study referred to at the beginning of Martin's article: the *Challenger* disaster. The case details the ethical dimensions of the *Challenger* disaster and relates the experience of senior scientist Roger Boisjoly and other colleagues who repeatedly tried to convince authorities of the fatal flaw in the design of the *Challenger*'s *O*-rings. Both before and after the disaster, Boisjoly found his knowledge questioned, ignored, and suppressed. As the authors note, "Boisjoly's experiences could well serve as a paradigmatic case study for . . . ethical problems, ranging from accountability to corporate loyalty and whistle-blowing."

THE LOYAL
AGENT'S
ARGUMENT

Alex C. Michalos

INTRODUCTION

According to the Report of the Special Review Committee of the Board of Directors of Gulf Oil Corporation:

> It is not too much to say that the activity of those Gulf officials involved in making domestic political contributions with corporate funds during the period of approximately fourteen years under review [1960–1974] was shot through with illegality. The activity was generally clandestine and in disregard of federal, as well as a number of state, statutes.[1]

Nevertheless, and more importantly for our purposes, the Committee apparently endorsed the following judgment, which was submitted by their lawyers to the U.S. Securities and Exchange Commission.

> No evidence has been uncovered or disclosed which establishes that any offi-

cer, director or employee of Gulf personally profited or benefited by or through any use of corporate funds for contributions, gifts, entertainment or other expenses related to political activity. Further, Gulf has no reason to believe or suspect that *the motive of the employee or officer* involved in such use of corporate funds was anything other than a *desire to act solely in what he considered to be the best interests of Gulf and its shareholders.*[2] [Emphasis added.]

If we accept the views of the Committee and their lawyers, then we have before us an interesting case of individuals performing illegal actions with altruistic motives. What they did was admittedly illegal, but they meant well. They had good intentions, namely, to further "the best interests of Gulf and its shareholders." Furthermore, there is no suggestion in these passages or in the rest

This paper was written for the Conference on Ethics and Economics at the University of Delaware, Newark, Delaware, November 10–12, 1977. Copyright © 1978 by Alex C. Michalos. Reprinted by permission of the author.

of the report that the officials were ordered to commit such acts. They were not ordered. On the contrary, the acts seem to have emerged as practically natural by-products of some employees' zeal in looking after their employer's interests. They are, we might say, the result of overzealous attempts of agents to fulfill their fiducial obligations.

In the following paragraphs I am going to pursue this apparently plausible account of overzealous behavior to its bitter end. That is, I'm going to assume for the sake of argument that there really are reasonable people who would and do perform immoral and illegal actions with altruistic motives, i.e., there are people who would and do perform such actions with reasons that they regard as good in some fairly general sense. It's not to be assumed that they are shrewd enough to see that their own interests lie in the advancement of their employer's or client's interests. They are not, I'm assuming, cleverly egoistic. If anything, they are stupidly altruistic by hypothesis. But that's beside the point now. What I want to do is construct a generalized form of an argument that I imagine would be attractive to such agents, whether or not any of them has or will ever formulate it exactly so. Then I want to try to demolish it once and for all.

THE ARGUMENT

What I will call the Loyal Agent's Argument (LAA) runs as follows:

1. *As a loyal agent of some principal, I ought to serve his interests as he would serve them himself if he had my expertise.*

2. He would serve his own interests in a thoroughly egoistic way.

   Therefore, as a loyal agent of this principal, I ought to operate in a thoroughly egoistic way in his behalf.

   Some clarification is in order. First, in order to make full use of the fairly substantial body of legal literature related to the *law*

of agency, I have adopted some of the standard legal jargon. In particular, following Powell, I'm assuming that "*an agent is a person who is authorised to act for a principal and has agreed so to act, and who has power to affect the legal relations of his principal with a third party.*"[3] The standard model is an insurance agent who acts in behalf of an insurance company, his principal, to negotiate insurance contracts with third parties. More generally, lawyers, real estate agents, engineers, doctors, dentists, stockbrokers, and the Gulf Oil zealots may all be regarded as agents of some principal. Although for some purposes one might want to distinguish agents from employees, such a distinction will not be necessary here. The definition given above is broad enough to allow us to think of coal miners, Avon Ladies, zoo attendants, and Ministers of Parliament as agents.

Second, as our definition suggests, there are typically three important relationships involved in agency transactions, namely, those between agent and principal, agent and third party, and principal and third party. The law of agency has plenty to say about each of these relationships, while LAA is primarily concerned with only the first, the fiducial relation between agent and principal. It would be a mistake to regard this as mere oversight. Few of us are immune to the buck-passing syndrome. Most of us are inclined to try to narrow the range of activities for which we are prepared to accept responsibility and, at the same time, widen the range of activities over which we are prepared to exercise authority. Notwithstanding the psychological theory of cognitive dissonance, most human beings seem to have sufficient mental magnanimity to accommodate this particular pair of incompatible inclinations. Like the insects, we are very adaptable creatures.

Third, I imagine that someone using an argument like LAA would, in the first place, be interested in trying to establish the fact that agents have a moral obligation to operate in a thoroughly egoistic way in their principals' behalf. If most LAA users in fact are primarily concerned with establishing their legal obligations, then perhaps what I have to say will be less interesting than I imagine to most people. Nevertheless, I'm assuming that the force of "ought" in the first premise and conclusion is moral rather than legal. For our purposes it doesn't matter what sort of an ontological analysis one gives to such obligations or what sort of a moral theory one might want to use to justify one's moral principles. It only has to be appreciated that LAA is designed to provide a moral justification for the behavior prescribed in its conclusion.

Fourth, an agent may be regarded as operating in a thoroughly egoistic way if all his actions are designed to optimize his own interests and he has no inclination at all to identify the interests of anyone else with his own. (Throughout the essay I usually let the masculine "he" abbreviate "he or she.") He may very well be a self-confident, self-starting, self-sustaining, and self-controlled individual. These are all commendable personal characteristics. But he must be selfish, self-centered, and/or self-serving. In conflict situations when there are not enough benefits to satisfy everyone, he will try to see that his own needs are satisfied, whatever happens to the needs of others. He is more interested in being first than in being nice, and he assumes that everyone else is too. He may harbor the suspicion that if everyone behaved as he does, the world's resources would be used in a maximally efficient way and everyone would be materially better off. But these are secondary considerations at best. His first consideration, which he regards as only prudent or smart, is to look out for *Numero Uno*, himself.

Fifth, to say that an agent is supposed to operate in a thoroughly egoistic way in behalf of his principal is just to say that the agent is supposed to act as he believes his principal would act if his principal were an egoist. The agent is supposed to conduct the affairs of his principal with the single-minded purpose of optimizing the latter's interests and not yielding them to anyone else's interests.

THE SECOND PREMISE

Now we should be talking the same language. The question is: Is the Loyal Agent's Argument sound? Can its conclusion be established or even well-supported by its premises? I think there are good reasons for giving a negative answer to these questions. Moreover, since the argument has been deliberately formulated in a logically valid form, we may proceed immediately to a closer investigation of the content of its premises.

Let's consider the second premise first. This premise can only be regarded as true of people *a priori* if one of the assumptions we have made for the sake of argument about human motivation is false. Following the quotations from the Special Review Committee, it was pointed out that the case involved agents who apparently performed illegal actions with altruistic motives. What they did wrong, they did in behalf of Gulf Oil Corporation. Fair enough. However, if it's possible to perform illegal but altruistically motivated acts, it must be possible to perform legal but altruistically motivated acts as well. The very assumption required to give the argument initial plausibility also ensures that its second premise cannot be assumed to be generally true *a priori*. Since some people can perform nonegoistically motivated actions, the second premise of LAA requires some defense. Moreover, broadly speaking there are two directions such a defense might take, and I will consider each in turn.

Granted that users of LAA cannot consistently regard every individual as a thoroughly egoistic operator and hence guarantee the truth of the second premise *a priori*, it is still possible to try to defend this premise as a well-confirmed empirical hypothesis. That is, admitting that there are exceptions, one might still claim that if one acted as if the second premise were true, much more often than not one would be right. This is the sort of line economists have traditionally taken toward their idealized rational economic man. They realize that people are capable of altruistic action, but they figure that the capability is seldom exercised and they design their hypotheses, laws, and theories accordingly.

So far as business is concerned, the egoistic line seems to be translated into profit maximization. According to Goodman, for example:

> The Wall Street rule for persons legally charged with the management of other people's money runs as follows: Invest funds in a company with the aim of gaining the best financial return with the least financial risk for the trust beneficiaries. If you later come to disagree with the company's management, sell the stock.[4]

Similarly, in a cautious version of LAA, Friedman has claimed that:

> In a free-enterprise, private-property system, a corporate executive is an employee of the owners of the business. He has a direct responsibility to his employers. That responsibility is to conduct the business in accordance with their desires, which generally will be to make as much money as possible while conforming to the basic rules of the society, both those embodied in law and those embodied in ethical customs.[5]

Instead of challenging the accuracy of these assessments of the motives of people generally or of businessmen in the marketplace in particular now, I want to grant it straightaway for the sake of the argument. The question is: How does that affect LAA?

As you may have guessed, users of LAA are not much better off than they were. If it's a good bet that the second premise is true, then it's an equally good bet that anyone inclined to defend his actions with LAA is not an altruistic operator. No one can have it both ways. Evidence for the empirical hypothesis that people generally act as egoists is evidence for the truth of the second premise and the falsehood of the alleged altruistic motives of anyone using LAA. In short, the premise is still self-defeating.

Corporate Principals

Instead of regarding the second premise as an empirical claim about real people and attempting to support it inductively, one might treat it as a logical claim justifiable by an appeal to the definitions of some of its key terms. This looks like a very promising strategy when one considers the fact that many contemporary principals, like Gulf Oil Corporation, for example, are abstract entities. Corporate persons are, after all, nothing but fictional persons invented by people with fairly specific aims. In particular, corporations have been invented to assist in the accumulation of material assets. While they typically accomplish many different tasks, the accumulation of assets is generally regarded as their basic aim. Thus, if one's principal happens to be a corporation, one might reasonably argue that it is by definition thoroughly egoistic. The business of such entities is certainly business, because that is their very reason for being, the very point of inventing them in the first place. So, the second premise of LAA could be substantiated by definitional fiat....

Apparently, then, morally conscientious corporate agents may find themselves facing lawsuits if they assume their principals are not self-serving profit maximizers and act accordingly. Legal niceties aside, there is a thought-provoking moral argument in favor of agents acting as if their principals were just as the designers of corporate law imagine them. That is, if any particular stockholder wants to give his money away or to pursue any aims other than profit maximization, he is free to do so. Investors should be and almost certainly are aware that corporations are designed to make money. If they have other aims, they shouldn't be investing in corporations. If they don't have other aims and they go into corporations with their eyes wide open, then they should appreciate and respect the interests of others who have gone in with them.

In principle, the defense of the second premise of LAA on the grounds of the defining characteristic of corporations may be challenged as before. Insofar as corporations are defined as egoistic corporate persons (a rough abbreviated definition, to be sure), a serious question arises concerning the morality of becoming an agent for them—not to mention inventing them in the first place. The evils of unbridled egoism are well known and they aren't mitigated by the fact that the egoist in question is a corporate person. If anything, they are magnified because of the difficulties involved in assigning responsibility and holding corporations liable to their activities. It is demonstrably certain that if everyone only attends to what he perceives as his own interests, a socially self-destructive result may occur. That is the clear message of prisoner's dilemma studies. It's also the message of two kids in a playpen who finally tear the toys apart rather than share them.

As before, it will not help to argue that in developed countries most people work for corporations or they don't work at all. Again, self-preservation is not altruism. To serve an evil master in the interests of survival is not to serve in the interests of altruism, and users of LAA are supposed to be motivated by altruism. On the other hand, insofar as corporations are not defined as egoistic corporate persons and are granted more or less benevolent if not downright altruistic aims, the truth of the second premise of LAA is again open to question. In either case, then, an agent trying to salvage LAA

with this sort of definitional defense is bound to find the task self-defeating.

THE FIRST PREMISE

Let's turn now to the first premise of LAA. In a way it's as innocuous as motherhood and apple pie. Every discussion I've read of the duties of agents according to agency law in North America and the United Kingdom has included some form of this premise. For example, Powell says, "An agent has a general duty to act solely for the benefit of his principal in all matters connected with the execution of his authority."[6] The *American Restatement of the Law of Agency* says that "an agent is subject to a duty to his principal to act solely for the benefit of the principal in all matters connected with his agency."[7] According to a standard Canadian textbook on business law, "Good faith requires that the agent place the interest of his principal above all else except the law."[8]

The only trouble with the premise is that its limitations are not clearly built into it. In this respect it is like most moral principles and rules of law. Short of turning every principle and rule into a self-contained treatise, it's impossible to indicate every possible exception.... However, the *American Restatement of the Law of Agency* makes it quite clear that "In no event would it be implied that an agent has a duty to perform acts which ... are illegal or unethical."[9] Moreover, "In determining whether or not the orders of the principal to the agent are reasonable ... business or professional ethics ... are considered."[10] Powell also remarks that agents have no duty "to carry out an illegal act."[11] ... Thus, there is no doubt at all that the first premise of LAA cannot be regarded as a licence to break the law. No respectable court would permit it. In fact, although the courts have no special jurisdiction over moral law, they have shown no reluctance to condemn immoral acts allegedly performed in the interests of fulfilling fiduciary obligations.

Illegality and immorality aside, the first premise still gives up much more than any sane person should be willing to give up. It virtually gives a principal licence to use an agent in any way the principal pleases, so long as the agent's activity serves the principal's interest. For example, suppose a life insurance agent agrees to sell State Farm Insurance on commission. It would be ludicrous to assume that the agent has also committed himself to painting houses, washing dogs, or doing anything else that happened to give his principal pleasure. It would also be misleading to describe such an open-ended commitment as an agreement to sell insurance. It would more accurately be described as selling oneself into bondage. Clearly, then, one must assume that the first premise of LAA presupposes some important restrictions that may have nothing to do with any sort of law.

Since they are apparently drawn from and applicable to ordinary affairs and usage, perhaps it would be instructive to mention some of the principles developed in the law of agency to address this problem. You may recall that the definition of an agent that we borrowed from Powell explicitly referred to a person being "authorised to act for a principal." An agent's duties are typically limited to a set of activities over which he is granted authority by his principal.... [This] ... would be sufficient to prevent the exploitation of the hypothetical insurance agent in the preceding paragraph.

Besides a carefully developed set of principles related to the granting of authority, the law of agency recognizes some other general duties of agents like the previously considered duty of good faith. For example, an agent is expected to "exercise due care and skill in executing his authority."[12] This obviously serves the interests of all concerned, and there are plenty of principles and precedents available to explain "due care and skill." ... He is expected to "keep proper accounts," i.e., accounts that clearly distinguish his principal's assets from his own....[13]

Keeping the preceding guidelines in mind, perhaps some form of LAA can be salvaged by tightening up the first premise. Let's suppose I'm in the advertising business and I want to use LAA by suitably restricting the scope of the first premise thus:

> 1a. *As a loyal advertising agent of some company, I ought to advertise its products as they would advertise them if they had my expertise.*

That would require a consistent modification of the second premise and conclusion, but we need not worry about that. The question is: Does this reformulated premise 1a escape the kinds of criticism leveled against premise 1?

Certainly not. If the company happens to be run by a bunch of thoroughly unscrupulous thugs, it could be immoral and illegal to advertise their products as they would if they had the agent's expertise. Even if the company is run by fools who really don't know what they make, it could be immoral and illegal to advertise their products as they would if they had the agent's expertise. For example, if the company's directors are smart enough to know that they can make more money selling drugs than they can make selling candy, but dumb enough to think that the candy they make is an effective drug, an agent could hardly be under any obligation to advertise their product as a marvelous new drug, i.e., assuming that the agent was smart enough to know that his employers were only capable of producing candy.

If you think the agent could have such an obligation, what would be its source? Clearly it is not enough to say that the agent is employed by the company. That would be tantamount to appealing to LAA in order to establish a version of its own first premise, i.e., it would be a circular salvaging effort. Something else is required to support premise 1a....

CONCLUSION

The announced aim of this essay was to destroy LAA once and for all. I think that has been done. It is perhaps worthwhile to emphasize that if people use LAA when, as we saw earlier, the real reason for their actions is fear (or job preservation) then they will be circulating a distorted view of the world and decreasing the chances of reform. Thus, in the interests of a clear perception and resolution of social problems related to responsible human agency, LAA deserves the sort of treatment it has received here.

ENDNOTES

1. J.J. McCloy, N.W. Pearson, and B. Matthews, *The Great Oil Spill* (New York: Chelsea House, 1976), p. 31.

2. Ibid., p. 13.

3. R. Powell, *The Law of Agency* (London: Sir Isaac Pitman and Sons, Ltd., 1965), p. 7.

4. W. Goodman, "Stocks Without Sin," Minneapolis Star and Tribune Co., Inc. Reprinted in R. Baum (ed.), *Ethical Arguments for Analysis* (New York: Holt, Rinehart & Winston, 1975), p. 206.

5. M. Friedman, "The Social Responsibility of Business Is to Increase Its Profits," see p. 41 ff. of this book.

6. Powell, *The Law of Agency*, p. 312.

7. Section 387 as quoted in P.I. Blumberg, "Corporate Responsibility and the Employee's Duty of Loyalty and Obedience: A Preliminary Inquiry," *The Corporate Dilemma*, ed. D. Votaw and S.P. Sethi (Englewood Cliffs, N.J.: Prentice-Hall, Inc., 1973), p. 87.

8. J.E. Smyth and D.A. Soberman, *The Law and Business Administration in Canada* (Toronto: Prentice-Hall of Canada, Ltd., 1968), p. 360.

9. Section 385 as quoted in Blumberg, "Corporate Responsibility," p. 86.

10. Ibid.

11. Powell, *The Law of Agency*, p. 302.

12. Ibid., p. 303.

13. Ibid., p. 321.

THE LOYAL AGENT'S
ARGUMENT REVISITED

Deborah C. Poff

Michalos has done an admirable job of illustrating the flaws in the reasoning of the "illogically altruistic" loyal agent. Though there may be some cases of such stupidly altruistic loyalty, I don't think that such altruism accounts for all or for the most interesting loyal agents. It is the more complex, intelligent loyal agent that I wish to discuss in this paper.

Michalos's naively altruistic loyal agent argues as follows:

1. As a loyal agent of some principal, I ought to serve his interests as he would serve them himself if he had my expertise.

2. He would serve his own interests in a thoroughly egoistic way.

    Therefore, as a loyal agent of this principal, I ought to operate in a thoroughly egoistic way in his behalf.[1]

It certainly does seem imprudent to accept this argument so unconditionally: it matters not what the interests of the principal are, the loyal agent will serve them. More interesting, I believe, are the cases of the intelligent misinformed (or willfully ignorant, or, even perhaps, evil) loyal agent. This loyal agent might argue as follows:

1. As a loyal agent of this specific principal (in whose aims and goals I believe) I ought to serve that principal's interests as she or he, given my expertise, would serve them.

2. The principal would serve them in a single-minded way to achieve her or his goals maximally.

    Therefore, as a loyal agent of this principal, I ought to operate in a single-minded way to achieve her or his goals maximally.

Now let's fill out our intelligently misinformed loyal agent's story. In this case, the ILA (Intelligent Loyal Agent) believes in the supremacy of the white race. The ILA be-

---

This article was written especially for the first edition of this book.

lieves that god and science have proven this to be true and is well-versed in both theological and bio-determinist accounts which support these beliefs. Consequently, the ILA has chosen to work for and help build a multinational corporation which exploits non-whites globally. This not only serves to maximize profit for white stockholders, it also serves to preserve the proper order of things. Let's further assume that the global community has finally resolved to condemn apartheid and through a global resolution begins court trials to assess the legal responsibility of key players in corporations which supported apartheid in South Africa. The ILA finds her/himself on the stand. The ILA trots out the ILAA (Intelligent Loyal Agent's Argument). Premise 1 of the ILAA states that as a loyal agent of this specific principal (in whose aims and goals I believe) I ought to serve her or his interests as she or he would serve them if she or he had my expertise. However, just as in Michalos' case, the ILA finds that Premise 1 of the ILAA will not absolve her/him from responsibility.

To the extent that this premise is appealed to solely on the grounds of loyal agency, it won't wash for the same reasons that Michalos cited. As Michalos argues, in addition to considerations of illegality and immorality, "the first premise gives up much more than any sane person should be willing to give up." If Premise 1 is accepted on the grounds of loyal agency, its perimeters are unlimited. Thus, Premise 1 implies that the loyal agent could give up all possibility of future rational decision-making (perhaps through the ingestion of loyal agents' loyalty potion). No premise with such unlimited scope can be appealed to on rational and moral grounds.

On the other hand, if the ILA appeals to Premise 1 because she or he personally be-lieves in what the principal stands for, then the ILA is stating a personal belief for which she or he can and should be held responsible. To appeal to loyal agency in such a case, is subterfuge. In this case, the alleged loyal agent is loyal because of that agent's acceptance of apartheid. Put another way, the agent's loyalty is fundamentally to apartheid and secondarily to her or his principal. The agent's primary interest is precisely the same as that of her or his principal, namely, apartheid. The agent's appeal to loyal agency is a misleading and unsuccessful (logically) attempt to win support for the morally unacceptable institution of apartheid.

Hence, both stupid and intelligent loyal agents find themselves on the hook. Michalos notes that in many discussions of loyal agency it is explicitly stated that there are limits to loyalty, whether these be stated as legal or ethical limitations. This is what we would and should expect. We have no evidence to believe that individuals as a rule become morally impaired when they work. However, we do have evidence to believe that some individuals find reason to join certain companies, to support certain practices and to benefit from certain immoral and/or illegal acts.

If we have reason to believe, which I doubt, that corporations brainwash those who enter them, we may have further reasons for substantially revising and strengthening our structures to ensure corporate moral accountability. In any case, we should demand that individuals, whether employed or not, assume responsibility for their decision making.

ENDNOTE

1. Alex C. Michalos, "The Loyal Agent's Argument." See p. 196 ff., this text.

ANONYMITY AND
WHISTLEBLOWING

Frederick A. Elliston

A. IDENTIFYING THE PHENOMENON

Whistleblowing is a practice that can be defined in various ways. In the literature to date, the following four definitions are among the clearest:

(a) going public with information about the safety of a product;[1]

(b) sounding an alarm from within the very organization in which [an employee] works, aiming to spotlight neglect or abuses that threaten the public interest;[2]

(c) (when) the employee, "without support or authority from his superiors ... independently makes known concerns to individuals outside the organization."[3]

(d) A whistleblower is an employee or officer of any institution, profit or nonprofit, private or public, who believes either that he/she has been ordered to perform some act or he/she has obtained knowledge that the institution is engaged in activities which (a) are believed to cause unnecessary harm to third parties, (b) are in violation of human rights or (c) run counter to the defined purpose of the institution and who informs the public of this fact.[4]

My purpose in this first section is not to appraise the practice but identify it. Accordingly, in discussing these definitions and other elements of the concept, I shall 'build in' no prejudices or biases—either in favor of or opposition to the practice, for otherwise the argument over justification becomes merely a verbal quibble.

To begin with, we must recognize we are dealing with a metaphor. Though 'whistleblowing' serves to connote an *action*, the reality is quite different. Typically several actions are involved in a *process* of

From the *Journal of Business Ethics*, Vol. 1, No. 3, 1982, pp. 167–177. Reprinted by permission of the author.

blowing the whistle—even if we exclude those events which lead up to the 'act' and follow it: someone calls a meeting of fellow employees, arranges interviews with the media, responds to questions, qualifies statements and counters objections.[5] Though we can treat whistleblowing as one act, to be more precise we should from the outset be aware that we are dealing much more with a *series of actions*, a process. With this caveat, what are the features of this process that distinguish it from others?

All four definitions refer to the transfer of information. Accordingly, whistleblowing can be characterized as a mode of *communication*. But it is distinctive in several respects.

First, what is communicated? De George identifies the subject of the communication as the *safety* of a product. Clearly this is one possible content, and typical for his domain of inquiry—engineering. But it is not the only one. Bok speaks of *abuses* and *neglect*. In view of Frank Serpico, the cop who blew the whistle on New York City's finest, one can add *corruption*.[6] And if one thinks of Ernest Fitzgerald, who blew the whistle on illegal or unwarranted payoffs to Lockheed, one can speak of *bribery*, *mismanagement*, and *inefficiency*.[7] Is there a more precise way to characterize the common elements in the above cases and definitions that is more informative than Chalk/von Hippel's 'concerns'? Bowie's definition attempts this.

He stipulates the information must concern activities believed to cause unnecessary harm to third parties. Consider each element of his definition in turn. First, the information deals with activities—not natural disasters, but human actions or practices: one may blow the whistle only on events or conditions that involve people as agents who are affected by or perform these activities. Second, these activities must be harmful, or more precisely, believed to be harmful; in fact they may not harm others and the whistleblower's dilemma is that the harm may not be actual but only threatened.

Accordingly, one must assess both the *amount* of harm, in terms both of the number of people harmed and the extent of the harm, and the *probability* of this harm's occurring.

What is meant by 'harm'? The second condition in Bowie's definition provides one answer: an action is harmful if it violates human rights. What these rights are is a difficult philosophical question to which we must return. De George's reference to safety suggests one kind of right-violation: putting others at risk—to their lives or health—without their consent, actual or proxy. Graft in the New York City Police Department violates another right: the public's right to fair value in police services for their tax dollar, distributed in an equitable way. Moreover, because this violation is typically hidden, their right to know whether paid government employees are doing their job is further violated.

Bowie stipulates this harm must be of a certain sort: '*unnecessary*, and to *third parties*.' Clearly, if the harm could be avoided at no cost, and hence is not necessary at all, it should not occur. But an organization may claim that its dumping toxic chemicals into public waters is necessary if it is to operate at a profit. Hence, more generally, whether one regards a harm as necessary depends on one's goals. It is the conflicting goals of institutions, their members and the public that generates the dilemma of the whistleblower. In claiming the harm is unnecessary one may have presupposed the priority of one group's interest—a third party or more generally the public.

From this it follows that I cannot accept Bowie's third condition, that the activities on which one blows the whistle "run counter to the defined purpose of the institution." If one of the purposes of private organizations is to make a profit (note I do not say this is the sole purpose, or that the profit must be maximized), then dumping toxic substances into the water may indeed be necessary for achieving this. Its consonance with institutional objectives is not relevant to either the definition or evaluation of whistleblowing—especially in private organizations. In public organizations the situation is different: their main objective (in principle) is to serve the public—at least some segment in some fashion. For this reason whistleblowers in public institutions have to take the interest of the public more seriously: private organizations may be allowed some small measure of harm to the public (e.g., dumping small amounts of toxic substances into the water, at a level below that judged to pose a threat to the health of citizens). To insist that they could not harm, or threaten to harm, the public in any way would curtail their activities too severely. Some measure of harm is allowed to be offset by the benefits from the activities of private organizations to the public generally. Inevitably, one is committed to a balancing act: how much harm to whom vs. how much benefit to whom. One must weigh both the net benefit in a utilitarian calculus and the distribution of benefits in a non-utilitarian deontological fashion to reach a decision on acceptable levels of harm to third parties.

So far I have analyzed whistleblowing as a *process*, which conveys *information* about activities producing a net harm to third parties. The information can be couched in different grammatical forms: (1) as a question, "Did you know that ...?" (2) as an exclamation, "That ... is terrible!" (3) as an injunction, "Do something about ...!" (4) or as a mere statement of fact, "It is the case that...." Typically, whistleblowing approximates the third, informing the public about an act or practice, and enjoining them to do something about it.

But if we think of whistleblowing only in these terms, we miss an important element. Consider the injunction: "Look out for the car!" It satisfies the four conditions listed so far—to inform third parties of an activity that threatens some harm. Clearly something is missing: what we have so far is not whistleblowing but warning.

The difference is that whistleblowing involves an *accusation*. It is directed to people—not just in the sense of warning those who are in danger, but in the sense of locating responsibility for the danger. The whistleblower need not identify one person who is responsible, though he may. Rather he may target a group who share responsibility, or who include someone likely to be responsible.

Responsibility has two dimensions. Consider an example. Someone in a chemical factory dumps toxic substances into the water which an engineer in the city's water department discovers is beyond acceptable risks. His boss tells him not to inform the residents, but when asked directly while testing the water in someone's house replies that he would not drink it—it's dangerous! He has blown the whistle—and gets fired.[8] His superior has the responsibility of informing the public when the water is unsafe, and the engineer blows the whistle on him for failing to perform his duties. But his superior is not responsible for the unsafe water in a causal sense: he did not put the toxic substances in it. Responsibility thus has two dimensions: a *descriptive* one referring to those who cause something to happen; and a *normative* one identifying those who should do something about it. The first sense looks to the past, as part of an explanation. The second looks to the future as a coping strategy. Whistleblowers must to some degree locate responsibility in at least one of these senses if their statements are to be more than mere warnings. Moreover, if one speaks purely of the past, one is not and cannot be a whistleblower. Of course, if one reveals a problem in the past which still persists, or the conditions which produced it still persist, then one warns of the recurrence of that problem in the future.

The whistleblower also differs from the spy: the latter belongs to the organization responsible for the harm, but owes his allegiance to another organization—one thinks of counter-espionage agencies and undercover police officers. In a sense he is a member of two organizations—spying on one to transmit information to the other. If one thinks of this other 'organization' as society, then the whistleblower is in a similar situation of divided loyalties: in the case of both public and private organizations, he owes allegiance to his co-workers and obedience to his superiors. But as a citizen in the society, he also owes allegiance to people outside the organization: he has a commitment to the public good. In public agencies, dependent on public funds and serving a public purpose, protecting the public interest is an even higher duty.

Organizational membership turns out to be a complicated issue. Consider the question many whistleblowers confront: Should I go public *before* or *after* I change jobs? The question raises issues like those raised by anonymity because the whistleblower who acts after he has left the organization (like the one who remains anonymous) does so to protect himself. Yet at the same time he risks loss of credibility: people may dismiss his accusations as the product of resentment and frustration in a disgruntled employee, an unfair counter-attack on those he has left behind. If the whistleblower has no choice in the matter because he has been fired, his charges may all too easily fall on deaf ears. In identifying whistleblowers, organizational membership must be taken broadly to include those who are no longer members of the organization on which they blow the whistle but who were in the not too distant past.

The central dilemma that defines whistleblowing has already been mentioned: the conflict in loyalty to one's employer (past or present) and to the public who has been or will (probably) be harmed.

Can one blow the whistle on one's employer without going public—restricting one's dissent to internal affairs? The issue of conflicting loyalties might then be recast: one owes obedience to one's immediate superior, but might blow the whistle on that

person by 'going over his head.' One could do this in several ways: by going to his boss; by going right to the top—the president or chairman of the board; by going to the stockholders; by going to watchdog agencies which in a public agency might be regarded as still part of one's organization. The conflict is then between loyalty to one's *immediate superior* and loyalty to one's *organization*. One blows the whistle on one's immediate superior when one goes to someone else within the organization.

A final point about whistleblowing can be made, citing Alan Westin's recent book.[9] As he points out, the classic whistleblowers within organizations differ from referees, linesmen and traffic cops. The latter have the authority to have their decisions enforced whereas figurative whistleblowers do not. In a football game, when the referee blows the whistle, the play is supposed to stop: if it does not, players can be penalized; if someone scores a touchdown [after the referee has blown the whistle], their team receives no points. In the case of the traffic officer, the motorist who deliberately disobeys his directions can be fined, and for refusing the fine, imprisoned. Such literal whistleblowers have the power to have their decisions enforced, and are recognized by others as having this power.[10]

In the case of metaphorical or figurative whistleblowers, this authority is lacking. Indeed, blowing the whistle is a 'power-play,' an effort to enlist the support of others to achieve social objectives. They act in the hope that if others co-operate, worthwhile ends can be accomplished. Their plight is typically that of the powerless: as employees they have very few rights and can be dismissed at will by most employers. Consequently, they have much to fear: those whom they oppose are much more powerful, and [the employee has] few defenses.

The public is a defense of sorts. Often people hesitate to do in public what they would otherwise do behind a veil of secrecy.

In going public in the act of whistleblowing, the individual not only seeks greater power, but seeks the protection that public scrutiny brings.

B. JUSTIFYING ANONYMITY

Should people who blow the whistle do so publicly? Are they obliged to make their identity known or may they remain anonymous? The prohibition on anonymity is pervasive and strong. My purpose is to sound out and assess alternative rationales for it.

Before turning to an appraisal of anonymous whistleblowing, we need to distinguish it from related phenomena. In general, someone acts anonymously when his (or her) identity is not publicly known. For example, a bomb threat is anonymous when no one knows who wrote the letter or made the telephone call. Yet clearly, to say literally that *no one at all* knows is mistaken: the writer himself knows he sent the letter, and therefore at least one person knows.

Is an action done anonymously when no one but the agent knows? This notion comes close to the extreme form of secrecy: the greatest secret concerns information I share with no one else. But secrecy in this sense is too extreme, for how did I come by this information? If someone told me, at least one other person knows. Paradigmatically, information is secret when shared among few people, with two as the limiting case. But it does not suffice that only these two people know and merely by chance no one else. Such 'accidental secrets' are not secrets in the strict sense. To qualify as a secret, there must be a conspiracy of silence. It is the exclusion of others, the denial of access by them to information, that marks a secret.

Yet something more is built into the notion of secrecy that becomes clearer if we consider a related concept—privacy. Information is private when I justifiably deny the right of others to share it. The facts about my sex life or income tax return are

private in that others (ordinarily) cannot demand access to them. The domain of privacy is one in which I claim a *right* to exclude others, unless they can invoke a higher right to override mine.[11]

In the case of privacy, the burden of proof rests with those who would secure access to what is protected under this rubric. In the case of secrecy, the burden of proof is reversed: those who would withhold information must provide the justification. In the case of privacy, the presumption is that others should not intrude. In the case of secrecy, the presumption is that something be shared. This presumption is countered by 'Top Secret' documents with an appeal to national security. In the case of secret acts or espionage, the presumption is not met: information not shared should be, but is wrongfully and deliberately kept from others.

Is anonymity more like privacy or secrecy? First one needs to note that the information kept from others is of a particular sort—namely about a person's identity. Moreover the sharing of this information may be limited or extensive. For one to be anonymous, the public must be precluded from knowledge of the individual's identity, but their exclusion does not entail no one else knows. Anonymity is neutral, lying in the middle ground between secrecy and privacy. It entails that the public does not know or have access to the identity of an individual, but does not locate the burden of proof in withholding this information.

Accordingly, one can ask: Does the public have a right to know the whistleblower's identity, or does he (or she) have a right to withhold it? Withholding such information strikes many as wrong. But why is it wrong, and in what sense?

A refusal to let one's identity be known could be construed as bad manners. Blowing the whistle anonymously is like snitching on someone behind his back. As kids we were all taught that such tattle-tailing is wrong. It is a paradigm of bad manners to say nasty things about people not present to defend themselves. Anonymity in whistle-blowers is a breach of manners—faulty etiquette in people who should know better as they act in the more consequential professional world. But why are such breaches of etiquette condemned so harshly, and is this harshness justified?

Typically, the answer is couched in terms of loyalty.[12] To be a faithful member of a group is to protect the interests of that group as a whole and of its members individually. Saying nasty things about people behind their backs disrupts the cohesion of the group, undermining trust in each other and threatening the group solidarity. As a threat to the welfare of the group, individually or collectively, as well as to the very basis of its existence, tattle-tailing is severely condemned.

Yet clearly a blanket prohibition on tattle-tailing is unwarranted, as three analogies can serve to demonstrate.

(1) Suppose my older sister is about to swallow some pills I think may be dangerous. To tell mother may not be wrong, but right and indeed obligatory. Though I have 'blown the whistle' on my sister, if I am doing so for her own good in a situation that is serious and urgent, it is not objectionable—even if I ask mother not to tell on me. Clearly, it is preferable to saying or doing nothing at all. My sister's ignorance may help us to live together, to get along in situations where her anger might be disruptive and counter-productive for each of us. Since my sister does not know what I did, I have acted anonymously—at least as far as she is concerned. Even though mother knows, her knowledge, like that of the closed Congressional Committee to which a whistleblower testifies in camera, does not totally dispel anonymity.

Typically the boyhood scenario is less serious: my sister takes a cookie from the cookie jar without asking, and I squeal on her. My action may be condemned because the incident is trivial. But as the *seriousness* of the incident increases, the condemnation of anonymous whistleblowing weakens. The extent of the harm threatened is one factor to be weighed in making a moral judgment. The seriousness of the harm the whistleblower seeks to disclose and thereby curtail may be measured in several ways: the number of people affected; the extent to which they are hurt, physically or psychologically. Alternatively one might appraise this seriousness in less consequentialist terms by invoking deontological principles: perhaps someone's rights are denied—such as the right to privacy—even though no physical or psychological harm ensues. Whichever approach one takes, the more serious the offense, the less stringent the prohibition on anonymity.

One might respond that my analogy confuses two different concepts: whistleblowing and anonymity. Conceding that one is more obliged to blow the whistle the greater the harm threatened, one could nevertheless insist that one should always do so publicly and never anonymously. Consider three possibilities: P_1 blowing the whistle publicly; P_2 blowing the whistle anonymously; and P_3 not blowing the whistle at all. *Prima facie* P_1 is morally preferable to P_2, and P_2 is morally preferable to P_3. Though this ranking holds at the *individual* level, one can adopt a rule-utilitarian perspective on the effects of the *practice* of whistleblowing from acting anonymously: anonymity is justified if it increases the number who with good reason blow the whistle, that is, if anonymity promotes the practice of effective warranted whistleblowing.[13] Accordingly, the first analogy asserts that blowing the whistle anonymously is preferable to not blowing it at all—especially when the particular harm threatened is serious; and it hypothesizes that if a veil of ignorance increases the number of effective and legitimate whistleblowers, the principle of anonymity has a rule-utilitarian defense. But the analogy does not show that anonymously blowing the whistle is always preferable to blowing the whistle publicly. Consider now a second case to elicit a second factor in addition to seriousness.

(2) The school bully is about to beat up a new kid who looks very frail and helpless. Since I am unable to stop him, I run to the teacher to report the incident. After the teacher has intervened, I ask him not to say I reported the incident: to protect myself from retaliation, I want to remain anonymous. If the bully is very strong and I am very weak, my request is justified: there is no moral reason why I too should suffer unfairly at his hands. By the same token, corporations bully employees who cannot easily defend themselves. Because of their vulnerability, anonymity is warranted. As a second thesis I propose that the greater the *probability of unfair retaliation*, the weaker the prohibition on anonymity should be.

The literature to date suggests that most whistleblowers—even those who act for good moral reasons—pay a very high price for dissenting.[14] In many cases they are fired or demoted, transferred to unattractive assignments or locales, ostracized by their peers and cast into psychological and professional isolation. Should they try to obtain another job in the same field, they often find they are 'blacklisted': many employers do not want to hire someone who 'caused trouble' on his (or her) last job. Moreover, under the prevailing legal doctrine of 'employment at will,' fired whistleblowers have only limited legal recourse: in most jurisdictions the courts uphold an employer's right to fire someone for almost any reason.[15] In the absence of such legal protection, the burden of defending himself falls very heavily on the shoulders of the whistleblower alone.

In asserting that the probability of unfair retaliation decreases the strength of the prohibition on anonymity, I do want to distinguish two concepts: permissible and obligatory. My point, to put it briefly, is that moral heroism is not and should not be mandated. Though we praise the courage of a professional engineer who speaks out regarding dangerous practices when he (or she) risks his job, to require extraordinary self-sacrifices demands too much. His unwillingness to risk his career, his personal livelihood and the means whereby he supports his family are perfectly understandable reasons for remaining silent. Indeed, they may justify silence. When such individual self-sacrifice is the only way to protect the public, one must look instead to the development of other mechanisms—the law, the courts, unions, the press, professional associations or watchdog agencies.

To return to the earlier threefold distinction, blowing the whistle publicly may be ideal but one cannot demand it. One cannot condemn the persons who act anonymously to protect themselves, those who depend on them, love them and care for them. There is a limit to what we can ask a person to give up in order to do the right thing. Insofar as anonymity reduces what may be an unfair burden to begin with, it reduces an evil promoting a good.

So far I have identified two factors that enter into an appraisal of anonymous whistleblowing: the seriousness of the harm threatened, and the probability of unfair retaliation.

(3) A third moral factor can be elicited with the following modification in the second analogy: Suppose the bully is my friend. This social relationship places an obligation on me to go to my friend. Even if I am frail and helpless, given that he is my friend, I am duty bound by friendship to ask him to stop. Even if he is not my friend but only is a member of my gang, I should not blow the whistle straight away but go to our leader first—ask him to intervene. If that is not possible or fails, recourse to an outside group may be warranted. My third thesis is that the strength of the prohibition on anonymity is a function of the social relationship: the closer the whistleblower stands to the accused, the stronger the prohibition on anonymity.[16]

Most whistleblowers feel an 'I vs. them' or 'us vs. them.' Within polarized groups, whistleblowers discuss problems with other members of their group, but hesitate—legitimately I contend—to go outside it without the protection anonymity brings.

This third factor is related to the second: social distance affects the probability of retaliation. If an intermediary can ensure that justice is done within the group, anonymity is less warranted—if not unwarranted. If the Federal Office of Professional Responsibility can guarantee that whistleblowers protecting unfair, illegal or corrupt practices will not suffer for their efforts to correct them, anonymity is less warranted. It is also less needed. But until employees' right are secure, a veil of ignorance is one of their few safeguards.

Anonymity may be condemned because it impedes the pursuit of truth. The person who levels accusations against another while withholding his own identity makes it difficult to determine whether what he charges is true or false: we cannot question him, ask for his sources of information, verify his accusations—or so it may be argued.

But to assert that we cannot verify anonymous charges at all, is too strong and unfounded. Verification, if it is to count as a proof, must be public and repeatable.[17] Consequently, the means whereby the whistleblower verified *to himself* that what he suspected was true must be available *to others* … if indeed he knows the truth. Those who would learn the truth can discover it by the same means the whistleblower used— even though they do not know his identity.

In the movie and book *All the President's Men*, the character called 'Deep Throat' played this role. Without revealing his own identity, he led the two reporters Bernstein and Woodward along a path that provided the evidence they needed to implicate the President in the Watergate break-ins. He did not need to reveal his own identity. It was enough that from the darkness he provided clues that would trace out a path, perhaps the one he followed but perhaps not, to the truth.

Admittedly, in some cases it may be difficult if not impossible for the whistleblower to provide any conclusive evidence that will not reveal his own identity. In such cases, the choice is not between blowing the whistle anonymously and blowing it publicly. Rather, the choice is between blowing it publicly and not blowing it at all. Accordingly, I do not assert that anonymity is always possible. But I do assert that where it is possible we cannot always fault it as a breach of professional etiquette or because it conceals the truth.

Therefore, I conclude that the blanket condemnation on anonymity is not warranted. Rather, its justification depends on three factors: the seriousness of the offense, the probability of unfair retaliation, and the social relationships. Let me now turn to some practical considerations.

C. ANONYMITY AND PERSONAL INTEGRITY

Perhaps anonymity is not a breach of professional etiquette or an obstacle to the truth but an act of foolishness. The individual who tries to shield himself may find anonymity makes his action *self-defeating*: to be effective one must act publicly—or so one argument may run. What can be said for or against it?

First, one must concede a paradox. The whistleblower attempts to draw public attention to an action he regards as wrong, yet is not willing to make his own identity public. His means and ends conflict: he uses ignorance to promote knowledge, identifies others while hiding himself. What he is trying to do is refuted by the way he does it. This paradoxical juxtaposition of means and ends raises our suspicions. It reminds us of those who make war to end war, who deceive to get at the truth, who use force to protect freedom.

Though our suspicions are justifiably aroused, they may turn out to be unjustified. Society may need an institution like the police, based on the legal use of physical force, to protect the freedom of its members. It may indeed be necessary to reveal less than the whole truth to determine if others are telling the truth. We are right to be suspicious when the means contradict the ends, but may find the contradiction only apparent: the whistleblower may succeed at uncovering abusive practices without blowing his cover.

Alternatively, our suspicions may be aroused not by the logical paradox but by the questions of motives: Why does the whistleblower conceal his identity—what does *he* have to hide? To show his intentions are pure, we demand that he stand up for his actions and not hide from public view. Hiding makes us uneasy that he seeks some private gain rather than the public good, that he himself may be implicated and protecting himself by pointing at others.

A sharp distinction can be drawn between reasons and causes,[18] the justification and the motivation, the evidence that proves a statement true or false and the personal considerations that lead a person to utter it. Anonymity calls the latter into question but need not affect the former. Whether the charges are true or false does not depend on the motivation of the individual who levies them. One can appraise the truth of accusations knowing nothing of motives. Whether the whistleblower draws attention to corruption out of spite or altruism makes no difference in one respect: if corruption exists, it should be ended.

Naturally our attitude towards the whistleblower depends very much on his motives. If he genuinely seeks the public good, he should be held in high esteem. If he does not benefit in any way, his altruism is commendable. In appraising his character, his motives are of the utmost importance. But in appraising his *charges*, his motives are logically irrelevant.[19] Anonymity helps guard against a fallacious counter-attack—

an *argumentum ad hominem*.[20] Individuals called to account by the whistleblower may try to protect themselves by diverting attention to him, by shifting the issue from what he says to why he says it. They may seek to redirect attention from the truth of his claims to the truthfulness of the claimant. But logicians have long recognized this strategy as fallacious: whether or not what someone says is true does not depend on his personal motive for saying it.

Anonymity may be treated as self-defeating because it calls into question the motives of the whistleblower, but I contend it is wrong to insist it must. However, one genuine issue is raised by this attack on anonymity: How do we distinguish the accusations that should be investigated from those that need not be? A filtering process is needed to make this determination. Anonymity is not and should not be the main factor in the filter: one should not decide to investigate a charge only if the person who makes it identifies himself publicly. One is less inclined to investigate anonymous charges because of difficulties anonymity creates—the problems of gathering data, identifying the relevant participants, fixing the time, location, and extent of the act or practice. But then it should be for these reasons, and not because of anonymity *per se*, that no further action is taken.

From what I have said already, several factors emerge in the determination of the point at which the whistleblower's charges should be investigated. The main factor is the seriousness of the harm to others if the charges are true. Clearly, if the risk to their lives and health is very great, steps must be taken to protect them. The first step is to determine whether the risk is real or imaginary—and this requires investigating the whistleblower's accusations. If he claims that money has been misspent, stolen or siphoned off for illegal purposes, then the greater the amount involved, the more serious the charge and the greater the need to verify it.

In judging the harm to be done, one must also weigh the costs of determining this harm. If an investigation is likely to destroy the morale of an otherwise socially useful and productive organization, an investigation is probably not warranted. If it is likely to cost more money than might be saved, then it is likewise unwarranted. It is the *net harm*, after the costs of an investigation have been subtracted, that must be given moral weight in fixing the threshold.

Should the likelihood that the charges are true be considered? The objection to giving this probability estimate any weight is that the whistleblower's dilemma arises precisely because people do not know. An estimate based on ignorance is unreliable, and acting on it irrational. But at the other extreme, to investigate charges that are preposterous, about events logically impossible or astronomically remote, will be wasteful if not harmful. Accordingly, the probability that the charges will prove unfounded should serve as a factor only to eliminate extreme cases of the preposterous, impossible, or improbable.

So far I have offered three interpretations of the thesis that whistleblowers should not remain anonymous. On the first, anonymity is in bad taste—it offends our sense of etiquette in saying nasty things about someone behind their back. On the second, it is a barrier to the truth. And on the third it is self-defeating. I want now to consider several moral objections.

Fair Play   It may be argued that everyone has a right to confront their accusers. If someone claims I have done something wrong, I should be allowed to question him face to face. It violates our sense of fairness to have accusations levelled against someone with no opportunity to defend themselves. Does this sense of fair play preclude anonymity among whistleblowers?

In fact we do not always regard concealing one's identity as morally bad. Quite the contrary, we sometimes regard it as good and

proper. For example, within academia blind reviewing is a widespread practice: members of an editorial board passing judgment on an article submitted for publication may find the author's name removed. Conversely, the reviewers of manuscripts for publication may not reveal their name. In the first case the practice is justified on the grounds that it equalizes the competition: established authors can less readily exploit their reputation, and the decision to accept or reject an article is made on the basis of quality alone. The second practice supposedly allows more candor: reviewers can offer an honest evaluation without fear of reprisals or alienating a colleague with whom they may need to cooperate in the future. Note that in the first case anonymity serves as an equalizer to factor out extraneous and unwarranted influences like reputation. And in the second case it produces harmony. Insofar as it promotes fairness, equality or harmony, the practice of concealing one's identity has a moral justification.

The objection to anonymity can likewise be rebutted on the grounds that it promotes other values, or that the rights of the accused can be protected in other ways. It allows individuals to come forward who would otherwise remain silent for fear of reprisals. In so doing it promotes the *public welfare* which may be subverted by abuses of power by government officials, or the *public safety*, which may be threatened by dangerous practices of private industry. It may also promote *honesty* and *accountability* among managers who know they will find it difficult to conceal their indulgences. Admittedly, individuals have a right to protect themselves against false accusations that can ruin their careers and compromise their good name. But to guarantee this right, the identity of whistleblowers need not be known: it is only necessary that accusations be properly investigated, proven true or false, and the results widely disseminated.

If the whistleblower and the accused confronted each other as equals, anonymity would be unnecessary. But typically the power differentials are enormous, and most whistleblowers pay dearly for the action: they lose their jobs, get transferred to a less attractive if not unattractive locale and assignment, find their family life disrupted and their friends and colleagues less amiable.[21] The taunt of the accused that the whistleblower come forward and 'face him like a man,' is a bully's challenge when issued by the powerful. In a court, where the judge, lawyers and legal process serve as an equalizer, anonymity is less warranted. The prohibition on anonymity denies employees one of their few safeguards from retaliation of powerful, aroused enemies. Until positive steps have been taken to protect employees' rights to dissent, the condemnation of anonymity discourages one of the few checks on the abuse of power by corporate or government officials.

The Slippery Slope Behind the prohibition on anonymity lurks the fear: What if everyone does that? The need to come forward and be identified acts as a check on a practice that threatens the day to day operation of bureaucracies, corporations and institutions. People have jobs to do, and precious time is wasted in unproductive activities if they go about secretly complaining of others—or so the argument may run. Furthermore, to continue this attack, damage is done to the moral fabric of an organization by anonymous whistleblowers who destroy the peace and harmony on which a smooth operation is based. To keep this practice within reasonable bounds and limit its corrosive impact, we must insist that whistleblowers publicly identify themselves. Without this restriction we slide down a slippery slope into corporate chaos and institutional anarchy.

What can be said against this slippery slope argument? First, it is important to maintain a realistic perspective: How many more employees are likely to blow the whistle if anonymity protected them? The simple answer is: We do not know. Clearly, to argue rationally against a practice, our argument should be based on information—not misinformation, suspicions and fears. Logically, the slippery slope contention is an *argumentum ad ignoratiam*,[22] a fallacious inference from our ignorance.

Second, it is important to locate clearly the burden of proof: Does it lie with the defenders of anonymity or its critics? As a form of dissent, whistleblowing is an exercise of a highly valued right—freedom of speech. Admittedly, the context is not political but bureaucratic, not dissent against one's government but against one's employer (though for some whistleblowers the two are the same). Insofar as whistleblowers are speaking out, the burden of proof rests with those who would restrict them from exercising their freedom of speech. Until they can demonstrate clear and present danger to society—and not just themselves, their fears or hysteria will not serve as an adequate moral basis for restricting the rights of others to dissent.

Third, it is important to be clear that this burden will be difficult to sustain for the right to dissent is not easily overridden. For example, though an organization might be destroyed by the actions of an anonymous whistleblower, proving this would not necessarily establish the moral right of the institution's executives to silence the whistleblower. For suppose the institution is a chemical company, polluting the water the public drinks with toxic substances. Given that they have no moral right to endanger the health of others to begin with, they have no right to silence the whistleblower from disclosing this danger—even if his actions threaten their corporate existence.

To establish a right of corporations to silence whistleblowers, one would have to show that society would be better off if corporations had such a right. The very claim that they do or should have it sounds dangerously close to the rhetorical flourish: What's good for General Motors is good for the country. Today we recognize the dangers of air pollution from automobiles, and the harm of gas-guzzlers to the nation's economy. Such claims can now more readily be seen for what they are: self-deluded or hypocritical attempts to equate corporate profits with the social good. For a utilitarian the burden of proof can be sustained only by demonstrating that restricting the whistleblower's right of dissent will work to the long-term advantage of society, rather than the corporation. I for one do not think that the empirical evidence can be marshalled to establish this claim.

ENDNOTES

1. Richard De George, "Ethical Responsibilities of Engineers in Large Organizations." Paper presented at the National Conference on Engineering Ethics; Troy, NY: June 20–22, 1980, p. 8.

2. Sissela Bok, "Whistleblowing and Professional Responsibility," *New York Univ. Educ. Quarterly XI* (1980), pp. 2–10.

3. Rosemary Chalk and Frank von Hippel, "Due Process for the Bearers of Ill Tidings: Dealing with Technical Dissent in the Organization," *Tech. Rev.* 81 (1979), pp. 49–55.

4. Norman Bowie, *Business Ethics* (Prentice-Hall, Englewood Cliffs, N.J., 1982).

5. Jackeline Varret's case follows this pattern. See Ralph Nader et al., *Whistleblowing* (Grossman Publishers, New York, 1972), pp. 90–97.

6. See Peter Maas, *Serpico* (Bantam Books, New York, 1974).

7. See Nader op cit., pp. 39–54, and Fitzgerald's autobiography *The High Priest of Waste* (Putnam and Sons, New York, 1968).

8. This case is adapted from Nader. See op cit. (Note 5).

9. Alan Westin, *Blowing the Whistle* (McGraw-Hill, New York, 1980).

10. I am here using Robert Paul Wolff's definition of authority. See his essay "On Violence" reprinted in *Obligation and Dissent*, ed. by Donald W. Hansen and Robert Booth Fowler (Little Brown & Co., Boston, 1971), pp. 242–258.

11. St. Augustine confuses this distinction between privacy and secrecy in his analysis of sexual intercourse, with the result that he regards all sex as evil. See Augustine's "Sexual Lust and Original Sin," in *The City of God* trans. by Philip Levine (Harvard Univ. Press, Cambridge, Ma., 1966), 4:345–401.

12. See *Divided Loyalties*, by Robert M. Anderson et al. (West Lafayette, Ind., Purdue U. Press, 1980).

13. The experience of France, where civil servants are encouraged to report abuses on government by calling an investigation office, has proven an effective curb on abusive actions and practices. A similar hotline exists in the United States Federal bureaucracy.

14. One has only to look to those cases cited by Nader (op. cit., Note 5 above) as well as those that typically make the newspaper headlines.

15. For an excellent discussion of this doctrine, see J.P. Christiansen's "A Remedy for the Discharge of Professional Employees Who Refuse to Perform Unethical or Illegal Acts: A Proposal in Aid of Professional Ethics," *Vanderbilt Law Review*, 28 (1975), 805–841.

16. Very little has been written on stratified moral obligations (and rights) that vary according to one's social relationship or role, though the issue is omnipresent in the fields of professional and applied ethics. For four notable exceptions, see R.S. Downie's *Roles and Values* (Methuen & Co., London, 1971) and

Stuart Hampshire (ed.), *Public & Private Morality* (Cambridge, N.Y., 1978), Charles Fried's "Rights & Roles," in *Right and Wrong* (Harvard Univ. Press, Cambridge, Ma.), pp. 167–195, and Alan Goldman's *The Moral Foundations of Professional Ethics* (Littlefield Adams, Totowa, N.J., 1980).

17. For a more detailed analysis of the philosophical issues involved in confirmation, see Carl G. Hempel's *Philosophy of Natural Science* (Prentice-Hall, Englewood Cliffs, N.J., 1966), Chap. 4.

18. For a discussion of these and related concepts see Richard Taylor's *Action & Purpose* (Prentice-Hall, Englewood Cliffs, N.J., 1966), Chap. 10.

19. John Stuart Mill recognizes this distinction between judgments about actions and judgments about agents. See Chapter II of his *Utilitarianism*, ed. by Samuel Gorovitz (Bobbs-Merrill, New York, 1971), p. 25.

20. See Irvin Copi's *Introduction to Logic*, 3rd edition (Collier Macmillan, New York, 1968), p. 61.

21. See Nader's examples (Note 5).

22. See Copi (op. cit.), p. 63.

WHISTLEBLOWING: Professionalism, Personal Life, and Shared Responsibility for Safety in Engineering

Mike W. Martin

... I want to take a fresh look at whistle-blowing in order to draw attention to some neglected issues concerning the moral relevance of personal life to understanding professional responsibilities. Specifically, the issues concern: personal right and responsibilities in deciding how to meet professional obligations; increased personal burdens when others involved in collective endeavors fail to meet their responsibilities; the role of the virtues, especially personal integrity, as they bear on "living with oneself"; and personal commitments to moral ideals beyond minimum requirements....

Let me bring to mind three well-known cases.

(1) In 1972 Dan Applegate wrote a memo to his supervisor, the vice-president of Convair Corporation, telling him in no uncertain terms that the cargo door for the DC-10 airplane was unsafe, making it "inevitable that, in the twenty years ahead of us, DC-10 cargo doors will come open and I would expect this to usually result in the loss of the airplane."[1] As a subcontractor for McDonnell Douglas, Convair had designed the cargo door and the DC-10 fuselage. Applegate was Director of Product Engineering at Convair and the senior engineer in charge of the design. His supervisor did not challenge his technical judgment in the matter, but told him that nothing could be done because of the likely costs to Convair in admitting responsibility for a design error that would need to be fixed by grounding DC-10s. Two years later, the cargo door on a Turkish DC-10 flying near Paris opened in flight, decompressurizing the cargo area so as to collapse the passenger floor—along which run the controls for the aircraft. All 346 people on board died, a record casualty figure at that time for a single-plane crash. Tens of millions of dollars were paid out in civil suits, but no one was

From *Business & Professional Ethics Journal*, Vol. 11, No. 2 (1992): 21–40. Reprinted by permission of the author.

charged with criminal or even unprofessional conduct.

(2) Frank Camps was a principal design engineer for the Pinto.[2] Under pressure from management he participated in coaxing the Pinto windshield through government tests by reporting only the rare successful test and by using a Band-Aid fix design that resulted in increased hazard to the gas tank. In 1973, undergoing a crisis of conscience in response to reports of exploding gas tanks, he engaged in internal whistleblowing, writing the first of many memos to top management stating his view that Ford was violating federal safety standards. It took six years before his concerns were finally incorporated into the 1979 model Pinto, after nearly a million Pintos with unsafe windshields and gas tanks were put on the road. Shortly after writing his memos he was given lowered performance evaluations, then demoted several times. He resigned in 1978 when it became clear his prospects for advancement at Ford were ended. He filed a lawsuit based in part on age discrimination, in part on trying to prevent Ford from making him a scapegoat for problems with the Pinto, and in part on trying to draw further attention to the dangers in the Pinto.

(3) On January 27, 1986, Roger Boisjoly and other senior engineers at Morton Thiokol firmly recommended that space shuttle *Challenger* not be launched.[3] The temperature at the launch site was substantially below the known safety range for the O-ring seals in the joints of the solid rocket boosters. Top management overrode the recommendation. Early in the launch, the *Challenger* boosters exploded, killing the seven crew members, to [sic] the terrified eyes of millions who watched because schoolteacher Christa McAuliffe was aboard. A month later Boisjoly was called to testify before the Rogers Commission. Against the wishes of management, he offered documents to support his interpretation of the events leading to the disaster—and to rebut the interpretation given by his boss. Over the next months Boisjoly was made to feel increasingly alienated from his coworkers until finally he had to take an extended sick leave. Later, when he desired to find a new job he found himself confronted with companies unwilling to take a chance on a known whistleblower.

As the last two cases suggest, there can be double horrors surrounding whistleblowing: the public horror of lost lives, and the personal horror of responsible whistleblowers who lose their careers. Most whistleblowers undergo serious penalties for "committing the truth." One recent study suggests that two out of three of them suffer harassment, lowered performance evaluations, demotions, punitive transfers, loss of jobs, or blacklisting that can effectively end a career.[4] Horror stories about whistleblowers are not the exception; they are the rule.

THREE APPROACHES TO WHISTLEBLOWING ETHICS

The literature on whistleblowing is large and growing. Here I mention three general approaches. The first is to condemn whistleblowers as disloyal troublemakers who "rat" on their companies and undermine teamwork based on the hierarchy of authority within the corporation. Admittedly, whistleblowers' views about safety concerns are sometimes correct, but final decisions about safety belong to management, not engineers. When management errs, the corporation will eventually pick up the costs in lawsuits and adverse publicity. Members of the public are part of the technological enterprise which both benefits them and exposes them to risks; when things go wrong they (or their surviving family) can always sue.

I once dismissed this attitude as callous, as sheer corporate egoism that misconstrues loyalty to a corporation as an absolute (unexceptionless) moral principle. *If*, however—and it is a big "if"—the public accepts this attitude, as revealed in how it expresses its will through legitimate political processes, then so be it. As will become clear later, I take public responsibilities seriously. If the public refuses to protect whistleblowers, it tacitly accepts the added risks from not having available important safety information. I hope the public will protect the jobs of whistleblowers; more on this later.

A second approach, insightfully defended by Michael Davis,[5] is to regard whistleblowing as a tragedy to be avoided. On occasion whistleblowing may be a necessary evil or even admirable, but it is always bad news all around. It is proof of organizational trouble and management failure; it threatens the careers of managers on whom the whistle is blown; it disrupts collegiality by making colleagues feel resentment toward the whistleblower, and it damages the important informal network of friends at the workplace; it shows the whistleblower lost faith in the organization and its authority, and hence is more likely to be a troublemaker in the future; and it almost always brings severe penalties to whistleblowers who are viewed by employers and colleagues as unfit employees.

I wholeheartedly support efforts to avoid the need for whistleblowing. There are many things that can be done to improve organizations to make whistleblowing unnecessary. Top management can—and must—set a moral tone, and then implement policies that encourage safety concerns (and other bad news) to be communicated freely. Specifically, managers can keep doors open, allowing engineers to convey their concerns without retribution. Corporations can have in-house ombudspersons and appeal boards, and even a vice-president for corporate ethics. For their part, engineers can learn to be more assertive and effective in making their safety concerns known, learning how to build support from their colleagues. (Could Dan Applegate have pushed harder than he did, or did he just write a memo and drop

the matter?) Professional societies should explore the possibility of creating confidential appeal groups where engineers can have their claims heard.

Nevertheless, this second approach is not enough. There will always be corporations and managers willing to cut corners on safety in the pursuit of short-term profit, and there will always be a need for justified whistleblowing. Labelling whistleblowing as a tragedy to be avoided whenever possible should not deflect attention from issues concerning justified whistleblowing.

We need to remind ourselves that responsible whistleblowing is not bad news all around. It is very good news for the public which is protected by it. The good news is both episodic and systematic. Episodically, lives are saved directly when professionals speak out, and lives are lost when professionals like Dan Applegate feel they must remain silent in order to keep their jobs. Systematically, lives are saved indirectly by sending a strong message to industry that legally-protected whistleblowing is always available as a last resort when managers too casually override safety concerns for short-term profits. Helpful pressure is put on management to take a more farsighted view of safety, thereby providing a further impetus for unifying corporate self-interest with the production of safe products. (In the DC-10, Pinto, and *Challenger* cases, management made shortsighted decisions that resulted in enormous costs in lawsuits and damaged company reputations.)

In this day of (sometimes justified) outcry over excessive government regulation, we should not forget the symbolic importance of clear, effective, and enforced laws as a way for society to express its collective vision of a good society.[6] Laws protecting responsible whistleblowing express the community's resolve to support professionals who act responsibly for the public safety. Those laws are also required if the public is to meet its responsibilities in the creation of safe technological products, as I will suggest in a moment.

A third approach is to affirm unequivocally the obligation of engineers (and other professionals) to whistleblow in certain circumstances, and to treat this obligation as paramount—as overriding all other considerations, whatever the sacrifice involved in meeting it. Richard De George gave the classical statement of this view.[7] External whistleblowing, he argued, is obligatory when five conditions are met (by an engineer or other corporate employee):

1. "Serious and considerable harm to the public" is involved;

2. one reports the harm and expresses moral concern to one's immediate superior;

3. one exhausts other channels within the corporation;

4. one has available "documented evidence that would convince a reasonable, impartial observer that one's view of the situation is correct"; and

5. one has "good reasons to believe that by going public the necessary changes will be brought about" to prevent the harm.

De George says that whistleblowing is morally *permissible* when conditions 1–3 are met, and is morally *obligatory* when 1–5 are met.

As critics have pointed out, conditions (4) and (5) seem far too strong. Where serious safety is at stake, there is some obligation to whistleblow even when there are only grounds for hope (not necessarily belief) that whistleblowing will significantly improve matters, and even when one's documentation is substantial but less than convincing to every rational person.[8] Indeed, often whistleblowing is intended to prompt authorities to garner otherwise unavailable evidence through investigations.

Moreover, having a reasonable degree of documentation is a requirement even for permissible whistleblowing—lest one make insupportable allegations that unjustifiably harm the reputations of individuals and corporations. So too is having a reasonable hope for success—lest one waste everyone's time and energy.[9] Hence, De George's sharp separation of requirements for permissibility and obligation begins to collapse. There may be an obligation to whistleblow when 1–3 are met and the person has some reasonable degree of documentation and reasonable hope for success in bringing about necessary changes.

My main criticism of this third approach, however, is more fundamental. I want to call into question the whole attempt to offer a general rule that tells us when whistleblowing is mandatory, *tout court*. Final judgments about obligations to whistleblow must be made contextually, not as a matter of general rule. And they must take into account the burdens imposed on whistleblowers.[10]

THE MORAL RELEVANCE OF PERSONAL LIFE TO PROFESSIONAL DUTY

In my view, there is a strong *prima facie* obligation to whistleblow when one has good reason to believe there is a serious moral problem, has exhausted normal organizational channels (except in emergencies when time precludes that), has available a reasonable amount of documentation, and has reasonable hope of solving the problem by blowing the whistle. Nevertheless, however strong, the obligation is only *prima facie*: It can sometimes have exceptions when it conflicts with other important considerations. Moreover, the considerations which need to be weighed include not only *prima facie* obligations to one's employer, but also consideration about one's personal life. Before they make all-things-considered judgments about whether to whistleblow, engineers may and should consider their responsibilities to their family, other personal obligations which depend on having an income, and their rights to pursue their careers.

Engineers are people, as well as professionals. They have personal obligations to their families, as well as sundry other obligations in personal life which can be met only if they have an income. They also have personal rights to pursue careers. These personal obligations and rights are moral ones, and they legitimately interact with professional obligations in ways that sometimes make it permissible for engineers not to whistleblow, even when they have a *prima facie* obligation to do so. Precisely how these considerations are weighed depends on the particular situation. And here as elsewhere, we must allow room for morally reasonable people to weigh moral factors differently.

In adopting this contextual approach to balancing personal and professional obligations, I am being heretical. Few discussions of whistleblowing take personal considerations seriously, as being morally significant, rather than a matter of non-moral, prudential concern for self-interest. But responsibilities to family and to others outside the workplace, as well as the right to pursue one's career, are moral considerations, not just prudential ones. Hence further argument is needed to dismiss them as irrelevant or always secondary in this context. I will consider three such arguments.

(i) The *Prevent-Harm Argument* says that morality requires us to prevent harm and in doing so to treat others' interests equally and impartially with our own. This assumption is often associated with utilitarianism, the view that we should always produce the most good for the most people. Strictly, at issue here is "negative utilitarianism," which says we should always act to minimize total harm, treating everyone's interests as equally important with our own. The idea is that even though engineers and their families must suffer, their suffering is outweighed by the lives saved through

whistleblowing. Without committing himself to utilitarianism, De George uses a variation of the impartiality requirement to defend his criteria for obligatory whistleblowing: "It is not implausible to claim both that we are morally obliged to prevent harm to others at relatively little expense to ourselves, and that we are morally obliged to prevent great harm to a great many others, even at considerable expense to ourselves."[11]

The demand for strict impartiality in ethics has been under sustained attack during the past two decades, and from many directions.[12] Without attempting to review all those arguments, I can indicate how they block any straightforward move from impartiality to absolute (exceptionless) whistleblowing obligations, thereby undermining the Prevent-Harm Argument. One argument is that a universal requirement of strict impartiality (as opposed to a limited requirement restricted to certain contexts) is self-demeaning. It undermines our ability to give our lives meaning through special projects, careers, and relationships that require the resources which strict impartiality would demand we give away to others. The general moral right to autonomy—the right to pursue our lives in a search for meaning and happiness—implies a right to give considerable emphasis to our personal needs and those of our family.

As an analogy, consider the life-and-death issues surrounding world hunger and scarce medical resources.[13] It can be argued that all of us share a general responsibility (of mutual aid) for dealing with the tragedy of tens of thousands of people who die each day from malnutrition and lack of medical care. As citizens paying taxes that can be used toward this end, and also as philanthropists who voluntarily recognize a responsibility to give to relief organizations, each of us has a *prima facie* obligation to help. But there are limits. Right now, you and I could dramatically lower our lifestyles in order to help save lives by making greater sacrifices. We could even donate one of our kidneys to save a life. Yet we have a right not to do that, a right to give ourselves and our families considerable priority in how we use our resources. Similarly, engineers' rights to pursue their meaning-giving careers, and the projects and relationships made possible by those careers, have relevance in understanding the degree of sacrifice required by a *prima facie* whistleblowing obligation.

(ii) The *Avoid-Harm Argument* proceeds from the obligation not to cause harm to others. It then points out that engineers are in a position to cause or avoid harm on an unusual scale. As a result, according to Kenneth Alpern, the ordinary moral obligation of due care in avoiding harm to others implies that engineers must "be ready to make greater personal sacrifices than can normally be demanded of other individuals."[14] In particular, according to Gene James, whistleblowing is required when it falls under the general obligation to "prevent unnecessary harm to others" and "to not cause avoidable harm to others," where "harm" means violating their rights.[15]

Of course there is a general obligation not to cause harm. That obligation, however, is so abstract that it tells us little about exactly how much effort and sacrifice is required of us, especially where many people share responsibility for avoiding harm. I have an obligation not to harm others by polluting the environment, but it does not follow that I must stop driving my car at the cost of my job and the opportunities it makes possible for my family. That would be an unfair burden. These abstract difficulties multiply as we turn to the context of engineering practice which involves collective responsibility for technological products.

Engineers work as members of authority-structured teams which sometimes involve hundreds of other professionals who share responsibility for inherently-risky technological projects.[16] Engineers are not the only team-members who have responsibilities to

create safe products. Their managers have exactly the same general responsibilities. In fact, they have greater accountability insofar as they are charged with the authority to make final decisions about projects. True, engineers have greater expertise in safety matters and hence have greater responsibilities to identify dangers and convey that information to management. But whatever justifications can be given for engineers to zealously protect public safety also apply to managers. In making the decision to launch the *Challenger*, Jerald Mason, Senior Vice President for Morton Thiokol, is said to have told Robert Lund, "Take off your engineering hat and put on your management hat." Surely this change in headgear did not alter his moral responsibilities for safety.

Dan Applegate and Roger Boisjoly acted responsibly in making unequivocal safety recommendations; their managers failed to act responsibly. Hence their moral dilemmas about whether to whistleblow arose because of unjustified decisions by their superiors. It is fair to ask engineers to pick up the moral slack for managers' irresponsible decisions—as long as we afford them legal protection to prevent their being harassed, fired, and blacklisted. Otherwise, we impose an unfair burden. Government and the general public share responsibility for safety in engineering. They set the rules that business plays by. It is hypocrisy for us to insist that engineers have an obligation to whistleblow to protect us, and then to fail to protect them when they act on the obligation.

(iii) The *Professional-Status Argument* asserts that engineers have special responsibilities as professionals, specified in codes of ethics, which go beyond the general responsibilities incumbent on everyone to prevent and avoid harm, and which override all personal considerations. Most engineering codes hint at a whistleblowing obligation with wording similar to that of the code of the National Society of Professional Engineers (NSPE):

Engineers shall at all times recognize that their primary obligation is to protect the safety, health, property and welfare of the public. If their professional judgment is over-ruled under circumstances where the safety, health, property or welfare of the public are endangered, they shall notify their employer or client and such other authority as may be appropriate.[17]

The phrase "as may be appropriate" is ambiguous. Does it mean "when morally justified," or does it mean "as necessary in order to protect the public safety, health, and welfare"? The latter interpretation is the most common one, and it clearly implies whistleblowing in some situations, no matter what the personal cost.

I agree that the obligation to protect public safety is an essential professional obligation that deserves emphasis in engineers' work. It is not clear, however, that it is paramount in the technical philosophical sense of overriding all other professional obligations in all situations. In any case, I reject the general assumption that codified professional duties are all that are morally relevant in making whistleblowing decisions. It is quite true that professional considerations require setting aside personal interests in many situations. But it is also true that personal considerations have enormous and legitimate importance in professional life, such as in choosing careers and areas of specialization, choosing and changing jobs, and deciding how far to go in sacrificing family life in pursuing a job and a career.

Spouses have a right to participate in professional decisions such as those involving whistleblowing.[18] At the very least, I would be worried about professionals who do not see the moral importance of consulting their spouses before deciding to engage in acts of whistleblowing that will seriously affect them and their children. I would be equally worried about critics who condemn engineers for failing to whistleblow without knowing anything about their personal situation.[19]

Where does all this leave us on the issue of engineers' obligations? It is clear there is a minimum standard which engineers must meet. They have strong obligations not to break the law and not to approve projects which are immoral according to standard practice. They also have a *prima facie* obligation to whistleblow in certain situations. Just how strong the whistleblowing responsibility is, all things considered, remains unclear—as long as there are inadequate legal protections.

What is clear is that whistleblowing responsibilities must be understood contextually, weighed against personal rights and responsibilities, and assessed in light of the public's responsibilities to protect whistleblowers. We must look at each situation. Sometimes the penalties for whistleblowing may not be as great as is usually the case, perhaps because some protective laws have been passed, and sometimes family responsibilities and rights to pursue a career may not be seriously affected. But our all-things-considered judgments about whistleblowing are not a matter of a general absolute principle that always overrides every other consideration.

Yes, the public has a right to be warned by whistleblowers of dangers—assuming the public is willing to bear its responsibility for passing laws protecting whistleblowers. In order to play their role in respecting that right, engineers should have a legally-backed *right of conscience* to take responsible action in safety matters beyond the corporate walls.[20] As legal protections are increased, as has begun to happen during the past decade,[21] then the relative weight of personal life to professional duty changes. Engineers will be able to whistleblow more often without the kind of suffering to which they have been exposed, and thus the *prima facie* obligation to whistleblow will be less frequently overridden by personal responsibilities.

CHARACTER, INTEGRITY, AND PERSONAL IDEALS

Isn't there a danger that denying the existence of absolute, all-things-considered, principles for whistleblowers will further discourage whistleblowing in the public interest? After all, even if we grant my claims about the moral relevance of personal rights and responsibilities, there remains the general tendency for self-interest to unduly bias moral decisions. Until adequate legal protection is secured, won't this contextual approach result in fewer whistleblowers who act from a sense of responsibility? I think not.

If all-things-considered judgments about whistleblowing are not a matter of general rule, they are still a matter of good moral judgment. Good judgment takes into account rules whenever they provide helpful guidance, but essentially it is a product of good character—a character defined by virtues. Character is a further area in which personal aspects of morality bear on engineering ethics, and in the space remaining I want to comment on it.

Virtues are those desirable traits that reveal themselves in all aspects of personality—in attitudes, emotions, desires, and conduct. They are not private merit badges. (To view them as such is the egoistic distortion of self-righteousness.[22]) Instead, virtues are desirable ways of relating to other people, to communities, and to social practices such as engineering. Which virtues are most important for engineers to cultivate?

Here are some of the most significant virtues, sorted into three general categories.[23]

(1) *Virtues of self-direction* are those which enable us to guide our lives. They include the *intellectual virtues* which characterize technical expertise: mastery of one's discipline, ability to communicate, skills in reasoning, imagination, ability to discern dangers, a disposition to minimize risk, and humility (understood as a reasonable perspective on one's abilities). They also include *integrity virtues* which promote coherence among one's attitudes, commitments, and conduct based on a core of moral concern. They include honesty, courage, conscientiousness, self-respect, and fidelity to promises and commitments—those in both personal and professional life. And *wisdom* is practical good judgment in making responsible decisions. This good moral judgment, grounded in the experience of concerned and accountable engineers, is essential in balancing the aspirations embedded in the next two sets of virtues.

(2) *Team-work virtues* include (a) loyalty: concern for the good of the organization for which one works; (b) collegiality: respect for one's colleagues and a commitment to work with them in shared projects; and (c) cooperativeness: the willingness to make reasonable compromises. Reasonable compromises can be integrity-preserving in that they enable us to meet our responsibilities to maintain relationships in circumstances where there is moral complexity and disagreement, factual uncertainty, and the need to maintain ongoing cooperative activities—exactly the circumstances of engineering practice.[24] Unreasonable compromises are compromising in the pejorative sense: they betray our moral principles and violate our integrity. Only good judgment, not general rules, enables engineers to draw a reasonable line between these two types of compromise.

(3) *Public-spirited virtues* are those aimed at the good of others, both clients and the general public affected by one's work. *Justice virtues* concern fair play. One is respect for persons: the disposition to respect people's rights and autonomy, in particular, the rights not to be injured in ways one does not consent to.

Public-spiritedness can be shown in different degrees, as can all the virtues. This helps us understand the sense of responsibility to protect the public that often motivates whistleblowers. Just as professional ethics has tended to ignore the moral relevance of personal life to professional responsibilities, it has tended to think of professional responsibilities solely in terms of *role responsibilities*—those minimal obligations which all practitioners take on when they enter a given profession. While role responsibilities are sufficiently important to deserve this emphasis, they are not the whole of professional ethics. There are also *ideals* which evoke higher aspirations than the minimum responsibilities.[25] These ideals are important to understanding the committed conduct of whistleblowers.

Depth of commitment to the public good is a familiar theme in whistleblowers' accounts of their ordeals. The depth is manifested in how they connect their self-respect and personal integrity to their commitments to the good of others. Roger Boisjoly, for example, has said that if he had it all to do over again he would make the same decisions because otherwise he "couldn't live with any self respect."[26] Similarly, Frank Camps says he acted from a sense of personal integrity.[27]

Boisjoly, Camps, and whistleblowers like them also report that they acted from a sense of responsibility. In my view, they probably acted beyond the minimum standard that all engineers are required to meet, given the absence of protective laws and the severity of the personal suffering they had to undergo. Does it follow that they are simply confused about how much was required of them? J.O. Urmson once suggested that moral heroes who claim to be meeting their duties are either muddled in their thinking or excessively modest about their moral zealousness, which has carried them beyond the call of duty.[28]

Urmson, like most post-Kantian philosophers, assumed that obligations are universal, and hence that there could not be personal obligations that only certain individuals have. I hold a different view.[29] There is such a thing as voluntarily assuming a responsibility and doing so because of commitments to (valid) ideals, to a degree beyond what is required of everyone. Sometimes the commitment is shown in career choice and guided by religious ideals: think of Albert Schweitzer or Mother Teresa of Calcutta. Sometimes it is shown in professional life in an unusual degree of *pro bono publico* work. And sometimes it is shown in whistleblowing decisions.

According to this line of thought, whistleblowing done at enormous personal cost, motivated by moral concern for the public good, and exercising good moral judgment is both (a) supererogatory—beyond the general call of duty incumbent on everyone, and (b) appropriately motivated by a sense of responsibility. Such whistleblowers act from a sense that they *must* do what they are doing.[30] Failure to act would constitute a betrayal of the ideal to which they are committed, and also a betrayal of their integrity as a person committed to that ideal.

Here, then, is a further way in which personal life is relevant to professional life. Earlier I drew attention to the importance of personal rights and responsibilities, and to the unfair personal burdens when others involved in collective enterprises fail to meet their responsibilities. Equally important, we need to appreciate the role of personal integrity grounded in supererogatory commitments to ideals. The topic of being able to live with oneself should not be dismissed as a vagary of individual psychology. It concerns the ideals to which we commit ourselves, beyond the minimum standard incumbent on everyone. This appreciation of personal integrity and commitments to ideals is compatible with a primary emphasis on laws that make it possible for professionals to serve the public good without having to make heroic self-sacrifices.[31]

ENDNOTES

1. Paul Eddy, Elaine Potter, Bruce Page, *Destination Disaster* (New York: Quandrangle, 1976), p. 185.

2. Frank Camps, "Warning an Auto Company About an Unsafe Design," in Alan F. Westin (ed.), *Whistle-Blowing!* (New York: McGraw-Hill, 1981), pp. 119–129.

3. Roger M. Boisjoly, "The Challenger Disaster: Moral Responsibility and the Working Engineer," in Deborah G. Johnson (ed.), *Ethical Issues in Engineering* (Englewood Cliffs, NJ: Prentice-Hall, 1991), pp. 6–14.

4. See, e.g., Myron P. Glazer and Penina Migdal Glazer, *The Whistleblowers* (New York: Basic Books, 1989).

5. Michael Davis, "Avoiding the Tragedy of Whistleblowing," *Business & Professional Ethics Journal* Vol. 8, No. 4 (Winter 1989): 3–19. Davis also draws attention to the potentially negative aspects of laws, as does Sissela Bok in "Whistleblowing and Professional Responsibilities," in D. Callahan and S. Bok (eds.), *Ethics Teaching in Higher Education* (New York: Plenum), pp. 277–295. Those aspects, which include violating corporate privacy, undermining trust and collegiality, and lowering economic efficiency, are serious. But I am convinced that well-framed laws to protect whistleblowers can take them into account. The laws should protect only whistleblowing that meets the conditions for the *prima facie* obligation I state at the beginning of section 3.

6. Robert Nozick drew attention to the symbolic importance of government action in general when he recently abjured the libertarian position he once defended vigorously. *The Examined Life* (New York: Simon and Schuster, 1989), pp. 286–288.

7. The quotes are from Richard T. De George's most recent statement of this view in *Business Ethics*, 3d ed. (New York: Macmillan Publishing, 1990), pp. 208–212. They parallel his view as first stated in "Ethical Responsibilities of Engineers in Large Organizations," *Business & Professional Ethics Journal* Vol. 1, No. 1 (Fall 1981): 1–14. As an example of a far higher demand on engineers see Kenneth D. Alpern, "Moral Responsibility for Engineers," *Business & Professional Ethics Journal* Vol. 2, No. 2 (Winter 1983): 39–47.

8. Gene G. James, "Whistle Blowing: Its Moral Justification," in W. Michael Hoffman and Jennifer Mills Moore (eds.), *Business Ethics*, 2d ed. (New York: McGraw-Hill, 1990), pp. 332–344.

9. David Theo Goldberg, "Tuning in to Whistle Blowing," *Business & Professional Ethics Journal* Vol. 7, No. 2 (Summer, 1988): 85–94.

10. As his reason for conditions (4) and (5), De George cites the fate of whistleblowers who put themselves at great risk: "If there is little likelihood of his success, there is no moral obligation for the engineer to go public. For the harm he or she personally incurs is not offset by the good such action achieves." ("Ethical Responsibilities of Engineers in Large Organizations," p. 7.) Like myself, then, he sees the personal suffering of whistleblowers as morally relevant to understanding professional responsibilities, even though, as I go on to argue, he invokes that relevance in the wrong way.

11. De George, *Business Ethics*, p. 214.

12. See especially Bernard Williams, "A Critique of Utilitarianism: in *Utilitarianism For and Against* (Cambridge: Cambridge University Press, 1973) and "Persons, Character, and Morality," in *Moral Luck* (New

York: Cambridge University Press, 1981). For samples of more recent discussions see the special edition of Ethics 101 (July 1991), devoted to "Impartiality and Ethical Theory."

13. Cf. John Arthur, "Rights and Duty to Bring Aid," in William Aiken and Hugh La Follette (eds.), *World Hunger and Moral Obligation* (Englewood Cliffs, NJ: Prentice-Hall, 1977).

14. Alpern, "Moral Responsibilities for Engineers," p. 39.

15. James, "Whistle Blowing: Its Moral Justification," pp. 334–335.

16. See Martin and Schinzinger, *Ethics in Engineering*, chapter 3. The emphasis on engineers adopting a wide view of their activities does not imply that they are culpable for all the moral failures of colleagues and managers.

17. National Society of Professional Engineers, *Code of Ethics*.

18. Cf. Thomas M. Devine and Donald G. Aplin, "Whistleblower Protection—The Gap Between the Law and Reality," *Harvard Law Journal* 31 (1988), p. 236.

19. I am glad that the NSPE and other professional codes say what they do in support of responsible whistleblowing, as long as it is understood that professional codes only state professional, not personal and all-things-considered obligations. Codes provide a backing for morally concerned engineers, and they make available to engineers the moral support of an entire profession. At the same time, professional societies need to do far more than most of them have done to support the efforts of conscientious whistleblowers. Beyond moral and political support, and beyond recognition awards, they need to provide economic support, in the form of legal funds and job-placement.

20. I defend this right in "Rights of Conscience Inside the Technological Corporation," *Conceptus-Studien*, 4: Wissen and Gewissen (Vienna: VWGO, 1986): 179–191.

21. Alan F. Westin offers helpful suggestions about laws protecting whistle-blowers in *Whistle-Blowing!* For a recent overview of the still fragmented and insufficient legal protection of whistleblowers see Rosemary Chalk, "Making the World Safe for Whistle-Blowers," *Technology Review* 91 (January 1988): 48–57; and James C. Petersen and Dan Farrell, *Whistle-blowing: Ethical and Legal Issues in Expressing Dissent* (Dubuque, Iowa: Kendall/Hunt, 1986).

22. Cf. Edmund L. Pincoffs, *Quandaries and Virtues* (Lawrence, KS: University Press of Kansas, 1986), pp. 112–114.

23. Important discussions of the role of virtues in professional ethics include: John Kultgen, *Ethics and Professionalism* (Philadelphia: University of Pennsylvania Press, 1988); Albert Fiores (ed.), *Professional Ideals* (Belmont, CA: Wadsworth, 1988); and Michael D. Bayles, *Professional Ethics*, 2d edition (Belmont, CA: Wadsworth, 1989). John Kekes insightfully discusses the virtues of self-direction in *The Examined Life* (Lewisburg: Bucknell University Press, 1988).

24. Martin Benjamin, *Splitting the Difference* (Lawrence, KS: University Press of Kansas, 1990).

25. On the distinction between moral rules and ideals see Bernard Gert, *Morality* (New York: Oxford University Press, 1988), pp. 160–178.

26. Roger Boisjoly, ibid., p. 14.

27. Frank Camps, ibid., p. 128.

28. J.O. Urmson, "Saints and Heroes," in A.I. Melden (ed.), *Essays in Moral Philosophy* (Seattle: University of Washington Press, 1958), pp. 198–216.

29. Cf. A.I. Melden, "Saints and Super-erogation," in *Philosophy and Life: Essays on John Wisdom* (The Hague: Martinus Nijhoff, 1984), pp. 61–81.

30. Harry Frankfurt insightfully discusses this felt "must" as a sign of deep caring and commitment in *The Importance of What We Care About* (New York: Cambridge University Press, 1988), pp. 86–88.

31. An earlier version of this paper was read in a lecture series sponsored by the Committee on Ethics in Research at the University of California, Santa Barbara (January 1992). I am grateful for the helpful comments of Jacqueline Hynes and Larry Badash, and also for conversations with Roland Schinzinger on this topic. I am especially grateful for the comments I received from the editor of this journal.

Author's Note: Some notes have been deleted and the remaining ones renumbered.

CASE 6 — Roger Boisjoly and the Challenger Disaster: The Ethical Dimensions

Russell P. Boisjoly

Ellen Foster Curtis

Eugene Mellican

Introduction

On January 28, 1986, the space shuttle *Challenger* exploded 73 seconds into its flight, killing the seven astronauts aboard. As the [American] nation mourned the tragic loss of the crew members, the Rogers Commission was formed to investigate the causes of the disaster. The Commission concluded that the explosion occurred due to seal failure in one of the solid rocket booster joints. Testimony given by Roger Boisjoly, Senior Scientist and acknowledged rocket seal expert, indicated that top management at NASA and Morton Thiokol had been aware of problems with the O-ring seals, but agreed to launch against the recommendation of Boisjoly and other engineers. Boisjoly had alerted management to problems with the O-rings as early as January, 1985, yet several shuttle launches prior to the *Challenger* had been approved without correcting the hazards. This suggests that the management practice of NASA and Morton Thiokol had created an environment which altered the framework for decision making, leading to a breakdown in communication between technical experts and their supervisors, and top level management, and to the acceptance of risks that both organizations had historically viewed as unacceptable. With human lives and the national interest at stake, serious ethical concerns are embedded in this dramatic change in management practice.

In fact, one of the most important aspects of the *Challenger* disaster—both in terms of the causal sequence that led to it and the lessons to be learned from it—is its ethical dimension. Ethical issues are woven throughout the tangled web of decisions, events, practices, and organizational structures that resulted in the loss of the *Challenger* and its seven astronauts. Therefore, an ethical analysis of this tragedy is essential for a full understanding of the event itself and for the implications it has for any endeavor where public policy, corporate practice, and individual decisions intersect.

The significance of an ethical analysis of the *Challenger* disaster is indicated by the fact that it immediately presents one of the most urgent, but difficult, issues in the examination of corporate and individual behavior today, i.e., whether existing ethical theories adequately address the problems posed by new technologies, new forms of organization, and evolving social systems. At the heart of this issue is the concept of responsibility. No ethical concept has been more affected by the impact of these changing realities. Modern technology has so transformed the context and scale of human action that not only do the traditional parameters of responsibility seem inadequate to contain the full range of human acts and their consequences, but even more fundamentally, it is no longer the individual that is the primary locus of power and responsibility, but public and private institutions. Thus, it would seem, it is no longer the character and virtues of individuals that determine the standards of moral conduct, it is the policies and structures of the institutional settings within which they live and work.

Many moral conflicts facing individuals within institutional settings do arise from matters pertaining to organizational structures or questions of public policy. As such, they are resolvable only at a level above the responsibilities of the individual. Therefore, some writers argue that the ethical responsibilities of the engineer or manager in a large corporation have as much to do with the organization as with the individual. Instead of expecting individual engineers or managers to be moral heroes, emphasis should be on the creation of organizational structures conducive to ethical behavior among all agents under their aegis. It would be futile to attempt to establish a sense of ethical responsibility in engineers and management personnel and ignore the fact that such persons work within a socio-technical environment which increasingly undermines the notion of individual, responsible moral agency (Boling and Dempsey, 1981; DeGeorge, 1981).

Yet, others argue that precisely because of these organizational realities individual accountability must be reemphasized to counteract the diffusion of responsibility within large organizations and to prevent its evasion under the rubric of collective responsibility. Undoubtedly institutions do take on a kind of collective life of their own, but they do not exist, or act, independently of the individuals that constitute them, whatever the theoretical and practical complexities of delineating the precise relationships involved. Far from diminishing individuals' obligations, the reality of organizational life increases them because the consequences of decisions and acts are extended and amplified through the reach and power of that reality. Since there are pervasive and inexorable connections between ethical standards and behavior or individuals within an organization and its structure and operation, "the sensitizing of professionals to ethical considerations should be increased so that institutional structures will reflect enhanced ethical sensitivities as trained professionals move up the organizational ladder to positions of leadership" (Mankin, 1981, p. 17).

By reason of the courageous activities and testimony of individuals like Roger Boisjoly, the *Challenger* disaster provides a fascinating illustration of the dynamic tension between organizational and individual responsibility. By focusing on this central issue, this article seeks to accomplish two objectives: first, to demonstrate the extent to which the *Challenger* disaster not only gives concrete expression to the ethical ambiguity that permeates the relationship between organizational and individual responsibility, but also, in fact, is a result of it; second, to reclaim the meaning and importance of individual responsibility within the diluting context of large organizations.

In meeting these objectives, the article is divided into two parts: a case study of Roger Boisjoly's efforts to galvanize management support for effectively correcting the high risk O-ring problems, his attempt to prevent the launch, the scenario which resulted in the launch decision, and Boisjoly's quest to set the record straight despite enormous personal and professional consequences; and an ethical analysis of these events.

Preview for Disaster

On January 24, 1985, Roger Boisjoly, Senior Scientist at Morton Thiokol, watched the launch of Flight 51-C of the space shuttle program. He was at Cape Canaveral to inspect the solid rocket boosters from Flight 51-C following their recovery in the Atlantic Ocean and to conduct a training session at Kennedy Space Center (KSC) on the proper methods of inspecting the booster joints. While watching the launch, he noted that the temperature that day was much cooler than recorded at other launches, but was still much warmer than the 18 degree temperature encountered three days earlier when he arrived in Orlando. The unseasonably cold weather of the past several days had produced the worst citrus crop failures in Florida history.

When he inspected the solid rocket boosters several days later, Boisjoly discovered evidence that the primary O-ring seals on two field joints had been compromised by hot combustion gases (i.e., hot gas blow-by had occurred) which had also eroded part of the primary O-ring. This was the first time that a primary seal on a field joint had been penetrated. When he discovered the large amount of blackened grease between the primary and secondary seals, his concern heightened. The blackened grease was discovered over 80 degree and 110 degree arcs, respectively, on two of the seals, with the larger arc indicating greater hot gas blow-by. Post-flight calculations indicated that the ambient temperature of the field joints at launch time was 53 degrees. This evidence, coupled with his recollection of the low temperature the day of the launch and the citrus crop damage caused by the cold spell, led to his conclusion that the severe hot gas blow-by may have been caused by, and related to, low temperature. After reporting these findings to his superiors, Boisjoly presented them to engineers and management at NASA's Marshall Space Flight Center (MSFC). As a result of his presentation at MSFC, Roger Boisjoly was asked to participate in the Flight Readiness Review (FRR) on February 12, 1985, for Flight 51-E, which was scheduled for launch in April, 1985. This FRR represents the first association of low temperature with blow-by on a field joint, a condition that was considered an "acceptable risk" by Larry Mulloy, NASA's Manager for the Booster Project, and other NASA officials.

Roger Boisjoly had twenty-five years of experience as an engineer in the aerospace industry. Among his many notable assignments were the performance of stress and deflection analysis on the flight control equipment of the Advanced Minuteman Missile at Autonetics, and serving as a lead engineer on the lunar module of Apollo at Hamilton Standard. He moved to Utah in 1980 to take a position in the Applied Mechanics Department as a Staff Engineer at the Wasatch Division of Morton Thiokol. He was considered the leading expert in the United States on O-rings and rocket joint seals and received plaudits for his work on the joint seal problems from Joe C. Kilminster, Vice President of Space Booster Programs, Morton Thiokol (Kilminster, July 1985). His commitment to the company and the community was further demonstrated by his service as Mayor of Willard, Utah, from 1982 to 1983.

The tough questioning he received at the February 12th FRR convinced Boisjoly of the need for further evidence linking low temperature and hot gas blow-by. He worked closely with Arnie Thompson, Supervisor of Rocket Motor Cases, who conducted subscale laboratory tests in March, 1985, to further test the effects of temperature on O-ring resiliency. The bench tests that were performed provided powerful evidence to support Boisjoly's and Thompson's theory: Low temperatures greatly and adversely affected the ability of O-rings to create a seal on solid rocket booster joints. If the temperature was too low (and they did not know what the threshold temperature would be), it was possible that neither the primary [n]or secondary O-rings would seal!

One month later the post-flight inspection of Flight 51-B revealed that the primary seal of a booster nozzle joint did not make contact during its two minute flight. If this damage had occurred in a field joint, the secondary O-ring may have failed to seal, causing the loss of the flight. As a result, Boisjoly and his colleagues became increasingly concerned about shuttle safety. This evidence from the inspection of Flight 51-B was presented at the FRR for Flight 51-F on July 1, 1985; the key engineers and managers at NASA and Morton Thiokol were now aware of the critical O-ring problems and the influence of low temperature on the performance of the joint seals.

During July, 1985, Boisjoly and his associates voiced their desire to devote more effort and resources to solving the problems of O-ring erosion. In his activity reports dated July 22 and 29, 1985, Boisjoly expressed considerable frustration with the lack of progress in this area, despite the fact that a Seal Erosion Task Force had been informally appointed on July 19th. Finally, Boisjoly wrote the following memo, labelled "Company Private," to R.K. (Bob) Lund, Vice President of Engineering for Morton Thiokol, to express the extreme urgency of his concerns. Here are some excerpts from that memo:

> This letter is written to insure that management is fully aware of the seriousness of the current O-ring erosion problem ... The mistakenly accepted position on the joint problem was to fly without fear of failure ... is now drastically changed as a result of the SRM 16A nozzle joint erosion which eroded a secondary O-ring with the primary O-ring never sealing. If the same scenario should occur in a field joint (and it could), then it is a jump ball as to the success or failure of the joint ... The result would be a catastrophe of the highest order—loss of human life ...

> It is my honest and real fear that if we do not take immediate action to dedicate a team to solve the problem, with the field joint having the number one priority, then we stand in jeopardy of losing a flight along with all the launch pad facilities (Boisjoly, July, 1985a).

On August 20, 1985, R.K. Lund formally announced the formation of the Seal Erosion Task Team. The team consisted of only five full-time engineers from the 2500 employed by Morton Thiokol on the Space Shuttle Program. The events of the next five months would demonstrate that management had not provided the resources necessary to carry out the enormous task of solving the seal erosion problem.

On October 3, 1985, the Seal Erosion Task Force met with Joe Kilminster to discuss the problems they were having in gaining organizational support necessary to solve the O-ring problems. Boisjoly later stated that Kilminster summarized the meeting as a "good bullshit session." Once again frustrated by bureaucratic inertia, Boisjoly wrote in his activity report dated October 4th:

> ... NASA is sending an engineering representative to stay with us starting Oct. 14th. We feel that this is a direct result of their feeling that we (MTI) are not responding quickly enough to the seal problem ... upper management apparently feels that the SRM program is ours for sure and the customer be damned (Boisjoly, October, 1985b).

Boisjoly was not alone in his expression of frustration. Bob Ebeling, Department Manager, Solid Rocket Motor Igniter and Final Assembly, and a member of the Seal Erosion Task Force, wrote in a memo to Allan McDonald, Manager of the Solid Rocket Motor Project, "HELP! The seal task force is constantly being delayed by every possible means ... We wish we could get action by verbal request, but such is not the case. This is a red flag" (McConnell, 1987).

At the Society of Automotive Engineers (SAE) conference on October 7, 1985, Boisjoly presented a six-page overview of the joints and the seal configuration to approximately 130 technical experts in hope of soliciting suggestions for remedying the O-ring problems. Although MSFC had requested the presentation, NASA gave strict instructions not to express the critical urgency of fixing the joints, but merely to ask for sugges-

tions for improvement. Although no help was forthcoming, the conference was a milestone in that it was the first time that NASA allowed information on the O-ring difficulties to be expressed in a public forum. That NASA also recognized that the O-ring problems were not receiving appropriate attention and manpower considerations from Morton Thiokol management is further evidenced by Boisjoly's October 24 log entry, "... Jerry Peoples (NASA) has informed his people that our group needs more authority and people to do the job. Jim Smith (NASA) will corner Al McDonald today to attempt to implement this direction."

The October 30 launch of Flight 61-A of the Challenger provided the most convincing, and yet to some the most contestable, evidence to date that low temperature was directly related to hot gas blow-by. The left booster experienced hot gas blow-by in the center and aft field joints without any seal erosion. The ambient temperature of the field joints was estimated to be 75 degrees at launch time based on post-flight calculations. Inspection of the booster joints revealed that the blow-by was less severe than that found on Flight 51-C because the seal grease was a grayish black color, rather than the jet black hue of Flight 51-C. The evidence was now consistent with the bench tests for joint resiliency conducted in March. That is, at 75 degrees the O-ring lost contact with its sealing surface for 2.4 seconds, whereas at 50 degrees the O-ring lost contact for 10 minutes. The actual flight data revealed greater hot gas blow-by for the O-rings on Flight 51-C which had an ambient temperature of 53 degrees than for Flight 61-A which had an ambient temperature of 75 degrees. Those who rejected this line of reasoning concluded that temperature must be irrelevant since hot gas blow-by had occurred even at room temperature

(75 degrees). This difference in interpretation would receive further attention on January 27, 1986.

During the next two and one-half months, little progress was made in obtaining a solution to the O-ring problems. Roger Boisjoly made the following entry into his log on January 13, 1986, "O-ring resiliency tests that were requested on September 24, 1985 are now scheduled for January 15, 1986."

The Day Before the Disaster

At 10 a.m. on January 27, 1986, Arnie Thompson received a phone call from Boyd Brinton, Thiokol's Manager of Project Engineering at MSFC, relaying the concerns of NASA's Larry Wear, also at MSFC, about the 18 degree temperature forecast for the launch of Flight 51-L, the *Challenger*, scheduled for the next day. This phone call precipitated a series of meeting within Morton Thiokol, at the Marshall Space Flight Center; and at the Kennedy Space Center that culminated in a three-way telecon involving three teams of engineers and managers, that began at 8:15 p.m. E.S.T.

Joe Kilminster, Vice President, Space Booster Programs, of Morton Thiokol began the telecon by turning the presentation of the engineering charts over to Roger Boisjoly and Arnie Thompson. They presented thirteen charts which resulted in a recommendation against the launch of the *Challenger*. Boisjoly demonstrated their concerns with the performance of the O-rings in the field joints during the initial phases of *Challenger*'s flight with charts showing the effects of primary O-ring erosion, and its timing, on the ability to maintain a reliable secondary seal. The tremendous pressure and release of power from the rocket boost-

ers create rotation in the joint such that the metal moves away from the O-rings so that they cannot maintain contact with the metal surfaces. If, at the same time, erosion occurs in the primary O-ring for any reason, then there is a reduced probability of maintaining a secondary seal. It is highly probable that as the ambient temperature drops, the primary O-ring will not seat; that there will be hot gas blow-by and erosion of the primary O-ring; and that a catastrophe will occur when the secondary O-ring fails to seal.

Bob Lund presented the final chart that included the Morton Thiokol recommendations that the ambient temperature including wind must be such that the seal temperature would be greater than 53 degrees to proceed with the launch. Since the overnight low was predicted to be 18 degrees, Bob Lund recommended against launch on January 28, 1986 or until the seal temperature exceeded 53 degrees.

NASA's Larry Mulloy bypassed Bob Lund and directly asked Joe Kilminster for his reaction. Kilminster stated that he supported the position of his engineers and he would not recommend launch below 53 degrees.

George Hardy, Deputy Director of Science and Engineering at MSFC, said he was "appalled at that recommendation," according to Allan McDonald's testimony before the Rogers Commission. Nevertheless, Hardy would not recommend to launch if the contractor was against it. After Hardy's reaction, Stanley Reinartz, Manager of Shuttle Project Office at MSFC, objected by pointing out that the solid rocket motors were qualified to operate between 40 and 90 degrees Fahrenheit.

Larry Mulloy, citing the data from Flight 61-A which indicated to him that temperature was not a factor, strenuously objected to Morton Thiokol's recommendation. He suggested that Thiokol was attempting to establish new Launch Commission Criteria at 53 degrees and that they couldn't do that the night before a launch. In exasperation Mulloy asked, "My God, Thiokol, when do you want me to launch? Next April?" (McConnell, 1987). Although other NASA officials also objected to the association of temperature with O-ring erosion and hot gas blow-by, Roger Boisjoly was able to hold his ground and demonstrate with the use of his charts and pictures that there was indeed a relationship: The lower the temperature the higher the probability of erosion and blow-by and the greater the likelihood of an accident. Finally, Joe Kilminster asked for a five minute caucus off-net.

According to Boisjoly's testimony before the Rogers Commission, Jerry Mason, Senior Vice President of Wasatch Operations, began the caucus by saying that "a management decision was necessary." Sensing that an attempt would be made to overturn the no-launch decision, Boisjoly and Thompson attempted to re-review the material previously presented to NASA for the executives in the room. Thompson took a pad of paper and tried to sketch out the problem with the joint, while Boisjoly laid out the photos of the compromised joints from flights 51-C and 61-A. When they became convinced that no one was listening, they ceased their efforts. As Boisjoly would later testify, "There was not one positive pro-launch statement ever made by anybody" (Report of the Presidential Commission, 1986, IV, p. 792, hereafter abbreviated as R.C.).

According to Boisjoly, after he and Thompson made their last attempts to stop the launch, Jerry Mason asked rhetorically, "Am I the only one who wants to fly?" Mason turned to Bob Lund and asked him to "take off his engineering hat and put on his management hat."

The four managers held a brief discussion and voted unanimously to recommend *Challenger*'s launch.

Exhibit I shows the revised recommendations that were presented that evening by Joe Kilminster after the caucus to support management's decision to launch. Only one of the rationales presented that evening supported the launch (demonstrated erosion sealing threshold is three times greater than 0.038" erosion experienced on SRM-15). Even so, the issue at hand was sealability at low temperature, not erosion. While one other rationale could be considered a neutral statement of engineering fact (O-ring pressure leak check places secondary seal in outboard position which minimizes sealing time), the other seven rationales are negative, anti-launch, statements. After hearing Kilminster's presentation, which was accepted without a single probing question, George Hardy asked him to sign the chart and telefax it to Kennedy Space Center and Marshall Space Flight Center. At 11 p.m. E.S.T. the teleconference ended.

Aside from the four senior Morton Thiokol executives present at the teleconference, all others were excluded from the final decision. The process represented a radical shift from previous NASA policy. Until that moment, the burden of proof had always been on the engineers to prove beyond a doubt that it was safe to launch. NASA, with their objections to the original Thiokol recommendation against the launch, and Mason, with his request for a "management decision," shifted the burden of proof in the opposite direction. Morton Thiokol was expected to prove that launching *Challenger* would not be safe (R.C., IV, p. 793).

The change in the decision so deeply upset Boisjoly that he returned to his office and made the following journal entry:

EXHIBIT 1

MTI assessment of temperature concern on SRM-25 (51L) launch

- CALCULATIONS SHOW THAT SRM-25 O-RINGS WILL BE 20° COLDER THAN SRM-15 O-RINGS
- TEMPERATURE DATA NOT CONCLUSIVE ON PREDICTING PRIMARY O-RING BLOW-BY
- ENGINEERING ASSESSMENT IS THAT:
- COLDER O-RINGS WILL HAVE INCREASED EFFECTIVE DUROMETER ("HARDER")
- "HARDER" O-RINGS WILL TAKE LONGER TO "SEAT"
- MORE GAS MAY PASS PRIMARY O-RING BEFORE THE PRIMARY SEAL SEATS (RELATIVE TO SRM-15)
- DEMONSTRATED SEALING THRESHOLD IS 3 TIMES GREATER THAN 0.038" EROSION EXPERIENCED ON SRM-15
- IF THE PRIMARY SEAL DOES NOT SEAT, THE SECONDARY SEAL WILL SEAT
- PRESSURE WILL GET TO SECONDARY SEAL BEFORE THE METAL PARTS ROTATE
- O-RING PRESSURE LEAK CHECK PLACES SECONDARY SEAL IN OUTBOARD POSITION WHICH MINIMIZES SEALING TIME
- MTI RECOMMENDS STS-51L LAUNCH PROCEED ON 28 JANUARY 1986
- SRM-25 WILL NOT BE SIGNIFICANTLY DIFFERENT FROM SRM-15

Joe C. Kilminster, Vice President Space Booster Programs

I sincerely hope this launch does not result in a catastrophe. I personally do not agree with some of the statements made in Joe Kilminster's written summary stating that SRM-25 is okay to fly (Boisjoly, 1987).

The Disaster and

its Aftermath

On January 28, 1986, a reluctant Roger Boisjoly watched the launch of the *Challenger*. As the vehicle cleared the tower, Bob Ebeling whispered, "[W]e've just dodged a bullet." (The engineers who opposed the launch assumed that O-ring failure would result in an explosion almost immediately after engine ignition.) To continue in Boisjoly's words, "At approximately T—60 seconds Bob told me he had just completed a prayer of thanks to the Lord for a successful launch. Just thirteen seconds later we both saw the horror of the destruction as the vehicle exploded" (Boisjoly, 1987).

Morton Thiokol formed a failure investigation team on January 31, 1986 to study the *Challenger* explosion. Roger Boisjoly and Arnie Thompson were part of the team that was sent to MSFC in Huntsville, Alabama. Boisjoly's first inkling of a division between himself and management came on February 13 when he was informed at the last minute that he was to testify before the Rogers Commission the next day. He had very little time to prepare for his testimony. Five days later, two Commission members held a closed session with Kilminster, Boisjoly, and Thompson. During the interview Boisjoly gave his memos and activity reports to the Commissioners. After that meeting, Kilminster chastised Thompson and Boisjoly for correcting his interpretation of the technical data. Their response was that they would continue to correct his version if it was technically incorrect.

Boisjoly's February 25th testimony before the Commission, rebutting the general manager's statement that the initial decision against the launch was not unanimous, drove a wedge further between him and Morton Thiokol management. Boisjoly was flown to MSFC before he could hear the NASA testimony about the pre-flight telecon. The next day, he was removed from the failure investigation team and returned to Utah.

Beginning in April, Boisjoly began to believe that for the previous month he had been used solely for public relations purposes. Although given the title of Seal Coordinator for the redesign effort, he was isolated from NASA and the seal redesign effort. His design information had been changed without his knowledge and presented without his feedback. On May 1, 1986, in a briefing preceding closed sessions before the Rogers Commission, Ed Garrison, President of Aerospace Operations for Morton Thiokol, chastised Boisjoly for "airing the company's dirty laundry" with the memos he had given the Commission. The next day, Boisjoly testified about the change in his job as-

signment. Commission Chairman Rogers criticized Thiokol management, "... if it appears that you're punishing the two people or at least two of the people who are right about the decision and objected to the launch which ultimately resulted in criticism of Thiokol and then they're demoted or feel that they are being retaliated against, that is a very serious matter. It would seem to me, just speaking for myself, they should be promoted, not demoted or pushed aside" (R.C., V, p. 1586).

Boisjoly now sensed a major rift developing within the corporation. Some co-workers perceived that his testimony was damaging the company image. In an effort to clear the air, he and McDonald requested a private meeting with the company's three top executives, which was held on May 16, 1986. According to Boisjoly, management was unreceptive throughout the meeting. The CEO told McDonald and Boisjoly that the company "was doing just fine until Al and I testified about our job reassignments" (Boisjoly, 1987). McDonald and Boisjoly were nominally restored to their former assignments, but Boisjoly's position became untenable as time passed. On July 21, 1986, Roger Boisjoly requested an extended sick leave from Morton Thiokol.

Ethical Analysis

It is clear from this case that Roger Boisjoly's experiences before and after the *Challenger* disaster raise numerous ethical questions that are integral to any explanation of the disaster and applicable to other management situations, especially those involving highly complex technologies. The difficulties and uncertainties involved in the management of these technologies exacerbate the kind of bureaucratic syndromes that generate ethical conflicts in the first place. In fact, Boisjoly's experiences could well serve as a paradigmatic case study for such ethical problems, ranging from accountability to corporate loyalty and whistleblowing. Underlying all these issues, however, is the problematic relationship between individual and organizational responsibility. Boisjoly's experiences graphically portray the tensions inherent in this relationship in a manner that discloses its importance in the causal sequence leading to the *Challenger* disaster. The following analysis explicates this and the implications it has for other organizational settings.

By focusing on the problematic relationship between individual and organizational responsibility, this analysis reveals that the organizational structure governing the space shuttle program became the locus of responsibility in such a way that not only did it undermine the responsibilities of individual decision makers within the process, but it also became a means of avoiding real, effective responsibility throughout the entire management system. The first clue to this was clearly articulated as early as 1973 by the board of inquiry that was formed to investigate the accident which occurred during the launch of Skylab 1:

> The management system developed by NASA for manned space flight places large emphasis on rigor, detail, and thoroughness. In hand with this emphasis comes formalism, extensive documentation, and visibility in detail to senior management. While nearly perfect, such a system can submerge the concerned individual and depress the role of the intuitive engineer or analyst. It may not allow full play for the intuitive judgment or past experience of the individual. An emphasis on management systems can, in itself, serve to separate the people engaged in the program from the real world of hardware (Quoted in Christiansen, 1987, p. 23).

To examine this prescient statement in ethical terms is to see at another level the serious consequences inherent in the situation it describes. For example, it points to a dual meaning of responsibility. One meaning emphasizes carrying out an authoritatively prescribed review process, while the second stresses the cognitive independence and input of every individual down the entire chain of authority. The first sense of responsibility shifts the ethical center of gravity precipitously away from individual moral agency onto the review process in such a way that what was originally set up to guarantee flight readiness with the professional and personal integrity of the responsible individuals, instead becomes a means of evading personal responsibility for decisions made in the review process.

A crucial, and telling, example of this involves the important question asked by the Rogers Commission as to why the concerns raised by the Morton Thiokol engineers about the effects of cold weather on the O-rings during the teleconference the night before the launch were not passed up from Level III to Levels II or I in the preflight review process. The NASA launch procedure clearly demands that decisions and objections methodically follow a prescribed path up all levels. Yet, Lawrence Mulloy, operating at Level III as the Solid Rocket Booster Project Manager at MSFC, did not transmit the Morton Thiokol concerns upward (through his immediate superior, Stanley Reinartz) to Level II. When asked by Chairman Rogers to explain why, Mr. Mulloy testified:

> At that time, and I still consider today, that was a Level III issue, Level III being a SRB element or an external tank element or Space Shuttle main engine element or an Orbiter. There was no violation of Launch Commit Criteria. There was no waiver required

in my judgment at that time and still today (R.C., I, p. 98).

In examining this response in terms of shifting responsibility onto the review process itself, there are two things that are particularly striking in Mr. Mulloy's statement. The first is his emphasis that this was a "Level III issue." In a formal sense, Mr. Mulloy is correct. However, those on Level III also had the authority—and, one would think, especially in this instance given the heated discussion on the effects of cold on the O-rings, the motivation—to pass objections and concerns on to Levels II and I. But here the second important point in Mr. Mulloy's testimony comes into play when he states, "[T]here was no violation of Launch Commit Criteria." In other words, since there was no Launch Commit Criteria for joint temperature, concerns about joint temperature did not officially fall under the purview of the review process. Therefore, the ultimate justification for Mr. Mulloy's position rests on the formal process itself. He was just following the rules by staying within the already established scope of the review process.

This underscores the moral imperative executives must exercise by creating and maintaining organizational systems that do not separate the authority of decision makers from the responsibility they bear for decisions, or insulate them from the consequences of their actions or omissions.

Certainly, there can be no more vivid example than the shuttle program to verify that, in fact, "an emphasis on management systems can, in itself, serve to separate the people engaged in the program from the real world of hardware." Time and time again the lack of communication that lay at the heart of the Rogers Commission finding that "there was a serious flaw in the decision making

process leading up to the launch of flight 51-L" (R.C., I, p. 104) was explained by the NASA officials or managers at Morton Thiokol with such statements as, "[T]hat is not my reporting channel," or "[H]e is not in the launch decision chain," or "I didn't meet with Mr. Boisjoly, I met with Don Ketner, who is the task team leader" (R.C., IV, p. 821, testimony of Mr. Lund). Even those managers who had direct responsibility for line engineers and workmen depended on formalized memo writing procedures for communication to the point that some "never talked to them directly" (Feynman, 1988, p. 33).

Within the atmosphere of such an ambiguity of responsibility, when a life threatening conflict arose within the management system and individuals (such as Roger Boisjoly and his engineering associates at Morton Thiokol) tried to reassert the full weight of their individual judgments and attendant responsibilities, the very purpose of the flight readiness review process, i.e., to arrive at the "technical" truth of the situation, which includes the recognition of the uncertainties involved as much as the findings, became subverted into an adversary confrontation in which "adversary" truth, with its suppression of uncertainties, became operative (Wilmotte, 1970).

What is particularly significant in this radical transformation of the review process, in which the Morton Thiokol engineers were forced into "the position of having to prove that it was unsafe instead of the other way around" (R.C., IV, p. 822; see also p. 793), is that what made the suppression of technical uncertainties possible is precisely that mode of thinking which, in being challenged by independent professional judgments, gave rise to the adversarial setting in the first place: groupthink. No more accurate description for what transpired the night before the launch of the *Challenger* can be given than the definition of groupthink as:

... a mode of thinking that people engage in when they are deeply involved in a cohesive in-group, when the members' strivings for unanimity override their motivation to realistically appraise alternative courses of action.

... Groupthink refers to the deterioration of mental efficiency, reality testing, and moral judgment that results from in-group pressures (Janis, 1972, p. 9).

From this perspective, the full import of Mr. Mason's telling Mr. Lund to "take off his engineering hat and put on his management hat" is revealed. He did not want another technical, reality-based judgment of an independent professional engineer. As he had already implied when he opened the caucus by stating "a management decision was necessary," he wanted a group decision, specifically one that would, in the words of the Rogers Commission, "accommodate a major customer" (R.C., I, p. 104). With a group decision the objections of the engineers could be mitigated, the risks shared, fears allayed, and the attendant responsibility diffused.[1]

This analysis is not meant to imply that groupthink was a pervasive or continuous mode of thinking at either NASA or Morton Thiokol. What is suggested is a causal relationship between this instance of groupthink and the ambiguity of responsibility found within the space shuttle program. Whenever a management system, such as NASA's, generates "a mindset of 'collective responsibility'" by leading "individuals to defer to the anonymity of the process and not focus closely enough on their individual responsibilities in the decision chain," (N.R.C. Report, 1988, p. 68) and there is a confluence of the kind of pressures that came to bear on the decision making process the night before the launch,

the conditions are in place for groupthink to prevail.

A disturbing feature of so many of the analyses and commentaries on the *Challenger* disaster is the reinforcement, and implicit acceptance, of this shift away from individual moral agency with an almost exclusive focus on the flaws in the management system, organizational structures and/or decision making process. Beginning with the findings of the Rogers Commission investigation, one could practically conclude that no one had any responsibility whatsoever for the disaster. The Commission concluded that "there was a serious flaw in the decision making process leading up to the launch of Flight 51-L. A well structured and managed system emphasizing safety would have flagged the rising doubts about the Solid Rocket Booster joint seal." Then the Commission report immediately states, "Had these matters been clearly stated and emphasized in the flight readiness process in terms reflecting the views of most of the Thiokol engineers and at least some of the Marshall engineers, it seems likely that the launch of 51-L might not have occurred when it did" (R.C., I, p. 104). But the gathering and passing on of such information was the responsibility of specifically designated individuals, known by name and position in the highly structured review process. Throughout this process there had been required "a series of formal, legally binding certifications, the equivalent of airworthiness inspections in the aviation industry. In effect the myriad contractor and NASA personnel involved were guaranteeing *Challenger*'s flight readiness with their professional and personal integrity" (McConnell, 1987, p. 17).

When the Commission states in its next finding that "waiving of launch constraints appears to have been at the expense of flight safety," the immediate and obvious question would seem to be: Who approved the waivers and assumed this enormous risk? And why? This is a serious matter! A launch constraint is only issued because there is a safety problem serious enough to justify a decision not to launch. However, the Commission again deflects the problem onto the system by stating, "There was no system which made it imperative that launch constraints and waivers of launch constraints be considered by all levels of management" (R.C., 1986, I, p. 104).

There are two puzzling aspects to this Commission finding. First, the formal system already contained the requirement that project offices inform at least Level II of launch constraints. The Commission addressed the explicit violation of this requirement in the case of a July 1985 launch constraint that had been imposed on the Solid Rocket Booster because of O-ring erosion on the nozzle:

NASA Levels I and II apparently did not realize Marshall had assigned a launch constraint within the Problem Assessment System. This communication failure was contrary to the requirement, contained in the NASA Problem Reporting and Corrective Action Requirements System, that launch constraints were to be taken to Level II (R.C., 1986, I, pp. 138–139; see also p. 159).

Second, the Commission clearly established that the individual at Marshall who both imposed and waived the launch constraint was Lawrence Mulloy, SRB Project Manager. Then why blame the management system, especially in such a crucial area as that of launch constraints, when procedures of that system were not followed? Is that approach going to increase the accountability of individuals within the system for future flights?

Even such an independent[ly] minded and probing Commission member as

Richard Feynman, in an interview a year after the disaster, agreed with the avoidance of determining individual accountability for specific actions and decisions. He is quoted as saying, "I don't think it's correct to try to find out which particular guy happened to do what particular thing. It's the question of how the atmosphere could get to such a circumstance that such things were possible without anybody catching on." Yet, at the same time Feynman admitted that he was not confident that any restructuring of the management system will ensure that the kinds of problems that resulted in the *Challenger* disaster—"danger signs not seen and warnings not heeded"—do not recur. He said, "I'm really not sure that any kind of simple mechanism can cure stupidity and dullness. You can make up all the rules about how things should be, and they'll go wrong if the spirit is different, if the attitudes are different over time and as personnel change" (Chandler, 1987, p. 50).

The approach of the Rogers Commission and that of most of the analyses of the *Challenger* disaster is consistent with the growing tendency to deny any specific responsibility to individual persons within corporate or other institutional settings when things go wrong. Although there are obviously many social changes in modern life that justify the shift in focus from individuals to organizational structures as bearers of responsibility, this shift is reinforced and exaggerated by the way people think about and accept those changes. One of the most pernicious problems of modern times is the almost universally held belief that the individual is powerless, especially within the context of large organizations where one may perceive oneself, and be viewed, as a very small, and replaceable, cog. It is in the very nature of this situation that responsibility may seem to become so diffused that no one person IS responsible. As the National Research Council committee, in following up on the Rogers Commission, concluded about the space shuttle program:

> Given the pervasive reliance on teams and boards to consider the key questions affecting safety, 'group democracy' can easily prevail ... in the end all decisions become collective ones ... (N.R.C. Report, pp. 68 and 70).

The problem with this emphasis on management systems and collective responsibility is that it fosters a vicious circle that further and further erodes and obscures individual responsibility. This leads to a paradoxical—and untenable—situation (such as in the space shuttle program) in which decisions are made and actions are performed by individuals or groups of individuals but not attributed to them. It thus reinforces the tendency to avoid accountability for what anyone does by attributing the consequences to the organization or decision making process. Again, shared, rather than individual, risk-taking and responsibility become operative. The end result can be a cancerous attitude that so permeates an organization or management system that it metastasizes into decisions and acts of life-threatening irresponsibility.

In sharp contrast to this prevalent emphasis on organizational structures, one of the most fascinating aspects of the extensive and exhaustive investigations into the *Challenger* disaster is that they provide a rare opportunity to re-affirm the sense and importance of individual responsibility. With the inside look into the space shuttle program these investigations detail, one can identify many instances where personal responsibility, carefully interpreted, can properly be imputed to NASA officials and to its contractors. By so doing, one can preserve, if only in a fragmentary way, the essentials

of the traditional concept of individual responsibility within the diluting context of organizational life. This effort is intended to make explicit the kind of causal links that are operative between the actions of individuals and the structures of organizations.

The criteria commonly employed for holding individuals responsible for an outcome are two: (1) their acts or omissions are in some way a cause of it; and (2) these acts or omissions are not done in ignorance or under coercion (Thompson, 1987, p. 47). Although there are difficult theoretical and practical questions associated with both criteria, especially within organizational settings, nevertheless, even a general application of them to the sequence of events leading up to the *Challenger* disaster reveals those places where the principle of individual responsibility must be factored in if our understanding of it is to be complete, its lessons learned, and its repetition avoided.

The Rogers Commission has been criticized—and rightly so—for looking at the disaster "from the bottom up but not from the top down," with the result that it gives a clearer picture of what transpired at the lower levels of the *Challenger*'s flight review process than at its upper levels (Cook, 1986). Nevertheless, in doing so, the Commission report provides powerful testimony that however elaborately structured and far reaching an undertaking such as the space shuttle program may be, individuals at the bottom of the organizational structure can still play a crucial, if not deciding, role in the outcome. For in the final analysis, whatever the defects in the *Challenger*'s launch decision chain were that kept the upper levels from being duly informed about the objections of the engineers at Morton Thiokol, the fact remains that the strenuous objections of these engineers so forced the decision process at their level that the four middle managers at Morton Thiokol had the full responsibility for the launch in their hands. This is made clear in the startling testimony of Mr. Mason, when Chairman Rogers asked him: "Did you realize, and particularly in view of Mr. Hardy's (Deputy Director of Science and Engineering at MSFC) point that they wouldn't launch unless you agreed, did you fully realize that in effect, you were making a decision to launch, you and your colleagues?" Mr. Mason replied, "Yes sir" (R.C., 1986, IV, p. 770).

If these four men had just said no, the launch of the *Challenger* would not have taken place the next day. Could there have been any doubt about what was at stake in their decision, or about the degree of risk involved? Not in view of the follow up testimony of Brian Russell, another Thiokol engineer present at the teleconference. Mr. Russell was asked by Mr. Acheson to give his recollection of the thought process followed in his mind "in the change of position between the view presented in the telecon that Thiokol was opposed to the launch, and the subsequent conclusion of the caucus within the company" (R.C., 1986, IV, p. 821). In the course of his response, Mr. Russell stated:

> But I felt in my mind that once we had done our very best to explain why we were concerned, and we meaning those in the camp who really felt strongly about the recommendation of 53 degrees, the decision was to be made, and a poll was then taken. And I remember distinctly at the time wondering whether I would have the courage, if asked, and I thought I might be, what I would do and whether I would be alone. I didn't think I would be alone, but I was wondering if I would have the courage, I remember that distinctly, to stand up and say no ... I was nervous ... there was a nervousness there that we were increasing the risk,

and I believe all of us knew that if it were increased to the level of O-ring burnthrough, what the consequences would be. And I don't think there's any question in anyone's mind about that (R.C., 1986, IV, pp. 822–823).

Some pertinent observations that have direct implications for managers in any organization must be made about where the principle of individual responsibility intersects with the structural flaws and organizational deterioration that have been attributed such a prominent role in the *Challenger* disaster. While it is on the basis of these flaws that the Rogers Commission absolved NASA officials of any direct responsibility for the disaster, it must nevertheless be pointed out that such officials "act in the context of a continuing institution, not an isolated incident, and they or other officials therefore may be culpable for creating the structural faults of the organization, or for neglecting to notice them, or for making inadequate efforts to correct them" (Thompson, 1987, p. 46). While it is true that attributing responsibility demands precision in determining the consequences of acts as much as in identifying the agents, this specificity of outcomes "does not preclude responsibility for patterns of decision and decision making" (Thompson, 1987, p. 48). Therefore, among the outcomes for which managers are held responsible, the continuing practices, standards, and structures of their organizations should be included.

Of all the descriptions of the flaws, break downs, and deterioration of NASA's managerial system, none point to any failures that fall outside the well-documented pathologies of bureaucratic behavior (e.g., lack of communication, distortion of information as it passes up the hierarchy, jealousy of existing lines of authority, bias in favor of the status quo, bureaucratic turf protection, power games, inclination to view the public interest through the distorted lens of vested interests, the "think positive" or "cando" syndrome), and, as such, they can be anticipated. That bureaucratic routines "have a life of their own, often roaming beyond their original purpose, is a fact of organizational behavior that officials should be expected to appreciate. The more the consequences of a decision fit such bureaucratic patterns, the less an official can plausibly invoke the excuse from [sic]ignorance" (Thompson, 1987, p. 61).

So much has been made of NASA's top officials not being fully informed of the extent of the problems with the O-rings, and specifically of the Thiokol engineers' objections to the *Challenger* launch in cold weather, that an analysis of the disaster in *Fortune* magazine had as its title, "NASA's Challenge: Ending Isolation at the Top" (Brody, 1986). The actual extent of their isolation has been questioned, and even the Rogers Commission is not consistent on this issue. In its findings for Chapter V, the Commission states, "A well structured and managed system emphasizing safety would have flagged the rising doubts about the Solid Rocket Booster joint seal." Nevertheless, it concludes in the next chapter that "the O-ring erosion history presented to Level I at NASA Headquarters in August 1985 was sufficiently detailed to require corrective action prior to the next flight" (R.C., 1986, I, pp. 104 and 148).

Whatever the extent of their ignorance, an important principle comes into play in determining the degree of individual responsibility. It is implied in Richard Feynman's position where he drew the line in not ascribing accountability for the *Challenger* disaster to specific individuals. Referring to Jesse Moore, Associate Administrator for Space Flight, the Level I manager with whom final approach for launch rested, Feynman maintained, "[T]he guy at the top should never have an excuse that nobody told him. It seemed to me he ought to go out and find out what's going on" (Chandler, 1987, p. 50). The moral principle underlying Feynman's position here and which must be considered in tracing the boundaries of individual responsibility vis-à-vis the question of ignorance is the principle of "indirect responsibility."

As applied to the issue of ignorance, this principle confronts anyone in any organization with the inherent expectations of his or her position of power and level of expertise. The contours of indirect responsibility follow in the wake of these expectations because the standards against which to measure a claim of ignorance are precisely the standards of a given position and requisite knowledge. Therefore, to reject an excuse from ignorance it is sufficient to say: You are indirectly responsible for what has transpired because, given your position and professional experience, if you didn't know, you should have (Rosenblatt, 1983).

Although this principle operates in a gray area where the difference between indirect responsibility and pardonable ignorance can be marginal, a tragic, complex event like the *Challenger* disaster demands its application. Like the law, ethical thought must not be willing to accept ignorance as a sufficient excuse when it can be reasonably established that those in the causal sequence or in positions of authority should have known, or found out before acting or rendering decisions. This is especially true for managers who become instruments of their own ignorance whenever they prevent the free and complete flow of information to themselves, either directly by their acts, or indirectly through the subtle messages they convey to their subordinates, in their management style, or by the organizational climate they help create (Thompson, 1987, pp. 60–61).

Although fragmentary and tentative in its formulation, this set of considerations points toward the conclusion that however complex and sophisticated an organization may be, and no matter how large and remote the institutional network needed to manage it may be, an active and creative tension of responsibility must be maintained at every level of the operation. Given the size and complexity of such endeavors, the only way to ensure that tension of attentive and effective responsibility is to give the primacy of responsibility to that ultimate principle of all moral conduct: the human individual— even if this does necessitate, in too many instances under present circumstances, that individuals such as Roger Boisjoly, when they attempt to exercise their responsibility, must step forward as moral heroes. In so doing, these individuals do not just bear witness to the desperate need for a system of full accountability in the face of the immense power and reach of modern technology and institutions. They also give expression to the very essence of what constitutes the moral life. As Roger Boisjoly has stated in reflecting on his own experience, "I have been asked by some if I would testify again if I knew in advance of the potential consequences to me and my career. My answer is always an immediate 'yes.' I couldn't live with any self-respect if I tailored my actions based upon the personal consequences …" (Boisjoly, 1987).

From *Journal of Business Ethics* 8: (1989) 217–230. © 1989 Kluwer Academic Publishers. Printed in the Netherlands. Reprinted by permission.

ENDNOTE

1. A contrasting interpretation of the meeting the night before the launch given by Howard Schwartz, is that NASA began to view itself as the ideal organization that did not make mistakes. According to Schwartz, "The organization ideal is an image of perfection. It is, so to speak, an idea of God. God does not make mistakes. Having adopted the idea of NASA as the organization ideal it follows that the individual will believe that, if NASA has made a decision, that decision will be correct" (Schwartz, 1987).

In his testimony before the Rogers Commission, Roger Boisjoly indicated the extent to which NASA procedure had changed: "This was a meeting (the night before the launch) where the determination was to launch, and it was up to us to prove beyond the shadow of a doubt that it was not safe to do so. This is the total reverse to what the position usually is in a preflight conversation or a flight readiness review" (Boisjoly, 1986).

As Schwartz indicates: "If it was a human decision, engineering standards of risk should prevail in determining whether it is safe to launch. On the other hand, if the decision was a NASA decision, it is simply safe to launch, since NASA does not make mistakes" (Schwartz, 1987).

REFERENCES

Boisjoly, Roger M.: 1985a, Applied Mechanics Memorandum to Robert K. Lund, Vice President, Engineering, Wasatch Division, Morton Thiokol, Inc., July 31.

Boisjoly, Roger M.: 1985b, Activity Report, SRM Seal Erosion Task Team Status, October 4.

Boisjoly, Roger M.: 1987, Ethical Decisions: Morton Thiokol and the Shuttle Disaster. Speech given at Massachusetts Institute of Technology, January 7.

Boling, T. Edwin and Dempsey, John: 1981, "Ethical Dilemmas in Government: Designing an Organizational Response," *Public Personnel Management Journal* **10**, 11–18.

Brody, Michael: 1986, "NASA's Challenge: Ending Isolation at the Top," *Fortune* **113** (May 12), pp. 26–32.

Chandler, David: 1987, "Astronauts Gain Clout in 'Revitalized' NASA," *Boston Globe* **1** (January 26), 50.

Christiansen, Donald: 1987, "A System Gone Awry," *IEEE Spectrum* **24** (3), 23.

Cook, Richard C.: 1986, "The Rogers Commission Failed," *The Washington Monthly* **18** (9), 13–21.

DeGeorge, Richard T.: 1981, "Ethical Responsibilities of Engineers in Large Organizations: The Pinto Case," *Business and Professional Ethics Journal* **1**, 1–14.

Feynman, Richard P.: 1988, "An Outsider's View of the Challenger Inquiry," *Physics Today* **41** (2), 26–37.

Janis, Irving L.: 1972, *Victims of Groupthink*, Boston: Houghton Mifflin Co.

Kilminster, J.C.: 1985, Memorandum (E000–FY86–003) to Robert Lund, Vice President, Engineering, Wasatch Division, Morton Thiokol, Inc., July 5.

McConnell, Malcolm: 1987, *Challenger, A Major Malfunction: A True Story of Politics, Greed, and the Wrong Stuff*, Garden City, NJ: Doubleday and Company, Inc.

Mankin, Hart T.: 1981, "Commentary on 'Ethical Responsibilities of Engineers in Large Organizations: The Pinto Case,'" *Business and Professional Ethics Journal* **1**, 15–17.

National Research Council: 1988, *Post-Challenger Evaluation of Space Shuttle Risk Assessment and Management*, Washington, D.C.: National Academy Press.

Report of the Presidential Commission on the Space Shuttle Challenger Accident: 1986, Washington, D.C.: U.S. Government Printing Office.

Rosenblatt, Roger: 1983, "The Commission Report: The Law of the Mind," *Time* **126** (February 21), 39–40.

Schwartz, Howard S.: 1987, "On the Psychodynamics of Organizational Disaster: The Case of the Space Shuttle Challenger," *The Columbia Journal of World Business*, Spring.

Thompson, Dennis F.: 1987, *Political Ethics and Public Office*, Cambridge: Harvard University Press.

Wilmotte, Raymond M.: 1970, "Engineering Truth in Competitive Environments," *IEEE Spectrum* **7** (5), 45–49.

SUGGESTED READINGS

Bok, Sisela. *Secrets: On the Ethics of Concealment and Revelation.* New York: Pantheon Books, 1983.

_____. *Lying: Moral Choice in Public and Private Life.* New York: Pantheon Books, 1978.

_____. "Whistleblowing and Professional Responsibilities." *New York University Education Quarterly*, Vol. II, 4, 1980.

Glazer, M. "Ten Whistleblowers and How They Fared." *The Hastings Center Report*, Vol. 13, December 1983.

Greenberger, David, Marcia Miceli and Debra Cohen. "Oppositionists and Group Norms: The Reciprocal Influence of Whistle-blowers and Co-workers." *Journal of Business Ethics*, Vol. 6, No. 7, 1987.

Isenberg, Arnold. "Deontology and the Ethics of Lying." In William Callahan (ed.) *Aesthetics and the Theory of Criticism: Selected Essays of Arnold Isenberg.* Chicago: The University of Chicago Press, 1973.

Jensen, J. Vernon. "Ethical Tensions in Whistle-blowing." *Journal of Business Ethics*, Vol. 6, No. 4, 1987.

Keenan, J. "Upper-level Managers and Whistle-blowing: Determinants of Perceptions of Company Encouragement and Information about Where to Blow the Whistle." *Journal of Business and Psychology*, 5, 2, 1990, pp. 223–235.

Larmer, R. "Whistleblowing and employee loyalty," *Journal of Business Ethics*, 11, 1992, pp. 125–128.

Loeb, S. and Suzanne Cory. "Whistleblowing and Management Accounting: An Approach." *Journal of Business Ethics*, Vol. 8, No. 12 (December 1989).

Miceli, M. and Janet Near. "The Relationship Among Beliefs, Organizational Position, and Whistle-blowing Status: A Discriminant Analysis." *Academy of Management Journal* 27, 1984.

Miceli, M., J. Near and C. Schwenk. "Who Blows the Whistle and Why?" *Industrial and Labor Relations Review* 45, 1991, pp. 113–130.

Murphy, K. *Honesty in the Workplace.* Belmont, California: Brooks/Cole, 1993.

Near, Janet and Marcia Miceli. "Organizational Dissidence: The Case of Whistle-blowing." *Journal of Business Ethics*, Vol. 4, No. 1, 1985.

Sims, R. and John Keenan. "Predictors of External Whistleblowing: Organizational and Intrapersonal Variables," *Journal of Business Ethics*, 17, 4, 1998, pp. 411–421.

Westin, A. *Blowing the Whistle.* New York: McGraw-Hill, 1980.

_____. *Whistleblowing: Loyalty and Dissent in the Corporation.* New York: McGraw-Hill, 1980.

P   a   r   t

DISCRIMINATION
AND EMPLOYEE
EQUITY

INTRODUCTION

On April 17, 1985, clause 15 of the *Canadian Charter of Rights and Freedoms* came into effect. Clause 15 states as follows:

(1) Every individual is equal before and under the law and has the right to the equal protection and benefit of the law without discrimination and, in particular, without discrimination based on race, national or ethnic origin, colour, religion, sex, age or mental or physical disability.

(2) Subsection (1) does not preclude any law, program or activity that has as its object the amelioration of conditions of disadvantaged individuals or groups including those that are disadvantaged because of race, national or ethnic origin, colour, religion, sex, age or mental or physical disability.

This clause has prompted considerable debate about its implications for hiring, promotion, training and retirement practices in Canada. The debate is not peculiar to the Canadian situation, however, and many of the issues that have been and will continue to be raised are familiar to both philosophers and those concerned with equality issues in law.

Some of the classic questions that arise, and which will be dealt with in this section, involve an examination of the rights of individuals to fair treatment in employment situations. Such questions as the following will be discussed: "What counts as equality in employment?" and "Do individuals have the right not to be discriminated against in hiring and promotion practices?" Other issues to be raised include the justifiability of affirmative action policy, and the imposition of quotas when such policy and quotas may inadvertently result in discrimination against otherwise qualified candidates. Is it justifiable to deny a qualified white male a position in senior management if a less-qualified member of a group that has been discriminated against applies for the same position? More

249

generally, the issue might be stated in terms of means and ends. Is policy that may be unjust to some individuals, justifiable as a means to achieving a more just society overall?

Another related issue is whether it is reasonable to try to remedy past injustices done to particular groups by preferentially treating members of those groups now. The principle appealed to as justification for such policy is called the *principle of compensatory justice* (i.e., the rule that one must rectify past wrongs). This principle is generally considered to be problematic, since those receiving the preferential treatment were not the ones initially discriminated against. A policy of preferential hiring for women, for example, if strictly applied, may result in the hiring of an upper-middle-class privileged woman over an under-privileged male.

Federal legislation imposes national employment equity policy on all Crown corporations and private companies with more than 100 employees and contracts in excess of $200 000. Legislation covers the four disadvantaged target groups identified by the Judge R. Abella's report, a description of which follows. None of the policies involve quotas for the target populations, and it is as yet unclear what these various policies will mean, if anything, with respect to changing Canadian views about employment equity and employee rights.

In "Defining Equality in Employment," Judge R. Abella provides an introduction to some of these issues. Abella begins with a discussion of the concept of equity as it relates to employment practices. This article is excerpted from the report of the Royal Commission on Employment Equity, which the Canadian government set up to examine the implications of clause 15 of the *Charter* on employment in Canada. As Abella notes, consensus about the definition of equality is difficult to achieve, and, in fact, what individuals have thought, and what nations have decided, was equitable

treatment for persons has changed radically over time and differs from nation to nation. Abella suggests that, minimally, equality is "freedom from adverse discrimination." However, what freedom from adverse discrimination means is not all that clear either.

To complicate things further, some people argue that no one has a right to non-discrimination. This position is represented in Jan Narveson's article, "Have We a Right to Non-Discrimination?" Narveson argues that there is no basic right to non-discrimination and that, in fact, "there is no such thing as obligatory basic non-discrimination." Narveson states further that "to require persons to perform all sorts of actions despite the fact that the actions they might instead prefer are not literally harmful to anyone is surely to violate their liberty."

This chapter ends with two case studies. The first, *Re Stelwire Ltd. and United Steelworkers of America, Local 5328,* raises the issue of discrimination on the basis of age. Specifically, the union argued that in requiring a mandatory physical examination of mobile equipment operators over the age of 40 (without conferring the company's right to do so in the collective agreement or by statute), the company was violating the *Human Rights Code* through age discrimination. The union also took the position that the medical examinations would constitute an invasion of the right to privacy. In ruling in favour of the company, the arbitrator accepted "the argument on behalf of the company . . . in its entirety . . ." In assessing this case, the reader should review both sides of this dispute including the reasonableness of imposing medical examinations in the context of the job in question.

The last case, *Central Alberta Dairy Pool v. Alberta Human Rights Commission,* involves adjudication of *bona fide* occupational requirements in a case in which an employee had claimed discrimination on the basis of religious belief, contrary to the *Alberta Individual's Rights Protection Act.* When a company discriminates on a prohibited ground, it is necessary for the employer to prove that the grounds for discrimination constitute a clear, *bona fide* requirement of doing the job. In this case, the appeal of the employee was upheld.

> The law, in its majestic equality, forbids the rich as well as the poor to sleep under bridges, to beg in the streets, and to steal bread.[1]

18

DEFINING EQUALITY
IN EMPLOYMENT

Rosalie Abella

The law in its majestic equality, forbids the rich as well as the poor to sleep under bridges, to beg in the streets, and to steal bread.[1]

Equality is, at the very least, freedom from adverse discrimination. But what constitutes adverse discrimination changes with time, with information, with experience, and with insight. What we tolerated as a society 100, 50, or even 10 years ago is no longer necessarily tolerable. Equality is thus a process—a process of constant and flexible examination, of vigilant introspection, and of aggressive open-mindedness.

One hundred years ago, the role for women was almost exclusively domestic; 50 years ago, some visible minorities were disenfranchised; 25 years ago, Native people lacked a policy voice; and 10 years ago, disabled persons were routinely kept dependent. Today, none of these exclusionary assumptions is acceptable.

But the goal of equality is more than an evolutionary intolerance to adverse discrimination. It is to ensure, too, that the vestiges of these arbitrarily restrictive assumptions do not continue to play a role in our society.

If in this ongoing process we are not always sure what "equality" means, most of us have a good understanding of what is "fair." And what is happening today in Canada to women, Native people, disabled persons, and visible minorities is not fair.

It is not fair that many people in these groups have restricted employment opportunities, limited access to decision-making processes that critically affect them, little public visibility as contributing Canadians, and a circumscribed range of options generally. It may be understandable, given history, culture, economics, and even human nature, but by no standard is it fair.

To attempt to unravel the complex tapestries that hang as a background to discriminatory attitudes can be an unproductive exercise. It is undoubtedly of interest to know why certain attitudes or practices were allowed to predominate; but in devising remedies to redress patently unfair realities, sorting through the malevolent, benevolent, or pragmatic causes of these realities is of little assistance. One can assume that the unfair results would not have occurred without the nourishing environment of limited sensitivities. But as we have these sensitivities educated, we must concentrate not on the motives of the past but on the best way to rectify their impact. And one of those ways is to appeal to our collective sense of fairness.

Equality in employment means that no one is denied opportunities for reasons that have nothing to do with inherent ability. It means equal access free from arbitrary obstructions. Discrimination means that an arbitrary barrier stands between a person's ability and his or her opportunity to demonstrate it. If the access is genuinely available in a way that permits everyone who so wishes the opportunity to fully develop his or her potential, we have achieved a kind of equality. It is equality defined as equal freedom from discrimination.

Discrimination in this context means practices or attitudes that have, whether by design or impact, the effect of limiting an individual's or a group's right to the opportunities generally available because of attributed rather than actual characteristics. What is impeding the full development of the potential is not the individual's capacity but an external barrier that artificially inhibits growth.

It is not a question of whether this discrimination is motivated by an intentional desire to obstruct someone's potential, or whether it is the accidental by-product of innocently motivated practices or systems. If the barrier is affecting certain groups in a disproportionately negative way, it is a signal that the practices that lead to this adverse impact may be discriminatory.

This is why it is important to look at the results of a system. In these results one may find evidence that barriers which are inequitable impede individual opportunity. These results are by no means conclusive evidence of inequity, but they are an effective signal that further examination is warranted to determine whether the disproportionately negative impact is in fact the result of inequitable practices, and therefore calls for remedial attention, or whether it is a reflection of a non-discriminatory reality.

Equality in employment is not a concept that produces the same results for everyone. It is a concept that seeks to identify and remove, barrier by barrier, discriminatory disadvantages. Equality in employment is access to the fullest opportunity to exercise individual potential.

Sometimes equality means treating people the same, despite their differences, and sometimes it means treating them as equals by accommodating their differences.

Formerly, we thought that equality only meant sameness and that treating persons as equals meant treating everyone the same. We now know that to treat everyone the same may be to offend the notion of equality. Ignoring differences may mean ignoring legitimate needs. It is not fair to use the differences between people as an excuse to exclude them arbitrarily from equitable participation. Equality means nothing if it does not mean that we are of equal worth regardless of differences in gender, race, ethnicity, or disability. The projected, mythical, and attributed meaning of these differences cannot be permitted to exclude full participation.

Ignoring differences and refusing to accommodate them is a denial of equal access and opportunity. It is discrimination. To reduce discrimination, we must create and maintain barrier-free environments so that individuals can have genuine access free from arbitrary obstructions to demonstrate and exercise fully their potential. This may mean treating some people differently by removing the obstacles to equality of opportunity they alone face for no demonstrably justifiable reason.

People are disadvantaged for many reasons and may be disadvantaged in a variety of ways—economically, socially, politically, or educationally. Not all disadvantages derive from discrimination. Those that do demand their own particular policy responses.

At present, society's disadvantages are disproportionately assumed by the four designated groups. Clearly, some distinctions have been made or overlooked in the past that have resulted in the disproportionate representation of Native people, visible minorities, disabled persons, and women on the lower rungs of the ladder to society's benefits. By reversing our approach and by using these same distinctions to identify, confront, and eliminate barriers these distinctions have caused in the past, we can reverse the trends, provide access, and open the door to equality.

To create equality of opportunity, we have to do different things for different people. We have to systematically eradicate the impediments to these options according to the actual needs of the different groups, not according to what we think their needs should be. And we have to give individuals an opportunity to use their abilities according to their potential and not according to what we think their potential should be. The process is an exercise in redistributive justice. Its object is to prevent the denial of access to society's benefits because of distinctions that are invalid.

Unless we reject arbitrary distinctions, these four groups will remain unjustifiably in perpetual slow motion. The objectives of breathing life into the notion of equality are to rectify as quickly as possible the results of parochial perspectives which unfairly restrict women, Native people, disabled persons, and visible minorities.

For women, equality in employment means, first, a revised approach to the role women play in the workforce....

For Native people, equality in employment means effective and relevant education and training, accommodation to cultural and geographic realities, a primary voice in the design of the education, training, and funding programs established for their benefit, meaningful support systems, and the delivery of services through Native-run institutions.

For visible minorities, we must begin with an attack on racism, which though sometimes inadvertent is nevertheless pervasive. For immigrants, there is a need for adequate language training, for some mechanism to fairly assess the qualifications of those with non-Canadian experience or education, and for a program of information and counselling to teach and assist them to adjust to Canadian culture....

For disabled persons, there must be as full accommodation as possible and the widest range of human and technical supports....

For all groups, equality means an effective communications network whereby potential employee and employer can become aware of each other, a commitment on the part of educators, employers, and government to revise where necessary those practices that unfairly impede the employment opportunities of women, Native people, disabled persons, and visible minorities, and an end to patronizing and stultifying stereotyping. It means an end to job segregation and the beginning of an approach that makes available to everyone, on the basis of ability, the widest range of options. It means accommodating differences....

If we do not act positively to remove barriers, we wait indefinitely for them to be removed. This would mean that we are prepared in the interim to tolerate prejudice and discrimination. By not acting, we unfairly ignore how inherently invalid these exclusionary distinctions are, and we signal our acceptance as a society that stereotypical attributes assigned to these four groups are appropriate justifications for their disproportionate disadvantages....

It is probable that absolute equality is unattainable.[2] But even if it is, no civilized society worthy of the description can afford not to struggle for its achievement. We may not be able to achieve absolute equality, but we can certainly reduce inequality.[3]

EMPLOYMENT EQUITY/ AFFIRMATIVE ACTION

The achievement of equality in employment depends on a double-edged approach. The first concerns those pre-employment conditions that affect access to employment. The second concerns those conditions in the workplace that militate against equal participation in employment.

Efforts to overcome barriers in employment are what have generally been called in North America affirmative action measures. These include making recruitment, hiring, promotion, and earnings more equitable. They concentrate on making adjustments in the workplace to accommodate a more heterogeneous workforce.

The Commission was told again and again that the phrase "affirmative action" was ambiguous and confusing....

The language that has collected around the issue of equality often produces overwhelming emotional responses. Positions are frequently taken that have not been thought through either to their logical origins or conclusions, and this is true regardless of which side of the argument is being presented; yet they are so strongly held that they leave little room for the introduction of information or contrary judgements....

People generally have a sense that "affirmative action" refers to interventionist government policies, and that is enough to prompt a negative reaction from many. For others, however, much depends on the degree and quality of the intervention. They may never agree to the concept, however reasonably argued, but at least a discussion of the issues will not have been foreclosed by the waving of the semantic red flag. In other words, there may be a willingness to discuss eliminating discriminatory employment barriers but not to debate "affirmative action" as it is currently misunderstood.

The Commission notes this in order to propose that a new term, "employment eq-uity," be adopted to describe programs of positive remedy for discrimination in the Canadian workplace. No great principle is sacrificed in exchanging phrases of disputed definition for newer ones that may be more accurate and less destructive of reasoned debate....

In default of some new verbal coinage, where this Report refers to affirmative action in the Canadian context, it is no more than a convenient way of identifying positive steps to correct discrimination in the workplace. Ultimately, it matters little whether in Canada we call this process employment equity or affirmative action, so long as we understand that what we mean by both terms are employment practices designed to eliminate discriminatory barriers and to provide in a meaningful way equitable opportunities in employment.

PURPOSE OF EMPLOYMENT EQUITY

Much legislative attention has been paid to eradicating and remedying discriminatory behaviour. Human rights acts, labour codes, and the *Charter of Rights and Freedoms* contain provisions to address the problem. By and large these provisions have been limited in two respects: they are restricted to individual allegations of discrimination; and they are potentially restricted, except under the *Ontario Human Rights Code* and the *Canadian Human Rights Act*, to cases of intentional discrimination.

This approach to the enforcement of human rights, based as it is on individual rather than group remedies, and perhaps confined to allegations of intentional discrimination, cannot deal with the pervasiveness and subtlety of discrimination.

Neither, by itself, can education. Education has been the classic crutch upon which we lean in the hopes of coaxing change in prejudicial attitudes. But education is an unreliable agent, glacially slow in movement and impact, and often completely ineffective in the face of intractable views. It promises no immediate relief despite the immediacy of the injustice.

The traditional human rights commission model, which valiantly signalled to the community that redress was available for individuals subjected to deliberate acts of discrimination, is increasingly under attack for its statutory inadequacy to respond to the magnitude of the problem. Resolving discrimination caused by malevolent intent on a case-by-case basis puts human rights commissions in the position of stamping out brush fires when the urgency is in the incendiary potential of the whole forest.

It is sometimes exceptionally difficult to determine whether or not someone intends to discriminate. This does not mean that there is no need for processes that provide remedies to individuals when intentional discrimination can be proven. On the contrary, the need is manifest, but these processes do not sufficiently address the complexity of the problem. There are those who are prejudiced in attitude but not in deed, and others who commit acts of flagrant discrimination out of obliviousness or misplaced benevolence. What we intend is sometimes far less relevant than the impact of our behaviour on others.

The impact of behaviour is the essence of "systemic discrimination." It suggests that the inexorable, cumulative effect on individuals or groups of behaviour that has an arbitrarily negative impact on them is more significant than whether the behaviour flows from insensitivity or intentional discrimination. This approach to discrimination was articulated in 1971 in the U.S. Supreme Court case of *Griggs v. Duke Power Co.*[4] The Court held that one should look at impact rather than motive in deciding whether or not discrimination has taken place. This approach has since been followed by the American courts and it is the one that should be followed here.

Systemic discrimination requires systemic remedies. Rather than approaching discrimination from the perspective of the single perpetrator and the single victim, the systemic approach acknowledges that by and large the systems and practices we customarily and often unwittingly adopt may have an unjustifiably negative effect on certain groups in society. The effect of the system on the individual or group, rather than its attitudinal sources, governs whether or not a remedy is justified.

Remedial measures of a systemic and systematic kind are the object of employment equity and affirmative action. They are meant to improve the situation for individuals who, by virtue of belonging to and being identified with a particular group, find themselves unfairly and adversely affected by certain systems or practices.

Systemic remedies are a response to patterns of discrimination that have two basic antecedents:

a) a disparately negative impact that flows from the structure of systems designed for a homogeneous constituency; and

b) a disparately negative impact that flows from practices based on stereotypical characteristics ascribed to an individual because of the characteristics ascribed to the group of which he or she is a member.

The former usually results in systems primarily designed for white able-bodied males; the latter usually results in practices based on white able-bodied males' perceptions of everyone else.

In both cases, the institutionalized system and practices result in arbitrary and extensive exclusions for persons who, by reason of their group affiliation, are systematically denied a full opportunity to demonstrate their individual abilities.

Interventions to adjust the systems are thus both justified and essential. Whether they are called employment equity or affirmative action, their purpose is to open the competition to all who would have been eligible but for the existence of discrimination. The effect may be to end the hegemony of one group over the economic spoils, but the end of exclusivity is not reverse discrimination, it is the beginning of equality. The economic advancement of women and minorities is not the granting of a privilege or advantage to them; it is the removal of a bias in favour of white males that has operated at the expense of other groups.[5]

Nor should we be ingenuous in believing that once access is expanded, the equal opportunity will translate into treatment as an equal. It is not enough merely to tantalize the excluded groups with the idea that the qualifying education and training by themselves will guarantee employment opportunities. Individuals must be assured that the metamorphosis includes equality not only of access to the opportunities, but to the opportunities themselves for which their abilities qualify them. This is meaningful equality of opportunity.

Equality demands enforcement. It is not enough to be able to claim equal rights unless those rights are somehow enforceable. Unenforceable rights are no more satisfactory than unavailable ones.

This is where we rely on employment equity—to ensure access without discrimination both to the available opportunities and to the possibility of their realization.

EQUALITY IN THE *CHARTER OF RIGHTS AND FREEDOMS*

The genuine pursuit of equality is a litmus test that gauges our success as a liberal democracy. Canada has affirmed its commitment to this pursuit by the inclusion of section 15 of the *Canadian Charter of Rights and Freedoms*.[6]

Section 15 protects every individual's right to equality without discrimination. It states:

(1) Every individual is equal before and under the law and has the right to the equal protection and equal benefit of the law without discrimination and, in particular, without discrimination based on race, national or ethnic origin, colour, religion, sex, age or mental or physical disability.

(2) Subsection (1) does not preclude any law, program or activity that has as its object the amelioration of conditions of disadvantaged individuals or groups including those that are disadvantaged because of race, national or ethnic origin, colour, religion, sex, age or mental or physical disability.

Although the body of section 15(2) refers to actions that have as their object "the amelioration of conditions of disadvantaged individuals or groups," the marginal notes to section 15(2) use the phrase "affirmative action."

Under the *Charter*'s legislative predecessor, the *Canadian Bill of Rights*, the Supreme Court of Canada restricted the definition of equality to "equality of process."[7] The wording of section 15(1) of the *Charter* attracts a more expansive interpretation, for it pronounces the right of equality to be one of process ("before and under the law") and also one of substance ("equal protection and equal benefit"). The law must not only be evenly available, it must be evenly applied.

Until any limits to equality are accepted as demonstrably justified by a court, the presumption is that equality as guaranteed by section 15(1) is unqualified. It is difficult in any case to see how equal freedom from discrimination in process or substance could be limited in a demonstrably justifiable way in a free and democratic society. Section 15 contains its own reasonable limits. It articulates the right to be equally free from discrimination.

As other parts of the *Charter* make clear, however, this does not mean that distinctions among individuals and groups are not to be recognized, or that everyone is necessarily to be treated identically. Honouring and protecting diversity is also one of our [i]deals as a liberal democracy.

Thus certain sections of the *Charter* reinforce the protection from enforced assimilation and provide rules of construction requiring that definitions of equality respect diversity. Section 23[8] protects language rights and freedoms, section 25[9] protects aboriginal rights and freedoms, and section 27[10] protects the diversity of cultural heritage. Section 28 reinforces gender equality. Section 36[11] reiterates Canada's commitment to the promotion of equal opportunity and the reduction of economic disparity. Equality under the *Charter*, then, is a right to integrate into the mainstream of Canadian society based on, and notwithstanding, differences. It is acknowledging and accommodating differences rather than ignoring and denying them.

This is a paradox at the core of any quest for employment equity: because differences exist and must be respected, equality in the workplace does not, and cannot be allowed to, mean the same treatment for all.

In recognition of the journey many have yet to complete before they achieve equality, and in recognition of how the duration of the journey has been and is being unfairly protracted by arbitrary barriers, section 15(2) permits laws, programs, or activities designed to eliminate these restraints. While section 15(1) guarantees to individuals the right to be treated as equals free from discrimination, section 15(2), though itself creating no enforceable remedy, assures that it is neither discriminatory nor a violation of the equality guaranteed by section 15(1) to attempt to improve the condition of disadvantaged individuals or groups, even if this means treating them differently.

Section 15(2) covers the canvas with a broad brush, permitting a group remedy for discrimination. The section encourages a comprehensive or systemic rather than a particularized approach to the elimination of discriminatory barriers.

Section 15(2) does not create the statutory obligation to establish laws, programs, or activities to hasten equality, ameliorate disadvantage, or eliminate discrimination. But it sanctions them, acting with statutory acquiescence....

In contrast to the American system, a finding of discrimination is not a condition precedent under the *Charter* for approving an affirmative action plan. The judicial inquiry, if any, would be into whether or not the group was disadvantaged. Such an inquiry, in the employment context, would probably look for evidence that members of a particular group had higher unemployment rates and lower income levels, and tended to be clustered in jobs with lower occupational status. These have been referred to as the "social indicators" of job discrimination. They can also be characterized as systemic discrimination....

ECONOMIC CONSIDERATIONS

... Full employment is desirable from every conceivable standpoint. In particular this Commission is aware of the advantages full employment would bring to the furtherance of its objectives. The fewer the jobs, obviously, the keener the competition, and the less probability of a generous and open-minded reception for proposals that the rules of the competition be changed. But the Commission must take the economy as it finds it. The fact that the economy is anaemic does not justify a listless response to discrimination.

The members of the four designated groups represent about 60 percent of Canada's total population.[12] They have a right, whatever the economic conditions, to compete equally for their fair share of employment opportunities. As it is, the recession has only intensified their long penalization in the form of undertraining, underemployment, underpayment, and outright exclusion from the labour force.

The competition for jobs must be made an impartial one, open to all who are qualified or qualifiable regardless of gender, ethnicity, race, or disability. It is hard to imagine a valid excuse for postponement, given our avowed ideals and the commitments entrenched in the *Canadian Charter of Rights and Freedoms*. As for awaiting better times, the economic millennium may be further away than anyone comfortably projects.

The pursuit of policies that permit everyone who so wishes access to the realization of his or her full employment potential is not one that ought to be tied to an economic divining rod. The most positive way to prevent further irreversible human and financial costs to these four groups from accumulating is to impose employment equity. Under section 15 of the *Charter* it is permissible, and, while it is not the whole solution, it is a major step.

THE DESIGNATED GROUPS

The Terms of Reference of this Commission encouraged it to look into the most effective means of responding to "deficiencies in employment practices" since "the measures taken by Canadian employers to increase the employability and productivity of women, Native people, disabled persons and visible minorities have as yet not resulted in nearly enough change in the employment practices which have the unintended effect of screening a disproportionate number of those persons out of opportunities for hiring and promotion."

The Terms of Reference also referred to the government's "obligation to provide leadership in ensuring the equitable and rational management of human resources within its organizations." Eleven Crown corporations were singled out for particular study.

In the cross-Canada meetings conducted by the Commission, much concern was expressed by the designated groups over the apparently restrictive focus of the mandate on Crown corporations. Other studies had shown that the problems were far more generalized and not exclusive to government corporations, agencies, and departments. In the face of intractable barriers throughout the marketplace, groups made it clear that they were deeply disappointed at the government's apparent unwillingness to tackle in a meaningful way the problems in the private sector. They felt the credibility of a government's commitment to equality was undermined by approaching the issue in a limited way rather than one sufficiently comprehensive to meet the demonstrated need.

Two facts in particular fuel this disappointment and skepticism. The first is that the federal government has forcefully intervened on behalf of the employment needs of francophones. This served as a direct example to the groups with whom the Commission met of a strong and effective political will. The government concluded rightly that francophones had been unfairly, and often arbitrarily, excluded from access to many of the opportunities available in Canada, and it took strong corrective measures. Fifteen years later, the positive results of this political intervention are apparent, a message to Canadians that a government is prepared to take remedial legislative measures to ensure equitable access to the distribution of the opportunities this country generates.

To the four designated groups from whom this Commission heard, the absence of similar political will and leadership with respect to their own exclusion from opportunities was the subject of much discussion. The fact that one group had been able to attract effective political action while others had only managed to attract repetitive research was both frustrating and inspiring as an example of the art of the politically possible....

The second pertinent fact to which these groups referred was that the country to which Canada has the closest physical and cultural proximity has had for two decades an intensive program of affirmative action. What was striking to them was that the American government had, for 20 years, made genuine efforts to rectify obvious employment inequities in the private sector, while Canadians were still wondering whether to take any steps at all.…

What follows is a consideration of the issues arising from the observations of the various groups. The issues concentrate on the observations members of these groups have about the way they are perceived by others. These collective perceptions were expressed as being determinatively inhibiting in defining the extent to which individuals felt they could maximize their employment opportunities.

A number of articulated employment barriers were common to all groups: insufficient or inappropriate education and training facilities; inadequate information systems about training and employment opportunities; limited financial and personal support systems; short-sighted or insensitive government employment counsellors; employers' restrictive recruitment, hiring, and promotion practices; and discriminatory assumptions.

Every study relevant to these groups in the past five years has urged the implementation of some form of interventionist measures to assist them in the competition for employment opportunities, yet in response, only peripheral adjustments to the system have been made. The progress for these groups has ranged from negligible to slow, yet there is an unexplained apparent reluctance on the part of governments to address squarely the conclusions of their own research.

Women

According to 1982 data, about 52 percent of Canadian women are in the paid labour force. They constitute 41 percent of the workforce. Year after year, women make the case for better childcare facilities, equal pay for work of equal value, equitable benefits, equal employment opportunities, unbiased educational options, and an end to job segregation. Year after year, they are told by governments that measures are being looked into and solutions being devised.…

One of the major impediments to women having adequate employment opportunities, articulated by both women and employers, has to do with the education choices made by females. If these choices are based on an assumption by females that they need not seek paid employment, that their economic security will flow from a marriage, then clearly they will not address the issue of which educational options will provide them with better employment skills. Where they are interested, and most are, in seeking employment, they must participate in the full range of available educational opportunities. This will require dramatic changes in the school system.

For women interested in joining or rejoining the workforce later in life, training and educational opportunities must be made available so that they have a chance to work at the widest range of jobs. Nor should they be neglected in the wake of technological change. Every effort must be made to attempt to break the mold that results in job and economic segregation.

What precedes employment may be just as important as what occurs once employment is obtained. The cultural ambience from which men and women emerge affects what takes place in the workplace. How men and women perceive one another as spouses and how children perceive their parents both determine what happens to women in the workforce. If women are considered economic and social dependents in the home, they will continue to be treated as subservient in the workplace. If, on the other hand, they are perceived as social and economic equals in a partnership in the home, this will be translated into the practices of the workplace. Two issues must therefore be addressed simultaneously: the way women are perceived generally in society, and the employment practices that affect women in any given corporation.

The problem is one of assumptions, almost religiously held, about the role and ability of women in Canada. Many men and women seem unable to escape from the perceptual fallout of the tradition that expects women to behave dependently and supportively toward men.

The historic and legally sanctioned role of women in Canada has been as homemaker. For more than a century, in every province, the legal doctrines around marriage required that the legal personae of husband and wife merge into that of the husband. This obliterated the wife's identity as an independent legal entity. It also required, rather than permitted, the husband to be the breadwinner, resulting in the allocation of the homemaking function to the wife.

Only in the recent past have provinces begun to impose an equal obligation on husband and wife to be responsible for their own support. The right of one spouse to support from the other now flows mainly from economic need arising from the spousal relationship and its division of labour rather than from gender. Marriage is to be considered a partnership of social and economic equals, and the division of labour in marriage between breadwinner and homemaker is to be considered a division of two equally valuable contributions to this partnership.

Notwithstanding the existence of this legal requirement that no one gender should expect the other automatically to provide financial support, childcare, or household services, it will likely be generations before the impact of this newly sanctioned approach to marriage is reflected in society's other institutions. Nevertheless, it immediately requires courts to consider that although one spouse, usually the wife, remains

at home, the homemaking contribution is to be considered equally valuable to the spousal relationship whether or not its efforts generate income. There is no longer an automatic division of household responsibilities based on gender in spousal relationships. The responsibilities of economic self-sufficiency and parenting are bilateral.

At the same time, it would be wrong to undervalue the role of homemaking and to ignore its economic contribution simply because it is not "employment" as it has been traditionally defined. Homemakers, who have made choices authorized by law and justified by their own spousal relationships, should not be penalized economically because the majority of women are now making different choices.

The essence of equality for women, now and in the future, is that in their options, which may or may not include the selection of a "traditional" role, they face no greater economic liability than would a man, and that in whatever "employment" environment they choose, they receive the same benefit for their contributions as would a man....

Although women have the same right to work and stay home as do men, until the legal directive in modern family law that each spouse is responsible for his or her own support takes root and inspires routinely in young girls and women the realization that they themselves, no less than any future spouse, must be financially self-reliant, women will likely be the gender performing the homemaking responsibilities.

In 1982, there were more than 70 000 divorces granted in Canada; about one in every three marriages now ends in divorce. Census figures show that the number of single-parent families increased from 477 525 in 1971 to 714 005 in 1981. Eighty-five percent of single-parent families in 1981 were headed by a woman, and Statistics Canada data show that three out of five female-headed families were living below the poverty line. Women who have functioned primarily as homemakers may suffer enormously heavy economic penalties when their marriages unravel, and they should be assisted in the form of tax and pension measures as well as enforceable maintenance and support systems to help them resist poverty and achieve financial viability. When they apply for jobs, their homemaking and volunteer work should be considered legitimate work experience. If they work part-time, they should not bear the unfair financial brunt of a perception that part-time work is not serious work. They should be remunerated and receive benefits on a pro-rated basis with workers employed full-time.

But for all women, whether they work at home or in the paid labour force, it is crucial that they not be deemed for policy purposes as economic satellites of their partners. Tax laws, pension schemes, the public perception of parental responsibilities—all these need to be examined, and in some cases drastically revised, to confirm for women their status as independent individuals, to negate the perception of their dependency, and to discredit the assumption that they have a different range of options than men have.

Notwithstanding that there is an equal right to work, there is no avoiding certain biological imperatives. Women rather than men become pregnant. Children require care. An environment must therefore be created that permits the adequate care of children while also allowing the equal right of men and women to maximize their economic potential. This environment, however, is not possible if the public continues to assume that the primary responsibility for the care of children belongs to women. There is no mysterious chemistry that produces in one gender an enhanced ability either to raise children or to work at a paid job....

Many women find that their current or prospective status as a mother is a powerful factor on a hidden agenda affecting hiring and promotion practices. Some companies fear hiring young women who,

though otherwise qualified, are potential childbearers. The prospect of maternity leave appears to inspire alarm in a way that training leaves, extended vacations, or even lengthy illnesses do not. This alarm is communicated throughout the female candidate pool and results in a form of psychological contraceptive blackmail....

Employers should presume no more about what mothers can, should, or should not do, than they do about fathers. Employers must operate on the assumption that their male and female employees have the same family responsibilities....

Most women work in the clerical, sales, and support services of any corporation. These are not only the lowest paying jobs, they also tend to be jobs limited in opportunities for promotion. Even where women perform managerial functions, as many secretaries do, they are not given credit for these responsibilities when candidates for promotion to management are sought. Nor do women get the same educational or training leaves in corporations as do men, and they are rarely selected by corporations for significant corporate policy task forces or committees. Women must train for, be hired in, and [be] given opportunities for the full range of occupational categories in order to break out of the economically limiting job segregation they now experience. This means more than an occasional token appointment of a woman to a management position; it means the routine hiring of qualified women throughout the occupational layers of a workforce.

Their work, wherever they perform it, should be valued and remunerated no differently than work done by men. There is no excuse for excluding paid domestic workers from the protection of human rights or employment legislation. At the workplace, women should be free from sexual harassment. When sexual harassment has been proven, women should have available an effective and early remedy. They should be encouraged to qualify and apply for the widest range of jobs and careers, but where they choose to work in jobs traditionally held by women they should not, by virtue of working in a predominantly female occupation, be paid less than is paid for work that is no more valuable but is done predominantly by men.

Women should be encouraged to set up their own businesses and be assisted by banks and other lending institutions with no less serious consideration than that accorded to men and no more onerous proof of the business potential than that required of men....

Unless concentrated attention is given to all of these issues, little will change. Human rights commissions must have the resources they need to fulfil their mandate; women must be encouraged by all political parties to play an equal and effective role both as candidates and as policy advisers; the media must become more self-conscious about how they portray issues they consider "female"; businesses must be made to examine their practices to identify and eliminate barriers facing women; and the public must be taught to stop thinking in terms of how a particular gender ought to behave and to start thinking in terms of equal options. Until all these initiatives are undertaken, women and men will be less than they could otherwise be....

Native People

Native people in Canada include Status and non-Status Indians, Métis, and Inuit.

It is not new that their economic conditions are poor. Study after study has documented the facts. The unemployment rate of Native people is more than twice that of other Canadians. Those in the labour force are concentrated in low-paid, low-skill jobs. The average employment income in 1980 for Native men was 60.2 percent of the average income for non-Native men; for Native women it was 71.7 percent of the average income for non-Native women.

Their economic plight has taken its inevitable toll on social conditions. Native people are angry over the disproportionate numbers of Native people who drop out of school, who are in prison, who suffer ill-health, who die young, who commit suicide. They are saddened by the personal, communal, and cultural dislocation of their people....

There are insufficient numbers of Native people teaching, resulting in an absence of role models for young children. Curricula in the public and high schools do not reflect the cultural differences of Native persons, and therefore a sense of either alienation or unreality inhibits the development of the minds of children who are being taught about a world that often seems inhospitable or irrelevant to them....

There is an inadequate supply of relevant training programs. Training programs designed with insufficient input from Native people often result in skills developed for jobs that are either unavailable or low-paying. Waiting lists are often as long as two years. There is a strong unmet demand for trades and technical training, as well as for basic literacy training and for upgrading and preparatory courses, such as basic job readiness. The lack of training programs specially designed for Native people means that many existing programs are ineffective for them. Educational requirements for many of these training programs are felt to be unrealistically and inappropriately high and therefore arbitrarily exclude less educated Native people from participating....

Native women feel that they are doubly disadvantaged—on one level because they are women and on another level because they are Native people. They feel that they are being constantly streamed into low-paying and irrelevant job opportunities....

For Native women, particularly those living on reserves and in rural and remote areas, the lack of childcare acts as a barrier to training and employment opportunities. These women are also concerned that where childcare facilities do exist they tend not to be run by Native people who can enhance the cultural environment found in the child's home.

... The government agencies that provide services to adult Native people are generally staffed by non-Native persons who are often unable to understand the needs of Native persons. The most frequent use of Native persons is made in the Outreach program, whose workers perform many of the same functions as do regular government employees but are employed on a year-to-year contract position, with no benefits or security. They are perceived by Native people to be critical to the delivery of government-run services for Native people. There is resentment that Native Outreach workers are being paid at a lesser rate than government employees, most of whom are not Native people.

Native people living in urban areas encounter numerous difficulties. For Status Indians, some of these difficulties stem from the fact that they are not entitled to benefits that accrue to them if they live on reserves. This limits their options and is a disincentive to seeking job opportunities off the reserves, even if job opportunities are severely limited on the reserves. Status Indians requested amendments to the tax system to soften the impact of living off the reserves....

Native people need better housing, services, and medical care. The Indian people want the paternalistic *Indian Act* abolished; it controls who can belong to Indian bands, the administration of reserves and reserve lands and resources, the ownership of reserve lands and education.

The central issues for Native people are their exclusion from relevant decision-making, the fragmented and uncoordinated programming, the problem of uncoordinated policy approaches, the absence of federal/provincial/municipal coordination of service delivery systems, and the constant sense that they are forever subject to the discretion of people who do not understand their culture....

Disabled Persons

The World Health Organization distinguishes among "impairment," "disability," and "handicap." An "impairment" embraces any disturbance of or interference with the normal structure and function of the body, including the systems of mental function.[13] Health and Welfare Canada statistics place the number of Canadians who have some form of mental or physical impairment at 5.5 million.[14]

"Disability," according to the World Health Organization, "is the loss or reduction of functional ability and activity" that results from an impairment. In other words, an impairment does not necessarily produce a disability, a fact reflected in the Health and Welfare Canada statistics estimating that fewer than half (2.3 million) of impaired Canadians can be termed disabled.

A "handicap" is defined by the World Health Organization as the disadvantage that is consequent upon impairment and disability.

Persons with disabilities experience some limitation of their work functioning because of their physical or mental impairment. But the extent to which their disability affects their lives on a daily basis—that is, handicaps them—is very often determined by how society reacts to their disability. A disabled person need not be handicapped.

The significance of these distinctions lies in the fact that we have tended to consider disabled persons as a uniformly incapacitated group of people. Disability may or may not lead to a handicap affecting employment.

The issue must be examined from the point of view of the individual who has the disability rather than from the point of view of the assumptions of the employer. This is not to suggest that an employer's needs and concerns are not relevant; in fact, they may be critically so. But it is to suggest that the way one deals with this issue is first to determine whether or not the disabled person is qualified or qualifiable, and secondly to determine what measures are necessary to maximize the ability of a qualified disabled individual to perform the job for which he or she is being employed....

There are many aspects of the systems and policy measures designed for disabled persons that have not been thought through. Generally, the problems include the fragmentation of policies, the short-term nature of many of the programs, the lack of continuity in these programs where they do exist, the uncoordinated approach among the various levels of government and within each level of government, and the lack of information about what programs in fact exist....

Where training programs do exist, the waiting period is too lengthy and the programs inadequate or irrelevant. They rarely result in jobs. Many disabled persons feel they would benefit from more on-the-job training.

There is an overwhelming problem for disabled persons in the way welfare and disability pension systems operate in this country. Programs have been devised that operate as a disincentive rather than an inducement to entering the labour force. Most welfare and disability pension schemes under which disabled persons receive income require that they choose between the income from these schemes and from employment. The loss of a pension, for example, often results in the loss of medical and social support benefits. These may no longer be affordable once a disabled person is employed because the work opportunities available are often part-time and usually in low-paying jobs. There is rarely enough income from these jobs to pay for the benefits formerly provided by welfare or disability pensions. This means as well that there is rarely enough money to pay for work-related expenses such as transportation.

Moreover, welfare and disability pension schemes normally are set up so that an individual no longer getting the benefit of these schemes disqualifies herself or himself for a substantial period of time before becoming again eligible for these benefits. If a job does not work out for a disabled indi-

vidual and he or she is again unemployed, there is the crucial problem of what the next source of income will be.

Unless these income systems are redesigned to take into account the financial reality disabled persons face, it is unreasonable to expect many disabled persons to risk economic security by seeking a job. When an individual has lived for years under the shadow of a public perception that he or she is incapable of functioning at the workplace in a meaningful way, that individual is likely to be insecure about having the ability to do so. The object of ameliorative programs, therefore, is to neutralize this insecurity, to encourage confidence, and to make the prospect of employment an economically and socially viable one....

More employment training must exist, and on-the-job support in the form of technical aids, personnel assistance, and a sensitized able-bodied workforce must all be offered to make employment possible for disabled persons. Transportation systems have to be devised to ensure that physical access to employment is possible, and buildings must be constructed or retrofitted to be physically accessible in all respects to disabled persons....

The problem of irrelevant job requirements affects all four designated groups. Job requirements that have a disparate impact on certain groups need to be analyzed to determine whether or not they are justified. Employment practices resulting in disparate impact are justifiable only if no reasonable alternative exists or if the practice is dictated by business necessity.

A related issue is the question of when an employer should be required to reasonably accommodate a disabled employee. Incentives must be given to employers to ensure that in those circumstances where accommodations should be made, it is economically feasible for the employer to make them. Amendments should be made to the *Income Tax Act* in order to permit employers to fully deduct these costs....

There is an additional concern that not enough emphasis is placed on preparing these workers for and facilitating their entry into the general workforce. Sheltered workshops, where they exist, should provide job placement services so that a greater number of disabled persons who are trained in these facilities are able to enter the workforce. Workshops must be encouraged to seek opportunities for more relevant long-term work for disabled workers. There should be defined guidelines as to the duration, quality, and evaluation of training in sheltered workshop programs so that an individual's successful completion of the program may be determined....

Although human rights statutes should continue to protect people with as wide a range of disabilities as possible from discriminatory acts or systems, employment equity programs should concentrate on attempting to increase employment opportunities for those persons whose permanent or long-term disabilities seriously handicap them in access to employment opportunities. Disabled persons should be defined for purposes of an employer's obligation to collect data under employment equity legislation as those persons whose general access to employment opportunities has been or has appeared to have been limited by the existence of a permanent or long-term disability. Because of the individualized approach employers must take in eliminating employment barriers for the different impairments a disabled employee may have, the emphasis in monitoring the success of employment equity systems for disabled persons should be less quantitative or data oriented. Disabled persons are so heterogeneous a group that each disability requires accommodation in a different way. This makes any emphasis on numerical change potentially unfair both to the disabled employee and to the employer....

Therefore, [there is a need] for restricted and careful use of medical examinations as a pre-employment selection process to en-sure that these examinations form only part of a *bona fide* occupational requirement and do not result in an arbitrary exclusion from employment....

For disabled persons, as for other individuals, two stages in employment equality are called for. The first stage is the preparation for their eligibility to compete fairly and equally for jobs—qualifying the qualifiable candidate for employment. In the education of the disabled child, for instance, the child should be made to feel that he or she is an equal social participant, with access to whatever services and systems exist for the general public.

The second stage is in preparing the work environment itself, where the effectiveness of the disabled person's performance may be determined by the extent to which the disability is either ignored, accommodated, or over-emphasized.

This emphasis on integration should be carried into an examination of which institutions are properly providing the care disabled persons need and which are unfairly isolating them from general opportunities. In addition, the public should be educated against making stereotypical judgements about disabled persons which prevent them from gaining access to those things to which they are otherwise entitled. The best education is the employment of a qualified disabled person who can, by doing a job, teach able-bodied fellow employees and employers that what was thought impossible is not only possible but inevitable.

It is not just the opportunity of becoming employed that is at issue, it is the opportunity, once employed, of being able to move through a corporation with the same facility as would any other employee with a disabled individual's qualifications....

Visible Minorities

Visible minorities were defined by this Commission for purposes of the questionnaire requesting data from the designated Crown corporations as "non-whites"....

Focusing on visible minority groups through employment equity programs does not relieve society of the responsibility to eradicate discrimination for all minority groups. It does not cancel the duty to provide for immigrants adequate language and skill training, bias-free mechanisms for determining the validity of foreign credentials and experience, and vigilant regard for whether employers are unreasonably making Canadian experience a job requirement. Nor does it absolve the school systems of their responsibility to ensure that minorities—visible or otherwise—are not being streamed routinely into certain types of courses. These are examples of the kind of measures that should be undertaken in any event to protect Canada's minorities from arbitrarily exclusionary systems....

The problems for newly arrived immigrants are enormous. There is little information given to them prior to their emigrating to prepare them for living in Canada, and they often arrive completely unfamiliar with Canadian life and institutions....

This has critical implications in employment contexts. In the interviewing process, for example, people are often hired on the basis of, among other things, an interviewer's perception of their ability to integrate easily into a given labour force. This may not be relevant either to the candidate's actual ability to integrate or to his or her qualifications.

Consistently across Canada the Commission heard that the language training an immigrant receives upon arrival is inadequate. The training tends to be too short; it tends to be English or French immersion which, for many immigrants, is an impossible pedagogical style; it is usually not taught by someone who speaks their own language; and it rarely provides instruction sufficient for them to be able to communicate with any degree of fluency. Moreover, an individual almost never receives language training in

his or her own skill or profession. The absence of technical language training practically guarantees that the immigrant's job opportunities are severely restricted and that whatever qualifications he or she brought to this country will be underutilized.

Not only was the language instruction itself deemed to be a problem, the fact that full-time programs are offered mainly to persons expected immediately to enter the paid labour force means that some immigrant women learn little or no English. If they subsequently join the paid workforce, their lack of language skills means that they are reduced to applying for low-paying, ghettoized jobs with little prospect of economic advancement. They are ripe for exploitation.

Immigrant women are disadvantaged, too, by the lack of adequate childcare facilities. Without access to childcare, some immigrant women who want to work cannot and many are unable to take language or training courses even when these courses are available.

A further difficulty is created by the absence of language training as an alternative to, or in conjunction with, employment opportunities. It is difficult to learn a language while employed. Once an immigrant has entered the labour force there is no financial assistance available for him or her to stop work temporarily, either to complete language training or to learn the language of his or her own profession or skill. Very little on-the-job language training exists, a system that would be exceptionally helpful to people anxious to integrate and contribute economically as quickly as possible. The result for many immigrants is that they tend to be locked into whatever jobs they obtain when they first arrive....

The problem of professional or career credentials from other countries is a serious one for many who try without success to find ways of satisfying an employer that their educational qualifications match those required to perform the job.

Many skilled and professional immigrants are frustrated by the absence of a mechanism to determine whether or not the professional qualifications they bring to this country qualify them to practise their profession in Canada or to determine what upgrading courses are necessary. The examinations and licencing requirements for many occupations and professions across Canada are prohibitively expensive. There is an additional problem of portability from province to province of professional qualifications. A system of qualification and credential assessment should be available so that recent as well as prospective immigrants can be advised accurately about exactly what is necessary in order to qualify them to practise their professions....

The problem is essentially one of racism. Strong measures are therefore needed to remedy the impact of discriminatory attitudes and behaviour flowing from this problem.

What is clear is that many groups of people living in Canada despair about ever being able to avail themselves of the economic, political, or social opportunities that exist in this country. They increasingly experience a sense of futility. Nothing short of strong legislative measures is necessary to reverse, or at least inhibit, the degree to which members of visible minorities are unjustifiably excluded from the opportunity to compete as equals....

ENDNOTES

1. Anatole France, *Le Lys Rouge (The Red Lily)*. Quoted in John Bartlett, *Familiar Quotations*. (Boston: Little Brown and Company, 1980), p. 655.

2. Jeremy Bentham, "Absolute Equality is Absolutely Impossible," in John Bowring (ed.), *The Works of Jeremy Bentham*. Vol. 1. (Edinburgh: William Tate, 1843), p. 361.

3. Ibid., p. 311.

4. *Griggs v. Duke Power Co.* 401 U.S. 424 (1971).

5. Robert Belton, "Discrimination and Affirmative Action: An Analysis of Competing Theories of Equality and Weber," 59 *North Carolina Law Review* (1981), p. 537, footnote 28. Belton argues that "reverse discrimination" is a legal fiction.

6. *The Constitution Act* 1982, C. 11 (U.K.) Section 15 does not come into force until after April 17, 1985.

7. R.S.C. 1970 Appendix III. See *Attorney General for Canada v. Lavell*, [1974] S.C.R. 1349; *Bliss v. Attorney General for Canada*, [1979] 1 S.C.R. 183.

8. Section 12(1) states:

   Citizens of Canada

   (a) whose first language learned and still understood is that of the English or French linguistic minority population of the province in which they reside, or

   (b) who have received their primary school instruction in Canada in English or French and reside in a province where the language in which they received that instruction is the language of the English or French linguistic minority population of the province, have the right to have their children receive primary and secondary school instruction in that language in that province.

9. Section 25 states:

   The guarantees in this *Charter* of certain rights and freedoms shall not be construed so as to abrogate or derogate from any aboriginal treaty or other rights or freedoms that pertain to the aboriginal people of Canada including

   (a) any rights or freedoms that have been recognized by the Royal Proclamation of October 7, 1763; and

   (b) any rights or freedoms that may be acquired by the aboriginal peoples of Canada by way of land claims settlement.

10. Section 27 states:

    This *Charter* shall be interpreted in a manner consistent with the preservation and enhancement of the multicultural heritage of Canadians.

11. Section 36(1) states:

    Without altering the legislative authority of Parliament or of the provincial legislatures, or the rights of any of them with respect to the exercise of their legislative authority, Parliament and the legislatures, together with the governments, are committed to

(a) promoting equal opportunities for the well-being of Canadians;

(b) furthering economic development to reduce disparity in opportunities; and

(c) providing essential public services of reasonable quality to all Canadians.

12. Women, Native males, and male members of visible minorities make up 57 percent of the Canadian population. (Statistics Canada, 1981 Census of Canada. Catalogue 92–911. Volume 1—National Series (Population).) Although there is no precise data on the number of disabled males in Canada, it is conservatively estimated that 10 percent of the Canadian population is disabled.

13. World Health Organization, Philip H.N. Wood, WHO/ICD9/REV. CONF/75.15.

14. Canada, Health and Welfare, *Disabled Persons in Canada* (Ottawa, 1981), p. 7.

HAVE WE A RIGHT TO NON-DISCRIMINATION?

Jan Narveson

1. PREFATORY

Discrimination stands very high on the list of what is currently accounted injustice. Indeed, the pages of North American journals, at least, tend to be filled with articles addressing the issue of whether *reverse* discrimination is justified or not; but that discrimination itself is unjust is scarcely ever questioned. The point of the present essay is to question it anyway. I largely share the tendency to regard much of what is currently regarded as discriminatory as a bad thing, something to condemn and certainly to avoid. I am much less certain, though, that it is in addition something to prohibit by the machinery of the law. At a minimum—and this is the motivation for the essay—I am puzzled. So the reader may construe the following investigation as an invitation to come forth with a clear account of the matter, at any rate, for I am quite sure

that none has as yet been given. And that seems to me to be a very bad thing. When we prohibit the activities of voluntary and rational human beings, we ought, one would think, to have a clear and compelling reason for it. The current tendency seems to be to assume that the wrongness of discrimination is self-evident. That attitude, I am sure we'll all agree, will not do.

2. INITIAL DEFINITIONS

Discrimination requires three persons at a minimum: (1) the Discriminator, (2) the Discriminatee, the person discriminated against, and (3) the parties who have been favored in comparison with the discriminatees; perhaps we can call this class the Beneficiaries. Further, there has to be some characteristic possessed by the second class of persons on account of which they are treated less well than the third; being black,

This article first appeared in the first edition of this text.

or a woman, or a foreigner, or non-Christian for instance. This property we might call the Discriminandum. Finally, note the expression 'discriminated *against*.' It is essential to the idea of discrimination, I take it, that the Discriminatee is treated badly, adversely, or at any rate less well than the Beneficiaries.

All these are necessary conditions. I believe we have a sufficient condition if we add that to discriminate against someone is to treat that person in the undesirable way in question *because* the person has the property in question. But we should perhaps make room for a notion, presumably lower on the scale of moral culpability, of inadvertent discrimination. Here, the persons badly treated are not intentionally singled out for their possession of the Discriminandum in question; but it turns out that the class distinguished by possession of it is, nevertheless, coming out on the short end of the stick just as if they were intentionally thus singled out.

As with so many of the expressions we employ in day-to-day moral activity, it would be possible to expend time and energy deliberating about whether the word 'discriminate' is logically condemnatory or not. I don't think this time would be well spent. Smith may be complimented for being a discriminating judge of wine, or of music; Jones may be condemned for his discriminatory practices in business. I believe we can readily enough identify a sense of 'discrimination' which is logically neutral on the moral issue, and indeed, the proposed definition assembled above really is so. Confining ourselves to the more dominant intentional sense of the term, let us begin as follows:

> D_1: A discriminates against B in relation to C by doing x = (def.). There is a property, K, such that B has K, C does not have K, and A treats B worse than C by doing x, and does so *because* B [has] K.

That A treats B worse than C is not, itself, a morally significant fact—a point I shall expand on below. And—as I shall also be at pains to point out—there are obvious cases of treatment fitting the above which no one would take to be unjust. There are two suggestions to consider for expanding the above in such a way as to bring it more nearly into line with the use of the term in which the current controversies are couched. Each deserves some further treatment of its own. Meanwhile, the partial definition given so far may serve as the basis for raising the important questions. What we want to know is: what values of K and x are such that to do x to a K *rather* than a non-K and *because* the person in question is a K rather than a non-K make the doing of x unjust?

Incidentally, I will tend to favor the term 'unjust' for these purposes because my main interest is in the moral status which would ground restrictive legislation. Whether some lesser charge than injustice might be brought against one who discriminates is not a matter I shall be much concerned to explore.

3. NON-BASIC DISCRIMINATION

One way in which D_1 can be expanded would be by restricting the value of our act-variable, x, in such a way as to guarantee that discrimination is unjust. There are two ways to do this (at least). One would go like this:

> D_2: A discriminates against B in relation to C by doing x = (def.). B is a K, C a non-K, and because B is a K, A does x and B *and x is unjust.*

This makes discrimination unjust by definition, but also trivializes the matter. What we want to know is whether there are acts, x, such that x is unjust because x is discriminatory. We do not wish to know whether there are acts, x, such that x is unjust because x is unjust.

A more interesting way might go like this:

D₃: A discriminates against B in relation to C by doing x = (def.). A does x to B and not to C because B is a K and C isn't a K, and x consists in harming B, e.g., by killing, torturing, maiming, depriving of rightful property, etc.

I leave an 'etc.' in this definition because my intention is to incorporate into the definition of discrimination a restriction on x to acts which are generally recognized to be morally wrong (and, indeed, are morally wrong, in my view). But I don't wish to incorporate a use of the term 'unjust' in the definition. The idea is to identify discrimination with the doing of evil acts, even though the evilness of those acts is not logically part of the description of those acts. (I have failed even so, in view of the reference to "depriving of rightful property"; finding a non-tendentious description of violations of property rights is not easy, and I request that this failing be overlooked for present purposes.)

D₃ makes discrimination wrong, all right, and it is not trivial either. But it has a different and crucial defect. For the restriction on the range of acts to be considered discriminatory acts are wrong, all right, but not *because* they are discriminatory. For they would be wrong even if they *weren't* discriminatory. We may call such acts, acts of "non-basic" discrimination. Now, there are plenty of examples of non-basic discrimination, and indeed, I think that most examples of discrimination which one might be inclined to go to as paradigm cases of it would be non-basic discriminations. Think of black people being lynched, or Jews sent to the gas chambers at Auschwitz, for instance. It is quite true that the reason why these people were thus treated is that they were black or Jews, and quite true that they were discriminatory. But surely what makes it wrong to lynch an innocent person is not that that's no way to treat a *black* person, but rather that it's no way to treat *any* innocent person.

A good deal of the progress which, I think we'd all agree, has been made in the treatment of other races in North America (at least) in the last few decades has taken the form of getting people to appreciate that the basic principles of morality are color-blind. We think there are basic human rights, held by everybody of whatever race, color, etc., and we are at the point where even sheriffs in small towns in Alabama could probably be got to subscribe to that thesis, at least in point of lip service and maybe to some degree in action as well. All this is very real progress, and insofar as the hubbub about discrimination is about this sort of thing, the hubbub is justified. The trouble is, it seems clear that what I have called non-basic discrimination is not the sort of thing which we need [in order] to show that discrimination as such is wrong—that there is anything that is wrong just *because* it is discriminatory. 'Discrimination,' given our new definition, D₃, has yet to signify a basic wrong, something which we have a right that others not do to us, which we wouldn't have had anyway.

There is, no doubt, an interesting question on the matter of whether non-basic acts of discrimination are *worse* because they are discriminatory. It has been suggested to me,[1] for instance, that if the Nazis had gassed people at random, or by lot, rather than picking on the Jews in particular, then that would strike us as being hideous and awful, but not *unjust*, or at least not as unjust as what actually happened. It is unclear to me whether this is so or not. Perhaps one reason why one might think so is that we tend to connect injustice with *unfairness*, and it may be agreed that it is unfair to gas people for being Jews, leaving non-Jews intact. And that defect could be rectified by establishing a lottery. But on the other hand, a just community will surely be just as concerned to prevent random gassing of innocent people as it will to prevent selective gassing of them, will it not?

Suppose that instead of gassing you because you are a Jew, I gas you because I dislike your taste in ties. Is this in the same boat, or not? Or suppose I gas you because I have embezzled your money and don't want you to tell the authorities I have done so. Gassing people at random is in one sense more terrible than any of these, in the same way that terrorism in general is terrible: it might befall anyone at any time. But all of these things are terrible, and I doubt that there's any point in trying to say in the abstract which is worst. In general, I suspect that the reason we are so impressed with the case of the Jews is twofold. First, antisemitism is popular, for some reason, whereas anti-tiewearing (to the point of gassing) is virtually unheard of, and random gassing is exceedingly rare, though random violence is not. And second, antisemitism is *divisive*. It sets people against each other. Policies of antisemitism will tend to produce in many people the attitude that there is actually something wrong with being Jewish, that Jewishness is a property which literally deserves extermination, or whatever. There is therefore a public interest reason for worrying about antisemitism that isn't there in regard to the other two practices.

4. MORAL IRRELEVANCE

The most popular candidate for a principle of non-discrimination, no doubt, would be one which makes use of the notion of "moral irrelevance." On this view, discrimination would be defined in some such way as the following:

> D4: A discriminates against B in relation to C by doing x = (def.). A does x to B and not to C because B is a K and C is not, and K-ness is *morally irrelevant* to treating people in way x.

What is meant by 'moral irrelevance' here? I suppose that a property of a person is morally relevant to a manner of treatment if it is the case that by virtue of having that property, one is morally entitled to a certain sort of treatment. And indeed, we do frame

some exceedingly high-level, abstract-sounding moral principles in some such manner as that. To use the words of Sidgwick, for instance: "If a kind of conduct that is right ... for me ... is not right ... for someone else, it must be on the ground of some difference between the two cases, other than the fact that I and he are different persons."[2] This suitably self-evident-seeming idea readily lends itself to evolution into a principle about the treatment of others: if I am to treat B differently from C, then there has to be some difference, other than the fact that B is B and C is C, which justified this difference of treatment.

Principles as abstract as this have some well-known demerits. Those, for instance, who practice racial discrimination are certainly not treating B differently from C just because C is a different person from B. They are treating B differently from C because (for instance) B is black and C isn't. Obviously a thicker theory about which properties are relevant to which sorts of treatment is required. But I think the plot can be thickened before we get into detail on that matter. We need at a minimum to distinguish two different levels of moral relevance. (1) A property might be morally relevant in the sense that we are morally required to treat people who have it differently from people who don't. Or (2) a property might be morally relevant only in the sense that it is morally permissible to treat people who have it differently from people who don't. And we may agree straight off that there must be morally relevant properties grounding any differences of treatment in the second sense. For after all, if it is not morally permissible to treat B differently from C, then no doubt it is wrong to treat them differently; and if we confine ourselves to the sorts of wrongnesses which ground restrictive laws, unjust-making wrongnesses, then it is obvious that moral relevance in sense (2) is a necessary condition for treating people justly. But it is also trivial to say that, after all. What, however, about sense (1)?

It does, I must say, seem perfectly obvious that in order to justify difference of treatment of two persons, B and C, there does not need to be a morally relevant difference between them in sense (1). I do not mean merely that we might find different ways of treating B and C which treat them equally well, so that neither has any complaint coming on the score of having been less well treated. I mean, more interestingly, that we may very well treat one person less well than another without a hint of injustice, and without appealing to any differences between them which are morally relevant in the stronger sense. Moreover, I think we can find examples of this type which are also frankly discriminatory in the sense not only of D4, but also relative to current thinking, in that they discriminate along the very lines which figure in many of our laws as well as private judgments.

Such, for instance, seems to me to be the case with marrying and offering to marry. It seems to me that there are virtually no morally relevant characteristics in this whole area. Suppose I decide to marry Jane on the ground that she has lovely blue eyes, whereas Nell has to make do with plain ol' brown ones. Well, where is the duty to marry blue-eyeds rather than brown-eyeds? Obviously nowhere: so do I perform an injustice to Nell in thus behaving? I think not. Nor is the situation any different if we think of the standard Discriminanda currently in the public eye. If I marry Amanda because she is black, I do not behave unjustly to Sue who is white; or if I marry Cathy because she is of the same religious persuasion as I—or because she is of a different persuasion, for that matter—I do not thereby wrong the unfortunate (or fortunate?) candidates who are thus rejected.

Similarly with friendship. If I like A because he is intelligent and charming, while refraining from befriending B because he is uninteresting, I do not thereby wrong B, despite the total lack of any moral duty to be-friend all and sundry, or to befriend the intelligent, or the charming. In short, I think it clear that the general claim that we can justify treating one person less well than another only by invoking "morally relevant" characteristics in the interesting sense distinguished above simply will not wash.

It is manifestly clear that we can act well or badly, and in particular, intelligently or unintelligently, in these contexts. You may certainly criticize my taste if I marry someone because of the color of her eyes, or her skin, or even her choice of religion, perhaps. These decisions may be personally justified or not. But morally? It would take a special background to bring morality into it. Perhaps you have been dating Jane all this time, leading her to expect that you like people such as her, indeed leading her to expect a proposal from you; and instead, you turn around and propose to some total stranger. You may owe her an explanation. Or perhaps you promised your dear ol' Mum that you'd marry a fellow Seventh Day Adventist, and now you've gone and proposed to a Buddhist, yet. There's no end of what might bring moral considerations into these matters. But my point is that so far as it goes, morality has no bearing on it: marry whom you like, and Justice will not blink an eye, though Prudence might turn around and quietly vomit.

5. IS THERE BASIC DISCRIMINATION?

Further reflection on the foregoing discussion of moral relevance raises the interesting question whether there really is any such thing as what I have implicitly identified as Basic discrimination. Non-basic discrimination, we recall, is where there is something wrong with what you are doing to B *anyway*; the fact that you do it to him because he is the possessor of some property (not common to all moral persons) which does not qualify him for that treatment is not needed in order to condemn the action in question. Basic discrimination, then, would be where your act of treating B worse than C is wrong, not because it is to do something to B which you have no right to do anyway, but because it unjustly discriminates between B and C. What we would need here, evidently, is a principle calling upon us to do certain things to certain people if we also do them to certain others, but where there is in itself nothing wrong with doing it to anyone.

Yet there seems something odd about this. Here is something I can do to someone, something which there is no inherent moral objection to doing. Call this act x. Often x will be some negative action, a *non*-action such as not offering the person in question a job. There is also, we are assuming, *no* moral duty to do not-x, to refrain from x, to *anyone*. How, then can it suddenly be unjust if I choose to do x to B, and not-x to C? Doing it, to anyone, is not wrong; nor is doing it, to anyone, a moral duty, required. Nobody has the right that I do it to him or refrain from doing it to him. How can it be that it is, under the circumstances, wrong to do it to B rather than C?

The most interesting current context, I take it, is employment. We have in general no obligation to hire anybody for anything; nor have we in general any obligation to refrain from hiring anybody for anything. Yet it is widely supposed that if A hires C rather than B because C is, say, a male, or white, despite B's equal competence, then A has done B an injustice, and the law may properly descend upon A and make him toe the line of equality. Why? So interesting are these contexts that I propose to discuss them on their own for a few pages.

6. PUBLIC/PRIVATE

To begin with, we had better immediately take account of a distinction plainly relevant in this connection, namely the distinction between hiring in the public sector and private hiring. I mean this to be a conceptual distinction. Some might argue that the public sector is a fraud, or at any rate, that there ought to be no such thing: you name it and "the public" has no business doing it. Others might say the same thing about the private sector. I do not intend either to affirm or deny either view here. I only wish to point out that if we acknowledge a public sector, it is easy enough to see why discrimination there would be something to make a fuss about.

The reason is simple enough. Suppose there are services which any member of the public has a right to, *vis-à-vis* the public generally. He has that right, then, *qua* member of the public. Moreover, those offering it to him are also acting as agents of the public. Now, the public consists of *everybody*. If, then, there is some service to which one is entitled *qua* member of the public, clearly it will be wrong for any agent of the public to give it to C but withhold it from B, so long as both are members of the relevant public. If there is a limited resource which the public is to expend—medical services, say—it is held that this is a public matter, so that all and only the medically needy have a claim on it, and demand exceeds supply, then it is also plausible to hold that the resources ought to be proportioned equally to the need, or perhaps that we ought to maximize the public health, but in any case not on a basis which favors some irrelevantly distinguished group in society. In fact, the criteria of relevance will be quite clear: if there is some need N to which some service S of the public is to cater, then factors other than N are irrelevant when it comes to administering S.

Prima facie, we also have a case for insisting that the agents administering S hire only on the basis of competence. If the idea is to maximize the satisfaction of N, then if applicant B promises to promote that goal better than C at the same cost, then the public would seem to have a right that B be hired rather than C. (The situation gets messy when we ask whether the public has the right that its servants reflect, say, the racial composition of the public they are to serve, particularly when perhaps the typical applicants from one readily distinguished group are less competent than those of some other, since now there will be a clash between considerations of efficiency, which the public has a right to, and the interest in an equal share of the action, which it may also have a right to. But we will not press these issues further here.)

What is important about the invocation of the public here is that it gives us a basis for nondiscrimination which again does not clearly show discrimination to be a *basic* injustice. For it seems, again, that if B can successfully claim to have been discriminated against in the public sector, there is also a claim on B's part to that which he was denied by virtue of the discriminatory act in question. It is not the case that there is no obligation to hire at all, nor that there is no obligation to provide the service for which hiring is being done. On the contrary, the thesis is that the public has the duty to provide the service, and is also entitled to it, on a basis that is equal as between persons of one color and another, one sex and another, etc.

But this is not true of the private sector in general. In that sector, the assumption is that those who hire do so in pursuit of private gain, or perhaps some other sort of private satisfaction. There is no obligation to set up any business whatever, no obligation to offer any particular service, or any service at all. That somebody didn't get hired by you, a private employer, is *prima facie* not something he can complain about, since you have no obligation to hire anybody at all—neither that person nor any other. More interestingly, it is by no means clear that he can complain even if he was of superior competence as compared with his competitors. Since you have no obligation to hire at all, it is hard to see why you should have an obligation to hire the most competent. What if

you don't care about competence? Perhaps you'd rather that your employees were attractive, or devout Catholics, or tee-totalers, or males. So what? Again, it seems to me: if there is no right to a job at all, how can there be a right that people like you be hired rather than people like anybody else, if anyone is hired at all?

Again, there are certainly considerations of prudence; and it is possible that some will see considerations of morality entering here too. Let us see, beginning in particular with prudence. We turn, briefly, to the question of the economics of discrimination. Too briefly, no doubt, but the matter can afford some instruction anyway.

7. DOLLARS AND DISCRIMINATION

Let us first consider the matter on what are usually thought of as classical assumptions, *viz.*, that everyone in the market is an economically rational agent interested in maximizing his dollar returns. (This assumption, as will be noted below, is unclear even if true; but one thing at a time. One good reason for starting with this assumption is that some people seem to think that discrimination is actually *caused* by the motive of gain.) Such agents will buy at the lowest price available for a given level of quality in the product, and will sell whatever they have to sell, e.g., their labour power, at the highest available price. If A wants an x and B, a black person, offers it to him at a lower price than C, who is white, then A will buy from the black person. (It should be noted that although, as I say, I will be questioning the above assumptions in some respects, there is plenty of empirical evidence that consumers, whether of labour or other things, will indeed buy from people they ostensibly despise if the price is right.)

Consider, then, the case of the Little Goliath Motor Company, a firm which makes no bones about its basic purpose:

profit. And consider any position in this firm, call it P, forwarding some function, F, within this noble enterprise. The primary purpose of making money will determine both which subordinate functions will be values of F and, together with an understanding of how F fits in with the rest of the operation, the criteria of better and worse performance at P. The more efficiently per unit of pay F is fulfilled, the lower will be the firm's cost per unit, or the higher the quality, or some mix of the two; in either case it will do better on the market, being able to sell cheaper or higher quality goods than the competition, if the latter don't do as well on these scores. Applicants for P, therefore, will rationally be judged by those criteria.

Enter another classical assumption, *viz.*, that such factors as race and sex make no difference to efficiency on the part of employees. (Again, it is an assumption which is often certainly false to fact, but, again, one thing at a time.) On this assumption, the people down at Little Goliath will not do well to have any interest in the race or sex of their applicants. For imagine what happens if they do. They begin, let us suppose, preferring males or whites. Preferring here means that they will hire them instead of females or blacks (or whatever). Now this presumably means that they will hire a less efficient white male at the same wage as they could get a more efficient black or female for the job at hand; which is equivalent, economically speaking, to paying more for an equally efficient one. On classical assumptions, what happens next? Well, the more persistently enterprising Universal Motor Co. up the road will begin to hire females and blacks, doing equally good work, for lower wages; it is in a position to do this, since the Goliath people insist on turning away perfectly good females with an interest in taking the best-paying job they can get. If this keeps up, and if, as our assumptions dictate, motor car purchasers are interested in quality for price rather than the

color or sex of those who put the product together, then we shall expect the Universal people to do well, and the Goliath people to do badly.

Perhaps a case at a somewhat classier level will be still more perspicuous. Most firms, we are told, much prefer males to females for executive positions; and we are also told that this is in fact sheer prejudice, females being equally capable. Under the circumstances, we should expect cagey firms to be soon staffed, in their higher reaches, with high-powered women at half the pay which their competitors have to offer to their all-male staffs. If all firms were rational and our assumption about the relative abilities of the sexes correct, we should eventually see executives of both sexes at the same salaries more or less everywhere.

The moral is generalizable: if the criterion of discrimination in hiring is that criteria other than those relevant to job-performance are used for the sorting of candidates, then in free-market conditions, with economically rational consumers, the non-discriminating firm will be better. Discrimination does not pay.

Might things go severely otherwise? Might the assumptions be badly wrong? The situation is unclear. We can certainly imagine cases in which consumers are not out to maximize their returns. If consumers insist on buying grapes picked by unionized labour, we are into another ball game: not that store-owners really *mind* customers who prefer paying more to paying less for the same goods, but it is all slightly puzzling. Likewise, it is possible that people would want to know whether the soap they buy was wrapped by lily-white rather than ebony hands. Possible, though unlikely. More likely, of course, is discrimination in service industries where the customer comes into direct contact with the supplier. People might like black waiters and butlers better than white ones, or pretty stewardesses better than plain though efficient ones, or whatever. In all such cases, economies will not erode discrimination. It will instead lead to the members of favoured classes being better off than members of unfavoured ones; and whether, for instance, wages in given industries will tend to equalize in a longish run is imponderable. But it should certainly be noted that there is no clear tendency toward reinforcing preexisting patterns of social discrimination, as anyone who has recently attempted to procure the services of Leontyne Price or Oscar Peterson will be acutely aware.

It is also essential to point out that the most scandalous cases in the past have been anything but cases of free market operation. Black slavery in the American South was not a free market institution. Neither is the situation in South Africa, where wage differentials between black and white workers are reinforced not only by law, but by unions.

I should like to explore this aspect of the matter much further, but space does not permit. Instead, I wish to turn to another crucial matter, closely related to that just discussed and, I think, offering perhaps the most puzzling challenge of all to those who think that there is a clear and straightforward underlying principle behind current attitudes about discrimination.

8. THE PURPOSES OF FIRMS

Competence is assessed by the criteria relevant to performance of the function which the position in question is to serve. Which functions are to be served, depends in turn on the ultimate purpose of the firm in which the position is situated. Some firms are out to make money; but not all. Let us address ourselves to a couple of relevant cases. One of my favorites, for starters, is a small nonprofit organization known as the Ecuadorian Friendship Society. The E.F.S. has as its purpose the forwarding of friendship among Ecuadorians, and this purpose is not notably served by hiring, say, Bolivian janitors and secretaries, or even French chefs. We may

well imagine that the management down at the E.F.S. will substantially prefer less competent Ecuadorians to more competent Bolivians when screening applications for those and other positions, right up to Vice President depending, no doubt, on the condition of its finances. But who is to say that the firm is acting irrationally in such practices? After all, it might be argued, given the purpose of this particular firm, that it is *not* efficient, looked at from the higher point of view, to hire Bolivian secretaries, however efficient they may be *qua* secretary. Under the circumstances, the hiring of Bolivians, however competent, is less than utterly Friendly.

Another of my favorites among these specialized nonprofit establishments is the Black Muslim Church of America, which may be presumed to look considerably askance at applicants of the Occidental persuasion for positions in their clergy, however eloquent and dedicated. The point, again, may be made that given the purposes of the firm, what would otherwise be discriminatory is legitimate, indeed efficient and thus mandatory. Thus it may be argued that these firms do not really violate the canon of hiring only on the basis of relevant competence: competence, as I say, is dictated by the purposes of the organization.

At this point, two questions loom before us. Both should tax us mightily, I think. The first point may be furthered by bringing up another example dear to my heart: the Irish-Canadian Distilleries Corporation. This amiable organization lets it be known to all and sundry that although it is happy to turn an honest dollar, it also has a pronounced interest in maximizing the percentage of persons of Irish descent amongst its employees, even if this should cut into profits a bit. For its purpose is not simply to make money— this, they imply, is a motive reserved for the low of mind, such as the denizens of the Highlands. It is, rather, to be a sort of marginally profitable Irish-Canadian Friendly

Society, a high purpose for which, indeed, its commercial product is peculiarly suitable. Its otherwise inefficient hiring practices, when viewed from this higher perspective, turn out to be perfectly efficient after all, and therefore, on the standard view which seems to prevail about what is "morally relevant," quite free of any taint of discrimination.

The second question follows naturally enough, *viz.*: what's so great about efficiency, anyway? Why not accuse those firms which hire exclusively on the basis of competence of discriminating unjustly against the incompetent? Why should competence be thought a "morally relevant characteristic"? It is not, incidentally, thought to be so when it comes to such elementary matters as the right to vote, or indeed, to stand for Parliament. From the point of view of the employer, of course, competence is highly desirable. So indeed is it from the point of view of the consumer. But why should only that point of view count? Aren't we supposed to be adumbrating an impartial standard of justice?

9. ADVERTISING OF POSITIONS

One possible account of the injustice thought to be inherent in discriminatory hiring, and to some extent applicable in other contexts as well, is that those who are excluded for apparently irrelevant reasons have been dealt badly with because their expectations, engendered by the advertisement for the position or such other description of the opportunity regarding which the discrimination has taken place, have been disappointed. An applicant may well say, "Look, I've come all this way, taken all this time and trouble to get this job interview, and now you tell me that no X-ians will be considered. Why didn't you say so in the first place?"

Complaints of this kind, where applicable, may certainly be well-taken, and sometimes could be a basis for a claim of compensation.

But so far as the general issue of a basic right to nondiscrimination is concerned, it is surely too weak to do the job many people feel there is to be done. For one thing, it would be hard to specify the number of factors on the basis of which a candidate might be rejected in any satisfactorily general way. After all, if there is just one job and many candidates, several are going to be disappointed, however excellent the reasons for their rejection. And more generally, it is surely not true that the case against discrimination, in the minds of the many who think it a major context for social concern, would always be settled just by wording advertisements appropriately. The claim is that it's wrong to impose the condition that No Irish Need Apply, however well advertised that condition may be. We shall have to look elsewhere to find any deep principles against discrimination. (Nor should it be assumed *a priori* that we will succeed.)

10. CURRENT PRACTICE

It is perhaps not entirely out of order to ask whether our current practices in this area make all that much sense, taken in large. For one thing, it does seem as though discrimination is in fact quite all right when practiced by the allegedly downtrodden against the allegedly mighty majority (though the term 'majority' has come to have a somewhat non-literal usage, in view of the fact that, e.g., white Anglo-Saxon males must by now make up rather a small percentage of the Canadian or American populace, and women an outright majority). And do we not tolerate, indeed expect and encourage, discrimination as between members of our own family and others when it comes to the distribution of various economic and social benefits, including jobs, education beyond what is provided by the public, and so forth?

Another area in a more public quarter has to do with the matter of nationalism. At one time, discrimination on grounds of nationality was one of the standard bad examples, along with discrimination on grounds of sex, race and religion. But recently, one hears less about nationality, perhaps for the reason that every government so flagrantly violates any principle along this line. Not only public employers, but also employers in the private sector, are routinely required to discriminate very strongly against citizens of other countries (in Canada, this is true even of immigrants, whom employers are often required to rank second to citizens for employment). Goods made by foreign firms are, of course, routinely discriminated against by means of tariffs and other restrictions. Even the freedom to marry foreigners has been abridged by some nations, and immigration restrictions having this effect are not uncommon.

I have already mentioned churches in connection with employment. But the existence of organizations with special purposes seem quite generally to raise a question about the intent of nondiscrimination principles; for do not organizations routinely distinguish between members and non-members, persons who share their goals and persons who do not? And why on earth shouldn't they—indeed, how could they not do so? But that is just the point. A clear principle distinguishing between all these myriad cases of intentionally prejudicial bestowing of important benefits and the ones popularly frowned upon as discriminatory is what we need and, it seems to me, do not have.

11. A NOTE ON UTILITARIANISM

Those who have felt that nondiscrimination is a basic right have often, I think, supposed that it is a right which exceeds the reach of utilitarianism. Partly for this reason, it is of some interest to observe that, while it is, if the foregoing arguments are as strong as I am so far persuaded they are, extremely dif-

ficult to find a plausible deep principle going beneath the level of utilitarian considerations, it is not difficult to give a pretty plausible account of our practices and currently professed principles in utilitarian terms. For one thing, the distinction between private and public in the hiring arena, which figures strongly in the foregoing, does not have all that much status for the utilitarian. From his point of view, one might say *all* activities are "public" in the sense that the public has a legitimate interest in how they are carried on. If there is to be a private sector at all, from that point of view, it is because the public interest is served better by making some things private. That the wealth of society is promoted by private enterprise, if true, is certainly important and creates a presumption in favor of private enterprise; but then, in cases where it is not so promoted, the utilitarian has no scruples about putting it back in the hands of the public. And if some other important public interest besides wealth comes into the picture, then the utilitarian will simply consider whether this other interest is sufficient to outweigh the lost prosperity resulting from catering to it, if indeed that is what would happen.

What other utilities might be at stake? Prominent among them, surely, are two, or perhaps two sides of a single one. First, there is the sheer fact that those discriminated against *feel* badly done by. If the public is upset by a certain practice—or indeed, if a smallish minority is upset by it, given that it is upset enough—then that creates at least some presumption in favor of altering the practice. And secondly, it is fair to argue that discriminatory practices, particularly in areas of such substantial concern to people as hiring, are socially divisive, as was noted in section 3 above. If sizable groups of people are clamoring for advancement, while others characteristically are preferred in those respects, even at some cost in efficiency, then the tendency will be for bad feeling to exist between the groups in question, and we may expect trouble. The fact that we can't identify, in principle and in general, any characteristics and range of practices such that the doing of those things to people with those characteristics and the nondoing of them to people without them is fundamentally wrong doesn't matter all that much; if we can deal with the situation pretty effectively with rather vague and unsatisfactorily messy principles, that is better than ignoring the problem.

It is to be expected, if utilitarianism is our guide, that there will be no stable list of Discriminanda such that nondiscrimination principles would always be stated in terms of them, nor any particular social context, such as hiring, where the wrongness of discrimination is permanently to be abhorred. It will depend on social conditions. Fifty years from now, perhaps some quite new contexts, new Discriminanda, will be where the focus of concern falls. And if we are interested in capturing current "intuitions" and predicting the way things will go, this aspect of utilitarianism seems likely to stand us in pretty good stead.

But there are some shortcomings. Naturally, the basic status of utilitarianism itself is one of them. Nor is it evident that the whole job to be done is to account for current practices; and if currently held beliefs are what are to be accounted for, then there is the widespread feeling that the right to nondiscrimination does not wait upon social interest for its confirmation to consider: is that part of what is to be accounted for, or isn't it? More importantly, however, is that it seems to me questionable what the real outcome of utilitarianism is on such issues. To see this, we need to distinguish between two views about the operation of utilitarianism, or perhaps about its application. We might call these the "crude" versus the "sophisticated" form. The crude variety, which I have tacitly appealed to above, has it that we weigh any old interest, however derived. If interests in straw-

berry jam count, and interests in Mahler symphonies, so do interests in wife-beating, in keeping up with the Joneses, and in one's neighbors all being attired in identical seersucker suits. The sophisticated type, however, does not easily allow such interests to count, or discounts them as compared with others. If interests in others' having such-and-such interests count, and if interests in others having such-and-such relations to oneself count equally, that seems to make way for the kind of objections to utilitarianism trotted out in the standard textbooks and Introductions to Philosophy. And the difficulty is that it seems that the kind of interests catered to in nondiscrimination principles are of that kind. In order to get very much weight behind the thesis that social utility will be further enhanced by A's electing to have B work for him rather than C, despite the fact that he'd prefer to have C, we have to attach a good deal of weight to the intensity of B's feelings of indignation at not being equally considered by A, and more weight to the fuss which will be caused by the objections of B's cohorts, etc. If, on the other hand, we simply attend to what appears to be the fact, that whichever A hires, A will be doing that person a favor, but if he hires the one he likes he will in addition create more utility for himself, then it is unclear that we should allow the further fact that B doesn't like the situation to count.

It is characteristic of utilitarianism that once one sees that there are competing sources of utility to take into account, and these are not easily estimated, the argument could be taken either way. And often, the very utility being counted is due to the preexisting moral beliefs of the persons involved. If B had the attitude that A has a perfect right to hire whomever he pleases, there wouldn't be the various political utilities to which the argument of crude utilitarianism appeals. And this means that utilitarianism may not be of much use in this matter after all.

12. AND A NOTE ON CONTRACTARIANISM

Another of the most important theoretical bases for social philosophy to have been taken seriously in recent times, as well as times past, is the suggestion that the principles of justice are the principles for the structuring of society which would be accepted by rational individuals on a long-term basis, or perhaps an impartial one. Indeed, I would be inclined to argue this way myself. But some who have been of this persuasion have evidently supposed that principles of nondiscrimination are among those which would most fundamentally be opted for in this way; and unfortunately, I fail to see that this is obvious.

Presumably a main source of the view that nondiscrimination would have such a status is the fact, which is not in dispute here, that the fundamental principles chosen would be, so to speak, color-blind (and sex-blind, etc.). Unfortunately, as has been in effect argued above, this is very far from supporting the very strong principles which are here being questioned. For it is one thing to say that the fundamental principles of morality will not favour any groups as compared with any other (except, of course, that it will disfavour those who don't comply with them), and quite another to say that those principles will require individuals not to favour other individuals on the basis of sex, color, race, religion, taste in wines, or whatever, when it comes to doing good things for them. When we are contracting for general rights, after all, we are contracting to give up certain liberties. The strategy of contractualism is to pick out those liberties which we are better off giving up, and thus to argue that the rational person will be prepared to do so, in exchange for certain benefits which cannot be had without giving up those liberties. In the case of the liberty to kill, or in general to inflict harms on people, it is plausible to argue that the advantage of being free from such depre-dations at the hands of others will outweigh, in any even modestly longish run, the disadvantage of giving up the liberty to commit them oneself. But it is a different story when what is at issue is how one is to dispose of one's various positive assets, one's capacity to benefit others. Here it is *not* plausible to argue that every rational person *must* find it to his or her advantage to forgo the liberty to decide who will be the beneficiary of such activities, in return for the benefit of being assured of having an equal chance, along with others who differ in various respects, of winding up as the beneficiary of some other people's similar activities.

It has been the habit of Rawls and of theorists persuaded by his general views to speak rather vaguely about opportunities for realizing the benefits which one's 'society' has to offer. The trouble with this, as Nozick was at pains to argue, is that it seems to assume that society is a kind of organized club with certain rather specific purposes which all members in good standing must be interested in promoting, and having a variety of assets at its disposal for the promotion of these purposes. But since this is fairly obviously not so, and fairly obviously therefore not something which we can simply assume, it is clear that one would have to argue for the claim that everyone ought to look at it that way. And I don't see how such an argument is to go through in general. But in 'general' is what we are talking about here. It is not to the point to observe that many people would see advantage in so viewing the matter; for manifestly some would not, and given that that is so, there is surely no prospect of a general agreement, reaching to all rational persons, on the point.

Even if we suppose that some progress along that line is possible, there is a further problem about the relevance of our results to the present issue. Suppose, for instance, that we can make some kind of case for, say, an assured minimal income for all—already an extremely implausible assumption. But still, although that would, by the reasoning of section 6 above, provide the basis for nondiscrimination in the administration of the program for securing that minimum to all, it does not seem possible that it would provide a basis for nondiscrimination as between candidates for very high-paying positions, or even most positions. Presumably the minimum must be set somewhere below the average income from employment, and then we have the question of why everyone's entitlement to this minimum should carry with it an entitlement to nondiscrimination at any of the levels above it.

Most contractualist arguments about social minima *et al.* in any case run up against another problem. If people were so interested in security, including the particular kinds of security which nondiscrimination laws provide, why wouldn't they buy into insurance which provided that kind of security? Or form clubs whose members would agree to boycott those who practiced the types of discrimination they wished to avoid? Why, in short, are the kinds of benefits which nondiscrimination presumably provides of a type which justifies coercive methods for seeing to it that *all* persons avoid practicing the types of discrimination in question—not only those who do see it as a benefit, but also those who see it as just the reverse? Given contractarian premises, one would have thought that if one has one's choice between enabling some good to be brought about by voluntary efforts among those who want it and a system of imposing it by force, if need be, on all alike, the former would be preferable. When we disagree, the rational thing for us both to do is agree to disagree—not agree that something called 'society' will declare one of us out of bounds and impose the other's view on him willy-nilly.

13. A NOTE ON LOGIC

The principal argument in the foregoing effort to establish that the foundations of our attitudes toward discrimination are insecure and obscure has been of the following general form: We do not (it is admitted) have any obligation to do anything of the kind in question—appointing to a position, say—to anybody at all; so why do we have an obligation not to do it to one person rather than another? If I don't owe *anybody* a certain benefit, x, how is it that I can owe it to everyone that if I do give it to some person other than he, it will not be because he has certain properties but rather because he has certain others? If I owe it to no one at all, then why can't I give it to whomever I please, since the option is to give it to nobody whatever?

The question arises how we are to formulate the principle thus implicitly appealed to. Very generally, no doubt, the idea is that found in Hobbes, to the effect that "Obligation and Liberty ... in one and the same matter are inconsistent." However, there is the question of specifying the 'matter' in question. Perhaps it is the case that even though I have no obligation to do x to A or to B, I have an obligation to do it to A in preference to B if at all, because in doing x to B I would not simply be doing x, but also something else, y, which is forbidden. The trouble is, though, that in the foregoing I have argued that the cases in which there clearly is this other description of my act, this other fact about it, in virtue of which it is obligatory on me not to do it, we have what I called "non-basic" discrimination, and this, I observed, doesn't seem to be sufficient to account for standard attitudes and practices on this subject. Were it the case that, in declining to give the job to A, one also hit him over the head or heaped insults upon him, that would be wrong; but that is not the behavior at issue. It is felt that it is wrong to decline to give it to A at all, if A is in fact "better qualified" than B and one simply prefers to have B for extraneous reasons such as that one simply likes B, or people like B in certain respects, better than A or people like A in certain respects.

A slightly formalized representation of the principle behind the argument would go, perhaps, something like this:

(1) A's preferring B to C in context H consists in A's doing x to B rather than to C, if at all.

(2) A's being obliged to prefer B to C in context H = A's being obliged to do x to B rather than C, if at all.

(3) A's not being obliged to do x at all = A's not being obliged to do x to any person whatever, for any reason; i.e., there is no class of persons such that A is obliged to do x to any member of that class.

(4) Context H involves some purpose, P, such that pursuit of P would give a reason to prefer B to C.

(5) But A has no obligation to pursue P *at all*. (If P were obligatory, then A would have some obligation to do x to someone, if available. But by hypothesis, A has no such obligation.)

(6) Therefore (by 5), A has no obligation to prefer anyone to anyone with respect to x; and hence not to prefer B to C.

If this is right, then it also appears that there is no such thing as obligatory *basic* nondiscrimination. If we were obliged to prefer one person to another *vis-à-vis* doing of some act x, that would imply that we had some obligation to do x, or pursue some purpose such that x promoted it, though other acts y could be done instead, or in general to perform kinds of acts of which x was an example.

Do we think this to be so? I am hard put to decide, but let us consider a few examples. Many of us would accept a general obligation to treat our children equally, for instance: if we have some limited resource— money, for instance—which we can devote to promoting their welfare, we feel some obligation to divide that resource equally, or in such a way as to promote their respective welfares equally. True: but it is also

true that we have an obligation to promote their welfare *at all*. How much is, of course, not entirely easy to say, but suppose that we say we are to promote each child's welfare maximally within some limit. If we have this for *each* of them, and the resources are only sufficient for some level short of what we would ideally like, then it is readily concluded that we should split the resource more or less equally, or aim at equal welfares. But if we had no such obligation at all, it is hard to see how any of them could reasonably complain if he or she were always passed over in favor of others.

In general, it seems to me that the claim to *equal treatment* rests on an assumption that there are equal *claims to that kind of treatment*; and hence, that there *are* claims to that kind of treatment. The right to *equal opportunity*, in particular, rests on an assumed *right to opportunity*. In the absence of the latter, it is hard to see how we can make much sense of the former.

14. A NOTE ON PREJUDICE

One final matter should be mentioned. Very often, certainly, treatment of different large groups that is markedly unequal in the various respects we have in mind when we talk of 'discrimination' is based on beliefs about the relative merits of those different groups. When those beliefs are without foundation, we bring in the notion of 'prejudice,' of judging people's merits before we actually know the relevant facts—if any. The subject of prejudice invites special comment; and doubtless some, though I think not all, of the prevailing beliefs about discrimination are accounted for on the basis of their relation to it. The following observations seem especially pertinent here.

(1) We must bear in mind that not all discrimination will be due to prejudice. Perhaps Brown doesn't believe that all X-ians are shiftless, immoral, or whatever: he may simply not much care for X-ians, or he

may care for members of his own race (etc.) more. There is a difference between an attitude based on an unreasoned or baseless belief, on the one hand, and on no belief at all, on the other.

(2) When the attitudes in question are based on beliefs, those beliefs are, of course, capable of being rationally appraised. Now sometimes—we ought to recognize—they might be based on pretty decent evidence. It may not be obvious that the different races, sexes, etc. do have the same degree of allegedly relevant properties. Possibly it is a matter on which reasonable people may differ. Where this is so, it is at least clear that one cannot convict, say, an employer who turns out to employ a quite different percentage of X-ians from that which X-ians bear to the whole population, of discrimination straight off. Perhaps the X-ians are a lot better, or a lot worse, at that sort of job than the average other person. (Obviously there might still be discrimination, for perhaps the employer follows a policy of not even considering non-Xians, when in fact a modest percentage of them are better at the job than a lot of X-ians. This raises further questions, prominent among them being how much trouble an employer could reasonably be required to go to to test persons directly rather than going by obvious qualities, such as sex, which are quite well correlated with them.) At any rate, the point is that we cannot assume *a priori* that various abilities and whatnot are distributed in a population independently of the popular Discriminanda; it simply isn't an *a priori* matter.

(3) Even where it is quite clear that prejudice is at work, there are two questions to raise about it. In the first place, there is the question whether it is right to persecute people for their beliefs. We do not do so, or at least we profess to believe that we have no right to do so, in the case of religious beliefs, even though those beliefs are always, strictly speaking, baseless, and even though they often lead to very substantial kinds of

discriminatory treatment. In the second place, and more important at least in practice, there is the fact that once the foundations, or lack of them, of a belief are out in the open where critics can assail them, it is not easy to maintain that belief with a perfectly straight face for very long. Why should we assume so readily that the proper way to deal with actions based on beliefs we think are baseless, illogical, or confused is by making laws against those actions? We can hardly think that generally appropriate. Do we not, after all, have a pretty well-grounded suspicion that most people's practical beliefs are baseless, illogical, and/or confused? (Including, it will doubtless turn out, most of our own?) And are we not agreed that one does not properly outlaw the entertaining of that belief: that in fact the proper way to deal with it is to *refute* it, much to the psychic stress of the person who holds it?

At the risk of being embarrassingly obvious, I would just note that if we were to take seriously the suggestion that it is unjust to hold baseless beliefs, then any principle of freedom of religion would evidently have to go by the boards. Most religions, after all, are almost self-consciously mysterious, and do not even pretend to offer sound reasons, persuasive to any rational being, for holding their main tenets. For all that, these beliefs are obviously dangerous. It takes little investigation of history to see that any number of wars, including perhaps most of the messier ones, have been fought partly or wholly on religious grounds. If the sort of prejudices often leading to discrimination are a public menace, surely religion is even more so. Yet which tenets of liberalism have pride of place over religious freedom?

It may be urged that there is a difference between allowing someone to hold a belief and allowing him to act on it. Anyone seriously urging a strong principle of freedom of thought or of speech needs to make such a distinction, since otherwise he will find himself in the embarrassing position of having to allow any degree of iniquity whenever the agent in question does it on conscientious grounds. In those cases, of course, we need to establish the iniquitousness of the acts in question on independent grounds; and by and large, my argument in this paper has been that it is unclear that we have such grounds. Meanwhile, it in any case remains that employers frequently cannot be said to have clearly unreasonable grounds for their discriminatory beliefs; and when this is so, it is difficult to see how we could proceed against them on the ground that their beliefs were, as we in our wisdom have decreed, false. And on the other hand, we do allow people to act on their religious beliefs, within broad limits, and those beliefs don't have nearly so much to be said for them as some of the beliefs on which prejudices are based.

There is one particular kind of prejudice-supporting belief of which we may, I would agree, make a special case. This is the kind which consists in holding that certain groups of people are, without further explanation, "morally inferior." A belief so expressed might, of course, be an empirically based one, to the effect that the incidence of certain standardly recognized types of immoral behavior is greater in that group than in others—which in any case, of course, would not in fact justify across-the-board discrimination against members of that group. But the case I have in mind does not involve an explicable belief of that kind. It consists instead of simply holding that the group in question is not morally deserving of normally good treatment or of ordinary rights. Such a belief, we may certainly agree, is not only unintelligible but almost immoral. It is unintelligible because it requires that there be a special, empirically undetectable property or set of properties that render their possessors eligible for inclusion in the moral community, and it is in principle erroneous to suppose that there is any such feature or features. And it is immoral because it would make it impossible for an accused person

to defend himself against the "charge" of "inferiority" of that kind, even though its purpose is to justify the kind of treatment that is only properly administered to persons guilty of genuinely immoral behavior. But as with the kind of beliefs discussed previously, it must again be pointed out that persons engaging in that kind of treatment of others without a supportable charge of that kind are themselves guilty of violating the rights of others. What is wrong with the behavior in question is not that that is its motive, and it is unclear that the motive in question *adds* to the iniquity of the behavior. But certainly the spreading of such "beliefs," since it *can* only be used to promote evil behavior, may be condemned strongly enough.

15. SUMMARY

The thesis of this essay is that the case for regarding discrimination, properly so called, as an injustice has not been clearly supported in western thought, despite its enormous impact on western practice. "Discrimination properly so called" marks an essential distinction here, for much discriminatory behavior, termed 'non-basic' in the foregoing, is undoubtedly wrong but not wrong by virtue of being discriminatory: killing or injuring people who are innocent of any morally sustainable crime is wrong, whatever the motive. But that leaves a great deal that *is* "properly so called," where the discrimination consists only in treating some people less well than others, and doing so for a reason that is not morally relevant, in the strong sense of that term in which a morally relevant distinction morally requires a corresponding distinction in treatment. Not giving one person rather than another a job in a company of which you are the owner, and where your reason for preferring the other has nothing to do with competence at that job, is an example. What is anomalous about classifying such behavior as unjust, I have argued, is that there seems to be no *duty* to give anyone the job, in general; how, then, can it be unjust not to give it to one person rather than another? That is the central puzzle, and it seems to me to remain unanswered.

Cases can be made for the wrongness of what is ordinarily called discrimination on indirect grounds having to do with social harmony and the like. But such cases, unlike what can be said in the case of nonbasic discrimination, run up against a serious barrier, *viz.*, the principle of liberty. To require persons to perform all sorts of actions despite the fact that the actions they might instead prefer are not literally harmful to anyone is surely to violate their liberty. It has been assumed throughout that that is a serious point against any requirement or prohibition, and perhaps some would be inclined to deny that it is. Arguing against those people would get us into another essay, and thus I let the case rest at this point.

ENDNOTES

1. In private conversation with G.A. Cohen.
2. Henry Sidgwick, *The Methods of Ethics*, 7th ed. (Indianapolis/Cambridge: Hacket, 1981), p. 379.

SAVE THE MALES:

Backlash in

Organizations

Ronald J. Burke

Susan Black

White male paranoia: Are they the newest victims ... or just bad sports?

(*Newsweek*, March 29, 1993)

White male and worried: White men still dominate corporate America. But in companies with aggressive diversity programs, they are beginning to feel angry and resentful. What should companies do?

(*Business Week*, January 31, 1994)

This paper deals with the subject of male backlash in organizations. Surprisingly, very little research attention has been devoted to understanding backlash, although stories about it have appeared in the media, a recent book has addressed the issue (Faludi, 1991), and individuals responsible for levelling the organizational playing field have observed it. The slogan "save the males" was recently seen adorning the front of a T-shirt. As a parody of the "save the whales" slogan, face-

tiously suggesting that men are becoming an endangered species, it suggests to us that the notion or concern that men are increasingly unfairly disadvantaged is gaining currency in mainstream society. This paper defines backlash, examines its causes and manifestations, describes who is likely to exhibit it and offers suggestions for addressing backlash in organizational settings. It reviews the limited writing on this topic, draws conclusions from this review and offers a research agenda.

Our motivations for writing this paper come from several sources. First, we were intrigued by isolated stories and reports on male backlash in the popular press, and in particular, the number of letters to the editor from aggrieved males. Second, Faludi's book (1991) pulled together instances of backlash in a wide variety of areas and provided an historical overview of the phenomenon. Finally, our involvement with four organizations in bringing about work-

Journal of Business Ethics 16: 933–942, 1997. © 1997 Kluwer Academic Publishers. Printed in the Netherlands.

place changes to support the career advancement of women has highlighted how difficult efforts towards the creation of a level playing field can be. One of these projects provided an opportunity to glimpse, first-hand, the reactions of several groups of men towards such efforts.

In reviewing the limited research on this topic, this paper considers the following questions:

Definition of backlash

- What is male backlash?
- Is backlash new?
- Why an increase in backlash now?
- How strong and pervasive is male backlash?

Backlash in the organizational context

- Is backlash warranted?
- Consequences of backlash?
- Who is most likely to exhibit male backlash?
- Should organizations care about backlash?
- How can organizations address backlash?

DEFINITION OF BACKLASH

What is Male Backlash?

Backlash can be defined as any form of resistance men exhibit towards policies, programs and initiatives undertaken by organizations to promote the hiring and advancement of marginalized employees (e.g., women, people of color, the handicapped, aboriginal people). This resistance can take many forms, both overt and covert.

Goode (1982) makes a distinction between two kinds of resistance typically shown by men. First, there are men who historically paid lip service to equality, but now disapprove of the way equality is being con-

cretely applied. Second, there are men who never believed in equality and now oppose it openly because it no longer is a trivial threat. Goode reserves the term backlash for the first group, those who now feel negatively about a policy they once thought was desirable. We believe the term covers both kinds of male resistance.

Is Backlash New?

Faludi (1991) suggests that male backlash is a recurring phenomenon with a long history. Every time women collectively make progress towards equality, instances of backlash arise. It is perhaps naive to believe that women's progress would not create a backlash since by definition, backlash is a reaction and can only exist in response to other forces.

We believe that backlash is not a male conspiracy at a conscious level. Men who exhibit backlash may be unaware of their attitudes, behavior and roles or if they are aware, do not realize the impact of their attitudes. Women have optimistically believed that once they demonstrated the merits of their case, male hostility to their claims and rights would disappear. Faludi (1991) concludes unfortunately, the women have always been disappointed.

Why an Increase in Backlash Now?

The following headlines (Table I), appearing during the past five years, illustrate the types of issues that have stimulated backlash. Typically, they convey a preference for hiring females and non-white males for jobs or changing job qualifications in an effort to include more females and non-white males.

Faludi (1991) believes that backlash is stronger now, though negative views on women's progress have always existed. She proposes several reasons for this. First, beginning with feminism in the 1970s, women have argued voraciously for equality. The anti-feminist backlash has been unleashed—not by women's achievement of full equality—but by the increased possibility that they may get it. Miller (1976) has suggested that male backlash is an indication that women may have really had an effect.

Second, there are now more challenges and obstacles to men's economic and social welfare, to their abilities to fulfil the male provider and breadwinner role, and ultimately to their masculinity (Pleck, 1987; Goode, 1982). These include:

- Retrenchment and decline in organizations leading to fewer employment opportunities

- Slower growth in organizations leading to fewer promotions

- Increased competition for jobs and promotions

- Smaller wage increases leading to a decreasing standard of living

- Politically correct environment foster[ing] perceptions of male-bashing

- Increased media attention to the notion of unfair advancement of women

- Increasing number of corporate and government initiatives supporting change (e.g., employment equity, diversity training)

Manhood is measured by power, health and success, and unfortunately for men, it is becoming harder to measure up. Kimmel (1993) writes that American men fear other men because these men may be seen by other men as less than manly. Since men derive much of their identity in the workplace, and it is increasingly more difficult for men to satisfy these needs, more men will feel like failures, inadequate and powerless. Women and non-white men serve as a convenient target at which to direct those frustrations, anxieties and anger.

Third, there are indications that women are/may be increasingly advantaged. This shows up in a variety of ways. When a job is posted, it is likely to state that applications from women (and other non-traditional

TABLE I	Issues that have stimulated backlash (1990–1994)
Headline	**Summary**
"Medical School anti-male bias alleged" *Globe & Mail*, October 18, 1994	Medical schools appear to be discriminating against men in the selection of new students.
"Ontario barring white applicants for senior position" *Globe & Mail*, November 11, 1993	The government of Ontario placed a job advertisement for a senior level position with the following statement: "This competition is limited to the following employment equity designated groups: aboriginal people, francophones, persons with disabilities, racial minorities and women."
"Art College will hire only women to balance male-dominated staff" *Toronto Star*, June 10, 1990	Ontario College of Art attempted to establish hiring criteria that would give preference to qualified women in a certain number of courses.
"Employment equity: bad news for young white males" *Globe & Mail*, June 15, 1993	Supported the conclusion that men seemed to be facing reverse discrimination.
"Burning issues: new rules for hiring minorities and women have Toronto firefighters up in arms" *Toronto Star*, January 31, 1993	Firefighting department attempted to increase the number of qualified minorities of women candidates at the expense of white male candidates.

groups) are particularly encouraged and that the firm is committed to employment equity. In addition, there have been a few well publicized announcements of positions specifically available only to women. Other well publicized stories have considered the hiring of women over men (e.g., police, firefighters, admissions to medical school, Ontario College of Art, the Ontario government advertisement).

Fourth, men are now sensing that, though not yet an endangered species, they may be becoming a minority. They are becoming increasingly aware of changing workforce demographics. In addition, if they examine the statistics carefully, women are slowly but surely making inroads and may even be gaining. We have found in most of our research and consulting sites, that although more men than women currently receive promotions, the percentage of women receiving promotions during the past five years has increased at a faster rate than the percentage of men. Some men now realize that the world around them has become more competitive. Men have historically only competed with other men; now men have to compete with an increasing number of women as well.

Fifth, some organizations are actively engaged in diagnosing their work environments to better understand the experiences of women (and men) and to identify barriers to women's (and men's) advancement. In an attempt to level the playing field these leading-edge firms are initiating policies and programs that involved removing advantages and exclusive privileges men have always had, as well as providing women with greater support. Backlash may be fostered by the very practices used to advance women (and other non-traditionals).

Sixth, it is obviously a time of change. And change—usually coupled with ambiguity, confusion and frustration—makes men anxious. In light of changing roles and changing rules, some men report greater fear

and resentment. Organizational discussion of targets or quotas, the increasingly popular establishment of women's groups, and the perception that women can now be placed on the "fast track" leave many men feeling passed over, ignored or excluded.

How Strong and Pervasive is Male Backlash?

There is little data that addresses this question. Astrachan (1986), in a seven year long study of American male attitudes in the 1980s, reported that only five to ten percent of the men he surveyed supported women's demands for equality. A later survey of about 3000 men (American Male Opinion Index, 1988) reported that only about twenty-five percent of men supported the women's movement. The majority favored traditional roles for women. As is often the case, men paid lip service to fairness, equal pay and working women until it was their wife that wanted to work. Faludi (1991) suggests that even these few men have in fact lost interest in feminist concerns. The pressure of male backlash is likely to reduce this support even further. As a result, the attitudinal gap between women and men continues to widen as more women come to support the goals of the push for equality.

BACKLASH IN THE ORGANIZATION CONTEXT

Is Male Backlash Warranted?

Begging the issue of whether male backlash is *ever* warranted, the answer to this question appears to be both yes and no. It may be understandable to the extent to which men *perceive* that women are making increasing gains, that women are hired and/or promoted though they lack qualifications or have lesser qualifications than men who are not hired (merit has gone by the boards), and that relatively more women are being promoted. Backlash may be a rational response to perceptions of reverse discrimination.

Backlash may also be irrational and an overreaction since more men than women continue to be promoted, men are still likely to be responsible for making the hiring and promotion decisions, and discriminations have always had to be made between similarly qualified applicants (e.g., men) using not only formal criteria (i.e., merit) but other factors as well. When one looks at the scarcity of women at the top levels of most organizations, the cry of "save the males" seems premature.

In addition men continue to have more advantage and privilege than do women. Perceptions of effective management (Schein, 1994) and aspects of organizational culture remain masculine in nature (Hearn, 1994; Maddock and Parkin, 1994).

Consequences of Backlash

Male backlash has consequences for women, men, and organizations. Male backlash influences the relationship of men and women resulting in increased tension between them. Male backlash confirms some women's views of the neanderthal attitudes of some men. These men "don't get it" and women may perceive them as the enemy. Male backlash solidifies the bonds between some men. They are under siege; they are an endangered species; they are now being discriminated against. This period, characterized by confusion, ambiguity, change, fear and attacks on male identity and masculinity, has increased some men's introspection and supported a growing interest in a men's movement (Bly, 1990; Keen, 1991; Lee, 1991). Women become the enemy for making men aware of the unfairness of the system. Men become suspicious of women if their firm has a women's group. The differences between women and men, the idea that they belong to two different worlds,

become reinforced (Tannen, 1990; Gray, 1993).

Male backlash also has an effect on women's relationship with women (Faludi, 1991). Backlash serves to drive a wedge between those women who have "made it" in the male system and those women who have not. Faludi indicates three ways in which this happens. First, successful women may defect from the women's movement. Second, successful women may give up their corporate careers. Third, women may become less interested in career advancement.

The recent writing and debate centering on political correctness can also be interpreted in the context of male backlash. Men now feel muzzled; previously acceptable conversation and behavior is now seen by some as in bad taste. If men display "politically incorrect" words or behaviors they may be centered out and punished. This serves to drive those conversations and actions underground. Solidarity between some men is heightened as they decry the new and venerate the old. Tensions between men and women are heightened, particularly by men who encounter women [who] support their concerns about the negative effects of the politically correct environment.

Male backlash also has an effect on organizations in a variety of insidious ways. Considerable energy may get dissipated in tension, anger, resentment and frustration. Men may rebel against and undermine the organizational efforts to support women's career advancement. Morrison (1992) found that backlash was cited as the biggest problem organizations faced in their efforts to support and advance non-traditional employees.

The following vignettes provide illustrations of male backlash we have observed in Canadian organizations.

Minefield

Minefield is a national professional services firm having a 2200 person workforce, 50%

of which are women. Although women make up half of the new professional hires, only 5% of the partnership were women. In focus groups exploring barriers to women's advancement at Minefield, women stated that male colleagues were critical of their participation in this activity and had told some of them not to gripe.

Redfield

Redfield is a financial services firm with a 35 000 person workforce, 75% of which are females. Some professional and manager-ial women belonging to a corporate women's network of about 150 choose not to reveal their membership in the network with male colleagues for fear of criticism. Some women believed that other women who were active in the creation of this group suffered setbacks in their careers as a result of their participation.

Bluefield

Bluefield is a computer manufacturing firm with an 8000-person workforce, 25% of which is female. Some men and women were critical of the formation of a women's advisory council.

Greenfield

Greenfield is another financial services firm employing over 30 000 people of whom ap-proximately 75% are female. The bank has few senior female executives and has be-come concerned with barriers to advance-ment faced by women. As a result it has undertaken a diagnosis of this issue and one method of gathering data has been a series of focus groups. The male-only groups have revealed considerable feelings of anxiety and anger by men, resulting in expressions of backlash. First, although some of the men acknowledged the absence of women at se-nior levels, few thought women at their lev-els faced any unique barriers. Second, when asked to identify benefits they hoped to come out of this diagnostic effort, many stated that they hoped that reverse discrim-ination would not be endorsed or under-taken. Several believed that women have already been given preferential treatment. For example, when asked specifically about what would help their career, the first an-swer given by a man in human resources was a "skirt." They shared a perception that promotion decisions were no longer based on merit, and moreover, membership in a designated group, such as "an MBA in a wheelchair" was a distinct advantage in one's career. The group believed the bank was under pressure to unfairly favor non-traditional groups from two sources. First, they were under the erroneous perception that the employment equity law must now be interpreted as hiring, supporting and pro-moting quotas in order to achieve a 50–50 distribution of men and women at the se-nior levels of the organization. Second, they believed that the bank was buckling under to political correctness pressure to maintain its image as a good corporate citizen.

Who is Likely to Exhibit Backlash?

Faludi (1991) suggests that backlash is more likely to be expressed by two groups of men. The first are blue collar workers. These men are typically less educated, less egalitarian men (more authoritarian) in their attitudes and more threatened by societal changes—those involving women in particular. The second group she identifies are men who are younger baby-boomers. These men face increasing competition in a more demanding world which offers fewer rewards. It will be more difficult for these men to achieve economic success and satisfy the provider role than their predecessors. Goode (1982) suggests that older men, less educated men, white men and men living in rural areas will have more negative reactions. Our work also indicates that older men who have been passed over (over 40, less educated) will have more negative attitudes towards women's equality and progress.

Do Two Wrongs Make a Right?

Some men will admit that women have been discriminated against in the past. A few will even admit that what is now happening to men (i.e., anti-male sentiments) has always happened to women. But these same men will report that men are now being discriminated against. As a result of their perceptions of feminism, some men believe they are viewed as the enemy. Male bashing, in their opinion, has become the order of the day. Some men believe they are prejudged as sexist, and that men are held responsible for creating and maintaining a sexist system. And to the extent to which these men perceive this to be the case, the question is then asked, "Do two wrongs make a right?"

Men resist the notion that they should be bashed or punished for a system that they did not create. An important distinction needs to be made between male bashing which truly bashes males from male bashing which calls into question the white male system that gives men privilege (i.e., unearned advantage). In addition men's reactions to male bashing deflects attention away from the ways in which men benefit/have benefitted and ways in which the playing field might be levelled.

Focus groups we have conducted with women, and with men in the same organization have supported the following conclusions. Women and men want organizations to make personnel decisions based on merit. Women believe that past decisions have not always been merit-based. Men believe that current personnel decisions are becoming less merit-based.

There is an emerging consensus in North America that the setting of goals or quotas to redress past wrongs, termed reverse discrimination by some, is still discrimination, however laudatory the intended consequences. Efforts are now underway to remove or weaken the legislative support for employment equity initiatives. The effects of such efforts on the continued advancement of women in the workplace is an open question at this point.

Dealing with Male Backlash

Organizations on the forefront in supporting the career aspirations of women have begun to develop strategies for dealing with male backlash, recognizing backlash is present, and is real. They conclude that backlash is better dealt with head on than swept under the rug. We have identified four options available to organizations who need to address the backlash problem.

- **Ignore It** The first suggests that male backlash be ignored. Backlash is inevitable and devoting energy to dealing with it may detract from the primary goal of advancing women. Martin Luther King advocated his followers to "keep their eyes on the prize."

- **Punish It** Another option is zero tolerance; backlash will be punished. The organization will work with you to acquire appropriate attitudes and behaviors, but only for a limited period. If you "don't get it," you will be terminated.

- **Co-opt Resisters** A third option is to co-opt men. This approach involves identifying concerns they (may) or do share with women such as bias and discrimination or work-family conflict. Both women and men become allies in changing the system.

- **Acknowledge and Educate** A fourth option is to acknowledge backlash and encourage its expression. It is important for organizations to help males understand that strict fairness (merit) has seldom been the only criterion for promotion. The underlying theory is that by allowing men to express their feelings they will become more open to appeals to reason through education. It would be possible to disabuse them of the myths underlying their fears and thereby diffuse the backlash.

Tips for Dealing with Male Backlash

The following tips were provided to us by a woman heading up the equality initiative in a major bank. We believe these tips are valuable in dealing with sceptics or individuals who draw the wrong conclusions from the efforts of organizations trying to create a level playing field.

- First, stress the benefits of supporting the advancement of non-traditional managers to all employees. This involves a commitment to continuous communication. Challenge the organization to get behind the initiative to help its success.

- Second, it is much better to prevent destructive myths than it is to react to them once they are full-blown. Table II indicates the most common myths and misunderstandings accompanied by suggested responses.

FUTURE RESEARCH DIRECTIONS

The field appears to be wide open since so little work has been done. Research could fruitfully be expanded in the following broad directions:

- men's attitudes towards women's equality
- overt and covert manifestations of male backlash

- role of one's peer group in maintaining backlash (Pope, 1993)
- the consequences of backlash
- the antecedents of backlash: societal, organizational, and personal
- evaluations of different initiatives for effectively addressing male backlash

We offer a preliminary research framework for future work. It suggests that the prevalence and depth of male backlash is a function of societal, organizational and personal characteristics. Personal characteristics predictive of male backlash would include such factors as age, level of education, organizational level, career progress compared to personal organization age norms, career satisfaction, years in present position, early socialization about male and female roles, ethnic group membership, attitudes towards women and attitudes toward equity.

Organizational characteristics predictive of male backlash would include type of industry, recent experiences of company growth versus decline, promotion opportunities, amount of government regulation and attention to employment equity (numbers), presence of initiatives (i.e., policies and/or programs) supporting women's career advancement, motivations for initiating such programs, credibility of senior management on equity issues, education and skill levels in the workforce, number and location of women in the organization and the existence of women's groups in the organization.

Societal factors predictive of male backlash would include aspects of the macroeconomy such as expansion, visibility of equity issues among the general public, visibility of male backlash symptoms among the general public and number and significance of events celebrating women's achievements or struggles.

We also need to develop some measures of backlash—that is, attitudes and behaviors indicating resistance. In addition, various consequences of backlash need to be

TABLE II	Common myths and misunderstandings
Myth	**Response**
Men are becoming an endangered species around here.	Men are not endangered. All that has changed is that men have lost their traditional advantages. Share the facts. Look at current executive and senior management. Look at promotions charts. Look at hiring rates.
If you want a job here these days you'd better be a member of the targeted groups.	We are concerned about the disadvantaged groups, but we only want to reflect their numbers in the population.
The bottom line is that we are really setting quotas, right?	There are no quotas and advancement is still based on merit. However we will actively promote the best women and minorities.
Workplace equity is just a buzz phrase to justify reverse discrimination.	Workplace equity—hopefully banishes all forms of discrimination not transfers it to women from men. Workplace equity is about removing special privileges from men, a traditionally privileged group, rather than transferring privilege to women.
Isn't it true that the government is forcing us to hire under-represented groups?	The government is not forcing us to do anything. We are aiming to have a workforce more representative of the community we serve because it makes good business sense.
Aren't we overlooking women's shortcomings because of our commitment to promoting women?	Women are as qualified as men—our data shows this. We are not forcing women to take promotions they don't want. Rather we are attempting to level the playing field.
How can we talk about a level playing field when we are so actively recruiting aboriginal people? Isn't that preferential treatment?	Seeking out aboriginals makes good business sense.
What if we hire (promote) a member of the designated groups that can't do the job?	Anyone who cannot perform in a job will face the same penalties as anyone else.

evaluated, monitored and understood and various strategies for addressing male backlash need to be evaluated. At a tactical level, the question of whether addressing male backlash focusses on men and their needs and responses (pouting, taking their ball and going home, passive-aggressive behavior, getting attention) once again giving them undue attention.

CONCLUSIONS

Although the focus of this paper was on male backlash in organizations, behavior in organizations reflects attitudes and values of the broader society. Events on December 6, 1989, at the University of Montreal suggests this connection with the larger context. Marc Lepine, blaming women—particularly feminist women—for spoiling his life, walked into a classroom at the University of Montreal's engineering building, ordered the men to leave and shot the women. It was probably not a coincidence that Lepine chose the engineering school, since these schools continue to provide a chilly climate for the small—but increasing—number of women choosing this specialization.

The text of Lepine's suicide letter stated that feminists wanted to keep the advantages of women while trying to grab those of men. Lepine reportedly shouted, "You're all a bunch of feminists" as he went on his rampage (*Globe and Mail*, December 7, 1989). Lepine undoubtedly absorbed his attitudes from the society around him. The sooner we begin to understand the seeds of male backlash and begin to address it at all levels of organization—from primary schools to the executive suite—the less likely such events will occur in the future.

ENDNOTE

1. Preparation of this manuscript was supported in part by the Faculty of Administrative Studies, York University. Bruna Gaspini prepared the manuscript. Our thinking about male backlash was influenced by discussions with our colleague Mark Maier.

REFERENCES

American Male Opinion Index (Condé Nast Publications, New York).

Astrachan, A.: 1986, *How Men Feel: Their Response to Women's Demands for Equality and Power* (Anchor Books, Garden City, N.Y.).

Bly, R.: 1990, *Iron John* (Reading, Mass., Addison-Wesley, New York).

Faludi, S.: 1991, *Backlash: The Undeclared War Against American Women* (Crown Publishers Inc., New York).

Goode, W.J.: 1982, 'Why Men Resist,' in B. Thorne and M. Yalom (eds.), *Rethinking the Family: Some Feminist Questions* (Longman, Inc., New York).

Gray, J.: 1993, *Women Are From Venus, Men Are From Mars* (Harper, New York).

Hearn, J.: 1994, 'Changing Men and Changing Managements: Social Change, Social Research and Social Research and Social Action,' in M.J. Davidson and R.J. Burke (eds.), *Women in Management: Current Research Issues* (Paul Chapman Publishing, London).

Keen, S.: 1991, *Fire In The Belly: On Being A Man* (Bantam Books, New York).

Kimmel, M.S.: 1993, 'Clarence, William, Iron Mike, Tailbook, Senator Packwood, Spur Posse, Magic ... and Us,' in E. Buchward, P.R. Fletcher and M. Roth (eds.), *Transforming A Rape Culture* (Milkweed Editions, Minneapolis, Minn.).

Lee, J.: 1991, *At My Father's Wedding: Reclaiming Our True Masculinity* (Bantam Books, New York).

Maddock, S. and D. Parkin: 1994, 'Gender Cultures: How They Affect Men and Women At Work,' in M.J. Davidson and R.J. Burke (eds.), *Women in Management: Current Research Issues* (Chapman Publishing, London).

Miller, J.B.: 1976, *Toward a New Psychology of Women* (Beacon Press, Boston).

Morrison, A.M.: 1992, *The New Leaders* (Jossey Bass, San Francisco).

Pope, B.S.: 1993, 'In The Wake of Tailbook: A New Order for The Navy,' in E. Buckwald, P.R. Fletcher and M. Roth (eds.), *Transforming A Rape Culture* (Minneapolis, Minn.).

Pleck, J.H.: 1987, 'The Contemporary Man,' in J. Scheer (ed.), *A Man's Handbook of Counselling and Psychotherapy For Men* (Sage Publications, Newbury Park, Calif.).

Schein, V.E.: 1994, 'Managerial Sextyping: A Persistent and Pervasive Barrier to Women's Opportunities,' in M.J. Davidson and R.J. Burke (eds.), *Women in Management: Current Research Issues* (Paul Chapman Publishing, London).

Tannen, D.: 1990, *You Just Don't Understand: Women and Men in Conversation* (Ballantine Books, New York).

CASE 7 — Re Stelwire Ltd. and United Steelworkers of America, Local 5328

Grievor Anderson was denied overtime opportunities operating the lift truck and was unsuccessful in applying for a job as a tractor operator; the basis of the company's denial was that he had refused to take most of the mandatory medical examination for mobile equipment operators. The policy regarding the medical examinations includes a requirement that operators over 40 undergo a physical examination either by a company doctor or the employee's own doctor (the latter at the employee's expense). Grievor Anderson filed six grievances and the union a policy grievance, all contesting the entitlement of the company to impose a mandatory examination ...

Evidence

The company is a fully owned subsidiary of Stelco Inc. The grievor is employed at the company's Parkdale Works where there are approximately 380 bargaining unit employees and 87 staff. The company is involved in the processing of steel rod into semi-finished and finished wire and nails. There is a lot of movement of materials within, and around, the plant (including shipping) through the use of cranes and mobile equipment such as lift trucks.

Many years ago (1970s or earlier) the Company implemented a policy of requiring medical tests for all mobile equipment operators, and a physical examination for operators over 40. In approximately 1984 there was a deviation from the policy and practice in that employees over 40 were not required to have a doctor perform the medical examination unless tests identified a particular problem which called for further investigation. The company said

that deviation from policy was in part due to the limited, or no, availability of a doctor or nurse on site. In December 1993, the company decided to revert to the full policy. The union says that it was never apprised of the actual policy.

The grievor commenced employment with the company in 1976. He was a vice-president and chief steward of the union in the late 1980s. He is a heat treat operator in the nail mill whose base job does not include the requirement to operate mobile equipment. However, he is qualified as a lift truck operator and has successfully applied for overtime work operating a lift truck. On February 25, 1994, he was requested by the company to report to the company's health unit. He had heard that employees had been going to the health unit (first aid) for tests. When he attended at first aid he advised the nurse that he was there for a vision test ("because I felt it was reasonable") but nothing else. The nurse told him he had no choice but to take all the tests and the physical examination. He refused to do so. Later that day he was told by Mr. Milner, the general foreman of the nail mill and shipping, that he had a choice of using his own doctor at his own expense for the medical examination and that if he chose to do so he should take his doctor a list of the tests and information required by the company ...

The grievor applied for overtime shifts operating the lift truck, and applied for a job posting as a tractor operator "hi-lift." He was denied the overtime shift and the position, on the basis that he had not taken the medical tests and examination.

The grievor testified that he had attended with his own doctor three to six months prior and had been given a number of blood tests, urinalysis, and electro-cardiogram and a physical examination. He said he was satisfied that he had no apparent physical or mental problem which would affect his ability to operate mobile equipment. He stated that when the issue arose he had read information relating to the *Occupational Health and Safety Act* and had spoken to a person in occupational health and safety at the Ontario Ministry of Labour; he believed, based on the information he received, that he was within (his) rights to decline. He had told Mr. Milner the next day that under the *Act* "I was declining any medical surveillance program. In cross-examination the grievor testified:

> "It [medical examination] was not necessary when I was having the testing done regularly myself … I've instructed health and safety courses. I have gone to school to learn more about the Act and what rights and duties I have. In my opinion I had a right not to subject myself to their testing."

Asked if his refusal was a matter of principle with him he responded: "It was a matter of expense so I opted for my rights." (It appeared to be generally agreed at the hearing that the cost of having a doctor complete the form, following a regular examination and test, would be approximately $20.) …

Dr. Cheung [Medical Director at Stelco] testified on behalf of the company … She emphasized that the examinations relate directly to the requirements of the job and particularly the potential risk to other employees. The examinations are also for the safety of the mobile equipment operators themselves. (Dr. Cheung also said that medical examinations are also made available to employees on a voluntary basis, free of charge.) She referred to the due diligence required

of employers under the *Occupational Health and Safety Act* to ensure the safety of workers. She explained the necessity of confirming on a regular basis the company's view about the fitness of the mobile equipment operators. Dr. Cheung explained the reasons for the tests such as vision (e.g., cataracts, deterioration in vision), blood pressure (e.g., potential for strokes, detection of heart problems), urinalysis for sugar, blood and protein (e.g., diabetes, kidneys: employees on insulin are checked more than once a year) …

Dr. Cheung testified that mandatory medical examinations of mobile equipment operators were considered important at the age of 40 because of the statistics and the proven greater health risks after that age; she said there are also mandatory medical examinations for managers over the age of 40 …

With reference to the *Occupational Health and Safety Act*, Dr. Cheung testified that because of a successful recent legal challenge to mandatory testing under the *Act*, based on violation of human rights, workers are not required to submit to testing if the danger (e.g., designated substances) is only to themselves. However, she said that employees who may be a danger to others (e.g., mobile equipment operators) are still required to submit to mandatory tests which are reasonable.

Argument of the Union

The issue is whether the company has the right to unilaterally impose a requirement on mobile equipment operators for medical examinations and, specifically, for a physical examination for operators over the age of 40. Any such right can only be conferred by the collective agreement or by statute. The union argues that no such right has been conferred and the company, in requiring the medical examinations, is violating the *Human Rights Code* by discriminating against operators over 40. The medical examinations are, furthermore, contrary to the common law in that they constitute an infringement upon the physical integrity of the person, i.e., an invasion of the right to privacy ...

The company has not established that its medical examination program for mobile equipment operators is a "reasonable" requirement. The union accepts that the company has a right, and a duty, to require a mobile equipment operator to "undergo a medical examination if [it] has reasonable and probably [sic] grounds for suspecting that the employee: (i) is a source of danger to himself, other employees or company property; or (ii) is unfit to perform his duties." [Dartmouth General Hospital] The uncontradicted evidence of grievor Anderson is that he has no apparent physical or mental problem which would affect his ability to do the job of a mobile equipment operator or the job of tractor operator for which he applied and was denied ...

The arbitration board should declare, as the remedy to the policy grievance, that the company's medical policy and program for mobile equipment operators are outside any statutory or collective agreement authority and must be rescinded. The overtime grievances of grievor Anderson should be sustained and damages awarded and the grievance regarding the posted position sustained; because the posted job has since been eliminated, the grievor should be awarded damages based on the difference in wage rates the grievor would have received in that position for as long as he should have been the incumbent ...

Argument for the Company

It is undisputed that for approximately 15 years, until 1984, the medical tests/examinations for mobile equipment operators were being regularly carried out, including physical examination by a doctor for operators over 40. The physical examination portion of the medicals was suspended for a few years for administrative reasons only (lack of staff). It is to be noted that the grievor ... had taken the tests on numerous occasions; the grievor did not operate mobile equipment between 1986 and 1994 and so was not required to take the tests/examinations. The grievor knew from his doctor that an annual medical is important; he could have got a certificate from his own doctor to satisfy the company's requirements but chose not to do so for whatever reason. The union witnesses agreed that it is important for the company to ensure the safety of works [sic], including ensuring the fitness of an employee to do his job where his actions could endanger others. The mobile equipment operators are using equipment which is inherently dangerous. It is essential that the operators' fitness be assured. It is also undisputed that the protocol for mobile equipment operators ... has been in place since the early 1970s ...

The company's position is:

(1) The company is entitled to require that the operators are medically fit to operate mobile equipment. The company places considerable emphasis on health and safety in the plant ...

The company and its directors have obligations under the *Occupational Health and Safety Act.* Under s. 32 every director and every officer of a corporation must take all reasonable care to ensure that the corporation complies with the act and the regulations. Under s. 66 every person who contravenes or fails to comply with a provision of the *Act* or the regulations is guilty of an offence and is liable to a fine or imprisonment; a corporation convicted of an offence is subject to a maximum fine of $500 000 ...

(2) The company is entitled to have medical examinations of mobile equipment operators to satisfy itself of the fitness of its employees ... Management has promulgated a reasonable rule. It is only applicable to mobile equipment operators, there is no requirement that the examination must be performed by a company doctor, and it is relevant to the position. In the job posting section ... physical fitness is a stated factor to be taken into consideration; the parties obviously contemplated some way of measuring physical fitness ...

(3) The mandatory physical examination for mobile equipment operators who have attained age 40 is a reasonable requirement and is not in violation of the *Human Rights Code*. The right to equal treatment with respect to employment without discrimination because of ... age ... is not infringed where it is a reasonable and bona fide qualification because of the nature of the employment. There was uncontradicted medical evidence of the importance of complete medical examinations for people over 40 years of age ...

(4) Management provides the medical tests and examinations free of charge. If an employee elects to have the examination performed by his or her own doctor management is not required to pay the cost. There is no requirement to do so under the collective agreement nor is there any such requirement under the *Occupational Health and Safety Act* ...

(5) Regarding the job posting grievance, the collective agreement states that physical fitness is one of the controlling factors. The company's requirement of proof of physical fitness is reasonable. The grievor refused to submit to the examination and therefore is not entitled to the job.

Decision

We accept, and adopt, the argument on behalf of the company (above), in its entirety ...

The standard to be met to satisfy an arbitration board that a rule unilaterally introduced by the company is proper, is that the rule not be unreasonable ... The question, therefore, is whether the company's requirement ... is a reasonable and bona fide requirement. If it is, it also satisfies the exception under the *Human Rights Code* to what would otherwise be discrimination because of age under s. 5. The relevant sections of the *Human Rights Code* provide:

Part 1
Freedom from Discrimination

> 5(1) Every person has a right to equal treatment with respect to employment without discrimination because of race, ancestry, place or origin, colour, ethnic origin, citizenship, creed, sex, sexual orientation, age, record of offences, marital status, family status, or handicap.

Special employment

> 24(1) the right under section 5 to equal treatment with respect to employment is not infringed where,

> (b) the discrimination in employment is [f]or reasons of age, sex, record of marital status if the age, sex, record

of offences or marital status of the applicant is a reasonable and bona fide qualification because of the nature of the employment.

The unchallenged evidence of Dr. Cheung is very compelling. The union's evidence, particularly of the grievor, in reference to his doctor recommending annual examination, tended to provide support for the company's position. As the doctor testified in *City of Mississauga Firefighters Assn:* "Almost any age chosen would be arbitrary to a certain extent, but age 60 constituted an appropriate compromise." We believe, in the circumstances of the present case, based on compelling evidence, that age 40 constituted an appropriate compromise ...

The rationale of arbitrator Swan in *City of Mississauga Firefighters Assn.* ... is pertinent to the present case:

> On the other hand, the fact that a medical examination may not provide a final answer as to the fitness of an employee for work is not conclusive of the value of requiring such an examination. An examination may well reveal evidence of coronary disease, just as it may indicate other disabling factors. It is thus not a perfect solution to individuation, but it may well be a way of identifying persons for whom continued employment as a firefighter is unsafe. As I have already indicated, I have also concluded that its value increases with the age of the individual, and although there is no particular magic in the age 60, the fact is that, on bal-

ance, medical examinations are of more value for 60-year-olds than for persons of any younger age.

> It is of interest that the association's plea here is for individuation in respect of the liability to a medical examination. Therefore, it is suggested that it would be quite reasonable to require medical examinations of persons, of whatever age, who had identifiable medical problems, but not to require them of all persons simply because they had reached a particular age. I do not find this argument convincing. Dr. Mymin's evidence was to the effect that apparent good health, whether through actual ignorance of underlying symptoms or deliberate concealment of those symptoms, could easily conceal serious disability and significant risk of death or incapacitation through continued strenuous work. To apply a requirement for medical examinations only to those persons who had already suffered from an identifiable medical condition would surely be to wait too long to assess the fitness of individuals for continued work. I have come to the conclusion, therefore, that age is an appropriate proxy for actual deterioration of medical condition.

> ... I have concluded that it is not a breach of the *Ontario Human Rights Code* for the employer to require annual medical examinations of employees after age 60."

Accordingly the grievances are denied.

54 L.A.C. 4th 303, March 25, 1996.

CASE 8	**Central Alberta Dairy Pool v. Alberta (Human Rights Commission)**

Per Wilson J.:—The principal question raised in this appeal is whether a particular attendance rule imposed by the respondent employer on an employee is a bona fide occupational qualification ("BFOQ") under the *Alberta Individual's Rights Protection Act*, R.S.A. 1980, c. I-2 ("the Act"). In the event that this court answers the question in the negative, we are further called upon by the parties to consider whether the respondent might defend itself from a charge of religious discrimination by proving that it accommodated the employee up to the point of undue hardship.

1. The Facts

The appeal arises out of a complaint launched by Jim Christie ("the complainant") against the respondent alleging that the respondent refused to continue to employ him because of his religion, contrary to s. 7(1) of the *Act*. His complaint was upheld by the board of inquiry but overturned by the Alberta Court of Queen's Bench. The Alberta Court of Appeal upheld the Queen's Bench decision.

The complainant was employed by the respondent from August 26, 1980 to April 4, 1983 in a number of positions in a [sic] production operations of the respondent's mil[k] processing plant in Wetaskiwin, Alberta. He became a prospective member of the World Wide Church of God in February 1983. The church recognizes a Saturday Sabbath, a five-day Fall Feast of the Tabernacle, and five other holy days during the year. Religious adherents are expected not to work on these days, although the church does not impose sanctions for disobedience.

The complainant requested to work the early shift on Friday in order that his work schedule not conflict with the onset of the Sabbath. This request was granted. He expressed a desire to schedule his vacation in the future to coincide with the Fall Feast of the Tabernacle but consideration of this request was superseded by subsequent events.

On March 25, 1983, Mr. Christie requested through his supervisor permission to take unpaid leave on Tuesday, March 29th and Monday, April 4th, in order to observe two holy days. The latter day was Easter Monday. He offered to work alternative days outside his regular schedule in consideration for his absence on the two hol[y] days. His supervisor responded that he would be allowed to be absent March 29th but for reasons of plant operating needs he would be required to work Monday, April 4th.

Mondays are especially busy days at the plant. Milk arrives seven days a week and mil[k] received on the week-end is prepared Sunday for canning on Monday. All milk that arrives on the week-end must be canned promptly on Monday to prevent spoilage. Mondays are also busy shipping days. In cases of employee absence on Mondays due to sickness or other emergencies the contingency arrangement contemplated under the collective agreement was to adjust work assignments and/or have the supervisor assist in maintaining operations.

The complainant reiterated his request and the reasons for it to his supervisor, his shop steward, and the branch manager. A meeting between these parties, as well as a union representative, took place on March 30th at which time the complaintant was advised by the branch manager that if he failed to report for work on April 4th his employment would be terminated. The complainant did not appear for work on April 4th. When he returned on April 5th he found his position occupied by a newly hired employee. He had been dismissed.

The board of inquiry established pursuant to the *Act* found that the respondent had discriminated against the complainant contrary to s. 7 of the *Act* and ordered the respondent to pay him partial compensation for Christie's lost wages. An appeal to the Alberta Court of Queen's Bench was allowed … and affirmed by the Alberta Court of Appeal.

2. The Relevant Legislation

Individual Rights Protection Act, **R.S.A. 1980 c.I-2:**
[Preamble]
WHEREAS recognition of the inherent dignity and equal and unalienable rights of all persons is the foundation of freedom, justice and peace in the world; and WHEREAS it is recognized in Alberta as a fundamental principle and as a matter of public policy that all persons are equal in dignity and rights without regard to race, religious beliefs, colour, sex, physical characteristics, age, ancestry or place o[f] origin; and WHEREAS it is fitting that this principle be affirmed by the Legislature of Alberta in an enactment whereby those rights of the individual may be protected: THEREFORE HER MAJESTY, by and with the advice and consent of the Legislative Assembly of Alberta, enacts as follows:

7(1) No employer or person acting on behalf of an employer shall

(a) refuse to employ or refuse to continue to employ any person, or

(b) discriminate against any person with regard to employment or any term or condition of employment,

because of the race, religious beliefs, colour, sex, physical characteristics, marital status, age, ancestry or place of origin of that person or on any other person.

(3) Subsection (1) does not apply with respect to a refusal, limitation, specification or preference based on a bona fide occupational qualification.

The *Individual Rights Amendments Act*, 1985 S.A. … amended s. 7(3) and replaced "qualification" with "requirement". The amendment also substituted the term "physical disability" for "physical characteristics".

Interpretation Act, **R.S.A. 1980, c. I-7:**

10. An enactment shall be construed as being remedial, and shall be given the fair, large and liberal construction and interpretation that best ensures the attainment of its objects.

12(1) The preamble of an enactment is a part of the enactment intended to assist in explaining the enactment.

3. The Decisions Below

Board of Inquiry (M. Johanson, Chairman)
… In the course of its decision the board considered the public policy underlying the *Act* (as expressed in the preamble) as well as the interaction of s. 7(1) and 7(3). It concluded, as did this court …, that intent is not a necessary prerequisite to a finding of discrimination in breach of a human rights statute.

In order to establish a *prima facie* case of discrimination the board held that the complainant had to prove:

(a) the existence of a bona fide religion with a genuine commitment to it;

(b) adequate notice of the employee's religious requirements to the employer; and

(c) an effort on the part of the employee to accommodate the employer as far as possible without being required to compromise his beliefs.

The first two points were not in dispute. The complainant's sincerity was not questioned at that time and the employer did not contend that more notice would have affected his decision. With respect to the complainant's attempt to accommodate his employer, the board found that his efforts were adequate and "other alternatives could have been explored if his employer had been open to discussion ..."

Alberta Court of Queen's Bench (MacNaughton)

MacNaughton J. held ... that the board erred in law in finding that the employer's action was not based on a bona fide occupational qualification:

> The complainant violated a term or condition of his employment which compelled him to attend regularly, and, in particular on April 4, 1983, at his place of employment in accordance with the work schedule established by the appellant. Such term or condition of employment was a bona fide occupational qualification ...

Having found the attendance in accordance with the employer's work schedule was a bona fide occupational qualification, MacNaughton J. ... ruled that the employer had no duty to accommodate once the BFOQ defence was established. He also held that in any event the employer had reasonably accommo-

dated the religious beliefs of the employee. Mr. Christie, on the other hand, had failed to take reasonable steps toward accommodating the employer's needs in that he "did not make diligent and complete inquiries of his church representatives to determine whether satisfactory solutions could be found." In coming to this conclusion, MacNaughton J. relied on evidence from a witness (who was also a member of the same church as Mr. Christie) that "if the requirement to work on holy days is an ongoing situation, a person has the responsibility to seek, over time, other employment which will allow observance of holy days." The witness was of the view that Mr. Christie's present occupation would present an ongoing conflict with his religious obligations ...

So much for way of preliminary comment. The issues raised in the appeal are as follows:

1. Can the employer's rule be upheld as a bona fide occupational qualification under s. 7(3) of the *Act*?

2. If question 1 is answered in the negative, was it still open to the respondent to demonstrate that it had accommodated the complainant's religious beliefs up to the point of undue hardship?

3. If question 2 is answered in the affirmative, did the respondent in fact reasonably accommodate the complainant's religious beliefs?

... The rule at issue in the case at bar pertains to mandatory Monday attendance subject to exceptions that do not include religious obligation. It bears the form of a neutral condition of general application and as a practical matter would be unlikely to impose any hardship on employees who adhere to the majority religious faiths. The adverse impact of the rule would be confined to adherents of minority religions or sects such as, in this case, a follower of the Worldwide Church of God.

... [W]e need only be concerned in this case with the criteria for establishing the defence of accommodation. Was the rule rationally connected to the performance of the job and, if so, did the respondent employer accommodate the employee up to the point of undue hardship?

McIntyre's judgment in *O'Malley* provides some guidance in identifying a rational connection between a given rule and the employment ... [H]e speaks of an "employment rule honestly made for sound economic or business reasons, equally applicable to all to whom it is intended to apply ...". As in the case at bar, the rule in *O'Malley* pertained to attendance on certain days, specifically two out of three Saturdays. The court in *O'Malley* concluded that the employer's rule satisfied the first branch of the test. McIntyre J. states ...

> To relate the principle of accommodation to the facts at bar, we must begin with the proposition that the employer is lawfully entitled to carry on business and to stay open for business on Saturdays. It is accordingly entitled to engage employees on the condition that they work on Saturdays.

I think it must follow from this that the respondent in the case at bar is equally entitled to organize its business by closing down its processor operation on the week-end resulting in Mondays being a particularly busy day. The respondent's work rule accordingly meets the test of being rationally connected to the job of being a dairy processor.

Turning to the question of a reasonable compromise, I adopt the observations made by McIntyre J. ... in *O'Malley* with respect to Mrs. O'Malley an[d] find here too that the complainant was lawfully entitled to pursue the practices of his religion and to be free of the compulsion to work on Monday, April 4, 1983, contrary to his religious beliefs. The onus is on the respondent employer to show that it made efforts to accommodate the religious beliefs of the complainant up to the point of undue hardship.

I do not find it necessary to provide a comprehensive definition of what constitutes undue hardship but I believe it may be useful to list some of the factors that may be relevant to such an appraisal. I begin by adopting those identified by the board of inquiry in the case at bar—financial cost, disruption of a collective agreement, problems of morale of other employees, interchangeability of work force and facilities. The size of the employer's operation may influence the assessment of whether a given financial cost is undue or the ease with which the work force and facilities can be adapted to the circumstance. Where safety is at issue both the magnitude of the risk and the identity of those who bear it are relevant considerations. This list is not intended to be exhaustive and the results which will obtain from a balancing of these factors against the right of the employee to be free from discrimination will necessarily vary from case to case.

In the case at bar the board of inquiry found as a fact that concerns of cost, disruption of a collective agreement, employee morale and interchangeability of work force did not pose serious obstacles to accommodating the complainant's religious needs by permitting him to be absent Monday, April 4, 1983. Indeed, it would be very difficult to conclude otherwise in light of the existence of a contingency plan for dealing with sporadic Monday absences. If the employer could cope with an employee's being sick or away on vacation on Mondays, it could surely accommodate a similarly isolated absence of an employee due to religious obligation. I emphasize once again that there is nothing in the evidence to suggest that Monday absences of the complainant would have become routine or that the general attendance record of the complainant was a subject of concern. The ability of the respondent to accommodate the complainant on this occasion was, on the evidence, obvious and, to my mind, incontrovertible. I therefore find that the respondent has failed to discharge its burden of proving that it accommodated the complainant up to the point of undue hardship....

Appeal allowed.

Supreme Court of Canada, 72 D.L.R. 4th 417; 22 A.C.S. 3d 1003, September 13, 1990.

SUGGESTED READINGS

Abella, Rosalie Silberman. *Equality in Employment: A Royal Commission Report.* Government of Canada, 1984.

_____. *Equality in Employment: A Royal Commission Report.* Government of Canada, 1985.

Blakely, John and Edward Harvey. "Socioeconomic Change and Lack of Change: Employment Equity Policies in the Canadian Context." *Journal of Business Ethics*, Vol. 7, No. 3, 1988.

Cahn, S. (ed.). *Affirmative Action Debate.* London and New York: Routledge, 1995.

Chegwidden, P. and Wendy Katz. "American and Canadian Perspectives on Affirmative Action: A Response to the Fraser Institute." *Journal of Business Ethics*, Vol. 2, No. 3, 1983.

Clairmont, Don and Richard Apostle. "Work: A Segmentation Perspective." In K. Lundy and B. Warme (eds.), *Work in the Canadian Context*, 2nd ed. Toronto: Butterworths, 1986.

Crosby, F. and S. Clayton. "Affirmative Action and the Issue of Expectancies." *Journal of Social Issues*, 42, 1–9, 1990.

Dworkin, Ronald. "What Is Equality? Part 1: Equality of Welfare." *Philosophy and Public Affairs*, Vol. 10, No. 3, Summer 1981.

Economic Council of Canada. *Towards Equity.* Ottawa, 1985.

Gold, S. (ed.). *Moral Controversies: Race, Class and Gender in Applied Ethics.* Belmont, Calif.: Wadsworth, 1993.

Groarke, Leo. "Beyond Affirmative Action." *Atlantis*, Vol. 9, No. 1, 1983.

Opotow, S. (ed.). "Affirmative Action and Social Justice." *Social Justice Research* (Special Issue), 5, 3, 1992.

Poff, Deborah. "Women and Economic Equity." *Canadian Issues*, Vol. 10, No. 1, 1988.

Singer, M. *Diversity-Based Hiring: An Introduction from Legal, Ethical and Psychological Perspectives.* London: Avebury, 1993.

Thompson, Judith Jarvis. "Preferential Hiring." *Philosophy and Public Affairs*, 1973.

Waluchow, W. "Pay Equity: Equal Value for Whom?" *Journal of Business Ethics*, Vol. 7, No. 3, 1988.

Winn, Conrad. "Affirmative Action for Women: More Than a Case of Simple Justice." *Canadian Public Administration*, Vol. 28, No. 1 (Spring 1985).

ENVIRONMENTAL
EFFECTS OF
BUSINESS ACTIVITIES

INTRODUCTION

You will recall the discussion of claim-rights from our introductory essay. Claim-rights are always paired with corresponding duties or obligations. A violation of a claim-right is always a violation of one person's duty towards another. Part 6 of this text focuses on such claim-rights. It focuses on the rights of individuals not to have their economic livelihood and physical health threatened by environmental contaminants. You may want to review the introductory essay, "Ethical Theory in Business," prior to reading the articles in this section. These articles also focus on the often competing interests of business, government, environmental groups, and private citizens.

In November 1985, two Native Indian bands secured a final out-of-court settlement worth $16.6 million in compensation for an environmental despoilment, the full extent of which has yet to be determined. Under the terms of this hard-fought settlement, two

companies, Reed Paper Company (Dryden Division) and its successor, Great Lakes Forest Products, agreed to pay $6.2 million to the Grassy Narrows band and $5.5 million to the Whitedog band. In addition, the Ontario government made a commitment to provide each band with $1.08 million; the federal government, $1.37 million.

The story behind this historic settlement is steeped in tragedy. Between 1962 and 1970, Dryden Chemicals Limited, a mercury cathode chlor-alkali plant producing chlorine and other chemicals for use in the adjacent pulp-and-paper mill of Reed Paper, dumped an estimated 20 tons (1 ton = 907.2 kilograms) of highly toxic inorganic mercury into the English-Wabigoon system of lakes and rivers (and discharged another 20 tons into the air). By March 1970, when the Ontario Ministry of Energy and Resource Management ordered a halt to the mercury discharges, extensive damage had already been done. In addition to the devastating effects of the methyl mercury poisoning on the health of their members, the Indian bands were forced to cope with the loss of their primary source of livelihood. Their rivers and lakes were closed to commercial fishing and their fishing lodges were shut down. As Anastasia Shkilnyk points out in "Mercury in the Environment," "[o]ver three hundred miles of the English-Wabigoon river system, with all its life, would probably remain poisoned for half a century." Yet, as Shkilnyk also notes, the devastation extended far beyond physical health and loss of economic livelihood. To a much greater extent than the majority of their fellow citizens, the Native peoples of Canada share an intimate relationship or "partnership" with their natural environment—a relationship that Reed Paper all but destroyed. The bands could, she writes, "no longer draw strength either from their relationship to the land or from the well of their faith, which had once given meaning and coherence to their lives."

The shameful case of the Grassy Narrows and Whitedog Indians serves is an all-too-vivid illustration of the potentially destructive effects of individual activities on our natural and social environments—on what some environmentalists have termed our "ecosystems." The threat of acid rain provides yet another. As Environment Canada points out in its 1985 *Status Report*, Atlantic salmon runs have disappeared from seven rivers in Nova Scotia. Toxic metals that the acid leaches from the soils find their ways into our lakes and rivers, deforming fish and other animals, clogging respiratory systems, and disrupting reproductive cycles. Metals, such as lead, mercury, and cadmium, find their way into the flesh of fish and ultimately onto our dinner plates. The list goes on and on.

Despite the clear and substantial threat it poses, however, industrial pollution is not easily curbed. In "Risks Versus Rights," Ted Schrecker outlines a number of forces that conspire to render environmental pollution an almost intractable problem. As Schrecker points out, a purely profit-oriented company

has little if any economic motive to pursue costly pollution control measures. "Indeed, unless it occupies a monopoly position, it has excellent economic reasons to avoid doing so: the higher prices or lower returns on capital which result mean that it would soon be driven out of business by less altruistic competitors." In short, from the point of view of sheer profit, it simply pays to pollute.

As a result, governments have felt the need to intervene to protect us from the undesirable and inevitable impact of unconstrained industrial activities. But as Schrecker demonstrates, the cards are stacked in favour of companies who often control, among other things, access to technical information essential to governments in the making of environmental policy. Companies are also able to exert considerable pressure on governments, the concerns of which must extend not only to the elimination of damaging environmental effects, but also to sustaining economic growth capable of providing income and employment for citizens, as well as essential funding for desirable state services of various kinds. Given these other serious interests, business can sometimes use implied threats of production cutbacks or plant closures (what some would like to call "job blackmail" or "extortion") to mobilize opposition to regulatory proposals on the part of governments—as well as affected workers and communities. As an example, Schrecker cites what for us is a highly relevant case. At hearings of an Ontario legislative committee held in 1979, the president of Reed Paper Company reportedly threatened that the firm would shut down its plant—Dryden's major employer—if the Ministry of the Environment held firm on a proposed deadline for pollution control measures. This clearly provides an example of what is aptly termed "the power position of business."

If economic forces conspire against morally responsible industrial activity, and we must rely instead on strong government intervention, then thorny moral and political questions arise. Precisely how do we, through our government agencies, determine the threshold of environmental despoilment beyond which companies will be prohibited from going? By what principles ought we to be guided, and upon whom should we place the burden of proof: businesses, government agencies, environmental groups, or private citizens? And how are we to balance the "costs" of pollution in terms of health, safety, and perhaps even a whole way of life (as in the case of the Grassy Narrows and Whitedog Indians) against the substantial costs of measures to reduce or eliminate pollution? These latter costs must be absorbed, not only by businesses but ultimately by consumers and employees who will inevitably be faced with higher prices, lower wages, and perhaps even the loss of a job. Some sort of balancing seems necessary here because, as the Law Reform Commission of Canada points out in "Crimes Against the Environment," it is generally acknowledged within our society that there are some valid social purposes that can justify, at least for periods of time and in varying degrees, industrial activities posing threats to our ecological systems. For instance, it is sometimes accepted that the only way to establish a new industry in an economically depressed area, and to develop and market local resources, is to permit it to do some widespread ecological damage— damage that would normally be beyond the limits of tolerance. According to the Commission, whose concern is to establish a new category of criminal activity involving environmental despoilment, it would be naive and unrealistic to think that all such judgments are equally defensible. (The case of Grassy Narrows should make this plain.) However, they go on to note, "[I]t would be equally naive and Utopian to expect that environmental decision-making can ever be completely insulated from economic and political considerations." So the economic

costs of pollution control measures must not be underestimated in our thinking about how best to police the environmental effects of business activities.

Together with these questions of balance go very difficult questions of measurement. Precisely how do we go about measuring the environmental and social costs of pollution so that these can be balanced against the economic costs of regulatory measures? Can these be measured at all? Or is this area one in which "incommensurable values (e.g., dollars versus lives) are being compared." Recall the position defended by Alan Gewirth in "Human Rights and the Prevention of Cancer" (see p.171) regarding the immeasurable value of human life. According to Gewirth, many of our social practices, e.g., our practice of sparing no effort to rescue trapped miners, reveal a commitment to the view that human life is "priceless, in the literal sense of being without price: it is incommensurable with, cannot be measured in terms of, money or any other material goods that might be needed to preserve the life or lives that are endangered." If this really is the case, and if we recognize the fact that environmental despoilment poses grave threats to our health and our lives (as well as to the quality of the lives we lead), then it is questionable whether we can rationally measure the costs of industrial pollution in a way that will enable us to carry out the delicate balancing that seems to be required.

These questions of measurement and balance are explored in some detail by Schrecker in his insightful and informative article. He both outlines and submits to critical scrutiny popular attempts to invoke cost-benefit analysis to solve the problems we have posed. This is a form of analysis developed by economists to help determine the most cost-efficient means of securing desired ends. Schrecker's conclusion regarding the use of cost-benefit analysis in this context is clearly stated. "Quite apart from such issues as the value implications of methods for valuing health benefits and criteria for resolving scientific uncertainty," he writes, "the 'bottom line' is how much do we, as a society, really care whether regulations guarding against this sort of effect are economically efficient?" There is nothing irrational, he argues, in deciding to forgo some wealth and some economic efficiency in favour of preventing adverse effects upon our fellow human beings—effects that may be incalculable or which we should not wish to inflict upon others at any cost. And this is especially clear when one considers that those affected adversely are sometimes people who (a) derive little, if any, of the off-setting benefits of industrial activities; (b) neither have chosen nor would have chosen to assume the risks they entail; and (c) can in no real measure ever be compensated for the harms they have endured. One might ask whether the Grassy Narrows and Whitedog tribes stood to benefit from the economic activities of Reed Paper, whether they would have chosen to assume the risks to which they were subjected, or whether they can ever really be compensated. As Chief Roy McDonald of the Whitedog band said, "No amount of money will ever right the wrongs that have happened here" (*Toronto Star*, Dec. 1, 1985, p. H1). Cases such as this confront us again with the issues of responsibility—indeed, criminality—of employees of polluting companies. In the light of continuing human-made disasters (Union Carbide's Bhopal plant, the Soviet Chernobyl radiation discharges), these questions demand answers.

Harriet Rosenberg introduces a different perspective on the environment, the household as "intimately linked to . . . [the] . . . global process of commodification and danger." Rosenberg's article deals with the household in two different ways. First, she details the fight of a number of women in Whitchurch-Stouffville, Ontario, who became worried about the unusually high rates

of miscarriage in their community and the possible link between those miscarriages and the "thousands of tons of toxic liquid industrial wastes . . . [which] . . . were poured into a farmer's field never designed as a landfill" between 1962 and 1969. She then goes on to discuss "exposure to less visible and less understood hazards stemming from the penetration of the home by the household products industry." Although causal relations between environmental contaminants and disease are often difficult to establish, there is continual and growing evidence of severe allergic reactions to the strong chemicals in household products. Rosenberg believes that women are the victims of advertising campaigns that equate "cleaning with caring," and which equate clean with industrially produced solvents and cleansers. Women increasingly put themselves and their families at risk by exposing them to noxious cleansers, and they do so because they are convinced that this makes them better homemakers, argues Rosenberg.

In the last article in this section, Singh and Carasco introduce a discussion of the relationship among business ethics, economic development, and the new world order. By new world order, the authors mean the post-Soviet Union, global economy context. The article essentially raises both the potential positive and negative directions that this new world order may take with respect to economic development and environmental protection and sustainability. In the end, the authors conclude by emphasizing the moral responsibility of the United States and other Western nations "to help stamp out environmental irresponsibility worldwide."

Since the first edition of this text was published, interest in and anxiety over the environment have spread. While environmentalists have been concerned for more than two decades about global indicators pointing to drastic erosion of the biosphere, dire warnings and predictions did not always result in action on the part of governments and businesses. The 1990s have been declared by many world leaders to require interventionist and radical attention to environmental issues.

This section ends with *R. v. Canadian Pacific Ltd.* Canadian Pacific Ltd. conducted controlled burns of dry grass and weeds that had injurious effects on both the health and the property of several Kenora residents. In its ultimate appeal to the Supreme Court, Canadian Pacific raised constitutional issues under section 7 of the *Canadian Charter of Rights and Freedoms*. The issues in this case provide the reader with the opportunity to explore issues ranging from the societal value of environmental protection to the right not to have legislation imposed that is so broad

and vague as to be unconstitutional under section 7 of the *Charter*.

When reading the articles in this section, you may wish to consider the reasons behind the increasing concern for the environment. Is it that the costs have risen so significantly that, according to any utilitarian calculation, the costs to the environment and human well-being far outweigh the benefits? Or is it that even the most narrowly focused, self-interested individuals and businesses recognize that there will be no profitable marketplace if the planet ceases to sustain life? Perhaps, as the so-called New Age thinkers would like us to believe, there has been a global shift in the orientation and value system of people with relation to their environment.

CRIMES AGAINST THE ENVIRONMENT

Law Reform
Commission of Canada

LATENCY, ACCUMULATION AND THE ECOSYSTEM APPROACH

In many cases, the pollution activities which are potentially the most harmful are those involving damage, destruction or injury which is not immediate and not harmful to identifiable aspects of the environment or identifiable human victims. Yet the damage can nevertheless be very grave. Two of the reasons why this can be so have to do with *latency* and *accumulation*. Latency is the delay between the release of, or exposure to, a hazard and the appearance of its injurious effects. Some of the most catastrophic effects can take the longest time to appear. An example is some carcinogens which can be latent for up to 30 years. The mutagenic effect of some hazardous chemicals may only show up several generations after the

initial exposure. The process of accumulation means, in effect, that while an individual release of a pollutant may not in some cases be seriously or obviously harmful, many such acts, from one or many sources, may in the aggregate produce an accumulated threat to the environment, health and property, one going well beyond the threshold of what a particular species, resource, ecosystem or human body can tolerate without serious harm. A lake can finally lose the ability to cope with accumulated acid rain, and will die. Or a child exposed to lead over a long period of time can finally become seriously ill and even die because too much lead has accumulated in the body.

One explanation of the mechanics and implications of environmental damage and destruction is that provided by the ecosystem approach. That approach is not without its limitations when pushed to extremes, and it

From Law Reform Commission of Canada, Working Paper 44, Protection of Life Series, *Crimes Against The Environment*. Copyright © Law Reform Commission of Canada, 1985. Reproduced with permission of the Minister of Supply and Services Canada.

is not our intention to promote it or to justify legal prohibitions and reforms purely on the basis of one or another environmental school of thought. Nevertheless, some findings of ecologists are not disputed, and the general lines of the approach help to underline the potential seriousness of some environmental pollution.

This relatively new approach is a synthesis of the insights and skills of a number of disciplines, especially biology, chemistry, geography, and climatology. Whereas those and other fields study the threads of nature, the ecosystem approach studies its "whole cloth." Its proponents insist especially upon two points. They argue first of all that it is erroneous to speak of man *and* environment, or of man as *external* to the natural environment. Rather, humans are internal to, and partners with, the rest of nature. They argue, secondly, that serious harm done to one element in an ecosystem will invariably lead to the damage or even destruction of other elements in that and other ecosystems.

What ecologists mean by an "ecosystem" is any relatively homogeneous and delineated unit of nature in which nonliving substances and living organisms interact with an exchange of materials taking place between the nonliving and living parts. The term "ecosystem" is somewhat flexible and the boundaries between them somewhat arbitrary. Those boundaries are generally based upon what is most convenient for measuring the movement of energy and chemicals into and out of the system. Typical and important interrelated and overlapping ecosystems are: units of land along with the surrounding air and water, or lakes, or river basins, or forests, or climatic zones, or the earth itself or the biosphere (the outer sphere of the earth inhabited by living organisms and including lakes, oceans, soil and living organisms, including man). Within each ecosystem there is, they maintain, a delicate balance and interdependence between all the elements. Systems can cope

with and adapt to some interferences, but not others. The overall long-range effect of some intrusions is not yet known with certainty or in detail. Ecologists argue that ecosystems are now known to be subject to very definable and immutable processes, which impose corresponding ecological constraints. They stress two organizational rules, namely, the first two of the three laws of thermodynamics. The first rule (that of conservation of matter and energy) is that matter and energy cannot be destroyed, only *transformed*. The second (the law of entropy) is that all energy transformations are *degradations*, whereby energy is transformed from more to less organized forms. In simpler terms, they explain those rules by the following principles and examples.

The first is that *everything in the environment or individual ecosystems is related*. If one breaks a link in the food-chain, for example, or introduces a substance not biodegradable, there are consequences for the entire ecosystem. Examples of the resulting serious and often irreversible harm are DDT and mercury. Since its massive use in the 1940s, the footsteps of DDT can be followed from wheat, to insects, to rodents, to larger animals and birds, and to man. In its wake it left whole species of animals more or less extinct or with serious reproductive problems. To illustrate the degree of interaction involved and the insignificance of time and distance, traces of DDT can now be found in the flesh of polar bears. The industrial discharge of *mercury* is another illustration. It has been followed from its discharge by pulp and paper industries into the air and water, to its transformation in the water into methylmercury by the water's micro-organisms, to its accumulation in the sediment of lakes or its absorption by the fish. Among its victims in the next stage, it is argued, have been the Indians of northern Ontario and Québec who eat those fish and are frequently inflicted with the horrors of what has come to be known as Minamata disease.

The second principle underlined by ecologists is that *unless neutralized, every contaminating substance remains harmful somewhere to something or someone* in the natural environment. Sooner or later we will pay, in some cases dearly, for discarding, for example, nonrecycled industrial toxins into rivers and dumps. Matter cannot be destroyed—only transformed. The atoms and molecules of matter are always preserved by ecosystems in some form. Moreover, if they are not or cannot be transformed, degraded, recycled or neutralized, it is an illusion to hope that that form will become a benign and harmless one.

LIMITATIONS OF AN UNQUALIFIED ECOSYSTEM APPROACH

From the perspective of harm, however, there may be some difficulties and limitations of the ecosystem approach pushed to its extreme. It has been observed that some (by no means all) of its proponents are unjustifiably pessimistic and too rigorous. Some imply that each now stable and healthy ecosystem has inherent worth, and must be preserved exactly as it is, that any harm or modification to it would be immoral, and that all human impacts upon, or changes to, an aspect of the environment are necessarily unnatural. However, that view has at least three limitations.

(1) Viruses and Diseases: Good or Bad?

First of all, if every ecosystem, every species, is to be preserved and protected "as is" in its natural state, if human values, human judgment and human benefit are to be considered irrelevant, we would be forced to *tolerate many threats and diseases* generally perceived to be themselves harmful if not attacked and even wiped out if possible. An unqualified ecosystem approach pushed to its logical extreme might, for example, force a conclusion that the extinction of the smallpox virus was not a good thing, or that grasshoppers, mosquitoes, noxious weeds, various pests and disease organisms should not be combatted but protected, or that the building of human settlements was wrong because some ecosystems were necessarily harmed in the process. Few if any ecologists seem actually to intend those conclusions, but they do perhaps illustrate the sort of dilemmas implicit in attempts to determine and evaluate environmental harm, and the need to qualify the "deep ecology" stance in the light of some other considerations.

(2) The Adaptive Capacity of the Environment

A second limitation of an extreme and rigorous ecosystem approach used to measure environmental harm, is that ecosystems are not only in many respects vulnerable, but also *adaptive and evolutionary*. Up to a point and in some respects, ecosystems can respond to and accommodate change. Some man-made alterations of an element of the environment can, in particular cases, trigger adaptive responses. Ecosystems are not in all respects fixed; there is a degree of rhythm and fluctuation. It becomes important in this regard to weigh impacts of polluting contaminants and activities as to whether they are degradable and noncumulative (for example, many pulp and paper wastes), nondegradable and cumulative (for example, mercury, lead, PCBs), reversible or irreversible, natural yet likely to cause damage to some environments in large concentrations (for example, sulphates, chlorides). There are undoubtedly good reasons for policy makers to give more attention to the "inherent worth" view of the natural environment, but this adaptive mechanism itself of ecosystems has an inherent worth and should be added to the calculations of harm. In some cases, the conclusion will be that a substance or activity goes well beyond the adaptive capacity of an ecosystem; in other cases it may not.

(3) Tolerating Pollution for Legitimate Social Purposes: Balancing the Human Health Standard

There is yet a third and most important factor to be weighed in calculations of serious pollution harm, a factor more or less incompatible with an ecosystem approach which is strict and absolute. It is generally acknowledged in our political and economic system, and in our environmental policies and laws, that there are a number of legitimate social purposes which can justify, at least for a period of time, varying degrees of pollution, deterioration and risk—which permit downgrading the pollution harm and risk from serious and intolerable to less-than-serious and tolerable. It is not, of course, uncommon for the law to conclude that what would be reckless and unacceptable behaviour in some circumstances, can be justified if socially desirable for one reason or another. For example, a very risky medical operation can, in some circumstances, be acceptable and even desirable if it offers the only chance to save a life.

Primary among the goals and purposes implicitly or explicitly underlying environmental policies, regulations and statutes are economic ones. An environmental agency may judge, for example, that a particular existing industry should be allowed to exceed, at least for a specified time, the statutory emission standard for a particular contaminant, because there may be good reason to believe the expense of strict compliance will bankrupt the company and cause widespread unemployment. Similarly, it may be judged

that the only way to secure the establishment of a new industry in an economically depressed area and to develop and market local resources is to permit it to do some widespread ecological damage, and/or, at least for a time, exceed by a considerable margin the statutory emission standards. It would, of course, be naive and unrealistic to assume that all such judgments are equally defensible, or that the economic viability and employment arguments of industry should be accepted uncritically by agencies. However, it would be equally naive and Utopian to expect that environmental decision making can ever be completely insulated from economic and political considerations.

It should be noted that the mere emission of a particular contaminating substance beyond the standard established in the relevant statute or regulations need not in itself always imply serious (or even minor) environmental and health harm. In the first place, the standard itself may be open to legitimate debate as to its accuracy and appropriateness. In some cases the standard may, by some criteria, be too strict, or based upon uncertain evidence. On the other hand, it may be felt by some to be not strict enough. Secondly, it is at least the intention of regulation and standard makers to build into the emission standards a certain margin of safety.

The "social utility" and other factors just indicated demonstrate that judgments before or after the event about the types and degrees of pollution which will be characterized and treated as serious and intolerable, as opposed to minor and tolerable within regulated limits, are not and cannot be strictly and exclusively "scientific" in nature. Determinations of harm and degree of harm are to a large degree value-judgments, rather than scientific calculations. More precisely, such judgments are based upon criteria which themselves imply or import value-judgments. Therefore, these judgments about the acceptability of harm and risk should not be made only by the scientist as scientist....

In any event, the life and health of others cannot be traded off for other apparent benefits, whether economic or other. We do not permit such a trade-off for other criminal offences involving serious harms or dangers to human life and bodily integrity. That being so, we may formulate the following by way of a general criterion: (1) the more certain is the evidence or likelihood of present or future harm and danger to human life and health, and the more serious the nature of that harm and danger, the less legitimate and persuasive should be other socially useful goals as justifications for the pollution or for reducing its classification from serious to minor, and the more compelling would be arguments for the criminal nature of that activity; (2) the less likely are the serious present and future human health harms and dangers, and the more likely the interests affected are exclusively those of the use and enjoyment of the environment, the more relevant and legitimate is the weighing of other societal goals by way of mitigating its classification as potentially serious harm.

RISKS VERSUS RIGHTS: Economic Power and Economic Analysis in Environmental Politics

Ted Schrecker

INTRODUCTION

Environmental pollution is one of the most striking and omnipresent impacts of industrial activity on society. Since the revelations concerning careless disposal of hazardous industrial wastes at Love Canal, it has become apparent that such corporate disregard for public health and safety is distressingly widespread, not only in the United States but in Canada as well.[1] Emissions of literally millions of tonnes per year of sulphur dioxide from non-ferrous smelters and electrical generating plants, and of nitrogen oxides from automobile exhausts and various industrial sources,[2] are transported over long distances and return to earth as the acid precipitation which threatens the life of lakes and rivers and, quite possibly, the health of forests in much of eastern North America.[3] And as this paper is being written, news stories about the "toxic blob" in the St. Clair river are drawing long-overdue attention to industry's use of the Great Lakes, which provide drinking water for millions of Canadians, as a convenient dumping ground for vast volumes of chemical waste.[4]

Economists refer to environmental impacts such as those described in the preceding paragraph as negative externalities. They are "costs of production," much like labour and raw materials. However, rather than being "internalized" in the sense that they are reflected in product prices and are therefore borne by either producers or consumers, they are borne by third parties (sometimes including future generations) who are not *directly* involved in the market transactions.[5] In an unregulated market, expenditures on pollution control would rarely be made. A purely profit-oriented firm has no economic motive to increase its production costs by internalizing the costs associated with its impacts on the environment. Indeed, unless it occupies a monopoly position, it has excellent economic reasons to avoid doing so: the higher prices or lower returns on capital which would result mean that it would soon be driven out of business by less altruistic competitors. Considerations other than profitability (such as the negative public image associated with being viewed as a major polluter) *may* temper this purely economic calculation somewhat. However, the concept of negative externalities emphasizes the fact that environmental protection requirements, like other forms of governmental intervention to protect health and safety, are inherently redistributive.[6] They represent attempts to shift some costs of production from those who are affected by environmental degradation to producers and consumers of the products and services whose production generates these externalities.

"Business" is, of course, not a homogeneous group which always speaks with one voice, although recent research has demonstrated a pattern of "classwide rationality" in which large corporations appear to defend at least a core set of common interests and priorities.[7] On strictly economic grounds, one of these common priorities clearly is opposing environmental control requirements, or (alternatively) minimizing their economic impact. The reason for this opposition is analogous to the reasons for resisting any other increase in costs of doing business which is unproductive from the point of view of the individual firm.

Part I of this paper is an extremely brief inventory of the political resources[8] which business brings to environmental policy and politics, in particular the leverage large corporations enjoy by virtue of their control over investment flows. In many cases, the deployment of these resources has enabled business successfully to resist potentially costly environmental regulation, to delay its implementation, and (when this is no longer possible) to shift the costs of compliance to the public purse rather than imposing them on shareholders or consumers.

A further, and philosophically more intriguing, aspect of environmental ethics and politics has to do with the way we (as citizens, as consumers, as decision-makers in business or government) think about the issue of environmental pollution. Cost-benefit analysis of environmental regulation is, superficially at least, a common-sense approach to setting or assessing objectives for environmental policy, and is attractive on that basis. However, Part II of the paper suggests that CBA contains a number of built-in biases which favor business's priorities—a fact which explains the frequent support for CBA of environmental regulations expressed by business, and by business's advocates within government.

Cost-benefit analysis, more generally, embodies an implicit (but by no means self-evident) conception of what environmental policy—indeed, public policy in general—ought to be about. Part III of the paper briefly critiques this conception, arguing that there is much more to environmental policy than just correcting for market failures, in economists' terminology. Cost-benefit analysis involves adopting the "conceptual lenses"[9] of economics in a way which essentially prejudges a number of important ethical and political questions, and which does so in a way which reinforces what might loosely be termed a business-oriented view of the political process as a whole. When we substitute other conceptual lenses, the relative importance of various aspects of environmental problems changes, as do problem definitions themselves. Exploring the biases of economics, *via* the implications of CBA, suggests the seriousness of some of the optical flaws in that particular set of lenses.

I. BUSINESS IN ENVIRONMENTAL POLITICS: HOW THE CARDS ARE STACKED

Given the economic analysis provided in the introduction to this paper, one would expect the relationship between business and environmental regulators to be an adversarial one. Yet despite occasionally bitter conflicts, it is generally characterized by a high degree of consultation and mutual accommodation between business and agencies charged with environmental protection.[10]

One reason for this coziness is information: regulated firms may control access to technical information which is essential to governments in the making of environmental policy. As an example of how this resource helps industry to defend its preferred status in the regulatory process, the head of Environment Canada's Environmental Protection Service (EPS) informed a Parliamentary committee in 1980 of EPS's fear that broadening public participation would "break down that relationship with industry that has served us very well in providing us with technical information."[11]

Another reason is the substantial financial and organizational resources of business, in particular of large corporations. The interests of these firms are articulated not just through individual representations to governments, but also by way of trade associations with substantial resources of their own. An extensive study of the 10 major chemical industry trade associations several years ago found that their average annual budget was roughly $350,000—not counting the value of the time of corporate staff spent on association business.[12] Few if any organizations representing the constituency for environmental protection have resources even approaching this magnitude. In addition, as illustrated in the chemical industry study,[13] trade associations have more or less on-going contacts with government concerning a variety of issues, of which the environment is only one—providing business with a valuable resource in terms of its contacts with government departments such as those responsible for industrial expansion or resource development. The success of policies and programs administered by these latter departments is more or less inseparable from the activities of industry,[14] a fact which may make them indifferent if not actively hostile to environmental concerns which threaten those activities.

One effect of business's wealth and organization is to enable it to monitor and respond to governmental initiatives on an on-going basis. The result is, arguably, environmental policy whose major impact is largely symbolic: "'tough' legislation to satisfy environmental groups and the general public, and weak enforcements with many complex exceptions to provide an accommodation with the pollution sources themselves."[15] At the level of implementation and enforcement, the financial resources of business firms allow them to delay implementation of costly environmental requirements by forcing regulators either to accept promises of compliance at some future date or to become involved in protracted and costly litigation. Relative to the costs (to polluters) of litigation, "[t]he benefits of delay are typically so great in comparison with the costs of complying that … a regulatory agency faces the possibility not of a handful of violators that it could reasonably handle, but of tacit noncompliance by large segments of an industry."[16] This observation helps to explain why (for example) throughout the 1970s firms in the Ontario pulp and paper industry persistently failed to meet the deadlines for meeting effluent limits which they had negotiated with the province's Ministry of the Environment.[17]

Another essential factor in explaining such situations is the way in which the legal framework for environmental policy reflects and reinforces business power and influence.[18] There are several dimensions to this problem, only two of which are discussed here. First, most environmental legislation in Canada is structured along the same lines as the criminal law—meaning that penalties can only be imposed following conviction. Preparing a successful prosecution is time-consuming and expensive, and the actual resolution of the case may take several years.[19] Yet until a conviction is registered, the cost of violating the law is limited to the costs of litigation, which (as noted earlier) may be trivial relative to the economic benefits of non-compliance. In addition, the economic penalties (fines) provided for by legislation need not bear any relationship to the economic benefits from violating environmental law.[20]

A number of alternative mechanisms for imposing sanctions on polluting firms have been proposed to overcome these difficulties.[21] For example, frustrated by the pulp and paper industry's continuing indifference to its effect on the environment, economists with Ontario's Ministry of the Environment in the mid-1970s proposed a regime of pollution control delay penalties, which would automatically be levied against any company which failed to meet a deadline (negotiated with the Ministry) for meeting pollution control objectives.[22] The penalties would be based on a formula taking into account both the amount by which effluent discharges exceeded allowable limits, and the duration of the violation. Perhaps not surprisingly,[23] this proposal was never implemented, despite the subsequent success of a similar approach to sanctioning polluters in the state of Connecticut.[24]

Second, the effectiveness of the potential constituencies for environmental protection (environmentalist organizations and the general public in affected areas) is seriously compromised by the general absence of legally guaranteed opportunities for participation in policy and enforcement decisions.[25] Whereas industry enjoys an ongoing consultative relationship with government, the situation in Ontario—in which public participation opportunities consist of meetings where audiences are treated to defences of positions previously negotiated between the Ministry of the Environment and the polluting firm—is more or less typical. As an extreme example of the effect of the absence of public participation on policy outcomes, in 1979 Amax Ltd. was given permission by Order-in-Council to dump more than 10,000 tonnes of heavy metal-laden tailings a day into the ocean from a mine in northern British Columbia, despite the fact that this dumping was clearly prohibited by one of the few sets of regulations under the federal *Fisheries Act*, and despite strong internal opposition within Environment Canada. The company was able to press its case in forums including a private meeting between its lawyers, Environment officials, and two Cabinet ministers; and the regulations permitting the dumping were developed on the basis of secret correspondence and exchanges of drafts between Environment Canada and Amax's lawyers.[26] Not only was there no "public participation" in this process, the very fact that there was a process going on was concealed from those outside the charmed government-industry circle until the regulations were published.

The law can provide for the public *some* portion of the status within the policy process which industry enjoys by virtue of wealth and organization. When the law fails to do this, as it does almost without exception in Canada, access to decision-making remains contingent on wealth, organization, and perceived legitimacy. Access therefore remains largely restricted to the industries whose activities create the need for government intervention in the first place. The extent of the perceived legitimacy of the priorities of business, and of business-government contacts, is indicated by the comments of Canada's Royal Commission on Corporate Concentration (the Bryce Commission) that:

> It is not surprising that there should be close contact between many businesses and the governments of Canada and the provinces in which they operate, for there is a common concern with a wide variety of economic and social problems and legislative and regulatory measures. The success of government measures requires knowledge of how they may be expected to affect particular industries or companies, while the success of business projects will require a knowledge of the laws and public policies that will apply to them. It is *in the public interest* that there should be consultation in these matters."[27] [Emphasis added]

But what are the roots of this equation of business priorities with the public interest, of the "common concerns" of business and government? And how do these affect environmental policy?

To address this question, it is necessary to consider the role of control over investment flows as a political resource for business (and for large corporations, in particular). In specific conflicts over environmental hazards, the ownership of capital (and its mobility) enable corporate polluters to use the implied or expressed threat of production cutbacks or plant closures to mobilize opposition to regulatory proposals on the part of affected workers and communities and to impose a particular set of tradeoffs between jobs and the environment on political decision-makers. Kazis and Grossman, who have analyzed this phenomenon extensively in the American context, refer to it as "job blackmail;"[28] and two Canadian examples suggest how the process works.

In the 1960s, the paper mill complex operated by Reed Ltd. at Dryden, Ontario, was responsible for the contamination of the English-Wabigoon river system in north-western Ontario with mercury, and the resulting destruction of the food supply of the local Native population.[29] The mercury problem was eventually remedied, but throughout the 1970s, Reed Ltd. made almost no changes to reduce its emissions of dissolved organic materials and suspended solids, with devastating effects on downstream waters, and the Ontario Ministry of the Environment made few serious efforts to induce such changes.[30] At hearings of an Ontario legislative committee held in 1979, partly to address Reed's pollution record, the president of Reed Ltd. threatened that the firm would shut down the plant (the community's major employer) if the Ministry of the Environment held firm on a proposed deadline for pollution control measures.[31] This threat, based on Reed's alleged financial weakness and the unwillingness of its British parent company to invest any additional money in its money-losing subsidiary, was effective in getting the legislators to recommend a compromise between the Ministry's proposed deadline and the three additional years Reed demanded for reducing discharges whose destructive efforts had been identified at least as early as 1968.[32]

Noranda, Inc., a firm indirectly controlled by one of the richest families in Canada,[33] operates a copper smelter in Rouyn, Quebec, which accounted in 1980 for roughly 11 percent of total Canadian emissions of sulphur dioxide, and roughly 30 percent of sulphur dioxide emissions from non-ferrous smelters.[34] Like other smelter operators (for example Inco Ltd. in Sudbury, Ontario[35]), Noranda has until recently been very successful in resisting public and governmental pressure for major emissions reductions, despite the contribution of smelter emissions to acid precipitation and despite evidence of elevated lung-cancer risk to residents of the Rouyn area.[36] The company's president warned in May 1984 that the firm "could find itself caught between the 'politically unacceptable' choice of closing a smelter that employs 1,200 people" or investing in modernization which would have the added effect of reducing SO_2 emissions.[37] The impact of such statements in terms of allocation of the costs of emission reduction is discussed below.

The threat of disinvestment may be invoked in discussions of general policy directions as well as in firm-specific conflicts. One of the executives interviewed by Silk and Vogel in their 1976 study of American business argued that it should be used more extensively: "We need political sophistication. We have to tell a state considering additional restrictions on business: 'The next plant doesn't go up here if that bill passes'."[38] Such a capital strike does not appear to have occurred in Canada in response specifically to environmental policy initiatives. However, the use of such a tactic by the mining industry in resisting the tax reform recommendations of the Carter Royal Commission on Taxation[39] suggests that it might be employed under some conditions in the environmental policy context.

In terms of the overall development of environmental policy, it is less important to enumerate specific cases of job blackmail than to understand that conflicts in which the overt threat of disinvestment is invoked in response to environmental requirements are the exception, rather than the rule. Here we come back to the Bryce Commission's definition of the "public interest." Governments in capitalist or mixed economies rely heavily on the continued flow of private investment to sustain the economic growth which both provides income and employment for their citizens and finances the provision of state services of various kinds. Public policy in various areas must therefore reflect an underlying latent tension between the state's various other functions, such as eliminating the damaging effects of industrial activity on the environment, and the need to sustain the conditions for capital accumulation—or, in

the more familiar terms often used by business organizations, to create and maintain a favorable business climate. Marxist analysts, of whom Offe is the most sophisticated,[40] have led the way in drawing attention to the importance of this constraint. At the same time, Lindblom's extremely perceptive account of the "privileged position of business" in public life[41] shows that it is possible to analyze the impact of corporate power on public policy starting from a thoroughly non-Marxist set of assumptions.

The powerful position of business is further enhanced when firms can allocate investment (and use their control over technology and expertise) in a way which maximizes returns on a transjurisdictional scale, whether the jurisdictions being played off one against another are provinces, states or nations. In the words of a leading text on international business: "Whenever a business has something of value that can be offered to several nations, the power to control can be eroded by competition between countries. And the limits on the exercise of this power are set by the weakest of the nations concerned."[42] This process becomes particularly significant in times of slow economic growth. Gladwin and Walter conclude, on the basis of extensive research on environmental conflicts involving large corporations, that "conditions of high unemployment [have] led to shifting environmental priorities and less opposition to new plant construction in some regions."[43]

An evocative illustration of the power of corporate managements and the shareholders they represent occurred in the United States, in 1983. Asarco, Inc. had threatened to shut down a copper smelter in Tacoma, Washington, if further reduction in the smelter's arsenic emissions were required by the Environmental Protection Agency (EPA). EPA solicited the views of area residents on whether or not they were willing to accept the (estimated) additional cancer risks associated with the arsenic emissions in re turn for the 500 jobs and associated economic benefits provided by the smelter.[44] This is job blackmail, but in a particularly subtle and revealing form. Government, *via* the EPA, was not in a position to challenge Asarco's right to shut down the smelter if the firm considered the returns from its operation to be inadequate. Thus, the terms of the jobs-versus-environment tradeoff imposed by the corporation's management and shareholders could not be altered except by compromising environmental and human health protection.

In the Canadian context, the control of emissions from copper and nickel smelters provides a fine illustration of another important aspect of business's power: the ability to recover from the public purse the cost of compliance with pollution restrictions. Copper and nickel smelters account for more than 40 percent of Canadian sulphur dioxide emissions[45]—the emissions which, along with nitrogen oxides emissions, are the chemical precursors of acid precipitation. The 1984 report of a Parliamentary Subcommittee on Acid Rain[46] pointed out that expenditures on modernizing Canadian nonferrous smelters would result both in emissions reductions and in major economic payoffs for the industry. According to the report, "process changes in a number of smelters can significantly reduce SO_2 emissions and still be justified on purely economic grounds. In other words, the portion of cost which is attributable to SO_2 control can, in some instances, approach zero."[47]

Yet despite such economic benefits to polluting firms, not *one* of the report's recommendations for controlling smelter emissions suggested a stricter or more effective regime of regulation to require emissions reductions at the expense of the smelter operators. Rather, citing the poor profit position of the smelter operators, the legislators recommended far more generous tax writeoffs for pollution control investments and research, as well as a system of direct capital grants to the non-

ferrous smelting industry for capital expenditures associated with pollution abatement.[48] Early in 1985, the Canadian government committed itself to providing up to $150 million in direct subsidies to smelter operators for pollution abatement, as part of an intergovernmental agreement under which provincial governments will be called on to provide further subsidies.[49]

As suggested earlier, direct job blackmail may have played a part in determining this outcome. Probably more important, however, was and is the fact that the redistributive nature of environmental policy means that it cannot be made in isolation—at least not for long, or not by a government which intends to remain in power. In Lindblom's words, "even the unspoken possibility of adversity for business operates as an all-pervasive constraint on governmental authority."[50] In the environment field, the most significant manifestation of business power is its effect in constraining the regulation of existing operations, or determining that some policy options (for example, requiring the shareholders of firms like Inco and Noranda or the consumers of their products, rather than the taxpaying public as a whole, to foot the bill for plant improvements which will reduce pollution levels) are *a priori* infeasible and therefore will not form part of the agenda of government. Feasibility in this context is defined not in a technical sense, or even on the basis of academic economic analysis, but rather by the wealth and power of the affected firms and industries.[51]

II. COST-BENEFIT ANALYSIS AND THE EFFICIENCY CRITERION

For most economists, the prevalence of environmental pollution is traceable to the absence of definable property rights to the use of common property resources like air and water, and to the consequent absence of a market in their use as a way of balancing competing uses.

> For example, people exposed to the effects of air pollution … have no recourse through the market to obtain financial compensation. This would not be the case if people owned a marketable right to clean air since, under those circumstances, industrialists wishing to pollute the air in their quest for profit would have to buy the right to do so in the same way as they must buy the right to use the other resources that are necessary for production."[52]

It is therefore plausible to take the view adopted by the Economic Council of Canada, in the final report of its Regulation Reference study, that "regulation has … to perform the function normally accomplished by market forces; that is, regulation must establish the relative values of alternative uses of the environment if appropriate trade-offs are to be made."[53]

Cost-benefit analysis (CBA) was originally developed as a technique for evaluating major public works projects involving water development, for many of whose benefits (e.g., flood control, improved recreational opportunities) no markets existed.[54] CBA "is a procedure through which the analyst simulates the workings of a perfectly competitive market system"; it "addresses the question of how the market would decide an issue, such as whether and in what way to use a new pesticide, if the market was perfectly competitive and all effects were accounted for."[55] There is a common-sensical appeal to CBA: would "we," as a society, want to incur costs for environmental protection which are not justified by the corresponding benefit? However, the implications are too seldom examined of the implied endorsement of markets as the preferred way of deciding the worth of benefits like the improvements in human health and longevity which may result from environmental protection initiatives.

Utilitarian philosophers have long been bedevilled by the abstract nature of the concept of utility, the absence of natural units for interpersonal comparisons of utility, and the consequent elusiveness of the ideal of the greatest good for the greatest number. The corresponding concept for economists is that of Pareto-optimal allocations of resources,[56] and markets provide a solution to the problem of interpersonal comparisons of utility by allowing all participants to define welfare or utility on the basis of their own preferences, and to maximize their welfare (within the context of their limited individual resources) on the basis of willingness to pay to satisfy those preferences.

> An exchange takes place only when both parties feel they benefit by it. When no additional exchanges can be made, the economy has reached a situation where each individual in it cannot improve his own situation without damaging that of another…. When no one can be made better off without someone else being worse off, Pareto optimality has been reached.[57]

In other words, perfectly functioning markets will generate optimal allocations of resources.

Situations in which no one is made any worse off (like perfectly functioning markets) are rare indeed in the real world of public policy. The response of welfare economists and policy analysts has been to evaluate policy alternatives on the basis of *potential* Pareto improvements. This criterion, known as the Kaldor-Hicks principle after its originators, requires only that aggregate welfare/utility gains outweigh aggregate losses, based on the ability of "gainers" to compensate "losers," once values have been attached to gains and losses. In theory, society could require that gainers compensate losers, thus achieving a Pareto-superior distribution of utility. However, the principle does not require that compensation actually be paid,[58] and is thus normatively indifferent to questions of distribution or entitlement. "This is the efficiency criterion of the new welfare economics."[59]

As applied to environmental pollution, this efficiency criterion defines an appropriate level of pollution abatement in terms of the level of pollution control or hazard control expenditures at which the sum of the costs of pollution abatement and of the damage done by the remaining externality is minimized. The next increment of environmental improvement "purchased" through installing additional pollution control devices will cost more than it is worth in terms of the value of damage reduction, and at this point:

> Despite passionate prose to the contrary, society will lose less, or gain more, if it puts [the remaining] waste in the river and takes the money (land, labor and capital) it would have spent treating these units of waste and devotes it to building hospitals, homes, and hula-hoop factories, or whatever people indicate they prefer by their spending habits.[60]

Pollution is thus only one among many competing uses of the natural environment, and pollution control just one among many competing uses of society's resources, the balance among which is best decided on the basis of market mechanisms.

For several years during the 1970s, executive agencies like the Council on Wage and Price Stability (COWPS) and the Office of Management and Budget (OMB) in the United States attempted to force regulatory agencies like the Environmental Protection Agency (EPA) and the Occupational Safety and Health Administration (OSHA) to attach greater importance to the costs of compliance with their proposed standards.[61] The rationale for these attempts was concern for the inflationary impacts of such regulations. The Reagan administration in February 1981 issued an Executive Order requiring formal CBA of major new regulations, specifically requiring that new regulations demonstrate

a favourable benefit-cost ratio.[62] Tolchin argues that this progression was a direct result of industry resistance to regulation-imposed costs:

> The rush to deregulate was industry's answer to double-digit inflation, and its leaders convinced the leaders of both political parties ... that they had a simple way of reducing product costs: reduce the onerous regulations, sometimes confusing and duplicative, and trust the free market to regulate itself.[63]

In Canada, CBA is a preferred, although not mandatory, technique for assessing the economic impacts of major new regulations under the Socio-Economic Impact Analysis (SEIA) requirements imposed by Treasury Board at the federal level.[64] Recent initiatives by a group of Canadian government departments including Environment, Agriculture, and Health and Welfare have strongly supported more extensive application of CBA to the choice of objectives in toxic substances policy.[65] Some of the reasons for the relatively less extensive reliance on CBA in Canadian regulatory decision-making, and for its attractiveness to industry, are discussed in Part III of this paper.

An extensive literature exists on the daunting practical limitations of trying to quantify the hazards of environmental pollution and the corresponding benefits of regulation—for instance, in terms of the improvements in water quality which will result from a specified level of effluent discharge reductions, or in terms of the reduced number of cases of lung cancer or premature mortality from respiratory disease which will be associated with controlling air pollution from a given source.[66] In the case of cancer, for example, uncertainties about actual human exposures are compounded by conflicting models of the relationship between disease incidence and exposure, meaning that numerical risk estimates may vary by several orders of magnitude.[67] In some instances, industries faced with absorbing the costs of regulation may argue that insufficient evidence exists for the existence of a health hazard. Industry spokesmen have claimed, for example, that insufficient evidence exists for a relationship among gasoline lead levels, blood lead levels in children, and behavior alterations and impairments in cognitive development in those exposed children[68] despite a large and growing body of scientific data.[69] In such situations of at least partial uncertainty about impacts (which are probably the rule rather than the exception in environmental policy) any CBA is only as good as the underlying quantitative risk estimates. The decisions which determine the outcome of the analysis do not involve readily and unequivocally quantified benefits. Rather, they involve policy decisions about how scientific uncertainty is to be treated for purposes of public decision-making.[70] The values brought to the resolution of such "science policy" questions,[71] crucial though they are, are not discussed further here. However, it must be emphasized that crucial value judgments about how to resolve scientific uncertainty—in situations where waiting for more evidence itself implies a particular normative balancing of risks and benefits[72]—are part of almost every assessment of human health risk or environmental impact.

When we make decisions about, for example, the appropriate level of pollution prevention on the basis of CBA or of the efficiency criterion which underlies it, we are saying that we would be satisfied with the outcomes of markets for such amenities as environmental quality, if such markets could be established. But this point is hardly self-evidence. We are uncomfortable with the implications of using "pure" markets to allocate such benefits (or hardships) as military service or scarce and expensive medical treatment,[73] largely because market-based resource allocations inevitably reflect the existing distribution of income and wealth.

Willingness to pay implies ability to pay. Thus in environmental planning, as Kapp has noted:

> The logical and practical result of using willingness to pay as a criterion would be that public parks or clean air in the ghetto sections of a large city would yield a lower benefit-cost ratio than the marina for top management personnel. A mode of reasoning which leads to or indirectly supports such an outcome reveals its hidden, basically unequalitarian [*sic*] value judgments inherent in the compensation principle as a criterion of evaluating the 'worth' of environmental goals.[74]

This inseparability of benefit valuations from distributions of wealth and income is one general source of bias in CBA. Another has to do with the issue of what is to count as a cost of regulation (or a benefit of the regulated activity). Such costs include not only the direct expenditures made on complying with the regulation or policy (compliance costs), but also the foregone returns that the funds thus expended could have been earning in some other use (e.g., producing more hula hoops rather than reducing emissions of the pollutants produced by their manufacture). Thus, Weidenbaum argues that the costs of regulation include "[t]he new investments in plant and equipment that are not made" and "the factors that are not built, the jobs that do not get created, the goods and services that do not get produced, and the incomes that are not generated"[75] because of the diversion of investment capital for purposes which are unproductive (in market terms).

The discounting of future benefits and costs is a corollary of this preference for market outcomes. Benefits which result in the future from the expenditure of funds today (for example, on proper disposal of industrial wastes) must be discounted in order to assess the efficiency of resource allocations, because otherwise the funds could be earning a return in some other use.[76] This is the rationale for the choice of a discount rate for purposes of CBA based on average private-sector rates of return on capital. It is possible, of course, to specify a lower discount rate for certain kinds of benefits, such as protection of human health. However, the choice of a discount rate remains inescapably value-laden. Since many environmental impacts and human health effects (e.g., from the improper disposal of hazardous industrial waste) may take many years to materialize, a point of particular importance is that extremely painful and undesirable future consequences may appear insignificant once their dollar cost is discounted to arrive at the present value of avoiding future disaster. In the occupational health context:

> … consider the economic decision faced by a businessman who would need $200,000 to 'design-in' carcinogenic exposure controls for workers at a particular worksite. Given a current [1981] discount rate in the private economy of at least 12 percent, if the businessman put only $11,800 into an investment opportunity affording 12 percent interest, at the end of 25 years there would be a check for $200,000 waiting for him. So, for the businessman, clearly the preference would not be to spend $200,000 now in prevention, but to bank $11,800 now for compensation and after-the-fact expenditures.[77]

Such discounting is, in the context of CBA, rational for society as well as for the individual firm.

Some further philosophical implications of this preference for marketed goods and services are explored in Part III of the paper. A more immediate issue is: how are dollar values attached to the benefits of environmental control for purposes of cost-benefit comparisons? Here, in particular, only an outline of a very extensive literature can be provided. The value of recreational amenities preserved or improved has often been inferred on the basis of the amount of time and money individuals are willing to spend to take advantage of such opportunities.[78] And the difference in property values between areas of (for example) high and low air pollution can be used to provide a proxy measure for the amount people are willing to pay for cleaner air.[79] Such measures are at least vaguely plausible, but they also illustrate (as Kapp points out) the biases which are related to income and wealth distribution. The fact that high-income areas generally enjoy cleaner air than poor areas of the same city[80] can be interpreted in terms of willingness to pay for air quality; it can also mean simply that the poor are victimized by their inability to pay the higher price of living in a cleaner, healthier area.

Benefit valuations become most questionable, and most contentious, when dollar values are determined for prevention of adverse effects on human life and health. One approach to valuing policy-related health improvements is to estimate direct cost savings on, e.g., doctors' fees, drugs, and hospital services.[81] Thus, the CBA produced by the U.S. EPA of its 1984 proposals for drastic reductions in allowable gasoline lead levels valued the benefits of regulation in terms of avoiding cognitive impairment among children with elevated blood lead levels in terms of the avoidance of costs for compensatory education and medical treatment which would otherwise be incurred.[82] Benefit valuations may also include the increased dollar earnings which are made possible by a healthier population—an approach which, admittedly, "discriminates against programs that improve the health of the non-working: children, the elderly, unemployed."[83] This is a specific variation of a general method for valuing the benefits of life-saving or health-protecting programs known as the "human capital approach," which values the saving of a life in terms of discounted future earnings. On this basis the lives of men are worth more than those of women (who earn less money), children's lives are worth less than those of young adults and middle-aged people (because of the effects of discounting on nominally larger, but more remote, future earnings), and the life of an 85-year-old nonwhite American woman, in 1972, was worth US $128.[84] Yet despite such conclusions, and despite its repudiation by at least some economists,[85] the human capital approach was endorsed by a Canadian governmental interdepartmental working group on toxic chemicals policy in 1984.[86]

The human capital approach is not, in fact, an estimate of willingness-to-pay: rather, "it is derived from an alternative value judgment, namely, that ... output is a measure of worth."[87] (It could, presumably, be argued that the maximum amount individuals will be able to pay for protection of life and health is a function of their discounted future earnings.[88]) Alternative approaches which attempt to generate estimates based on willingness to pay do not attach a value directly to life; rather, they assess expenditures directed toward improving health or incrementally reducing the risk of death—a subtle but important distinction.[89] As an extreme and barbaric example of such inferences, it has been seriously suggested that cosmetic losses resulting from illness or injury could be value based on "an implicit price of personal attractiveness" based on "expenditures wholly designed to increase one's own attractiveness."[90] (A moment's reflection on the application of this criterion in a CBA of, say, a product safety standard designed to prevent disfiguring injury is sufficient to illustrate its absurdity). More humanely, analysts have attempted to infer valuations from the amounts people spend to protect their life and health (for example, by investing in home smoke detectors[91]) or, alternatively, from the amount they appear to demand as compensation for increased risk as measured by the wage differentials between more and

less hazardous occupations.[92] (The "payment" in this case is not a direct one, but rather the foregone earnings in higher-paid, but more hazardous occupations.)

Full information on the effectiveness of, e.g., smoke detectors may not be available. And full information on work-related hazards is probably never available.[93] (Indeed, employers have an obvious economic motive to restrict the supply of such information.[94]) The "choice" facing workers may be seriously limited by such factors as skills, geographical location, the cyclical nature and dominant labour market position of local industries (alternative employment for uranium miners in Elliot Lake, Ontario; asbestos miners in Thetford Mines or Asbestos, Quebec; or loggers and pulp mill workers in northwestern Ontario and much of British Columbia may be hard to come by[95]) and regional and national unemployment levels. Since the distribution of wealth in economies like Canada's means that most individuals must work for a living, many of those who enter risky occupations may have little *effective* choice in the matter.[96] A related weakness of wage differential studies, almost universally ignored, is that they have focussed on hourly-rated or working-class occupations[97] and have therefore restricted their scope to individuals whose alternative employment options are far less extensive than those of, say, senior managers (or university economists). People in these latter occupations might demand far higher compensation in return for additional increases in work-related risk. Indeed, it may well be that such occupations are not only much better paid but also safer than those included in wage differential studies. This observation illustrates the class bias of such studies, and suggests that "risk premiums" for hazardous work, if and when they exist at all, probably reflect only the relative power of buyers and sellers in a particular labour market. Here, again, valuations of life and health are "molded by the current distribution of wealth because behaviour and perceived opportunities depend on ability to pay. Thus, these methods have a status quo bias and cannot be expected to produce socially equitable resource allocations."[98]

III. COST-BENEFIT ANALYSIS, ETHICS, AND POLITICAL THEORY

An economist might respond to these criticisms, and others, by pointing out that society's material resources are finite. In one respect, society implicitly attaches a dollar value to human life and health (the most frequent criticism of CBA) every day, for example in deciding on the level of expenditure which will be made (or required) on various life- or health-protecting initiatives, ranging from occupational health standards to purchases of medical equipment for hospitals or improvements in highway guardrails.[99] Cost-benefit analysis, then, is merely a source of information which can be used to improve the "return" (in terms of protecting life, health and the environment) from the use of limited resources.

Few would deny the problem posed by finite resources, although (as suggested in Part I) limits to available resources in specific contexts are often a function of the wealth and power of those who might be adversely affected by the redistributive impact of a particular policy. However, there are several reasons to reject invocations of resource limitations in defence of CBA. First, Calabresi and Bobbitt have coined the phrase "tragic choices" to describe such decisions as the allocation of life-saving expenditures or scarce medical treatment.[100] CBA attempts to simulate the market allocation, but markets are only one of several ways of making tragic choices. (The choice of a market mechanism rather than some other kind is itself a value-laden and political one.) At best, then, CBA is instructive

as a way of determining how resources might be allocated *if* markets were used to make a particular tragic choice. And in the course of doing so, it arguably serves to camouflage the importance of the fact that incommensurable values (e.g., dollars versus lives) are being compared.

This weakness is important even in cases where CBA is only used (as some economists say it should be) to "organize available information"[101] for purposes of policy decisions. A second weakness emerges in cases where CBA is used as the basis for an actual decision rule—i.e., where market valuations are implicitly favoured as the basis of allocating resources. Requirements that policy measures show a favourable benefit-cost ratio foreclose serious consideration of the merits of decisions which would reduce the aggregate wealth of society but improve the situation of a particular set of victims. For example, a CBA might conclude that the costs of regulations which reduce or eliminate the use of lead additives in gasoline are not exceeded by the dollar benefits of associated improvements in the cognitive abilities of children who now are exposed, via a number of pathways, to considerable amounts of lead which originates from gasoline combustion.[102] Quite apart from such issues as the value implications of methods for valuing health benefits and criteria for resolving scientific uncertainty, the "bottom line" is: how much do we, as a society, really care whether regulations guarding against this sort of effect are economically efficient? There is nothing irrational about a society which decides to forgo some wealth in favour of preventing adverse health effects of this sort, unless "rationality" is *a priori* equated with wealth-maximization.[103]

To state this problem in another way, the efficiency criterion as embodied in CBA of environmental policy implies that the creation of any "cost," including pain, illness and death, can be justified (at least in principle) by the demonstrable creation of an offsetting benefit *somewhere* within the society or the economy, once both benefits and costs have been properly monetized. On the basis of the Kaldor-Hicks principle, this state of affairs is justifiable since losers *could* be compensated for their losses. But what if no mechanism exists for them to assert a claim for such compensation? (The inadequacy of existing legal entitlements to compensation for pollution damages in Canada has been extensively documented.[104]) Or, more seriously, what if the losers consider their losses non-compensable and would as individuals choose not to incur them, whatever the greater good in whose pursuit the costs are imposed? In such cases, a cost-benefit approach to choosing environmental policy objectives constitutes a form of technological conscription. As Bogen notes, the process "… goes farther than merely placing life on the market, it perforce places *all* lives on the market—in effect, transforming life into currency or legal tender which society is of right free to collect, like taxes, in order to pay off its technological debts."[105]

CBA, then, solves the problem posed for resource allocation (according to economists' analysis) by the absence of property rights in resources like air and water. But it does so by way of a powerful, implicit assignment of rights to the creators of environmental hazards, as a category, rather than to the potential recipients or victims of hazards, as long as economic benefits can be claimed to offset these risks. This is the same bias which is evident within the implementation of environmental policy, as typified by the case of Canadian non-ferrous smelter emissions, where the choice of accepting continued environmental destruction or bearing at least part of the cost of reducing those impacts is imposed by industry on other "users" of the natural environment.

At least some environmentalists have argued that the problem should be solved in quite a different way: some form of substantive and enforceable right to environmental quality, analogous in at least some respects to property rights, should be entrenched in law.[106] Examining the implications of this alternative approach serves to highlight the biases of the efficiency criterion. When a regulation prohibiting the release of a hazardous pollutant is not adopted because it cannot be shown to have a favourable benefit-cost ratio, government in effect allows the expropriation of the health of those individuals whose health may deteriorate as a result of exposure to the pollutant, based on an analyst's inference of the fair market value of their lives and health. The process is analogous to that of expropriation of real property. However, until and unless specific procedures for expropriation have been followed, our society defends your right to refuse to sell your house, whatever an economist's opinion of its fair market value. In Sax's words, society does not "leave the enforcement of an individual's property rights to some bureaucrat to vindicate when, and if, he determines them to be consistent with the public interest."[107] Procedural safeguards against unfair or arbitrary expropriation of property may be inadequate, but their perceived inadequacy highlights our general unwillingness to abandon a conception of property as an issue of *rights* for an alternative conception in which the entitlements to exclusion which constitute property rights are less firmly entrenched.

Why might industry support the application of CBA to environmental policy? The preceding analysis of the assignment of rights to the use of the environment suggests one important reason. Related, but probably more significant, is the way in which CBA's implied skepticism about the worth of benefits such as health protection which are inherently difficult to quantify and value serves to focus attention on the more "solid" and readily quantifiable costs (to industry) of regulation. In a perceptive comparison of American and British regimes of environmental regulation, Vogel notes that the informal, consultative nature of the British regulatory process allows industry ample scope for articulating its priorities. On the other hand:

> American corporate executives, and academics sympathetic to them, urge the use of cost-benefit analysis precisely because so much of American environmental regulation is written and enforced without reference to the costs of complying with it. In a sense, the use of cost-benefit analysis represents a surrogate for the inability of American industry to have its interests taken more seriously.[108]

Tolchin similarly notes that CBA provides "a respectable methodological rationale" for opposition to the redistributive impacts of social regulations.[109] Vogel's analysis also suggests a reason for the relative scarcity of formal CBA requirements in Canadian regulatory mechanisms. The role played by CBA in the American context is made superfluous in Canada (as in Britain) by the routinely high degree of industry involvement in the policy process, and by the associated deference accorded to its priorities.

Related to the ethical assumptions embedded in CBA are implied propositions concerning political theory and the proper form of public decision-making. Environmental regulation is routinely justified as a necessary corrective for market failures. However, it is not self-evident that public policies which control environmental pollution should be evaluated on this basis. An alternative view, which emphasizes the redistributive aspects of environmental protection initiatives, is that "[t]he real purpose of government regulation in this field is not and never has been to correct deficiencies of markets but to transcend markets altogether." From this point of view, environmental policy "can be said to advance a conception of the public interest apart from,

and often opposed to, the outcomes of the market place."[110] Beauchamp has made a similar point in analyzing public health policy: he contrasts the allocations of resources which result from the highly unequal distribution of market power ("market-justice") with what he sees as the basic direction of public health policy. That direction is "ultimately rooted in an egalitarian tradition that conflicts directly with the norms of market-justice."[111]

To oversimplify a highly complex set of comparisons, markets differ in several ways from non-market mechanisms (such as electoral politics) for making decisions and allocating resources. Although within an electoral system the impact of all franchised individuals is theoretically equal,[112] in a market setting power is directly proportional to wealth. One person, one vote as a basis for decision-making can yield outcomes strikingly different from those generated based on the (market) principle of one dollar, one vote.

More subtly, markets allocate resources based on the aggregation of (wealth- or income-weighted) individual preferences. Unlike at least some political decision-making mechanisms, they do not offer the opportunity for decisions based on collective choices about the proper direction and values of the community. This point has often been made with respect to decisions about the preservation of wilderness (whose direct economic worth may be relatively low) as opposed to its destruction for purposes of building dams or vacation resorts.[113] A dramatic contrast may well exist between individuals' willingness to pay for environmental protection (or to finance environmentally destructive activity!) as individual consumers, and their willingness as *citizens* to make decisions incurring a collective obligation (for example, preserving wilderness).[114] In Tribe's words, a decision-making process based on the "instrumental rationality" of which CBA is typical

… could help the community draw various inferences from an assessment of how much its inhabitants do in fact value birds and other wildlife as compared, say, with boating and other activities; that is, the analysis could spin out of the logical and empirical entailments of the value systems with which the community begins. But the analysis could not enable the community's inhabitants to think about *what those value systems ought to be*—about the extent to which their *should* be a wildlife-valuing community, with all that this might entail for how its members view and value both nature and one another.[115]

Similarly, members of a community might decide on the need to guard against the health and environmental dangers of improper industrial waste disposal (for example) for reasons unrelated to the inferred willingness of any individual or set of individuals to pay for the benefits of those objectives as consumers, and unrelated to the number of dollars which can be saved for society (e.g., via reductions in health care expenditures).

It is not suggested here that political choice mechanisms in Canada routinely operate in the way idealized by Tribe. But they *can* do so, whereas markets cannot. The presuppositions underlying CBA and its application to public policy are therefore important as what Mueller has called a para-ideology.[116] For Mueller, ideologies in the traditional sense "justify the use of force to maintain the status quo, to initiate social change, and to suppress revolutionary activities."[117] Para-ideologies substitute, in functional terms, for such "integrated system[s] of meaning providing sociopolitical interpretations"[118]; they consist of "collective imagery rooted in material and social compensations"[119] which has the effect of structuring individuals' perceptions about the social order.

As an example of the contemporary significance of the concept of para-ideology,

Mueller uses the acceptance of "rational" solutions derived by analogy with scientific and technological conclusions as a substitute for the outcome of conscious political choice. He is particularly concerned with the way such "rationality" can be used to obscure class conflicts—in Mueller's own words, to depoliticize politics.[120] The "rationality" embodied in CBA arguably has a similar effect, at the level of issue definitions, by (a) legitimizing existing distributions of wealth and rights, and (b) obscuring the potential for making tragic choices on some basis other than the aggregation of individual preferences.

There is nothing vicious or conspiratorial in business's defence of CBA and the associated norms of the marketplace. These are the norms according to which business must function, and according to which its success or failure is judged. One executive interviewed by Silk and Vogel succinctly argued that: "In the marketplace, every person gets a vote every day. The market is more democratic than the government."[121] There are a number of objections to this claim, only some of which have been discussed in this paper. More detailed examination would lead into a critical scrutiny of the concept of "democracy" itself.[122] The quotation is cited here to underscore the depth of potential conflict between markets and politics as alternative—if not competing—ways of making decisions about the direction of society, and the allocation of its admittedly finite resources. The greatest weakness of CBA as applied to environmental policy is simply that it presupposes the proper resolution of this competition. It does so in a way which reinforces, at the conceptual level, existing inequalities of wealth and power and which fails to acknowledge the legitimacy of views of public life as discerned through conceptual lenses other than those of economics.

ENDNOTES

1. J. Jackson and P. Weller, *Chemical Nightmare: The Unnecessary Legacy of Toxic Wastes* (Waterloo, Ont.: Between the Lines Press, 1982); S. Wolf, "Hazardous Waste Trials and Tribulations," *Environmental Law* 13 (1983), pp. 367–491. The province of Ontario alone generates more than 1.5 million tonnes of industrial wastes per year: D. Chant, "Ontario Generates 1.5 million Tonnes of Industrial Waste Annually," *Water and Pollution Control* (Directory and Buyers' Guide issue, 1983), pp. 17–21, 87–88.

2. *Still Waters: The Chilling Reality of Acid Rain*, Report of the Sub-Committee on Acid Rain, House of Commons Standing Committee on Fisheries and Forestry (Ottawa: Supply and Services Canada, 1981), pp. 19–47.

3. Ibid., pp. 51–59. See also M. Havas et al., "Red Herrings in Acid Rain Research," *Environmental Science and Technology* 18:6 (June 1984), pp. 176A–186A; G. Likens et al., "Acid Rain," *Scientific American* 241:4 (October 1979), pp. 43–51; G. Tomlinson II, "Air Pollutants and Forest Decline," *Environmental Science and Technology* 17:6 (June 1983), pp. 246A–256A.

4. Great Lakes Water Quality Board, International Joint Commission, *Inventory of Major Municipal and Industrial Point Source Dischargers in the Great Lakes Basin* (Windsor, Ontario: IJC, July 1979); M. Comba and K. Kaiser, "Volatile Hydrocarbons in the Detroit River and their Relationship with Contaminant Sources," *Journal of Great Lakes Research* 11:3 (1985), pp. 404–418; Y. Hamdy and L. Post, "Distribution of Mercury, Trace Organics and Other Heavy Metals in Detroit River Sediments," *Journal of Great Lakes Research* 11:3 (1985), pp. 353–365.

5. P. Victor, "Economics and the Challenge of Environmental Issues," in *Ecology versus Politics in Canada*, ed. W. Leiss (Toronto: University of Toronto Press, 1979), pp. 36–37.

6. R. A. Kagan, "On Regulatory Inspectorates and Police," in *Enforcing Regulation*, ed. K. Hawkins and J. Thomas (Boston: Kluwer-Nijhoff, 1984), p. 43.

7. M. Useem, "Classwide Rationality in the Politics of Managers and Directors of Large Corporations in the United States and Great Britain," *Administrative Science Quarterly* 27 (1982), pp. 199–226; M. Useem, *The Inner Circle* (New York: Oxford University Press, 1984).

8. R. Dahl defines political resources as "means by which one person can influence the behavior of another. Political resources therefore include money, information, food, the threat of force, jobs, friendship, social standing, the right to make laws, votes, and a great variety of other things." *Modern Political Analysis*, 4th ed. (Englewood Cliffs, NJ: Prentice-Hall, 1984), p. 31.

9. A concept drawn from G. Allison, *Essence of Decision* (Boston: Little, Brown, 1971), p. v.

10. J. Castrilli and C. Lax, "Environmental Regulation-Making in Canada: Towards a More Open Process," in *Environmental Rights in Canada*, ed. J. Swaigen (Toronto: Butterworths, 1981); R. Gibson, *Control Orders and Industrial Pollution Abatement in Ontario* (Toronto: Canadian Environmental Law Research Foundation, 1983), esp. chapter 4; J. W. Parlour, "The Politics of Water Pollution Control: A Case Study of the Canadian Fisheries Act Amendments and the Pulp

and Paper Effluent Regulations, 1970," *Journal of Environmental Management* 13 (1980), pp. 127–149; W. Sullivan, "An Overview of the Background and Development of the Canadian Mercury Chlor-Alkali Air Emission Regulation," paper presented at the 73rd Annual Meeting, Air Pollution Control Association (Montreal, 1980), reproduced in Proceedings of the meeting.

11. Comments of R. Robinson, Assistant Deputy Minister, Environmental Protection Service, Environment Canada, in *Minutes of Proceedings* no. 6, House of Commons Special Committee on Regulatory Reform (September 24, 1980), p. 7.

12. W. Coleman and H. Jacek, "The Political Organization of the Chemical Industry in Canada," paper presented to the Canadian Political Science Association (Hamilton, Ont.: McMaster University, mimeo, 1981), pp. 36–37.

13. Ibid., pp. 24–29.

14. On such "functional relationships" between government departments and specific private-sector interests, see R. Presthus, *Elite Accommodation in Canadian Politics* (Toronto: Macmillan, 1973), pp. 212–216.

15. D. Dewees, "Evaluation of Economic Policies for Regulating Environmental Quality," Regulation Reference Working Paper No. 4 (Ottawa: Economic Council of Canada, 1980), p. 24.

16. F. Anderson, *Environmental Improvement Through Economic Incentives* (Baltimore: Johns Hopkins University Press, 1977), p. 16.

17. P. Victor and T. Burrell, *Environmental Protection Regulation, Water Pollution and the Pulp and Paper Industry*, Regulation Reference Technical Report no. 14 (Ottawa: Economic Council of Canada, 1981).

18. See generally T. Schrecker, "Mobilization of Bias in Closed Systems: Environment and Regulation in Canada," *Journal of Business Administration* 15:1, 1985, pp. 43–63.

19. See, e.g., "Long-Drawn Trial of Lead Company Adjourned Again," *Winnipeg Free Press*, October 18, 1984, p. 10; "Lead-Emission Case Goes to Judge," *Winnipeg Free Press*, December 7, 1984, p. 1 (on a prosecution under the federal *Clean Air Act* over regulations covering secondary lead smelters, which had dragged on for more than four years).

20. Gibson, note 10 above, p. 83; J. Swaigen, "Sentencing in Environmental Cases: A View from the Bar," in *Environmental Enforcement: Proceedings of the National Conference on the Enforcement of Environmental Law*, ed. L. Duncan (Edmonton: Environmental Law Centre, 1984).

21. For an overview see S. Baumol and W. Oates, *Economics, Environmental Policy and the Quality of Life* (Englewood Cliffs, NJ: Prentice-Hall, 1979), pp. 241–281 (on effluent charges); Dewees, note 15 above; Economic Council of Canada, *Reforming Regulation* (Ottawa, Supply and Services Canada, 1981), pp. 92–93; Peat, Marwick and Partners, *Economic Incentive Policy Instruments to Implement Pollution Control Objectives in Ontario* (Toronto: Ontario Ministry of the Environment, 1984), chapter III.

22. J. Donnan and P. Victor, *Alternative Policies for Pollution Abatement: The Ontario Pulp and Paper Industry* (Toronto: Ontario Ministry of the Environment, October 1976).

23. The cynical explanation is quite simply that such penalties would work—i.e., they would create much more reliable and consistent economic disincentives to the externalization of cost via pollution of the environment than do current legal

regimes. See G. Majone, "Choice Among Policy Instruments for Pollution Control," *Policy Analysis* 2 (1976), pp. 590–613.

24. W. Drayton, "Economic Law Enforcement," *Harvard Environmental Law Review* 4 (1980), pp. 1–40.

25. Castrilli and Lax, note 10 above; Gibson, note 10 above; A. Lucas, "Legal Foundations for Public Participation in Environmental Decision Making," *Natural Resources Journal* 16 (January 1976), pp. 73–102; M. Rankin, "Information and the Environment: The Struggle for Access," in *Environmental Rights in Canada*, ed. J. Swaigen (Toronto: Butterworths, 1981).

26. This case is discussed in greater detail in K. Boggild, "The Amax Controversy," *Alternatives: Perspectives on Society and Environment* 10:2/3 (1982), pp. 40–46, 54; Schrecker, note 18 above, pp. 45–46, 54.

27. *Report of the Royal Commission on Corporate Concentration* (Ottawa: Supply and Services Canada, 1978), pp. 338–339.

28. R. Kazis and R. Grossman, *Fear at Work: Job Blackmail, Labor, and the Environment* (New York: Pilgrim Press, 1982).

29. W. Troyer, *No Safe Place* (Toronto: Clarke, Irwin, 1977).

30. *Final Report on Acidic Precipitation, Abatement of Emissions from the International Nickel Company Operations at Sudbury, Pollution Control in the Pulp and Paper Industry, and Pollution Abatement at the Reed Paper Mill in Dryden*, Standing Committee on Resources Development, Legislature of Ontario (Toronto, October 1979), pp. 85–90.

31. Ibid., pp. 94–95.

32. Ibid., pp. 115, 119–120.

33. B. Jorgensen, "Noranda Will Stick it Out Despite Debt," *The Globe and Mail*, June 29, 1985, p. 81.

34. *Still Waters*, note 2 above, pp. 19, 24.

35. B. Felske and R. Gibson, *Sulphur Dioxide Regulation and the Canadian Non-Ferrous Metals Industry*, Regulation Reference Technical Report No. 3 (Ottawa: Economic Council of Canada, 1980).

36. S. Cordier, et al., "Mortality Patterns in a Population Living near a Copper Smelter," *Environmental Research* 31 (1983), pp. 311–322.

37. K. Noble, "Noranda Links Pollution Control Costs to Fate of Its Smelters," *The Globe and Mail*, May 31, 1984, p. 84.

38. L. Silk and M. Vogel, *Ethics and Profits: The Crisis of Confidence in American Business* (New York: Simon & Schuster, 1976), p. 66.

39. M. Bucovetsky, "The Mining Industry and the Great Tax Reform Debate," in *Pressure Group Behavior in Canadian Politics*, ed. P. Pross (Toronto: McGraw-Hill-Ryerson, 1975).

40. C. Offe, *Contradictions of the Welfare State*, ed. J. Keane (Cambridge, MA: MIT Press, 1984).

41. C. Lindblom, *Politics and Markets* (New York: Basic Books, 1977), pp. 170–221.

42. S. Robock et al., *International Business and Multinational Enterprises*, rev. ed. (Homewood, IL: Irwin, 1977), p. 260. See also A. Martinelli, "The Political and Social Impact of Transnational Corporations," in *The New International Economy*, ed. H. Makler et al. (London/Beverly Hills: Sage, 1982).

43. T. Gladwin and I. Walter, *Multinationals Under Fire: Lessons in the Management of Conflict* (New York: Wiley/ Interscience, 1980), p. 433.

44. P. Davis, "Arsenic and Jobs Trade-Off," *Nature* 304 (July 21, 1983), p. 200; B. Kalikow, "Environmental Risk: Power to the People," *Technology Review* 87:7 (October, 1984).

45. *Still Waters*, note 2 above, p. 19.

46. *Time Lost: A Demand for Action on Acid Rain*, Report of the Sub-Committee on Acid Rain, House of Commons Standing Committee on Fisheries and Forestry (Ottawa: Supply and Services Canada, 1984).

47. Ibid., p. 32.

48. Ibid., pp. 34–36.

49. J. Sallot, "$150 Million Slated for Smelter Cleanup," *The Globe and Mail*, March 7, 1985.

50. Lindblom, note 41 above, p. 178.

51. "[T]he power position of private investors includes the power to define reality. That is to say, whatever they consider an intolerable burden in fact is an intolerable burden which will in fact lead to a declining propensity to invest...." (Emphasis in original.) C. Offe, "Some Contradictions of the Modern Welfare State," in *Contradictions*, note 40 above, p. 152.

52. Victor, note 5 above, pp. 36–37.

53. *Reforming Regulation*, note 21 above, p. 83.

54. A. Kneese and R. d'Arge, "Benefit Analysis and Today's Regulatory Problems," *The Benefits of Health and Safety Regulation*, ed. A. Ferguson and P. LeVeen (Cambridge, MA: Ballinger, 1981).

55. P. Victor, "Techniques for Assessment and Analysis in the Management of Toxic Chemicals," paper prepared for Agriculture Canada National Workshop on Risk-Benefit Analysis (Toronto: Victor & Burrell Research and Consulting, mimeo, March 1985), p. 7.

56. For a succinct explanation of the concept and its philosophical foundations, see N. Rescher, "Economics versus Moral Philosophy: The Pareto Principle as a Case Study," in Rescher, *Unpopular Essays in Technological Progress* (Pittsburgh: University of Pittsburgh Press, 1980).

57. A. Kneese, *Economics and the Environment* (New York: Penguin, 1977), p. 20.

58. A. M. Freeman, *The Benefits of Environmental Improvement: Theory and Practice* (Baltimore: Johns Hopkins University Press, 1979), pp. 54–57.

59. Ibid., p. 55.

60. H. Macaulay and B. Yandle, *Environmental Use and the Market* (Lexington, MA: D. C. Heath, 1977), p. 49.

61. D. McCaffrey, *OSHA and the Politics of Health Regulation* (New York: Plenum, 1982), pp. 89–94, 113–122, 128–131; S. Tolchin, "Cost-Benefit Analysis and the Rush to Deregulate," *Policy Studies Review* 4:2 (November 1984), pp. 212–218; D. Whittington and W. N. Grubb, "Economic Analysis in Regulatory Decisions: The Implications of Executive Order 12291," *Science, Technology and Human Values* 9:1 (1984), pp. 63–71.

62. 46:33 *Federal Register* (February 19, 1981), pp. 13191–13198.

63. Tolchin, note 61 above, p. 212.

64. Treasury Board of Canada, *Administrative Policy Manual*, Chapter 490, "Socio-Economic Impact Analysis" (Ottawa: Supply and Services Canada, December 1979).

65. *Risk-Benefit Analysis in the Management of Toxic Chemicals* (Ottawa: Agriculture Canada, 1984).

66. Summarized in N. Ashford and C. Hill, *Benefits of Environmental, Health and Safety Regulation*, prepared for

Committee on Government Affairs, U.S. Senate, 96th Cong., 2nd Sess. (Washington, D.C.: U.S. Government Printing Office, 1980). See also J. Haigh et al., "Benefit-Cost Analysis of Environmental Regulation: Case Studies of Hazardous Air Pollutants," *Harvard Environmental Law Review* 8 (1984), pp. 395–434.

67. L. Fishbein, "Overview of Some Aspects of Quantitative Risk Assessment," *Journal of Toxicology and Environmental Health* 6 (1980), pp. 1275–1296.

68. Canadian Energy and Emissions Committee, International Lead Zinc Research Organization, "Response of the Canadian Lead Industry to Environment Canada's Proposal to Further Restrict Gasoline Lead Usage" (Toronto: ILZRO, mimeo, March 1984); H. Kelly, "The Misdirected War Against Leaded Gasoline," *ACSH News and Views* 6:1 (January/February 1985), pp. 1, 12–13 (New York: American Council on Science and Health).

69. See, e.g., *Low Level Lead Exposure: The Clinical Implications of Current Research*, ed. H. Needleman (New York: Raven Press, 1980); *Lead versus Health*, ed. M. Rutter and R. Russell Jones (London: John Wiley, 1983). A detailed discussion of the treatment of scientific uncertainty with respect to controlling lead pollution is provided in T. Schrecker, "Environmental Lead Pollution: A Public Health Issue in Social Context," submission to the Royal Society of Canada Commission on Lead in the Environment (Ottawa: Friends of the Earth, Canada, December 1985).

70. T. Page, "A Generic View of Toxic Chemicals and Similar Risks," *Ecology Law Quarterly* 7:2 (1978), pp. 207–244; T. McGarity, "Substantive and Procedural Discretion in Administrative Resolution of Science Policy Questions," *Georgetown Law Journal* 67 (1979), pp. 729–810 (see particularly pp. 731–749).

71. McGarity, note 70 above.

72. Page, note 70, above; S. Jellinek, "On the Inevitability of Being Wrong," in *Management of Assessed Risk for Carcinogens*, ed. W. Nicholson, Annals of the New York Academy of Sciences 363 (1981); H. Latin, "The 'Significance' of Toxic Health Risks: An Essay on Legal Decisionmaking Under Uncertainty," *Ecology Law Quarterly* (1982), pp. 339–395.

73. G. Calabresi and P. Bobbitt, *Tragic Choices* (New York: W. W. Norton, 1977), pp. 32–41.

74. K. W. Kapp, "Social Costs, Non-Classical Economics, and Environmental Planning: A Reply" [to W. Beckerman], *Political Economy of Environment: Problems of Method, Environment and Social Sciences* 2 (Paris/The Hague: Mouton, 1971), p. 120. (See also Kapp's essay "Environmental Disruption and Social Costs," in the same volume).

75. M. Weidenbaum, "The Continuing Need for Regulatory Reform," in *Use of Cost-Benefit Analysis by Regulatory Agencies*, Joint Hearings before the Subcommittee on Oversight and Investigations and the Subcommittee on Consumer Protection and Finance, Committee on Interstate and Foreign Commerce, U.S. House of Representatives, Serial 96–157 (Washington, D.C.: U.S. Government Printing Office, 1980), pp. 330–331.

76. T. Page, *Conservation and Economic Efficiency* (Baltimore: Johns Hopkins University Press, 1977), pp. 152–155.

77. R. Ruttenberg and E. Bingham, "A Comprehensive Occupational Carcinogen Policy as a Framework for Regulatory Activity," in *Management of Assessed Risk for Carcinogens*, ed. W. Nicholson, Annals of the New York Academy of Sciences 363 (1981), p. 18.

78. Freeman, note 58 above, pp. 195–233; E. Hyman, "The Valuation of Extramarket Benefits and Costs in Environmental Impact Assessment," *Environmental Impact Assessment Review* 2:3 (1981), pp. 227–264 (see pp. 228–232); D. Tihansky, "A Survey of Empirical Benefit Studies," in *Cost-Benefit Analysis and Water Pollution Policy*, ed. H. Peskin and E. Seskin (Washington, D.C.: The Urban Institute, 1975).

79. Freeman, note 58 above, pp. 108–164; Hyman, note 78 above, pp. 233–235.

80. See, e.g., F. Handy, "Income and Air Quality in Hamilton, Ontario," *Alternatives: Perspectives on Society and Environment* 6:3 (1977), pp. 18–26; F. Muller, "Distribution of Air Pollution in the Montreal Region," *Canadian Public Policy* 3 (1977), pp. 199–204.

81. Freeman, note 58 above, p. 191; G. Torrance and D. Krewski, "Risk Assessment and the Evaluation of Toxic Chemical Control Programs," paper prepared for Agriculture Canada National Workshop on Risk-Benefit Analysis (Ottawa: Health and Welfare Canada, mimeo, March 1985), p. 9.

82. *Costs and Benefits of Reducing Lead in Gasoline: Final Regulatory Impact Analysis* (Washington, D.C.: Economic Analysis Division, Office of Policy, Planning and Evaluation, U.S. Environmental Protection Agency, February 1985). For another example of such an approach, see R. Dardis, et al., "Cost-Benefit Analysis of Flammability Standards" [for children's sleepwear], *American Journal of Agricultural Economics* 60 (November 1978), pp. 695–700.

83. Torrance and Krewski, note 81 above, p. 9. The authors note that such calculations do, however, "provide a measure of *productive* resources returned to society as a result of allocating other resources ... to the program" [Emphasis added].

84. Freeman, note 58 above, pp. 169–172.

85. E.g., Kneese and d'Arge, note 54 above, p. 85.

86. *Risk-Benefit Analysis*, note 65 above, p. 6.

87. Freeman, note 58 above, p. 171.

88. Ibid., p. 170.

89. R. Howard, "On Making Life and Death Decisions," in *Societal Risk Assessment: How Safe is Safe Enough?* ed. R. Schwing and A. Albers (New York: Plenum, 1980); Kneese and d'Arge, note 54 above, pp. 84–85.

90. J. Bishop and C. Cicchetti, "Some Institutional and Conceptual Thoughts on the Measurement of Indirect and Intangible Benefits and Costs," in *Cost-Benefit Analysis and Water Pollution Policy*, ed. H. Peskin and E. Seskin (Washington, D.C.: The Urban Institute, 1975), p. 121.

91. R. Dardis, "The Value of a Life: New Evidence from the Marketplace," *American Economic Review* 70 (December 1980), pp. 1077–1082.

92. Freeman, note 58 above, pp. 185–189; R. Thaler and S. Rosen, "The Value of Saving a Life," *Household Production and Consumption*, ed. N. Terleckyj, *Studies in Income and Wealth* 40 (New York: National Bureau of Economic Research/Columbia University Press, 1975); W. K. Viscusi, "Labor Market Valuations of Life and Limb: Empirical Evidence and Policy Implications," *Public Policy* 26 (Summer 1978), pp. 359–386. Viscusi has defended the validity of this approach as a basis for standard-setting in "Setting Efficient Standards for Occupational Hazards," *Journal of Occupational Medicine* 24:12 (December 1982), pp. 969–976.

93. Economic Council of Canada, note 21 above, p. 101; Viscusi, note 92 above, p. 365.

94. G. Reschenthaler, *Occupational Health and Safety in Canada: The Economics and Three Case Studies* (Montreal: Institute for Research on Public Policy, 1979), p. 11.

95. For a discussion and inventory of Canadian one-industry communities such as those named, see Department of Regional Economic Expansion, *Single-Sector Communities*, rev. ed. (Ottawa: Supply and Services Canada, 1979).

96. M. MacCarthy, "A Review of Some Normative and Conceptual Issues in Occupational Safety and Health," *Boston College Environmental Affairs Law Review* 9 (1981–82), pp. 773–814 (see esp. pp. 778–781).

97. Thaler and Rosen, note 92 above, pp. 287–289; Viscusi, "Valuations," note 92 above, p. 364.

98. Hyman, note 78 above, p. 252.

99. Freeman, note 58 above, p. 166; J. Graham and J. Vaupel, "Value of a Life: What Difference Does It Make?" *Risk Analysis* 1:1 (1981), pp. 89–95.

100. Calabresi and Bobbitt, note 73 above.

101. Freeman, note 58 above, p. 6.

102. The U.S. EPA's analysis of the costs and benefits of further limits on lead additives in gasoline (note 82 above) in fact found a strongly favourable benefit-cost ratio for further reductions in allowable lead levels.

103. N. Ashford, "Alternatives to Cost-Benefit Analysis in Regulatory Decisions," in *Management of Assessed Risk for Carcinogens*, ed. W. Nicholson, Annals of the New York Academy of Sciences 363 (1981), p. 137.

104. S. Chester, "Class Actions to Protect the Environment," in *Environmental Rights in Canada*, ed. J. Swaigen (Toronto: Butterworths, 1981); P. Elder, "Environmental Protection Through the Common Law," *University of Western Ontario Law Review* 12 (1973), pp. 107–171; J. Swaigen, Compensation of Pollution Victims in Canada (Ottawa: Economic Council of Canada, 1981).

105. K. Bogen, "Public Policy and Technological Risk," *IDEA: Journal of Law and Technology* 21:1 (1980), pp. 37–74 (at p. 56).

106. J. Swaigen and R. Woods, "A Substantive Right to Environmental Quality," in *Environmental Rights in Canada*, ed. J. Swaigen (Toronto: Butterworths, 1981).

107. J. Sax, *Defending the Environment: A Strategy for Citizen Action* (New York: Knopf, 1971), p. 60. Sax was the principal drafter of a statute (the *Michigan Environmental Protection Act*) which is widely cited as an adventurous attempt to extend to citizens the legal right to use the courts in defence of environmental quality: see Swaigen and Woods, note 106 above, pp. 212–223.

108. D. Vogel, "Cooperative Regulation: Environmental Protection in Great Britain," *The Public Interest* no. 72 (June 1983), pp. 88–106 (at p. 97).

109. Tolchin, note 61 above, p. 212.

110. D. Caplice, Regional Director, Central Region, Ontario Ministry of the Environment, "Role of the Senior Regulator: Practicalities and Pressures," presented to Canadian Environmental Law Research Foundation conference on Environmental Regulation: The Burdens and the Benefits, February 1981 (Toronto: Ontario Ministry of the Environment, mimeo), p. 5.

111. D. Beauchamp, "Public Health as Social Justice," in *Public Health and the Law: Issues and Trends*, ed. L. Hogue (Rockville, MD: Aspen Systems Corp., 1980), p. 6.

112. This equality seldom obtains in practice, because (for example) of the way in which electoral results in systems where legislators are elected individually by geographically defined constituencies tend to reward regional concentrations of support, but not to respond to diffuse national increases in party support. See R. Landes, *The Canadian Polity: A Comparative Perspective* (Scarborough, Ont.: Prentice-Hall, 1984).

113. M. Sagoff, "We Have Met the Enemy and He is Us, or, Conflict and Contradiction in Environmental Law," *Environmental Law* 12 (Winter 1982), pp. 283–315; L. Tribe, "Technology Assessment and the Fourth Discontinuity: The Limits of Instrumental Rationality," *Southern California Law Review* 46 (1973), pp. 617–660.

114. Sagoff, note 113 above; M. Sagoff, "Economic Theory and Environmental Law," *Michigan Law Review* 79 (June 1981), pp. 1393–1419.

115. Tribe, note 113 above, p. 656.

116. C. Mueller, *The Politics of Communication* (New York: Oxford University Press, 1973), p. 108.

117. Ibid.

118. Ibid.

119. Ibid.

120. Ibid., pp. 109–111.

121. Silk and Vogel, note 38 above, p. 49.

122. J. Schaar, "Legitimacy in the Modern State," in Power and Community: *Dissenting Essays in Political Science*, ed. P. Gren and S. Levinson (New York: Vintage, 1970).

THE KITCHEN AND THE MULTINATIONAL CORPORATION:

An Analysis of the Links Between the Household and Global Corporations

Harriet Rosenberg

INTRODUCTION

This paper will explore certain relatively unstudied aspects of the relationships between multinational corporations and the unwaged work that women do in their households. The activities of multinational corporations since the 1930s but especially in the last two decades have pushed them into far-flung areas of the world. This process of global penetration has seen pesticides, pharmaceuticals, chemical and nuclear wastes dumped in Africa, Asia and the Pacific (Melrose, 1982; Bull, 1982; Dinham and Hines, 1983). The Bhopal disaster is one horrifying example of the implications of this process but smaller-scale events occur on a daily basis. The Third World is not alone in being a dumpsite for global corporations. The household in North America is also intimately linked to this global process

of commodification and danger. In large part it has been the unwaged workers within the household who have come face to face with the contradictory tasks of trying to do their jobs as housewives and mothers, while encountering life-threatening hazards.

The social relationships that women manage in the home, especially as caregivers, are not commodified, for the most part, even under the advanced capitalist conditions of North American society.[1] This separation from the commodity sphere has facilitated the mystification that the home is a haven from outside hazards and is protected from danger by the power of love, reciprocal human feelings, and kinship obligations. But the home is not really a private fortress: it is a sieve, open to all the excesses of industrial development. The household and its environment are a dumpsite for thousands of untested, or undertested chemical products[2]

From *Journal of Business Ethics* 6 (1987) 179–194. © 1987 by D. Reidel Publishing Company. Reprinted by permission.

which endanger the health and safety of its members. And since the sexist gender division of labour in North America has designated women as primary caregivers it is women—wives and mothers—who are responsible for the health and safety of household members. Women confront the contradictions of trying to do their unwaged work of nurturing while being undermined by the dangerous products and practices of capitalist industrial production. The confrontations that these contradictions produce usually come as great surprises to women who may have heard of health and safety dangers in factories or offices but have felt secure and protected in their own homes. Nevertheless, it is in their homes that women begin to piece together the statistics on local miscarriage rates, on high incidences of birth defects and chronic illnesses in the neighbourhood. It is over cups of coffee in their kitchens that women have mobilized and found themselves taking on some of the most powerful forces in our society.

Part I of this article deals with the household's exposure to external dangers such as chemical waste dumps. Part II concerns exposure to less visible and less understood hazards stemming from the penetration of the home by the household products industry. In both cases the household will be analyzed in terms of its relationship to global corporations.

PART I

The Household as a Dumpsite: Prelude to Consciousness and Action

Across the United States and Canada, thousands of housewives and mothers have become political activists. They have left their homes to become collectors and analysts of health statistics, writers of briefs, organizers of press conferences, public speakers,

agitators and demonstrators. In Hardeman County, Tennessee; Rutherford, New Jersey; Pine Ridge Reservation, South Dakota; Alsea, Oregon; Harlem, New York; rural Nova Scotia; Niagara Falls, New York; Scarborough, Ontario; and Whitchurch-Stouffville, Ontario,[3] women have found their households exposed to toxins and pollutants. Their houses have been found to be built on or near nuclear waste dumps (Scarborough, Ont.; Pine Ridge Reservation), they have found deadly pesticides blowing into their windows (Alsea, Oregon; rural Nova Scotia) and chemical residues seeping into homes and schools (Love Canal, Niagara Falls, New York). They have found their air and their water contaminated by lead, PCBs and dioxin[4] (Rosenberg, 1984, Table 2). Women have miscarried at alarmingly high rates, have seen their children born with defects or die of leukemia at early ages.

The women who pieced together the evidence of these disasters and organized grassroots movements have been for the most part unwaged, full-time housewives. (See for example Freudenberg and Zaltzberg's 1984 survey of 110 grass-roots groups in the U.S. and Jackson and Weller, 1984, for a discussion of some Canadian housewife/activists.) Those housewives from white middle class backgrounds rarely had any previous political experience and began their inquiries assuming that government agencies were on their side—and would support them. (Black and native women began with no such trust for politicians and bureaucrats.) These women soon became disillusioned with local and national politicians who treated housewives dismissively and sided with the large corporations. Encountering male dominated 'realpolitik' was a bitter but also energizing experience for many of the women involved in neighbourhood coalitions. They frequently became tougher and more self-confident in their own organizational and political abilities. The political implications of this transformation from isolated housewife to activist has had an important personal impact on the lives of many of the participants and is also an important area for socialist/feminist analysis.

Let us consider in more detail the experiences of one such grass-roots alliance and trace out the course of events which brought housewives out of their kitchens and into major confrontations with big business and big government. My example is drawn from the Concerned Citizens of Whitchurch-Stouffville Inc.

Whitchurch-Stouffville is a small Ontario community just north of Toronto. Between 1962 and 1969 thousands of tons of toxic liquid industrial wastes were poured into a farmer's field never designed as a landfill (i.e., no liners were used) near the community.[5]

> One particular site was called a "garbageman's delight" because "you could pour stuff in one day and when you came back the next it was empty." (Cited in Jackson and Weller, 1982, 62.)

For years, local women who constantly used the water in their domestic routines, asked the Ministry of the Environment about the impact of the dump on their water supply. Groundwater was only 100 feet below the dump and supplied residents' wells and the town of Whitchurch-Stouffville. In the spring of 1981, a group of Stouffville mothers conducted a health survey and found an unexpectedly high number of miscarriages. Like their concerned counterparts in Oregon, Nova Scotia, New Jersey and Niagara Falls, New York, they went to what they thought would be the appropriate government agency with their health survey of the area. Except for one member of the group who had been vice-president of the Scarborough Progressive Conservative Association, they had had no previous political experience. "We were just your average Joe Citizen." Many have since come to the conclusion that "... government is nothing but bullshit and baffling brainlessness" (Interview, April 1984).

The group began as a Moms and Tots meeting in a United Church basement. Before they changed their name to the Concerned Citizens of Whitchurch-Stouffville they called themselves Concerned Mothers and conducted a health survey of a quarter of the homes in Stouffville. They found that the town's miscarriage rate was 26% compared to the provincial rate of 15%. Another survey within a two mile radius of the dump found 37 cases of cancer, 11 miscarriages, seven cases of birth defects and four cases of thyroid problems (*Globe and Mail*, May 12, 1982). Despite repeated statements by the Ministry of the Environment that the water was safe the group was far from reassured and decided to hire independent scientists to test the water. They raised money in the ways in which women raise money, through bake sales and entertainment shows, and spent between $10 000 and $15 000 on tests whose findings were at complete odds with the Ministry's.[6] Furthermore the Citizen's group protested that the government was trying to intimidate them with wiretaps and threats (*Toronto Star*, March 10, 1982) and a barrage of demeaning remarks about housewives. One member of the group dealt with the pressure by wearing a T-shirt to meetings which read: THIS IS NO ORDINARY HOUSEWIFE YOU ARE DEALING WITH. Other grass-roots groups in the U.S. and Canada experienced similar anti-housewife attacks. In Alsea, Oregon, for example, women were organized in opposition to aerial spraying of forests with the herbicide 2, 4, 5–T manufactured by the Dow Chemical Company. Dow countered with accusations that the high miscarriage rates in the region were caused by alleged marijuana use among the mothers of Alsea (Freudenberg and Zaltzberg, 1984, 250).

In Whitchurch-Stouffville housewives have regarded themselves as fighting for life. "Our kids could get cancer ... and that's a crime" (Interview, April 1984). Like their counterparts in other areas of Canada and the U.S. they soon realized that they had to form alliances with other groups (there are about 100 Environmental Non-Government Organizations in Ontario); they had to find out more about government,[6a] about power and about Waste Management Inc. (WMI), the multinational that they charged was polluting their neighbourhood.

Many people in Whitchurch-Stouffville no longer trust the Government of Ontario. They believe in ways that they never understood or believed before that the government is serving the interests of big corporations and finds the housewives to be a nuisance.[7] Said one member of the group protesting the dumpsite:

> Certain people had the rough luck to be situated near a landfill. Are they expendable because of that? (Fran Sainsbury cited in Jackson and Weller, 1981, 66.)

The Household and the Multinational Corporation

The question raised in Whitchurch-Stouffville is the crux of a global problem, in terms of health, responsibility and regulation. Capitalism has developed a new service—the disposal of dangerous industrial waste products. The corporations that deal in this service are enormously powerful in terms of size and profit margins. They view the world in terms of cheap and easily accessible dumpsites. They are "not in business for their health" as the saying goes; they are in business to make a profit. Here is a direct contradiction between the needs of capitalist accumulation and the needs of social reproduction: this contradiction pits the housewife and mother doing her unwaged job against global corporations.

It takes a great deal of digging to find out about such corporations. They purposefully keep very low profiles, and count on the fact that the average citizen is not an investiga-

tive reporter and will not be able to identify the dangerous cargo moving through their community in virtually unmarked trucks.

The company that the people of Whitchurch-Stouffville have been concerned about is called York-Sanitation and is a subsidiary of Waste Management Inc. (WMI). WMI of Oak Brook, Illinois, is currently the largest waste disposal company in the world. The company had a profit margin of 20.4% in 1980 representing $54.9 million (US) of revenue in excess of expenditures (*Moody's Handbook of Common Stocks*). WMI has contracts for waste disposal all over the world including Venezuela, Argentina and Saudi Arabia where they recently signed a $380 million (US) contract. In 1983 WMI purchased Chemical Nuclear Systems and is now involved in the disposal of nuclear wastes.

The corporation has been investigated and sued many times. For example, the state of Illinois has charged [them] with concealment of illegal toxic waste shipments and they are currently being prosecuted in Vickery, Ohio, in a $400 000 suit which alleges that they violated environmental laws in relation to the disposal of PCBs and dioxin (*Wall Street Journal*, 29 March, 1983). In November (4th) 1984 both *Business Week* and *Fortune* reported that the U.S. Environmental Protection Agency had launched a $1.1 million suit against WMI for price fixing and illegal dumping. A year before (27 Dec. 1983) an Australian court refused to allow a WMI contract with Queensland to stand and they were not permitted to operate in that state (*Wall Street Journal*, 27 Dec. 1983). WMI's incinerator ships have been investigated by the United States Environmental Protection Association and even WMI shareholders have brought a suit against their company which "alleges failure to disclose environmental liabilities" (*Wall Street Journal*, 29 March 1983).

Because WMI operates around the world it can offset the problems caused by lawsuits in one place by new deals in another and can count on the fact that there is very little communication between the people of the different areas where it operates. Furthermore WMI has the money and power to launch appeals when and where it wants to. And as in the case of Whitchurch-Stouffville it has continued to operate while appeals are pending. In fact in this Ontario community residents have been greeted with the following picture since 1977. As the Hughes Commission Report put it:

> There is no doubt in my mind (Hon. S.H.S. Hughes) that a great deal of justifiable public resentment was occasioned by the spectacle of the dump trucks rattling past the building where a hearing was convened to entertain an application for authority to do what their owners were doing without any authority whatsoever, and by open violation of orders made by a ministry of the government on the grounds that either an appeal was pending or the officers of the ministry were trying to coax a recalcitrant operator into a mood of compliance with what had been ordered.

(... *Royal Commission ... into WMI*, 1978, 60–61)

The dumptrucks are continuing to operate in Whitchurch-Stouffville but the housewives have not given up. They are still concerned and still want the dumping to stop and they are willing to continue pushing public authorities to serve what they see as being the interests of the citizens rather than the multinational corporations. They still want regular health surveys of the region to test for changes in the levels of diseases and birth defects and they still want their water tested for mutagenicity and carcinogenicity. And they say, because they see the issue in terms of the health and lives of their children, that they have no intention of quitting their fight.

Politics

One of the most ingenious mystifications of capitalism has been to separate ideologically the economic from the political, making it appear as though power, the essence of politics, were somehow outside the realm of the process of capital accumulation (Wood, 1981). Companies as large as WMI control enormous financial, legal and political resources. Compared to the millions that companies like this take in profits a year, the Concerned Mothers of a small Ontario community have very little in the way of resources. WMI, in an uncharacteristic breech of silence concerning their activities once accused the Whitchurch-Stouffville group of being "political elements"—clearly the most negative epithet they could come up with (*Globe and Mail*, 14 May 1982). And in essence the company was quite right, even though what they meant to imply was that the women of Whitchurch-Stouffville were using emotional pressure tactics to press their position with the ministry. The 'politics' of this grass-roots organization go well beyond such petty accusations. Lois Gibbs, the mother/housewife who was president of the Love Canal Homeowners Association, a group that argued that 56% of the children born near the site were mentally or physically disabled has said, "Birth defects have become a political issue'" (Cited in Norwood, 1985, 16).

Gibbs, who has now become a full-time activist, is involved with The Citizen's Clearing House for Hazardous Wastes (Arlington, Virginia) in the United States. This group has pressed for fuller studies of links between residential proximity to chemical dumpsites and birth defects. Thus far, U.S. Centers for Disease Control have been unwilling to undertake such surveys and have attributed higher rates of teratagenicity to improved reporting techniques by doctors. Gibbs' interpretation is different. She has argued that public health officials are deliberately refusing to continue monitoring hot spots, because epidemiological surveys may in fact confirm that industrial wastes are heavily implicated in causing birth defects (Norwood, 1985, 16).

If such correlations were confirmed the findings would be explosive. They would raise questions about the sanctity of the home—a discourse thus far staked out by political conservatives. The conservative symbolic geography of private home and safe family life separated from public and workplace activities is based on the image of home as reward for hard work and law-abiding (i.e., non-militant) habits. (See Wynn, 1985, for a brief history of separate spheres ideology.) Whitchurch-Stouffville, Love Canal and other activist groups have challenged that ideology and have shown that the home is not necessarily a sanctuary or a reward. They have argued that industry and government have lined up to attack the home, not defend it.

PART II

This section discusses factors that contributed to the social isolation of the housewife in the home and facilitated the household's colonization by home products manufacturers. I will analyze how the home came to be a dumpsite in which women/consumers have been actively and successfully encouraged to purchase large quantities of potentially hazardous substances in the belief that they are fulfilling supposedly innate feminine caregiving functions. The marketing of these products has involved the development of costly advertising campaigns but has also produced extremely high profits for multinational corporations who are among the largest and most powerful companies in the world.

The Mortgage-Holding Husband/ Consumerist Wife Ideal: "Because cleaning is caring."

The home products industry began actively expanding in the 1920s and 1930s. Its development was intertwined with political and

ideological trends which devalued collectivist movements in relation to domestic labour. In post World War I North America, anything other than the isolated housewife managing her domestic world alone, came to be identified as politically subversive. The imagery and symbols of these decades continue to have profound effects on how domestic labour is organized and carried out today, and influence what has and what has not been problematized in relation to domestic labour in both personal and theoretical terms.

Extremely significant for Canadian and American domestic life had been the defeat of the collectivist branch of the home economics movement, which since the late 19th century had developed models of co-operative solutions to the problems of housework, food distribution (consumer's co-operatives) and preparation (co-operative dining clubs and cooked food delivery services) and childcare (daycare). By the 1920s individualist trends among home economists were in the ascendancy presenting models of the home as a private, feminized and isolated domestic sphere. The model of the private home paid for by the male breadwinner in long term installments and the female un-waged caregiver who maintained the home and raised children by herself became the dominant model, in North America, in conscious opposition to collectivist models which were being developed in Russia after the 1917 Revolution.

The concept of the mortgage-holding male appealed to industrialists who saw it as a way of taming an increasingly radicalized and militant labour force. In 1919 when over 4 000 000 workers were involved in demonstrations in the U.S. (and major strikes in Canada as well as mass rallies of unemployed veterans), industrialists became intrigued by the idea that labour peace could be bought by making small suburban homes available to white male workers. Representatives of the housing industry phrased it this way:

Happy workers invariably mean bigger profits, while unhappy workers are never a good investment ... A wide diffusion of home ownership has long been recognized as fostering a stable and conservative habit ... The man owns his own home but in a sense his home owns him, checking his impulses. (Industrial Housing Associates, 1919, *Good Homes Make Contented Workers* cited in Hayden 1982, 283–4).

By 1931, this approach had been institutionalized in U.S. public policy. That year President Hoover convened the Conference on Home Building and Home Owning, which put government support behind a national strategy of home ownership for men "'of sound character and industrious habits'" (Cited in Hayden, 1982, 2896). The coalition of those who favoured this policy included former campaigners against slums and even some feminists. But for the most part backing came from real estate speculators, housing developers and the manufacturers of consumer goods.

The involvement of this latter group is significant because the move to cheap urban housing which aimed at tying men to long-term mortgages also aimed at tying women to consumerism or 'consumptionism' as one of its leading advocates (Christine Frederick) in the 1920s and 30s called it (Hayden, 1982. See also Ewen, 1976). The gendered social division of labour was to work as follows. Men were to be breadwinners and homeowners able to liberate their wives and children from the evils and hazards of the workplace. The dependent-wife family (Cameron, 1983) meant not only the demobilization of women from the workforce and the closure of wartime daycare centres but the possibility that working class women could devote themselves full-time to domestic tasks. Higher steady wages for husbands were still too small to pay for servants to help with the childcare and housework but North American industry in combina-

tion with the teaching of home economics in schools and community centres (see for example, Parkers, 1899, "Training for Housework in Canada") would create a class of "scientific household engineers" who did not need servants or collective social supports (Hayden, 1982, 386). Each woman was to become the epitome of Taylorist efficiency, alone, in her own home. (See for example Frederick's *Household Engineering: Scientific Management in the Home*, 1920).

It has been pointed out that Taylorist techniques of efficiency were logically impossible in the home since scientific management required scale, specialization and the division of labour while the essence of privatized housework is precisely its isolated unspecialized character (Hayden, 1982; Wynn, 1985). Efficiency was a smokescreen, according to Hayden, for the real aim of the home economics movement as developed by Frederick and her colleagues which was to turn the household into a unit of consumption. Frederick and others worked as consultants to large corporations and advertising agencies becoming specialists on how to sell things to women, and developing advertising techniques aimed at women's supposed suggestibility, passivity and inferiority complexes. (See *Selling Mrs. Consumer*, 1928, dedicated to Herbert Hoover and for a later era see Janet Wolff, 1958, *What Makes Women Buy*.)

The world, in which men earned and women bought, did not become a widespread reality until the post-Second World War boom of cheap suburban housing supported by government policy in both the U.S. and Canada in the 1950s. The image of women's domesticated role which preceded that boom had decades to spread and fix itself in popular consciousness. Since the 1920s advertising and the household products industry had worked hard to stereotype housework as an extension of the feminine role, an expression of love of family and not socially useful work that could potentially be organized in a variety of different ways. Housework became conceptualized as a personal task made easier by the purchase of an ever-increasing array of products which women bought because they wished to care for their families in the best, most modern way possible.

An ironic boon to advertisers was the fact that despite it all women did not seem always to love isolated housework and often yearned to find ways to involve others, even though this upset the social conventions of a male-female division of labour. Colgate-Palmolive, for example, hit upon the sales advantages of this discontent years ago with its ads for a home cleaner that was symbolized by a white knight.[8] A Colgate vice-president explained the significance of the ad this way:

> We believe that every women has a white knight in her heart of hearts. To her he symbolizes a good powerful force that can enter her life and clean up that other man in her life, her husband, who symbolizes exactly the opposite of what the white knight stands for (*Printer's Ink*, 1966, 85).

In the isolation of their housework, while serving their families women have been encouraged by advertisers to fantasize about other men but in ways that are not a threat to marital stability. The somewhat ambiguous figure of Mr. Clean has been consciously portrayed by advertisers as being a eunuch, and, therefore not a problem in terms of female alliances or male egos (*Ibid.*).

While variations on this theme of fantasy domesticity have continued to appear, one theme is never raised: women are discouraged from asking any questions about the safety of the products they buy. They are to concentrate on "ring around the collar," extra moist cake mixes and shiny floors that never yellow. They are never to ask questions about the chemicals used to attain these dazzling effects. They are never to ask questions about the unsafe and toxic qualities of what they

bring into their homes because otherwise the whole myth of the home as separate sanctuary and reward might crumble.

Let the Buyer Beware

The development of the mortgage-holding consumerist household ideal has permitted manufacturers to dump an enormous variety of virtually untested chemicals into the home and to shift the responsibility for product safety onto the consumer rather than the producer. There are literally thousands of products that one could discuss. In the area of food, for example, housewives and health activists have been concerned with the issue of food additives—everything from salt, sugar, preservatives, artificial colours and flavours to lead leeching out of the solder of evaporated milk cans to hormones and antibiotics in meat.[9] These are not simple issues of the kind with which public health officials deal. These are issues which lead to the heart of major world corporations such as plantations, agribusinesses and food processing companies, and also have to do with the most fundamental organizational structures of production, advertising, distribution, and health. The presence of sugar, salt, caffeine, BHA, BHT, and pesticide residuals in food has raised key questions about social, economic and political organization as well as health concerns.

Other areas of concern are the dumping of pesticides, asbestos, lead, PCBs, formaldehyde, aerosols, vinyl chloride and appliances which pose carbon monoxide and radiation hazards in the home. (See Rosenberg, 1984, for a discussion of these hazards.) Also of concern are the products we use to clean our homes—the soaps, detergents, softeners, and polishes. This latter category will be discussed in some detail because these products are usually viewed as benign and the hazards they pose are generally unknown as are the connections between these products and multinational corporations.

I have argued that, for the last 50 years, the notion of the isolated housewife fulfilling her feminized caregiving destiny has been developed, used and refined to facilitate the dumping of mountains of unsafe products in the home. What is known about these products is that they are supposed to make women feel satisfied in the thought that they are creating comfortable happy homes.[10] (Of course we also know that a large percentage of women hate doing housework. See, for example, Oakley, 1975; Luxton, 1980; Proulx, 1978.)

I have written about the health and safety problems that detergents, polishes and cleaners pose in the home elsewhere (Rosenberg, 1984). Table I (pp. 361) summarizes my findings. What is not known and as far as I can tell [is] not being studied is what the impact of long term exposure to these products might mean. If two ounces of dishwashing detergent can be lethal to a small child, what is the health outcome of 30 years of exposure to detergent residue? If one or two drops of furniture polish can be fatal if ingested, if aspiration can cause a form of chemical pneumonia, if some products are routinely contaminated by cancer-causing nitrosamines; then what are the long term effects of spraying and inhaling while cleaning the dining room table? If a fifth of an ounce of disinfectant can kill a small child, which is more dangerous in the long run: the microbe or the disinfectant? And finally what are the combined effects of these cleaners, sprays, and pesticides?

The success of advertising in directing women away from health and safety questions is in large part attributable to the enormous size of the advertising budgets available to these corporations.

Soap Business: Harvesting Profits in Households

Proctor and Gamble (as of 1978) is the biggest advertiser in the United States, spending $554 million (US) a year. This is more money than such major corporations as General Motors, AT&T or Gulf and Western spend in a year on advertising (Moskowitz et al., 1980, 359). Proctor and Gamble harvests enormous profits in the kitchens of the world. As of 1980, its sales were estimated at $9.3 billion (US), with profits at $557 million (US) (*Ibid.*, 499). In the United States Proctor and Gamble is the largest manufacturer of bar soap, cake mixes, laundry detergent, toilet tissue, toothpaste, diapers and deodorants and the third largest producer of mouthwash, salad and cooking oils, and coffee (*Ibid.*, 355). Its products are sold under a variety of different names suggesting to consumers that they are actually choosing from a variety of different products. However, only the names are different—the products are essentially the same.[11]

Most of the home cleaning and bar soap market is controlled by only three corporations: Proctor and Gamble, Colgate-Palmolive and Unilever. These three corporations accommodate each other and do not compete; the fiction of competition is maintained within the differently named soaps and detergents produced by each conglomerate. The real aim of advertising is not to promote Tide over Cheer but to constantly assert the need for these products.

Enormous profits have been made, but only by those companies that were big enough to market and promote them. Thus when chemists at Monsanto (the fifth largest chemical company in the U.S.) invented a low-sudsing detergent in 1957, they found that even they were too small to capitalize the marketing programme necessary to sell the detergent. "Monsanto people blanched" at the price and sold the product to Lever Bros. (Moskowitz et al., 1980, 611). Monsanto bowed out of sales and promotion and focussed its attention on making most of the chemicals which are used by the major manufacturers of soaps and detergents.[12]

In the past the advertising industry has expressed concern about the fact that there was very little difference between the products on the market. *Printer's Ink*, a leading journal of the United States advertising industry, noted in 1966:

> Is such advertising an economic waste—a drain on society? The differences in scents and the amount of chemical brighteners among brands are not regarded by many economists as justification for spending millions on advertising [just] to establish brand preferences.
>
> (*Printer's Ink*, 1966, 85)

The article went on to predict that the advertising structure as it then existed would inevitably collapse. Instead it has expanded. This is not only due to the expansion of selling techniques and the development of new "needs" and new products in North America but to the expansion of activities in the Third World.

In sales to the Third World it is the Unilever Corporation which dominates,[13] through its subsidiaries Hindustan Lever and United Africa Company (Pedlar, 1974). On a world scale the Unilever Corporation is the ninth largest corporation on the globe, just after the major oil corporations. Women were from the beginning (1885) targeted by this international empire. Unilever (formerly Lever Brothers) was among the pioneers of market research. Between 1885 and 1905 Lever Brothers spent the sum of £2 million in advertising—an unheard of amount in those days, in campaigns directed against working class housewives.[14] Lever exhorted his managers to try to achieve "hypnotic effect" with their advertising, and to "build a halo around the product" (cited in Counter Information Services, n.d., 92). By 1899 soap advertising was directed at children "... so they will bother their mothers to buy some" (*Ibid.*, 23).

Unilever, with over 800 subsidiaries, has rarely identified itself as the parent company. Unlike the Nestlé Corporation for example, it has striven for a policy of anonymity so that workers and consumers in different areas rarely know with whom they are dealing. The company's activities range from owning plantations that supply palm oil, cocoa, tea and coffee to companies trading in agricultural commodities, shipping lines, warehouses; they own factories processing primary products into margarine, cooking oils and of course detergent, soaps and other cleaning products. They own supermarket chains and marketing organizations which distribute their products. Their subsidiaries handle every imaginable level of production, distribution and marketing from growing timber to designing wallpaper. They have a network of laboratories producing pesticides and conducting genetic engineering projects (*Ibid.*, 8). Unilever is the largest food company in the world. It has over 1000 products on the market; none of which bears the name Unilever.[15]

This company which touches the daily lives of millions amassed sales to third parties (i.e., excluding intracompany trading) in 1979 of £9 842 million—"an amount roughly equivalent to the GNP of Angola, Benin, Botswana, Berundi, the Central African Empire, Chad, Congo, Gabon, Gambia, Guinea, Guinea-Bissau, Lesotho, Malawi, Mali, Mauritania, Mauritius, Mozambique, Niger, Rwanda, Senegal, Sierra Leone, Somalia, Swaziland, Togo, and Upper Volta" (Dinham and Hines, 1983, 167).

Politics

What have been the responses to such power? In North America we often see the small scale skirmishes between mother/housewives and these major corporations acted out in women's pages of our local newspapers. Women write in to complain about faulty pouring spouts on bleach containers, or lung irritations caused by cleaning the oven, or baby bottle nipples contaminated by cancer-causing nitrosamines[16] (Fishbein, 126–127). The "consumer or

TABLE I	Dangers of home-cleaning products	
Product	**Dangers**	**Alternatives**
Drain cleaner (lye)	The most dangerous product in home use. Can eat through mouth, skin, stomach, or damage eyes. There is no effective antidote.	Rubber plunger or plumber's snake. Prevent clogging with drain strainer. Use hot water + $1/4$ cup washing soda.
Toilet bowl cleaner (ammonia)	Can burn skin on contact, or respiratory tract if inhaled. Liquid from intank cleaner harmful if swallowed. Fumes fatal if mixed with chlorine bleach.	Scrub with stiff brush.
Scouring powder	Rapidly absorbed through mucous membranes and scraped skin. Can cause red rash in any area that comes in contact with product.	Salt or baking soda clean and disinfect effectively.
Oven cleaner (lye)	Extremely dangerous. Can burn skin and eyes. Inhaling fumes is hazardous. Some brands don't have childproof closures.	Damp cloth and baking soda. Scrape hardened material with a knife. One commercial product contains no lye.
Chlorine bleach	Can cause corrosive burns if swallowed. Fumes fatal if mixed with ammonia.	Safer when diluted.
Window or glass cleaner	Swallowing can cause nausea or vomiting. Can irritate eyes. Lethal dose for a child is over one pint.	Warm tap water alone or $1/2$ cup white vinegar mixed with 1 quart cool water. For chrome, use flour and a dry cloth.
Disinfectants	May irritate skin and eyes. Spray can irritate throat. May cause nausea and diarrhea if swallowed. Lethal dose for small child is $1/5$ oz.	Soap and water.
All-purpose cleaner	Hazardous to eyes. Can burn throat and stomach lining if swallowed. Products containing petroleum distillates can cause a fatal lung condition.	Diluted bleach or detergent. A slice of potato removes fingerprints on painted wood.
Dishwashing detergent	A lethal dose for a small child is 2 oz. Enzymes can be highly irritating.	Use less. Rinse dishes immediately after use. Scour with a stiff brush and/or salt and baking soda. Soak burned pots overnight, boil, cool, and scour.
Automatic dishwashing detergent	Major cause of poisoning in children. Irritating to skin, eyes, respiratory tract. Residue on dishes may have long-term effects.	Use less. Vinegar in rinse cuts spotting, leaves less residue to be ingested.
Laundry detergent	A lethal dose for a small child is $1/7$ oz. Swallowing can cause nausea, vomiting, diarrhea. A few grains can damage eye cornea if left untended.	Soap powders are safer. Liquid laundry detergents do not contain sodium carbonate, a corrosive present in detergent powders.
Furniture polish	A drop or two of solvent fatal if swallowed. Flammable. Aspiration can cause a form of chemical pneumonia. Nitrosamines (present in some brands) can be absorbed through skin and cause cancer in laboratory animals.	Tsp. of vinegar in a cup water; buff with a dry cloth for wood furniture. Use material [sic] oil for shine.

Sources: On drain cleaners, see *Calpirg Reports* (June 1981). "Factsheet." Center for Science in the Public Interest, *The Household Pollutants Guide* (Garden City, N.Y.: Anchor Books, 1978), pp. 180–90. Joanne Robertson, "Housework is Hazardous to Your Health," Pollution Probe (Toronto), 1982, Women's Occupational Health Resource Center. "Factsheet for Women Who Work in the Home," January 1979. "Alkali Products Dangerous to Eyes," *Occupational Health Bulletin* 26, nos. 1–2 (1971): 4.
On toilet bowl cleaners, see Robertson *op. cit.*, *Housework is Hazardous to Your Health, op. cit.*, Center for Science in the Public Interest. Household Pollutants Guide, *op. cit.*, "Toilet Bowl Cleaners," *Consumer Reports* (4, 3), March 1975: 157.
On scouring powder, see Robertson, *op. cit.*
On oven cleaners, see Robertson, *op. cit.*, "Oven Cleaners," *Consumer Reports* (45, 10), October 1980: 598–99.
On chlorine bleach, see *Calpirg Reports, op. cit.*, Robertson, *op. cit.*
On window and glass cleaners, see *Calpirg Reports, op. cit.*, Robertson, *op. cit.*
On disinfectants, see Robertson, *op. cit.*, "Household Cleaners," *Consumer Reports* (39, 9), September 1974: 677.
On all-purpose cleaners, see *Calpirg Reports, op. cit.*, Robertson, *op. cit.*, "All-purpose Cleaners," *Consumer Reports* (44, 2), February 1979: 81.
On dishwashing detergent, see *Calpirg Reports, op. cit.*, Robertson, *op. cit.*
On automatic dishwashing detergent, see Robertson, *op. cit.*
On laundry detergent, see *Calpirg Reports, op. cit.*: Center for Science in the Public Interest, *op. cit.*, pp. 149–50: Emmanuel Sommers, "Risk Assessment for Environmental Health," *Canadian Journal of Public Health* (7), November/December 1979: 389.
On furniture polish, see *Calpirg Reports, op. cit.*, Robertson, *op. cit.*, "Furniture Polishes," *Consumer Reports* (44, 7), July 1979: 496.

perts" hired by local papers treat each issue as an isolated problem. Consumer objections of this sort are easily absorbed into the mythology that corporations will always try to make their products better and safer if concerns are pointed out to them.

More subversive to the ideology of consumerism are public education activities carried out by ecology groups who are not dependent on advertising dollars for their existence. In this context just naming names and pointing out some of the dangers of these products can be very effective. It has been because of alliances between consumer groups, legal groups and ecology groups that such dangerous products as Captan, a fungicide, have come under government scrutiny and may eventually be banned.[17]

Other effective alliances have come from the international sphere where organizations like the International Organization of Consumers' Unions operate. In 1981 for example the IOCU with head offices in Brussels and Penang, launched Consumer Interpol.[18] There are about 52 groups working in 32 countries which are actively participating in this network. They are also in close contact with other highly successful coalitions like the International Babyfood Network, and Health Action International, which coordinated an informal grapevine of about 200 groups working on pharmaceutical issues and which is in contact with Pesticides Action Network, itself representing about 50 working groups. It is clear to Third World health activists that the multinationals are using their countries as dumpsites for hazardous wastes, for untested or banned pharmaceuticals, for toxic pesticides and for dangerous consumer products. In the summer of 1985, North American non-government organization (NGOs) delegates met with their Third World counterparts in the context of the Nairobi Conference to share information and discuss strategies in dealing with global corporations.[19] These coalitions are concrete examples of how

groups have developed ways to expand and attack the practice of the multinationals of turning the home into a dumpsite.

CONCLUSION

Health issues and consumer issues have come to be defined as women's issues, because women act as our principal caregivers and are seen as being responsible for the reproduction of non-commodified reciprocal relationships in the home. Mothers, and wives are under social obligations to keep the family safe and nurture human feelings of intimacy, sharing and security. But this caregiving work is not done in a vacuum: world economic systems are dominated by capital accumulation and the spread of commodified relationships.

This process has been resisted in a variety of ways, as people have confronted not only exploitation in the workplace but also threats to themselves and their families at home. Love, attachment and security are still highly valued and these values in relation to the home have been politicized. The New Conservatives have characterized the discourse in terms of a defence of home and family as a private feminized sanctuary apart from the public masculinized domain. Separation of spheres and of gender roles are crucial to this conception. The New Right has attributed problems within the family to feminists defined by them as women who want abortions, sex-education, day care and non-gendered division of labour in the home and in the workplace (Freudenberg and Zaltzberg, 1984; Harding, 1978).

But the activities of the people and groups discussed in this paper have the potential for shifting the locus of the discourse to an examination of capitalism and the responsibilities of democratic governments. Environmentalist, consumer and health groups, dealing with essentially the same issues as the New Right in terms of concern with life, health, and caregiving have identified different enemies and are forging a different political discourse. They have found the home to be a contrived and inauthentic refuge and attribute this finding not to feminism but to corporate greed, and inadequate government regulation.

Such groups are amorphous; they do not form a coherent social movement. Often group structure is decentralized. Such groups, by their very existence provide lived alternatives to the alienating and oppressive conditions around them. Because they are usually composed of society's less powerful people, they are rarely taken seriously by those with power. Such grass-roots groups are like social guerrillas who deal in localized hit and run operations, not full-fledged battles. But herein may lie their advantage. They are harder for power structures to define, locate, co-opt or eradicate. They may be suppressed in one place but reform and reappear in another. They have the weapons of ridicule and embarrassment using the sacredness of motherhood ideology to confound their enemies. In the past (see for example, Kaplan, 1982) as well as in the present women transcending their domestic roles formed coalitions and formulated radical social visions which have brought women into large scale collective action against economic and political power holders. Whether these actions are mobilized by the right or the left is historically contingent but the capacity of housewives to draw on social networks and personal resources holds out the promise of new patterns of empowerment and new alliances for social change.

Paper presented at *Women and the Invisible Economy*, Conference, Institute Simone de Beauvoir, Concordia University, Montreal, Quebec, Feb. 22, 1985.

ENDNOTES

1. There are certain highly significant exceptions. Much that now relates to birth control, the management of dying and death is commodified, for example, in the marketing of contraceptives by multinational pharmaceutical companies or the franchising of profit-making nursing homes. Also significant is the relatively new phenomenon of surrogate motherhood, although certain kinds of adoption, especially from Native reserves and overseas, has been and continues to be a means by which relatively wealthy white middle class people purchase children from the poor. While the sale of sex in the form of prostitution is ancient, the recent expansion of pornography has made it a major growth industry.

2. In the wake of the Bhopal disaster the *New York Times* published an article on potential chemical hazards. Citing a survey by the U.S. National Academy of Science, March 1984, the *Times* listed the following estimates about the quality of information available on the potential health hazards of selected chemicals, expressed as a percentage of the chemicals in each of the groups.

Group	Quality of Information			No. of Chemicals Studied
	A	**B**	**C**	
Pesticide Ingredients	10%	52%	38%	3,350
Pharmaceuticals	18%	42%	56%	3,410
Food Additives	5%	49%	46%	8,627
Other Commercial Chemicals (with sales of at least one million pounds a year)	11%	11%	78%	12,880

A = Adequate Information

B = Incomplete Information

C = No Information

Source: *New York Times*, Dec. 16, 1984; National Academy of Sciences 1984. Toxicity Testing: Strategy to Determine Needs and Priorities, Washington: National Academy Press.

3. *Hardeman County, Tennessee,* was the site of chemical dumping by Velsicol Chemical Company. Local wells were contaminated with 12 chemicals including five known carcinogens—benzene, chlordane, heptachlor, endrin, dioxin. Eighty residents have launched a $2.5 billion class action suit against the company (Freudenberg and Zaltzberg, 1984, 246–7).

Rutherford, New Jersey, is a cancer hot spot. In this comfortable middle class suburb, the leukemia rate for children ages 5 to 19 was six times higher than the U.S. national average. Causes for high cancer rates in this community include: 42 industrial concerns using organic chemicals including known carcinogens within three miles of the local school; intensive mosquito spraying yearly, including the use of DDT until 1967; exposure to high levels of automobile exhaust; exposure to microwave radiation from two airports and an industrial research facility. Parent activists in this community have forced a plant using benzene to shut down and with the support of labour and environmentalist groups have forced the state of New Jersey to establish a cancer registry to aid in epidemiological research (Freudenberg and Zaltzberg, 1984, 247–249).

Pine Ridge Reservation, South Dakota, has been the site of high rates of miscarriage (38% in 1979 compared to generally acceptable rates of 10% to 20%). A local hospital has also reported extremely high rates of birth defects. Other studies have shown that the reservation had higher than average rates of bone and gynecological cancers. Widespread spraying of pesticides and herbicides and exposure to uranium tailings and nuclear waste have been implicated in these health disorders. WARN (Women of All Red Nations) has been active in

trying to improve health conditions on this reservation (Freudenberg and Zaltzberg, 1984, 249–250).

Alsea, Oregon, is a rural logging community where high levels of herbicidal spraying have been linked to an elevated miscarriage and birth defects rate. Women in that community have taken on the Dow Chemical Corporation, manufacturers of the defoliant 2, 4, 5–T, the United States Forest Service and the United States Environmental Protection Agency to have spraying banned (Freudenberg and Zaltzberg, 1984, 251–252). A comparable event has occurred in rural Cape Breton, Nova Scotia, where local residents have recently fought and lost a court case to prevent the spraying of a 2, 4, 5–T and 2, 4–D mixture. This mixture was known as Agent Orange when it was used by the United States army as a defoliant during the Vietnam war. It has been sprayed in Nova Scotia by Nova Scotia Forest Industries, a Swedish multinational, to destroy competing hardwoods in areas reforested with the softwood cash crop. Herbicide efficacy has never been demonstrated. Critics contend that its use and putative value are aimed primarily at justifying unecological forest harvesting practices. Dioxin, a byproduct of this herbicide, is a carcinogen (Labonté, 1984, 4–9).

Recently Dow Chemical, involved in a major class action suit brought by veterans of the Vietnam war who were exposed to Agent Orange, settled out of court. Dow agreed to pay the veterans and/or their survivors $180 million. The plight of women nurses exposed to Agent Orange during the Vietnam war is discussed in *Family Circle* magazine (Distelheim, 1985).

In addition, the U.S. government has purchased the entire town of Times

Beach, Missouri, for $30 million. The town had been exposed to dioxin-laden oil which was sprayed on its streets to keep dust levels down (Labonté, 1984, 4). Niagara Falls, New York, site of Love Canal, Bloody Run Creek and other chemical dumps has been identified as releasing toxins into Lake Ontario. Dioxin may be among them. Citizens Rebelling Against Wastes in Ontario, Inc. and Operation Clean Niagara have been active on the Canadian side of the Niagara River (Jackson and Weller, 1984, 30).

The Love Canal Home Owners Association was influential in forcing the United States government to evacuate 239 families closest to a chemical dumpsite in 1980. Research at the Rosewell Park Memorial Institute in Buffalo, New York, indicated higher than accepted rates of miscarriage and birth defects including mental retardation (Orwen, 1985, Toronto Star, 26 January). Some Love Canal area residents who relocated three kilometres away now find themselves exposed to toxins from the Cecos dumpsite (Orwen, 1985, *Toronto Star*, 2 February).

In *Harlem, New York City*, mothers concerned over high levels of asbestos fibres in their children's school forced the city to spend $100 000 on repairs. A survey by the New York City Board of Education in 1977 showed that 400 New York schools had asbestos problems (Freudenberg and Zaltzberg, 1984, 252–253). Asbestos is a potent carcinogen found in insulation products, drywall patching compounds, ceiling tiles, as well as some baby powders, some hair dryers, oven mitts and ironing board covers (Rosenberg, 1984, Table II). The hazards of asbestos are well-documented. As early as 1913 both United States and Canadian insurance companies refused to sell life policies to asbestos workers (Epstein, 1978, 83–4). Johns-Manville is a leading manufacturer of asbestos products. Workers in its Scarborough plant have sustained high rates of disabling chronic respiratory diseases including lung cancer (Ibid., 85). This multinational has recently been accused of dumping 300 000 tons of crushed asbestos in Scarborough near Highland Creek, a small stream flowing into Lake Ontario (*Toronto Clarion*, 1984, Vol. VIII, No. 4).

4. Concern over PCB exposure has mobilized citizens in the west-end of Toronto (who live near a CGE plant). Recently, high levels of PCBs have been identified in Pottersburg Creek in London, Ontario. Joseph Cummins, a geneticist at the University of Western Ontario, has called Pottersburg Creek one of Canada's largest environment disasters. "It's unprecedented to have PCBs loaded with dioxins running through residential neighbourhoods," according to Cummins (Kenna, 1985, *Toronto Star*, 2 February).

5. In Dec. 1979 the *Globe and Mail* reported that the government had found 800 previously unrecorded dumpsites in southern Ontario (*Globe and Mail*, Dec. 11, 1979). The research team making that survey also estimated that there may be between 2000 and 3000 unrecorded dumps in Ontario as a whole. In 1979 the U.S. Environmental Protection Agency estimated that there were 50 000 chemical dumps in the U.S. Between 1200 and 2000 are thought to pose significant dangers (Hart 1979, 25). In the U.S., it has been argued that 125 billion pounds of hazardous wastes were produced in 1980—enough to fill 2000 Love Canals (Brownstein, 1981). In Canada, the federal government has estimated that as of 1982, there are 3.2 million tonnes of toxic wastes generated

in this country (Environment Canada, 1982, Vol. 3, 8). About half of these wastes come from Ontario which produces 1 650 107 tonnes annually (Waste Management Corporation, 1982, 58).

6. The Minister of the Environment (Ontario) Keith Norton stated in 1981 that on the basis of "the most comprehensive testing of any water supply in the history of this province using some of the most sophisticated methods available to us," that there was "outstanding water quality in the community" of Whitchurch-Stouffville (Legislature of Ontario, Legislative Debates, 11 June 1981, p. 1486 and 16 June 1981, p. 1650).

6a. One thing they discovered was that York Sanitation, a subsidiary of Waste Management Inc. of Oakbrook, Ill., had made a $35 000 contribution to the Progressive Conservative party of Ontario in 1977 which was laundered through Chicago, Luxembourg and Italy. The Royal Commission which investigated this unseemly donation in 1978 admitted that it contravened the *Election Finance Act* of 1975 but laid no criminal charges (Ontario, Report of the Royal Commission Appointed to Inquire Into Waste Management Inc. etc., The Hon. S.H. Hughes, March 30, 1978).

7. Not all members of the community supported the efforts of the Concerned Citizens groups. According to Fran Sutton, some Stouffville residents thought of the women as "'mouthy dames,' and wished '... they would go ... look after their pots and pans and children and keep out of this. They are just hysterical women'" (Jackson and Weller, 1984, 30).

8. Advertisement (television) for Pinesol cleaner, March 1985.

9. See for example, Hall, 1974, on the issues of additives overprocessing and the destruction of nutrition, carcinogens (DES) and antibiotics in meat; Consumer Reports on lead in evaporated milk, lowering sugar and salt content in baby foods etc. The Nestlé boycott has generated important literature on multinational corporations, food and health. See also Weir and Schapiro, *Circle of Poison*, on the return of banned pesticides in food imported into North America from the Third World.

10. What is also mystifying about these products is the conditions under which they are made and distributed both in terms of the working conditions inside the factories which produce them and in terms of the health and safety concerns within those factories. We don't normally pick up a box of detergent and ask what the hourly wage of the worker who made it was. In fact we have little knowledge of the production process involved in making laundry detergent. The whole process is socially and culturally camouflaged. Our schools do not tour detergent plants, or the chemical companies that make the dyes, emulsifiers and solvents that go into the detergent. There are no TV documentaries about the men or women in these plants. Are they unionized, do they have adequate health and safety equipment? These are questions totally absent from public discourse and in fact very hard for the specialist to investigate. The barriers preventing problematization and investigation are socially constructed. Once questions are asked about the working conditions of lettuce pickers, for example, alarming truths about exploitation, child labour or the unsafe use of pesticides may emerge. Thus manufacturers must make a concerted effort to prevent consumers from asking: "Who made this? How did it get to my kitchen?"

One strategy of deflection has been to present the labour process as a fairy tale.

Advertisements tell the public that products are made by elves, "Crans," giants or benign patriarchs like "Mr. Kraft," "Mr. Christie," and "Aunt Beatrice." Fantasy labour complements fantasy housework symbolized by blonde middle class mothers dancing or singing in glowingly well appointed homes as camera angles pan to describe the intense satisfaction they feel in cleaning " ... because cleaning is caring ...".

11. Among dish detergents P&G produces Ivory Liquid, Joy and Dawn. In laundry detergents P&G makes Bold, Cheer, Dash, Duz, Era, Gain Oxydol, Tide, Dreft and Ivory Snow. In bar soap Ivory, Camay, Coast, Lava and Safeguard are all made by P&G. And in general cleaners and softeners, P&G makes Mr. Clean, Spic and Span, Top Job. P&G toothpastes are Crest and Gleem; deodorants are Secret and Sure; diapers are Pampers and Luvs.

12. Monsanto is also a major producer of pesticides for agribusinesses and in this regard has become involved in advertising. As the pesticide industry came under increasing attack by environmentalists and health activists, Monsanto has launched a $45 million (US) campaign to assure consumers that chemicals are 'natural' and that its herbicides, like Vegadex discussed in TV commercials, are beneficial. In independent studies, Vegadex has been shown to be carcinogenic to rats and mice, including breast cancers in the females of both species, tumors of the stomach in male rats and of the lung in male mice. It is considered to be unsafe for agricultural workers (Epstein, 1978, 394).

13. In the United States, Proctor and Gamble, Colgate-Palmolive and Unilever control 90% of the market, Unilever has only 18% of detergent sales, Proctor and Gamble has 50% and Colgate-Palmolive has 22% (Counter Information Services, n.d. 12–13).

14. Global market penetration seems boundless. In the summer of 1983, while I was doing research in a remote corner of the Kalahari desert in Botswana, I found Bingo detergent available on the virtually barren shelves of a small store.

15. In some African countries a large percentage of the waged workforce is in some way dependent on Unilever (*Ibid.*, 7. See also R. Howard, 1978).

16. Former Consumer Affairs Minister Judy Erola set a limit for nitrosamines of 30 parts per billion in baby bottle nipples to be lowered to 10 p.p.b. in Jan. 1985 (*Toronto Star*, 16 February 1984).

17. Captan, a fungicide, is hazardous to pregnant woman and young children. It has been found to cause cancer and birth defects in pregnant animals. It is used by home gardeners as well as commercial florists and gardeners and unbeknownst to most people, it is also found in cosmetics, wallpaper paste, vinyl textiles, and polyethylene garbage bags (Rosenberg, 1984).

Captan has been tested and approved by Industrial Bio-Test Laboratories in the United States and their findings on this and over 100 other chemicals were used by Canadian regulators to grant registration for the use of these chemicals in this country. Unfortunately IBT officials have been tried and found guilty of having falsified tests on more than 100 chemicals allowed for use in Canada by the departments of Agriculture and Health and Welfare (Hall, 1981; Vigod and Woodsworth, 1982; Schneider, 1983). The Canadian government knew of this problem in 1977 but did not release details to the public until 1980 (Toronto Health Advocacy Unit, City Hall, 1981). Pressure by ecology groups after the IBT affair finally forced the

Ontario Ministry of the Environment to act on Captan.

18. When a Consumer Interpol member learns of a potential hazard in his or her country, the member will investigate and if convinced that something is amiss, will notify the Consumer Interpol coordinator in Penang, sending along whatever evidence has been gathered. The coordinator drawing on the advice of experts on such issues as food, drugs, pesticides, consumer law will sift the evidence. If the suspected hazard is confirmed, the coordinator sends out Alert notices to all groups in the network. The message that goes out directs activists to contact manufacturers or distributors immediately, to contact the relevant government agencies and agitate loudly in the press (*New Internationalist*, 1983; 28–29).

19. Personal communication from a delegate from the Manitoba Council for International Co-operation on joint efforts between MCIC, IOCU, and HAI.

20. For a fuller discussion of recent patterns of organization in the United States see Freudenberg, 1984.

REFERENCES

Brownstein, Richard: 1981, "The Toxic Tragedy," in R. Nader et al. (eds.), *Who's Poisoning America?* Sierra Club Books: San Francisco.

Bull, David: 1982, *A Growing Problem: Pesticides and the Third World Poor*, Oxfam: Oxford, U.K.

Cameron, Barbara: 1983, "The Sexual Division of Labour and Class Struggle," *Social Studies/Études Socialistes: A Canadian Annual*, pp. 40–50.

Cyng-Jones, T.W.: n.d., Unilever, Geneva: International Union of Food and Allied Workers' Association.

Counter Information Service: n.d., "Unilever's World," Report No. 1.

Dinham, Barbara and Colin Hines: 1983, *Agribusiness in Africa*, Earth Resources Research: Birmingham, U.K.

Distelheim, Rochelle: 1985, "There's a Time Bomb Ticking Inside My Body," *Family Circle*, Oct. 89 (14): 46 and ff.

Dowie, Mark: *Circle of Poison*

Epstein, Samuel S.: 1978, *The Politics of Cancer*, Sierra Club Books: San Francisco.

Ewen, Stuart: 1976, *Captains of Consciousness*, McGraw-Hill: New York.

Fishbein, Laurence: "An Overview of Potential Mutagenic Problems Posed by Some Pesticides and Their Trace Impurities," *Environmental Health Perspectives* 27, 126–127.

Freudenberg, Nicholas and Ellen Zaltzberg: 1984, "From Grassroots Activism to Political Power: Women Organizing Against Environmental Hazards," in E. Chavkin (ed.), *Double Exposure: Women's Health Hazards on the Job and at Home*, Monthly Review Press: New York.

Freudenberg, Nicholas: 1984, *Not in Our Backyards*, Monthly Review Press: New York.

Gore and Storrie Limited: 1982, *Canadian National Inventory of Hazards and Toxic Wastes*, Ottawa: Environment Canada.

Hall, Ross Hume: 1974, *Food for Nought: The Decline in Nutrition*, Harper and Row: New York.

Hall, Ross Hume: 1981, "A New Approach to Pest Control in Canada," Canadian Environmental Advisory Council, Report No. 10, July: 48.

Hart, Fred C. Associates Inc.: 1979, *Preliminary Assessment of Cleanup Costs for National Hazardous Waste Problems*.

Hayden, Dolores: 1981, *The Grand Domestic Revolution: A History of Feminist Designs for American Homes, Neighborhoods, and Cities*. MIT Press: Cambridge, Mass.

Howard, Rhoda: 1978, *Colonialism and Underdevelopment in Africa*, Croom Helm: London.

Jackson, John, Phil Weller and the Ontario Public Interest Group: 1982, Chemical Nightmare: *The Unnecessary Legacy of Toxic Wastes*, Between the Lines: Toronto.

Jackson, John and Phil Weller: 1984, "Focus: Chemical Nightmare," *Homemaker's*, Oct. 19(8).

Labonté, Ron: 1984, "Chemical Justice: Dioxin's Day in Court," *This Magazine* 17(16), 4–9.

Luxton, Meg: 1980, *More Than a Labour of Love*, Women's Press: Toronto.

Kaplan, Temma: 1982, "Female Consciousness and Collective Action: The Case of Barcelona. 1910–1918," *Signs* 7(3), 545.

Melrose, Dianna: 1982, *Bitter Pills: Medicines and the Third World Poor*, Oxfam: Oxford, U.K.

Moskowitz, Milton, Michael Katz and Robert Levering (eds.): 1980, *Everybody's Business: An Almanac*, Harper and Row: San Francisco.

Norwood, Christopher: 1985, "Terata," *Mother Jones*, Jan. X(1), 15–21.

Oakley, Anne: 1975, *The Sociology of Housework*, Pantheon: New York.

Ontario Waste Management Corporation: 1982, Waste Quantities Study.

Ontario: Report of the Royal Commission Appointed to Inquire Into Waste Management Inc., et cetera: 1978, The Hon. S.H.S. Hughes, March 30.

Pedler, Frederick: 1974, *The Lion and the Unicorn in Africa: The United Africa Company, 1787–1931*, Heinemann: London.

Proulx, Monique: 1978, *Five Million Women: A Study of the Canadian Housewife*, Advisory Council on the Status of Women: Ottawa.

Rosenberg, Harriet: 1984, "The Home is the Workplace: Hazards, Stress and Pollutants in the Household," in W. Chaukin (ed.), *Double Exposure*, Monthly Review Press: New York.

Schneider, Keith: 1983, "Faking It," *Amicus Journal* 4(4), 14–26.

Vigod, Toby and Anne Woodsworth: 1982, "Captan: The Legacy of the IBT Affair," Submission on Pesticide Law and Policy to the Consultative Committee on IBT Pesticides on Behalf of the Canadian Environmental Law Association and Pollution Probe.

Weir, David and Mark Schapiro: 1981, *Circle of Poison*, Institute for Food and Development Policy: San Francisco.

Wolff, Janet: 1958, What Makes Women Buy?: *A Guide to Understanding and Influencing the New Woman to [sic]Today*, McGraw-Hill: New York.

Wood, Ellen: 1981, "The Separation of the Economic and the Political in Capitalism," *New Left Review* 127, 66–95.

Wynn, Mona: 1985, "Selling Mrs. Consumer: Corporate Capitalism and the Domestic Labour Process," paper presented at the Women and the Invisible Economy Conference. Simone de Beauvoir Institute, Montreal, February 20–22.

BUSINESS ETHICS, ECONOMIC DEVELOPMENT, AND PROTECTION OF THE ENVIRONMENT IN THE NEW WORLD ORDER

Jang B. Singh

Emily F. Carasco

As dramatically presented in the final report of the World Commission on Environment and Development (the Brundtland Report) (1987), one of the most serious threats to our civilization is the accelerating deterioration of our environment. A conference on the Brundtland Report held in Toronto in 1988 issued the following warning:

> Humanity is conducting an uncontrolled, globally pervasive experiment whose ultimate consequences could be second only to a global nuclear war. The best predictions available indicate potentially severe economic and social dislocation ... which will worsen international tensions and increase the risk of conflicts among and within nations. These ... changes may well become the major non-military threat to international security and the future of the global economy.
>
> (MacNeill, 1989: 4)

In varying degrees, governments, businesses, non-governmental organizations and individuals are taking measures to ward off the threat of environmental disasters. Kirpatrick (1990) characterizes this new environmentalism as being global, more cooperative than confrontational—and with business at the center (p. 55). This paper focuses on the role of business in protection and restoration of the environment in what President Bush called the New World Order.

OUR MORAL OBLIGATION TO PROTECT THE ENVIRONMENT

The desire for a clean, safe and ecologically balanced environment implicitly recognizes the right to a livable environment. This right of an individual to a livable environment is

Journal of Business Ethics 15: 297–307, 1996. © 1996 Kluwer Academic Publishers. Printed in the Netherlands.

easily established at the theoretical level. Blackstone (1983), in a widely cited article, discusses the right to a livable environment as a human right and a legal right. He argues that the right to a clean, safe environment is a human right since this condition is essential for fulfilling one's human capacities.

> Each person has this right qua being human and because a livable environment is essential for one to fulfil his/her human capacities. And given the danger to our environment today and hence the danger to the very possibility of human existence, access to a livable environment must be conceived as a right which imposes upon everyone a correlative moral obligation to respect.

(Blackstone, 1983: 413)

Guerrette (1986: 409) illustrates this position by arguing that since people simply cannot live in a chemically toxic area, experience freedom in an industrially polluted environment or be happy while worrying about the quality of air they breathe and since life, liberty and the pursuit of happiness are defined by the Constitution of the United States as inalienable rights—then a livable environment is also an inalienable right. Moreover, some argue that this right extends to future generations (e.g., Feinberg, 1983) and that the present generation has a moral obligation to pass on a clean safe environment to them. This belief is the driving force behind the Brundtland Report (1987) and its focus on sustainable development. Stone (1983) proposes that to effectively protect the environment, it should be granted standing in its own right. He argues that just as courts appoint trustees to oversee the affairs of "sick" corporations, we should have a system in which, when a friend of a natural object perceives it to be endangered, he/she can apply to a court for the creation of a guardianship (p. 566).

While it is a fairly simple exercise to philosophically establish the rights of present and future generations to a livable environment, and the rights of the environment itself, it is more difficult to establish these as legal rights. The establishment of legal rights requires the formulation and adoption of appropriate legislation and the arrangement of a legal framework through which remedies may be sought. Unlike the philosophical establishment of the right to a livable environment, legal establishment of environmental rights must consider the competing views of both environmentalists and non-environmentalists. The debate then becomes one involving costs and benefits. Proponents of this view argue that protection of the environment is not without costs and that one has to view such costs against possible benefits. Thus, while children in Mezibori, Czechoslovakia, sometimes wear filters to protect them from dirty air (Cook, 1991: D5) the cost of quickly solving this environmental problem may include closing the factories where many of their parents work. Beckerman (1988) grudgingly conceded that there is a one percent grain of truth in what he calls the anti-growth movement and proposes that pollution should only be cut to the point where the benefits from reducing it further no longer offset the costs to society of doing so (p. 370). In further developing an extreme anti-environmentalist position, he suggests that since most of humanity lead lives full of pain and suffering, the extinction of the human race would not matter—since, by and large, the human race stinks, the sooner it is extinct, the better (Beckerman, 1988: 374).

Of course, the extreme position of Beckerman is shared by few; as is the position of extreme environmentalists. Governments, organizations and individuals throughout the world, as illustrated by the positive reaction to the Brundtland Report, have recognized the danger posed to present and future generations by a deteriorating environment. The prevailing opinion now seems to be that while development is necessary, it must be sustainable. Sustainable development is now part of the parlance of politicians of both developed and developing countries and a small industry has sprung up around this term. For example, at one of Canada's leading graduate schools of Business Administration, one can now take a course in sustainable development. Hearteningly, it is not all rhetoric. Many governments are enacting legislation aimed at protecting the environment. However, the developing countries and the former Eastern block countries are lagging behind in this process. This is significant, for the collapse of socialist systems around the world, the ascendancy of the free enterprise ideology and the resulting domination of world affairs by the United States of America in what some are calling the New World Order, may likely lead to increased business activity in many parts of the world. The implications of the New World Order for the protection of the Environment warrants examination.

THE NEW WORLD ORDER AND IMPLICATIONS FOR THE ENVIRONMENT

The term New World Order is not new. For example, it was used by Hitler to describe his perceived domination of international affairs and more recently by analysts, to describe the bipolar world dominated by the United States and the Soviet Union. The withdrawal of the Soviet Union from this bipolar world leaves a unipolar world dominated by the United States. This new reality is what President Bush called the New World Order. Krauthammer (1991: 36) claims that Bush liked this phrase so much that he used it constantly from August 1990 to the end of his term in office and would have liked the New World Order to be as much his legacy as the New Deal was FDR's. The implications of the New World

Order for the environment are twofold. On the one hand, the new acceptance of the free enterprise system may lead to uncontrolled business activities which are harmful to the environment. On the other hand, the United States and other nations may be in a position to influence consensus building on international environmental law while sharing advanced environmental protection technology and scientific information with the rest of the world.

The danger posed to the environment by increased, unhampered business activities has been addressed by Greenpeace. Commenting on the issue in April, 1990 it noted that Western investments in Eastern Europe consist largely of the type of grimy industries that the environmental movement in Western Europe and North America spends much of its time hounding: car and chemical manufacturing, McDonald's restaurants and toxic pesticides (*No Time to Waste*, 1990: 1). The organization further argues that of the more than 2000 "joint development projects" between Western firms and Eastern European countries, many are similar to the industries that have contributed to high levels of pollution in Poland, Romania, East Germany and Czechoslovakia. The danger illustrated by the situation in Eastern Europe is that governments, especially in industrially developing countries, anxious to demonstrate their faith in the free enterprise system and in their zest to attract foreign investment, may tolerate business activities which are unacceptably harmful to the environment.

A more optimistic outlook on the environment in the New World Order would see positive aspects of environmental policies in the United States and other Western countries being transferred to other nations. This may happen in a number of ways. First, the United States could use its considerable influence in the New World Order to build international consensus aimed at establishing new environmental protection agreements and strengthening international law in this area. The lessons gained in the last two decades of attempting to reconcile the need for environmental protection with the need of developing countries for rapid development may prove invaluable in the New World Order. Second, Western companies doing business in industrially developing countries may apply values learned in their home countries where environmental legislation and awareness are advanced, to their operations abroad. Third, a world-wide educational program on environmental protection must be undertaken if wide-scale change is to occur.

INTERNATIONAL ENVIRONMENTAL LAW

Following upon the Stockholm Declaration of 1972, the last 21 years have witnessed a flurry of activities relating to the protection of the environment through international law. The indisputable fact that the nations of the world are indivisible components of one ecosystem has led to relatively quick action in the field of international environmental law. However neither customary international law nor conventional law has responded effectively to the urgent need to create a system that would prevent one or more States from damaging the ecological basis for development/survival in other states. The classical international legal system was founded on the sovereignty of states and was a minimal system for the co-existence of states (Kindred, 1987: 819). Although recognition of the unity of the global physical environment has found expression in modern international law, it remains questionable as to whether a system premised on the independence, equality and self-preservation of individual states is the appropriate vehicle to respond to the crisis of environmental protection. Can sovereignty give way to co-operation? The President of the International Court of Justice has posed the challenge in these terms:

The crucial problem is to bring about a crystallization of international co-operation into the field of enforceable law—an aspect calling for a great deal more than efforts solely directed towards the formulation of new laws or rights without any method or machinery to enforce them.

(Gaines, 1991: 782)

The 1972 Declaration on the Human Environment (Stockholm Declaration) restated the existing rule of international law which imposes upon states a "responsibility to ensure that activities within their jurisdiction and control do not cause [significant] damage to the environment of other states" or to the environment of any area beyond their jurisdiction (Principle 21, Stockholm Declaration) but stopped short of progressive development of existing principles. The Stockholm Declaration is merely declaratory of the substantive conclusions of a conference and since it lacks the formal requirements of a treaty, it lacks the binding legal force of a treaty. Even proponents of the assertion that Principle 21 is reflective of a norm of customary international law or has itself evolved into a norm of customary international law, would concede that the norm is short on clarity. Stockholm Principle 22 does require States to co-operate to develop further the international law regarding liability and compensation with regard to transboundary pollution, but twenty years later it is clear that very little progress has been made in the rules of customary international law on the subject. The frustrating slow pace of development in this area has aptly been termed the "Stillborn Regime of International Liability" for transnational pollution (Note, H.L.R. 1991: 1498).

Traditional principles of state sovereignty and conflicting state interests have been blamed for the failure to develop unambiguous standards of liability vis-a-vis clearly stated substantive norms of conduct.

O'Riordan (1981: 294) identifies the reluctance of states to relinquish or appear to relinquish their territorial sovereignty as the chief barrier to effective international institutions of environmental protection. Ntambirweki (1991) points out that as far back as the Stockholm Conference, industrially developing countries presented the dilemma between conserving the environment and fulfilling the developmental needs of the Third World. The Head of the Brazilian delegation stated: "A country that has not yet reached minimum satisfactory levels in the supply of essentials is not in a position to divert considerable resources to environmental protection" (Tolba, 1988: 135). The Ugandan delegate made the equally important point that developing countries face environmental problems different in degree from those encountered in developed countries: "… [W]e are not confronted with an environment that has degenerated into pollution as a result of development. On the contrary, we are faced with an environment many of whose inherent aspects are prohibitive to development and injurious to human comfort" (Tolba, 1988: 342). The Stockholm Declaration in recognizing the concerns of these countries (Principles 8, 9, 10, 11, 12) promoted the notion advanced at the 1971 Founex Seminar that environmental concerns should not be a barrier to development—that the goal was to foster ecologically sound development.

Formation and development of rules of customary international law requires in any area, the uniformity of practice by states and *opinio juris*, a sense that one is legally compelled to act in accordance to a certain norm. When the players in the international scheme of law-making were restricted to relatively homogeneous, Western, Christian states with similar economic/political states and outlook, consensus on the establishment norms for international conduct was not uncommon, e.g., many of the laws relating to the sea now found in treaties, were first established through the practice of states as rules of customary international law. Today however, international law is "no longer the almost exclusive preserve of the peoples of European blood" by whose consent it used to be said, "it exists and for the settlement of whose differences it is applied or at least invoked" (Anand, 1987: 23). The players in the international community have increased and their economic status and goals being significantly different from that of the earlier players, it is not surprising that there is very little agreement on substantive rules relating to international environmental protection. With the economic priorities and needs of the Eastern European countries being similar to those of the developing countries, this tension is likely to continue.

The virtual dearth of international adjudication based upon rules of customary international environmental law (even the most notable exceptions, the Trail Smelter Arbitration (1938), the Lac Lanoux arbitration (1956), the Gut Dam Claims (1969) and the Nuclear Tests Case (1974) provide little precedential value) reflect the difficulties of relying upon an archaic, slow-moving regime to obtain redress. In the absence of a binding treaty entitling one party to seek redress before an international tribunal, both State parties must freely consent to the adjudication, an uncommon occurrence. Individuals and organizations who are victims of prohibited transboundary pollution are particularly vulnerable in this flawed regime. Only states have standing before the International Court of Justice (ICJ) and therefore if the national State of a victim is unwilling to espouse an individual's claim before the ICJ, the victim is left without any effective international remedy. Furthermore as some have pointed out, the whole concept of international adjudication is inadequate for transboundary pollution because any proposed regime would necessarily operate *ex post facto* (Schneider, 1979: 50). In response to these inherent weaknesses in the traditional liability regime, a movement has arisen to develop rules of state conduct designed to prevent environmental harm before the event giving rise to it occurs (Note, H.L.R., 1991: 1512). Various treaties and charters now impose duties on states to assess transboundary environmental dangers and to inform potentially affected states of dangers (Kirgis, 1983). Critics point out that the trend towards vague and essentially toothless procedural obligations does little to actually reduce transboundary environmental harm. The absence of any liability standards or cause of action prior to the infliction of harm make failure to comply with the duty to inform meaningless as a means of asserting a right to an unspoiled environment (Magraw, 1986: 312).

Failure to relinquish outmoded concepts of sovereignty that are a stumbling block to a co-operative, comprehensive regulation of the environment has led to a piecemeal treaty/convention approach towards issues of international environmental protection. States are bound by the terms of treaties they sign and breach of treaty obligations results in international state responsibility for the consequences of that breach. The treaty/convention method is time-consuming, restricting and expensive but it has allowed for the expression of important differences among states and the creation of innovative responses to these differences. Recent successes such as the 1987 Montreal Protocol on Substances that Deplete the Ozone Layer and the 1989 Basel Convention on the Control of Transboundary Movements of Hazardous Wastes and their Disposal have led to new hope for international co-operation in the creation of international environmental law.

The Montreal Protocol has been hailed as a landmark agreement demonstrating a spirit of international co-operation (Morrisette, 1989: 793). The Protocol, which lies within the framework of the 1985 Vienna Convention for the Protection of the Ozone Layer, seeks to protect the stratospheric ozone layer through the control of deleterious emissions, especially chloroflourocarbons

(CFCs) and halons. Recognition was given to the position of industrially developing countries by allowing them to delay compliance with the mandated control measures for 10 years, as long as each state consumed less than 0.03 kilograms per capita (Art. 5). It has been stated that the sensitivity of the international community to their domestic needs has encouraged the developing countries to respond positively to the Vienna Convention and the Montreal Protocol by becoming parties to the two treaties (Ntambirweki, 1991: 911). Not all the developing countries were immediately convinced. India and China (representing over 1/3 of humanity) indicated at the 1987 Montreal Protocol that they would not become parties to the Protocol because of its failure to provide adequate assistance to developing countries (Caron, 1991: 761). Two years later when the London Meeting adopted amendments to the Protocol that provided for technology transfer and established a fund to help developing countries phase out ozone depleting chemicals, the representatives of China and India indicated that their countries would sign the Protocol in 1992 (Caron, 1991: 763).

The Montreal Protocol sought to avoid hold-out problems (which often result in lowest common denominator solutions), by permitting flexibility. Higher regulatory requirements were imposed on industrialized states than on developing countries— allowing for an agreement that was acceptable to all states and still provided substantial CFC reductions. Hold-outs were also discouraged by the attempt to remove any advantage from remaining outside the Convention. The baseline calculation from which reductions are to be made are fixed and technical assistance is provided to those who accede to the Convention. Finally, there was no trade advantage in remaining outside the Convention since it restricts members from trading in areas involving the regulated substances with those outside the regime.

In response to the unchecked transboundary movement of hazardous wastes, 116 nations met in Basel in March 1989 and authored the Basel Convention on the Control of Transboundary Movements of Hazardous Wastes and their Disposal. In creating a system of stringent requirements for export agreements and extensive monitoring of the movements of hazardous waste, the Convention's focus was on regulation and not on prohibition of international transportation of hazardous waste. While the creation of a global system of regulation of international transportation of hazardous wastes is in itself an achievement, the various unresolved issues and significant omissions are a sharp reminder that the interests of the already industrialized states and the newly industrialized states may not always be identical. Outright banning of international transportation of hazardous wastes, funding, liability rules—major areas of concern to less powerful economies—were not included in the Basel Convention. However, certain aspects of both the Montreal/London and the Basel meetings signify a new awareness of what is necessary to obtain active participation of newly industrializing countries in environmental treaty negotiations.

In 1990, when a fund was established to help less developed countries switch to chloroflourocarbon alternatives, a new era of linkages between international environmental management and international finance and trade was set in motion (Moltke, 1991: 974). This linkage finds expression in many different forms, e.g., The Global Environmental Facility—intended to assist developing countries implement programs which protect the global environment; debt-for-nature programs—generally a bank exchanges part of the debt of a less economically developed country for that country's bonds or currency, which the bank sells or donates to an environmental conservation organization (Caron, 1991: 974). Indirect financial linkage may be found in the guise of guidelines for the exchange of scientific information (London Guidelines, 1989 U.N. Doc. A/44/25), provision of funds for the transfer of technology or for technical assistance. Under the Basel Convention, technical assistance is used to promote public awareness in developing countries of low-waste technologies, as well as sound management of hazardous and other wastes (Art. 10, para. 4).

REFLECTIONS ON THE ROLE OF LAW

The traditional system of international law was designed for survival rather than cooperation (Kindred, 1987: 819). Environmental protection demands the latter.

Customary international law with its emphasis on state practice, and of necessity, the unilateral relinquishing of sovereignty, makes it an inappropriate vehicle for the formulation of rules on a subject with profound economic consequences particularly on newly industrializing countries. The role that the cost of eliminating even current levels of transboundary pollution has played in the failure to develop rules of liability, cannot be minimized. Witness the reluctance of the United States and Canada to act upon the acid rain crisis. In 1980 the two countries signed a Memorandum of Intent (Memorandum of Intent Between the United States and Canada Concerning Transboundary Pollution, 1980). Canada has asserted that both countries need to adopt interim measures to protect the environment from irreversible damage while scientists conduct further research; the United States has maintained that it would be better to increase resources for research rather than to adopt (costly) regulation that might not solve the problem. This impasse does raise the important question of who bears the cost of eliminating from [sic] or curtailing harmful economic activities. It has been suggested that Canada could pay the U.S. to install pollution control equipment (Note, 1991: 1566).

In failing to create rules of liability, customary international law fails to provide solutions for the restoration of the environment to its pre-damaged state and/or for reparation for injury caused by pollution. To paraphrase from the Brundtland Report, it is a legal regime that is being rapidly outdistanced by the accelerating pace and expanding scale of impacts on the environmental base of development (The World Commission on Environment Development, 1987: 330).

The Convention/Treaty route to international environmental protection has enjoyed some measure of success in recent years. It should be noted however that the truly multi-lateral conventions have been very few and have had a narrowly defined focus and have dealt with subject areas which are chiefly the concerns of the industrialized West. Environmental problems related to rapid urbanization, provision of safe drinking water, soil improvement, waste management, inadequate housing and food have not received the global priority they deserve. Furthermore, the specifically focussed treaties that do exist do not necessarily incorporate some of the most basic principles deemed necessary (see The World Commission on Environment and Development, 1987: 348–351) to protect the environment e.g., liability/compensation.

It may be that consolidation and extension of existing legal principles in the form of a Universal Declaration on Environmental Rights is timely. The Brundtland Report suggests that such a Declaration would provide the basis for a Convention setting out the sovereign rights and reciprocal responsibilities of all states on environmental protection and sustainable development (The World Commission on Environment and Development, 1987: 332). For the benefit of sceptics it should be noted that the current U.N. system of human rights (the Convenant on Civil and Political Rights and the Convenant on Economic and Social Rights)

had its origins in the 1948 Universal Declaration of Human Rights. The global acceptance of the notion of international protection of human rights would not have been anticipated in 1948. With the right commitment and adequate resources being directed at this goal, the idea of international protected environmental rights could well receive global acceptance.

The advantages of a binding convention incorporating basic principles are too numerous to examine in any detail in this paper. We would suggest going a step further and declaring certain principles to be *jus cogens*, i.e., allowing for no derogation by treaty even by non-signatories of the Convention. It is important to establish certain basic principles of environmental protection as *jus cogens*. The Basel Convention in permitting Member States to enter into bilateral treaty agreements outside the parameters of the Convention allows for situations where a country in need of foreign currency may well risk the lives of its citizens (Howard, 1990: 243). If one of the principles to be enshrined in a Convention is the right of every human being to an environment adequate for her/his health and well-being (The World Commission on Environment and Development, 1987: 348), then governments should not be permitted to enter treaties which deny their nationals this right. If the right of every human being to an environment adequate for their health and well-being is to be given effective protection, it must be enforceable by both individuals and states. A victim of environmental pollution such as would be protected in the proposed Convention should not have to be dependent on the goodwill of a government to pursue a claim on her/his behalf. Moreover, it may well be that the victim's national state is partially or fully responsible for the alleged wrongful act or omission. An individual must be able to allege a breach of environmental law both against other individuals as well as states. Again, there is precedent for individuals being granted a right to allege wrongdoing either against their own or another government in the human rights protection arena. Direct access to an adjudicative body is particularly important in those situations where the victim's national judicial system does not provide adequate protection.

The fact that the destruction of the environment impacts indiscriminately upon all nations of the world should not necessarily mean that the cost of environmental protection should be borne equally by all the nations of the world. There has been much discussion about intergenerational equity with regard to environmental protection (Weiss, 1989: 22). It has been pointed out by some who find the costs of environmental protection burdensome that intergenerational equity is just as important (Ntambirweki, 1991: 924). Environmental protection must not, as many now argue, be at the expense of development—it must be part of the process of sustainable development. This clearly requires some notion of those with the ability to pay having the greater responsibility to bear the costs involved. Furthermore, the notion of intergenerational equity must necessarily take into account what has happened in the past as much as what may happen in the future. This would require companies and states with a history of pollution to be held responsible for a larger share of the clean-up operation, directly or indirectly. Some aspect of the municipal law concept of "the polluter pays" must be incorporated into the international system but it must be a liability concept based on a broad notion of equity.

Clearly, consensus on the notion of an international Convention or Charter of Environmental Rights is not an immediate prospect. Other methods of achieving environmental protection must concurrently be explored. These may include, *inter alia,* corporate codes of conduct and widescale educational endeavors.

CODES OF CONDUCT

Ethical codes or codes of conduct may be used to guide the activities of firms and industries vis-a-vis the environment. An ethical code is defined as part of that middle ground between internalized societal values on the one hand and law on the other, where formal social and economic sanctions of a social group—a profession, an industry, a firm, etc.—act to ensure conformity with acceptable standards of behaviour and penalize deviance (Molander, 1987: 619–620). Codes are obeyed because individuals subject themselves to standards above their own or fear penalties which may be imposed on violators. Murphy (1989) proposes that ethical business practices stem from an ethical corporate structure and corporate credos: ethics programs and ethical codes enhance such a structure. It is submitted that the inclusion of environmental protection clauses in codes of conduct and similar documents will aid in the establishment of a corporate culture that is environmentally responsible. The true value of such an orientation would be demonstrated in jurisdictions where environmental protection regulations are either lax or non-existent. Research to date has shown that few corporate codes of ethical conduct include clauses dealing with the environment. Of 202 codes of conduct of major American corporations analyzed by Mathews (1987) 176 (87.1%) do not discuss environmental affairs. A similar study of 75 codes of conduct of Canadian corporations (Lefebvre and Singh, 1990) found that 59 (78.7%) do not discuss environmental issues. These results clearly indicate the need for more corporations to include environmental concerns in their credos, ethics programs and codes of conduct. However, some corporations now emphasize environmental matters and, for example, the important chemical industry in North America has formulated a Guided Principles Statement on the environment, the signing of which is an obligation of members of the Chemical Manufacturers Association in the United States and the Chemical Producers Association in Canada (Farha, 1990).

If more corporations include clauses dealing with the environment in their codes of conduct and if these have an impact on corporate cultures worldwide then such codes will have a positive effect on the international effort to achieve a clean and safe environment.

EDUCATION

Ultimately, our environmental crisis will be solved not by grand studies such as the Brundtland Report but by ecologically literate citizens of all countries acting in an environmentally responsible way. Ecological literacy implies a broad understanding of how people and societies relate to one another and to natural systems, and how they might do so sustainably (Orr, 1990: 51). Ecological illiteracy is a prime cause of pollution. People who pour anti-freeze into the sewer, the retired African who accepted barrels of hazardous wastes for storage in his backyard and the South American who poured pesticide into a lake to make fishing easy are all manifestations of ecological illiteracy. Any normal human being who has the knowledge necessary to understand that all of nature is interrelated will not only desist from actions harmful to the environment but will be alert to the actions of the environmentally irresponsible. Clearly, worldwide environmental education should not be limited to schools but should also be aimed at the community at large. But, according to Lewis (1990), even in the United States, environmental education is still a subject on the fringe. She argues that there is very little room in the curriculum for a subject viewed as being on the fringe of science. Moreover, few teachers in the West, and less in the developing countries, have an understanding of and are committed to environmental edu-

cation. Stone (1990: 43) proposes that in the ideal situation separate courses designed to teach environmental education competencies should be required for teacher education majors. Since it is difficult to add new courses to the curricula of Faculties of Education, the alternative is to infuse environmental education into existing courses.

A global initiative in training environmental educators, adding ecological education to the curriculum and community education on environmental issues will decrease ecological illiteracy. This in turn will decelerate the rate of deterioration of the environment and eventually assist in its restoration. In the New World Order, where information flows more easily, a global initiative in environmental education should be less difficult than during the Cold War. The newly vitalized United Nations has the facilities and knowledge to encourage and/or initiate a worldwide educational program.

CONCLUSION

The end of the cold war has elevated environmental issues to the highest level of concern for humanity while creating a world order dominated by the United States and other Western nations. In this new power structure, these nations have a compelling moral responsibility to help stamp out environmental irresponsibility worldwide. By using their power and influence in international affairs, they should build consensus to strengthen international environmental law. Moreover, Western transnational corporations which now have expanded opportunities to do business in previously inaccessible locations should ensure that their corporate cultures reflect concern for the environment. Transnational corporations should operate on the basic premise that conduct unacceptable in their home country is unacceptable in their host countries. However, a massive global environmental education campaign will contribute more to a clean safe environment than either of the above stated measures. In the final analysis, the best safeguard against environmental damage is an ecologically literate population.

REFERENCES

Anand, R.P.: 1987, 'Attitude of the Asian-African States', in F.E. Snyder and S. Sathirathai (eds.), *Third World Attitudes Toward International Law* (Martinus Nijhoff Publishers, Dordrecht), pp. 5–22.

Beckerman, W.: 1988, 'The Case for Economic Growth', in T. Donaldson and P. Werhane (eds.), *Ethical Issues in Business: A Philosophical Approach*, 3rd ed. (Prentice Hall, Englewood Cliffs, New Jersey), pp. 369–375.

Blackstone, W.T.: 1988, 'Ethics and Ecology', in T. L. Beauchamp and N. E. Bowie (eds.), *Ethical Theory and Business* (Prentice Hall, Englewood Cliffs, New Jersey), pp. 411–424.

Caron, D.: 1991, 'Protection of the Stratospheric Ozone Layer and the Structure of International Environmental Lawmaking', *Hastings International and Comparative Law Review* 14, 755-777.

Cook, P.: 1991, 'Eastern Europe Get Full Marx for Disaster', *Globe and Mail*, Oct. 19, D5.

Farha, A.: 1990, 'The Corporate Conscience and Environmental Issues: Responsibility of the Multinational Corporation', *Northwestern Journal of International Law and Business* 10, 379–396.

Feinberg, J.: 1983, 'The Rights of Animals and Unborn Generations', in T.L. Beauchamp and N.E. Bowie (eds.), *Ethical Theory and Business* (Prentice Hall, Englewood Cliffs, New Jersey), pp. 428–436.

Gaines, S.E.: 1991, 'Taking Responsibility for Transboundary Environmental Effects', *Hastings International and Comparative Law Review* 14, 781–809.

Guerrette, R.H.: 1986, 'Environmental Integrity and Corporate Responsibility', *Journal of Business Ethics* 5, 405–415.

Howard, K.: 1990, 'The Basel Convention: Control of Transboundary Movements of Hazardous Wastes and Their Disposal', *Hastings International and Comparative Law Review* 14, 223–246.

Kindred, H. (General Editor): 1987, *International Law*, 4th ed. (Emond Montgomery Publications Ltd., Canada).

Kirgis, F.: 1983, *Prior Consultation in International Law: A Study of State Practice* (University Press of Virginia, Charlottesville).

Kirpatrick, D.: 1990, 'Environmentalism: The New Crusade', *Fortune*, Feb. 12, 55.

Krauthammer, C.: 1991, 'The Lonely Superpower', *The New Republic*, July 29, 23–27.

Lefebvre, M. and J. Singh: 1990, 'The Content and Focus of Canadian Corporate Codes of Ethics', Unpublished Manuscript.

Lewis, A.C.: 1990, 'Education and the Environment', Phi Delta Kappa, April, 580–581.

London Guidelines: 1989, U.N. Environmental Programme, Environmental Law Guidelines and Principle No. 10: Exchange of Information on Chemicals in International Trade adopted by UNEP Governing Council, Dec. 15/30, 44 U.N. GAOR Supp. (No. 25) at 157, U.N. Doc. A/44/25.

MacNeill, J.: 1989, 'Towards 2000: Add Environmental Refugees to the List of Things to Worry About as We Proceed', *Policy Options* 10(3), April, 3–6.

Magraw, D.: 1986, 'The International Law Commission's Study of International Liability for Non-prohibited Acts as It Relates to Developing States', *Washington Law Review* 61(1041).

Mathews, M.: 1987, 'Codes of Ethics', *Organizational Behaviour and Misbehaviour Research in Corporate Social Performance and Policy: Empirical Studies of Business Ethics and Values* 19, 107–130.

Memorandum of Intent Between the United States and Canada Concerning Transboundary Pollution, Aug. 5, 1980, 32 U.S.T. 2521, 2524, T.I.A.S. No. 9856, at 4.

Molander, E.: 1987, 'A Paradigm for Design, Promulgation and Enforcement of Ethical Codes', *Journal of Business Ethics*, 6, 619–631.

Moltke, K.: 1991, 'Review-for-Nature: The Second Generation', *Hastings International and Comparative Law Review* 14, 973–987.

Morrisette, P.: 1989, 'The Evolution of Policy Responses to Stratospheric Ozone Depletion', *Natural Resources Journal* 29, 793–820.

Murphy, P.: 1989, 'Creating Ethical Corporate Structure', *Sloan Management Review* 30(2), 81–87.

Note: 1991, 'Developments in the Law— International Environmental Law', Harvard *Law Review* 104, 1484–1639.

No Time To Waste: 1990, *Greenpeace Waste Trade Update* 3(1), April, 1–2.

Ntambirweki, J.: 1991, 'The Developing Countries in the Evolution of an International Environmental Law', *Hastings International and Comparative Law Review* 14, 905–928.

O'Riordan, T.: 1981, *Environmentalism*, 2nd ed. (Pion, London).

Orr, D.W.: 1990, 'Environmental Education and Ecological Literacy', *Education Digest*, May, 49–53.

Schneider, J.: 1979, *World Public Order of the Environment* (University of Toronto Press, Toronto).

Stone, C.D.: 1983, 'Should Trees Have Standing?—Toward Legal Rights for Natural Objects', in Beauchamp and Bowie (eds.), pp. 563–567.

Stone, J. M.: 1990, 'Preparing Teachers as Environmental Educators', *Education Digest*, Jan., 43–45.

The World Commission on Environment and Development: 1987, *Our Common Future* (Oxford University Press, Oxford).

Tolba, M. (ed.): 1988, *Evolving Environmental Perception from Stockholm to Nairobi* (Butterworths, Boston).

Weiss, E.: 1989, *In Fairness to Future Generations* (Dobbs Ferry, New York).

CASE 9 Mercury in the Environment

Anastasia M. Shkilnyk

Pijibowin is the world for poison. It is used by the people of Grassy Narrows to describe the mercury that now contaminates their sacred English–Wabigoon River. Between 1962 and 1970, Dryden Chemicals Limited, a pulp and paper mill located about eighty miles upstream from Grassy Narrows, dumped over 20,000 pounds [1 pound = .45 kilograms] of mercury into the river system as effluent from its chlor-alkali plant. By March 1970, when the Ontario Minister of Energy and Resource Management ordered the company to stop discharging mercury into the environment, the dam-

age was complete and irreversible. Over three hundred miles [1 mile = 1.6 kilometres] of the English–Wabigoon river system, with all its biological life, would probably remain poisoned for half a century or more.

An environmental disaster can be assessed in many ways. One can measure the sheer force of the impact, the extent of the damage, the effects on human health, the economic losses sustained, or the length of recovery time. Any major disruptive event, however, should also be judged by looking at the vulnerability of the people who are exposed to it. It seems logical that a community that has just suffered a traumatic upheaval in its way of life will experience the effects of yet another crisis much more acutely. In such a situation, environmental contamination can no longer be measured in isolation, for its impact interacts with previous events in a complex manner to form a pattern of cumulative injury.

Coming only a few years after the relocation, the discovery of mercury dealt a devastating blow to the community of Grassy Narrows. Having just been wrenched from their moorings on the old reserve, the people were ill prepared to cope with yet another misfortune. They had but a precarious hold on the conditions of their existence on the new reserve. They could no longer draw strength either from their relationship to the land or from the well of their faith, which had once given meaning and coherence to their lives. In the context of their traditional religious beliefs, the contamination of the river could only be interpreted as punishment by the Great Spirit for some serious violation of the laws governing man's relationship to nature. People had great difficulty comprehending this "unseen poison" of mercury, whose presence in the water and in the fish they could not see or taste or smell. They could not understand how something that happened so far away from them could hurt them. Many could not believe that the natural environment, which had nurtured them both spiritually and materially could suddenly betray them. To accept the fact that their "River of Life" had turned into a river of poison meant to lose forever their faith in nature and in the source of life itself.

In the community, the suspicion of *pijibowin* and the feeling of loss of control over the environment ran like a strong undercurrent beneath the tangible and measurable effects of the contamination. The tangible effects—the disruption in guiding, the loss of commercial fishing, the warnings against taking fish for food—struck a further blow to the people's already weakened ability to produce their own food and make an independent living from the resources of the land. Just as important were the intangible effects—the massive intrusion of outsiders, the confusion and misunderstanding about the effects on human health, the political manipulation of the mercury issue and the acceleration of government intervention in community life. Far from being just a medical and an economic problem, the pollution of the river became a serious psychological problem. The way in which the governments of Canada and Ontario handled the mercury issue and the exploitation of the Grassy Narrows people by self-seeking groups and individuals were in the end as severely demoralizing as the fact of the poison itself. Any analysis of the impact of this environmental disaster, therefore, has to take into account the relationship of Indian people to the Canadian society as a whole. Indeed, the way in which the mercury issue was defined, managed, and politicized mirrors much of what is so wrong with our own mainstream society.

While there is no way to measure with any precision how much of the current crisis at Grassy Narrows is attributable to mercury and how much to the collapse of a way of life, the people's own perception of the importance of mercury is significant. They speak of mercury poisoning as the event that pushed them over the edge of their ability to feel secure in nature, to relate to each other and to the world around them, and to be self-reliant in providing for their material needs. They call mercury "the last nail in the coffin."

Mercury is one of the oldest metals known to us. Aristotle described it as "liquid silver" in the fourth century B.C. Its ore cinnabar was used to make the red dye found in prehistoric cave paintings in

Europe. During Roman times, it was used to purify gold and silver. In the first century A.D., Greek physicians used it to heal open sores and burns. Centuries later, mercury ointment became a treatment for syphilis. But the hazards of mercury, as well as its uses, were also well known from early times. The miners of this metal, for example, developed violent tremors, muscular spasms, and character disorders. The Romans therefore chose convicts and slaves to mine the metal, and this precedent of using forced labor was followed by the Spaniards in the mercury mines they developed in the New World.

Miners, however, were not the only ones susceptible to the toxic effects of exposure to mercury. In the eighteenth century, a physician called Ramazzini wrote that goldsmiths using mercury in their craft "very soon become subject to vertigo, asthma, and paralysis. Very few of them reach old age, and even when they do not die young, their health is so terribly undermined that they pray for death."[1] Of artisans who used mercury to coat the backs of mirrors, he wrote: "You can see these workmen scowling and gazing reluctantly into their mirrors at the reflection of their own suffering and cursing the trade they have adopted."[2]

The popular expression "mad as a hatter" grew out of the observation of tremors, manic-depressive behavior, and temperamental instability among hatmakers who used mercuric nitrate to improve the felting quality of wool and fur. The toxic and potentially fatal effects of working with metallic or inorganic mercury, therefore, have been well established in recorded history.

Today, mercury and its compounds are used in about three thousand industrial processes by over eighty industries. Mercury is a valuable element because it is the only metal that is liquid at room temperature, and it also has special electrical properties that make it almost irreplaceable. It is used in making dental fillings, paints, electronic controls, thermometers, disinfectants, preservatives, and lotions. It is a catalyst in many metallurgical processes, and it is used in the production of vinyl chloride, a component in the manufacturer of plastics. The single most important use of mercury (prior to 1970) was in chlor-alkali plants that served the huge pulp and paper industry. Here, mercury was used in the electrolytic production of caustic soda and chlorine, and it was this industry that "lost" mercury in great volume both in wastewater and through exhaust gases.[3] While individual cases of industrial mercury poisoning have been fairly well documented,[4] it took the massive epidemic of poisoning in Minamata, Japan, in the late 1950s and 1960s to shake the world out of its complacency about the dangers of discharging mercury as industrial waste.

An Insidious Poison

Minamata is a village of about forty thousand persons, located on the southernmost island of Japan, Kyushu, on the bay of the Shiranui Sea. Its inhabitants make their living by commercial fishing, tourism, and working in the giant petrochemical complex owned by the Chisso Corporation. The town is associated with Minamata disease, which is known to have taken 107 lives and by 1970 had left over a thousand people with irreversible neurological damage, crippled limbs, blindness, paralysis, internal disorders, and loss of bodily functions. The disease fell most heavily on the poorest people of the area, who were most dependent on a steady diet of fish and shellfish.

Signs of the poison appeared in 1950, when fish in the bay began to float to the surface, swim erratically, and thrash about wildly before dying. Two years later, cats began to leap up in the air and turn in feverish circles, like whirling dervishes, before dying. People call it "the cat-dancing disease." In April 1956, two victims of what was at first diagnosed as cerebral palsy were admitted to the Chisso Factory Hospital. By mid-summer, so many similar cases had been reported that the director of the hospital, Dr. Hosokawa, declared that "an unclarified disease of the central nervous system had broken out." By the autumn of that year, a research team of the Kumamoto University Medical School suspected that the mass poisoning was traceable to a heavy metal concentrated in the flesh of fish and shellfish taken from Minamata Bay. It took years of research to identify organic mercury as the cause of the disaster and to provide conclusive evidence that the source of the poison was the effluent from the chemical plant of the Chisso Corporation. Indeed, a full decade passed before enough evidence could be accumulated to establish Chisso's legal liability for the damages caused by industrial pollution. Meanwhile, the company's executives refused to cooperate with the scientists, continued to dump mercury as effluent until 1968, and used their considerable economic and political influence to stifle criticism and frustrate the research effort.[5] In the end, the Chisso Corporation was forced to pay compensation to the victims of mercury poisoning, but the cost in human life was staggering. It is estimated that, aside from the actual and potential cases of congenital mercury poisoning, the number of Minamata disease victims may ultimately exceed ten thousand because of the long-term effects of past exposure.

Although outbreaks of mercury poisoning have occurred elsewhere,[6] the disease is always associated with the Minamata experience. This tragedy was followed by an extensive investigation of the causal links between inorganic mercury dumped as industrial waste, the contamination of the marine food chain by methyl mercury, and the onset of clinical symptoms of poisoning in humans. Scientists discovered a rather extraordinary natural phenomenon whereby inorganic (or metallic) mercury, which settles into the sediment of a body of water, is transformed into the much more toxic form of organic (or methyl) mercury in a process known as biomethylation.[7] What happens is that microorganisms living in the sediment, in order to protect themselves, convert the inorganic mercury into methyl mercury, which is much less toxic to them. The transformed mercury is then absorbed by microscopic underwater life such as plankton or algae, which serve as food for insect larvae. The insects are consumed by little fish; the little fish are consumed by bigger fish; and in this manner, the burden of methyl mercury in fish increases in concentration and toxicity as it passes up the food chain. Once inorganic mercury has been added to a water system, it takes a very long time for the mercury to clear the marine biosystem. Scientists estimate that only about 1 percent of the sediment's burden of inorganic mercury is converted into methyl mercury each year. Further, the biological half-life of methyl mercury in fish is very long. As a result, the process of contamination of marine life is continuous, persistent, and irreparable.

Of the two kinds of mercury, methyl mercury is more dangerous to human beings. Structurally, it differs from inorganic mercury simply through the addition of one or more carbon atoms to the mercury atom. Although both types are toxic, inorganic mercury does not do as much damage when taken by mouth. It is not as readily absorbed by the body; it is much more easily expelled from the body; and it does not accumulate in the body's vital organs and brain. Methyl mercury, on the other hand, is quickly carried by the blood through body tissues, concentrating in the heart, intestine, liver, and kidneys. But its greatest damage is reserved for the brain, and most of the clinical symptoms of mercury poisoning are related to brain and nerve lesions.[8] Methyl mercury destroys cells in the cerebellum, which regulates balance, and the cortex, which influences vision. It finds its way to other regions of the brain like the frontal lobe, where it may cause disturbances in personality. The toxin is singularly difficult to trace as a cause of illness because the symptoms of poisoning are not very specific and may be simulated by alcoholism, diabetes, severe nutritional deficiencies, old age, and many other disorders of the central nervous system. Therefore, a complete assessment of mercury poisoning can be made only at autopsy. Postmortem studies of the brains of Japanese victims, for example, revealed a marked atrophy or shrinkage of the brain caused by the destruction of nerve cells; the remaining nerve cell tissue was characterized by a sponge-like quality.

Neurologists have identified the clinical symptoms of Minamata disease as follows: numbness of the mouth, lips, tongue, hands, and feet; tunnel vision, sometimes accompanied by abnormal blind spots and disturbances in eye movement; impairment of hearing; speech disorders; difficulty in swallowing; loss of balance; a stumbling, awkward gait; clumsiness in handling familiar objects; disturbances in coordination; loss of memory, inability recall basic things like the alphabet; loss of the ability to concentrate; apathy; feelings of extreme fatigue; mental depression; emotional instability; and a tendency to fits of anxiety and rage. These initial symptoms of mercury poisoning may eventually lead

to severe disability, uncontrollable tremors and convulsions, deformity, paralysis, coma, and death. There are no remedies or therapy for the victims of mercury poisoning; the disease is considered to be irreversible.

Aside from these dreadful symptoms, methyl mercury has other characteristics that make it a particularly insidious poison. In the first place it has a special affinity for unborn children. In the body of a pregnant woman, not only is the mercury immediately passed from the placenta to the fetus, but the fetus actually concentrates the lethal toxin. In Japan, blood concentrations of methyl mercury in infants at birth averaged about 30 percent higher than in the mother. There were many cases of infants born with what seemed like cerebral palsy; some had deformed limbs, showed uncontrollable muscle spasms, and were seriously mentally retarded. These were the congenital victims of Minamata disease who had acquired the poison prenatally. Postmortem studies of such children showed massive atrophy in brain size and underdeveloped and malformed tissues in the central nervous system. To illustrate: the normal brain weight for a two-year-old child is about 960g; for a three-year-old child, about 1125. Minamata disease victims aged two and three registered brain weights of only 650 and 630 g, respectively.

Second, mercury continues to affect brain cells even after a person has stopped eating contaminated food. It has a half-life of at least seventy days in human blood and perhaps longer in the brain. This means that after seventy days, half of the burden of methyl mercury still exists in the body; it takes another seventy days to eliminate half of the remaining burden, and the balance is halved again every seventy days. Yet brain damage can be caused by minute amounts of mercury.

Third, individuals have different tolerances for the toxin; some are so sensitive to methyl mercury that even very brief exposure to contaminated food can cause significant damage to the brain. Some people also retain the poison in the body for a much longer time than others. So there are no guarantees that an individual who is exposed to small amounts of mercury over a long period of time will escape the pitiless and progressive degeneration of the nervous system.

Fourth, methyl mercury is a poison that follows no specific timetable between the time of exposure and the onset of symptoms of neurological injury. The damage done to the brain may not be manifest for several years.[9] In Japan, some patients diagnosed initially as chronic cases of low-level mercury intoxication developed symptoms of acute poisoning three or four years later. Thus there are no assurances that cases of low-grade or subacute poisoning will not worsen later on.

Finally, since many of the first symptoms of mercury poisoning (a "pins and needles" sensation in the arm and legs, tunnel vision, tremors) are also characteristics of other illnesses and nervous afflictions, it is very difficult to make a positive and early diagnosis of Minamata disease. No wonder, then, that the correlation between levels of exposure to methyl mercury and neurological symptoms of mercury poisoning has presented scientists with a formidable analytical challenge. It does not help matters when different laboratories use different units to measure the burden of mercury in the body or when significant differences appear in the interpretation of symptomatic evidence. But all scientists agree on one point: the amount of mercury in the blood is positively correlated with the potential health risk a person bears. Blood levels of mercury are indicated by the ratio of

mercury to whole blood calibrated in parts per billion (ppb). In Canada, the norm for the level of mercury in the blood of persons who are not fish-eaters is considered to be about 5 ppb; this rises to about 20 ppb for people who eat a lot of fish. Some countries recognize 200 ppb of mercury in blood as a "safe" level. Others (for example, Canada, the United States, Sweden, Finland, and Japan) accept 100 ppb as a "safe" level; anyone with more than 100 ppb is considered to be at risk.

The body burden of mercury can also be measured by the analysis of mercury values in human hair. It so happens that as hair is being formed on the head, mercury is being incorporated from the bloodstream. Thus there is a constant concentration ratio between the amount of mercury in the hair and in the blood. Once in the hair, methyl mercury remains there unchanged. Since hair grows at the rate of about one centimeter per month, scientists have an inbuilt and permanent record of previous levels of exposure to the toxin.[10]

Because of individual variations in tolerance and in the length of the retention period, it has been very difficult to establish the precise relationship between blood concentrations of mercury and the incidence of symptoms of Minamata disease. The available data, gathered from an outbreak of mercury poisoning in Iraq, are shown in the table.[11]

Symptoms of poisoning, then, begin to appear when levels of mercury in blood fall in the range of 500–1000 ppb. Studies published by the World Health Organization confirm that lower levels of exposure are associated with a significantly decreased degree of risk; at mercury blood levels in the 200–500 ppb range, there is presumed to be a 5 percent chance that adults will show the initial symptoms of Minamata disease.[12] It is worth repeating that very little is known about the long-term effects of even very modest concentrations of mercury in the human brain. In Japan, a few particularly sensitive individuals developed initial symptoms of mercury intoxication at blood levels close to 200 ppb; in Sweden, some chromosome breakage was observed at the 400-ppb level. Autopsies have shown brain damage in individuals whose exposure to methyl mercury was considered insufficient to provoke actual symptoms. In general, however, fully developed methyl mercury poisoning will occur only when the concentration of mercury in the blood is in the range of 1230–1840 ppb.[13] With prenatal exposure to the toxin, the risks of poisoning are considerably higher, perhaps three or four times.

An Environmental Disaster

Following the dreadful experiences of Minamata and Iraq, a series of interna-

tional conferences on heavy metals took place in the late 1960s to publicize the link between the industrial uses of mercury and the potential dangers of mercury contamination. At about the same time, Swedish scientists described the process of biomethylation and established that abnormally high levels of mercury found in fish and wildlife were related to upstream chlor-alkali and pulp and paper plants. In Canada, early warnings to government health officials about the hazards of mercury spills seem to have gone unheeded.[14] Then, in 1967–68, Norvald Fimreite, a Norwegian graduate student at the University of Western Ontario, studied the effects of industrial mercury losses on birds and fish. He found very high levels of mercury in the fish of the southern part of the Saskatchewan River, downstream from a pulp and paper mill and chlor-alkali plant. In 1969, he alerted the officials of the Ontario Water Resources Commission that the fish of Lake St. Clair had unac-

TABLE I	Relation of clinical symptoms of methyl mercury poisoning in Iraq to blood levels of mercury					
Whole Blood Methyl Mercury Concentration Levels (ppb)	**Percentage of Patients Showing Symptoms**					
	Paresthesia	**Ataxia**	**Visual Changes**	**Dysarthria**	**Hearing Defects**	**Death**
0– 100[a]	9.5	5	0	5	0	0
101– 500	5	0	0	5	0	0
501–1 000	42	11	21	5	5	0
1 001–2 000	60	47	53	24	0	0
2 001–3 000	79	60	56	25	12.5	0
3 001–4 000	82	100	58	75	36	17
4 001–5 000	100	100	83	85	66	28

Source: From F. Bakir, S.F. Damluji, L. Amin-Zaki *et al.* "Methylmercury Poisoning in Iraq: An Inter-University Report," *Science* 181 (1973), as reproduced in David Shephard, "Methyl Mercury Poisoning in Canada," *Canadian Medical Association Journal* 114 (March 1976): 463–72.

[a]The data from Iraq suggest that the range of 0–100 ppb of mercury in whole blood is associated with a 9.5 percent incidence of paresthesia (numbness in the extremities) and a 5 percent incidence of ataxia (stumbling gait) and dysarthria (slurred speech). Medical authorities concluded, however, that at this concentration, the symptoms were probably caused by factors other than methyl mercury.

ceptably high concentrations of methyl mercury. It did not take long to confirm that fish taken downstream from all the chlor-alkali plants in Ontario carried body burdens of mercury that were sometimes more than forty times the standard of 0.5 ppm set for export and human consumption by the federal government. The Lake St. Clair fishery was closed. In March 1970, the Ontario Minister of Energy and Resource Management ordered all the companies in the province with substantial industrial mercury losses to stop discharging mercury into the environment. One of these companies was Dryden Chemicals Limited, a subsidiary of Reed Paper Limited. In May 1970, the Ontario government banned commercial fishing on all lakes and tributaries of the English–Wabigoon river system.

There was cause for concern. Fish in the 300-mile river system, from Dryden to the Manitoba border, were found to contain mercury burdens comparable to those found in the fish of Minamata Bay. Levels of methyl mercury in the aquatic food chain of the system, including plankton, bottom-dwelling organisms, fish, wildfowl, and fish-eating mammals, were found to be ten to fifty times higher than those in surrounding waterways off the system. The greatest concentration of mercury was found among the organisms dwelling on the sediment bottom, particularly crayfish. In 1970, the average value of mercury in crayfish was 10 ppm, a value about twenty times greater than that in crayfish from unpolluted adjacent lakes and rivers.[15] Comprehensive studies of the mercury burden in fish in the early 1970s revealed levels of contamination so high that no species of fish from any lake on the river system was fit for human consumption. The range of mean mercury concentration (measured in parts per million, ppm) in the three most commercially viable species of fish found in

the English–Wabigoon river system was as follows (1975 data): pike, 2.31–5.18 ppm; walleye, 1.58–5.98 ppm; whitefish, 0.47–2.01 ppm. The mean level of mercury in the same species and size of fish taken from off-system lakes was, by contrast, several times lower: pike, 0.47–1.39 ppm; walleye, 0.38–1.08 ppm; whitefish, 0.04–0.24 ppm.[16]

Since these peak values were recorded, in the early 1970s, there has been a decline in the amount of mercury in fish, but it has not been of sufficient magnitude to inspire confidence that the river system will heal itself quickly.[17] Not only is the process of biomethylation singularly unenergetic, but there is also a great deal of inorganic mercury sitting on the bottom of the riverbed. It may therefore take anywhere from fifty to seventy years for the poison to clear the system. The pressing question is: Who is responsible for an environmental disaster of such proportions?

Between March 1962 and October 1975, Dryden Chemicals operated a mercury cathode chlor-alkali plant that produced chlorine and other chemicals for use as bleach in the adjacent pulp and paper mill of Reed Paper Limited (Dryden Division). During that period, scientists estimated that about 40 000 pounds of inorganic mercury were "lost" to the environment via aquatic and aerial discharges, of which about 20 000 pounds entered the English–Wabigoon river system.[18] Prior to the promulgation of the 1970 government control order to stop all mercury discharges into water systems, all the waste from the mercury cells was going into the air and the Wabigoon River. In 1970–71, treatment systems were installed to isolate the heavy metal in the effluent. Although this resulted in a significant decline in the amount of mercury going into the river, aerial emissions continued. The loss of mercury to the environment was finally halted in 1975, when the company changed the technology in its chlor-alkali plant.

Executives of Dryden Chemicals and Reed Paper Limited have repeatedly insisted that mercury occurs naturally in the environment of the Canadian Shield and that therefore the effluent from the mill was not the only source of mercury in the river. But the sheer volume of mercury discharged as waste and the fact that fish taken from the polluted waters show much higher mercury levels than fish caught in adjacent lakes and rivers undermine this argument. After studying the problem, scientists of the Ontario government came to the conclusion that "factors such as mineralization, mining activities, and aerial fallout cannot account for the elevated mercury levels found in fish from the Wabigoon–English system of lakes. The major source of mercury pollution in the area is the chlor-alkali plant/pulp and paper complex in Dryden, Ontario."[19]

Throughout the 1970s, corporate executives continued to deny any culpability for the contamination. They pleaded ignorance of the process of biomethylation. They argued that the mercury in the Wabigoon system was less harmful than the mercury discharged in Minamata Bay. And they insisted that they had no records of how much mercury was purchased, used, or discharged into the environment. The litany of rationalizations in their public pronouncements sometimes bordered on the absurd.[20] But the strongest line of defense was marshalled around the idea that the company had "a license to pollute" from the Ontario government. It had, after all, respected existing environmental regulations and standards; therefore, it could not be held exclusively liable for the disaster.

Robert Billingsley, president of Reed Paper Limited, succinctly asserted the company's position in an interview filmed in September 1975. "I think there are many instances in our society where people are harmed in one way or another through no fault of their own, and it's particularly difficult where blame is not exclusive, where there is [sic] complicating factors; and since we operate on a principle of law in this country, then you almost have to define [blame] in the courts, split up where is the responsibility, do it on a legal basis and assign ... the consequences.... I don't know exactly what we've done. Nobody has told us what the consequences of our actions were." The company's defense, then as now, rested on the premise that mercury pollution was a societal responsibility and that any claims for damages would have to be fought out in the courts. But as we come to understand the kind of injury and loss sustained by the Indian people, we will recognize the immense hurdles of definition, proof, and lack of precedent that would have to be overcome to obtain justice through the Canadian courts.

From Anastasia M. Shkilnyk, *A Poison Stronger Than Love: The Destruction Of An Ojibwa Community* (New Haven, Connecticut: Yale University Press, 1985). Copyright © Yale University. Reprinted by permission.

ENDNOTES

1. Bernardino Ramazzini, 1731 A.D., as quoted in Warner Troyer, *No Safe Place* (Toronto: Clark, Irwin and Company Limited, 1977), p. ix.

2. Quoted in "Mercury and Its Compounds," *Occupational Health Bulletin* 25, no. 7–8 (1970).

3. Data on the volume of mercury emissions in Canada show that in 1970 the chlor-alkali industry accounted for about 32.1 percent of the total volume of mercury losses from all industrial plants. Inadvertent emissions of mercury from petroleum combus-

tion constituted about 24.3 percent of the total. Paints, dental amalgams, instrumentation and electrical equipment, print manufacture, battery cathodes, pharmaceuticals, fungicides, and the recovery of gold, zinc, copper, and lead accounted for the remainder. Total emissions of mercury into the atmosphere in 1970 have been documented as 74.6 metric tons. Environment Canada, "National Inventory of Sources and Emissions of Mercury: 1970," Internal report APCD 73–6, 1973. See also L.M. Azzaria and F. Habashi, "Mercury Pollution—An Examination of Some Basic Issues," *CIM Bulletin* (August 1976), pp. 101–107.

4. Between 1955 and 1975, in the province of Ontario, for example, the Workmen's Compensation Board paid compensation to twenty-two workers who developed mercury poisoning. These workers held jobs in the following industries: hat manufacturing, gold refining, fungicides, battery manufacturing, and the electrical industry. Other cases of poisoning stemmed from working with mercury in a dental laboratory and from inhaling mercury vapor while firefighting. Two other cases of poisoning involved workers exposed to mercury in a chlor-alkali plant. It is inorganic mercury that is most often responsible for mercury poisoning among industrial workers (Troyer, p. 10).

5. In 1969, attorneys representing disease victims came to see Hosokawa, who had retired as the director of the Chisso Factory Hospital. He was very ill and dying, but he made a sworn statement that in 1959 he had informed Chisso executives that his research had demonstrated a direct link between Chisso effluent discharges and Minamata disease. In response to this information, management had stopped him from doing any further research and had clamped down on scientists trying to take samples of the effluent water. In public and during the court case, the company continued to deny that it had any previous knowledge of the link between its chemical operations and Minamata disease.

6. In 1956, 1960 and 1971–72, there were outbreaks of mercury poisoning in Iraq, where seed grain treated with mercury to prevent spoilage was diverted and milled for flour. Smaller outbreaks caused by eating mercury-treated seed grain occurred in Guatemala (1963–65), Ghana (1967), and Pakistan (1969). In 1964, in Niigata, Japan, 120 persons died from eating poisoned fish and shellfish in an outbreak similar to that at Minamata.

7. The process of biomethylation was first described in 1965 by two Swedish scientists, Alf Johnels and M. Olsson, who suggested that inorganic mercury of the kind used in chlor-alkali plants could be converted to methyl mercury in muddy lake bottoms. Within a few years, two more researchers documented more precisely how biomethylation works. See Soren Jensen and Arne Jernelov, "Biological Methylation of Mercury in Aquatic Organisms," Institute of Analytical Chemistry, University of Stockholm, 1969. In Canada, there is a continuing controversy as to when Canadian scientists were made aware of biomethylation and the dangers of polluting waterways with inorganic mercury.

8. A complete description of the type and distribution of lesions in the human brain caused by methyl mercury can be found in D. Hunter and

D. Russell, "Focal Cerebral and Cerebellar Atrophy in a Human Subject due to Organic Mercury Compound," *Journal of Neurology, Neurosurgery, and Psychiatry* 17 (1954):235–41; and T. Takeuchi, "Biological Reactions and Pathological Changes in Human Beings and Animals Caused by Organic Mercury Contamination," in *Environmental Mercury Contamination*, ed. R. Hartung and B.D. Dinman (Ann Arbor: Ann Arbor Science Publishers, 1972), pp. 247–89.

9. In 1953, in Niigata, Japan, a boy who had eaten large amounts of contaminated fish and shellfish over a period of only ten days was, seven years later, so severely affected by the poison that he could not attend school. Department of National Health and Welfare Canada, "Task Force on Organic Mercury in the Environment: Final Report (1973)," p. 6.

10. The level of mercury in hair is given in units of parts per million (ppm). The criteria for "safe" levels of mercury vary for hair as they do for blood, but generally, for persons having minimal environmental exposure to mercury, levels in hair are about 6 ppm. In Japan, people who had hair values of 200 ppm or more in 1965 are now seriously ill with Minamata disease; some of those who had hair levels between 100 and 200 ppm are now certified patients; and a few with hair levels between 50 and 100 ppm have the initial symptoms of mercury poisoning. Memorandum from the Mercury Team, National Indian Brotherhood, to the Standing Committee on Mercury in the Environment, October 9, 1975.

11. Iraq has had three outbreaks of organic mercury poisoning, two of which were major. In 1960, approximately 1000 persons were affected; in 1971 and 1972, 6430 cases were recorded, of which 459 were fatal. The 1971–72 outbreak followed the ingestion of bread made from grain treated with methyl mercurial fungicide. The symptoms of poisoning were similar, but not identical, to those found at Minamata. Whereas blood concentrations of Japanese victims were not fully documented at the time of exposure, in Iraq, blood samples were taken an average of sixty-five days after people stopped eating contaminated food.

An important question is whether the Iraqi data are relevant as a baseline for other populations. What the data show is that there is a risk of neurological damage for persons whose blood levels of methyl mercury are in the range of 100–500 ppb. The difference between the Iraqi situation and that in northwestern Ontario lies in the temporal nature of the exposure to mercury. In Iraq, the exposure was a brief one, with relatively large doses of mercury ingested over a period of one to three months. In Canada, the exposure of the Indian people is seasonal, with the highest blood levels of mercury falling at the end of the summer guiding period.

12. World Health Organization, Environmental Health Criteria: Mercury (Geneva: World Health Organization, 1976), pp. 23–24.

13. B.D. Dinman and L.H. Hecker, "The Dose-Response Relationship Resulting from Exposure to Alkyl Mercury Compounds," in *Environmental Mercury Contamination*, p. 290.

14. In 1966 and 1967, the Department of Health and Welfare was apparently warned by several sources that mer-

cury contamination could be a serious health hazard. Scientists from the National Research Council approached federal health authorities but were told that there was no problem. That same year, direct communication from the World Health Organization in Geneva failed to move the federal bureaucrats in Ottawa to action. Yet a full account of Minamata disease had been published in English as early as September 1961 (Troyer, pp. 22–23).

15. A comprehensive survey of mercury accumulation by all organisms in the system was carried out by the staff of the Freshwater Institute of the Fisheries Marine Service in Winnipeg. See A.L. Hamilton, "A Survey of Mercury Levels in the Biota of a Mercury-Contaminated River System in Northwestern Ontario," The Freshwater Institute, report No. 1167, 1972. In 1971, Norvald Fimreite studied fish-eating birds and waterfowl on the English–Wabigoon river system. He found very high levels of mercury in the tissues of the birds. Similar mercury values were found in another study of birds around Clay Lake (K. Vermeer, F. A. J. Armstrong, and D. Hatch, "Mercury in Aquatic Birds at Clay Lake, Western Ontario," *Journal of Wildlife Management* 37[1973]: 58–61).

16. J.N. Bishop and B.P. Neary, *Mercury Levels in Fish from Northwestern Ontario 1970–1975*, Inorganic Trace Contaminants Section, Laboratory Services Branch, Ontario Ministry of the Environment,, April 1976, p. 78.

17. After mercury discharges into a river system cease, natural restorative processes help to reduce the concentration of mercury in the sediment. These include the trapping and isolation of mercury by further sedimentation, the "flushing" of the system by the natural seasonal flow of water, and the transport of mercury further downstream. Between 1970 and 1975, for example, the level of mercury in the sediment twenty miles from the source of pollution in Dryden had decreased by half; further downstream, however, the level had increased. Recent indications are that the mercury burden continues to travel westward, downstream, away from the original source of the pollution.

18. J.A. Spence, "Inorganic Mercury Discharges and Emissions by the Dryden Chemical Col. Ltd., March 1962 to October 1975" (Unpublished paper, April 1977), p. 9. Estimates of mercury losses to the English–Wabigoon river system were based on known empirical relationships between chlorine production, mercury consumption, and mercury losses per ton of chlorine produced. Mercury was lost to the environment in wastewater from the plant, in sludge resulting from the precipitation of impurities in brine, and in atmospheric emissions from the mercury cell room. No direct estimate of aerial emissions of mercury has been made, although studies at similar plants have shown that such discharges form a substantial proportion of total losses; furthermore, they occur in the immediate vicinity and are then washed into the adjacent river system. The total inorganic mercury available to the English–Wabigoon river system (from both aerial and direct aquatic emissions) was estimated to be between 30 000 and 46 000 lbs (1962–75); the remainder (from estimated total losses of 50 000 lbs) was trapped in special disposal pits and buried.

19. Bishop and Neary, p. 78.

20. In describing the attempts to white-wash "the crimson history of mercury," Troyer includes the following excerpt from a press release prepared by Dryden Chemicals Limited: "To dispell [sic] the notion that we have wantonly dumped mercury into the river, we should point out that the effluent from our plant even before the installation of the treatment system had a mercury concentration in the order of 1/30 the concentration of mercury in normal human urine." Troyer quips back: "The logic is not much better than the spelling—few of us manage to excrete 33 million gallons* of urine daily" [1 gallon = 3.8 litres] (Troyer, p. 98).

CASE 10   R. v. Canadian Pacific Ltd.

Per Gonthier J. (La Forest, L'Heureux-Dube, McLachlin, Iacobucci and Major JJ. concurring)

Factual Background

On April 6 and 11, 1988, Canadian Pacific Limited ("C.P.") conducted controlled burns of the dry grass and weeds on its railway right-of-way in the Town of Kenora, Ontario. The purpose of the controlled burns was to clear the right-of-way of combustible material which posed a potential fire hazard. Both burns discharged a significant amount of thick, dark smoke, which adversely affected the health and property of nearby residents. One resident suffered an asthma attack in his driveway after being exposed to the smoke. The smoke filled the home of another man, with the result that he had to clean the interior walls and furniture thoroughly. Another resident discovered that the shrubs, grass and trees in her backyard had been damaged by the fire and smoke.

The smoke from the April 11, 1988 controlled burn was not only injurious to the health and property of several Kenora residents, but also hampered visibility on a 200-foot stretch of an adjacent road.

One driver was forced to engage his vehicle lights and brakes because the smoke was so heavy that he was unable to see the other side of the road.

Following complaints from residents of the town, C.P. was charged with unlawfully discharging or permitting the discharge of a contaminant namely, smoke, into the natural environment that was likely to cause an adverse effect, contrary to s. 13(1)(a) of the Ontario *Environmental Protection Act* ("E.P.A.").

On October 22, 1991, C.P. was acquitted by Daub J.P. of the Provincial Offences Court of Ontario, who concluded that, although the respondents had established the essential elements of the offence under s. 13(1)(a) of the E.P.A., the appellant's defence of due diligence raised a reasonable doubt. On June 22, 1992, the respondent's appeal to the Ontario Court of Justice, Provincial Division, was allowed, and C.P.'s acquittal was overturned ...

C.P. appealed to the Ontario Court of Appeal, raising two constitutional issues. First, C.P. advanced an interjurisdictional immunity claim, arguing that, because it is a federal undertaking, s. 13(1)(a) of the *Ontario E.P.A.* is not constitutionally applicable to emissions from controlled burns on its railroad right-of-way. Second, C.P. alleged that s. 13(1)(a) was unconstitutionally vague, and therefore in violation of s. 7 of the *Charter*. On May 19, 1993, the Court of Appeal dismissed C.P.'s appeal ...

C.P. then appealed both constitutional issues to this court. In reasons delivered from the bench on January 24, 1995, this court dismissed the interjurisdictional immunity claim ... Judgment on the s. 7 claim was reserved.

Relevant Statutory Provisions

Environmental Protection Act, R.S.O. 1980, c. 141, as amended S.O. 1983, c. 52

1(1) in this Act,

(viii)

(c) "contaminant" means any solid, liquid, gas, odour, heat, sound, vibration, radiation or combination of any of them resulting directly or indirectly from the activities of many [sic] that may,

(i) impair the quality of the natural environment for any use that can be made of it,
(ii) cause injury or damage to property or to plant or animal life,
(iii) cause harm or material discomfort to any person,
(iv) adversely affect the health or impair the safety of any person,
(v) render any property or plant or animal life unfit for use by man,
(vi) cause loss of enjoyment of normal use of property, or
(vii) interfere with the normal conduct of business.

(k) "natural environment" means the air, land, and water, or any combination or part thereof, of the Province of Ontario;

13(1) Notwithstanding any other provision of this Act or the regulations, no person shall deposit, add, emit or discharge a contaminant or cause or permit the deposit, addition, emission or discharge of a contaminant into the natural environment that,

(a) causes or is like[ly] to cause impairment of the quality of the natural environment for any use that can be made of it;
(b) causes or is likely to cause injury or damage to property or to plant or animal life;
(c) causes or is likely to cause harm or material discomfort to any person;
(d) adversely affects or is like[ly] to adversely affect the health of any person;
(e) impairs or is likely to impair the safety of any person;
(f) renders or is likely to render any property or plant or animal life unfit for use by man;
(g) causes or is likely to cause loss of enjoyment of normal use of property;
(h) interferes or is likely to interfere with the normal conduct of business.

(2) Clause (1)(a) does not apply to animal wastes disposed of in accordance with normal farming practices.

Analysis

... Section 13(1)(a) constitutes a broad and general pollution prohibition. In this respect, it is not unusual, as the E.P.A. contains several broadly worded prohibitions. For example, Part VIII of the E.P.A. prohibits "littering," and "litter" is broadly defined in s. 73 to include,

73 ... any material left or abandoned in a place other than a receptacle or place intended or approved for receiving such material and "littering" has a corresponding meaning.

Another example is found in s. 23(2) of the E.P.A., which prohibits the discharge or deposit of any "waster upon or over the ice over any water." "Waster" is defined in s. 23(1)(c) as "human excrement or any refuse."

Environmental protection laws in other provinces contain similarly broad pollution prohibitions. Nova Scotia's *Environmental Protection Act* ... prohibits pollution generally... and "pollution" is defined in part as a "detrimental alteration or variation ... that causes or is likely to cause impairment of the quality of the environment for any use that can be made of it ..." (S. 3(f)(i)(A)).

Quebec's *Environmental Quality Act* ... contains the following prohibition:

> 20. No one may emit, deposit, issue or discharge or allow the emission deposit issuance or discharge into the environment of a contaminant in a greater quantity or concentration than that provided for by regulation of the Gouvernement.

The same prohibition applies to the emission, deposit, issuance or discharge of any contaminant the presence of which in the environment is prohibited by regulation of the Gouvernement or is likely to affect the life, health, safety, welfare or comfort of human beings, or to cause damage to or otherwise impair the quality of the soil, vegetation, wild life or property ...

What is clear from this brief review of Canadian pollution prohibitions is that our legislators have preferred to take a broad and general approach, and have avoided an exhaustive codification of every circumstance in which pollution is prohibited. Such an approach is hardly surprising in the field of environmental protection, given the nature of the environment (its complexity, and the wide range of activities which might cause harm to it) is not conducive to precise codification. Environmental protection legislation has, as a result, been framed in a manner ca-

pable of responding to a wide variety of environmental harmful scenarios, including ones which might not have been foreseen by the drafters of the legislation. This has left such legislation open to allegations of unconstitutional vagueness ...

C.P.'s vagueness and overbreadth claims in relation to s. 13(1)(a) of the Ontario *E.P.A.* could, in my view, be raised against any of the provincial and federal pollution prohibitions which I have mentioned above. Thus, a finding in C.P.'s favour in the instant case would place these prohibitions, and potentially many others, in constitutional jeopardy. Such a finding would obviously impede the ability of the legislature to provide for environmental protection, and would constitute a significant social policy set-back. However,... I find that C.P.'s constitutional challenge must fail. The terms of s. 13(1)(a) of the *E.P.A.* are not vague, but in fact apply quite clearly to pollution activity which is appropriately the subject of legislative prohibitions. Moreover, while s. 13(1)(a) applies broadly, the objective of environmental protection is ambitious in scope. The legislature is justified in choosing equally ambitious means for achieving this objective.

... In the context of environmental protection legislation, a strict requirement of drafting precision might well undermine the ability of the legislature to provide for a comprehensive and flexible regime ... [G]enerally framed pollution prohibitions are desirable from a public policy perspective ... In my view, the generality of s. 13(1)(a) ensures flexibility in the law, so that the *E.P.A.* may respond to a wide range of environmentally harmful scenarios which could not have been foreseen at the time of its enactment.

Moreover, the precise codification of environmental hazards in environmental protection legislation may hinder, rather than promote, public understanding of what conduct is prohibited, and may fuel uncertainty about the areas of risk created by legislation ... In the area of environmental protection, legislators have two choices. They may enact detailed provisions which prohibit the release of particular quantities of enumerated substances into the natural environment. Alternatively, they may choose a more general prohibition of pollution, and rely on the courts to determine whether, in a particular case, the release of a substance into the natural environment is of sufficient magnitude to attract legislative sanction. The latter option is, of course, more flexible and better able to accommodate developments in our knowledge about environmental protection. However, a general enactment may be challenged (as in the instant case) for failing to provide adequate notice to citizens of prohibited conduct. Is a very detailed enactment preferable? In my view, in the field of environmental protection, detail is not necessarily the best means of notifying citizens of prohibited conduct. If a citizen requires a chemistry degree to figure out whether an activity releases a particular contaminant in sufficient quantities to trigger a statutory prohibition, then that prohibition provides no better fair notice than a more general enactment. The notice aspect of the vagueness analysis must be approached from an objective point of view: would an average citizen, with an average understanding of the subject matter of the prohibition, receive adequate notice of prohibited conduct? If specialized knowledge is required to understand a legislative provision, then citizens may be baffled.

Of course, the question remains as to whether sufficient notice is provided to meet the standard demanded of s. 7 [of the *Canadian Charter of Rights and Freedoms*]. On this point, in *Nova Scotia Pharmaceutical Society* ... I observed that there are two aspects to the fair no-

tice requirement: procedural and substantive. Procedural notice involves the mere fact of bringing the text of a law to the attention of citizens ... [T]he idea of giving fair notice to citizens would be rather empty if procedural notice were sufficient, particularly since citizens are presumed to know the law. Therefore, whether or not citizens are familiar with the text of a law is not a central concern of vagueness analysis. Instead the focus of the analysis is the substantive aspect of fair notice, which I described ... as an understanding that some conduct comes under the law.

Whether citizens appreciate that particular conduct is subject to legislative sanction is inextricably linked to society values. As I stated in *Nova Scotia Pharmaceutical Society* ...

> The substantive aspect of fair notice is therefore a subjective understanding that the law touches upon some conduct, based on the substratum of values underlying the legal enactment and on the role that the legal enactment plays in the life of the society.

Societal values are highly relevant in assessing whether a general pollution prohibition such as s. 13(1)(a) of the *E.P.A.*, provides fair notice to citizens of prohibited conduct. It is clear that over the past two decades, citizens have become acutely aware of the importance of environmental protection, and of the fact that penal consequences may flow from conduct which harms the environment. Recent environmental disasters, such as the Love Canal, the Mississauga train derailment, the chemical spill at Bhopal, the Chernobyl nuclear accident, and the Exxon Valdez oil spill, have served as lightening [sic] rods for public attention and concern. Acid rain, ozone depletion, global warming and air quality have been highly publicized as more general environmental issues. Aside from high-profile environmental issues with a national or international scope, local environmental issues have been raised and debated widely in Canada. Everyone is aware that individually and collectively, we are responsible for preserving the natural environment ...

In 1988, when the pollution in the instant case took place, few citizens would have been aware of the actual terms of s. 13(1)(a) of the *E.P.A.* However, the average citizen in Ontario would have known that pollution was statutorily prohibited. It therefore would not have come as a surprise to citizens that *E.P.A.* prohibited the emission of contaminants into the environment that were likely to impair a use of the natural environment. In my view, the purpose and terms of s. 13(1)(a) are so closely related to the society value of environmental protection that substantive notice of the prohibition in s. 13(1)(a) is easy to demonstrate ...

I therefore conclude that the purpose and subject-matter of s. 13(1)(a) of the *E.P.A.*, the society values underlying it, and its nature as a regulatory offence, all inform the analysis of C.P.'s vagueness claim. Legislators must have considerable room to manoeuvre in the field of environmental regulation, and s. 7 must not be employed to hinder flexible and ambitious legislative approaches to environmental protection.

Keeping this is mind, it is now necessary to consider the actual terms of s. 13(1)(a). In order to secure a conviction under s. 13(1)(a), the Crown must prove three elements: (1) that the accused has emitted, or caused or permitted the emission of a contaminant; (2) that the contaminant was emitted into the natural environment; and (3) that the contaminant caused or was likely to cause the impairment of the quality of the natural environment for any use that can be made of it ...

Like the lower courts, I have no difficulty in concluding that C.P.'s conduct

in Kenora on April 6 and 11, 1988, fell squarely within the pollution prohibition contained in s. 13 (1)(a) of the *E.P.A.* C.P. emitted noxious smoke which contaminated the natural environment, and which interfered with its use by several homeowners and drivers in a manner which was more than trivial or minimal. In fact, I do not understand C.P.'s argument to be that s. 13(1)(a) is vague in relation to the conduct which gave rise to the charges in the instant case. C.P. argues instead that the expression for any use than [sic] can be made of "the natural environment" is vague because it is not qualified as to time, degree, space or user, and thus fails to delineate clearly an area of risk for citizens generally.

C.P. is advancing an argument based on peripheral vagueness, which arises where a statute applies without question to a core of conduct, but applies with uncertainty to other activities. C.P.'s conduct fell within the core of polluting activity prohibited by s. 13(1)(a), yet C.P. is relying on hypothetical fact situations which fall at the periphery of s. 13(1)(a), and to which it is uncertain whether liability attaches. I would note that the core-periphery problem is encountered in relation to virtually every legislative provision, and is an inevitable result of the imprecision of human language ...

Having dispensed with C.P.'s vagueness claim, it is now necessary to turn to the issue of overbreadth. In its submissions, C.P. argued in part that s. 13(1)(a) of the *E.P.A.* is vague because it is overbroad. In light of my reasons above, however, I think that this submission must fail.

Environmental protection is a legitimate concern of government, and as I have already observed, it is a very broad subject-matter which does not lend itself to precise codification. Where the legislature is pursuing the objective of environmental protection, it is justified in choosing equally broad legislative language in order to provide for a necessary degree of flexibility. Certainly, s. 13(1)(a) captures a broad range of polluting conduct. However, my reasons in relation to the vagueness claim illustrate that the provision does not capture pollution with only a trivial or minimal impact on a use of the natural environment. Moreover, the "use" condition limits the application of s. 13(1)(a) by requiring the Crown to establish not only that a polluting substance has been released, but also that an actual or likely use of the environment, which itself has some significance, has been impaired by the release. Speculative or purely imaginary uses of the environment are not captured by the provision. These limits on the application of s. 13(1)(a) prevent it from being deployed in situations where the objective of environmental protection is not implicated. In my view, then, the breadth of s. 13(1)(a) matches the breadth of the objective of environmental protection. There is no overbreadth ...

Conclusion

... s 13(1)(a) of the *E.P.A.*, and specifically the expression "for any use that can be made o[f] the natural environment," are not unconstitutionally vague or overbroad.

Section 13(1)(a) is sufficiently precise to provide a meaningful legal debate, when the provision is considered in light of the purpose and subject matter of the *E.P.A.*, the nature of the provision as a regulatory offence, the societal value of environmental protection, related provisions of the *E.P.A.*, and general interpretive principles. Section 13(1)(a) is also proportionate and not overbroad. The objective of environmental protection is itself broad, and the legislature is justified in choosing broad, flexible language to give effect to this objective. I would therefore dismiss this appeal and answer the second and third constitutional questions as follows:

> 2. Is s. 13(1)(a) of the *Environmental Protection Act* so vague as to infringe s. 7 of the *Canadian Charter of Rights and Freedoms*?

A. No.

> 3. If the answer to Question 2 is in the affirmative, is s. 13(1)(a) nevertheless justified by s. 1 of the *Charter*?

A. This question does not arise.

Appeal dismissed.

Supreme Court of Canada, 99 C.C.C. 3d 97, July 20, 1995.

SUGGESTED READINGS

Blackstone, William (ed.). *Philosophy and the Environmental Crisis*. Athens, Georgia: University of Georgia Press, 1974.

Dobell, R. "The Global Bargain." *Options*, Vol. 10, No. 10, 1989.

Doern, G.B. *Regulatory Processes and Jurisdictional Issues in the Regulation of Hazardous Products in Canada*. Background Study No. 41, Ottawa: Science Council of Canada, 1977.

Goodland, R. and H. Daley. "Environmental Sustainability: Universal and Non-Negotiable." In L. Westra and J. Lemons (eds.), *Perspectives on Implementing Ecological Integrity*. Cordrecht, The Netherlands: Kluwer Publishing, 1995.

Goodpaster, K. and K. Sayre (eds.). *Ethics and Problems of the 21st Century*. Notre Dame, Ind.: University of Notre Dame Press, 1979.

Holm, Wendy (ed.). *Water and Free Trade*. Toronto: James Lorimer and Co., 1988.

Leiss, W. (ed.) *Ecology Versus Politics in Canada.* Toronto: University of Toronto Press, 1979.

Passmore, J.E. *Man's Responsibility for Nature.* New York: Charles Scribner's Sons, 1974.

Roemer, John. "A Public Ownership Resolution of the Tragedy of the Commons." *Social Philosophy & Policy*, Vol. 6, No. 2, Spring 1989.

Scherer, D. and T. Attig (eds.). *Ethics and the Environment.* Englewood Cliffs, NJ: Prentice-Hall, 1983.

Schrader-Frechette, K. and E McCoy. *Method in Ecology.* Cambridge: Cambridge University Press, 1993.

Schrecker, T. "Political Economy of Environmental Hazards." Law Reform Commission of Canada Study Paper: Protection of Life Series, 1984.

Sentes, Ray. "The Asbestos Albatross." *Options*, Vol. 10, No. 10, December 1989.

Singer, P. *Practical Ethics,* 2nd ed. New York: Cambridge University Press, 1993.

Singh, Jang. "Business Activity and the Environment: The Case of Guyana Sugar Corporation and Thallium Sulphate." *Journal of Business Ethics*, Vol. 7, No. 5, 1988.

Swaigen, John (ed.). *Environmental Rights in Canada.* Toronto: Butterworths, 1981.

Westra, L. "Corporate Responsibility and Hazardous Products." *Business Ethics Quarterly*, 4, 1, 1994, pp. 47–110.

BUSINESS IN A

GLOBAL ECONOMY

INTRODUCTION

Some people argue that a corporation is fulfilling its moral responsibility if it maximizes profit for its stockholders and obeys
the law. As we saw in Part 1, this is essentially the view defended by Milton
Friedman. Others, however, while they agree
that corporations should obey the law, point
out that the law is often an inadequate guide
to morally responsible behaviour.

In this section, we examine this debate in
the context of international business.
Companies often choose to operate in countries where the law is far less protective of
workers than in Canada. With a new world
economic order of free-trade pacts, multinational corporations negotiate globally for the
most competitive work environments in which
to operate. This frequently means moving factories to countries where salaries are lower
and worker benefits less onerous than in developed and industrialized nation states. Many
fashion houses have garments sewn in developing countries, where women work for

far less than the minimum wage in Canada,
and where the law does not protect them from
having to work long hours without overtime
pay. Are Canadian companies that faithfully
obey the laws of these host countries, and
which dutifully maximize the profits of their
stockholders, fulfilling their moral responsibilities? Should there perhaps be universal
guidelines or laws by which all companies
must abide, regardless of the particular laws of
their host country? Many answer "yes" to the
first question and "no" to the second. In defence of this view, some simply reiterate the
arguments of capitalists such as Friedman.
Others argue that universalized laws would
not in fact benefit workers in underdeveloped
countries. Still others believe that offering
wages similar to those received by the rest of
the citizens in the country not only allows for
the possibility of more jobs, which benefits
the country as a whole, but also serves to prevent unrest among employees not working
for the company. Others counter that this is
merely a smoke-screen argument made by
those who wish to exploit cheap labour in un-

derdeveloped countries. What is clear is that the world has become in many respects a "global assembly line." The third edition of this text goes to press as Canadians debate the next phase of international free trade, the Multilateral Agreement on Investment (MAI). As with the North American Free Trade Agreement (NAFTA), Canadians are embroiled in a debate about whether this proposed agreement will increase Canada's competitive edge in the global economy, or erode the quality of life both for Canadians and citizens in other countries. In a recent text, Clarke and Barlow (1997) argue in a manner similar to Poff, in an article in this chapter, that such agreements threaten Canadian sovereignty and democracy by eroding the authority of nation states.

In the first article in this chapter, Donaldson attempts to solve the issue of differing legal and moral standards, and the dilemmas these pose for multinational corporations, by constructing an ethical algorithm for multinational managers to use in reconciling international normative conflicts. While Donaldson is skeptical about the likelihood of corporations adopting such an ethical algorithm, he believes both in the possibility of this occurring and the value of this contribution in improving the ethical performance of multinational corporations.

In our second article, a different issue in international business negotiations is introduced. Bribery, while a crime in many nation states, has been common practice in others. Is it acceptable to offer bribes to obtain contracts in another country if the practice is not only commonplace there but seems essential to any successful business negotiation? In our second selection, Henry Lane and Donald Simpson address this question and relate some of their own personal experiences. They also clearly outline the basic sides taken in the debate. On the one hand, some argue, "it is an accepted business practice in [some] countries, and when you are in Rome you have to do as the Romans do. 'Moralists,' on the other hand, believe that cultural relativity is no excuse for unethical behavior." Lane and Simpson provide a theoretical discussion of the multifaceted nature of bribery in global terms, and argue that bribery is not only unnecessary for successful negotiation, but may not even be in one's own self-interest or the interests of one's company.

In a related article, Carson analyses both bribery and extortion in international business. He begins by offering definitions of these two activities. Bribery, he suggests, "is a payment of money (or something of value) to another person in exchange for his giving one special consideration that is incompatible with the duties of his office, position, or role." Carson contrasts this with extortion, which "is the act of threatening someone with harm (that one is not entitled to inflict on him), in order to obtain benefits to which one has no prior right." Although Carson believes that his definition is inadequate to cover all types of extortion, his claim is that anyone who does act in accordance with it would indeed be guilty of extortion. After providing his useful definitions, Carson proceeds to offer a conceptual analysis of the similarities and differences between bribery and extortion. He then makes an interesting case for the claim that although we have strong *prima facie* reasons to believe that bribery is wrong, it is not so clear that succumbing to extortion is always morally wrong.

Chapter 25

MULTINATIONAL DECISION-MAKING: Reconciling International Norms

Thomas Donaldson

Jurisprudence theorists are often puzzled when, having thoroughly analyzed an issue within the boundaries of a legal system, they must confront it again outside those boundaries. For international issues, trusted axioms often fail as the secure grounds of legal tradition and national consensus erode. Much the same happens when one moves from viewing a problem of corporate ethics against a backdrop of national moral consensus to the morally inconsistent backdrop of international opinion. Is the worker who appeals to extra-national opinion while complaining about a corporate practice accepted within his or her country, the same as an ordinary whistleblower? Is a factory worker in Mexico justified in complaining about being paid three dollars an hour for the same work a U.S. factory worker, employed by the same company, is paid eight dollars?[1] Is he justified when in Mexico the practice of paying workers three dollars an hour—and even much less—is widely accepted? Is an asbestos worker in India justified in drawing world attention to the lower standards of in-plant asbestos pollution maintained by an English multinational relative to standards in England, when the standards in question fall within Indian government guidelines and, indeed, are stricter than the standards maintained by other Indian asbestos manufacturers?

What distinguishes these issues from standard ones about corporate practices is that they involve reference to a conflict of norms, either moral or legal, between home and host country. This paper examines the subclass of conflicts in which host country norms appear substandard from the perspective of home country, and evaluates the claim often made by multinational executives that the prevalence of seemingly lower

From *Journal of Business Ethics* 4 (1985), 357–366. © 1985 by Thomas Donaldson. Reprinted by permission.

standards in a host country warrants the adoption by multinationals of the lower standards. It is concerned with cases of the following form: A multinational company (*C*) adopts a corporate practice (*P*) which is morally and/or legally permitted in *C*'s host country (*B*), but not in *C*'s home country (*A*). The paper argues that the presence of lower standards in *B* justifies *C*'s adopting the lower standards only in certain, well-defined contexts. It proposes a conceptual test, or ethical algorithm, for multinationals to use in distinguishing justified from unjustified applications of standards. This algorithm ensures that multinational practice will remain faithful at least to the enlightened standards of home country morality.

If *C* is a non-national, that is to say a multinational, corporation, then one may wonder why home country opinion should be a factor in *C*'s decision-making. One reason is that although global companies are multinational in doing business in more than one country, they are uninational in composition and character. They are chartered in a single country, typically have over ninety-five percent of their stock owned by citizens of their home country, and have managements dominated by citizens of their home country. Thus, in an important sense the term 'multinational' is a misnomer. For our purposes it is crucial to acknowledge that the moral foundation of a multinational, i.e., the underlying assumptions of its managers infusing corporate policies with a basic sense of right and wrong, is inextricably linked to the laws and mores of the home country.

Modern textbooks dealing with international business consider cultural relativity to be a powerful factor in executive decision-making. Indeed they often use it to justify practices abroad which, although enhancing corporate profits, would be questionable in the multinational's home country. One prominent text, for example, remarks that "In situations where patterns of dominance-subordination are socially determined, and

not a function of demonstrated ability, management should be cautioned about promoting those of inferior social status to positions in which they are expected to supervise those of higher social status."[2] Later, referring to multiracial societies such as South Africa, the same text offers managers some practical advice: "... the problem of the multiracial society manifests itself particularly in reference to promotion and pay. And equal pay for equal work policy may not be acceptable to the politically dominant but racial minority group ..."[3]

Consider two actual instances of the problem at issue:

Charles Pettis In 1966 Charles Pettis, employee of Brown and Root Overseas, Inc., an American multinational, became resident engineer for one of his company's projects in Peru: a 146 mile, $46 million project to build a highway across the Andes. Pettis soon discovered that Peruvian safety standards were far below those in the United States. The highway design called for cutting channels through mountains in areas where rock formations were unstable. Unless special precautions were taken, slides could occur. Pettis blew the whistle, complaining first to Peruvian government officials and later to U.S. officials. No special precautions were taken, with the result that thirty-one men were killed by slides during the construction of the road. Pettis was fired for his trouble by Brown and Root and had difficulty finding a job with another company.[4]

American bank in Italy A new American bank in Italy was advised by its Italian attorneys to file a tax return that misstated income and expenses and consequently grossly underestimated actual taxes due. The bank learned, however, that most other Italian companies regarded this practice as standard operating procedure and merely the first move in a complex negotiating process with the Italian Internal Revenue Service. The bank initially refused to file a fallacious return on moral grounds and submitted an 'American style' return instead. But because the resulting tax bill was many times higher than what comparable Italian companies were asked to pay, the bank changed policy in later years to agree with 'Italian style.'[5]

A. THE MORAL POINT OF VIEW

One may well decide that home country standards were mandatory in one of the above cases, but not in the other. One may decide that despite conforming to Peruvian standards, Peruvian safety precautions were unacceptable, while at the same time acknowledging that however inequitable and inefficient Italian tax mores may be, a decision to file 'Italian style' is permissible.

Despite claims to the contrary, one must reject the simple dictum that whenever P violates a moral standard of country A, it is impermissible for C. Arnold Berleant has argued that the principle of equal treatment endorsed by most U.S. citizens requires that U.S. corporations pay workers in less developed countries exactly the same wages paid to U.S. workers in comparable jobs (after appropriate adjustments are made for cost of living levels in the relevant areas).[6] But most observers, including those from the less developed countries, believe this stretches the doctrine of equality too far in a way detrimental to host countries. By arbitrarily establishing U.S. wage levels as the benchmark for fairness one eliminates the role of the international market in establishing salary levels, and this in turn eliminates the incentive U.S. corporations have to hire foreign workers. If U.S. companies felt morally bound to pay Korean workers exactly the wages U.S. workers receive for comparable work, they would not locate in Korea. Perhaps U.S. firms should exceed market rate for foreign labor as a matter of moral principle, but to pay strictly equal rates would freeze less developed countries out of the international labor market.[7] Lacking, then, a simple formula of the sort, 'P is wrong when P violates A's norms,' one seems driven to undertake a more complex analysis of the types and degrees of responsibilities multinationals possess.

The first task is to distinguish between responsibilities that hold as minimum conditions, and ones that exceed the minimum. We are reminded of the distinction, eloquently articulated by Kant, between perfect and imperfect duties. Perfect duties are owed to a specific class of persons under specified conditions, such as the duty to honor promises. They differ from imperfect duties, such as the duty of charity, which although mandatory, allow considerable discretion as to when, how, and to whom they are fulfilled. The perfect-imperfect distinction, however, is not appropriate for corporations since it is doubtful whether economic entities such as corporations must assume the same imperfect burdens, e.g., of charity, as individual persons.

For purposes of discussing multinationals, then, it is best to recast the distinction into one between 'minimal' and 'enlightened' duties, where a minimal duty is one the persistent failure of which to observe would deprive the corporation of its moral right to exist, i.e., a strictly mandatory duty, and an enlightened duty is one whose fulfillment would be praiseworthy but not mandatory in any sense. In the present context, it is the determination of minimal duties that has priority since in attempting to answer whether P is permissible for C in B, the notion of permissibility must eventually be cashed in terms of minimal standards. Thus, P is not impermissible for C simply because C fails to achieve an ideal vision of corporate conduct; and C's failure to contribute generously to the United Nations is a permissible, if regrettable, act.

Because minimal duties are our target, it is appropriate next to invoke the language of rights, for rights are entitlements that impose minimum demands on the behavior of others.

B. THE APPEAL TO RIGHTS

Theorists commonly analyze the obligations of developed to less developed countries in terms of rights. James Sterba argues that "distant peoples" (e.g., persons in Third World countries) enjoy welfare rights that members of the developed countries are obliged to respect.[8] Welfare rights are defined as rights to whatever is necessary to satisfy "basic needs", and "basic needs", in turn, as needs "which must be satisfied in order not to seriously endanger a person's health and sanity".[9] It follows that multinationals are obliged to avoid workplace hazards that seriously endanger workers' health.

A similar notion is advanced by Henry Shue in his book, *Basic Rights*. The substance of a basic right for Shue is "something the deprivation of which is one standard threat to rights generally."[10] He considers it a "minimal demand" that "no individuals or institutions, including corporations, may ignore the universal duty to avoid depriving persons of their basic rights."[11] Since one's physical security, including safety from exposure to harmful chemicals or pollution, is a condition for one's enjoyment of rights generally, it follows that the right to physical security is a basic right that imposes specific obligations on corporations.

Equally important for our purposes is Shue's application elsewhere of the "no harm" principle to the actions of U.S. multinationals abroad.[12] Associated with Mill and traditional liberalism, the "no harm" principle reflects a rights based approach emphasizing the individual's right to liberty, allowing maximal liberty to each so long as each inflicts no avoidable harm on others. Shue criticizes as a violation of the no-harm principle a plan by a Colorado based company to export millions of tons

of hazardous chemical waste from the U.S. for processing and disposal in the West African nation of Sierra Leone.[13] Using the same principle, he is able to criticize any U.S. asbestos manufacturing corporation which, in order to escape expensive regulations at home, moves its plant to a foreign country with lower standards.[14]

Thus the Shue-Sterba rights based approach recommends itself as a candidate for evaluating multinational conduct. It is irrelevant whether the standards of *B* comply or fail to comply with home country standards; what is relevant is whether they meet a universal, objective minimum. In the present context, the principal advantage of a rights based approach is to establish a firm limit to appeals made in the name of host country laws and morals—at least when the issue is a clear threat to workers' safety. Clear threats such as in-plant asbestos pollution exceeding levels recommended by independent scientific bodies, are incompatible with employees' rights, especially their right not to be harmed. It is no excuse to cite lenient host country regulations or ill-informed host country public opinion.

But even as a rights oriented approach clarifies a moral bottom line for extreme threats to workers' safety, it leaves obscure not only the issue of less extreme threats, but of harms other than physical injury. The language of rights and harm is sufficiently vague so as to leave shrouded in uncertainty a formidable list of issues crucial to multinationals.

When refined by the traditions of a national legal system, the language of rights achieves great precision. But left to wander among the concepts of general moral theory, the language proves less exact. Granted, the celebrated dangers of asbestos call for recognizing the right to workers' safety no matter how broadly the language of rights is framed. But what are we to say of a less toxic pollutant? Is the level of sulfur-dioxide air pollution we should demand in a struggling nation, say, one with only a few fertilizer plants working overtime to help feed its malnourished population, the same we should demand in Portland, Oregon? Or taking a more obvious case, should the maximal level of thermal pollution generated by a poor nation's electric power plants be the same as West Germany's? Since thermal pollution raises the temperature of a given body of water, it lowers the capacity of the water to hold oxygen and in turn the number of 'higher' fish species, e.g., Salmon and Trout. But whereas the trade-off between more Trout and higher output is rationally made by the West German in favor of the Trout, the situation is reversed for the citizen of Chad, Africa. This should not surprise us. It has long been recognized that many rights, e.g., the right to medical care, are dependent for their specification on the level of economic development of the country in question.[15]

Nor is it clear how a general appeal to rights will resolve issues that turn on the interpretation of broad social practices. For example, in the Italian tax case mentioned earlier, the propriety of submitting an 'Italian' vs. 'American' style tax return hinges more on the appraisal of the value of honesty in a complex economic and social system, than on an appeal to inalienable rights.

C. AN ETHICAL ALGORITHM

What is needed, then, is a test for evaluating *P* more comprehensive than a simple appeal to rights. In the end nothing short of a general moral theory working in tandem with an analysis of the foundations of corporate existence is needed. That is, ultimately there is no escape for the multinational executive from merging the ordinary canons of economic decision-making, of profit maximization and market share, with the principles of basic moral theory.[16] But this formidable task, essential as it is, does not preclude the possibility of discovering lower-order moral concepts to clarify the moral intuitions already in use by multinational decision-makers. Apart from the need for general theories of multinational conduct there is need for pragmatic aids to multinational decision-making that bring into relief the ethical implications of views already held. This suggests, then, the possibility of generating an interpretive mechanism, or algorithm, that managers of multinationals could use in determining the implications of their own moral views about cases of the form, "Is *P* permissible for *C* when *P* is acceptable in *B* but not in *A*?"

The first step in generating such an ethical algorithm is to isolate distinct senses in which *B*'s norms may conflict with the norms of *A*. Now, if *P* is morally and/or legally permitted in *B*, but not in *A* then either:

1. The moral reasons underlying *B*'s view that *P* is permissible refer to *B*'s relative level of economic development; or

2. The moral reasons underlying *B*'s view that *P* is permissible are independent of *B*'s relative level of economic development.

Let us call the conflict of norms described in (1) a 'type #1' conflict. In such a conflict, an African country that permits slightly higher levels of thermal pollution from electric power generating plants, or a lower minimum wage, than those prescribed in European countries would do so not because higher standards would be undesirable *per se*, but because its level of economic development requires an ordering of priorities. In the future when it succeeds in matching European economic achievements, it may well implement the higher standards.

Let us call the conflict of norms described in (2) a 'type #2' conflict. In such cases levels of economic development play no role. For example, low level institutional nepotism, common in many underdeveloped countries, is justified not on economic grounds, but on the basis of clan and family loyalty. Presumably the same loyalties should be operative even after the country has risen to economic success—as the nepotism prevalent in Saudi Arabia would indicate. The Italian tax case also reflects an Italian cultural style with a penchant for personal negotiation and an unwillingness to formalize transactions, more than a strategy based on level of economic development.

When the conflicts of norms occur for reasons other than relative economic development (type #2), then the possibility is increased that there exists what Richard Brandt has called an "ultimate ethical disagreement." An ultimate disagreement occurs when two cultures are able to consider the same set of facts surrounding a moral issue while disagreeing on the moral issue itself. An ultimate disagreement is less likely in a type #1 case since after suitable reflection about priorities imposed by differing economic circumstances, the members of *A* may come to agree that given the facts of *B*'s level of economic development, *P* is permissible. On the other hand, a type #2 dispute about what Westerners call "nepotism" will continue even after economic variables are discounted.[17]

The status of the conflict of norms between *A* and *B*, i.e., whether it is of type #1 or #2, does not fix the truth value of *B*'s claim that *P* is permissible. *P* may or may not be permissible whether the conflict is of type #1 or #2. This, however, is not to say that the truth value of *B*'s claim is independent of the conflict's type status, for a different test will be required to determine whether *P* is permissible when the conflict is of type #1 than type #2. In a type #1 dispute, the following formula is appropriate:

> *P* is permissible if and only if the members of *A* would, under conditions of economic development relevantly similar to those of *B*, regard *P* as permissible.

Under this test, excessive levels of asbestos pollution would almost certainly not be tolerated by the members of *A* under relevantly similarly economic conditions, whereas higher levels of thermal pollution would be. The test, happily, explains and confirms our initial moral intuitions.

Yet, when as in type #2 conflicts the dispute between *A* and *B* depends upon a fundamental difference of perspective, the step to equalize hypothetically the levels of economic development is useless. A different test is needed. In type #2 conflicts the opposing evils of ethnocentricism and ethical relativism must be avoided. A multinational most forgo the temptation to remake all societies in the image of its home society, while at the same time rejecting a relativism that conveniently forgets ethics when the payoff is sufficient. Thus, the task is to tolerate cultural diversity while drawing the line at moral recklessness.

Since in type #2 cases *P* is in conflict with an embedded norm of *A*, one should first ask whether *P* is necessary to do business in *B*, for if not, the solution clearly is to adopt some other practice that is permissible from the standpoint of *A*. If petty bribery of public officials is unnecessary for the business of the Cummins Engine Company in India, then the company is obliged to abandon such bribery. If, on the other hand, *P* proves necessary for business, one must ask whether *P* constitutes a direct violation of a basic human right. Here the notion of a right, specifying a minimum below which corporate conduct should not fall, has special application. If Polaroid, an American company, confronts South African laws that mandate systematic discrimination against non-whites, then Polaroid must refuse to comply with the laws. Thus, in type #2 cases, *P* would be permissible if and only if the answer to both of the following questions is 'no.'

a. Is it possible to conduct business successfully in *B* without undertaking *P*?

b. Is *P* a clear violation of a basic human right?

What sorts of practice might pass both conditions (a) and (b)? Consider the practice of low-level bribery of public officials in some underdeveloped nations. In some South American countries, for example, it is impossible for any company, foreign or national, to move goods through customs without paying low-level officials a few dollars. Indeed, the salaries of such officials are sufficiently low that one suspects they are set with the prevalence of the practice in mind. The payments are relatively small, uniformly assessed, and accepted as standard practice by the surrounding culture. Here, the practice of petty bribery would pass the type #2 test and, barring other moral factors, would be permissible.

A further condition, however, should be placed on multinationals undertaking *P* in type #2 contexts. The companies should be willing to speak out against, and be willing to work for change of *P*. Even if petty bribery or low-level nepotism passes the preceding tests, it may conflict with an embedded norm of country *A*, and as a representative of *A*'s culture, the company is obliged to take a stand. This would be true even for issues related exclusively to financial practice, such as the Italian tax case. If the practice of underestimating taxes due is (1) accepted in *B*, (2) necessary for successful business, and (3) does not violate any basic human rights, then it satisfies the necessary conditions of permissibility. Yet insofar as it violates a norm accepted by *A*, *C* should make its disapproval of the practice known.

To sum up, then, two complementary tests have been proposed for determining the ultimate permissibility of *P*. If *P* occurs in a type #1 context, then *P* is not permissible if:

> The members of *A* would not, under conditions of economic development relevantly similar to those of *B*, regard *P* as permissible.

If *P* occurs in a type #2 context, then *P* is not permissible if either:

1. It is possible to conduct business successfully in *B* without undertaking *P*, or

2. *P* is a direct violation of a basic human right.

Notice that the type #1 criterion is not reducible to the type #2 criterion. In order for the two criteria to have equivalent outcomes, four propositions would need to be true: (1) If *P* passes #1, it passes #2; (2) if *P* fails #1, it fails #2; (3) if *P* passes #2, it passes #1; and (4) if *P* fails #2, it fails #1. But none of these propositions is true. The possibility matrix below lists in rows *A* and *B* the only combinations of outcomes that are possible on the assumption that the two criteria are equivalent. But they are not equivalent because the combinations of outcomes in *C* and *D* are also possible. To illustrate, *P* may pass #2 and fail #1; for example, the practice of petty bribery may be necessary for business, may not violate basic human rights, but may nonetheless be unacceptable in *A* under hypothetically lowered levels of economic development; similarly, the practice of allowing a significant amount of water pollution may be necessary for business, may not violate basic rights, yet may be hypothetically unacceptable in *A*. Or, *P* may fail #2 and pass #1; for example, the practice of serving alcohol at executive dinners in a strongly Moslem country may not be necessary for business in *B* (and thus impermissible by criteria #2) while being thoroughly acceptable to the members of *A* under hypothetically lowered economic conditions. It follows, then, that the two tests are not mutually reducible. This underscores the importance of the preliminary step of classifying a given case under either type #1 or type #2. The prior act of classification explains, moreover, why not all cases in row *C* or in row *D* will have the same moral outcome. Consider, for example, the two Fail–Pass cases from row *C* mentioned above, i.e., the cases of water pollution and petty bribery. If classified as a type

#1 case, the water pollution would *not* be permissible, while petty bribery, if classified as a type #2 case, *would* be.

	Criterion #1	Criterion #2
A	Fail	Fail
		equivalent outcomes
B	Pass	Pass
C	Fail	Pass
		non-equivalent outcomes
D	Pass	Fail

D. SOME PRACTICAL CONSIDERATIONS AND OBJECTIONS

The algorithm does not obviate the need for multinational managers to appeal to moral concepts both more general and specific than the algorithm itself. It is not intended as a substitute for a general theory of morality or even an interpretation of the basic responsibilities of multinationals. Its power lies in its ability to tease out implications of the moral presuppositions of a manager's acceptance of 'home' morality and in this sense to serve as a clarificatory device for multinational decision-making. But insofar as the context of a given conflict of norms categorizes it as a type #1 rather than type #2 conflict, the algorithm makes no appeal to a universal concept of morality (as the appeal to basic human rights does in type #2 cases) save for the purported universality of the ethics endorsed by culture *A*. This means that the force of the algorithm is relativized slightly in the direction of a single society. When *A*'s morality is wrong or confused, the algorithm can reflect this ethnocentricity, leading either to a mild paternalism or to the imposition of parochial standards. For example, *A*'s oversensitivity to aesthetic features of the environment may lead it to reject a given level of thermal pollution even under hypothetically lowered economic circumstances, thus yielding a paternalistic refusal to allow such levels in *B*, despite *B*'s acceptance of the higher levels and *B*'s belief that tolerating such levels is necessary for stimulating economic development. Or, *A*'s mistaken belief that the practice of hiring twelve year olds for full-time, permanent work, although happily unnecessary at its relatively high level of economic development, would be acceptable and economically necessary at a level of economic development relevantly similar to *B*'s, might lead it both to tolerate and undertake the practice in *B*.

Nor is the algorithm a substitute for more specific guides to conduct such as the numerous codes of ethics now appearing on the international scene. A need exists for topic-specific and industry-specific codes that embody detailed safeguards against self-serving interpretations. Consider the Sullivan Standards, designed by the black American minister, Leon Sullivan, drafted for the purpose of ensuring non-racist practices by U.S. multinationals operating in South Africa. As a result of a lengthy lobbying campaign by U.S. activists, the Sullivan principles are now endorsed and followed by almost one third of all American multinationals with South African subsidiaries. Among other things, companies complying with the Sullivan principles must:

Remove all race designation signs.

Support the elimination of discrimination against the rights of Blacks to form or belong to government registered unions.

Determine whether upgrading of personnel and/or jobs in the lower echelons is needed (and take appropriate steps).[18]

A variety of similar codes are either operative or in the process of development, e.g., the European Economic Community's Vredeling Proposal on labor-management consultations; the United Nation's Code of Conduct for Transnational Corporations and its International Standards of Accounting and Reporting; the World Health Organization's Code on Pharmaceuticals and Tobacco; the World Intellectual Property Organization's Revision of the Paris Convention for the Protection of Industrial Patents and Trademarks; the International Chamber of Commerce's Rules of Conduct to Combat Extortion and Bribery; and the World Health Organization's Infant Formula code against advertising of breast-milk substitutes.[19]

Despite these limitations, the algorithm has important applications in countering the well documented tendency of multinationals to mask immoral practices in the rhetoric of 'tolerance' and 'cultural relativity'. Utilizing it, no multinational manager can naively suggest that asbestos standards in Chile are permissible because they are accepted there. Nor can he infer that the standards are acceptable on the grounds that the Chilean economy is, relative to his home country, underdeveloped. A surprising amount of moral blindness occurs not because people's fundamental moral views are confused, but because their cognitive application of those views to novel situations is misguided.

What guarantees that either multinationals or prospective whistleblowers possess the knowledge or objectivity to apply the algorithm fairly? As Richard Barnet quips, "On the 56th floor of a Manhattan skyscraper, the level of self-protective ignorance about what the company may be doing in Colombia or Mexico is high."[20] Can Exxon or Johns Manville be trusted to have a sufficiently sophisticated sense of 'human rights,' or to weight dispassionately the hypothetical attitudes of their fellow countrymen under conditions of 'relevantly similar economic development'? My answer to this is 'probably not,' at least given the present character of the decision-making procedures in most global corporations. I would add, however, that this problem is a contingent and practical one. It is no more a theoretical flaw of the proposed algorithm

that it may be conveniently misunderstood by a given multinational, than it is of Rawl's theory that it may be conveniently misunderstood by a trickle-down capitalist.

What would need to change in order for multinationals to make use of the algorithm? At a minimum they would need to enhance the sophistication of their decision-making mechanisms. They would need to alter established patterns of information flow and collection in order to accommodate moral information. The already complex parameters of corporate decision-making would become more so. They would need to introduce alongside analyses of the bottom line analyses of historical tendencies, nutrition, rights, and demography. And they would need to introduce a new class of employee to provide expertise in these areas. However unlikely such changes are, I believe they are within the realm of possibility. Multinationals, the organizations capable of colonizing our international future, are also capable of looking beyond their national borders and applying—at a minimum—the same moral principles they accept at home.

This is a revision of a paper entitled 'International Whistleblowing', to be published in *Conflicting Loyalties in the Workplace*, ed. by Frederick Elliston (Notre Dame, Indiana: University of Notre Dame Press).

ENDNOTES

1. An example of disparity in wages between Mexican and U.S. workers is documented in the case-study, 'Twin-Plants and Corporate Responsibilities', by John H. Haddox, in *Profits and Responsibility*, ed. Patricia Werhane and Kendall D'Andrade (New York: Random House, 1985).

2. Richard D. Robinson, *International Business Management: A Guide to Decision Making*, Second Edition (Hinsdale, Ill.: The Dryden Press, 1978), p. 241.

3. Robinson, p. 241.

4. Charles Peters and Taylor Branch, *Blowing the Whistle: Dissent in the Public Interest* (New York: Praeger Publishers, 1972), pp. 182–185.

5. Arthur Kelly, 'Italian Bank Mores', in Case-Studies in *Business Ethics*, ed. T. Donaldson (Englewood Cliffs: Prentice-Hall, Inc., 1984).

6. Arnold Berleant, 'Multinationals and the Problem of Ethical Consistency', *Journal of Business Ethics* 3 (August 1982), 185–195.

7. One can construct an argument attempting to show that insulating the economies of the less developed countries would be advantageous to the less developed countries in the long run. But whether correct or not, such an argument is independent of the present issue, for it is independent of the claim that if *P* violates the norms of *A*, then *P* is impermissible.

8. James Sterba, 'The Welfare Rights of Distant Peoples and Future Generations: Moral Side Constraints on Social Policy', in *Social Theory and Practice* 7 (Spring, 1981), p. 110.

9. Sterba, p. 111.

10. Henry Shue, *Basic Rights, Subsistence, Affluence, and U.S. Foreign Policy* (Princeton, N.J.: Princeton University Press, 1981), p. 34.

11. Shue, *Basic Rights*, p. 170.

12. Henry Shue, 'Exporting Hazards', *Ethics* 91 (July 1981): 579–606.

13. Shue, 'Hazards', pp. 579–580.

14. Considering a possible escape from the principle, Shue considers whether inflicting harm is acceptable in the event overall benefits outweigh the costs. Hence, increased safety risks under reduced asbestos standards might be acceptable insofar as the economic benefits to the country outweighed the costs. The problem, as Shue correctly notes, is that this approach fails to distinguish between the no-harm principle and a naive greatest happiness principle. Even classical defenders of the no-harm principle were unwilling to accept a simple-minded utilitarianism that sacrificed individual justice on the altar of maximal happiness. Even classical utilitarians did not construe their greatest happiness principle to be a 'hunting license' (Shue, 'Hazards', pp. 592–593.) Still another escape might be by way of appealing to the rigors of international economic competition. That is, is it not unreasonable to expect firms to place themselves at a competitive disadvantage by installing expensive safety equipment in a market where other firms are brutally cost conscious? Such policies, argue critics, could trigger economic suicide. The obligation not to harm, in turn, properly belongs to the government of the host country. Here, too, Shue's rejoinder is on-target. He notes first that the existence of an obligation by one party does not cancel its burden on another party; hence, even if the host country's government does not have an obligation to protect their citizens from dangerous workplace conditions, its duty does not cancel that of the corporation. (Shue, 'Hazards', p. 600.) Second, governments of poor countries are themselves forced to compete for scarce foreign capital by weakening their laws and regulations, with the result that any 'competitive disadvantage' excuse offered on behalf of the corporation would also apply to the government. (Shue, 'Hazards', p. 601.)

15. Sterba himself reflects this consensus when he remarks that for rights "... an acceptable minimum should vary over time and between societies at least to

some degree". (Sterba, 'Distant Peoples', p. 112.)

16. For the purpose of analyzing the moral foundations of corporation behavior, I prefer a social contract theory, one that interprets a hypothetical contract between society and productive organizations, and which I have argued for in my book, *Corporations and Morality*. Thomas Donaldson, *Corporations and Morality* (Englewood Cliffs: Prentice-Hall, 1982); See especially Chapter 3. There I argue that Corporations are artifacts; that they are in part the products of our moral and legal imagination. As such, they are to be molded in the image of our collective rights and societal ambitions. Corporations, as all productive organizations, require from society both recognition as single agents, and the authority to own or use land and natural resources, and to hire employees. In return for this, society may expect that productive organizations will, all other things being equal, enhance the general interests of consumers and employees. Society may reasonably ex-pect that in doing so corporations honor existing rights and limit their activities to accord with the bounds of justice. This is as true for multinationals as it is for national corporations.

17. Richard Brandt, 'Cultural Relativism', in *Ethical Issues in Business*, Second Edition, ed. T. Donaldson and P. Werhane (Englewood Cliffs, N.J.: Prentice-Hall, 1983).

18. See 'Dresser Industries and South Africa', by Patricia Mintz and Kirk O. Hanson, in *Case Studies in Business Ethics*, ed. Thomas Donaldson (Prentice-Hall, 1984).

19. For a concise and comprehensive ac-count of the various codes of conduct for international business now under con-sideration, see 'Codes of Conduct: Worry over New Restraints on Multinationals', *Chemical Week* (July 15, 1981), 48–52.

20. Richard J. Barnet and Ronald Muller, *Global Reach: The Power of Multi-national Corporations* (New York: Simon and Schuster, 1974), p. 185.

BRIBERY IN INTERNATIONAL BUSINESS: Whose Problem Is It?

Henry W. Lane
Donald G. Simpson

INTRODUCTION

No discussion of problems in international business seems complete without reference to familiar complaints about the questionable business practices North American executives encounter in foreign countries, particularly developing nations. Beliefs about the pervasiveness of dishonesty and the necessity of engaging in such practices as bribery vary widely, however, and these differences often lead to vigorous discussions that generate more heat than light. Pragmatists or 'realists' may take the attitude that "international business is a rough game and no place for the naive idealist or the faint-hearted. Your competitors use bribes and unless you are willing to meet this standard, competitive practice you will lose business and, ultimately, jobs for workers at home. Besides, it is an accepted business

practice in those countries, and when you are in Rome you have to do as the Romans do." 'Moralists', on the other hand, believe that cultural relativity is no excuse for unethical behavior. "As Canadians or Americans we should uphold our legal and ethical standards anywhere in the world; and any good American or Canadian knows that bribery, by any euphemism, is unethical and wrong. Bribery increases a product's cost and often is used to secure import licenses for products that no longer can be sold in the developed world. Such corrupting practices also contribute to the moral disintegration of individuals and eventually societies."

The foregoing comments represent extreme polar positions but we are not using these stereotypes to create a 'straw-man' or a false dichotomy about attitudes toward practices like bribery. These extreme viewpoints, or minor variations of them, will be

From the *Journal of Business Ethics*, Vol. 3, No. 1 (Feb. 1984), pp. 35–42. © 1984 D. Reidel Publishing Co., Dordrecht, Holland. Published by permission.

encountered frequently as one meets executives who have experience in developing countries. Some 'realists' and 'moralists' undoubtedly are firm believers in their positions, but many other executives probably gravitate toward one of the poles because they have not found a realistic alternative approach to thinking about the issue of bribery, never mind finding an answer to the problem.

The impetus for this article came from discussions with executives and government officials in Canada and in some developing nations about whether a North American company could conduct business successfully in developing countries without engaging in what would be considered unethical or illegal practices. It was apparent from these talks that the question was an important one and of concern to business executives, but not much practical, relevant information existed on the issue. There was consensus on two points: first, there are a lot of myths surrounding the issue of pay-offs, and second, if anyone had some insights into the problem, executives would appreciate hearing them.

In this article we would like to share what we have learned about the issue during the two years we have been promoting business (licensing agreements, management contracts, joint ventures) between Canadian and African companies. Our intention is not to present a comprehensive treatment of the subject of bribery nor a treatise on ethical behavior. Our intention is to present a practical discussion of some dimensions of the problem based on our experience, discussions and in some cases investigation of specific incidents.

THE PROBLEM IS MULTI-FACETED

It can be misleading to talk about bribery in global terms without considering some situational specifics such as country, type of business and company. Our discussions with businessmen indicate that the pay-off problem is more prevalent in some countries than in others. Executives with extensive experience probably could rank countries on a scale reflecting the seriousness of the problem. Also, some industries are probably more susceptible to pay-off requests than others. Large construction projects, turn-key capital projects, and large commodity or equipment contracts are likely to be most vulnerable because the scale of the venture may permit the easy disguise of pay-offs, and because an individual, or small group of people, may be in a strategic position to approve or disapprove the project. These projects or contracts are undoubtedly obvious targets also because the stakes are high, the competition vigorous and the possibility that some competitors may engage in pay-offs increased. Finally, some companies may be more vulnerable due to a relative lack of bargaining power or because they have no policies to guide them in these situations. If the product or technology is unique or clearly superior, and it is needed, the company is in a relatively strong position to resist the pressure. Similarly, those firms with effective operational policies against pay-offs are in a position of strength. Many senior executives have stated, with pride, that their companies have reputations for not making pay-offs and, therefore, are not asked for them. These were executives of large, successful firms that also had chosen not to work in some countries where they could not operate comfortably. These executives often backed up their claims with specific examples in which they walked away from apparently lucrative deals where a pay-off was a requirement.

Two other elements of the situational context of a pay-off situation that vary are the subtlety of the demand and the amount of money involved. All pay-off situations are not straightforward and unambiguous, which may make a clear response more difficult. Consider, for example, the case of company that was encouraged to change its evaluation of bids for a large construction project. Some host-country agencies were embarrassed by the evaluation results since Company *X*, from the country providing significant financing for the project, was ranked a distant third. The agencies sought a re-evaluation on questionable technicalities. The changes were considered but the ranking remained the same. At this point pressure began to build. Phone calls were made berating the firm for delaying the project and hinting that the large follow-on contract, for which it had the inside track, was in jeopardy. [But] no one ever said [explicitly,] make Company *X* the winner or you lose the follow-on.

Although no money was to change hands, this situation was similar to a pay-off request in that the company was being asked to alter its standard of acceptable business practices for an implied future benefit. The interpretation of the "request," the response, and the consequences, were left entirely to the company's management. Refusal to change may mean losing a big contract, but giving in does not guarantee the follow-on and you leave the company vulnerable to further demands. In ambiguous situations, factors such as corporate policies and the company's financial strength and its need for the contract enter into the decision. In this case the company had firm beliefs about what constituted professional standards and did not desperately need the follow-on contract. Although it refused to change, another company might find itself in a dilemma, give in to the pressure, and rationalize its behavior.

Finally, pay-offs range in size from the small payments that may help getting through customs without a hassle up to the multi-million dollar bribes that make headlines and embarrass governments. The pay-off situations we discuss in this article are more significant than the former, but much smaller and far less dramatic than the latter. These middle-range pay-offs (tens of thousands of dollars) may pose a problem for corporations. They are too big to be ignored but possibly not big enough to be referred to corporate headquarters unless the firm has clear guidelines on the subject. Regional executives or lower level managers may be deciding whether or not these 'facilitating payments' are just another cost of doing business in the developing world.

ON THE OUTSIDE LOOKING IN: THE NORTH AMERICAN PERSPECTIVE

"It's a corrupt, pay-off society. The problem has spread to all levels. On the face it looks good, but underneath it's rotten." Comments such as these are often made by expatriate businessmen and government officials alike. The North American executive may arrive in a Third World Country with a stereotype of corrupt officials and is presented with the foregoing analysis by people on the spot who, he feels, should know the situation best. His fears are confirmed.

This scenario may be familiar to some readers. It is very real to us because we have gone through that process. Two cases provide examples of the stories a businessman may likely be told in support of the dismal analysis.

The New Venture Company *Y*, a wholly-owned subsidiary of a European multinational, wished to manufacture a new product for export. Government permission was required and Company *Y* submitted the necessary applications. Sometime later one of the Company *Y*'s executives (a local national) informed the Managing Director that the application was approved and the consultant's fee must be paid. The Managing Director knew nothing about a consultant or such a fee. The executive took his boss to a meeting with the consultant—a government official who sat on the application review committee. Both the consultant and the executive claimed to remember the initial meeting at which agreement was reached on the $10 000 fee. A few days later the Managing Director attended a cocktail party at the home of a high ranking official in the same agency. This official recommended that the fee be paid. The Managing Director decided against paying the fee and the project ran into unexpected delays. At this point the Managing Director asked the parent company's legal department for help. Besides the delay, the situation was creating a problem between the Managing Director and his executives as well as affecting the rest of the company. He initially advised against payment but after watching the company suffer, acquiesced with the approval of the parent company. The fee was re-negotiated downward and the consultant paid. What was the result? Nothing! The project was not approved.

The Big Sale Company *Z*, which sold expensive equipment, established a relationship with a well placed government official on the first trip to the country. This official, and some other nationals, assured Company *Z* representatives that they would have no trouble getting the contract. On leaving the country, Company *Z* representatives had a letter of intent to purchase the equipment. On the second trip Company *Z* representatives brought the detailed technical specifications for a certain department head to approve. The department head refused to approve the specifications and further efforts to have the government honour its promise failed. The deal fell through. Company *Z*'s analysis of the situation, which became common knowledge in business and government circles, was that a competitor paid the department head to approve its equipment and that the government reneged on its obligation to purchase Company *Z* equipment.

While in the country, the visiting executive may even have met Company *Z*'s

agent in the Big Sale who confirms the story. Corruption is rampant, and in the particular case of the Big Sale he claims to know that the department head received the money and from whom. The case is closed! An honest North American company cannot function in this environment—or so it seems.

ON THE INSIDE LOOKING OUT: THE DEVELOPING COUNTRY'S PERSPECTIVE

During his visit the executive may have met only a few nationals selected by his company or government representatives. He probably has not discussed bribery with them because of its sensitive nature. If the businessmen and the officials he met were dishonest, they would not admit it; if they were honest he probably felt they would resent the discussion. Also, he may not have had enough time to establish the type of relationship in which the subject could be discussed frankly. It is almost certain that he did not speak with the people in the government agencies who allegedly took the pay-offs. What would he say if he did meet them? And more than likely he would not be able to get an appointment with them if he did want to pursue the matter further. So the executive is convinced that corruption is widespread, having heard only one side of the horror stories.

Had the visitor been able to investigate the viewpoints of the nationals, what might he have heard? "I would like to find a person from the developed world that I can trust. You people brought corruption here. We learned the concept from you. You want to win all the time, and you are impatient so you bribe. You offer bribes to the local people and complain that business is impossible without bribing."

Comments like these are made by local businessmen and government officials alike. If the visiting executive heard these comments he would be confused and would wonder whether or not these people were talking about the same country. Although skeptical, his confidence in the accuracy of his initial assessment would have been called into question. Had he been able to stay longer in the country, he might have met an old friend who knew the department head who allegedly was paid off in the Big Sale. His friend would have made arrangements for the visitor to hear the other side of the story.

The Big Sale Re-Visited After the representatives of Company Z received what they described as a letter of intent to purchase the equipment they returned home. On the second visit they had to deal with the department head to receive his approval for the technical specifications.

At the meeting they told the department head that he need not worry about the details and just sign-off on the necessary documents. If he had any questions regarding the equipment he could inspect it in two weeks time in their home country. The department head's initial responses were: (1) he would not rubber stamp anything, and (2) how could this complex equipment which was supposedly being custom made for his country's needs be inspected in two weeks when he had not yet approved the specifications.

As he reviewed the specifications he noticed a significant technical error and brought it to the attention of Company Z's representatives. They became upset with this 'interference' and implied that they would use their connections in high places to ensure his compliance. When asked again to sign the documents he refused, and the company reps left saying that they would have him removed from his job.

After this meeting the Premier of the country became involved and asked the company officials to appear before him. They arrived with the Premier's nephew for a meeting with the Premier and his top advisors. The Premier told his nephew that he

had no business being there and directed him to leave. The company officials then had to face the Premier and his advisors alone.

The Premier asked if the company had a contract and [said] that if it had, it would be honoured. The company had to admit that it had no contract. As far as the Premier was concerned the issue was settled.

However, the case was not closed for the Company Z representatives. They felt they had been promised the deal and that the department had reneged. They felt that someone had paid off the department head and they were quite bitter. In discussions with their local embassy officials and with government officials at home they presented their analysis of the situation. The result was strained relations and the department head got a reputation for being dishonest.

Well, the other side of the story certainly has different implications about whose behaviour may be considered questionable. The situation is now very confusing. Is the department head honest or not? The executive's friend has known the department head for a long time and strongly believes he is honest; and some other expatriate government officials have basically corroborated the department head's perception of the matter. But the businessmen and government officials who first told the story seemed reputable and honest. Who should be believed? As the visiting executive has learned, you have to decide on the truth for yourself.

PATTERNS OF BEHAVIOUR

The preceding vignettes illustrate our position that bribery and corruption is a problem for North American and Third World businessmen alike. We also have observed two recurring behaviour patterns in these real, but disguised, situations. The first is the predisposition of the North American businessman to accept the premise that bribery is the way of life in the developing world and a necessity in business transactions. The second behavioural pattern occurs in situations where payments are requested and made.

We believe that many executives visit Third World countries with an expectation to learn that bribery is a problem. This attitude likely stems from a number of sources. First, in many cases it may be true. In some countries it may be impossible to complete a transaction without a bribe and the horror stories about the widespread disappearance of honesty are valid. However, in some instances the expectations are conditioned by the 'conventional wisdom' available in international business circles. This conventional wisdom develops from situations like the ones we have described. As these situations are passed from individual to individual accuracy may diminish and facts be forgotten. This is not done intentionally but happens since it is rare that the story-tellers have the complete story or all the facts. Unverified stories of bribery and corruption circulate through the business and government communities and often become accepted as true and factual. The obvious solution, and difficulty, is learning how to distinguish fact from fiction.

Another factor influencing initial expectations is the unfavourable impressions of developing countries and their citizens that are picked up from the media. Often only the sensational, and negative, news items from these countries are reported in North America. We learn of bombings, attacks on journalists and tourists, alleged (and real) coup d'états, and major scandals. These current events and the conventional wisdom combined with an executive's probable lack of knowledge of the history, culture, legal systems or economic conditions of a country all contribute to the development of unfavourable stereotypes that predispose the executive toward readily accepting reports that confirm his already drawn conclusions: all Latin American or African countries, for example, are the same and corruption is to be expected.

The stories that constitute evidence of corruption may be tales of bribery like the New Venture or the Big Sale, or they may take other forms. The story we have heard most often has the "protect yourself from your local partner" theme. It goes like this: "If you are going to invest in this country, particularly in a joint venture, you have to find a way to protect yourself from your partner. He is likely to strip all the company's assets and leave you nothing but a skeleton. Just look what happened to Company *A*."

On hearing the evidence, particularly from expatriates in the foreign country, a visiting businessman most likely accepts it without further investigation. He has forgotten the old adage about there being two sides to every story. His conclusions and conviction are most likely based on incomplete and biased data.

Is there another viewpoint? Certainly! Many nationals have expressed it to us: "The Europeans and North Americans have been taking advantage of us for decades, even centuries. The multinationals establish a joint venture and then strip the local company bare through transfer pricing, management fees and royalties based on a percentage of sales rather than profits. They have no interest in the profitability of the company or its long-term development."

The situation is ironic. Some local investors are desperately looking for an honest North American executive whom they can trust at the same time the North American is searching for them. Our experience indicates that this search process is neither straightforward, nor easy. And while the search continues, if it does, it is difficult for the North American to maintain a perspective on the situation and remember that there are locals who may share his values and who are equally concerned about unethical and illegal practices.

In summary, we would characterize the first observed pattern of behaviour as a preparedness to accept 'evidence' of corruption and the simultaneous failure to examine critically the evidence or its source.

The second behavioural pattern appears in the actual pay-off process. The request very likely comes from a low- or middle-level bureaucrat who says that his boss must be paid for the project to be approved or for the sale to be finalized. Alternatively, it may be your agent who is providing similar counsel. In either case you are really not certain who is making the demand.

Next, the pay-off is made. You give your contact the money, but you never really know where it goes.

Your expectations are obvious. You have approached this transaction from a perspective of economic rationality. You have provided a benefit and expect one in return. The project will be approved or the sale consummated.

The result, however, may be very different than expected. As in the case of the New Venture, nothing may happen. The only outcome is indignation, anger, and perhaps the loss of a significant amount of money. Now is the time for action, but what recourse do you have? Can you complain? You may be guilty of bribing a government official. And, you certainly are reluctant to admit that you have been duped. Since your direct options are limited, your primary action may be to spread the word: "This is a corrupt, pay-off society."

WHY DOES IT HAPPEN?

There are numerous explanations for corruption in developing nations. First, and most obvious is that some people are simply dishonest. A less pejorative explanation is that the cost of living in these countries may be high and salaries low. Very often a wage earner must provide for a large extended family. The businessman is viewed opportunistically as a potential source of extra income to improve the standard of living. Finally, some

nationals may believe strongly that they have a right to share some of the wealth controlled by multi-national corporations.

Besides being familiar to many readers, these explanations all share another common characteristic. They all focus on the other person—the local national. Accepting that there may be some truth in the previous explanations, let us, however, turn our focus to the visiting North American to see what we find. We could find a greedy, dishonest expatriate hoping to make a killing. But, let us give him the same benefit of the doubt we have accorded to the local nationals so far.

On closer examination we may find a situation in which the North American executive is vulnerable. He has entered an action vacuum and is at a serious disadvantage. His lack of knowledge of systems and procedures, laws, institutions, and the people can put him in a dependent position. Unfamiliarity with the system and/or people makes effective, alternative action such as he could take at home difficult. A strong relationship with a reputable national could help significantly in this situation. Quite often the national knows how to fight the system and who to call in order to put pressure on the corrupt individual. This potential resource should not be dismissed lightly. Although the most powerful and experienced MNCs may also be able to apply this pressure, most of us must be realistic and recognize that no matter how important we think we are, we may not be among those handful of foreigners that can shake the local institutions.

Time also can be a factor. Often the lack of time spent in the country either to establish relationships, or to give the executive the opportunity to fight the system contributes to the problem. Because the North American businessman believes that time is money and that his time, in particular, is very valuable, he operates on a tight schedule with little leeway for unanticipated delays. The pay-off appears to be a cost-effective solution. In summary, the executive might not have the time, knowledge, or contacts to fight back and sees no alternative other than pay or lose the deal.

SOME REAL BARRIERS

If, as we think, there are many honest businessmen in North America and in the developing world looking for mutually profitable arrangements and for reliable, honest partners, why is it difficult for them to find each other? We believe a significant reason is the inability of both sides to overcome two interrelated barriers—time and trust.

Trust is a critical commodity for business success in developing countries. The North American going to invest in a country far from home needs to believe he will not be cheated out of his assets. The national has to believe that a joint venture, for example, will be more than a mechanism for the North American to get rich at his expense. But, even before the venture is established, trust may be essential if the prospective partners are ever to meet. This may require the recommendation of a third party respected by both sides.

Establishing good relationships with the right people requires an investment of time, money and energy. An unwillingness of either party to make this investment is often interpreted as a lack of sincerity or interest. The executive trying to do business in four countries in a week (the 'five-day wonder') is still all too common a sight. Similarly, the successful local businessman may have an equally hectic international travel schedule. Both complain that if the other was really serious he would find time to meet. Who should give in? In our opinion, the onus is on whichever party is visiting to build into his schedule the necessary time to work on building a relationship or to find a trusted intermediary. Also, both parties must be realistic about the elapsed time required to establish a good relationship and negotiate a mutually satisfactory deal. This

will involve multiple trips by each party to the other's country and could easily take 12 to 18 months.

THE COST OF BRIBERY

The most quantifiable costs are the financial ones. The cost of the 'service' is known. The costs of not bribing are also quantifiable: the time and money that must be invested in long-term business development in the country, or the value of the lost business. However, there are other costs that must be considered.

(1) You may set a precedent and establish that you and/or your company are susceptible to pay-off demands.

(2) You may create an element in your organization that believes pay-offs are standard operating procedure and over which you may eventually lose control.

(3) You or your agents may begin using bribery and corruption as a personally non-threatening, convenient excuse to dismiss failure. You may not address some organizational problems of adapting to doing business in the developing world.

(4) There are also personal costs. Ultimately you will have to accept responsibility for your decisions and actions, and those of your subordinates. At a minimum it may involve embarrassment, psychological suffering and a loss of reputation. More extreme consequences include the loss of your job and jail sentences.

CONCLUSION

It is clear that bribery can be a problem for the international executive. Assuming you do not want to participate in the practice, how can you cope with the problem?

(1) Do not ignore the issue. Do as many North American companies have done. Spend time thinking about the tradeoffs and your position prior to the situation arising.

(2) After thinking through the issue, establish a corporate policy. We would caution, however, that for any policy to be effective, it must reflect values that are important to the company's senior executives. The policy must also be used. Window dressing will not work.

(3) Do not be too quick to accept the 'conventional wisdom.' Examine critically the stories of bribery and the source of the stories. Ask for details. Try to find out the other side of the story and make enquiries of a variety of sources.

(4) Protect yourself by learning about the local culture and by establishing trusting relationships with well-respected local businessmen and government officials.

(5) Do not contribute to the enlargement of myths by circulating unsubstantiated stories.

Finally, we would offer the advice that when in Rome do as the *better* Romans do. But, we would add, do not underestimate the time, effort, and expense it may take to find the better Romans and establish a relationship with them.

The authors wish to acknowledge the support of the Plan for Excellence and the Centre for International Business Studies at the University of Western Ontario's School of Business Administration, and the Industrial Cooperation Division of the Canadian International Development Agency.

BRIBERY AND EXTORTION IN INTERNATIONAL BUSINESS

Thomas L. Carson

BRIBERY

Webster's New World Dictionary (1962) defines a bribe as a payment or inducement for someone to do something illegal or unethical. This definition is too broad; not all instances of paying someone to do something illegal or immoral count as cases of bribery. Hiring someone to murder one's spouse is not a case of bribery. Talk of bribery only makes sense in the context of positions or roles having special obligations. Central cases of bribery involve paying or inducing others to violate the fiduciary obligations of their offices or positions. Consider the following examples: (1) Paying a judge or juror to decide in one's favour; (2) Paying a policeman not to give one a traffic ticket; and (3) Paying a government official not to report violations of health and safety standards.

One can imagine cases of bribery in which the person being paid is not an agent or employee of a specific party. For example, it would be possible to bribe a self-employed professional tennis player or boxer to lose a match.[1] Bribery is also possible in the case of amateur athletics. However, in these cases the recipient of the bribe still has specific obligations attaching to his role that he is being paid to ignore. An athlete performing in public competition has an obligation (assignable to the sponsors of the competition, his fellow competitors, and to those who follow the sport) to do his best to win in that competition. Athletes participate in such competition on the understanding that they will do their best to win. On my view, it would not be a bribe for one to pay an athlete to lose a private match that was not represented as being a real competition. For ex-

From T.L. Carson, "Bribery, Extortion, and 'The Foreign Corrupt Practices Act,'" *Philosophy and Public Affairs*, Vol. 14, No. 1 (Winter 1985). Copyright © 1985 by Princeton University Press. Reprinted by permission of Princeton University Press.

ample, it would not be a bribe if I paid Bjorn Borg to lose to me in a secret tennis match. Nor would it be a bribe if I paid him to lose to me in public, provided that our agreement was a matter of public record and the match was not represented to anyone as a true competition. I don't think that conventional usage of the word "bribe" gives us decisive reasons for either accepting or rejecting the consequences of my view for this kind of case. However, the fact that there is clearly nothing morally objectionable about paying someone to lose in a private athletic match that is not represented as true competition is a strong reason for thinking that a correct definition of the word "bribe" should not count such cases as bribes. I propose the following definition of bribery:

> A bribe is a payment of money (or something of value) to another person *in exchange for* his giving one special consideration that is incompatible with the duties of his office, position, or role.[2]

There are uses of the terms "bribe" and "bribery" that do not fit this definition. We speak of parents "bribing" their children to be quiet or to behave themselves. Children do not have any special position that obligates them to be noisy or misbehave. If we allow this as a genuine case of bribery then the foregoing definition is untenable. However, it seems more plausible to say that this is not a genuine case of bribery but rather an extended use of the term analogous to the use of the word "murder" in "your father is going to murder you when he sees this mess." Consider another possible objection to my definition. Suppose that I call a *self-employed* plumber and ask him to come and fix my pipes. He refuses to come on account of its being the weekend. Then I offer him extra money to come out anyway. Many would describe this case by saying that I bribed the plumber. However, I believe that this is just an extended use of the term "bribery." In any case, the kinds

of examples considered here are not morally worrisome cases of bribery. Surely there is nothing morally objectionable about either my offering the plumber payment or his accepting it. My definition may not be adequate to all of the everyday uses of the word "bribery," but it covers all of the cases of bribery that raise ethical questions.

BRIBERY AND EXTORTION

Here I will attempt to define "extortion" and contrast it with bribery. Before doing this, however, we should first have before us some clear cases of extortion: a gangster threatening to blow up my store unless I pay him for "protection" each month, and a policeman threatening to frame someone for a crime unless he pays him money. Extortion is sometimes construed in a very narrow sense as an official's demanding payment for services that he is obligated to perform without payment.[3] In cases of bribery someone offers an officer payment for doing something contrary to the duties of his position. According to the present definition, extortion occurs when an official demands payment for doing something that he ought to do without being paid. The proposed definition of extortion, however, seems excessively narrow. For as we ordinarily use the term "extortion" it is possible for someone who does not hold any official position to extort money from others. For example, the criminal who demands money from a merchant in exchange for not burning down his store is committing extortion even though he is not acting in any official capacity. Consider the following definition of extortion:

> Extortion is the act of threatening someone with harm in order to obtain payment or other benefits to which one has no prior entitlement.[4]

The expression "benefits to which one has no prior entitlement" in the above definition should be read as "benefits to which one has no prior *legal* right" as opposed to "benefits to which one has no prior moral right" or "benefits to which one has no prior moral or legal right." It is not a case of extortion if a slaveowner threatens his slaves with a beating unless they work hard, even though he is not morally entitled to the fruits of their labour. Similarly, a banker who threatens a poor family with foreclosure is not committing an act of extortion, even if he has no moral right to repossess their home. This definition is not intended to suggest that extortion is a purely legal concern; it may be morally wrong to threaten to inflict harm on someone unless he gives one something to which one is not legally entitled. It is also worth noting that this definition does not imply that it is necessarily illegal to extort things from others. Unless the harms threatened are either illegal for independent reasons or forbidden by specific statutes concerning extortion, extortion (as defined here) is not illegal.

There seem to be clear counterexamples to the proposed definition. Suppose that I threaten to leave your employ unless you give me a 100-percent pay raise. I am threatening you with economic harm and I am not entitled to the extra money that I am demanding (I have no cause for complaint if you don't pay me), so this counts as a case of extortion according to the preceding definition. However, this is clearly not an instance of extortion, just fair bargaining. There is nothing morally or legally objectionable about my threatening to leave unless you pay me more since you have no right to my continued services. We might say that this is also what accounts for the fact that the case in question is not an instance of extortion. This suggests the following definition of extortion:

> Extortion is the act of threatening someone with harm (that one is not entitled to inflict on him), in order to obtain benefits to which one has no prior right.

However, this definition is also inadequate. Although the harms threatened in extortion are often ones that an individual is neither morally nor legally entitled to inflict, for example, murder or arson, this needn't be the case. My threatening to expose the official misconduct of a high government official unless he pays me $100 000 constitutes a case of extortion, even though exposing him would be both morally and legally permissible.

I am unable to formulate a fully adequate definition of extortion. However, nothing that I say in this article is dependent on my being able to do so.... All that I need to do is make the unproblematic claim that threatening someone with harm (that one is neither morally nor legally entitled to inflict on him) unless he gives one benefits to which one is neither morally nor legally entitled is *sufficient* for extortion. Given this, it follows that, contrary to most press reports, some of the most notorious foreign payments were not bribes, but rather extortion payments.[5]

Many of the most troubling cases ... seem to lie near the border between bribery and extortion. Therefore, it would be helpful to inquire as to the nature of the difference or differences. Typically, in cases of bribery the payment in question is suggested or offered by the party who makes the payment; in cases of extortion the payment is usually suggested or demanded by the party who receives it. However, these differences cannot serve as a basis for distinguishing between bribery and extortion. For an official might suggest payment of a bribe to him without threatening any harm for nonpayment, that is, without it being the case that this suggestion constitutes extortion.

Let us consider one of the sorts of cases that has been a matter of particular controversy.... Suppose that a salesman is told by the purchasing agent of another company that he (the purchasing agent) won't consider the salesman's product unless he receives a payment. To offer payment here would not constitute bribery since the salesman is not paying the officer to disregard his fiduciary obligations—to the contrary, the salesman is paying him to fulfill them by giving his product fair consideration. In this case the payment is merely for fair consideration and is not understood to guarantee one any special privileges. (To offer a larger payment than is requested and stipulate that one expects this payment to guarantee that one's own products will be purchased would constitute bribery.) Since the payment is a) for something to which one is legally entitled (one is entitled not to have it be the case that one's competitors gain an advantage over one through bribery), and b) made for the purpose of avoiding threatened harm, it constitutes an extortion payment. I am assuming that the purchasing agent will demand payment from all potential suppliers and then make an impartial decision from among those suppliers who pay. Perhaps a more likely scenario is that the purchaser will make an impartial rank ordering of suppliers, then demand payment from the leading candidate and buy from the first supplier on the list who is willing to pay. In neither case, however, can making the payment be considered bribery.

My contention that this is not bribery is somewhat vitiated by the following considerations. While the payment is not a case of paying someone to fail to fulfill his fiduciary obligations, it is presumably contrary to his fiduciary obligations for him to accept payments of any sort from potential suppliers. His firm may have explicit regulations forbidding such payments. Does this compel me to grant that payment here would constitute bribery? I think not. Not every inducement or temptation for one to violate one's fiduciary obligations is a case of bribery. It is not a bribe if I induce you to abandon your post and come and get drunk with me. A bribe must be a payment for actions that violate the recipient's fiduciary obligations.

Consider a slightly different case. Suppose that some of one's competitors, for whatever reasons, are not making the payments. Wouldn't offering payments in this sort of case constitute bribery? Payment would secure one special consideration over those competitors who don't pay and therefore it would be payment for acts that are contrary to the fiduciary obligations of the recipient. However, this argument is not entirely convincing. For it is not clear that a payment that can be foreseen to give one an unfair advantage over certain competitors always counts as payment for the purchaser to give one this advantage. Perhaps it is also necessary that the payment be intended to give one these advantages. Whatever one says about all of this (and I prudently propose to say nothing more), it is clear that one could offer the payment in such a way that it didn't constitute a bribe by stipulating that one doesn't want the payment to give one any advantages over those competitors who don't pay.

AN ECONOMIC ANALYSIS OF BRIBERY AND EXTORTION

Here I will propose an economic analysis of several common types of bribery and extortion.

Case 1 Suppose that a *firm* or *government* demands a substantial payment from a supplier as a condition of sale. This demand is not a solicitation for a bribe or an extortion demand; it is, in effect, a demand for a lower price. Therefore, for a supplier to offer payment in this case would not constitute either a bribe or an extortion payment; it would simply be tantamount to giving the firm or government a "rebate" or a lower price. (Similarly, for a supplier to offer payments to another company or government would not be an offer of bribery, but only an offer of a lower price. Only payments to individuals who have specific duties attaching to their positions or roles can constitute bribes.) There is no particular moral or economic objection to payments of the sort described in this case.

Case 2 Suppose that I am a sales representative for an aircraft corporation that is trying to market its products abroad. My company's planes are costlier and less fuel efficient than those of our major competitor. There are no significant respects in which our aircraft is preferable to theirs. If things function the way that they are supposed to according to economic theory, then our company's planes will not be sold. If I offer a substantial bribe to the government or corporate officer who is responsible for purchasing aircraft then he may decide to purchase our planes instead. In this kind of case a company that is willing to engage in bribery can gain considerable advantages over its competitors. It is precisely this kind of advantage that makes bribery such a tempting option. From a purely economic point of view such bribery is undesirable—optimal results will occur if agents act in the best interests of those whom they represent and make purchases that best further the economic interests of their principals.

Case 3 This is a variation of the preceding example. Suppose that our planes are the best buy, all things considered, and that the purchasing agent will probably choose them without receiving any payment from us. But just to be on the safe side we make him a payment. In that case the "right" decision from an economic point of view will still be made—they will buy the best planes. However, our costs will be higher than they should have been and the purchasing agent will get the extra money—this is also undesirable: if anyone gets the money it should be his firm or government.

Case 4 Suppose that I know that all of our competitors are offering bribery or extortion

payments and that the person in charge of purchasing the aircraft is corrupt so that we cannot expect to sell our aircraft unless we do the same. In this case our offering payments will not disrupt the usual competitive constraints of the marketplace. In fact, it might serve to restore the competition. For, in this case, the purchasing agent might attempt to buy the best product from those suppliers who are willing to make him payments. (This is arguably a case of extortion. Although the purchasing agent doesn't actually threaten harm for non-payment, one can expect to suffer harm unless one pays.) Assuming that the purchaser will attempt to make the best choice from those companies that are willing to offer payments, an individual company can make it more likely that the "correct choice" will be made, that is, that the best product, all things considered, will be chosen, by being willing to make such payments itself. For it is conceivable that its product is the best or at least the best of those companies that are willing to pay and the company can sell its product only if it is willing to pay. If all potential suppliers offer payments (of roughly equal size), then there is no reason to suppose that the final decision reached will be any different from the one obtained under perfect competition. The scenario described here differs from a perfect market only in that the supplier will receive a lower net price (the difference between the selling price and the amount of the bribery or extortion payment) than he would have in a perfect market and the purchasing agent pockets the difference. Perhaps the fact that suppliers were willing to offer substantial payments shows that the selling price was pegged too high. In that case, the difference between our present scenario and a perfect market is that in a perfect market the company or government purchasing the product would reap the benefits of the lower net selling price.

Case 5 Suppose that only *some* of one's competitors are willing to make payments and that the individuals in charge of purchasing are corrupt and will only buy from a supplier who is willing to pay them. In this case it would also seem to be preferable (economically speaking) to offer payments oneself. Regardless of what one does oneself, the product purchased will be chosen from one of the companies that is willing to make payments. By offering payments oneself one increases the number of firms whose products will be given consideration, and thereby increases the probability that the "best" product will be purchased. (There is some chance that one's own product is the best, or if not, one's product might still be better than those of the companies whose willingness to pay has kept them in the running.)

Case 6 Suppose that the purchasing agent informs us that he will purchase our product, but only on the condition that we make him a substantial payment.[6] Assume also that it is in the economic interest of our company to make the deal in spite of the payment. Then, if at least one of our competitors is willing to pay, it seems probable that the economic consequences of our making the payment will be preferable to those of our not making it. The product purchased will presumably be the one judged best of those companies that are willing to make extortion payments. If we don't pay, then the product chosen will be one judged to be inferior to ours.

From the foregoing it can be concluded that there are situations in which there would be good economic consequences if a company made bribery or extortion payments in order to help sell its products. Bribery and/or extortion payments to help make sales cannot be faulted on economic grounds if the following conditions are satisfied:

1. The person who is making the purchasing decision is corrupt and, if possible, will purchase only from firms that offer him payments.

2. At least some of one's competitors are willing to make payments so that the purchasing agent is in a position to refuse to buy from any company that doesn't offer him payment.

3. The supplier finds it advantageous to make the payment rather than not do business at all.

4. The payments that one makes are not greatly in excess of those made by one's competitors, so that making the payments does not put one in a position to get preference over other suppliers making smaller payments who may have better products.

It is worth noting here that it may often be difficult for a company to *know* whether or not these conditions are satisfied. This suggests that the economic status of foreign payments (and their status as either bribes or extortion payments) is often unclear (see n. 5). I am assuming that no individual company has the power to end the practice of extortion and that any such attempt on the part of an individual company would be futile. (For further consideration of this assumption, see Section V.)

So far I have only considered examples of paying someone to purchase a product. There are many other types of payments that space does not permit an adequate discussion of here. However, I would like to consider briefly the economic consequences of three other important kinds of payments to government officials....

1. "Grease payments" offered in order to facilitate or speed up routine bureaucratic decisions of a nondiscretionary nature, e.g., hastening the passage of goods through customs....

2. Payments to insure nonenforcement of laws or regulations....

3. Payments intended to influence officials possessing substantial discretionary powers in their interpretation of laws and regulations affecting one's business....

1. In much of the world it is simply impossible for companies to do business without making grease payments to cut red tape and obtain routine governmental services within a reasonable amount of time. Clearly, the decision to make such payments cannot be considered undesirable from an economic point of view. Grease payments do not necessarily constitute bribes. If government officials routinely violate their duties by providing slow and inefficient services, then payments to insure more efficient service cannot be considered bribes; they would only be payments in exchange for the officials' fulfillment of their fiduciary obligations. There are some countries in which nominal payments to government officials are tantamount to tips. The payments are expected in exchange for the performance of routine tasks. They are not taken to entitle one to any special or unfair advantage over others, and (most importantly) the payments are tacitly condoned by those governments in question. The practice of tipping as we are familiar with it in the context of restaurants and taxicabs differs from grease payments in that it is at least semi-voluntary; since the tip is paid after the services are rendered it is possible to receive the services in question without making the payment. The involuntary nature of grease payments argues in favour of viewing them as extortion payments and, no doubt, they often are. However, when modest grease payments are tacitly condoned by foreign governments as a means for civil servants to supplement their incomes, such payments would be more plausibly viewed as fees paid for services to be rendered. (The withholding of services in the absence of such payments is a kind of harm that the officials have both a moral and a [*de facto*] legal right to inflict on one.) Not only is there no economic or moral objection to making grease payments when they are tantamount (or nearly tantamount) to tips, there is nothing inherently ineffi-

cient or immoral about a system in which government officials are paid in part through "tips." On the other hand it must be conceded that such a system is easily abused. There is a slippery slope leading from mere tips to payments intended to secure one special consideration over others.

2. If a company pays a government official not to enforce a particular law or regulation against it, then it is spared the costs of complying with the law or regulation. Often the social costs of noncompliance with regulations, for example, increased pollution, are greater than the costs of compliance. In such cases the payments will result in a net economic harm. However, there are presumably some costly regulations that are undesirable from an economic point of view, that is, regulations that are such that the cost of compliance with them greatly exceeds the benefits of compliance. Payments intended to secure the nonenforcement of such regulations may have desirable economic consequences.

3. There are situations in which government officials have very wide discretionary powers in interpreting laws and regulations affecting businesses. For example, in Italy tax collectors have great discretionary power in determining the tax liabilities of individuals and corporations. Corrupt officials have the power to impose extremely heavy tax burdens on those who are unwilling to placate them with special favours.[7] It's hard to see how payments intended to avoid unfair treatment can be considered undesirable from an economic point of view. Of course, payments intended to give one favoured treatment in the interpretation of the law are most likely undesirable from an economic point of view.

WHAT'S WRONG WITH BRIBERY?

To accept a bribe is *prima facie* wrong because it involves violating the fiduciary obligations (or other obligations) attaching to one's office or role. The following are examples of fiduciary obligations. Attorneys are expected to act in the best interests of their clients; government regulatory officers are expected to enforce regulations impartially. Fiduciary obligations are central to cases of conflict of interest. It is thought to be wrong merely to allow oneself to be in a position in which one would be tempted to violate one's fiduciary obligations or fail to act in the best interests of one's principal. I take it that fiduciary obligations have their basis in implicit or explicit agreements. An employee works on the implicit or explicit understanding that he will do certain things. Other types of "positional obligations" also have their basis in agreements or understandings. A tennis player who participates in public competition does so on the understanding that he will do his best to win. So, accepting a bribe is wrong, in part, because it is a case of breaking an understanding or agreement. It is also wrong on account of the bad consequences that may result from it. There are two types of bad consequences that often result when people accept bribes: (a) Accepting bribes causes one to corrupt one's moral character; (b) The actions that the recipient is being paid to perform are likely to have bad economic consequences. For example, if a businessman accepts a bribe to purchase a product or service that is either inferior to or costlier than something else that he could have purchased, then he is hampering the efficiency of his company and the efficiency of the marketplace itself. The acceptance of bribes by government officials may also lead to undesirable consequences such as the pollution of the environment, the endangerment of the health and safety of workers, or the noncollection of taxes.

There are several reasons for thinking that it is wrong or *prima facie* wrong to *offer* bribes in business contexts: (a) The bribery payments may be an attempt to gain an unfair advantage over one's competitors; (b) Bribery offers often serve to corrupt the character of those to whom they are made; (c) Bribery offers often cause the recipient to do things that have bad economic consequences. The bad consequences of the action that the recipient is being paid to perform also count as bad consequences of the bribery offer itself. In assessing the responsibility of the briber for the bad consequences of what the bribed party does, we need to ask what would have happened if the briber had not made his offer. Suppose that the bribed party has received other bribery offers to do things having the same sorts of bad economic consequences that he actually brought about by accepting the briber's offer. Suppose also that he would have accepted one of these other bribery offers, if he hadn't received the offer from the actual briber. In this case, the briber is not responsible for bringing about bad economic consequences that would not have occurred, were it not for him. Further, he is not responsible for any harm to the moral character of the bribed party that would not have occurred otherwise. However, if the briber makes the only bribery offer that the bribed party is willing to accept, then the briber is the cause of both harm to the bribed party's character and of economic harm that would not have occurred otherwise. (d) Offering bribes is wrong, because it compels one to falsify financial records in order to keep the bribery secret.[8] (e) It is often morally wrong for someone to fail to fulfill the obligations of his position. Therefore, offering bribes often involves enticing others to do what is morally wrong. As a general principle, if it is wrong for *S* to do *x*, then it is wrong to entice or induce him to do *x*. (This principle will be discussed and qualified at some length below.) So, it is probable that it is at least *prima facie* wrong to offer someone a bribe if what he is being paid to do is itself morally wrong. (Offering a bribe to a guard to let one out of a concentration camp would presumably not be *prima facie* wrong in this way.)

THE MORAL STATUS OF EXTORTION PAYMENTS

Let us consider our example of offering extortion payments to corrupt officials in cases in which one knows that some of one's competitors are willing to offer similar payments, so that one has little chance of doing business unless one pays. What, if anything, is wrong with making such payments oneself? Are any of our four reasons for thinking that it is wrong to offer bribes also reasons for thinking that it is wrong to offer extortion payments?

(a) Making the payment in this case would not constitute an attempt to gain an unfair advantage over one's competitors for, by hypothesis, they are making, or are willing to make, the payments themselves.

(b) Making an extortion payment cannot corrupt the extortionist's character, for the extortionist has demonstrated that he already has a bad character by demanding the payment. Paying him cannot cause him to be corrupted.

(c) Such payments are not harmful from an economic point of view; to the contrary, they may help to restore a "fair" competitive balance. The corrupt officials may make a perfectly objective and impartial decision after receiving payment (or offers of payment) from all potential suppliers. (A more probable scenario is that the officials will compile a rank ordering of potential suppliers in an impartial manner and then purchase from the first of those on their list who is willing to make extortion payments.) From an economic point of view it would be best if there were no extortion at all. But no one company can eliminate the practice of extortion on its own and, given that others are willing to make extortion payments, it may be preferable that one do so as well.

(d) The practice of making extortion payments to corrupt officials may require companies to conceal or withhold certain information, but it does not require that they falsify their financial records. Companies involved in making extortion payments can make a full accounting of the existence and cost of such payments to stockholders. The experiences of those companies whose payments to foreign officials were revealed during the Watergate scandals suggest that such revelations have little effect on investor confidence and the value of stock.[9] Of course, a company may not be able to reveal the details of extortion payments. In particular, it may be unable to reveal the identities of the recipients of its payments; for most extortionists will presumably demand that their identities be kept secret. (There is nothing morally objectionable about withholding such information, except perhaps when the information in question can be used to remove extortionists from positions of authority—see below.) Given that there are laws against payments to foreign officials for "economic extortion," any company that makes such payments must falsify its books in order to avoid prosecution.…

(e) Do extortion payments of this sort constitute inducements for others to act immorally? It seems that they would not, provided that they are only intended to insure that one's own product will be given fair consideration. (If the payment is intended to give one special consideration over one's competitors, then that is another matter.) One is only paying the officials to do what they are morally obligated to do anyway. They aren't being paid to do anything that is either immoral or contrary to the duties of their positions. However, it might be objected that accepting the payment is itself both immoral and contrary to the duties of their positions. So, even if the money isn't offered as payment for doing anything wrong, the very act of offering the money is an inducement to do wrong. Offering someone money constitutes enticing him to violate his promise not to accept such payments. Generally speaking, if it's wrong for S to do x, then it's wrong to induce him to do *x*. However, we need to examine the status of this principle in some detail. Does it constitute an "ultimate" ground of obligation or is it merely a derivative principle? Consider the following:

> (1) The act of inducing someone to do something that is morally wrong, all things considered, is itself *prima facie* wrong, that is, the fact that an act is one of inducing another person to do wrong is always a *prima facie* reason for thinking that the act is wrong.

Unless (1) is true, there is no reason to think that the payment to the corrupt foreign official is *prima facie* wrong on account of its being a case of inducing someone to do wrong. There is no way to make a fully adequate assessment of (1) in the absence of a thorough inquiry into general questions of normative ethics, which extends far beyond the scope of this article. Still, I think that it is possible to give cases that show that (1) is inconsistent with our considered moral intuitions. According to our considered moral intuitions, it is not *prima facie* wrong to induce someone to do wrong unless doing so has bad consequences (such as the corruption of the recipient's character), or constitutes a violation of some *other* ultimate moral principle.

Case 1 *Y* is the flagrantly adulterous husband of *X*. *Z* meets *Y* at a singles bar and invites him to have sex with her. *Y* would have had sex with someone on that occasion, even if he hadn't received an invitation from *Z*. *Z* has not done anything to corrupt *Y*. She hasn't harmed his character or caused him to perform any wrong actions that he wouldn't have performed otherwise. (There is a pickwickian sense in which this just isn't so. *Z* has caused *Y* to perform the act of "committing adultery with *Z*" and this is an act that *Y* would not have performed if it hadn't been for *Z*. However, the wrongness of this act is derived *entirely* from its being a case of "committing adultery with someone" and

this is an act that *Y* would have performed that night, regardless of what *Z* did.) There may be other reasons for thinking that what *Z* does is morally wrong, but we can't say that it's wrong on account of what she does to *Y*.

Case 2 In city *q* police protection is almost nonexistent in certain neighbourhoods on account of the corruption and inefficiency of the higher officials of the department. Merchants in these areas receive little, if any, police protection. A merchant offers the police chief a large sum of money in exchange for a promise of protection. Even though the merchant is entitled to the protection, the offer is an inducement to do something that is wrong—the chief has a fiduciary obligation not to accept such payments. However, there is no moral presumption whatever against making the payment and it follows that (1) is false.

Should these arguments against (1) fail—and I do not concede this for a moment—I still have one further argument to show that the sorts of economic extortion payments considered in our example are permissible. Let us grant for the sake of argument that making extortion payments to corrupt foreign officials is *prima facie* wrong on account of being a case of inducing others to do wrong. The presumption against paying is still rather weak and can be easily overridden by the economic considerations that weigh in favor of paying. The economic extortion payments in question are analogous to the case of paying a corrupt police officer for protection that he ought to provide without receiving the payment. Although in each case offering the payments constitutes enticing someone to do something that he ought not to do, i.e., accept the payment, the recipients are still being *paid to do* things that they ought to do anyway—give one's product fair consideration or provide one with police protection. Since it is clearly permissible to pay the police, we are entitled to conclude that it is permissible to pay economic extortion in cases of the sort in question. It might be objected that there are relevant differences between the two cases; the harms averted by the payment to the police are much greater than those involved in the case of extortion payments. But this isn't necessarily the case. The merchant is justified in making payments to the police officers, even if the harms that he is seeking to avoid are of a relatively minor nature. For example, it is permissible to pay in order to help avoid vandalism or attract new customers who might otherwise be kept away out of fear of crime in the area.

None of the reasons proposed earlier for thinking that it is wrong to make bribery payments is a strong reason to think that it is wrong to make extortion payments.... However, one might argue that making bribery or extortion payments is morally wrong in this case because it abets and contributes to the harmful practice of extortion.[10] This argument raises the question of how much one is obligated to sacrifice to help eliminate harmful practices. For the sake of argument, let us suppose that a corporation is obligated to sacrifice whatever profits it obtains from making bribery or extortion payments in order to combat these practices. This may be conceding too much. However, I believe that I can defend my view without denying this. As stated, the foregoing principle is in need of qualification. It is plausible only if we make the further stipulation that no firm is obligated to keep its hands clean if doing so is completely futile (see principle *P* below). Suppose that a supplier is being subjected to extortion demands by an employee of another company. There is a very strong presumption against making the payments. Instead of paying him off, one should expose him to his employer. In ordinary contexts this is very likely to be effective—it is safe to assume that the other company doesn't want its employees to either demand or accept such payments. By revealing the extortion demands one can probably succeed in removing the corrupt employee and thereby the extortion itself.

The same remarks apply to many cases of extortion payments demanded by government officials. If the official in question is likely to be dismissed or reprimanded if exposed, then, allowing for exceptions in unusual cases, one should refuse to make the payment and expose the demand to the government in question. If a company makes extortion payments in these circumstances, we have good reasons to suspect that it is seeking to obtain special advantages from the payments. For, by hypothesis, it can nullify the extortion demand simply by exposing it. However, there are many situations in which corrupt officials have little to fear from having the wrongdoing brought to light. In such cases the aforementioned remedies and recourses may be of no avail. In a limiting case, the corrupt official in question may be the head of a non-democratic regime and thus invulnerable to unfavorable publicity. Perhaps one should try to get all of one's competitors to refuse to do business with him. Failing this, one could pressure other ... companies by threatening to report their violations.... However, in cases in which one is dealing with large numbers of foreign competitors this does not seem to be a viable option. (It is worth remarking here that if there were effective [and enforceable] international laws against bribery and extortion, then it might be nearly impossible to justify extortion payments for the purpose of making sales. Alas, however, there are no such laws.)

There seem to be cases in which any attempt on the part of an individual company to curb the practice of extortion will be completely futile. In such cases I believe that a company has no obligation to refrain from engaging in the practice itself. But, no doubt, there are many who would disagree. At issue is the following principle:

P. A company or individual has no *special obligation* to sacrifice its own interests in order to refrain from participating in harmful practices if doing so will not help to curb those practices.

Let me consider some examples that might be thought to constitute objections to *P*:

1. A man in the deep South in the 1930s refuses to allow blacks to use the restrooms in his service station.

2. A soldier in the Waffen-SS takes active part in the massacre of civilians in a small village in Poland.

3. Following the example of his colleagues, a business executive "pads" his expense account for a business trip.

P might seem to commit me to saying that the actions described in 1, 2, and 3 are morally permissible. However, as I shall now argue, this is not the case. In all three cases the agent has the option to refuse to participate in a harmful practice. But his own nonparticipation is likely to be futile; he can do nothing to effectively curb these practices. *P* commits me to saying that the conduct described in 1, 2, and 3 cannot be criticized simply on the grounds that the agents are participating in practices that are generally harmful. However, it is perfectly open to me to say that there are other reasons for thinking that the conduct in question is morally wrong. The actions described in these three examples are wrong for reasons that are independent of their being instances of harmful practices. The agents in 1 and 2 are unjustly harming others and denying them their rights. Case 3 involves lying, breach of promise, and the act in question results in direct economic harm to the agent's company. The cases of extortion payments in dispute are very different. As our earlier arguments have shown, it is only the fact that the acts in question are part of the harmful practice of extortion that makes it at all plausible to hold that they are morally wrong. Apart from their place in the practice of extortion, we have failed to find any reason for thinking that it is morally wrong to make the payments.

Example 2 deserves one further comment. It is quite possible that massacre of the people in the village will occur no matter what one does. Therefore in this case a utilitarian might reason as follows: "No matter what I do the people in the village will be killed, so I don't have a duty to refrain from participating in the massacre and thus risk my own life just to keep my hands clean." While this line of reasoning is consistent with *P*, *P* does not commit me to this. *P* does not commit me to be a utilitarian; it is consistent with principles that imply that one has a special duty not to be the immediate cause of harm or injustice oneself, as opposed to simply having the duty to minimize the incidence of harm or injustice.[11] *P* only says that one has no special duty to refrain from participating in practices that are generally harmful.

It remains for us to consider briefly a slightly different and, perhaps, more common sort of case. Suppose that most, but not all, of one's competitors are willing to make extortion payments to a corrupt foreign official who demands the payments as a necessary (but not sufficient) condition of doing business and that any attempt on one's own part to limit this practice will prove to be unavailing. The only morally relevant difference between this case and the one considered earlier is that in this case making the payment will give one an unfair advantage over some of one's competitors. Is this sufficient reason for saying that it would be wrong to offer the payments? I think not. Making the payment oneself will not harm those companies that don't pay; they will be unable to do business regardless of what one does. However, this is not enough to settle the issue, as the example of the soldier who is deliberating about whether to take part in the massacre should make clear. Still, in this case all companies are justified in making payments to avoid being placed at an unfair disadvantage relative to other companies, and no company is obligated to refrain from making payment. Those companies that don't pay might be motivated by moral considerations, but refusing to pay is not morally required. They cannot blame those companies that do pay for their unfair disadvantage relative to them. It is possible for them to remedy that situation, themselves, without doing anything that is morally wrong. By making payments in a case in which some of one's competitors do not pay, one is not placing them in the unacceptable situation of being forced to choose between being at an unfair disadvantage relative to others and acting immorally.

ENDNOTES

1. This example is taken from Michael Philip's article, "Bribery" (*Ethics*, 94, July 1984, pp. 621–636).

2. This is similar to one of the definitions given in *Black's Law Dictionary* (St. Paul, MN: West Publishing Company, 1968): "The offering, giving, receiving, or soliciting of anything of value to influence actions as official or in discharge of legal or public duty." See also the second definition of "bribe" in *The Oxford English Dictionary*, "a reward given to prevent the judgment or corrupt the conduct."

3. This sort of definition is also given in *Black's*. On this broader definition of extortion, blackmail counts as a special case of extortion. Blackmail is extortion in which the harm threatened involves damage to one's reputation. (See the definition of "blackmail" in *Black's*.)

4. See *Black's Law Dictionary*.

5. Between 1966 and 1970 the Gulf Oil Corporation paid $4 million to the ruling Democratic-Republican Party of South Korea. The late party chairman S.K.

Kim once demanded $10 million from Gulf, warning that Gulf's continued prosperity and survival in Korea depended on its making this payment. (See Jacoby et al., pp. 107–108, and Yerachmiel Kugel and Gladys W. Gruenberg, *International Payoffs* [Lexington, MA: D.C. Heath & Co., 1977], p. 68.) Northrop Corporation's board member, Richard Miller, claimed that his company's highly publicized foreign payments were necessary for its sales and thus a form of blackmail or extortion. (See Kugel and Gruenberg, p. 13.) At the very least it seems plausible to suppose that its payments in the Middle East were extortion payments. (See Jacoby et al., pp. 8–9.)

The most notorious case of foreign political payments is that of Lockheed's payments in Japan to help sell its L1011 aircraft. The rough outlines of the case are as follows. In 1972 the two major Japanese airlines JAL and ANA were planning to make large purchases of the then new wide-bodied aircraft. Lockheed was in very bad financial shape, having only just recently avoided bankruptcy by receiving a government guaranteed loan. It was competing with Boeing and McDonnell Douglas for the lucrative Japanese market. Lockheed hired several highly connected Japanese agents to handle the sale. The agents suggested several times that Lockheed make them large payments which would be channeled to high government officials, including Prime Minister Tanaka. Lockheed made all of these payments totaling about $7 million. The sale to ANA was completed in the following way. Lockheed's vice-president and head in charge of the Japanese sale, Carl Kotchian, was informed by the company's principal agent that the sale would be made provided that Lockheed did the following:

1. guarantee that its maintenance and fuel consumption estimates would not be exceeded; 2. assign 100 technical and maintenance personnel to ANA for a short period of time; and 3. make a final payment of about $400 000 to officials in ANA and the Japanese government. (Carl Kotchian, "Lockheed's 70-day Mission to Tokyo," *Saturday Review*, July 9, 1977, and Robert Shaplen, "The Annals of Crime: The Lockheed Incident," *The New Yorker*, Jan. 23 and 30, 1978.) From the facts of the case as we know them it cannot be determined whether it was a case of bribery or extortion. Did Lockheed's payments give it special advantages over Boeing and McDonnell Douglas or did the payments just insure it equal consideration? (In other words, would the Japanese officials have requested and received payments from either of the other companies if none had been forthcoming from Lockheed?) Lockheed made no attempt to answer these questions and can therefore be faulted for its *willingness* to make bribery payments—for all it knew its payments were bribes. However, Lockheed is not guilty of making payments that it *knew* to be bribes. It had reason to suppose that if it declined to pay it would lose the contract to another company from whom payment would be demanded and received. Boeing's history of foreign payments makes this supposition probable. (See Jacoby et al., pp. 117 and 256, and "How Boeing Passed $52 Million Under the Table," *Business and Society Review* [Winter 1978–79].)

6. This is apparently what happened in the case of Lockheed's sale of its L1011 aircraft to Japan.

7. Jacoby et al., pp. 37 and 112; Arthur Kelly, "Italian Tax Mores," in *Ethical Theory in Business*, 1st ed., Donaldson and Werhane, eds. (Englewood Cliffs, NJ: Prentice-Hall, 1979).

8. Jacob Zamansky, "Preferential Treatment, Payoffs and the Antitrust Laws: Distortion of the Competitive Process Through Commercial Bribery," *Commercial Law Journal* 83, no. 10 (December 1978): 559, and Judson Wambold, "Prohibiting Foreign Bribes: Criminal Sanctions for Corporate Payments Abroad," *Cornell International Law Journal* 10, no. 2 (May 1977): 234.

9. Jacoby et al., p. 57.

10. Cf. Kenneth Alpern, "Moral Dimensions of the Foreign Corrupt Practices Act: Comments on Hooker and Pastin," in *Ethical Issues in Business*, Donaldson and Werhane, eds. (Englewood Cliffs, NJ: Prentice-Hall, 1982).

11. Bernard Williams attacks utilitarianism on the grounds that it denies that one has special duties to avoid harming others or acting unjustly *oneself*. According to Williams, a utilitarian only recognizes the duty to minimize instances of harm and injustice. Among other things a utilitarian seems to be committed to the view that it would be permissible for an SS soldier to murder innocent civilians, provided that they will be killed by someone else regardless of what he does himself. Cf. *Utilitarianism For and Against* (with J.J.C. Smart) (Cambridge: Cambridge University Press, 1972), pp. 93–100 and "Utilitarianism and Moral Self-Indulgence," in *Moral Luck* (Cambridge: Cambridge University Press, 1982).

RECONCILING THE IRRECONCILABLE: The Global Economy and the Environment

Deborah C. Poff

For the past decade, we have been listening to a number of inconsistent and irreconcilable recommendations for solving the serious economic and environmental problems in both domestic and international economies. Our current language with respect to the significant sea changes we have witnessed in the global economy over the past decade is filled with, to use that most appropriate euphemism of the 1980s, disinformation.

This discussion will focus on how the relationship among structural adjustment policies and practices, the business activities of transnational corporations and what Robert Reich has called "the coming irrelevance of corporate nationality" makes environmental sustainability impossible. To begin, a brief discussion of the global economy and its relation to the diminishing significance of national boundaries will set the context.

THE GLOBAL ECONOMY AND THE EROSION OF STATEHOOD

In their 1989 book, *For the Common Good*, Daly and Cobb argued that if Adam Smith were alive today, he would probably not be preaching free trade. Their argument is based on what they believe to have been a necessary commitment of the 18th century capitalist to a sense of community and to an identification with his own nationhood. On this point, Smith is perhaps most universally known. He states, "By preferring the support of domestic to that of foreign industry, he (i.e., the capitalist) intends only his own security; and by directing that industry in such a manner as its produce may be of the greatest value, he intends only his own gain, and he is in this, as in many other cases, led by an invisible hand to promote an end which

Journal of Business Ethics 13: 439–445, 1994. © 1994 Kluwer Academic Publishers. Printed in the Netherlands.

has no part of his intention" (Smith, 1776, p. 423). Daly and Cobb argue that the cornerstone of the free trade argument, capital immobility, that factored so strongly into Smith's belief that the capitalist was committed to investing in his or her own domestic economy has been eroded by

> [a] world of cosmopolitan money managers and transnational corporations which, in addition to having limited liability and immortality conferred on them by national governments, have not transcended those very governments and no longer see the national community as their residence. They may speak grandly of the 'world community' as their residence, but in fact, since no world community exists, they have escaped from community into the gap between communities where individualism has a free reign (Daly and Cobb, p. 215).

These capitalists, as Daly and Cobb rightly note, have no disinclination to move their capital abroad for the slightest favourable preferential rate of return. The concern which Daly and Cobb articulate here is frequently posed as a question or series of questions. For example, "with the globalization of the economy are we living in a world system in which national economies are merely vestigial remnants of modernity or the earlier industrial period?", or, "are nations as political and social regulatory systems necessary agents for global economic negotiation and cooperation?" And what we've had as answers to these questions is essentially political positioning in two oppositional camps. As MacEwan and Tabb (1989) summarize this debate,

> The extreme globalist position often carries the implication that no change is possible except on the international level, and since there is no political mechanism for such change—aside from that of formal relations among governments—oppositional political activity is easily seen as useless. On the other ex-

treme, those who view the national economic system as a viable unit are led to formulate programs that ignore the importance of economic forces which transcend national boundaries. Such an outlook can lead to both unrealistic programs which fail because of capital's international flexibility and implicit alliances with reactionary nationalist groups to advocate, for example, increased 'competitiveness' (p. 24).

Now while I will later argue that both of these alternatives are inadequate, I'd like first to spend some time discussing how we've gotten into our current economic crisis and that means a brief sojourn into the world of structural adjustment, the world we have essentially been living in for much of the past decade.

STRUCTURAL ADJUSTMENT

I am going to address structural adjustment only as a consequence of the debt crisis and the stagnation and economic insecurity of the 1980s. Those familiar with the literature on the current economic crisis know that a complete picture starts with the Bretton Woods conference of 1944 which set guidelines for what was to become the International Monetary Fund and the International Bank for Reconstruction and Development (the World Bank as it is now known). Bretton Woods also guaranteed the dominance of the United States in the world economy. As Jamie Swift notes, "the U.S. dollar, linked to gold, would be the world's most important reserve currency and the United States effectively became banker to the Western world, with the right to print and spend the principle currency" (p. 82). What ensued in the next forty plus years is too complex to examine here. It is sufficient to note that during that time, Japan and Germany rebuilt, the United States faced with a growing trade deficit and budget deficits abandoned the gold standard, and an unprecedented exchange of world currency as commodities ensued. This was followed by extensive loans to third world countries. And with those loans went conditionality, that conditionality being structural adjustment.

Structural adjustment as the salvation from national and international economic insecurity was a natural by-product of the Reagan-Thatcher-Mulroney era posited as it is on an idealized 19th century laissez-faire. It comes from, as Foster (1989) notes, a "renewed faith in the rationalizing effect of market forces in the face of economic stagnation" (p. 281)

Structural adjustment involves, in fact, a number of complementary actions, all mutually targeted to producing on a global scale, a so-called level playing field. These actions include privatization, deregulation and liberalization of national economies. Much of this is familiar to Canadians for this is precisely what the Canadian government has been pursuing in concert with the Canadian-American Free Trade agreement and with the North American Free Trade Agreement. The impact of structural adjustment it is assumed will remove the supposed artificial obstacles and allow for the rational correction of the current crisis by removing the obstructions to natural market forces. Part of adjusting to create a level playing field, however, means, to quote Rosenberg (1986) "a weakened, restructured labour force with lowered expectations" (as quoted in Foster, p. 281). Thus, part of the restructuring for global competitiveness has meant deregulating or decertifying unions in the United Kingdom, New Zealand and elsewhere in the developed world. In the developing world, it has meant devalued domestic currencies, high unemployment, increased poverty and starvation, inflation of the cost of living and, as a strategy for global competitiveness, the establishment of free trade zones within a number of these countries.

Furthermore, within the developing nations all of these factors have lead to disproportionately increased poverty among women. This appears somewhat paradoxical given that much of this increase in poverty happened during the second half of the United Nations Decade for Women. However, since women are the poorest and most politically and economically vulnerable members of the global community (the UN 1980 data argued that women do 2/3rds of the world's labour, earn 1/10th of the world's income and own 1/100th of the world's property), they also represent the largest so-called surplus labour force. Hence we have the incongruity that while both nationally and internationally, more equity legislation was introduced into charters and constitutions and international agreements than ever before in recorded history, at the same time, the transnational corporations of advanced economies were utilizing the world's poor women as an avenue out of the stagnation of their own domestic economies by moving some of their operations to free trade zones. As Beneria (1989) states,

> The existence of a large pool of female labour at a world scale is being used to deal with the pressures of international competition, profitability crises, and economic restructuring that characterize the current reorganization of production. The availability of cheap female labour has also been an instrumental factor in the export-led policies of their world countries shifting from previous import-substitution strategies (p. 250).

The United Nations World Survey on Women (1989) concludes that "[t]he bottom line shows that, ...economic progress for women has virtually stopped, social progress has slowed, social well-being in many cases has deteriorated and, because of the importance of women's social and economic role, the aspirations of them in current development strategies will not be met" (p. xiv).

ENVIRONMENTAL SUSTAINABILITY

Having briefly outlined the parameters of structural adjustment, we can now ask: "What does it mean for environmental sustainability?" Well, if it is not already evident, any attempt to repay debts and remain competitive in such a global market under such conditions is almost impossible for a third world country and increasingly difficult for developed nations like Canada. To look first at the seemingly more favourable conditions in Canada, consider that environmental protection in developed nations like our own is only a relatively recent phenomenon. Snider (1993) argues that even within the boundaries of a nation state where a conflict arises between business interests and environmental protection, business wins. Thus, she states that both in Canada and the United States "environmental protection varies from poor to nonexistent, basically...because of the power of business." (p. 194) When we add to this the power of transnational corporations which take on supernumerary roles, traversing the globe and engaging in negotiations that change the quality of life and laws in various domestic economies, we begin to realize the resistance which any attempt to protect the environment meets. To again quote Snider with respect to the situation in Canada,

As with occupational health and protection laws, provinces and countries fear they will be at a competitive disadvantage if they strengthen environmental regulations unilaterally. Industries have always tried to minimize the costs of operation by moving to the cheapest locations they can find. Free trade between Canada and the United States has often resulted in industries from Canada and northern U.S. states relocating to the less regulated south...With an extension of the free trade agreement to Mexico, many can be expected to join the already extensive migration..., taking advantage of cheap labour and lax environmental regulations there. (p. 194)

In developing countries, the situation is exacerbated by the very nature of their so-called competitive edge as outlined by Snider (i.e., cheap labour, lax environmental regulations). The result of a heavy debt load, structural adjustment, and a radical change in the basis of domestic economies in third world nations guarantees that such nations cannot put the environment before economic survival. As Swift (1991) summarizes the problem.

It is simply not possible to push the idea of sustainable development while insisting also on debt repayment, favourable access to minerals and agricultural resources for transnational corporations, and cuts in the public sector and lower levels of social spending by Third World governments. Such an economic model is bound to focus not on environmental safeguards but on achieving a better trade and payments balance—the kind of policy package known as 'structural adjustment'. The notion that the same ideologies of industrial growth that created the environmental crisis can bring about 'sustainable growth' is, in the end, not only puzzling but also dangerous. (pp. 215–216)

The perversity of food-aid distribution over the past decade to countries where predictably famine follows deforestation and desertification and developed nation dogooders attempt to teach starving people in the third world modern farming methods to previously agrarian peoples who destroyed their environment cash-cropping for markets in the developed world, is sufficiently mind-boggling as to make us search for alternative, more coherent explanations to the problem. Essentially, we have here three cycles of activity. The first is the externally imposed requirement within a third world country to move from traditionally agrarian subsistence farming to large-scale cash crop farming.

This results in a cycle of famine. And this, in turn, results in foreign food-aid and the attempt by non-profit organizations from industrialized countries to bring modern agricultural farming methods to the famine-stricken area along with the food-aid as a means of eliminating starvation. The latter cycle is initially done in relative ignorance by well-intentioned individuals who are unaware that the cycle of famine was predictable —engineered by previous development strategies. Rather, it assumed that there is an inability among poor nations to deal with what are believed to be natural disasters like famine in Ethiopia or flooding in Bangladesh. However, as Berlan (1989) notes these disasters are not caused by whims of nature. Nor are they caused by the ignorance of peoples who merely need instruction in ecological conservation. Rather, "Third World countries are caught up in a desperate and vicious process of destroying their natural resources simply to service debt and allow short-term survival" (p. 222). And they are doing so because they have lost control of their domestic economy and of national self-governance. The environmental damage seems reminiscent and evocative. It brings to mind images of the pollution and environmental degradation which was endemic to the Industrial Revolution. The difference here is that the negotiations and damages incurred by development have been transnational in nature and have seemingly gone beyond the capacity of nation-states to effectively control. This is not just a difference in scale but a difference in kind. As Berlan summarizes the problem,

> Transnational companies are involved in all manner of hazardous ventures in Third World countries. They are building nuclear power plants, constructing massive dam projects, undertaking large mining and mineral-processing ventures, and investing in manufacturing that uses dangerous chemicals and produces hazardous wastes. In most Third World countries health and safety regulations inside plants are either non-existent or weak. Environmental standards to govern industry are just starting to be taken seriously. Most Third World governments are so desperate to attract investment that companies are in a good position to reduce their costs by saving on expensive pollution controls and health and safety equipment for workers (pp. 221–222).

Such radical shifts in power from national economies to transnational corporations and supranational monetary funds has led some intellectuals to embrace a new political cynicism and existential ennui captured by the general heading, post-modernism. David Harvey summarizes this state as a loss of faith in progress, science and technology and a total agnosticism with respect to any political or collective solutions. At least psychologically, if not epistemologically, this is similar to the political inertia noted at the beginning of this paper, the position of the extreme globalist which "carries the implication that no change is possible except on the international level, and since there is no political mechanism for such change—aside from that of formal relations among governments—oppositional political activity is easily seen as useless" (p. x).

THE REMNANT STATE?

This brings us to the final questions: "Do we have both conceptually and factually or descriptively an erosion of nationhood or statehood?" And, if so, "What does this mean for such global problems as environmental sustainability?"

Robert Reich (1991) argues that it is no longer meaningful to speak of nations in terms of national economies because the emerging global economy has rendered those economies irrelevant. He states,

> As almost every factor of production— money, technology, factories, and equipment—moves effortlessly across borders, the very idea of an American

economy is becoming meaningless, as are the notions of an American corporation, American capital, American products, and American technology. A similar transformation is affecting every other nation, some faster and more profoundly than others (p. 8).

This perspective is echoed in the discussion of national governance in the UN World Investment Report (1991). The report notes:

One of the trends highlighted in the present volume is the growing regionalization of the world economy. National economies are becoming increasingly linked in regional groupings, whether through initiatives at the political level, as in the case of the integration of the European Community, or through activities at the private-sector level ... As described in this report, regionalization is one of the important factors behind the recent growth of foreign direct investment and its growing role in the world economies (p. 40).

For those concerned with Canada's involvement in free trade agreements and the protection of Canada's natural resources in those agreements, the question of Canadian sovereignty is central. As Bienefeld (1991) notes with respect to financial deregulation, "the political content of financial regulation is usually entirely neglected when the multilateral agencies stress the importance of international regulation while advocating national deregulation even though this "means giving up a large degree of autonomy in domestic ... policy" (p. 50). To this, Easter (1992) adds, "In Canada, our true sovereignty as a nation is being lost as we replace political debate and decision-making for community goals, with the absolute rule of the market ... Almost all ... [good policies] ... are now being lost or rendered useless under the 'competitiveness' and 'open borders'" (p. 93).

But there is something to remain cognizant of when we look at the literature on the loss of national economic autonomy and sovereignty and that is that it is nations that are the key agents in negotiating deregulation, privatization and free trade deals. In the worst literature on the globalization of the economy it is as if Adam Smith's invisible hand had been replaced by the invisible man for all we hear about are global economic forces that require structural adjustments.

Nation states which, in liberal democracies, we view as protectors of basic rights, both positive and negative, and basic civil liberties are, in fact, involved in global negotiations which may erode the very principles on which they are based. And this not only affects rights meant to ensure the quality of life, including the right to live in a clean and sustainable environment, within given nations but also diminishes the possibility for the growth of democracy and democratic rights on a global scale. As Foster points out, "as each state makes its economy leaner and meaner to enlarge its own internally generated profits and export the crisis to others, the stress on the world economy intensifies, and international cooperation—always a dim possibility—becomes more remote" (p. 294). Interestingly, as regional deprivation within developed economies more and more mirrors the economies in developing nations, we witness what we previously only saw in countries, like India, where prior to Bhopal, the prime minister of the country was willing to put jobs at any cost before anything else; safety, environment, quality of work life, etc. As we add the nations of the former Soviet Union to this mix, we observe with seeming fatalism the bottom-rung position which both environmental protection and quality of life issues take in the turmoil of establishing political and economic security.

Not only, however, do forward-looking principles of rights and benefits get undermined as nation after nation positions for a competitive advantage that results in levelling to the lowest common denominator, but global negotiation coupled with financial deregulation and the development of information technology has resulted in unbridled corruption and crime. As chief financial officer of the Bank of Montreal noted,

> I can hide money in the twinkling of an eye from all of the bloodhounds that could be put on the case, and I would be so far ahead of them that there would never be a hope of unravelling the trail ... Technology today means that that sort of thing can be done through electronic means. (quoted in Naylor, 1987, p. 12)

In a related argument, Thomas (1989) claims that "the contradictory development of bureaucracy in the face of ideological assaults on the state ... includes a burgeoning growth of corruption, which has reached such staggering proportions that some social scientists see it as an 'independent productive factor'" (p. 337).

With respect to the environment, this level of corruption coupled with desperation has been evidenced in the Third World as nations vie for position to accept toxic waste from developed countries in contravention to international law.

So, does all of this mean that indeed the notion of statehood has shifted, diminished or been eroded? I would say unequivocally not. What has been eroded here is not statehood but democracy and the ability for citizens within democratic states to exercise democratic rights. Democracy has been undermined or subverted and people have been disempowered, but states have not. And this is not only true with respect to developed countries which have some type of democratic governance but it also bodes ominously for the establishment of new fledgling democracies. Not only is Canada less democratic to the extent that deregulation, privatization and economic liberalization has been ac-

complished, but to the extent that nations are willing to use such factors as economic bargaining chips, so is the possibility for democracy in other nations. With deregulation, privatization and economic liberalization, environmental sustainability becomes one more barrier to competitiveness, as do social programs and other quality of life indicators.

Assuming as I do that democracy is a good thing, what should be done about this? At the beginning of this paper, I pointed out what I thought were false alternatives, on the one hand extreme globalism that accepts the world defeat of nationhood and, on the other, naive nationalism which we encounter frequently in Canada these days as Canadians try to claw back Canada's social democracy from its recent demise. So, what's my solution? Well, it is not a new idea. Essentially all nations need to negotiate internationally from a position where they can set their own national priorities with respect to the social, political and economic needs of their citizens. This is something that increasingly has been given up even in nations like Canada where there is still the possibility of exercising collective political will. All nations have to negotiate from a position of national self-sufficiency. Transnational corporations have a political and undemocratic message that citizens in all nations have to be more competitive and that that is to be accomplished by dismantling national institutions, social programs and environmental protections. The fact that competitiveness without the protection of our natural resources, our infrastructure and social programs amounts to mass suicide is rarely considered. And what I am going to conclude with here may sound reminiscent of the cultural imperialism of a former era but it behooves those of us with the privilege to still resist global degradation and the erosion of basic rights and freedoms to do so and not allow our nations to bargain away the world. As Keynes noted in 1933,

The divorce between ownership and the real responsibility of management is serious within a country when, as a result of joint-stock enterprise, ownership is broken up between innumerable individuals who buy their interest today and sell it tomorrow and lack altogether both knowledge and responsibility towards what they monetarily own. But when this same principle is applied internationally, it is, in times of stress, intolerable—I am irresponsible towards what I own and those who operate what I own are irresponsible towards me (p. 193).

And the solution to the problem of divorce here is reconciliation rather than resignation and resistance to the false and alarming rhetoric of global greed that has benumbed our better sensibilities.

REFERENCES

Berlan, J.P.: 1989, 'Capital Accumulation, Transformation of Agriculture, and the Agricultural Crisis: A Long-Term Perspective', in *Instability and Change in the World Economy*.

Bienefeld, M.: 1992, 'Financial Deregulation: Disarming the Nation State,' *Studies in Political Economy* 37, 31–58.

Daly, H. and J. Cobb: 1989, *For the Common Good: Redirecting the Economy Toward Community, the Environment and a Sustainable Future* (Beacon Press, Boston).

Easter, W.: 1992, 'How Much Lower is Low Enough?', in J. Sinclair (ed.), *Crossing the Line* (New Star Books, Vancouver).

Foster, J.B.: 1989, 'The Age of Restructuring', in *Instability and Change in the World Economy*.

Keynes, J.M.: 1933, 'National Self-Sufficiency', in D. Moggeridge (ed.), *The Collected Writings of John Maynard Keynes*, Vol. 21 (Cambridge University Press, London).

MacEwan, A. and W. Tabb (eds.): 1989, *Instability and Change in the World Economy* (Monthly Review Press, New York).

Naylor, R.: 1987, *Hot Money and the Politics of Debt* (McClelland and Stewart, Toronto).

Reich, R.: 1991, *The Work of Nations: Preparing Ourselves for 21st Century Capitalism* (Alfred Knopf, New York).

Snider, L.: 1993, *Bad Business: Corporate Crime in Canada* (Nelson, Toronto).

Swift, J. and the Ecumenical Coalition for Economic Justice: 1991, 'The Debt Crisis: A Case of Global Usury', in J. Swift and B. Tomlinson (eds.), *Conflicts of Interest: Canada and the Third World* (Between the Lines, Toronto).

Swift, L.: 1991, 'The Environmental Challenge: Towards a Survival Economy', in *Conflicts of Interest: Canada and the Third World*.

Thomas, C.: 1989, 'Restructuring of the World Economy and its Political Implications for the Third World', in A. MacEwan and W. Tabb (eds.), *Instability and Change in the World Economy* (Monthly Review Press, New York).

United Nations: *1989, 1989 World Survey on the Role of Women in Development* (United Nations, New York).

United Nations: 1991, *World Investment Report: The Triad in Foreign Direct Investment* (United Nations, New York).

Wood, R.: 1989, 'The International Monetary Fund and the World Bank in a Changing World Economy', in *Instability and Change in the World Economy*.

ADVERTISING ETHICS

INTRODUCTION

What constitutes the good life? From the time of Plato and Aristotle to the current day, philosophers have posed, and continue to pose, this question. The relevance of this question to Part 8 of this text may not at first be obvious. Yet when you think about advertising for a moment, you will realize that, for the most part, advertising introduces products to consumers that they either need or want. There are philosophical debates and a considerable literature about the difference between needs and wants. Presumably in the case of both needs and wants, the assumption is that their satisfaction will improve the quality of life and, hence, make for a better life.

But what is a better life? Is it the same as a good life? Would a good life mean not caring about material goods as much as we do in Western industrialized countries, and

caring more about humanity? And what if we are deluded into believing falsehoods about products? What if I believe that product X will make my face look younger, when it is in fact a common moisturizer? Does it matter that I am deluded— living in a fool's paradise—as long as I am happy? Or is it better to know the truth and be miserable than be fooled but content? Does false advertising matter if the consumer is satisfied with the product, be it moisturizer or floor cleaner or laundry detergent that promises to get your clothes "cleaner than clean" and "whiter than white"? And what if we all actually shared the same vision of the minimal requirements for the "good life," but denied access to those who could not afford to meet those requirements?

This issue is further complicated if we believe, as does John Kenneth Galbraith, that advertising can actually *create* wants or desires. Galbraith argued that the central function of advertising is not to provide information about how antecedently existing needs and desires might be satisfied, but to create desires and needs, which it then offers to satisfy. Many of our desires and needs, on this view, are dependent on the processes by which they are designed to be satisfied.

This theory of "the dependence effect" has sparked considerable controversy among economists, philosophers, and advertisers. Of particular interest to the philosopher is the question whether, in manufacturing desires and needs, as well as in the products to satisfy them, advertisers are manipulating and controlling us in ways that violate our dignity and autonomy. In the words of Robert Arrington, "Puffery, indirect information transfer, subliminal advertising—are these techniques of manipulation and control whose success shows that many of us have forfeited our autonomy and become a community, or herd, of packaged souls?" Arrington's answer is a qualified "no." The creation of desires through advertising may, but does not always or even frequently, control behaviour or create wants that are not rational or are not truly ours. More often than not, he submits, advertising creates and is intended to create the desire "for a particular object given that the purchaser has other desires." Given our antecedently existing "basic desire" for a youthful appearance, the advertiser influences, but does not control us, by creating the desire for Grecian Formula 16. She leads us to desire this particular object as a means of fulfilling the more basic desire. It is perhaps worth noting that on this view, a beer company violates our autonomy only if, in addition to creating a desire to drink a particular brand of beer, it also helps create the desire to drink beer (or alcohol). And this is just what the typical beer ad is designed to do according to some of its critics. In their defence against this charge, many beer companies assert that their aim is merely to capture a larger share of existing markets, not to create new ones. Their aim, they say, is not to encourage drinking *per se*, only to encourage the drinking of their particular brand.

So according to Arrington, the creation of desires through advertising is not in and of itself morally wrong. It is wrong only when it creates within the consumer desires that are foreign to her nature.

Barbara Phillips takes a different stance from Arrington, arguing that the criticisms of advertising are misdirected. The real problem, she states, is Capitalism and the corollary false belief that happiness comes from material goods.

In the next selection in these readings, John Waide adds a complementary analysis of the self and how advertising affects our understanding of who we are. The next article provides a content analysis of how men and women are portrayed in advertising by Canadian magazines. Zhou and Chen are particularly interested in whether advertising captures women's and men's changing roles in society as women become more equitably treated in the workplace and more represented in the professions. In general, the authors' conclusions are positive. However, they add that advertisers must continue to recognize that they have a social responsibility as corporate citizens to ensure that advertising reflects the continuing improvement of women's socioeconomic status and power.

This section of the text ends with a famous Canadian case study, *R. J. MacDonald v. Canada (Attorney General)*. In this case, the rights of freedom of expression are discussed in the context of advertising. It raises important questions about the right of freedom of expression and its relevance to corporations (i.e., corporate persons) and advertising. Also raised are issues of the responsibility of the state to protect Canadian citizens from the health risks associated with tobacco use.

John Waide argues that his main concern with advertising is with the quality of values created by advertising. Waide believes that what he calls "associative advertising" desensitizes those qualities in advertisers that we believe to be virtuous (e.g., compassion, concern, and sympathy for others), and also influences consumers to neglect the non-market-oriented values of humanity. Thus, argues Waide, associative advertising diminishes the quality of human virtue and what is most praiseworthy and good in human life.

ADVERTISING AND BEHAVIOR CONTROL

Robert L. Arrington

Consider the following advertisements:

(1) "A woman in *Distinction Foundations* is so beautiful that all other women want to kill her."

(2) Pongo Peach color from Revlon comes "from east of the sun ... west of the moon where each tomorrow dawns." It is "succulent on your lips" and "sizzling on your finger tips (And on your toes, goodness knows)." Let it be your "adventure in paradise."

(3) "Musk by English Leather—The Civilized Way to Roar."

(4) "Increase the value of your holdings. Old Charter Bourbon Whiskey—The Final Step Up."

(5) Last Call Smirnoff Style: "They'd never really miss us, and it's kind of late already, and it's quite a long way, and I could build a fire, and you're looking very beautiful, and we could have another martini, and it's awfully nice just being home ... you think?"

(6) A Christmas Prayer. "Let us pray that the blessings of peace be ours—the peace to build and grow, to live in harmony and sympathy with others, and to plan for the future with confidence." New York Life Insurance Company.

These are instances of what is called puffery—the practice by a seller of making exaggerated, highly fanciful or suggestive claims about a product or service. Puffery, within ill-defined limits, is legal. It is considered a legitimate, necessary, and very successful tool of the advertising industry. Puffery is not just bragging; it is bragging carefully designed to achieve a very definite effect. Using the techniques of so-called motivational research, advertising firms first

From *Journal of Business Ethics* 1 (1982) 3–12. Copyright © 1983 by D. Reidel Publishing Company, Dordrecht, Holland. Reprinted by permission.

identify our often hidden needs (for security, conformity, oral stimulation) and our desires (for power, sexual dominance and dalliance, adventure) and then they design ads which respond to these needs and desires. By associating a product, for which we may have little or no direct need or desire, with symbols reflecting the fulfillment of these other, often subterranean interests, the advertisement can quickly generate large numbers of consumers eager to purchase the product advertised. What woman in the sexual race of life could resist a foundation which would turn other women envious to the point of homicide? Who can turn down an adventure in paradise, east of the sun where tomorrow dawns? Who doesn't want to be civilized and thoroughly libidinous at the same time? Be at the pinnacle of success—drink Old Charter. Or stay at home and dally a bit—with Smirnoff. And let us pray for a secure and predictable future, provided for by New York Life, God willing. It doesn't take very much motivational research to see the point of these sales pitches. Others are perhaps a little less obvious. The need to feel secure in one's home at night can be used to sell window air conditioners, which drown out small noises and provide a friendly, dependable companion. The fact that baking a cake is symbolic of giving birth to a baby used to prompt advertisements for cake mixes which glamorized the 'creative' housewife. And other strategies, for example involving cigar symbolism, are a bit too crude to mention, but are nevertheless very effective.

Don't such uses of puffery amount to manipulation, exploitation, or downright control? In his very popular book *The Hidden Persuaders*, Vance Packard points out that a number of people in the advertising world have frankly admitted as much:

> As early as 1941 Dr. Dichter (an influential advertising consultant) was exhorting ad agencies to recognize themselves for what they actually

were—"one of the most advanced laboratories in psychology." He said the successful ad agency "manipulates human motivations and desires and develops a need for goods with which the public has at one time been unfamiliar—perhaps even undesirous of purchasing." The following year *Advertising Agency* carried an ad man's statement that psychology not only holds promise for understanding people but "ultimately for controlling their behavior."[1]

Such statements led Packard to remark: "With all this interest in manipulating the customer's subconscious, the old slogan 'let the buyer beware' began taking on a new and more profound meaning."[2]

B.F. Skinner, the high priest of behaviorism, has expressed a similar assessment of advertising and related marketing techniques. Why, he asks, do we buy a certain kind of car?

> Perhaps our favorite TV program is sponsored by the manufacturer of that car. Perhaps we have seen pictures of many beautiful or prestig[ious] persons driving it—in pleasant or glamorous places. Perhaps the car has been designed with respect to our motivational patterns: the device on the hood is a phallic symbol; or the horsepower has been stepped up to please our competitive spirit in enabling us to pass other cars swiftly (or, as the advertisements say, 'safely'). The concept of freedom that has emerged as part of the cultural practice of our group makes little or no provision for recognizing or dealing with these kinds of control.[3]

In purchasing a car we may think we are free, Skinner is claiming, when in fact our act is completely controlled by factors in our environment and in our history of reinforcement. Advertising is one such factor.

A look at some other advertising techniques may reinforce the suspicion that Madison Avenue controls us like so many puppets. T.V. watchers surely have noticed that some of the more repugnant ads are shown over and over again, *ad nauseam.* My favorite, or most hated, is the one about A-1 Steak Sauce which goes something like this: Now, ladies and gentlemen, what is hamburger? It has succeeded in destroying my taste for hamburger, but it has surely drilled the name of A-1 Sauce into my head. And that is the point of it. Its very repetitiousness has generated what ad theorists call *information.* In this case it is indirect information, information derived not from the content of what is said but from the fact that it is said so often and so vividly that it sticks in one's mind—i.e., the information yield has increased. And not only do I always remember A-1 Sauce when I go to the grocers, I tend to assume that any product advertised so often has to be good—and so I usually buy a bottle of the stuff.

Still another technique: On a recent show of the television program *Hard Choices* it was demonstrated how subliminal suggestion can be used to control customers. In a New Orleans department store, messages to the effect that shoplifting is wrong, illegal, and subject to punishment were blended into the Muzak background music and masked so as not to be consciously audible. The store reported a dramatic drop in shoplifting. The program host conjectured whether a logical extension of this technique would be to broadcast subliminal advertising messages to the effect that the store's $15.99 sweater special is the "bargain of a lifetime." Actually, this application of subliminal suggestion to advertising has already taken place. Years ago in New Jersey a cinema was reported to have flashed subthreshold ice cream ads onto the screen during regular showings of the film—and yes, the concession stand did a landslide business.[4]

Puffery, indirect information transfer, subliminal advertising—are these techniques of manipulation and control whose success shows that many of us have forfeited our autonomy and become a community, or

herd, of packaged souls?[5] The business world and the advertising industry certainly reject this interpretation of their efforts. *Business Week*, for example, dismissed the charge that the science of behavior, as utilized by advertising, is engaged in human engineering and manipulation. It editorialized to the effect that "it is hard to find anything very sinister about a science whose principal conclusion is that you get along with people by giving them what they want."[6] The theme is familiar: businesses just give the consumer what he/she wants; if they didn't they wouldn't stay in business very long. Proof that the consumer wants the products advertised is given by the fact that he buys them, and indeed often returns to buy them again and again.

The techniques of advertising we are discussing have had their more intellectual defenders as well. For example, Theodore Levitt, Professor of Business Administration at the Harvard Business School, has defended the practice of puffery and the use of techniques depending on motivational research.[7] What would be the consequences, he asks us, of deleting all exaggerated claims and fanciful associations from advertisements? We would be left with literal descriptions of the empirical characteristics of products and their functions. Cosmetics would be presented as facial and bodily lotions and powders which produce certain odor and color changes; they would no longer offer hope or adventure. In addition to the fact that these products would not then sell as well, they would not, according to Levitt, please us as much either. For it is hope and adventure we want when we buy them. We want automobiles not just for transportation, but for the feelings of power and status they give us. Quoting T.S. Eliot to the effect that "Human kind cannot bear very much reality," Levitt argues that advertising is an effort to "transcend nature in the raw," to "augment what nature has so crudely fashioned." He maintains that "everybody everywhere wants to modify, transform, embellish, enrich and reconstruct the world around him." Commerce takes the same liberty with reality as the artist and the priest—in all three instances the purpose is "to influence the audience by creating illusions, symbols, and implications that promise more than pure functionality." For example, "to amplify the temple in men's eyes, (men of cloth) have, very realistically, systematically sanctioned the embellishment of the houses of the gods with the same kind of luxurious design and expensive decoration that Detroit puts into a Cadillac." A poem, a temple, a Cadillac—they all elevate our spirits, offering imaginative promises and symbolic interpretations of our mundane activities. Seen in this light, Levitt claims, "Embellishment and distortion are among advertising's legitimate and socially desirable purposes." To reject these techniques of advertising would be "to deny man's honest needs and values."

Philip Nelson, a Professor of Economics at SUNY-Binghamton, has developed an interesting defence of indirect information advertising.[8] He argues that even when the message (the direct information) is not credible, the fact that the brand is advertised, and advertised frequently, is valuable indirect information for the consumer. The reason for this is that the brands advertised most are more likely to be better buys—losers won't be advertised a lot, for it simply wouldn't pay to do so. Thus even if the advertising claims made for a widely advertised product are empty, the consumer reaps the benefit of the indirect information which shows the product to be a good buy. Nelson goes so far as to say that advertising, seen as information, does not require an intelligent human response. If the indirect information has been received and has had its impact, the consumer will purchase the better buy even if his explicit reason for doing so is silly, e.g., he naively believes an endorsement of the product by a celebrity. Even

though his behavior is overtly irrational, by acting on the indirect information he is nevertheless doing what he ought to do, i.e., getting his money's worth. "'Irrationality' is rational," Nelson writes, "if it is cost-free."

I don't know of any attempt to defend the use of subliminal suggestion in advertising, but I can imagine one form such an attempt might take. Advertising information, even if perceived below the level of conscious awareness, must appeal to some desire on the part of the audience if it is to trigger a purchasing response. Just as the admonition not to shoplift speaks directly to the superego, the sexual virtues of TR-7s, Pongo Peach, and Betty Crocker cake mix present themselves directly to the id, by bypassing the pesky reality principle of the ego. With a little help from our advertising friends, we may remove a few of the discontents of civilization and perhaps even enter into the paradise of polymorphous perversity.[9]

The defense of advertising which suggests that advertising simply is information which allows us to purchase what we want, has in turn been challenged. Does business, largely through its advertising efforts, really make available to the consumer what he/she desires and demands? John Kenneth Galbraith has denied that the matter is as straightforward as this.[10] In his opinion the desires to which business is supposed to respond, far from being original to the consumer, are often themselves created by business. The producers make both the product and the desire for it, and the "central function" of advertising is "to create desires." Galbraith coins the term 'The Dependence Effect' to designate the way wants depend on the same process by which they are satisfied.

David Braybrooke has argued in similar and related ways.[11] Even though the consumer is, in a sense, the final authority concerning what he wants, he may come to see, according to Braybrooke, that he was mistaken in wanting what he did. The statement 'I want *x*', he tells us, is not incorrigible but is "ripe for revision." If the consumer had more objective information than he is provided by product puffing, if his values had not been mixed up by motivational research strategies (e.g., the confusion of sexual and automotive values), and if he had an expanded set of choices instead of the limited set offered by profit-hungry corporations, then he might want something quite different from what he presently wants. This shows, Braybrooke thinks, the extent to which the consumer's wants are a function of advertising and not necessarily representative of his real or true wants.

The central issue which emerges between the above critics and defenders of advertising is this: do the advertising techniques we have discussed involve a violation of human autonomy and a manipulation and control of consumer behavior, or do they simply provide an efficient and cost-effective means of giving the consumer information on the basis of which he or she makes a free choice. Is advertising information, or creation of desire?

To answer this question we need a better conceptual grasp of what is involved in the notion of autonomy. This is a complex, multifaceted concept, and we need to approach it through the more determinate notions of (a) autonomous desire, (b) rational desire and choice, (c) free choice, and (d) control or manipulation. In what follows I shall offer some tentative and very incomplete analyses of these concepts and apply the results to the case of advertising.

(a) Autonomous Desire Imagine that I am watching T.V. and see an ad for Grecian Formula 16. The thought occurs to me that if I purchase some and apply it to my beard, I will soon look younger—in fact I might even be myself again. Suddenly I want to be myself! I want to be young again! So I rush out and buy a bottle. This is our question: was the desire to be younger manu-

factured by the commercial, or was it 'original to me' and truly mine? Was it autonomous or not?

F.A. von Hayek has argued plausibly that we should not equate nonautonomous desires, desires which are not original to me or truly mine, with those which are culturally induced.[12] If we did equate the two, he points out, then the desires for music, art, and knowledge could not properly be attributed to a person as original to him, for these are surely induced culturally. The only desires a person would really have as his own in this case would be the purely physical ones for food, shelter, sex, etc. But if we reject the equation of the nonautonomous and the culturally induced, as von Hayek would have us do, then the mere fact that my desire to be young again is caused by the T.V. commercial—surely an instrument of popular culture transmission—does not in and of itself show that this is not my own, autonomous desire. Moreover, even if I never before felt the need to look young, it doesn't follow that this new desire is any less mine. I haven't always liked 1969 Alixe Corton Burgundy or the music of Satie, but when the desires for these things first hit me, they were truly mine.

This shows that there is something wrong in setting up the issue over advertising and behavior control as a question whether our desires are truly ours or are created in us by advertisements. Induced and autonomous desires do not separate into two mutually exclusive classes. To obtain a better understanding of autonomous and nonautonomous desires, let us consider some cases of a desire which a person does not acknowledge to be his own even though he feels it. The kleptomaniac has a desire to steal which in many instances he repudiates, seeking by treatment to rid himself of it. And if I were suddenly overtaken by a desire to attend an REO [a "heavy metal" rock band—ED] concert, I would immediately disown this desire, claiming possession or momentary madness. These are examples of desires which one might have but with which one would not identify. They are experienced as foreign to one's character or personality. Often a person will have what Harry Frankfurt calls a second-order desire.[13] In such cases, the first-order desire is thought of as being nonautonomous, imposed on one. When on the contrary a person has a second-order desire to maintain and fulfill a first-order desire, then the first-order desire is truly his own, autonomous, original to him. So there is in fact a distinction between desires which are the agent's own and those which are not, but this is not the same as the distinction between desires which are innate to the agent and those which are externally induced.

If we apply the autonomous/nonautonomous distinction derived from Frankfurt to the desires brought about by advertising, does this show that advertising is responsible for creating desires which are not truly the agent's own? Not necessarily, and indeed not often. There may be some desires I feel which I have picked up from advertising and which I disown—for instance, my desire for A-1 Steak Sauce. If I act on these desires it can be said that I have been led by advertising to act in a way foreign to my nature. In these cases my autonomy has been violated. But most of the desires induced by advertising I fully accept, and hence most of these desires are autonomous. The most vivid demonstration of this is that I often return to purchase the same product over and over again, without regret or remorse. And when I don't, it is more likely that the desire has just faded than that I have repudiated it. Hence, while advertising may violate my autonomy by leading me to act on desires which are not truly mine, this seems to be the exceptional case.

Note that this conclusion applies equally well to the case of subliminal advertising. This may generate subconscious desires which lead to purchases, and the act of purchasing these goods may be inconsistent with other conscious desires I have, in which case I might repudiate my behavior and by implication the subconscious cause of it. But my subconscious desires may not be inconsistent in this way with my conscious ones; my id may be cooperative and benign rather than hostile and malign.[14] Here again, then, advertising may or may not produce desires which are 'not truly mine.'

What are we to say in response to Braybrooke's argument that insofar as we might choose differently if advertisers gave us better information and more options, it follows that the desires we have are to be attributed more to advertising than to our own real inclinations? This claim seems empty. It amounts to saying that if the world we lived in, and we ourselves, were different, then we would want different things. This is surely true, but it is equally true of our desire for shelter as of our desire for Grecian Formula 16. If we lived in a tropical paradise we would not need or desire shelter. If we were immortal, we would not desire youth. What is true of all desires can hardly be used as a basis for criticizing some desires by claiming that they are nonautonomous.

(b) Rational Desire and Choice
Braybrooke might be interpreted as claiming that the desires induced by advertising are often irrational ones in the sense that they are not expressed by an agent who is in full possession of the facts about the products advertised or about the alternative products which might be offered him. Following this line of thought, a possible criticism of advertising is that it leads us to act on irrational desires or to make irrational choices. It might be said that our autonomy has been violated by the fact that we are prevented from following our rational wills or that we have been denied the 'positive freedom' to develop our true, rational selves. It might be claimed that the desires induced in us by ad-

vertising are false desires in that they do not reflect our essential, i.e., rational, essence.

The problem faced by this line of criticism is that of determining what is to count as rational desire or rational choice. If we require that the desire or choice be the product of an awareness of *all* the facts about the product, then surely every one of us is always moved by irrational desires and makes nothing but irrational choices. How could we know all the facts about a product? If it be required only that we possess all of the *available* knowledge about the product advertised, then we still have to face the problem that not all available knowledge is *relevant* to a rational choice. If I am purchasing a car, certain engineering features will be, and others won't be, relevant, *given what I want in a car*. My prior desires determine the relevance of information. Normally a rational desire or choice is thought to be one based upon relevant information, and information is relevant if it shows how other, prior desires may be satisfied. It can plausibly be claimed that it is such prior desires that advertising agencies acknowledge, and that the agencies often provide the type of information that is relevant in light of these desires. To the extent that this is true, advertising does not inhibit our rational wills or our autonomy as rational creatures.

It may be urged that much of the puffery engaged in by advertising does not provide relevant information at all but rather makes claims which are not factually true. If someone buys Pongo Peach in anticipation of an adventure in paradise, or Old Charter in expectation of increasing the value of his holdings, then he/she is expecting purely imaginary benefits. In no literal sense will the one product provide adventure and the other increased capital. A purchasing decision based on anticipation of imaginary benefits is not, it might be said, a rational decision, and a desire for imaginary benefits is not a rational desire.

In rejoinder it needs to be pointed out that we often wish to purchase subjective effects which in being subjective are nevertheless real enough. The feeling of adventure or of enhanced social prestige and value are examples of subjective effects promised by advertising. Surely many (most?) advertisements directly promise subjective effects which their patrons actually desire (and obtain when they purchase the product), and thus the ads provide relevant information for rational choice. Moreover, advertisements often provide accurate indirect information on the basis of which a person who wants a certain subjective effect rationally chooses a product. The mechanism involved here is as follows.

To the extent that a consumer takes an advertised product to offer a subjective effect and the product does not, it is unlikely that it will be purchased again. If this happens in a number of cases, the product will be taken off the market. So here the market regulates itself, providing the mechanism whereby misleading advertisements are withdrawn and misled customers are no longer misled. At the same time, a successful bit of puffery, being one which leads to large and repeated sales, produces satisfied customers and more advertising of the product. The indirect information provided by such large-scale advertising efforts provides a measure of verification to the consumer who is looking for certain kinds of subjective effect. For example, if I want to feel well dressed and in fashion, and I consider buying an Izod Alligator shirt which is advertised in all of the magazines and newspapers, then the fact that other people buy it and that this leads to repeated advertisements shows me that the desired subjective effect is real enough and that I indeed will be well dressed and in fashion if I purchase the shirt. The indirect information may lead to a rational decision to purchase a product because the information testifies to the subjective effect that the product brings about.[15]

Some philosophers will be unhappy with the conclusion of this section, largely because they have a concept of true, rational, or ideal desire which is not the same as the one used here. A Marxist, for instance, may urge that any desire felt by alienated man in a capitalistic society is foreign to his true nature. Or an existentialist may claim that the desires of inauthentic men are themselves inauthentic. Such concepts are based upon general theories of human nature which are unsubstantiated and perhaps incapable of substantiation. Moreover, each of these theories is committed to a concept of an ideal desire which is normatively debatable and which is [as] distinct from the ordinary concept of a rational desire as one based upon the relevant information. But it is in the terms of the ordinary concept that we express our concern that advertising may limit our autonomy in the sense of leading us to act on irrational desires, and if we operate with this concept we are driven again to the conclusion that advertising may lead, but probably most often does not lead, to an infringement of autonomy.

(c) Free Choice It might be said that some desires are so strong or so covert that a person cannot resist them, and that when he acts on such desires he is not acting freely or voluntarily but is rather the victim of irresistible impulse of an unconscious drive. Perhaps those who condemn advertising feel that it produces this kind of desire in us and consequently reduces our autonomy.

This raises a very difficult issue. How do we distinguish between an impulse we *do* not resist and one we *could* not resist, between freely giving in to a desire and succumbing to one? I have argued elsewhere that the way to get at this issue is in terms of the notion of acting for a reason.[16] A person acts or chooses freely if he does so for a reason, that is, if he can adduce considerations which justify in his mind the act in question. Many of our actions are in fact free because

this condition frequently holds. Often, however, a person will act from habit, or whim, or impulse, and on these occasions he does not have a reason in mind. Nevertheless he often acts voluntarily in these instances, i.e., he could have acted otherwise. And this is because if there *had been* a reason for acting otherwise of which he was aware, he would in fact have done so. Thus acting from habit or impulse is not necessarily to act in an involuntary manner. If, however, a person is aware of a good reason to do x and still follows his impulse to do y, then he can be said to be impelled by irresistible impulse and hence to act involuntarily. Many kleptomaniacs can be said to act involuntarily, for in spite of their knowledge that they likely will be caught and their awareness that the goods they steal have little utilitarian value to them, they nevertheless steal. Here their 'out of character' desires have the upper hand, and we have a case of compulsive behavior.

Applying these notions of voluntary and compulsive behavior to the case of behavior prompted by advertising, can we say that consumers influenced by advertising act compulsively? The unexciting answer is: sometimes they do, sometimes not. I may have an overwhelming T.V.-induced urge to own a Mazda Rx-7 and all the while realize that I can't afford one without severely reducing my family's caloric intake to a dangerous level. If, aware of this good reason not to purchase the car, I nevertheless do so, this shows that I have been the victim of T.V. compulsion. But if I have the urge, as I assure you I do, and don't act on it, or if in some other possible world I could afford an Rx-7, then I have not been the subject of undue influence by Mazda advertising. Some Mazda Rx-7 purchasers act compulsively; others do not. The Mazda advertising effort *in general* cannot be condemned, then, for impairing its customers' autonomy in the sense of limiting free or voluntary choice. Of course, the question remains what should be done about the fact that advertising may and does *occasionally* limit free choice. We shall return to this question later.

In the case of subliminal advertising we may find an individual whose subconscious desires are activated by advertising into doing something [of which] his calculating, reasoning ego does not approve. This would be a case of compulsion. But most of us have a benevolent subconsciousness which does not overwhelm our ego and its reasons for action. And therefore most of us can respond to subliminal advertising without thereby risking our autonomy. To be sure, if some advertising firm developed a subliminal technique which drove all of us to purchase Lear jets, thereby reducing our caloric intake to the zero point, then we would have a case of advertising which could properly be censured for infringing our right to autonomy. We should acknowledge that this is possible, but at the same time we should recognize that it is not an inherent result of subliminal advertising.

(d) Control or Manipulation Briefly let us consider the matter of control and manipulation. Under what conditions do these activities occur? In a recent paper 'Forms and Limits of Control,' I suggested the following criteria.[17] A person C controls the behavior of another person P if

(1) C *intends* P to act in a certain way A;

(2) C's intention is causally effective in bringing about A; and

(3) C intends to ensure that all of the necessary conditions of A are satisfied.

These criteria may be elaborated as follows. To control another person it is not enough that one's actions produce certain behavior on the part of that person; additionally one must intend that this happen. Hence control is the intentional production of behavior. Moreover, it is not enough just to have the intention; the intention must give rise to the conditions which bring about the intended effect. Finally, the controller must

intend to establish by his actions any otherwise unsatisfied necessary conditions for the production of the intended effect. The controller is not just influencing the outcome, not just having input; he is as it were guaranteeing that the sufficient conditions for the intended effect are satisfied.

Let us apply these criteria of control to the case of advertising and see what happens. Conditions (1) and (3) are crucial. Does the Mazda manufacturing company or its advertising agency intend that I buy an Rx-7? Do they intend that a certain number of people buy the car? *Prima facie* it seems more appropriate to say that they *hope* a certain number of people will buy it, and hoping and intending are not the same. But the difficult term here is 'intend.' Some philosophers have argued that to intend A it is necessary only to desire that A happen and to believe that it will. If this is correct, and if marketing analysis gives the Mazda agency a reasonable belief that a certain segment of the population will buy its product, then, assuming on its part the desire that this happen, we have the conditions necessary for saying that the agency intends that a certain segment purchase the car. If I am a member of this segment of the population, would it then follow that the agency intends that I purchase an Rx-7? Or is control referentially opaque? Obviously we have some questions here which need further exploration.

Let us turn to the third condition of control, the requirement that the controller intend to activate or bring about any otherwise unsatisfied necessary conditions for the production of the intended effect. It is in terms of this condition that we are able to distinguish brainwashing from liberal education. The brainwasher arranges all of the necessary conditions for belief. On the other hand, teachers (at least those of liberal persuasion) seek only to influence their students—to provide them with information and enlightenment which they may absorb *if they wish.* We do not normally think of teachers as controlling their students, for the students' performances depend as well on their own interests and inclinations.

Now the advertiser—does he control, or merely influence, his audience? Does he intend to ensure that all of the necessary conditions for purchasing behavior are met, or does he offer information and symbols which are intended to have an effect only *if* the potential purchaser has certain desires? Undeniably advertising induces some desires, and it does this intentionally, but more often than not it intends to induce a desire for a particular object, *given* that the purchaser already has other desires. Given a desire for youth, or power, or adventure, or ravishing beauty, we are led to desire Grecian Formula 16, Mazda Rx-7s, Pongo Peach, and Distinctive Foundations. In this light, the advertiser is influencing us by appealing to independent desires we already have. He is not creating those basic desires. Hence it seems appropriate to deny that he intends to produce all of the necessary conditions for our purchases, and appropriate to deny that he controls us.[18]

Let me summarize my argument. The critics of advertising see it as having a pernicious effect on the autonomy of consumers, as controlling their lives and manufacturing their very souls. The defense claims that advertising only offers information and in effect allows industry to provide consumers with what they want. After developing some of the philosophical dimensions of this dispute, I have come down tentatively in favor of the advertisers. Advertising may, but certainly does not always or even frequently, control behavior, produce compulsive behavior, or create wants which are not rational or are not truly those of the consumer. Admittedly, it may in individual cases do all of these things, but it is innocent of the charge of intrinsically or necessarily doing them or even, I think, of often doing so. This limited potentiality, to be sure, leads to the question whether ad-

vertising should be abolished or severely curtailed or regulated because of its potential to harm a few poor souls in the above ways. This is a very difficult question, and I do not pretend to have the answer. I only hope that the above discussion, in showing some of the kinds of harm that can be done by advertising and by indicating the likely limits of this harm, will put us in a better position to grapple with the question.

ENDNOTES

1. Vance Packard, *The Hidden Persuaders* (Pocket Books, New York, 1958), pp. 20–21.

2. Ibid., p. 21.

3. B.F. Skinner, 'Some Issues Concerning the Control of Human Behavior: A Symposium,' in Karlins and Andrews (eds.), *Man Controlled* (The Free Press, New York, 1972).

4. For provocative discussions of subliminal advertising, see W.B. Key, *Subliminal Seduction* (The New American Library, New York, 1973), and W.B. Key, *Media Sexploitation* (Prentice-Hall, Inc., Englewood Cliffs, N.J., 1976).

5. I would like to emphasize that in what follows I am discussing these techniques of advertising from the standpoint of the issue of control and not from that of deception.

6. Quoted by Packard, op. cit., p. 220.

7. Theodore Levitt, 'The Morality (?) of Advertising', *Harvard Business Review* 48 (1970), 84–92.

8. Phillip Nelson, 'Advertising and Ethics', in Richard T. De George and Joseph A. Pichler (eds.), *Ethics, Free Enterprise, and Public Policy* (Oxford University Press, New York, 1978), pp. 187–198.

9. For a discussion of polymorphous perversity, see Norman O. Brown, *Life*

Against Death (Random House, New York, 1969), Chapter III.

10. John Kenneth Galbraith, *The Affluent Society*; reprinted in Tom L. Beauchamp and Norman E. Bowie (eds.), *Ethical Theory and Business* (Prentice-Hall, Englewood Cliffs, 1979), pp. 496–501.

11. David Braybrooke, 'Skepticism of Wants, and Certain Subversive Effects of Corporations on American Values,' in Sidney Hook (ed.), *Human Values and Economic Policy* (New York University Press, New York, 1967); reprinted in Beauchamp and Bowie (eds.), op. cit., pp. 502–508.

12. F.A. von Hayek, "The Non Sequitur of the 'Dependence Effect,'" *Southern Economic Journal* (1961); reprinted in Beauchamp and Bowie (eds.), op. cit., pp. 508–512.

13. Harry Frankfurt, 'Freedom of the Will and the Concept of a Person', *Journal of Philosophy* LXVIII (1971), 5–20.

14. For a discussion of the difference between a malign and a benign subconscious mind, see P.H. Nowell-Smith, 'Psycho-analysis and Moral Language', *The Rationalist Annual* (1954); reprinted in P. Edwards and A. Pap (eds.), *A Modern Introduction to Philosophy*, Revised Edition (The Free Press, New York, 1965), pp. 86–93.

15. Michalos argues that in emphasizing a brand name—such as Bayer Aspirin—advertisers are illogically attempting to distinguish the indistinguishable by casting a trivial feature of a product as a significant one which separates it from other brands of the same product. The brand name is said to be trivial or unimportant "from the point of view of the effectiveness of the product or that for the sake of which the product is purchased." This claim ignores the role of indirect information in advertising. For example, consumers want an aspirin they can trust (trustworthiness being part of "that for the sake of which the product is purchased"), and the indirect information conveyed by the widespread advertising effort for Bayer aspirin shows that this product is judged trustworthy by many other purchasers. Hence the emphasis on the name is not at all irrelevant but rather is a significant feature of the product from the consumer's standpoint, and attending to the name is not at all an illogical or irrational response on the part of the consumer.

16. Robert L. Arrington, 'Practical Reason, Responsibility and the Psychopath', *Journal for the Theory of Social Behavior* 9 (1979), 71–89.

17. Robert L. Arrington, 'Forms and Limits of Control', delivered at the annual meeting of the Southern Society for Philosophy and Psychology, Birmingham, Alabama, 1980.

18. Michalos distinguishes between appealing to people's tastes and molding those tastes, and he seems to agree with my claim that it is morally permissible for advertisers to persuade us to consume some article if it suits our tastes. However, he also implies that advertisers mold tastes as well as appeal to them. It is unclear what evidence is given for this claim, and it is unclear what is meant by tastes. If the latter are thought of as basic desires and wants, then I would agree that advertisers are controlling their customers to the extent that they intentionally mold tastes. But if by molding tastes is meant generating a desire for the particular object they promote, advertisers in doing so may well be appealing to more basic desires, in which case they should not be thought of as controlling the consumer.

IN DEFENSE OF ADVERTISING: A Social Perspective

Barbara J. Phillips

Advertisements are a pervasive part of the American aural and visual environment. It is impossible to ignore their wider role in providing people a general education in goods, status, values, social roles, style, and art (Schudson, 1984, p. 207).

For as long as there have been advertisements, there have been critics of advertising who have contended that advertising is harmful to society. Although this topic has been argued from many perspectives, often the critics and the defendants appear to [be] talking at cross-purposes—each arguing narrow points with little regard for the overarching question: what are the social effects of advertising? That is, what impact does advertising have on the collective attitudes, beliefs, and behaviors of our society? Critics tend to fixate on the common argument against advertising—that it manipulates or forces consumers to buy unneeded or un-

wanted products. Supporters counter that advertising plays an important role in providing information, and cannot force sceptical consumers to buy anything that they do not want already. Stalemate.

Both this criticism and its rebuttal focus attention on the *individual* effect of advertising—that is, on its power over each consumer's market behavior. It diverts attention from the more fundamental and perhaps more important issue concerning advertising's *collective* effect on society. The purpose of this paper is to critically examine three negative collective effects that have been attributed to advertising:

(a) the elevation of consumption over other social values,

(b) the use of goods to satisfy social needs, and

(c) general dissatisfaction with one's life.

Journal of Business Ethics 16: 109–118, 1997. © 1997 Kluwer Academic Publishers. Printed in the Netherlands.

These three effects can be grouped under the umbrella of increased materialism in society.

This paper will present a defense of advertising which argues that advertising is not the underlying cause of these negative effects. It will be argued that a larger social factor, *capitalism*, is responsible for the growing materialism in our society. Few critics or defenders of advertising have addressed materialism from this perspective. Thus, the primary contribution of this paper is its explanation of the crucial role that a capitalistic economic system plays in creating the negative social effects that have attributed to advertising.

Before this argument is developed in greater detail, however, it is necessary to understand how advertising came to be seen as the institution responsible for society's rampant materialism. The next section of this paper explains how advertising gained its social influence. The third section examines the three social criticisms of advertising discussed above, and builds the argument that the underlying cause of these social conditions is capitalism. The final section offers suggestions for reducing the impact of capitalism's negative social effects.

A BRIEF HISTORY OF THE RISE OF ADVERTISING

There is no single point in history before which we were all nature's children, after which we became the sons and daughters of commerce (Schudson, 1984, p. 179).

In traditional societies of the past, the family and the community were the most important social units. Because the social environment changed little from generation to generation, older community members had valuable knowledge about the opportunities and dangers in the outside world (Becker, 1981) and they instructed young people in the tasks and roles that they would be required to perform in society. Social guidance was provided by the family and the extended community, including the religious and educational authorities of the day.

At the beginning of the twentieth century, however, these social institutions began to change in the United States. Industrialization and urbanization split individuals from their communities as workers rushed to cities and factories (Harriss, 1991). Individuals were physically separated from their families, plucked from their isolated communities, and exposed to the wider world (Bell, 1976). In this rapidly changing society, older community members found that their experiences were out-dated and devalued (Bell, 1976); they had little relevant advice to offer. As geographic and social mobility increased, individuals became increasingly detached from traditional sources of cultural influence and authority, such as families, churches, and schools. Individuals were required to look elsewhere to receive the information that these institutions once had provided (Bell, 1976; Pollay, 1989).

Industrialization also caused a separation between individuals and the products they used. Because the manufacturing process was removed from individuals' daily lives, they had less personal knowledge of a product's production and of its qualities. Consumers did not know how goods were made, nor by whom, nor for what purpose. At the same time, individuals had less time to spend seeking information about the increasingly complex goods in the market (Schudson, 1984). Consequently, consumers had a difficult time assigning social meanings to goods (Jhally, 1989).They were unsure what the goods they bought "said" about them; what messages were communicated to others by their choice of food, clothing, transportation, and gifts.

The sweeping social changes described above left individuals clamoring for a source of social guidance, and advertisers were happy to step into the void left by the decline of other institutions (Leiss, et al., 1986). As the tremendous consumer demand for advice grew, advertising in the U.S. began to change its focus from product attributes to the social meaning of goods (Leiss et al., 1986). Around 1920, advertising began to take on a social guidance function, advising consumers in matters of morality, behavior, social roles, taste, style, and dress (Bell, 1976; Marchand, 1985). Consumers could turn to advertising for desperately-needed information that could help them reduce their anxiety in a complex and confusing world (Dyer, 1982). Although traditional sources of social guidance still exerted an influence, consumers responded to advertising because it was highly visible, readily available, and because it emanated authority and certainty (Cushman, 1990). "It tells us what we must do in order to become what we wish to be" (Berman, 1981, p. 58).

Since the 1920s, the importance of family, community, and tradition has continued to decline and the world has become more complex (Berman, 1981), while advances in technology have made advertising more pervasive and given it more impact (Leiss et al., 1986). As a social institution with cultural influence and authority, advertising has a collective effect on society which Goldman (1992, p. 2) describes:

> Cultural hegemony refers to those socially constructed ways of seeing and making sense of the world around us that predominate in a given time and place. In the latter twentieth-century U.S. the supremacy of commodity relations has exercised a disproportionate influence over the ways we conceive our lives. Every day that we routinely participate in the social grammar of advertisements, we engage in a process of replicating the domain assumptions of commodity hegemony. These domain assumptions are important because they condition and delimit the field of discourse within

which our public and private conversations take place.

That is, advertising helps to create our social reality (Dyer, 1982), thereby affecting the framework through which we view the relationships between society and ourselves (Berman, 1981), ourselves and others (Schudson, 1984), and ourselves and objects (Leiss et al., 1986). By influencing our culture, advertising has the potential to affect our attitudes and values regarding the most fundamental issues in our lives, even when it does not affect our buying habits (Schudson, 1984).

It is important to note that advertising's collective effects on society, as opposed to its individual effects on buying behavior, do not require our belief in its claims (Schudson, 1984). For example, one advertisement for Dow bathroom cleaner presents a straightforward "reason-why" claim for this low-involvement product: Dow clean[er] makes cleaning the bathroom easier. At the individual level, a consumer can accept or reject the product claim, and they may choose whether or not to purchase the product. Regardless of whether consumers accept or reject the advertising message, they have been exposed to social information while viewing the ad. For example, the Dow ad implies that a sparkling clean bathroom is an important goal, and that this goal can be more easily reached through the purchase of a commodity. Even if consumers reject the advertising message as unbelievable, they are unlikely to reject, or even examine, the social information presented (Dyer, 1982). That information is implicitly accepted as "reality." And although a single ad may have little impact, consumers are exposed to similar social messages in hundreds of ads each day.

Thus, one of advertising's collective effects is that it helps to shape consumers' social reality. Consumers tend to accept the values and assumptions presented through advertising as "normal" without question because they live within the reality that advertising has helped to create (Pollary, 1989; Goldman, 1992). In the future, advertising's social influence may become more pervasive. The overused and often meaningless phrase of the 1990s, the "information superhighway," conjures up images of the future—a solitary individual barricaded in a room lit only by a flickering TV screen, isolated from the rest of society except for the information he or she receives through the surrounding mass-media. In modern U.S. society, individuals are increasingly isolated from others. Technology has contributed to the separation of the individual from traditional sources of social information. Perhaps in the future, all of our social guidance will be mass-mediated.

But putting science fiction scenarios aside, what does it matter if advertising is a major source of social guidance? The next section of this paper will examine the negative social effects that have been attributed to advertising because of its social guidance function, and will argue that these collective effects are not caused by advertising, but by capitalism.

CAPITALISM: THE INVISIBLE UNDERLYING CAUSE

Critics faulted advertising for its espousal of "materialism"—a venerable criticism, somewhat akin to criticizing a football player for aggressiveness or a model for concern with her appearance (Gold, 1987, p. 31).

As discussed in the preceding section, advertisers did not wrest control away from other social institutions in a calculated attempt to overthrow the traditional social order (Schudson, 1984); advertising gained social importance almost through default by responding to consumer demand for social

information. Schudson (1984) notes that the religious, educational, and family forces that have lost much of their influence were often unwelcome and coercive, while advertising's growing influence on socialization was desired by consumers.

Despite Schudson's argument, however, critics contend that while advertising has immense social influence, it has no explicit social goals or social responsibility (Pollary, 1989). Advertising purports to have no social values beyond economic gain. We do not really know what advertising "believes" (Berman, 1991). This is in direct contrast with other social institutions such as educational systems or religions that explicitly state the social values they are trying to impart, and thereby open these values to public scrutiny and debate.

Defendants of advertising state that the primary job of advertising is to sell goods. Understandably, then, advertising practitioners concentrate on the effect advertising has on individual behavior and do not examine the collective effect that they are creating on society. However, they are transmitting a powerful social message. Every ad "addresses the dilemmas of modern life with a single, all-purpose solution: Buy something" (Gold, 1987, p. 25). And it is this collective message that critics say has unintended negative effects on society.

As discussed earlier, three negative social effects have regularly been attributed to advertising: (a) the elevation of consumption over other social values, (b) the use of goods to satisfy social needs such as the needs for self-identity and relationships with others, and (c) general dissatisfaction. Advertising can defend itself against these compelling accusations only by showing that a social factor larger than advertising is responsible for these social conditions. There is such a factor—capitalism.

Capitalism is the accepted economic system that functions to maximize total productive output and relies on the self-interest of the individual who is intent on satisfying his or her own needs (Leiss, 1976; Rotzoll et al., 1989). Our own capitalistic economic system directly causes the negative social conditions which lead to increased materialism. Advertising, as the mouthpiece for capitalism, presents values and assumptions that color consumers' perceptions of reality. Therefore, advertising becomes a target for social criticism. However, advertising does not create the values it presents. Capitalism is the creator, and the cause of the negative social conditions underlying materialism, perhaps encouraged by basic human nature.

Again, because individuals live within a capitalistic system, they take its "realities" for granted. That is, individuals are not aware of capitalism's effects on their cultural attitudes and beliefs because the capitalistic framework is largely invisible to those who operate within it. In addition, there are few alternative frameworks for contrast and comparison. Thus, individuals tend to displace capitalism's negative social effects onto more visible institutions, such as advertising. The sections below will examine the role of capitalism in the three materialistic trends that have been attributed to advertising.

The Elevation of Consumption

Because the ultimate purpose of advertising is to sell products, each advertisement promotes consumption of a specific brand. This may help consumers make individual market choices. However, on a social level, the promotion of consumption in many ads over time leads to a representation of goods as the solution to all of life's problems, and the way to achieve the "good life" of happiness and success (Pollay, 1989). Dyer (1982, p. 1) states that "Advertisers want us to buy things, use them, throw them away, and buy replacements in a cycle of continuous and conspicuous consumption." Beyond the negative environmental impact of this strategy, the promotion of aggregate consumption may

lead to a preoccupation with material concerns at the expense of other values in society (Schudson, 1984). This is because individuals' attention is a scarce resource that social institutions organize and direct, and advertising directs attention towards consumption (Schudson, 1984). It tends to select and promote attitudes and lifestyles that are compatible with acquisition and consumption, and the unity and the pervasiveness of this message focus consumer attention on those chosen lifestyles (Dyer, 1982; Pollay, 1989). By directing consumers' attention towards consumption, advertising may contribute to the neglect of other social values considered important by family, government, or religious institutions. That is, this first criticism of advertising states that advertising makes individuals materialistic by focusing their attention on the consumption of goods and ignoring other values.

However, there is some evidence that our capitalist culture had materialistic leanings long before the rise of modern advertising (Pollay, 1989). Historians state that the belief in the worth of superior goods is an inherent part of American culture, and as early as 1830 writers note the rampant materialism of the colonies (Schudson, 1984). The production and consumption of goods are the most important activities in a capitalist economy, and a "capitalist society, in its emphasis on accumulation, has made that activity an end in itself" (Bell, 1976, p. xii). Capitalism directs attention towards consumption because it requires that a vast number of diverse commodities be produced and sold (Jhally, 1989). This cycle of consumption is necessary because the stability and authority of our society is not founded on inherited privilege or traditional associations, but on the achievements of economic production (Leiss, 1976). Therefore, permanently rising consumption is necessary for our capitalist society to retain its legitimacy and power (Leiss, 1976).

Capitalism requires that consumers' attention be directed to goods. In an expanding economy where all types of goods are widely available, this creates an inherent tendency for consumers to become fixated on exclusively material objects instead of seeking a more balanced mix of objects and other satisfiers such as interesting work or creativity (Leiss, 1976). Therefore, it appears that it is the importance of consumption and the abundance of products in a *capitalist* society that causes materialism; advertising is not the underlying cause.

Of course, there is no denying that advertising is one *tool* that capitalism uses to keep consumers' attention focused on goods. However advertising, as a tool, can be used to focus attention on any social value. This conclusion is supported by the rare instances when advertising is not used as a consumption tool, but instead is used to further a different social agenda. For example, the American Heart Association created print ads to encourage parents to turn off the TV and help their children exercise. In this case, advertising was used to promote *less* consumption of the mass media, and to focus attention on non-consumption based activities. There are several other instances where advertising has been used to direct attention away from consumption and onto competing social values. For example, anti-smoking, [anti-]drunk driving, and recycling campaigns have been successful in achieving these goals. These examples support the argument that advertising is just a tool for directing consumer attention; on what our attention is focused depends on who is controlling the advertising. In most cases, advertising serves capitalism, suggesting that a capitalist agenda is the underlying cause of increasing materialism in our society.

The Use of Goods to Satisfy Social Needs

The second major criticism of advertising is that it presents goods not only as the solution to concrete problems (e.g., "Tough grass stains? Try Wisk!") but also as the solution to social problems. Ads tell us that we can buy happiness, success, and love, and over time, consumers may come to believe that their social needs can be satisfied by purchasing commodities (Schudson, 1984). Consumers may start to believe that they can use goods to define themselves, or their relationships with others.

As discussed in the previous section, advertising tells consumers what the goods they use "say" about them. Ads tell consumers that they can express their identities through a pattern of preferences for the goods they consume (Leiss et al., 1986). For example, recent Nike ads present the personalities of the individuals who wear each type of shoe. A Nike sandal wearer is "quiet yet aggressive" while a running shoe wearer is "strong and spunky." In this way, ads state that we tell the world who we are and to which groups we belong by purchasing certain goods. In addition, ads show us what we can become (Leiss, Kline and Jhally, 1986). For example, milk commercials show children that by drinking milk they can grow up to be strong, attractive, and popular. Consumption is extolled as a way of elevating ourselves into a superior position (Berman, 1981); we are not just buying a product, we are buying a way of life (Dyer, 1982).

The problem with this message is that when we think we can buy a self, we focus on the external trappings of identity instead of internal character. Critics contend that advertising finds reality in appearances (Bell, 1976; Leiss et al., 1986). A focus on identity through consumption leads to building a life-style, not a character, and this means that our identity and perhaps our self-worth are directly related to our purchasing power. An example of equating self-worth with consumption occurred in the 1980s, when several boys in U.S. inner-cities were killed for their athletic shoes (Grimm, 1990). Although many social and environmental factors played a part in this behavior, it is an example of the consumption ethic taken to the streets. The perpetrator could not afford to buy an identity, so he stole one.

Advertising also presents consumption as the mediator in another social relationship—that between ourselves and others. Goldman (1992, p. 32) observes that "Ads obscure the fact that social relations, traits, and experiences are made by humans, suggesting that they come to us ready-made as part of the goods we purchase." Products become means for fulfilling social needs; when we buy a product we are also buying love, friendship, or respect from others. We will be able to "kiss a little longer," for example, if we buy Big Red gum. In addition, we can show our feelings for others through goods (Dyer, 1982). For example, a man can proclaim his devotion to his fiancée by buying her an expensive diamond ring. Many ads promise to both create a social relationship, and make that relationship explicit to the rest of the world. One example of this type of advertising is a Coors Light ad which shows three young women painting a room. It suggests that buying the right beer will lead to closer friendships, and will also let your friends know how much you care.

The problem with ads that promote consumption as the way to social relationships is that consumers may ultimately come to believe that goods are the *only* means to this end. That is, social needs such as love, esteem, and friendship can be acquired or expressed only through purchasing a product, and not through other avenues such as concern for others and shared activities. The main point emphasized by advertising is that individuals' relationships have nothing to do with their personalities or characters; it is the product that makes it happen (Goldman, 1992). Therefore, individuals cannot build relationships; they must buy them. Again, this equates individuals' social worth with their purchasing power, and may focus attention on consumption to the detriment of actual relationship-builders such as communication.

Thus, the second major criticism of advertising states that advertising teaches us to define ourselves and our relationships with others through goods; that it, that advertising gives social meaning to goods. Critics of advertising feel that it causes us to buy products as means to social ends rather than as commodities that can perform utilitarian functions. In defense of advertising, however, researchers generally agree that every society establishes object meanings through which individuals can relate themselves to the world (Bell, 1976; Leiss et al., 1986). This means that all needs are socially constructed in all human societies (Schudson, 1984), even when that society has no advertising.

The most basic human needs are socially constructed. For example, our culture dictates arbitrary rules about what is and is not an acceptable satisfier for our need for food. We are taught what we can eat, where, when, and with whom, and all of these rules are based on objects. For example, in American culture, we do not eat horse meat, brains, or insects. We cannot eat in a church, but it is fine for us to eat in our cars. If we invite guests over to eat with us in the dining room using fine china, silverware, and candles, we don't serve hamburgers. However, if we eat in the back yard on the picnic table, hamburgers would be perfectly acceptable. Jhally (1987, p. 4) sums up this view by stating:

> The contention that goods should be important to people for what they are *used* for rather than their *symbolic* meaning is very difficult to uphold in light of the historical, anthropological and cross-cultural evidence. In all cultures at all times, it is the relation between use and symbol that provides the concrete context for the playing out of the universal person–object relation.

It is a basic human practice to assign social values and social meanings to objects. For example, every society gives status to certain objects, whether they are beads or sports cars. All of these social meanings are transmitted through the social guidance institutions of the time (Schudson, 1984). Previously, social meanings were taught through religion, education, and family. Currently, they are taught also through advertising. The problem is not that advertising transmits social information about products, but that critics take exception to the type of social information that is being transmitted.

Once again, we see that the underlying social meanings being promoted by advertising are those that are required by capitalism. Capitalism organizes and specializes these social meanings according to its needs (Goldman, 1992) and dictates them to consumers to meet the market economy's requirements for continually expanding commodities (Leiss, 1976). A capitalist system would prefer all needs, including consumers' identities and relationships, to be purchased through the market. Again, advertising is a tool that capitalism uses to reach this goal; it is not the underlying cause. In support of this view, advertising has been used successfully to promote the social meanings dictated by other institutions. One example is a long-running television campaign for the Church of Jesus Christ of Latter Day Saints. These spots promote family relationships based on religious values and non-consumption based activities. One commercial shows parents and children building a relationship by having a water-fight while washing their car. As with the first criticism, if advertising can present different social meanings based on its sponsor, it cannot be held solely responsible if the majority of those meanings promote consumption as a means of satisfying social goals.

Dissatisfaction

Advertising's purpose is to continually sell goods, which means that consumers have to continually buy them. To accomplish this,

advertising must create "successive waves of associations between persons, products, and images of well-being" for possible routes to happiness and success (Leiss et al., 1986, p. 239). For example, in the 1980s a "successful" woman, in general, was portrayed in ads as excelling in her career, helped by specific products like Charlie perfume or Secret deodorant. In the 1990s, a successful woman nurtures her family and the environment, and thus needs a whole new set of products. Just when consumers think they may have reached their consumption goals, advertising shows them new consumption goals. Thus, the third social criticism of advertising states that it causes general dissatisfaction with one's lot in life. Advertising tells us to search diligently and ceaselessly among products to satisfy our needs, implying that we should be somewhat dissatisfied with what we have or are doing now (Leiss, Kline and Jhally, 1986).

Consumers accept this command because the payoff is so appealing. We would all like to be the person and live the life that we see in advertisements. On some level, consumers know that ads idealize and falsify reality, but on another level, they know that such a reality is at least a possibility (Schudson, 1984). Moog (1990, p. 15) says about one of her patients: "Those brilliant commercials that were intended to make people like Amy thirsty for Pepsi were *actually* making people like Amy thirsty for a fantasy of a life." Our own lives pale in comparison to what ads show us we could have (Pollay, 1989), and so we become dissatisfied enough to buy the next product and the next.

The problem with crediting advertising for the creation of dissatisfaction is that dissatisfaction seems to be a basic human condition; comparing oneself to others has been occurring since the time of Cain and Abel. Dissatisfaction occurs because wants are psychological, not biological, and so are unlimited (Bell, 1976). To determine if their wants are being satisfied, consumers turn to their neighbors and define their needs relative to the standards of their society (Schudson, 1984). That is, we compare our consumption patterns to an average consumption norm to determine whether or not we are satisfied (Jhally, 1987). The problem with this method is that we take past increases in wealth and comfort for granted (Leiss, Kline and Jhally, 1986); as average national income increases over time, average levels of happiness and satisfaction stay the same (Jhally, 1987). Therefore, the manner in which we make comparisons dictates that many individuals will be somewhat dissatisfied.

Some critics may accept that advertising is not the fundamental cause of dissatisfaction, but may contend that advertising exacerbates it. However, increasing dissatisfaction appears to be directly related to a more basic aspect of capitalism; there are an increasing number of products available on the market to satisfy our needs. As the number of available products grows, each aspect of a consumer's needs is broken down into smaller and smaller components (Leiss, 1976). Think of the countless products, such as soap, moisturizer, and sunscreen, created just to meet the needs of one consumer's skin. It becomes hard to integrate all of these tiny subneeds into a coherent ensemble of needs, and it becomes increasingly difficult to determine if all of these complex subneeds are being met (Leiss, 1976). Consumers may become dissatisfied because they cannot monitor nor meet all of the various subneeds they have; at any time there will always be some subneeds that are not being satisfied. Thus it appears that the root of dissatisfaction is our basic method of comparison that only considers relative, and not absolute, satisfaction. The dissatisfaction that arises from this comparison is exacerbated by the availability of too many products in our capitalist economy that each address only one fragmented subneed.

Overall, it appears that the above three conditions of materialism are levelled at ad-

vertising because it is a visible target of attack, while ignoring the true cause of these social conditions—capitalism. In a capitalist system, there is an abundance of goods in the market and the manufacture and consumption of goods are the most visible and important activities in society. The prominence of consumption in a capitalistic society causes a focus on these activities. Because an expanding economy is the source of its legitimacy and power, a capitalist system also prefers that all needs, including social, be mediated through the market. It uses advertising as one tool to achieve a fixation on goods above all else. Advertising, however, can also be used by other social institutions to achieve competing social goals. It is therefore a tool for directing consumer attention, but does not make the ultimate decision about where attention should be focused. In addition, capitalism is responsible for a flood of products in the market which fragment our needs to the point where we can no longer integrate these subneeds into a coherent ensemble, and dissatisfaction results.

Critics may be quick to point out that this argument seems to be splitting hairs—does it really matter whether advertising causes negative social effects or if capitalism causes these effects through advertising? It does matter, because by discovering the actual cause of these social problems we can begin to explore viable solutions to address them.

THE NEXT STEP

One should not underestimate the elementary common sense of the general population just as one should not underestimate the degree to which individuals are dependent on social cues for guidance on how to consume things (Leiss, Kline, and Jhally, 1986, p. 242).

This paper has argued that capitalism is the underlying cause of several social problems that have been blamed on advertising.

However, it is not enough to make this observation. The criticisms discussed above stem from growing materialism in our society that must be addressed. The overarching problem with materialism is that "commodities themselves, and the income to purchase them, are only weakly related to the things that make people happy: autonomy, self-esteem, family, felicity, tension-free leisure, friendship" (Leiss et al., 1986, p. 252). Capitalism obscures this fact and focuses consumers' attention on goods as the solutions to *all* of their needs. There are no easy answers to the problem of growing materialism in society.

Many critics of advertising call for increased regulation or an outright ban on advertising. However advertising is just one tool that capitalism uses to reach its goals. Other tools include the mass media, popular culture, and other economic enterprises (Schudson, 1984). Policies that only impact advertising would not affect the root of the problem; if advertising is stripped of its power to accomplish capitalist objectives, other tools will be used. However, it is also unlikely that we can attack the root of the problem by removing capitalism. In the modern world, there appear to be no viable alternatives. In addition, such an idea is untenable because it can create far more social problems than it can hope to correct. For better or for worse, we live in a capitalist economic system, and have to work within it to solve its problems.

One way to address these social problems is to create awareness of the capitalistic framework inside which we live. As discussed in the introduction to this paper, consumers tend to take for granted the social assumptions embedded in advertisements that reflect capitalist values (Goldman, 1992). By making these assumptions explicit, consumers are able to see how their attitudes, values, and actions are affected by the capitalist agenda espoused by advertising and other institutions. One way to create awareness is through consumer education, especially for children through the school system. Classes in understanding advertising and media are currently offered in some schools; an expanded program could bring about widespread awareness of the social values transmitted through the media. These programs would emphasize that individuals are not passive absorbers of ads but actively participate in constructing their meanings (Dyer, 1982). Consumers have the ability to look at ads and other sources of information critically, and accept or reject not only the product claims, but also the social assumptions. Information, education, and critical reasoning are the keys to solving these social problems (Moog, 1990).

Another way to combat these social effects is to create a greater number of advertisements that are based on alternative value systems. Several ads that present the values of religious and governmental institutions have been mentioned in this paper, but these types of ads make up a very small percentage of all of the ads seen. More non-consumption based advertising is needed to present a balanced picture of the alternative ways consumers can satisfy their needs. A simple way to begin this remedy is for each advertising agency to increase the number of public service announcements that it creates and airs.

Both of these alternatives address the underlying cause of materialism, the requirements of capitalism, with viable and effective solutions that can work within the capitalist system. As researchers concentrate on the actual roots of the negative social effects described above, many other remedies will follow. As Moog (1990, p. 221) says, "more can be done to deal effectively with the reality of advertising rather than cursing its pervasiveness."

REFERENCES

Becker, G.S.: 1981, *A Treatise on the Family* (Harvard University Press, Cambridge, MS).

Bell, D.: 1976, *The Cultural Contradictions of Capitalism* (Basic Books Inc., New York, NY).

Berman, R.: 1981, *Advertising and Social Change* (Sage Publications, Inc., Beverly Hills, CA).

Cushman, P.: 1990, 'Why the Self is Empty: Toward a Historically Situated Psychology', *American Psychologist* 45(5), 599–611.

Dyer, G.: 1982, *Advertising as Communication* (Methuen, Inc., New York, NY).

Gold, P.: 1987, *Advertising, Politics, and American Culture: From Salesmanship to Therapy* (Paragon House Publishers, New York, NY).

Goldman, R.: 1992, *Reading Ads Socially* (Routledge, New York, NY).

Grimm, M.: 1990, 'New Games to Play, New Rules to Learn', *Adweek* 31(38), S172.

Harriss, J. (ed.): 1991, *The Family: A Social History of the Twentieth Century* (Oxford University Press, New York, NY).

Jhally, S.: 1987, *The Codes of Advertising: Fetishism and the Political Economy of Meaning in the Consumer Society* (St. Martin Press, Inc., New York, NY).

Jhally, S.: 1989, 'Advertising as Religion: The Dialectic of Technology and Magic', in I. Angus and S. Jhally (eds.), *Cultural Politics and Contemporary America* (Routledge, New York, NY), pp. 217–229.

Leiss, W.: 1976, *The Limits to Satisfaction: An Essay on the Problems of Needs and Commodities* (University of Toronto Press, Toronto, ON).

Leiss, W., S. Kline and S. Jhally: 1986, *Social Communication in Advertising: Persons, Products, & Images of Well-Being* (Methuen Publications, New York, NY).

Marchand, R.: 1985, *Advertising and the American Dream: Making Way for Modernity*, 1920–1940 (University of California Press, CA).

Moog, C.: 1990, 'Are They Selling Her Lips?', *Advertising and Identity* (William Morrow and Company, Inc., New York, NY).

Pollay, R.W.: 1989, 'The Distorted Mirror: Reflections on the Unintended Consequences of Advertising', in R. Hovland and G.B. Wilcox (eds.), *Advertising in Society: Classic and Contemporary Readings on Advertising's Role in Society* (NTC Business Books, Lincolnwood, IL), pp. 437–476.

Rotzoll, K., J.E. Haefner and C.H. Sandage: 1989, 'Advertising and the Classical Liberal World View', in R. Hovland and G. B. Wilcox (eds.), *Advertising in Society: Classic and Contemporary Readings on Advertising's Role in Society* (NTC Business Books, Lincolnwood, IL), pp. 37–41.

Schudson, M.: 1984, *Advertising, the Uneasy Persuasion: Its Dubious Impact on American Society* (Basic Books, Inc., New York, NY).

THE MAKING OF
SELF AND WORLD
IN ADVERTISING

John Waide

In this paper I will criticize a common practice I call associative advertising. The fault in associative advertising is not that it is deceptive or that it violates the autonomy of its audience—on this point I find Arrington's arguments persuasive.[1] Instead, I will argue against associative advertising by examining the virtues and vices at stake. In so doing, I will offer an alternative to Arrington's exclusive concern with autonomy and behavior control.

Associative advertising is a technique that involves all of the following:

1. The advertiser wants people[2] to buy (or buy more of) a product. This objective is largely independent of any sincere desire to improve or enrich the lives of the people in the target market.

2. In order to increase sales, the advertiser identifies some (usually) deep-seated non-market good for which the people in the target market feel a strong desire. By

"non-market good" I mean something which cannot, strictly speaking, be bought or sold in a marketplace. Typical non-market goods are friendship, acceptance and esteem of others. In a more extended sense we may regard excitement (usually sexual) and power as non-market goods since advertising in the U.S.A. usually uses versions of these that cannot be bought and sold. For example, "sex appeal" as the theme of an advertising campaign is not the market-good of prostitution, but the non-market good of sexual attractiveness and acceptability.

3. In most cases, the marketed product bears only the most tenuous (if any) relation to the non-market good with which it is associated in the advertising campaign. For example, soft drinks cannot give one friends, sex, or excitement.

4. Through advertising, the marketed product is associated with the non-market desire it cannot possibly satisfy. If possible,

From *Journal of Business Ethics* 6 (1987) 73–79. © 1987 by D. Reidel Publishing Company. Reprinted by permission.

the desire for the non-market good is intensified by calling into question one's acceptability. For example, mouthwash, toothpaste, deodorant, and feminine hygiene ads are concocted to make us worry that we stink.

5. Most of us have enough insight to see both (a) that no particular toothpaste can make us sexy and (b) that wanting to be considered sexy is at least part of our motive for buying that toothpaste. Since we can (though, admittedly, we often do not bother to) see clearly what the appeal of the ad is, we are usually not lacking in relevant information or deceived in any usual sense.

6. In some cases, the product actually gives at least partial satisfaction to the non-market desire—but only because of advertising.[3] For example, mouthwash has little prolonged effect on stinking breath, but it helps to reduce the intense anxieties reinforced by mouthwash commercials on television because we at least feel that we are doing the proper thing. In the most effective cases of associative advertising, people begin to talk like ad copy. We begin to sneer at those who own the wrong things. We all become enforcers for the advertisers. In general, if the advertising images are effective enough and reach enough people, even preposterous marketing claims can become at least partially self-fulfilling.

Most of us are easily able to recognize associative advertising as morally problematic when the consequences are clear, extreme, and our own desires and purchasing habits are not at stake. For example, the marketing methods Nestlé used in Africa involved associative advertising. Briefly, Nestlé identified a large market for its infant formula—without concern for the well-being of the prospective consumers. In order to induce poor women to buy formula rather than breastfeed, Nestlé selected non-market goods on which to base its campaign—love for one's child and a desire to be acceptable by being modern. These appeals were effective (much as they are in advertising for children's clothing, toys, and computers in the U.S.A.). Through billboards and radio advertising, Nestlé identified parental love with formula feeding and suggested that formula is the modern way to feed a baby. Reports indicate that in some cases mothers of dead babies placed cans of formula on their graves to show that the parents cared enough to do the very best they could for their children, even though we know the formula may have been a contributing cause of death.[4]

One might be tempted to believe that associative advertising is an objectionable technique only when used on the very poorest, most powerless and ignorant people and that it is the poverty, powerlessness, and ignorance which are at fault. An extreme example like the Nestlé case, one might protest, surely doesn't tell us much about more ordinary associative advertising in the industrialized western nations. The issues will become clearer if we look at the conceptions of virtue and vice at stake.

Dewey says "the thing actually at stake in any serious deliberation is not a difference of quantity [as utilitarianism would have us believe], but what kind of person one is to become, what sort of self is in the making, what kind of a world is making [sic]."[5] Similarly, I would like to ask who we become as we use or are used by associative advertising. This will not be a decisive argument. I have not found clear, compelling, objective principles—only considerations I find persuasive and which I expect many others to find similarly persuasive. I will briefly examine how associative advertising affects (a) the people who plan and execute marketing strategies and (b) the people who are exposed to the campaign.

(a) Many advertisers[6] come to think clearly and skillfully about how to sell a marketable item by associating it with a non-market good which people in the target market desire. An important ingredient in this process is lack of concern for the well-being of the people who will be influenced by the campaign. Lloyd Slater, a consultant who discussed the infant formula controversy with people in both the research and development and marketing divisions of Nestlé, says that the R&D people had made sure that the formula was nutritionally sound but were troubled or even disgusted by what the marketing department was doing. In contrast, Slater reports that the marketing people simply did not care and that "those guys aren't even human" in their reactions.[7] This evidence is only anecdotal and it concerns an admittedly extreme case. Still, I believe that the effects of associative advertising[8] would most likely be the same but less pronounced in more ordinary cases. Furthermore, it is quite common for advertisers in the U.S.A. to concentrate their attention on selling something that is harmful to many people, e.g., candy that rots our teeth, and cigarettes. In general, influencing people without concern for their well-being is likely to reduce one's sensitivity to the moral motive of concern for the well-being of others. Compassion, concern, and sympathy for others, it seems to me, are clearly central to moral virtue.[9] Associative advertising must surely undermine this sensitivity in much of the advertising industry. It is, therefore, *prima facie* morally objectionable.

(b) Targets of associative advertising (which include people in the advertising industry) are also made worse by exposure to effective advertising of this kind. The harm done is of two kinds:

(1) We often find that we are buying more but enjoying it less. It isn't only that products fail to live up to specific claims about service-life or effectiveness. More often, the motives ('reasons' would perhaps not be the right word here) for our purchases consistently lead to disappointment. We buy all the right stuff and yet have no more friends, lovers, excitement or respect than before. Instead, we have full closets and empty pocket books. Associative advertising, though not the sole cause, contributes to these results.

(2) Associative advertising may be less effective as an advertising technique to sell particular products than it is an ideology[10] in our culture. Within the advertising which washes over us daily we can see a number of common themes, but the most important may be "You are what you own."[11] The quibbles over which beer, soft drink, or auto to buy are less important than the overall message. Each product contributes its few minutes each day, but we are bombarded for hours with the message that friends, lovers, acceptance, excitement, and power are to be gained by purchases in the market, not by developing personal relationships, virtues, and skills. Our energy is channeled into careers so that we will have enough money to be someone by buying the right stuff in a market. The not very surprising result is that we neglect non-market methods of satisfying our non-market desires. Those non-market methods call for wisdom, compassion, skill, and a variety of virtues which cannot be bought. It seems, therefore, that insofar as associative advertising encourages us to neglect the non-market cultivation of our virtues and to substitute market goods instead, we become worse and, quite likely, less happy persons.

To sum up the argument so far, associative advertising tends to desensitize its practitioners to the compassion, concern, and sympathy for others that are central to moral virtue and it encourages its audience to neglect the cultivation of non-market virtues. There are at least five important objections that might be offered against my thesis that associative advertising is morally objectionable.

First, one could argue that since each of us is (or can easily be if we want to be) aware of what is going on in associative advertising, we must want to participate and find it unobjectionable. Accordingly, the argument goes, associative advertising is not a violation of individual autonomy. In order to reply to this objection I must separate issues.

(a) Autonomy is not the main, and certainly not the only, issue here. It may be that I can, through diligent self-examination neutralize much of the power of associative advertising. Since I can resist, one might argue that I am responsible for the results—*caveat emptor* with a new twist.[12] If one's methodology in ethics is concerned about people and not merely their autonomy, then the fact that most people are theoretically capable of resistance will be less important than the fact that most are presently unable to resist.

(b) What is more, the ideology of acquisitiveness which is cultivated by associative advertising probably undermines the intellectual and emotional virtues of reflectiveness and self-awareness which would better enable us to neutralize the harmful effects of associative advertising. I do not know of specific evidence to cite in support of this claim, but it seems to me to be confirmed in the ordinary experience of those who, despite associative advertising, manage to reflect on what they are exposed to.

(c) Finally, sneer group pressure often makes other people into enforcers so that there are penalties for not going along with the popular currents induced by advertising. We are often compelled even by our associates to be enthusiastic participants in the consumer culture. Arrington omits consideration of sneer group pressure as a form of compulsion which can be (though it is not always) induced by associative advertising.

So far my answer to the first objection is incomplete. I still owe some account of why more people do not complain about associative advertising. This will become clearer as I consider a second objection.

Second, one could insist that even if the non-market desires are not satisfied completely, they must be satisfied for the most part or we would stop falling for associative advertising. This objection seems to me to make three main errors:

(a) Although we have a kind of immediate access to our own motives and are generally able to see what motives an advertising campaign uses, most of us lack even the simple framework provided by my analysis of associative advertising. Even one who sees that a particular ad campaign is aimed at a particular non-market desire may not see how all the ads put together constitute a cultural bombardment with an ideology of acquisitiveness—you are what you own. Without some framework such as this, one has nothing to blame. It is not easy to gain self-reflective insight, much less cultural insight.

(b) Our attempts to gain insight are opposed by associative advertising which always has an answer for our dissatisfactions—buy more or newer or different things. If I find myself feeling let down after a purchase, many voices will tell me that the solution is to buy other things too (or that I have just bought the wrong thing). With all of this advertising proposing one kind of answer for our dissatisfactions, it is scarcely surprising that we do not usually become aware of alternatives.

(c) Finally, constant exposure to associative advertising changes[13] us so that we come to feel acceptable as persons when and only when we own the acceptable, fashionable things. By this point, our characters and conceptions of virtue already largely reflect the result of advertising and we are unlikely to complain or rebel.

Third, and perhaps most pungent of the objections, one might claim that by associating mundane marketable items with deeply rooted non-market desires, our everyday lives are invested with new and greater meaning. Charles Revlon of Revlon once said that "In the factory we make cosmetics; in the store we sell hope."[14] Theodore Levitt, in his passionate defense of associative advertising, contends that[15]

> Everyone in the world is trying in his [or her] special personal fashion to solve a primal problem in life—the problem of rising above his [or her] own negligibility, of escaping from nature's confining, hostile, and unpredictable reality, of finding significance, security, and comfort in the things he [or she] must do to survive.

Levitt adds: "Without distortion, embellishment, and elaboration, life would be drab, dull, anguished, and at its existential worst."[16] This objection is based on two assumptions so shocking that his conclusion almost seems sensible.

(a) Without associative advertising would our lives lack significance? Would we be miserable in our drab, dull, anguished lives? Of course not. People have always had ideals, fantasies, heroes, and dreams. We have always told stories that captured our aspirations and fears. The very suggestion that we require advertising to bring a magical aura to our shabby, humdrum lives is not only insulting but false.

(b) Associative advertising is crafted not in order to enrich our daily lives but in order to enrich the clients and does not have the interests of its audience at heart. Still, this issue of intent, though troubling, is only part of the problem. Neither is the main problem that associative advertising images somehow distort reality. Any work of art also is, in an important sense, a dissembling or distortion. The central question instead is whether the specific appeals and images, techniques and products, enhance people's lives.[17]

A theory of what enhances a life must be at least implicit in any discussion of the morality of associative advertising. Levitt appears to assume that in a satisfying life one has many satisfied desires—*which* desires is not important.[18] To propose and defend an alternative to his view is beyond the scope of this paper. My claim is more modest—that it is not enough to ask whether desires are satisfied. We should also ask what kinds of lives are sustained, made possible, or fostered by having the newly synthesized desires. What kind of self and world are in the making?, Dewey would have us ask. This self and world are always in the making. I am not arguing that there is some natural, good self which advertising changes and contaminates. It may be that not only advertising, but also art, religion, and education in general, always synthesize new desires.[19] In each case, we should look at the lives. How to judge the values of these lives and the various conceptions of virtue they will embody is another question. It will be enough for now to see that it is an important question.

Now it may be possible to see why I began by saying that I would suggest an alternative to the usual focus on autonomy and behavior control.[20] Arrington's defense of advertising (including, as near as I can tell, what I call associative advertising) seems to assume that we have no standard to which we can appeal to judge whether a desire enhances a life and, consequently, that our only legitimate concerns are whether an advertisement violates the autonomy of its audience by deceiving them or controlling their behavior. I want to suggest that there is another legitimate concern—whether the advertising will tend to influence us to become worse persons.[21]

Fourth, even one who is sympathetic with much of the above might object that associative advertising is necessary to an industrial society such as ours. Economists since Galbraith[22] have argued about whether, without modern advertising of the sort I have described, there would be enough demand to sustain our present levels of production. I have no answer to this question. It seems unlikely that associative advertising will end suddenly, so I am confident that we will have the time and the imagination to adapt our economy to do without it.

Fifth, and last, one might ask what I am proposing. Here I am afraid I must draw up short of my mark. I have no practical political proposal. It seems obvious to me that no broad legislative prohibition would improve matters. Still, it may be possible to make small improvements like some that we have already seen. In the international arena, Nestlé was censured and boycotted, the World Health Organization drafted infant formula marketing guidelines, and finally Nestlé agreed to change its practices. In the U.S.A., legislation prohibits cigarette advertising on television.[23] These are tiny steps, but an important journey may begin with them.

Even my personal solution is rather modest. First, if one accepts my thesis that associative advertising is harmful to its audience, then one ought to avoid doing it to others, especially if doing so would require that one dull one's compassion, concern, and sympathy for others. Such initiatives are not entirely without precedent. Soon after the surgeon general's report on cigarettes and cancer in 1964, David Ogilvy and William Bernbach announced that their agencies would no longer accept cigarette accounts and New Yorker magazine banned cigarette ads.[24] Second, if I am even partly right about the effect of associative advertising on our desires, then one ought to expose oneself as little as possible. The most practical and effective way to do this is probably to banish commercial television and radio from one's life. This measure, though rewarding,[25] is only moderately effective. Beyond these, I do not yet have any answers.

In conclusion, I have argued against the advertising practice I call associative advertising. My main criticism is two-fold: (a) Advertisers must surely desensitize themselves to the compassion, concern, and sympathy for others that are central emotions in a virtuous person, and (b) associative advertising influences its audience to neglect the non-market cultivation of our virtues and to substitute market goods instead, with the result that we become worse and, quite likely, less happy persons.

An earlier draft of this paper was presented to the Tennessee Philosophical Association, 10 November 1984. I am indebted to that group for many helpful comments.

ENDNOTES

1. Robert L. Arrington, "Advertising and Behavior Control," *Journal of Business Ethics* **1**, pp. 3–12.

2. I prefer not to use the term "consumers" since it identifies us with our role in a market, already conceding part of what I want to deny.

3. Arrington, p. 8.

4. James B. McGinnis, *Bread and Justice* (New York: Paulist Press, 1979), p. 224. McGinnis cites as his source *INFACT Newsletter*, September 1977, p. 3. Formula is often harmful because poor families do not have the sanitary facilities to prepare the formula using clean water and utensils, do not have the money to be able to keep up formula feeding without diluting the formula to the point of starving the child, and formula does not contain the antibodies which a nursing mother can pass to her child to help immunize the child against common local bacteria. Good accounts of this problem are widely available.

5. John Dewey, *Human Nature and Conduct* (New York: Random House, 1930), p. 202.

6. This can be a diverse group including (depending upon the product) marketing specialists, sales representatives, or people in advertising agencies. Not everyone in one of these positions, how-

ever, is necessarily guilty of engaging in associative advertising.

7. This story was told by Lloyd E. Slater at a National Science Foundation Chatauqua entitled "Meeting World Food Needs" in 1980–81. It should not be taken as a condemnation of marketing professionals in other firms.

8. One could argue that the deficiency in compassion, concern, and sympathy on the part of advertisers might be a result of self-selection rather than of associative advertising. Perhaps people in whom these moral sentiments are strong do not commonly go into positions using associative advertising. I doubt, however, that such self-selection can account for all the disregard of the audience's best interests.

9. See Lawrence A. Blum, *Friendship, Altruism and Morality* (Boston: Routledge and Kegan Paul, 1980) for a defense of moral emotions against Kantian claims that emotions are unsuitable as a basis for moral judgement and that only a purely rational good will offers an adequate foundation for morality.

10. I use "ideology" here in a descriptive rather than a pejorative sense. To be more specific, associative advertising commonly advocates only a part of a more comprehensive ideology. See Raymond Geuss, *The Idea of a Critical Theory* (Cambridge: Cambridge University Press, 1981), pp. 5–6.

11. For an interesting discussion, see John Lachs, "To Have and To Be," *Personalist* 45 (Winter, 1964), pp. 5–14; reprinted in John Lachs and Charles Scott, *The Human Search* (New York: Oxford University Press, 1981), pp. 247–255.

12. This is, in fact, the thrust of Arrington's arguments in "Advertising and Behavior Control."

13. I do not mean to suggest that only associative advertising can have such ill effects. Neither am I assuming the existence of some natural, pristine self which is perverted by advertising.

14. Quoted without source in Theodore Levitt, "The Morality (?) of Advertising," *Harvard Business Review*, July–August 1970; reprinted in Vincent Barry, *Moral Issues in Business* (Belmont, CA: Wadsworth Publishing Company, 1979), p. 256.

15. Levitt (in Barry), p. 252.

16. Levitt (in Barry), p. 256.

17. "Satisfying a desire would be valuable then if it sustained or made possible a valuable kind of life. To say this is to reject the argument that in creating the wants he [or she] can satisfy, the advertiser (or the manipulator of mass emotion in politics or religion) is necessarily acting in the best interests of his [or her] public." Stanley Benn, "Freedom and Persuasion," *Australasian Journal of Philosophy* 45 (1969); reprinted in Beauchamp and Bowie, *Ethical Theory and Business*, 2nd ed. (Englewood Cliffs, NJ: Prentice-Hall, 1983), p. 374.

18. Levitt's view is not new. "Continual success in obtaining those things which a man from time to time desires—that is to say, continual prospering—is what men call felicity." Hobbes, *Leviathan* (Indianapolis: Bobbs-Merrill, 1958), p. 61.

19. This, in fact, is the principal criticism von Hayek offered of Galbraith's argument against the "dependence effect." F.A. von Hayek, "The Non Sequitur of the 'Dependence Effect'," *Southern Economic Journal*, April 1961; reprinted in Tom L. Beauchamp and Norman E. Bowie, *Ethical Theory and Business*, 2nd ed. (Englewood Cliffs, NJ: Prentice-Hall, 1983), pp. 363–366.

20. Taylor R. Durham, "Information, Persuasion, and Control in Moral Appraisal of Advertising," *The Journal of Business Ethics* 3, p. 179. Durham also argues that an exclusive concern with issues of deception and control leads us into errors.

21. One might object that this requires a normative theory of human nature, but it seems to me that we can go fairly far by reflecting on our experience. If my approach is to be vindicated, however, I must eventually provide an account of how, in general, we are to make judgments about what is and is not good (or life-enhancing) for a human being. Clearly, there is a large theoretical gulf between me and Arrington, but I hope that my analysis of associative advertising shows that my approach is plausible enough to deserve further investigation.

22. The central text for this problem is *The Affluent Society* (London: Houghton Mifflin, 1958). The crucial passages are reprinted in many anthologies, e.g., John Kenneth Galbraith, "The Dependence Effect," in W.Q. Michael Hoffman and Jennifer Mills Moore, *Business Ethics: Readings and Cases in Corporate Morality* (New York: McGraw-Hill, 1984), pp. 328-333.

23. "In March 1970 Congress removed cigarette ads from TV and radio as of the following January. (The cigarette companies transferred their billings to print and outdoor advertising. Cigarette sales reached new records.)" Stephen Fox, *The Mirror Makers: A History of American Advertising and Its Creators* (New York: William Morrow and Co., 1984), p. 305.

24. Stephen Fox, pp. 303–304.

25. See, for example, Jerry Mander, *Four Arguments for the Elimination of Television* (New York: Morrow Quill Paperbacks, 1977).

A CONTENT ANALYSIS OF MEN AND WOMEN IN CANADIAN CONSUMER MAGAZINE ADVERTISING: Today's Portrayal, Yesterday's Image?

Nan Zhou

Mervin Y.T. Chen

INTRODUCTION

A stereotype can be defined as an often false over-generalization of characteristics of a group of people without regard to differences among members of that group (Mackie, 1973; Williams and Best, 1982, 1990). Stereotypes are often used in advertising to convey images with which potential buyers may identify so as to increase advertising effectiveness. Since the feminist movement in the 1960s, critics have charged that advertising stereotypes women in traditional roles, resulting in undesirable social consequences (Royal Commission on the Status of Women in Canada, 1970; Darmon and Laroche, 1991). This is because that advertising is also a means of social communication. From the perspective of social learning and socialization, people at a very young age begin learning gender pre-scriptions. These prescriptions are said to be resistant to change later on, because they have been with people for so long that people have formed gender role expectations based on them (Bromley, 1993; Fiske and Stevens, 1993; Williams and Best, 1990). If people often "observe" a particular group of people engaging in a particular behavior in mass media, they are likely to believe that the abilities and personality attributes required to carry out that activity are typical for that group of people (Golombok and Fivush, 1994; Stroebe and Insko, 1989). Thus, the repeated observations of women in traditional roles or "working" at jobs of low socioeconomic status in advertising could lead an audience to believe that these roles or jobs are typical of women. They could also affect women's self-images and self-concepts negatively and limit their behavior. They could particularly place working

Journal of Business Ethics 16: 485–495, 1997. © 1997 Kluwer Academic Publishers. Printed in the Netherlands.

women in a sensitive situation which results in a prejudice against them (Fiske and Stevens, 1993; Stroebe and Insko, 1989).

Research in several countries has, in general, confirmed the validity of critics' charges. In the United States, Courtney and Lockeretz's (1971) pioneering study found that magazine advertising showed four traditional stereotypes of women: a woman's place was in the home while a man's was working outside the home; women did not make important decisions and do important things; women were dependent on men and needed men's protection; and women were sex objects. Replications of this study and other studies conducted during the 1970s found that advertising did not convey the elevated roles of women in society adequately (Courtney and Whipple, 1983). For example, women were often found in home settings (Dominik and Rauch, 1972; Wagner and Banos, 1973); women were mainly shown as product users, not authorities (Dominik and Rauch, 1972; Courtney and Whipple, 1974; McArthur and Resko, 1975; O'Donnell and O'Donnell, 1978); women were often portrayed as subordinated and inferior to men (Goffman, 1979). Several studies compared advertisements from different time periods since the pre-women's movement era. Sexton and Haberman (1974), Venkatesan and Losco (1975), and Belkaoui and Belkaoui (1976) found that stereotypes had remained and that advertising was not keeping up with the times. Wolheter and Lammers (1980) examined advertisements in 1958, 1968, and 1978 and reported that male and female portrayal in family roles had changed very little; Weinberger et al. (1979), using a somewhat different sample of advertisements, found that between 1972 and 1978 there had been a significant gain in the portrayal of women in professional occupations. Later studies in the 1980s (Ruggiero and Weston, 1985; Sullivan and O'Connor, 1988) also revealed that advertising had become more likely to

project an image of women in positions of power and responsibility. A recent study (Ferguson et al., 1990), however, reported that advertisements in *Ms.* Magazine had increasingly portrayed women as sex objects during its first 15 years of publication since the early 1970s. Another study (Klassen et al., 1993), using a sample from 1972 to 1989, concluded that a disproportionately high number of advertisements portrayed women in traditional poses, although the traditional depictions were decreasing and the "quality portrayals" were increasing. In studies of images of older characters in advertising, older females were portrayed more negatively than older males (Harris and Feinberg, 1977; Ursic et al., 1986; Swayne and Greco, 1987). In a cross-cultural study, negative gender stereotypes were reported in U.S., Mexican, and Australian TV commercials (Gilly, 1988).

In the United Kingdom, Lysonski (1985, p. 49) found that between 1976 and 1983 "British [magazine] advertising's role portrayals [had] undergone some metamorphoses ... although these shifts were not dramatic." Mitchell and Taylor's (1990, p. 3) research concluded that "advertisers have become increasingly sensitive to the issue of stereotyping" and that female images in advertising were polarized: one towards a more traditional, home-related, dependent image; the other towards a non-traditional, career-oriented, authority image. In Italy and Australia, gender roles in TV commercials were reported to be similar to those in North America and the United Kingdom (Mazzella et al., 1992).

CANADIAN RESEARCH ON GENDER PORTRAYAL IN ADVERTISING

A Canadian study of TV commercials in the early 1970s (Toronto Women's Media Committee, 1973) found that more men were present as voice-overs, and that females dominated in domestic occupations and products while males dominated in non-domestic occupations. The Canadian Radio-Television and Telecommunications Commission (CRTC), a federal government regulatory body, commissioned two major studies on the portrayal of gender roles in TV and radio commercials in 1984 and 1988. In TV commercials for both years, few males and fewer females were in the 36–65 age range and even fewer people were beyond age 65; in English TV commercials there was a significantly greater proportion of male characters and voice-overs, and a significantly greater proportion of females in preparing and consuming food or beverages and in a consumer role, and there were no significant differences in these categories in 1984 and 1988. Over that time period, however, the proportions of males and females depicted in family settings and in professional/managerial occupations changed from being significantly different in 1984 to becoming closer to the point that on the basis of 1988 data alone, there were no statistically significant gender differences. Similar findings were reported in French TV and English and French radio commercials (ERIN Research, 1990).

There are only a few Canadian studies on gender portrayal in print media available. One cross-national study using a 1975 sample of magazine advertisements from Canada, the U.S., the U.K., and France found that women were not caricatured as useless, decorative sex objects any more than men (Pasold, 1976). Kinda (1982) analyzed advertisements carried in U.S. and Canadian magazines published in the week of January 21, 1981 and concluded that "although the portrayal of women in traditional roles has declined, their projected image continues to be narrow and limited" (Kindra, 1982, p. 109).

The Canadian public has reacted strongly to women's negative images in advertising. When advertisements for feminine-hygiene

products first appeared during 1978–79, over a period of two months, over 1200 petitions and letters were sent to the Advertising Standards Council (ASC) and to the CRTC to complain about the existence, styles, and tone of those advertisements which "demeaned women" (Courtney and Whipple, 1974). In CRTC's (1978) survey during the same time period, 59% of the 3000-plus respondents believed TV commercials to be insulting to women, and 40% thought they were insulting to men. A recent survey of 175 female adults over the age of 18 years found that the respondents did not believe that women were accurately portrayed in advertising in Canada, although 55% of them believed that the portrayal would change for the better in the future (DeYoung and Crane, 1992). Another survey of 179 university students reported that the attitudes of both male and female respondents toward the portrayal of women in advertising were moderately critical, with females being more critical than males (Zhou and Burris, 1992).

Mainly as a result of public reaction, a CRTC Task Force on Sex-Role Stereotyping in the Broadcast Media was set up in 1979. The Task Force proposed a two-year period of CRTC-monitored self-regulation for broadcast and advertising industries (CRTC, 1982). The CRTC also published two studies, mentioned previously, as an assessment of the effectiveness of self-regulation (ERIN Research, 1990). While acknowledging that "considerable work [had] been done to sensitize and educate the industry and the public to the issue," the CRTC concluded that "self-regulation [had] been only partially successful." It also published a "Policy on Sex-Role Stereotyping in the Broadcast Media" in 1986 (CRTC, 1990a).

The Canadian advertising industry's self-regulatory body, the Advertising Advisory Board (AAB), conducted its own study in the mid-1970s and acknowledged that there was a problem (AAB, 1997). As a result, it instituted an Advisory Commission on Sex-

Role Stereotyping in 1982. Later, it indicated that "the advertising industry has failed to implement a guideline that dictates the use of more women in television and radio commercials" (AAB, 1983). Representing the advertising industry's recent major self-regulatory effort, the Canadian Advertising Foundation published guidelines about gender-role stereotyping in 1987. The guidelines have been endorsed by the major advertising associations in the country (Darmon and Laroche, 1991).

THE STUDY

Courtney and Whipple (1983, p. 172) suggested that "Canada has taken one of the world's strongest stances concerning the improvement of the sexes in advertising." Wyckham (1987, p. 89) also suggested that

> [t]he Canadian self-regulation of sex role stereotypes in advertising should be considered a qualified success. Progress has been made. The [advertising] industry has recognized the existence of a problem and has taken steps to adjust its behavior.

If so, how is the progress reflected in the current gender portrayal in Canadian advertising? Our knowledge about the subject is mostly derived from broadcast media and little from print media. Almost a decade had passed since Kindra's (1982) study. As part of a larger project on images of people in Canadian advertising and an update of Kindra's study, this paper attempts to examine the portrayal of males and females in Canadian magazine advertisements in 1990. The three research questions addressed were: (1) How frequently did advertisements present adult (18 years an older) male and female characters? (2) For each gender, how were the characters portrayed? (3) Did the portrayal of male and female characters differ? If the stance Canada has taken has improved the situation, we should expect that the proportions of male and female characters

in magazine advertisements would represent their respective proportions in the population, that non-stereotypical portrayals for both genders would be used to a great extent, and that there would be no significant difference between the portrayal of the genders.

METHODOLOGY

Sample

The ten largest circulating consumer magazines in Canada in 1990, as listed in the *Canadian Media Directors' Council Media Digest 1990/91* (Maclean-Hunter, 1990), were intended to be used for the study. All geographic editions of all December 1990 issues of these magazines were ordered from the publishers. Then, all national advertisements (i.e., identical advertisements in all editions of each issue) were identified. Next, all national advertisements containing a picture of at least one human character were retained. All regional advertisements were excluded because they could distort the results of a national study (Zhou et al., 1990).

Several magazines published more than one issue and some also published multiple regional editions for one issue during the month. The resultant sample included 198 editions from 8 magazines (see Table I). Of the magazines used in the study, *Maclean's* is mainly a "men's" magazine, *Canadian Living, Chatelaine* and *Homemaker's* are considered mainly "women's" magazines, and others are general interest or entertainment magazines. There were no national advertisements in the other two, *Leisure Ways/West World* and *Starweek*. In selecting characters to be analyzed, clearly analyzable complete human figures and close-up shots were counted. Blurry shots, shadow figures, and very small characters in crowded scenes were not included. Of the 255 analyzable human characters, 188 were judged to be 18 or older and used in the study (see Table I).

TABLE I	National advertisements sample								
Magazine	**A** Total number of geographic editions used in the study	**B** Ads with analyzable characters		**C** Ads with analyzable older characters		**D** All analyzable characters in the ads		**E** All analyzable older characters	
		n	(%)	n	(% of B)	n	(%)	n	(% of D)
Canadian Living	6	34	(26.6)	1	(2.9)	61	(23.9)	1	(1.6)
Chatelaine	11	28	(21.9)	1	(3.6)	56	(22.0)	3	(5.4)
Homemaker's	5	10	(7.8)	0	(0.0)	19	(7.4)	0	(0.0)
Maclean's	60	29	(22.7)	5	(17.2)	64	(25.1)	8	(12.5)
Prime Time	3	1	(0.8)	0	(0.0)	4	(1.6)	0	(0.0)
Reader's Digest	6	6	(4.7)	1	(16.7)	15	(5.9)	1	(6.7)
TV Guide	75	18	(14.0)	0	(0.0)	34	(13.3)	0	(0.0)
TV Times[1]	32	2	(1.5)	0	(0.0)	2	(0.8)	0	(0.0)
Total	198	128	(100.0)	8	(6.3)	255	(100.0)	13	(5.1)

[1]Some issues were unavailable.

Categories of Analysis

Categories for analysis were formulated after an extensive review of relevant literature and pilot studies (see Table II). For each category, a character was classified into the proper sub-category through an examination of the whole content of the advertisement, both written and pictorial. The more criteria that could be applied to a character, the greater the possibility that the character could be classified into a sub-category. If unable to be classified, the character would be put into the "indeterminate" sub-category.

Coding

Two trained coders, a male and female, content analyzed the data. For initial analysis, both coders were given 25 randomly selected, identical characters. Their judgements were compared and disagreements were resolved through discussions between themselves and consultations with the researchers. Depending on the items coded, inter-coder agreements ranged from 90 to 100 percent, which was acceptable in this type of study (Kassarjian, 1977). They subsequently analyzed the remaining characters during a period of two weeks. Several reasons attributed to the high inter-coder agreements: (1) extensive training and the pilot study; (2) coordinated coding process by an experienced coder with coding experience from a previously published advertising content analysis product; and (3) close supervision by the researchers. One month after the completion of the analysis, 5% of the characters were re-analyzed and the test-retest agreements were 98%.

RESULTS

Distribution of Characters by Gender

Forty-two percent of the characters were males and 58% were females (see Table III). When compared with their relative proportions in the Canadian population in 1990, males were underrepresented and females were overrepresented in the advertisements as a whole.

In terms of age, when compared with their relative proportions in the Canadian population, the younger age group (18–49) characters were overrepresented (93.1% of the characters, vs. 49.7% of the population), and the older age group (50 and over) characters were underrepresented (6.9% of the characters, vs. 25.3% in the population) see Table III). In the younger age group characters, when compared to their relative proportions in the population, females were overrepresented (61.1% of the characters, vs. 49.9% of the population) and males were underrepresented (38.9% of the characters,

vs. 50.1% of the population) (see Table III). In the older age group characters, when compared to their relative proportions in the population, in contrast, females were underrepresented (15.4% of the characters, vs. 54.2% of the population) and males were overrepresented (84.6% of the characters, vs. 45.8% of the population) (see Table III). It should be noted that there was no character of either gender identified to be 65 years of age or older at all in the advertisements.

In terms of race, although 4.3% of the characters were non-white, none of them was female. Further, while in the white male group 93.3% were in the 18–49 age group and 6.7% were in the 50 and over group, all

TABLE II	Categories of analysis
Category	**Subcategories and criteria**
Gender	Male and female.
Age	Age groups: 18–49, 50–64, 65 and older.
	Criteria: mentioned; not mentioned but known (such as a life celebrity); "look" age: face, hair, hand, wrinkles; clothes; posture.
Race	White and non-white (Aboriginal, black, and Asian)
	Criteria: mentioned; features of face; color of skin.
Occupation	Domestic and non-domestic occupations. Domestic occupations include cooking, house cleaning, taking care of children at home, etc. Non-domestic occupations include high level (top level manager, professional, entertainer, etc.), middle level (middle level white collar occupation, etc.), and low level (service, clerical, construction worker, student, etc.).
	Criteria: mentioned; task performed; tool used; surrounding; background; relation with others in the illustration.
Role importance to ad's theme/layout	Important, equally important, less important and unimportant.
	Criteria: mentioned; strategic physical position in illustration (front vs. back, centre vs. side); shot size relative to others in illustration; focal point of attention or not; product expert vs. non-expert, giving advice/help vs. receiving advice/help.
Location (setting)	Residential, business, neither (such as outdoor), and no background.
	Criteria: surroundings and background of the character.
Product association	Domestic products and non-domestic products. Domestic products include food, household products, home remedies, personal care products, clothing, jewelry, home furnishings, etc. Non-domestic products include car and related products, financial services, etc. Twenty-nine product/service categories in all.
Sex appeal	Sex is related to the product (e.g., character used as sexual stimulus in a perfume ad) vs. sex is unrelated to the product (decorative-character used as attention getting, but otherwise irrelevant, object).

TABLE III	Ad characters and Canadian population by gender and age								
Gender	Number in ads			Percentage in ads			Percentage in population in 1990		
	Male	Female	Total	Male	Female	Total	Male	Female	Total
Total	79	109	188	42.0	58.0	100.0	49.4[a]	50.6[a]	75.0
Age group									
18–49	68	107	175	38.9	61.1	93.1	50.1[a]	49.9[a]	49.7[a]
50 and +	11	2	13	84.6	15.4	6.9	45.8[a]	54.2[a]	25.3[a]
Race									
White	71	109	178	39.4	60.6	100.0	—[b]	—[b]	—[b]
Non-white	8	0	8	100.0	0.0	0.0	—[b]	—[b]	—[b]

[a]Calculated from Statistics Canada (1990b).
[b]Unavailable.

of the non-white males belonged to the 18–49 age group. Although no direct demographic statistics on racial composition for 1990 was available to compare with our sample, aboriginal, Asian, and black accounted for 6.25% of the Canadian population in 1986 (Statistics Canada, 1990a).

Portrayal of Males

Table IV shows that there were no male characters shown in domestic occupations; for those shown in non-domestic occupations, a significantly larger proportion was depicted in high/middle level occupations than in low level ones based on the chi-square test ($p < 0.05$). While no one was shown as a sex-related-to-the-product model, 8.9% were shown as sex-unrelated-to-the-product (decorative) models. A significantly greater proportion of men were cast in important/equally important roles to an advertisement's theme than in less important/unimportant ones ($p < 0.001$). But, there was no significant difference between the proportions shown in home and business settings.

Portrayal of Females

Table IV also indicates that there were no female characters shown in domestic occu-

pations and for those shown in non-domestic occupations, the proportion depicted in high/middle level occupations was about the same as in low level ones. Unlike men, women were shown as both sex-related-to-the-product (5.5%) and sex-unrelated-to-the-product (3.7%). Like males, a significantly larger proportion of females were cast in important/equally important roles to the advertisement's theme than in less important/unimportant ones ($p < 0.001$). There was also a significant difference between the proportions of females shown in home and business settings with the larger proportion in home ($p < 0.001$).

Differences Between Portrayal of Males and Females

Table IV shows that there were no significant differences between the proportions of male and female characters in terms of low level non-domestic occupations, role importance to the advertisement's theme, home setting, and as decorative models. However, significantly larger proportions of men than women were cast in high/middle level occupations ($p < 0.01$) and business settings ($p < 0.01$) and only women were used as sex-related-to-the-product models.

TABLE IV	Portrayal of the characters	
Category	Males %	Females %
Occupation[a]		
Domestic occupations	0	0
Non-domestic occupations		
High/middle level	15.2*	3.7 ***
Low level	5.1*	2.8
Importance[a]		
Most important/equally important	67.1**	67.9**
Less important/unimportant	8.9**	8.3**
Place (setting)[a]		
Home	22.8	29.4**
Business	17.7	5.5** ***
Sex appeal[a]		
Sex related to the product	0	5.5
Sex unrelated to the product	8.9	3.7

[a] The total is not equal to 100% because some characters are coded in the "indeterminate" sub-category.

* It indicates a same gender difference at the 0.05 level using chi-square test.

** It indicates a same gender difference at the 0.001 level using chi-square test.

*** It indicates a between gender difference at the 0.01 level using chi-square test.

tion of both genders depicted in important or unimportant roles to the advertisement's theme and in sex appeal themes, men were used as decorative models only and women were used as both types of sex appeal models. Also, a significantly larger proportion of men than women was shown in high/middle level occupations and in business settings. Women were also more likely to be associated with domestic products. Moreover, men were underrepresented in the 18–49 age group (while this age group as a whole was overrepresented with respect to its proportion in the population), in the white category, and in the advertisements as a whole relative to their proportion in the population. In contrast, women were not represented in the non-white category, underrepresented in 50 and older age group (while this age group as a whole was already much underrepresented with respect to its proportion in the population), but were overrepresented in the advertisements as a whole.

Men were associated with 15 (including "others") and women were associated with 17 (including "others") product categories. Table V lists all product categories with which each gender was associated with 2% or more characters. It shows that a significantly smaller proportion of males than females was associated with domestic products ($p < 0.05$). There was no significant difference between the two genders in terms of their association with non-domestic products.

CONCLUSION

Summary

While no males or females were shown in domestic occupations, and no significant difference was found in the propor-

TABLE V	Characters' association of products	
Product category	Males %	Females %
Domestic products		
Personal care products/ services	2.5	22.9
Jewelry	0.0	11.0
Clothing	13.9	15.6
Food	6.3	3.7
Home furnishings	3.8	2.8
Liquor	21.5	13.8
Sub-total	48.0	69.8*
Non-domestic products		
Car and related products/ services	8.9	3.7
Financial services	2.5	4.6
Sub-total	11.4	8.3
Others	40.6	21.9
Total	100.0	100.0

*It indicates a difference at the 0.05 level using Chi-Square Test.

Discussion

These results suggest that in 1990 Canadian consumer magazine advertising portrayed women more positively than a decade before. In several areas, however, advertising still portrayed men more favourably than women.

The Canadian government takes the position of giving "fair and equitable portrayal of women and men" in advertising (CRTC, 1990b). Its main concern is the negative social impact of traditional gender stereotyping, which reflects male-dominated attitudes and roles in the society. Sociologists are also concerned. Their studies in the 1980s found continued use of stereotyped messages about genders in advertising in Canada (Singer, 1986). Men were still portrayed as voices of authority but also became more narcissistic (Wernick, 1987). Males as well as females were objectified and sexually exploited (Posner, 1987). Sociologists in general have been critical of gender images in advertising.

Advertisers and writers in the field of marketing communication, in contrast, are struggling with whether advertising "should promote new ideas and/or fight undesirable social stereotypes or should communicate effectively with markets," as suggested by Darmon and Laroche (1991, p. 485). Whipple and Courtney (1985), based on their extensive research, point out that the communication effectiveness of gender role portrayal in advertising is a function of the following: First, model-gender/product congruence. For them, "consumers' previously made judgments of the products' gender image are important determinants of model gender choice." Second, appropriate role setting to match specific product usage situation, e.g., a female model for female cosmetics. And third, liberatedness and realism. Here they emphasize the importance of "realistic and natural, rather than false and stereotyped" role depiction.

Research, mainly conducted in the U.S. in the 1970s, has shown that no one mode of portrayal, traditional or nontraditional or liberated, is preferred by men and women. Both Wortzel and Frisbie's (1974) and Duker and Tucker's (1977) studies indicated that both female college students who expressed pro-feminist attitudes, and those who did not, held similar positions toward women's roles in advertising. Lundstrom and Sciglimpaglia (1977, p. 78) suggested that "[m]ore specific and detailed targeting ... will allow selective marketing strategies ... instead of one which is stereotypically traditional." Recently, Leigh et al. (1987), Mitchell and Taylor (1990), and Jaffe (1991) also reported evidence to support the marketing segmentation view. Nonetheless, according to Whipple and Courtney (1985, p. 8), "[w]ithin any chosen role setting, modern, liberated depictions are generally more effective than traditional ones (e.g., a woman in the paid labour force is an effective depiction for both working and non-working women)."

Today, over half of the Canadian women aged 15 or over have paid employment outside the home. Many of them already occupy important positions comparable to those held by men. Advertising should reflect these changes and improvement of women's socioeconomic status and power. Our study has found that advertising does portray these changes and improvement to a certain extent, although the results of the study cannot be generalized due to the limited scope of the sample used. Advertisers should continue to remind themselves that advertising is a marketing communication medium which has significant sociocultural consequences. They should remember that they have a social responsibility as corporate citizens in ensuring that advertising continues to reflect these changes and improvement. At the same time, we should realize that efforts of the advertising industry, the public and the government are all needed to ensure that the trend will continue.

REFERENCES

Advertising Advisory Board: 1977, *Women and Advertising, Today's Message—Yesterday's Images?* (CAAB, Toronto) (November).

Advertising Advisory Board: 1983, Press Release (March 21), cited in Ronald H. Rotenberg: 1986, *Advertising: A Canadian Perspective* (Allyn and Bacon, Toronto), p. 197.

Belkaoui, A. and J.M. Belkaoui: 1976, 'A Comparative Analysis of the Role Portrayal by Women in Print Advertisements: 1958, 1970, 1972', *Journal of Marketing Research* XIII (May), 168–172.

Bromley, D.B.: 1993, *Reputation, Image and Impression Management* (Wiley, Chichester).

Canadian Radio-television and Telecommunications Commission: 1978, *Attitudes of Canadians Toward Advertising on Television* (Supply and Services Canada, Hull, Quebec).

Canadian Radio-television and Telecommunications Commission: 1982, *Images of Women*, Cat. # BC92-26/1982E (Minister of Supply and Services, Ottawa).

Canadian Radio-television and Telecommunications Commission: 1990a, News Release (CRTC Calls for Comments on Sex-Role Portrayal in Broadcast Media) (December 28).

Canadian Radio-television and Telecommunications Commission: 1990b, Public Notice, CRTC 1990-114 (December 28).

Courtney, A.E. and S.W. Lockeretz: 1971, 'A Woman's Place: An Analysis of the Roles Portrayed by Women in Magazine Advertisements', *Journal of Marketing Research* VIII (February), 92–95.

Courtney, A.E. and T.W. Whipple: 1974, 'Women in TV Commercials', *Journal of Communication* (Spring), 110–118.

Courtney, A.E. and T.W. Whipple: 1983, *Sex Stereotyping in Advertising* (Lexington Books, Lexington, MA).

Darmon, R. Y. and M. Laroche: 1991, *Advertising in Canada: A Managerial Approach* (McGraw-Hill Ryerson, Toronto).

DeYoung, S. and F.G. Crane: 1992, 'Females' Attitudes Toward the Portrayal of Women in Advertising: A Canadian Study', *International Journal of Advertising* 11, 249–255.

Dominik, J.R. and G.E. Rauch: 1972, 'The Image of Women in Network TV Commercials', *Journal of Broadcasting* 16(3), 259–265.

Duker, J. M. and L. R. Tucker: 1977, 'Women's Libbers' Versus Independent Women: A Study of Preferences for Women's Roles in Advertisements', *Journal of Marketing Research* XIV (November), 469–475.

ERIN Research: 1990, *The Portrayal of Gender in Canadian Broadcasting*—Summary Report 1984–1988, Cat. BC92-46, (Minister of Supply and Services, Ottawa).

Ferguson, J.H., P.J. Kreshel and S.F. Tinkham: 1990, 'In the Pages of *Ms.*: Sex Role Portrayals of Women in Advertising', *Journal of Advertising* 19(1), 40–51.

Fiske, S. and L.E. Stevens: 1993, 'What's So Special about Sex? Gender Stereotyping and Discrimination', in S. Oskamp and M. Costanzo (eds.), *Gender Issues in Contemporary Society* (Sage, Newbury Park), pp. 173–196.

Gilly, M.C.: 1988, 'Sex Roles in Advertising: A Comparison of Television Advertisements in Australia, Mexico, and the United States', *Journal of Marketing* 52 (April), 75–85.

Goffman, E.: 1979, *Gender Advertising* (Harper and Row, New York).

Golombok, S. and R. Fivush: 1994, *Gender Development* (Cambridge University Press, Cambridge).

Harris, A.J. and J.F. Feinberg: 1977, 'Television and Aging: Is What You See What You Get?', *The Gerontologist* 17(5), 464–468.

Jaffe, L.J.: 1991, 'Impact of Positioning and Sex-Role Identity on Women's Responses to Advertising', *Journal of Advertising Research* 31 (June/July), 57–64.

Kassarjian, H.H.: 1977, 'Content Analysis in Consumer Research', *Journal of Consumer Research* 4 (June), 8–18.

Kindra, G.S.: 1982, 'Comparative Study of the Roles Portrayed by Women in Print Advertising', in Michel LaRoche (ed.), Marketing 1982, Proceedings, Annual Conference of the Administrative Sciences Association of Canada (Concordia University, Montreal), pp. 109–116.

Klassen, M.L., C.R. Jasper and A.M. Schwartz: 1993, 'Men and Women: Images of Their Relationships in Magazine Advertisements', *Journal of Advertising Research* 33 (March/April), 30–39.

Leigh, T.W., A.J. Rethans and T.R. Whitney: 1987, 'Role Portrayals of Women in Advertising: Cognitive Responses and Advertising Effectiveness', *Journal of Advertising Research* 27 (October/November), 54–63.

Lundstrom, W.J. and D. Sciglimpaglia: 1977, 'Sex Role Portrayals in Advertising', *Journal of Marketing* (July), 72–79.

Lysonski, S.: 1985, 'Role Portrayals in British Magazine Advertisements', *European Journal of Marketing* 19(7), 37–55.

Mackie, M.: 1973, 'Arriving at "Truth" by Definition: The Case of Stereotype Inaccuracy', *Social Problems* 20, 431–447.

Maclean-Hunter: 1990, *Canadian Media Directors' Council Media Digest* 1990/91 (Maclean-Hunter, Toronto).

Mazzella, C., K. Durkin, E. Cerini and P. Buralli: 1992, 'Sex Role Stereotyping in Australian Television Advertisements', *Sex Roles* 26(7/8), 243–259.

McArthur, L.Z. and B.G. Resko: 1975, 'The Portrayal of Men and Women in American Television Commercials', *The Journal of Social Psychology* 97, 209–220.

Mitchell, P.C.N. and W. Taylor: 1990, 'Polarising Trends in Female Role Portrayals in U.K. Advertising', *European Journal of Marketing* 24(5), 41–49.

O'Donnell, W.J. and K.J. O'Donnell: 1978, 'Update: Sex-Role Messages in TV Commercials', *Journal of Communication* (Winter), 156–158.

Pasold, P.W.: 1976, 'Role Stereotyping in Magazine Advertising of Different Countries', in Proceedings, Canadian Association of Administrative Sciences, Marketing Division (Université Laval, Quebec), pp. 41–60.

Posner, J.: 1987, 'The Objectified Male: The New Male Image in Advertising', in G. J. Nemiroff, ed., *Women and Men: Interdisciplinary Readings on Gender* (Fitzhenry and Whiteside, Toronto).

Royal Commission on the Status of Women in Canada: 1970, Report (Information Canada, Ottawa).

Ruggiero, J.A. and L.C. Weston: 1985, 'Working Options for Women in Women's Magazine: The Medium and the Message', *Sex Roles* 12(5/6), 535–547.

Sexton, D.E. and P. Haberman: 1974, 'Women in Magazine Advertisement', *Journal of Advertising Research* 14 (August), 41–46.

Singer, B.D.: 1986, *Advertising and Society* (Addison–Wesley, Don Mills, Ont.).

Statistics Canada: 1990a, *Market Research Handbook* 1991 (Minister of Supply and Services Canada, Ottawa).

Statistics Canada: 1990b, *Postcensal Annual Estimates of Population by Marital Status, Age, Sex and Components of Growth for Canada, Provinces and Territories, 1990* (Minister of Supply and Services, Ottawa).

Stroebe, W. and C.A. Insko: 1989, 'Stereotype, Prejudice, and Discrimination: Changing Conceptions in Theory and Research', in D. Bar-Tal, C. F. Graumann, A. W. Kruglanski and W. Stroebe (eds.), *Stereotyping and Prejudice: Changing Conceptions* (Springer–Verlag, New York), pp. 3–34.

Sullivan, G.L. and P.J. O'Connor: 1988, 'Women's Role Portrayals in Magazine Advertising: 1958–1983', *Sex Roles* 18(3/4), 181–188.

Swayne, L.E. and A.J. Greco: 1987, 'The Portrayal of Older Americans in Television Commercials', *Journal of Advertising* 16(1), 47–54.

Toronto Women's Media Committee: 1973, Study of the Image of Women in Toronto Area Television Commercials, cited in A. E. Courtney and T. W. Whipple: 1974, 'Women in TV Commercials', *Journal of Communication* (Spring), 110–118.

Ursic, A.C., M.L. Ursic and V.L. Ursic: 1986, 'A Longitudinal Study of the Use of the Elderly in Magazine Advertising', *Journal of Consumer Research* 13 (June), 131–133.

Venkatesan, M. and J. Losco: 1975, 'Women and Magazine Advertisements', *Journal of Advertising Research* 15(5), 49–54.

Wagner, L.C. and J.B. Banos: 1973, 'A Woman's Place: A Follow-Up Analysis of the Roles Portrayed by Women in Magazine Advertisements', *Journal of Marketing Research* X (May), 213–214.

Wernick, A.: 1987, 'From Voyeur to Narcissist: Imaging Men in Contemporary Advertising', in M. Kaufman (ed.), *Beyond Patriarchy* (Oxford University Press, Toronto).

Weinberg, M.G., S.M. Petroshius and S.A. Westin: 1979, 'Twenty Years of Women in Magazine Advertising: An Update', in Neil Beckwith et al. (eds.), Proceedings, American Marketing Association Annual Educators' Conference, pp. 373–377.

Whipple, T.W. and A.E. Courtney: 1985, 'Female Role Portrayals in Advertising and Communication Effectiveness: A Review', *Journal of Advertising* 14(3), 4–8.

Williams, J.E. and D.L. Best: 1982, *Measuring Sex Stereotypes: A Thirty-Nation Study* (Sage, Beverly Hills).

Williams, J.E. and D.L. Best: 1990, *Sex and Psyche: Gender and Self Viewed Cross-Culturally* (Sage, Newbury Park).

Wolheter, M. and H.B. Lammers: 1980, 'An Analysis of Male Roles in Print Advertisements Over a 20-Year Span: 1958–1978', *Advances in Consumer Research* VII, 760–761.

Wortzel, L.H. and J.M. Frisbie: 1974, 'Women's Role Portrayal Preferences in Advertisements: An Empirical Study', *Journal of Marketing* 38(4), 41–46.

Wyckham, R.G.: 1987, 'Self-Regulation of Sex Role Stereotyping in Advertising: The Canadian Experience', *Journal of Public Policy and Marketing* 6, 76–92.

Zhou, N. and M.B. Burris: 1992, 'University Student Attitude Toward the Portrayal of Women in Advertising', Proceedings of the 22nd Annual Atlantic Schools of Business Conference, p. 112.

Zhou, N., R. Sparkman and S. Follows: 1990, 'Geographic Culture, Regional Advertising, and the Myth of the Nine Nations of North America: A Content Analysis of Canadian and U.S. Magazine Advertisements', in N. E. Synodinos, C. F. Keown, T.H. Becker, T.G. Grunert, T.E. Muller and J.H. Yu (eds.), The Proceedings of the Third Symposium on Cross-cultural Consumer and Business Studies (University of Hawaii, Honolulu), pp. 1 6.

CASE 11   R.J. MacDonald Inc. v. Canada (Attorney General)

The *Tobacco Products Control Act* (the "Act") broadly prohibited (with specific exceptions) all advertising and promotion of tobacco products and the sale of a tobacco product unless its package includes prescribed unattributed health warnings and a list of toxic constituents. The legislative scheme targeted three distinct categories of commercial activity: adver-tising, promotion and labelling. The Act, except for a prohibition on the distribution of free samples of tobacco products, did not proscribe the sale, distribution or use of tobacco products …

Held (La Forest, L'Heureux-Dube, Gonthier and Cory JJ. dissenting): The appeals should be allowed. The first constitutional question dealing with the legislative competence of Parliament to enact the legislation under the criminal law power or for the peace, order and good government of Canada should be answered in the positive. With respect to the second constitutional question, ss. 4 (re advertising), 8 (re trade mark use) and 9 (re unattributed health warnings) of the Act are inconsistent with the right of freedom of expression as set out in 2(b) of the [*Canadian Charter of Rights and Freedoms*] and do not constitute a reasonable limit on that right as can be demonstrably justified [in a free and democratic society] pursuant to s. 1 thereof. La Forest, L.Heureux-Dube, Gonthier and Cory JJ. would find that they constitute a reasonable limit ...

Per Sopinka, McLachlin and Major JJ.: The appropriate test in a s. 1 analysis is that found in s. 1 itself: whether the infringement is reasonable and demonstrably justified in a free and democratic society ... The word "demonstrably" in s. 1 is critical: the process is neither one of mere intuition nor of deference to Parliament's choice. While remaining sensitive to the social and political context of the impugned law and allowing for difficulties of proof inherent in that context, the courts must nevertheless insist that, before the state can override constitutional rights, there be a reasoned demonstration of the good which the law may achieve in relation to the seriousness of the infringement.

Context, deference and a flexible and realistic standard of proof are essential aspects of s. 1 analysis. The *Oakes* test must be applied flexibly, having regard to the factual and social context of each case. This contextual approach does not reduce the obligation on the state to demonstrate that the limitation on rights imposed by the law is reasonable and justified. The deference accorded to Parliament may vary with the social context but must not be carried to the point of relieving the government of its *Charter*-based burden of demonstrating the limits it has imposed on guaranteed rights to be reasonable and justifiable. To do so would diminish the role of the courts in the constitutional process and weaken the structure of rights ...

The objective [of relevant sections of the Act] should not be overstated ... The advertising ban and trade mark usage restrictions are to prevent people in Canada from being persuaded by advertising and promotion to use tobacco products. The mandatory package warning is to discourage people who see the package from tobacco use. Both constitute important objectives. The critical question, however, is not the evil tobacco works generally in our society, but the evil which the legislation addresses ...

The impugned provisions mandating a complete ban and [sic] unattributed package warnings do not minimally impair the right to freedom of expression. Under the minimal impairment analysis, the trial judge did not rely on problematic social science data, but on the fact that the government had adduced no evidence to show that less intrusive regulation would not achieve its goals as effectively as on [sic] outright ban. Nor had the government adduced evidence to show that attributed health warnings would not be as effective as unattributed warnings on tobacco packaging.

The causal relationship between the infringement of rights and the benefit sought may sometimes be proved by scientific evidence showing that as a matter of repeated observation, one affects the other. Where, however, legislation is directed at changing human behaviour, as in the case of the *Tobacco Products Control Act,* the causal relationship may not be scientifically measurable. In such cases, this Court has been prepared to find a causal connection between the infringement and benefit sought on the basis of reason or logic, without insisting on direct proof of a relationship between the infringing measure and the legislative objective. Here, no direct evidence of a scientific nature showed a causal link between advertising bans and decrease in tobacco consumption. A link, established on a balance of probabilities and based on reason, existed between certain forms of advertising, warnings and tobacco consumption. No causal connection existed, however, whether based on direct evidence or logic and reason, between the objective of decreasing tobacco consumption and s. 8's absolute prohibition on the use of a tobacco trade mark on articles other than tobacco products. Section 8 failed the rational connection test.

A complete ban on a form of expression is more difficult to justify than a partial ban. The government must show that only a full prohibition will enable it to achieve its objective. Where, as here, no evidence is adduced to show that a partial ban would be less effective than a total ban, the justification required by s. 1 to save the violation of free speech is not established.

As a matter of reason and logic, lifestyle advertising is designed to increase consumption. Purely informational or brand preference advertising, however, has not been shown to have this effect. Several less intrusive alternative measures would be a reasonable impairment of the right to free expression, given the important objective and the legislative context.

Allowing Parliament to choose such measures as it sees fit by contrasting the importance of Parliament's objective with the low value of the expression at issue raises a number of concerns ... [J]ust as care must be taken not to overvalue the legislative objective beyond its actual pa-rameters, so care must be taken not to undervalue the expression at issue ... [A] great deal of reliance is placed on the fact that the appellants are motivated by profit. Motivation to profit is irrelevant to the determination of whether the government has established that the law is reasonable or justified as an infringement of freedom of expression ...

The Dissenting View

Per La Forest, L'Heureux-Dube, Gonthier and Cory JJ.: The infringement [of s. 2(b) of the *Charter*] was justifiable under s. 1. Protecting Canadians from the health risks associated with tobacco use, and informing them about these risks, is a pressing and substantial objective ... The courts are to determine whether an infringement is reasonable and can be demonstrably justified in a "free and democratic society" and must strike a delicate balance between individual rights and community needs. This balance cannot be achieved in the abstract ... The section 1 inquiry is an unavoidably normative inquiry, requiring the courts to take into account both the nature of the infringed right and the specific values and principles upon which the state seeks to justify the infringement ...

The nature and scope of the health problems raised by tobacco consumption are highly relevant to the s. 1 analysis, both in determining the appropriate standard of justification and weighing the relevant evidence. Despite the lack of definitive scientific explanations of the causes of tobacco addiction, clear evidence does exist of the detrimental social effects of tobacco consumption. Overwhelming evidence was introduced at trial that tobacco consumption is a principal cause of deadly cancers, heart disease and lung disease, and that tobacco is highly addictive. The most distressing aspect of the evidence is that tobacco consumption is most widespread among the most vulnerable, the young and the less educated, at whom much of the advertising is specifically directed.

The significant gap between an understanding of the health effects of tobacco consumption and of the root causes of tobacco consumption raises a fundamental institutional problem that must be taken into account in undertaking the s. 1 balancing ...

Expression, depending on its nature, is entitled to varying levels of constitutional protection and requires a contextual, as opposed to an abstract, approach. Although freedom of expression is a fundamental value, other fundamental values are also deserving of protection and consideration by the courts. When these values come into conflict, the courts must make choices based not upon abstract analysis, but upon a concrete weighing of the relative significance of each of the relevant values in our community in the specific context. Freedom of expression claims must be weighed in light of their relative connection to a set of even more fundamental or core values which include the search for political, artistic and scientific truth, the protection of individual autonomy and self-development, and the promotion of public participation in the democratic process. State action placing such values in jeopardy is subject to a searching degree of scrutiny. Where the expression in question is farther from the "core" of freedom of expression values, a lower standard of justification may be applied.

The harm engendered by tobacco and the profit motive underlying its promotion place this form of expression as far from the "core" of freedom of expression values as prostitution, hate-mongering and pornography. Its sole purpose is to promote the use of a product that is harmful and often fatal to the consumer by sophisticated advertising campaigns often specifically aimed at the young and most vulnerable. This form of expression must then be accorded a very low degree of protection under s. 1 and an attenuated level of justification is appropriate. The Attorney General need only demonstrate that Parliament had a rational basis for introducing the measures contained in this Act ...

The legislative means chosen under the Act must be rationally connected to the objective of protecting public health by reducing tobacco consumption, not according to a civil standard of proof [the balance of probabilities], but only to the extent that there was a reasonable basis for believing such connection. A rational connection obviously exists between ... the prohibition on advertising and promotion of tobacco products under ss. 4, 5, 6 and 8 and the objective of reducing tobacco consumption. Notwithstanding the want of a definitive study connecting tobacco advertising and tobacco consumption, sufficient evidence was adduced at trial to conclude that the objective of reducing tobacco consumption is logically furthered by the prohibition on tobacco advertising and promotion under the Act. The large advertising budgets of the tobacco companies of themselves suggest that advertising not only helps to maintain brand loyalty but also to increase consumption and to induce smokers not to quit. The government's concern with the health effects of tobacco can quite reasonably extend to both potential smokers and current smokers who would prefer to quit but cannot. Three categories of evidence capable of substantiating this rational connection were disregarded at trial: internal tobacco marketing documents, expert reports, and international materials. The internal marketing documents introduced at trial strongly suggest that the tobacco companies perceive advertising to be a cornerstone of their strategy to re-assure current smokers and expand the market by attracting new smokers, primarily among the young. The expert reports introduced at trial attest, at the very least, to the existence of a "body of opinion" supporting the existence of a causal connection between advertising and consumption. It is also significant that by 1990, over 40 countries had adopted measures to restrict or prohibit advertising.

... [T]he legislative means chosen impair the right in question as little as possible, notwithstanding the fact that it imposes a complete prohibition on tobacco advertising and promotion rather than a partial one. The relevance of context is important in s. 1 balancing ... because it does not require that the least intrusive measures be used but only that the measures employed were the least intrusive in light of both the legislative objective and the infringed right. The measures taken here to control tobacco products, given the legislative context and the fact that this profit-generated type of expression is far from the "core" of the freedom of expression, satisfied the ... minimal impairment requirement. While a complete prohibition on a type of expression is more difficult to justify than a partial prohibition, ample evidence was adduced at trial to demonstrate the government's decision that a full prohibition on advertising was justified and necessary. The measures were the product o[f] an intensive 20-year period of experimenting with less intrusive measures with the cooperation of the provinces and expensive consultation with an array of national and international health groups. Over the course of this period the government adopted a variety of less intrusive measures before determining a full prohibition on advertising was necessary. Parallel developments in the international community have taken place. There has been overwhelming legislative and judicial acceptance of this type of prohibition by other democratic countries. Where governments have instituted partial prohibitions, tobacco companies have devised ingenious tactics to circumvent them. International health organizations support this kind of prohibition.

A proportionality must exist between the deleterious and the salutary effects of the measures. The legislative objective of reducing the number of direct inducements for Canadians to consume these products outweighs the limitation on tobacco companies to advertise inherently dangerous products for profit ...

Supreme Court of Canada, [1995] 3 S.C.R.

SUGGESTED READINGS

Aaker, David, Douglas Stayman, and Michael Hagerty. "Warmth in Advertising: Measurement, Impact and Sequence Effects." *Journal of Consumer Research*, Vol. 12, 1986.

Beauchamp, Tom. "Manipulative Advertising." *Business and Professional Ethics Journal*, Vol. 3, Nos. 3 and 4 (Spring/Summer 1984), pp. 1–23.

Bella, David. "Organized Complexity in Human Affairs: The Tobacco Industry." *Journal of Business Ethics*, 16, 10, 1997, 977–999.

Bennett, J.R. "Saturday Review's Annual Advertising Awards." *Journal of Business Ethics*, Vol. 2, No. 2 (May 1983), pp. 73–79.

Bok, Sissela. Lying: *Moral Choice in Public and Private Life*. New York: Pantheon Books, 1978.

Calfee, J. and D. Ringold. "The 70% Majority: Enduring Consumer Beliefs About Advertising." *Journal of Public Policy and Marketing*, 13, 1994, 228–238.

Clasen, Earl. "Marketing Ethics and the Consumer." *Harvard Business Review*, January/February 1967.

Consumer and Corporate Affairs Canada. *The Misleading Advertising Bulletin*. Ottawa.

Edell, Julie and Marian Chapman Burke. "The Power of Feelings in Understanding Advertising Effects." *Journal of Consumer Research*, Vol. 14, 1987.

Goldman, A. "Ethical Issues in Advertising." In Tom Regan (ed.) *Just Business*. New York: Random House, 1984.

Gowans, Christopher. "Integrity in the Corporation: The Plight of Corporate Product Advocates." *Journal of Business Ethics*, Vol. 3, No. 1 (February 1984), pp. 21–29.

Gratz, J.E. "The Ethics of Subliminal Communication." *Journal of Business Ethics*, Vol. 3, No. 3 (August 1984), pp. 181–185.

Held, Virginia. "Advertising and Program Content." *Business and Professional Ethics Journal*, Vol. 3, Nos. 3 and 4 (Spring/Summer 1984), pp. 61–77.

Hyman, M. and Richard Tansey. "The Ethics of Psychoactive Ads." *Journal of Business Ethics*, Vol. 9, No. 2, Feb. 1990.

Hyman, M., R. Tansey, and J. Clark. "Research on Advertising Ethics: Past, Present and Future." *Journal of Advertising*, 23, 1994, 5–15.

Latour, Michael and Shaker Zahra. "Fear Appeals as Advertising Strategy: Should They Be Used?" *Journal of Consumer Marketing*, Vol. 6, 1989.

Leiser, Burton. "Professional Advertising." *Business and Professional Ethics Journal*, Vol. 3, Nos. 3 and 4 (Spring/Summer 1984), pp. 93–109.

Levitt, Theodore. "The Morality (?) of Advertising." *Harvard Business Review*, 48, 1970, pp. 84–92.

Millum, Trevor. *Images of Woman: Advertising in Women's Magazines*. Totowa, NJ: Rowman and Littlefield, 1975.

Nelson, Philip. "Advertising and Ethics." In Richard deGeorge and Joseph Pichler (eds.) *Ethics, Free Enterprise, and Public Policy*. Oxford: Oxford University Press, 1978, pp. 187–198.

Paine, Lynda. "Children as Consumers." *Business and Professional Ethics Journal*, Vol. 3, Nos. 3 and 4 (Spring/Summer 1984).

Preston, I. *The Tangled Web They Weave: Truth, Falsity and Advertisers*. Madison, Wisconsin: University of Wisconsin Press, 1994.

Sautter, Elise Truly and Nancy A. Oretskin. "Tobacco Targeting: The Ethical Complexity of Marketing to Minorities." *Journal of Business Ethics*, 16, 10, 1997, 1–1011–1017.

Sexty, Robert. *Issues in Canadian Business*. Scarborough, Ontario: Prentice-Hall Canada Ltd., 1979.

Stuart, Frederick (ed.). *Consumer Protection from Deceptive Advertising*. Hampstead, NY: Hofstra, 1975.

Toronto School of Theology. *Truth in Advertising*. Toronto: Fitzhenry and Whiteside Ltd., 1992.

Wyckham, R., P. Banting and A. Wensley. "The Language of Advertising: Who Controls Quality?" *Journal of Business Ethics*, Vol. 3, No. 1 (February 1984), pp. 45–55.

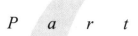

HONESTY AND
DECEPTION IN
BUSINESS

INTRODUCTION

Generally speaking, most of us agree that lying is morally wrong. Of course, we can always think of exceptions—situations in which we believe that it may be good to tell a lie (e.g., we might tell a suicidal friend that we don't own a gun when he asks to borrow one), but such cases confirm our general belief by illustrating their unique features. However, despite our consensus with respect to lying and truth-telling, many people are unclear as to what constitutes lying in business, and what its moral import is in that context. Also, there is some debate about the nature of misrepresentation that doesn't fall under the category of lying but does involve not telling all that you know, with the intent to deceive. Further, there is the issue of who is responsible for lies or deceptions done for the good of the corporation or the union. Many of these issues have already been addressed

in preceding sections. Here they are considered in the specific context of commercial negotiation.

Before proceeding with a discussion of how all of this relates to business negotiations, it is useful to define our terms. In the first article in Part 9, Carson, Wokutch, and Murrmann provide various candidates as definitions of lying. The definition that they believe most plausibly and completely captures what is meant by a lie is as follows: "a deliberate false statement which is either intended to deceive others or foreseen to be likely to deceive others." This definition presupposes intent and purpose, knowledge of the truth, and freedom from constraint. Thus, the individual who lies is one who knowingly and freely tells someone a false statement that they wish the listener to believe. If we morally condemn most lies, it would seem that we would morally condemn anyone who in business negotiations knowingly and freely states a falsehood that she wishes to be believed. However, the case may be more complex than it appears.

In 1968, A.Z. Carr argued in "Is Business Bluffing Ethical?" that making false statements in negotiation is all part of the "game" in business. The difference here, according to Carr, is that—as in any game, but unlike life generally—everyone is playing by the same rules. Hence, a consultant telling a company that he would not work for less than $1000 per day, even though that was false, would be considered morally acceptable because the company would assume that the consultant was not going to be truthful. Similarly, the company's stated position might be that $500 per day was the upper acceptable salary that they were prepared to pay even though they knew that their final offer could go as high as $750 per day. Consequently, Carr distinguishes between lying and *bluffing* on the grounds that the presuppositions are different. Lying presupposes that, other things being equal, people are going to be truthful. Bluffing suggests that the partners in negotiation both implicitly accept that false statements will be offered as truths.

Carson, Wokutch, and Murrmann do not agree. There may be justifications for some instances of bluffing, but that does not mean that bluffing is not lying. It also means that people can and often should be morally blamed for lying in business negotiations. Carson et al. argue that "competitive arrangements do not cause people to become dishonest, treacherous, etc." Consequently, to bluff or not to bluff is ultimately a personal decision for which one must take personal responsibility.

Part of the discussion by Carson et al. concerns the nature of lying and deception. This discussion is to illustrate their claims that 1) bluffing involves lying; 2) other types of deception may be equally reprehensible; and finally, 3) bluffing and other forms of deception may be justifiable "in the absence of any special reasons for thinking that one's negotiating partners are not bluffing (e.g., when one is dealing with an unusually naive or scrupulous person)."

Although James Michelman doesn't disagree with the definition proposed by Carson et al., his emphasis is slightly different. While Carson et al. argue that bluffing can be justified if everyone is operating by the same rules, they also suggest that bluffing is not necessary for successful negotiation. Michelman, on the other hand, believes that "under certain conditions, given the constraints of economic competition, one must negotiate by means of deception." The disagreement may not be moot, however, for Michelman concludes that to participate in such practices is morally wrong, and in fact "diminishes" the humanity of the players in such deceit.

Michelman defines commercial negotiation as "that interchange between buyer and seller in which they attempt to reach price agreement within implicit boundaries on the grounds of their common desire to consummate a deal and in the face of their diametrically opposed price goals." Since the goal of the seller is to sell for the highest price she can get, and the goal of the buyer is to buy for the lowest price he can offer, the negotiators are in a stalemate position if they truthfully state what is the optimal price for each, respectively. Since both want to "win," any compromise means failure. However, "deception offers a way out of this dilemma." If the negotiating buyer and seller lie about what the actual optimal price is, then both parties can appear to concede and still win. The result is "a peculiar kind of deception in which both parties are aware that each is trying to deceive the other, and . . . [making] . . . a sad mockery of protestations of truth and fidelity."

Patricia Werhane adds to this discussion by adding another, albeit different, element —insider trading. Werhane takes an interesting stance on insider trading, namely that insider trading is contrary to the efficiency of a laissez-faire free market, and consequently violates both the raison d'être of the free market, economically and morally.

This section of the text ends with two case studies. In the first, *Hollis v. Dow Corning Corp.,* the highly publicized issue of breast implants, and in particular the issue of the duty to warn, is discussed. As noted in the case, "it is well established in Canadian law that a manufacturer of a product has a duty to warn consumers of dangers inherent in the use of its product of which it has knowledge or ought to have knowledge . . ." In the case of Dow Corning, the duty to warn involved the potentiality of breast implants to

rupture—a phenomenon of which the company was clearly aware.

The second case involves what many would consider petty: white collar crime or, perhaps less seriously, misconduct. The behaviour involved the joint collusion of two employees in knowingly and fraudulently manufacturing expense claims. While such behaviour is clearly illegal, some employees seem to think that it is just one of the perks of the job. In assessing the case, the reader is asked to consider whether the same standards need to be applied to the employee as to the corporation.

BLUFFING IN LABOR NEGOTIATIONS: Legal and Ethical Issues

Thomas L. Carson
Richard E. Wokutch
Kent F. Murrmann

More than a decade ago a *Harvard Business Review* article entitled "Is Business Bluffing Ethical" (Carr, 1968) created a storm of controversy when the author defended bluffing and other questionable business practices on the grounds that they are just part of the game of business. The controversy over the ethics of bluffing and alleged deception in business negotiations erupted again recently with the publication of the *Wall Street Journal* article, "To Some at Harvard, Telling Lies Becomes a Matter of Course" (Bulkeley, 1979). This [article] detailed a negotiations course taught at Harvard Business School in which students were allowed to bluff and deceive each other in various simulated negotiation situations. Students' grades were partially determined by the settlements they negotiated with each other, and hence some alleged that this course encouraged and taught students to

bluff, lie to, and deceive negotiating partners. These controversies raised issues concerning the morality, necessity, and even the legality of bluffing in business negotiations which were never adequately resolved. It is the aim of this paper to shed some light on these issues.

In the first section of the paper we will describe briefly the nature of the collective bargaining process and then examine the role of bluffing in that process. The second section of the paper is a discussion of labor-law as it relates to bluffing. Then, in the third and fourth sections of the paper we will argue that bluffing and other deceptive practices in labor negotiations typically do constitute lying. Nevertheless, we will argue that bluffing is typically morally permissible but for different reasons than those put forth by Carr. In our conclusion we consider whether it is an indictment of our present

From the *Journal of Business Ethics*, Vol. 1, No. 1, February 1982, pp. 13–22. © 1982, D. Reidel Publishing Company, Dordrecht, Holland. Reprinted by permission.

negotiating practices and our economic system as a whole that, given the harsh realities of the marketplace, bluffing *is* usually morally acceptable.

THE NATURE OF COLLECTIVE BARGAINING

Collective bargaining is fundamentally a competitive process in which labor and management dispute and eventually decide the terms of employment. Through bargaining each party attempts to reach an agreement which each perceives to be at least minimally acceptable if not highly favorable, in light of its vital interests.

Typically there is a range of possible settlement points on wages (and other bargained issues) that each party would accept rather than fail to reach an agreement. This range exists with respect to wages, for instance, because the minimum wage that an employer could pay and still attract the needed employees is typically lower at any point in time than the maximum wage the employer could pay and still manage to operate a competitive business. Neither party knows the exact location of these extreme points. And ordinarily there is no one economically optimal wage level within the range that can be established through reference to objective criteria that are acceptable to both parties.[1] Each party attempts to move the wage agreement toward its preferred end of the range. Also, each attempts to define a point on the range beyond which it would rather endure a work stoppage than accept a settlement. Thus, in practice, the top end of the range becomes the highest wage that management would pay rather than endure a work stoppage. The bottom end of the range becomes the minimum wage that labor would accept rather than endure a work stoppage. These extreme positions are the parties' respective "sticking points."

Factors Affecting Bargaining Success

Two factors are instrumental to the ability of either party to negotiate a favorable agreement, i.e., an agreement that both perceive to be more than minimally acceptable. The first factor is the ability to impose significant costs on the other party, or to credibly threaten the imposition of such costs, in order to pressure the other party to make concessions. Thus, in order to bargain successfully, labor must be able to instill in management the belief that labor would initiate a work stoppage, or other form of costly noncooperation, in order to secure what it considers to be reasonable terms of employment. Likewise, in order for management to bargain successfully, it must convey to labor the perception that it would endure a work stoppage rather than accept what it believes to be unreasonable conditions.

The other key factor that affects one's bargaining success is the ability to accurately discern the other party's minimum acceptable conditions while vigilantly concealing one's own minimum terms. Such knowledge enables one to confidently drive the bargain to more favorable terms without risking an unwanted and costly work stoppage.

Bluffing and Bargaining Success

Bluffing typically plays a very important part concerning both of these factors. Bluffing is an act in which one attempts to misrepresent one's intentions or overstate the strength of one's position in the bargaining process. This is possible because neither party knows for sure the other party's true intentions or "sticking point." Bluffing often involves making deceptive statements. For instance, the union bargaining representative may boldly state, "There is no way that our people will accept such a small wage increase," when he/she knows full well that they would gladly accept management's offer rather than go out on strike. However, bluffing can be entirely nonverbal. Nodding confidently as one raises the bet while holding a poor hand in a game of poker is a paradigm case of bluffing. Getting up from the bargaining table in a huff and going out the door is another example of nonverbal bluffing. Through these and similar types of statements and behavior either party can convey to the other an exaggerated portrayal of its ability to impose or endure costs, and thereby can increase its actual ability to gain concessions in the bargaining process.

In addition, aggressive bluffing can be used to test the other party's resolve or otherwise prod the other party to concede certain points. This use of bluffing on different bargaining issues over a period of time, say spanning several bargaining sessions, can significantly increase one's understanding of the other party's true strength, and thus can enhance one's ability to accurately estimate the other party's sticking points on various issues.

There can be no doubt that bluffing is an important bargaining tool. It can be employed to create impressions of enhanced strength as well as to probe the other party to find out the level of its critical sticking points. Through these methods either party can attempt to gain a more favorable settlement than the other party would otherwise be willing to allow. Labor and management alike are more apt to fully abide by those terms of employment that they know were established through a free and vigorous use of their best bargaining skills.

The Alleged Necessity of Bluffing

While bluffing can obviously be advantageous in labor negotiations, one might ask whether it is "economically necessary." This does not appear to be the case. Where one of the parties has an extremely strong negotiating position (e.g., an employer in a one company town with a high unemployment rate, a slavemaster, or a surgeon who is the only one capable of performing a new surgical procedure necessary to save one's life) wages and working conditions can simply be dictated by the stronger party.

What about the claim that bluffing is a necessary part of the negotiation of any *voluntary* labor agreement between parties of relatively equal power? This also seems false. Suppose that two very scrupulous parties are attempting to reach a wage settlement and neither wants to engage in bluffing. Assuming that they trust each other and honestly reveal their 'sticking points', they could agree to some formula such as splitting the difference between the sticking points. This is of course unlikely to occur in real life, but only because few individuals are honest or trusting enough for our assumptions to hold.

THE LEGAL STATUS OF BLUFFING

The *National Labor Relations Act* (U.S.), as amended (1970), provides the legal framework within which the collective bargaining process in the private sector of our economy is carried out. Sections 8(a)(5) and 8(b)(3) of the *National Labor Relations Act* provide that it shall be an unfair labor practice for a union or an employer in a properly constituted bargaining relationship to fail to bargain in good faith. The statute left it to the National Labor Relations Board and the courts to establish criteria for determining whether a party is bargaining in good faith. Over the years numerous such criteria have been established by the Board and the courts.

The Honest Claims Doctrine

Of particular interest with respect to the legal status of bluffing is the "honest claims" doctrine, established by the U.S. Supreme Court in its *Truitt Mfg. Co.* decision (*NLRB c. Truitt Mfg. Co., 1956*). This states that "good faith necessarily requires that claims made by either party should be honest claims." The central issue in the *Truitt* case was whether the employer would be required to substantiate its claim that it could not afford to pay a certain wage increase. In addition to enunciating its "honest claims" doctrine, the court declared that if an "inability to pay argument is important enough to present in the give and take of bargaining it is important enough to require some sort of proof of its accuracy" (*NLRB v. Truitt Mfg. Co.*, 1956, p. 152). This "honest claims" policy has been consistently upheld and applied in numerous court decisions to this day. Thus, it is clear that the law requires honesty in collective bargaining. However, the "honest claims" requirement applies only to those types of claims that pertain directly to issues subject to bargaining and the employer's ability to provide certain conditions of employment. Thus, the "honest claims" policy requires a union to refrain from presenting false information to management concerning the level of wages and fringe benefits provided by employers under other union contracts. Likewise, the employer must refrain from falsely claiming an inability to provide a certain benefit.

Bluffing and the Honest Claims Doctrine

How does the honest claims doctrine apply to the practice of bluffing? It is clear that bluffing that involves the presentation of false information about issues subject to bargaining (i.e., wages, hours, and condition of employment) is a violation. However, bluffing about objective issues not subject to negotiation such as one's ability to withstand a strike (e.g., the size of the union strike fund, or the union membership's vote on the question of whether or not to go out

on strike) is allowable. Also, bluffing that is limited to representatives of one's bargaining intentions or one's willingness to impose or endure costs in order to win a more favorable contract does not constitute a violation. Of course, this type of bluffing is more effective and more prevalent because it can not be as easily discredited through reference to objective information as can false statements about working conditions. In sum, though the *Truitt* decision requires honesty with regard to the making of claims concerning bargaining topics, it does not proscribe the more effective and important forms of bluffing commonly used in bargaining today.

BLUFFING AND THE CONCEPT OF LYING

Suppose, example (1), that I am a management negotiator trying to reach a strike settlement with union negotiators. I need to settle the strike soon and have been instructed to settle for as much as a 12% increase in wages and benefits if that is the best agreement I can obtain. I say that the company's final offer is a 10% increase. Am I lying? Consider also whether any of the following examples constitute lying:

(2) Management negotiators misstating the profitability of a subsidiary to convince the union negotiating with it that the subsidiary would go out of business if management acceded to union wage demands.

(3) Union officials misreporting the size of the union strike fund to portray a greater ability to strike than is actually the case.

(4) Management negotiators saying, "We can't afford this agreement," when it would not put the firm out of business but only reduce profits from somewhat above to somewhat below the industry average.

(5) Union negotiators saying, "The union membership is adamant on this issue," when they know that while one half of

the membership is adamant, the other half couldn't care less.

(6) Union negotiators saying, "If you include this provision, we'll get membership approval of the contract," when they know they'll have an uphill battle for approval even with the provision.

Defining Lying

What is lying? A lie must be a false statement[2], but not all false statements are lies. If I am a salesman and say that my product is the best on the market and *sincerely believe this to be the case*, my statement is not a lie, even if it is untrue. A false statement is not a lie unless it is somehow deliberate or intentional. Suppose that we define a lie as an intentional false statement. According to this definition, I am telling a lie when I say, "This aftershave will make you feel like a million bucks." This definition implies that we lie when we exaggerate, e.g., a negotiator representing union workers making $10/hour but seeking a substantial raise says, "These are slave wages you're paying us." When I greatly exaggerate or say something in jest, I know that it is very improbable that the other person(s) will believe what I say. The reason that these examples do not appear to be lies is that they do not involve the intent to deceive. This suggests the following definition of lying:

> D1   A lie is a deliberate[3] false statement intended to deceive another person.

This definition is inadequate in cases in which a person is compelled to make false statements. For example, I may lie as a witness to a jury for fear of being killed by the accused. But it doesn't follow that I hope or intend to deceive them.[4] I may hope that my statements don't deceive anyone. We might say that what makes my statements lies is that I realize or foresee that they are likely to deceive others. This then suggests the following definition of lying:

> D2   A lie is a deliberate false statement which is thought to be likely to deceive others by the person who makes it.

This definition is also lacking because a person can lie even if he or she has almost no hope of being believed. A criminal protesting his or her innocence in court is lying no matter how unlikely it is that he/she thinks the argument will be convincing to the judge or jury. The following definition is more plausible than either D1 or 2:

> D3   A lie is a deliberate false statement which is either intended to deceive others or foreseen to be likely to deceive others.

Implications for Bluffing

It appears that this definition implies that the statements in our first three examples constitute lies. In examples (1) and (2) one is making deliberate false statements with the intent of deceiving others about matters relevant to the negotiations. In the first case I am making a deliberate false statement with the intent to deceive the other party into thinking that I am unwilling to offer more than 10%. One might object that this needn't be my intent in example (1). No one familiar with standard negotiating practices is likely to take at face value statements which a person makes about a "final offer." One might argue that in the two cases in question I intend and expect my statement that 10% is my best offer to be taken to mean my highest possible offer is something around 12%. If this is my intention and expectation, then my bluffing does not constitute a lie. To this we might add the observation that such intentions are quite uncommon in business negotiations. Even if I don't *expect* you to believe that 10% is my final position, I probably still *hope* or intend to deceive you into thinking that I am unwilling to offer as much as 12%. Examples (2) and (3) are clear instances of lying—they involve deliberate false statements intended to deceive others. It's not so clear, however, that examples (4), (5) and (6) constitute instances of lying. These cases do seem to involve the intent to deceive, but the statements involved are sufficiently ambiguous that it is not clear that they are untrue. We can still say that these are cases in which one affirms (or represents as true) statements which one knows to be dubious with the intent to deceive others. Morally speaking this may be just as bad or wrong as straightforward instances of lying.

An Alternative Definition of Lying

Our proposed definition of lying implies that bluffing in standard negotiation settings constitutes lying. There is at least one other approach to defining the concept of lying which does not have this consequence and it would be well for us to consider it here. In his *Lecture on Ethics*, Immanuel Kant (1775–1780) holds that a deliberate false statement does not constitute a lie unless the speaker has "expressly given" the other(s) to believe that he/she intends to speak the truth.[5] According to Kant's original view, when I make a false statement to a thief about the location of my valuables, I am not lying because "the thief knows full well that I will not, if I can help it, tell him the truth and that he has no right to demand it of me" (1775–1780, p. 227). According to this view, false statements uttered in the course of business negotiations do not constitute lies except in the very unusual circumstances that one promises to tell the truth during the negotiations. Kant's definition is open to serious objections. It seems to rule out many common cases of lying. For example, suppose that a child standing in line to see an X-rated movie claims to be 18 when he or she is only 15. This is a lie in spite of the fact that no explicit promise to tell the truth was made to the ticket seller. There does seem to be one relevant difference between the two cases in question. The ticket taker has a right to be

told the truth and the right to the information in question, the thief has no right to the information on one's valuables. This suggests the following revision of Kant's definition:

> D4   A lie is a deliberate false statement which is (i) either intended to deceive others or foreseen to be likely to deceive others, and (ii) either the person who makes the statement has promised to be truthful or those to whom it is directed have a right to know the truth.

Many would take it to be a virtue of D4 that it implies that deliberate false statements made during the course of certain kinds of competitive activities do not constitute lies. Carr quoted the British statesman Henry Taylor who argued that "falsehood ceases to be falsehood when it is understood on all sides that the truth is not expected to be spoken" (1968, p. 143). Carr argued that in poker, diplomacy, and business, individuals (through mutually implied consent) forfeit their rights to be told the truth. It seems at least plausible to say this with respect to standard cases of negotiation. However, it is surely not the case in situations in which one of the parties is unfamiliar with standard negotiating procedures (e.g., children, immigrant laborers, naive individuals or the mentally impaired), and enters into the discussion assuming that all of the parties will be perfectly candid.

If D4 is a correct definition of lying, then it does seem plausible to say that bluffing typically does not amount to lying. So, in order to defend our earlier claim that bluffing usually involves lying we need to give reasons for thinking that D3 is preferable to D4. We are inclined to think that deliberate falsehoods uttered in the course of games and diplomacy as well as business do constitute lies, and are thus inclined to prefer D3 to D4. This is a case about which people have conflicting intuitions; it cannot be a decisive reason for preferring D3 to D4 or vice versa. A more decisive consideration in favor of D3 is the following case.

Suppose that a management negotiator asks a union negotiator the size of the union strike fund. The union negotiator responds by saying it is three times its actual amount. Definition (4) implies that this statement is not a lie since the management negotiator didn't have a right to know the information in question and the union didn't explicitly promise to tell the truth about this. But surely this is a lie. The fact that management has no right to know the truth is just cause for withholding the information, but responding falsely is a lie nonetheless.

There is, to the best of our knowledge, no plausible definition of lying which allows us to say that typical instances of bluffing in labor and other sorts of business negotiations do not involve lying. We should stress that it is only bluffing which involves making false statements which constitutes lying. One is not lying if one bluffs another by making the true statement "We want a 30% pay increase." Similarly, it is not a lie if one bluffs without making any statements as in a game of poker or overpricing (on a price tag) a product where bargaining is expected (e.g., a used car lot or antique store).

The Concept of Deception

At this point it would be useful to consider the relationship between lying and the broader concept of deception. Deception may be defined as intentionally causing another person to have false beliefs. (It is not clear whether preventing someone from having true beliefs should count as deception.) As we have seen, lying always involves the intent to deceive others, or the expectation that they will be deceived as a result of what one says, or both. But one can lie without actually deceiving anyone. If you don't believe me when I lie and tell you that 10% is our final offer, then I haven't succeeded in deceiving you about anything. It is also possible to deceive another person without telling a lie. For example, I am not lying

when I deceive a thief into thinking that I am at home by installing an automatic timer to have my lights turned on in the evening. Only deception which involves making false statements can be considered lying.

It seems that one can often avoid lying in the course of a business negotiation simply by phrasing one's statements very carefully. In negotiations, instead of lying and saying that 10% is the highest wage increase we will give, I could avoid lying by making the following true, but equally deceptive statement: "Our position is that 10% is our final offer" (without saying that this position is subject to change). It is questionable whether this is any less morally objectionable than lying. Most people prefer to deceive others by means of cleverly contrived true statements, rather than lies. Some who have strong scruples against lying see nothing wrong with such ruses. It is doubtful, however, whether lying is any worse than mere deception. Consider the following example. I want to deceive a potential thief into thinking that I will be at home in the late afternoon. I have the choice between (i) leaving my lights on, and (ii) leaving a note on the door which says "I will be home at 5 p.m." Surely this choice is morally indifferent. The fact that (ii) is an act of lying and (i) isn't, is not, itself, a reason for thinking that (i) is morally preferable to (ii).[6]

MORAL ISSUES IN LYING

Common sense holds that lying is a matter of moral significance and that lying is *prima facie* wrong, or wrong everything else being equal. This can also be put by saying that there is a presumption against lying, and that lying requires some special justification in order to be considered permissible. Common sense also holds that lying is not always wrong, it can sometimes be justified (Ross, 1930). Almost no one would agree with Kant's (1797) later view in "On the Supposed Right to Tell Lies from Benevolent

Motives," that it is wrong to lie even if doing so is necessary to protect the lives of innocent people. According to this view it would be wrong to lie to a potential murderer concerning the whereabouts of an intended victim. Common sense also seems to hold that there is a presumption against simple deception.

Assuming the correctness of this view about the morality of lying and deception, and assuming that we are correct in saying that bluffing involves lying, if follows that bluffing and other deceptive business practices require some sort of special justification in order to be considered permissible.

We will now attempt to determine whether there is any special justification for the kind of lying and deception which typically occurs in labor and other sorts of business negotiations.

Bluffing and other sorts of deceptive strategies are standard practice in these negotiations and they are generally thought to be acceptable. Does the fact that these things are standard practice or "part of the game" show that they are justified? We think not. The mere fact that something is standard practice, legal, or generally accepted is not enough to justify it. Standard practice and popular opinion can be in error. Such things as slavery were once standard practice, legal and generally accepted. But they are and were morally wrong. Bluffing constitutes an attempt to deceive others about the nature of one's intentions in a bargaining situation. The *prima facie* wrongness of bluffing is considerably *diminished* on account of the fact that the lying and deception involved typically concern matters about which the other parties have no particular right to know. The others have no particular right to know one's bargaining position—one's intentions. However, there is still some presumption against lying or deceiving other people, even when they have no right to know how old I am. I have no obligation to provide him/her with this information. Other things being

equal, however, it would still be wrong for me to lie to this stranger about my age.

In our view the main justification for bluffing consists in the fact that the moral presumption against lying to or deceiving someone holds only when the person or persons with whom you are dealing is/are not attempting to lie to or deceive you. Given this, there is no presumption against bluffing or deceiving someone who is attempting to bluff or deceive you on that occasion. The prevalence of bluffing in negotiations means that one is safe in presuming that one is justified in bluffing in the absence of any special reasons for thinking that one's negotiating partners are not bluffing (e.g., when one is dealing with an unusually naive or scrupulous person).

CONCLUSIONS

Granted that bluffing and deception can be permissible given the exigencies and harsh realities of economic bargaining in our society, isn't it an indictment of our entire economic system that such activities are necessary in so many typical circumstances? Even those who defend the practice of bluffing (Carr, 1968) concede that a great deal of lying and deception occurs in connection with the economic activities of our society. Much of this (particularly in the area of bargaining or negotiating) is openly condoned or encouraged by both business and labor. While lying and deception are not generally condoned in other contexts, they often occur as the result of pressures generated by the highly competitive nature of our society. For example, few would condone the behavior of a salesperson who deliberately misrepresents the cost and effectiveness of a product. However, a salesperson under pressure to sell an inferior product may feel that he/she must either deceive prospective customers or else find a new job.

Many people would argue that our economic system is flawed in that it allegedly encourages dishonesty and thus corrupts our moral character and makes us worse persons than we would have been otherwise. Such criticisms are frequently found in Marxist literature. This kind of criticism can be extended into other areas as well. The competitive arrangements of our economic system are not only blamed for encouraging dishonesty, but other kinds of allegedly unethical conduct as well. The so-called competitive business "rat race" has been cited as a cause of personal treachery, backbiting, and sycophantic behavior. This, it seems to us is a very serious criticism which warrants careful consideration. We suggest the following three lines of response.

(1) One could concede that the economic arrangements of our society are such as to elicit a great deal of unethical conduct, but argue that this is the case in any viable economic system—including various forms of socialism and communism. If this is so, then the existence of immoral conduct which is associated with economic activities in our own society cannot be a reason to prefer some other sort of economic system. The record of the major socialist and communist countries would tend to support this view. There is deception in the bargaining involved in such things as the allocation of labor and raw materials for industry and setting production quotas for industry. There is also the same kind of gamesmanship involved in competing for desirable positions in society and (by all accounts) much greater opportunity and need for bribery. However, there have been viable feudalistic and caste societies which were much less competitive than our own which functioned with much less deception or occasion for deception. If one's place in society is determined by birth, then one will simply not have occasion to get ahead by deception.

(2) While it must be conceded that there are other types of economic systems which involve less dishonesty than our own, these systems have other undesirable features

which outweigh this virtue. In a feudal society or a centrally planned "command" economy there might well be less occasion for bargaining about wages and prices and thus also less occasion for deceiving other people about such things. But such a society is surely less free than our own and also very likely to be less prosperous. There are strong reasons to desire that wages be determined by voluntary agreements, even if that allows for the possibility of dishonesty in negotiations.

(3) It can be argued that the present objections to competitive economic systems such as our own rest on a mistaken view about the nature of moral goodness and the moral virtues. One's moral goodness and honesty are not a direct function of how frequently one tells lies. Thor Heyerdahl did not tell any lies during the many months in which he was alone on the Kon-Tiki. But we would not conclude from this that he was an exceptionally honest man during that period of time. Similarly, the fact that a businessperson who has a monopoly on a vital good or service does not misrepresent the price or quality of his/her goods or services does not necessarily mean that he/she is honest. There is simply no occasion or temptation to be dishonest. The extent to which a person possesses the different moral virtues is a function of how that person is disposed to act in various actual and possible situations. My courage or cowardice is a function of my ability to master fear in dangerous situations. Suppose that I am drafted into the Army and sent to serve in the front lines. If I desert my post at the first sign of the enemy we would not say that being drafted into the army has made me a more cowardly person. Rather, we could say that it has uncovered and actualized cowardly dispositions which I had all along. Similarly, competitive economic arrangements do not usually cause people to become dishonest or treacherous, etc. However these arrangements often actualize dispositions to act dishonestly or

treacherously which people had all along. This is not to deny that the economic institutions of our society can in some cases alter a person's basic behavioral dispositions and thereby also his/her character for the worse. For example, the activities of a negotiator may cause him/her to be less truthful and trusting in his/her personal relationships. Our claim is only that most of the "undesirable moral effects" attributed to our economic institutions involve actualizing pre-existing dispositions, rather than causing any fundamental changes in character.

ENDNOTES

1. It could, however, be argued on utilitarian grounds that, given a decreasing marginal utility for money, there is a presumption to settle as favorably as possible for the employees since they are *generally* poorer than the stockholders.

2. Arnold Isenberg, however, disputes this in "Conditions for Lying," in *Ethical Theory and Business*, Tom Beauchamp and Norman Bowie (eds.) (Prentice-Hall, Englewood Cliffs, N.J., 1979), pp. 466–468. He holds that a true statement can be a lie provided that one does not believe it. He defines a lie as follows: "A lie is a statement made by one who does not believe it with the intention that someone else be led to believe it. This definition leaves open the possibility that a person could be lying even though he says what is true" (p. 466). We feel that this is most implausible. For if what one says is true, this is always sufficient to defeat the claim that it is a lie.

3. There is however some question here as to what it means to make a deliberate false statement. Must one believe that what one says is false or is it enough that one not believe it? Roderick Chisholm and Thomas Feehan hold that

the latter is all that is necessary in "The Intent to *Deceive,*" *Journal of Philosophy* 74 (1977), 143–159. This makes the concept of lying broader than it would otherwise be.

4. Frederick Siegler considers this kind of example in "Lying," *American Philosophical Quarterly* 3 (1966), 128–136. But he argues that it does not count against the view that a necessary condition of a statement's being a lie is that it is intended to deceive someone. The example only shows that it is not necessary that the liar, him/herself, intend to deceive the others. But it does not count against the view that the lie must be intended *by someone* to deceive others. For, in our present example, *the criminal intends* that the witness's statements deceive others. However, a slight modification of the present example generates a counter-example to his claim that a lie must be intended by someone or other to deceive. Suppose that a witness makes a deliberate false statement, *x*, for fear of being killed by the friends of the accused. He/she is lying even if the accused's friends believe that *x* is true, in which case neither they nor anyone else intend that the witness's statements deceive the jury.

5. Kant's analysis of lying offered here differs from the one presented in Kant's later and more well known work, "On the Supposed Right to Tell Lies from Benevolent Motives" (1797) in Barauch Brody (ed.), *Moral Rules and Particular Circumstances* (Prentice-Hall, 1970), pp. 31–36. There he says that any intentional false statement is a lie (p. 32). Kant also gives a different account of the morality of lying in these two works. His well-known absolute prohibition against lying is set forth only in the latter work.

6. We owe this example to Bernard Gert.

DECEPTION IN COMMERCIAL NEGOTIATION

James H. Michelman

"… I hate, detest, and can't bear a lie, not because I am straighter than the rest of us, but simply because it appalls me. There is a taint of death, a flavor of mortality in lies …" — Joseph Conrad, *Heart of Darkness*

I observe that deception seems to be a recurring concomitant of commercial negotiation. My observation leads me to wonder if these deceptions are merely aberrations, reflecting only the moral frailty of the performers; or whether they stem from a different—or additional—cause, one that has to do with the nature of commercial negotiation itself. If the latter is true, then we might find that the logic of commercial negotiation forces those who engage in it to become liars.[1]

In the investigation that follows I attempt to analyze in some depth the notion of a negotiating range. There is nothing novel in the concept itself. In their article, 'Bluffing in Labor Negotiations: Legal and Ethical Issues,' … Professors Carson, Wokutch, and Murrman … also explore the negotiating range.[2] Their conclusions as to its nature agree with mine.[3] We do not agree, however, on an equally fundamental matter. Professor Carson et al. state that "competitive arrangements do not usually *cause* [emphasis theirs] people to become dishonest, treacherous, etc." My contrary conclusion is that, under certain conditions, given the constraints of economic competition, one *must* negotiate by means of deception. At the end of this paper I briefly sketch some consequences.

I

The term 'commercial negotiation' carries a firm implication that price is involved; and indeed price may be the only factor being

Journal of Business Ethics, Vol. 2, No. 4, November 1983, pp. 255–262. © 1983 D. Reidel Publishing Company, Dordrecht, Holland. Reprinted by permission.

negotiated. The environment in which commercial negotiation takes place is one of freedom with respect to price. If the price were fixed there would be no need for—and could not be—any price negotiation. And although quantities, qualities, and dates of delivery may also be the subjects of commercial negotiation, these most often, in the last analysis, involve price. Quality always does; and since quantities and delivery dates affect both seller's costs and purchaser's 'buying power', these factors may be looked on generally as other ways of expressing price. Thus buyer and seller come to the bargaining table not knowing at what price the deal finally will be made.

Consider the respective viewpoints of the negotiators. Without immediately examining the reason why this should be so, it seems clear that the buyer's goal is to buy as cheaply as he can, and the seller's to sell as dearly. Since technically there is no top limit (or at best it is undefined) to the seller's price if he wishes to sell as dearly as possible, and since the buyer's desire to purchase as cheaply as possible is limited only by no cost at all, it is obvious that there is a wide differential between the seller's desired price and the buyer's desired cost. If there is to be a transaction this differential must be narrowed, and finally eliminated, by commercial negotiation. Thus, *commercial negotiation* may be thought of as *that interchange between buyer and seller in which the parties attempt to reach price agreement on the grounds of their common desire to consummate a deal and in the face of their diametrically opposed price goals.* Let this definition stand for the moment. Before modifying it, it will be helpful to identify those situations which are excluded from this analysis. I wish to emphasize, for example, that what we are investigating are those interchanges that take place when the price is not set. For example, we are not concerned with the following scenario: Small supplier, atomistic or nearly so, con-

fronts large powerful buyer—say major retail chain operation. Large powerful buyer tells small, weak supplier—and means it—that the price which he is offering is 'not subject to negotiation', a common enough phrase. The supplier can take the proffered deal or leave it. There is no coercion because the supplier is not being threatened. He may infer a threat but the inference would be incorrect. Nor, since this particular deal is spread out on the table unconcealed, is there deception. It is true that there may be deception in a more subtle sense. Perhaps the buyer is not sure of how cheap he can buy what he wants and is using his power in order to test the market, to explore how low his costs might be. In this case the seller becomes sort of a guinea pig in an experiment. Nevertheless, there has been no negotiation offered, and in the immediate sense, no concealment or deception. This is not the situation with which we are concerned. By contrast, the subject of my analysis lies only in those circumstances in which the parties expect and agree, for the most part tacitly, to truly negotiate.

II

In order to determine those markets that might be candidates for deceptive practice it will be helpful to scan briefly an array of markets. Consider this array as a spectrum starting with perfect competition at one end, shading by degrees into bilateral monopoly at the other. Save for bilateral monopoly (or bilateral oligopoly), microeconomists view all these markets, even those served by a monopolist, or defined as monopsony, as impersonal. That is, the seller (or in the case of monopsony, the buyer) calculates that at a given price, the market—rather than a buyer—will purchase (or provide) a determinable quantity of his product. This calculation may be very complex indeed since, except for conditions of perfect competition on the one hand or pure monopoly on the other, it must take into account the manner in which other suppliers will respond to the seller's actions. Nevertheless it is a *market* that the seller views; and the concept of markets, in this sense, excludes negotiation. A market, in this sense, is a public, impersonal collection of individual buyers that *in the aggregate*, given a certain price, over a certain period of time will buy a certain quantity of the offered product.

Now, for the most part, this is not the way the commercial world works. What we actually find are nominated buyers dealing with nominated sellers over prices that are not fixed, but negotiable. It is these negotiations and negotiators with which we are finally concerned. But even if these transactions all share in elements of a bilateral market, they do so in different degrees. To make this point clearer, we now eliminate from the spectrum all those (conceptual or real) situations which are truly impersonal, leaving for examination those in which an actual buyer confronts an actual seller. This truncated spectrum remains, as before, fixed at one end described by bilateral monopoly. But the opposite end, the new starting point, no longer is the impersonal, general construct known as perfect competition. Instead, it is that market comprised of real individuals which retains more elements of generality than any other. I will define one such polar example as being made up of a large, but countable and namable, set of suppliers providing a similar set of users with more or less fungible material.

This market with large numbers of suppliers and users, although it cannot be described as (economically) perfect, does have—imperfectly—some of the characteristics of perfect competition. Information is widespread and mostly, but not entirely, complete and accurate. Traders can never be sure that they possess all pertinent facts, nor can they be sure that what they do know is wholly correct. Nevertheless, since there are many buyers and sellers there are many

trades, and approximate market levels are commonly known. Under these conditions there is not much negotiating room and outright deception is not only difficult but probably counterproductive. Yet since the market is not general, trading skills must be employed in order to conclude transactions. The negotiators exploit the incompleteness and uncertainty of information. Accompanying their price designations, they marshall and present facts. They are engaged in a process of persuasion in which each tries to make his case compelling to the other. Pertinent data usually includes recent trades—not necessarily known to both; the level of present and projected supply; an assessment of present and projected demand; general economic considerations. Each uses those pieces of information which advance his argument and ignores those which do not. If the buyer is aware of a recent trade close to the price he is bidding, he will certainly inform the seller. If he also knows of a trade significantly higher, he will, of course, not convey this information. Now a command of the facts and their shrewd selection are not the only skills traders use. There also, for example, can be open or implied threats of loss of continuity or custom; but in active, publicized markets these tactics can be employed only occasionally: otherwise they lose force. The traders are concerned to maintain credibility and this concern constrains their actions.

But if we now skip over all the intervening shades of the market spectrum and examine purely bilateral markets, we find a very different set of considerations. By definition these markets have just a few participants, perhaps only two. There are not very many transactions; thus common information is limited or non-existent. And the traders have no escape. They must deal with each other for they have nowhere else to go. In fact, either might try to deceive the other with respect to his own abilities to deal elsewhere. Negotiating room is probably very extensive since it is determined only by the price limits below which it is not rational for the supplier to sell and above which for the user to buy. Since this information only can be surmised of his opposite by each trader, considerations of credibility become much less of a constraint.

In what follows, it is important to keep in mind that what I am attempting to analyze are those transactions that occur in markets that lie on the bilateral, or less general, side of our truncated spectrum. They need not, of course, conform to the limiting case I have just described. How important they are as compared to more general markets is a separate question.

III

We have already excluded from our analysis take-it-or-leave-it offers; and, even limiting our inquiry to less general markets, there seems to be no reason to relax this exclusion. But there may be circumstances which fall between take-it-or-leave-it and clear negotiation. We can try to exemplify this 'in-between' case: Buyer and seller meet to discuss a deal. There exists a reasonable range—perhaps sharply, but more likely fuzzily, defined—in which there is tacit agreement that a transaction will take place. Buyer makes the initial move. He offers the seller a price at or near the bottom of this range. Seller responds by naming a price closer to the top of the range. Buyer accepts. Now either this has been a 'ritual' negotiation performed out of custom, but with no real conviction, or the range has been so narrow that any further negotiation would have served no purpose, perhaps would not have been worth the time of the negotiators. My observation is that this is a situation more common to more general markets; but even in those less general it occurs often enough to be of more than trifling importance. In it the range, not the single-mindedness or skill of the negotiators, is the overriding consideration, and within it no concealment

will occur—merely an offer, counter-offer, and acceptance. But we must take a closer look at this idea of a range.

We will think of it as that price differential in which a transaction can take place. The top of the range is not so high as to make it unacceptable to the buyer, nor is the bottom so low as to make it unacceptable to the seller. In fact we might say that the range is defined by these limits of acceptability. That there really must be limits on the lowest price at which the buyer can hope to buy and the highest price a seller can hope to sell becomes apparent when we consider them both as bidders in the immense economic auction. If the buyer will not pay that price which otherwise could conveniently be commanded by the seller, the seller is free to sell his wares elsewhere.[4] If the seller will not set his price at that level which the buyer could find elsewhere, the buyer is free to part with his dollars at another place.[5] So in the end, both buyer and seller are constrained to be reasonable and the deal will fall within a range somehow defined.

It will be helpful at this point to return to our consideration of the respective viewpoints of the buyer and the seller. These clearly are shaped by participation of buyer and seller in the market scheme. (And they hold true regardless of where the actors fall on the market spectrum.) Now any (free) market scheme needs to be fueled by incentives. These incentives, I believe, are resolvable into eight categories, not all confined to free market economics. They are:

(1) the material rewards stemming from doing the job well one is paid to do;

(2) the avoidance of loss of material well-being stemming from doing the job poorly one is paid to do. The consequence of poor performance might even be discharge;

(3) the material rewards stemming from contributing to, and association with, a successful enterprise;

(4) the avoidance of loss of material well-being which comes from being associated with an unsuccessful enterprise;

(5) the psychic satisfaction of contributing to the success of a team (the firm) and reaping the recognition therefrom;

(6) the avoidance of pain of an awareness of having let the team down by performing poorly;

(7) the satisfaction, similar to that experienced by a craftsman, of a job well done; and

(8) the avoidance of discomfort common to those who do a job badly or sloppily.

Although incentives (5) through (8) could apply to non-market economies, they definitely do apply to market economies; and all eight powerfully influence both buyer and seller to do their jobs well—to buy low and sell high. It is true, of course, that after a point buying low and selling high are not the only factors which contribute to the success of a firm. Volume is an important factor and so is monopoly power. It is interesting to note, however, that rationality—the necessity that under competition the participants act so as to maximize profits—demands that given a determined quantity, the parties buy as cheaply as possible and sell as dearly as possible.

There are other influences on the negotiators which act in the opposite manner to those which I enumerated. For example, the bonds of friendship between two negotiators. Or simply feelings of beneficence between two fellow humans. Or, not impossibly feelings of pity toward the weaker (for whatever reason) from the stronger. But to the degree that the negotiators allow these other influences to affect their performance in negotiation they are failing in that capacity. Moreover, if all other negotiators in the economic scheme do their jobs as best they can, those who do not are doomed to certain failure. Further, if they negotiate at less than their best, the nego

tiators are failing their fellow firm members who, whether they realize it consciously or not, depend upon them to do that best job. So, we may take it that the negotiators, because it is the essence of their responsibilities and because they benefit from doing so both materially and psychically, will do their best, in the one case to sell as dearly as possible, and in the other to buy as cheaply. In commercial negotiation there is no mutual search for value. No one discussed marginal costs and optimum quantities. It should be understood that we are not examining negotiation from the standpoint of ascertaining whether an efficient transaction takes place, nor are we concerned with the contract curve. What I am concerned with is *what takes place between the negotiators, not what results from the transaction.*

If we accept this outline of the motivation and purpose of the negotiators, recall that in the markets we are examining credibility is not easily ascertainable, and now turn again to a consideration of the range in which the negotiations will take place, we find that its limits must be implicit rather than explicit. There are two arguments:

(1) Suppose that the necessary information was supplied by each negotiator to his opposite and thus the limits were made explicit. The buyer would then know—and the seller would know that he knew—the lowest selling price acceptable to the seller; and this would be the best possible price from the standpoint of the buyer, his lowest possible cost. Similarly the seller would know—and the buyer would know that he knew—the highest purchasing cost acceptable to the buyer; and this would be the best possible price from the standpoint of the seller.

Under these conditions the buyer and seller, each (by hypothesis) of equal bargaining 'power' and so neither constrained to cede an advantage to the other, would split the difference. Perhaps an economically efficient purchase, expeditiously concluded, would result. But, *given the aims of the negotiators*, each would have lost. For once either budged from the (opposite) limits of the range he would no longer have the best deal, but only an acceptable deal. His job as a negotiator, however, is precisely to get the best deal, not less.

(2) Even if one of the parties gave accurate information to the other, he could never be sure he was getting accurate information in return. His personal predilection for trusting or not trusting would be of no account. His responsibility remains to look out for his firm's interests and he must assume the same of his trading partner. I do not believe this to be a circular argument—one that states that because the parties engage in deception, commercial negotiation must be deceptive. My claim is different. It is that, given the duties and aims of the negotiators and the difficulty of verifiability, it would be illogical of one to assume the veracity of the other and so illogical of himself to be truthful. But in any case the first argument seems to be sufficient.

Now since negotiators work within a range, set out to conclude, and do successfully conclude negotiations, it must be that the range has described an implicit, rather than explicit, set of boundaries. We now qualify our provisional definition of commercial negotiation to be more precisely a definition of *commercial negotiation in less general markets* and to read as *that interchange between buyer and seller in which they attempt to reach price agreement within implicit boundaries on the grounds of their common desire to consummate a deal and in the face of their diametrically opposed price goals.* The adding of the words 'within implicit boundaries' (or similar phraseology) brings the definition into the realm of common experience; but this addition also carries with it its own implication with respect to my original question of whether commercial negotiation necessarily entails deception.

A summary will help. I have eliminated non-negotiable situations from considera-

tion. These could either be fixed-price arrangements, or they could stem from one party simply announcing that he will not negotiate—by virtue of size conferring power, for example. I have also eliminated offer-counter offer-acceptance deals which can be thought of as a kind of ritual negotiation. Thus we are left with what we might call 'true negotiation' in which the interests of the parties are in opposition, and in which both intend to make the deal at the best possible level—different, of course, for each. Further, we have determined that the parties are negotiating within a range that is tacitly assumed by both and that is wide enough to allow meaningful negotiation. Bids and offers outside this range would be considered to be frivolous, not to be taken seriously. The buyer takes pretty much for granted that:

(a) the seller's opening offer defines the top of the range, that

(b) this is the seller's idea of the highest cost which would be acceptable to the buyer though not best for the buyer, but

(c) best for the seller.

Analogously the seller takes pretty much for granted that

(a) the buyer's opening bid defines the bottom of the range, which

(b) is the buyer's idea of the lowest price which would be acceptable to the seller though not best for the seller, but

(c) best for the buyer.

Now if this description of the negotiating stage is accurate, it is hard to see how there could be any negotiation. Each party would feel that his opening bid (offer) was acceptable to the other. And each party has entered the negotiation with the intention of making the best deal and knows that the best deal for him is an acceptable deal for the other. That is, the other will accept the deal if he can not improve on it. Thus if we rule out coercion or bribery we are left with a set of constraints which prevent any movement at all. For once either party moves from his original position he has lost: he can no longer get the best deal. What he has done is redefine the range to the benefit of his adversary.

The fact that the range limits are implicit rather than explicit informs us at once—as a tautology—that concealment and negotiation are inseparable. It makes sense, for example, for the buyer to tell the seller that although he would like to conclude the deal at *P* which is the lowest cost that he can reasonably hope to attain, he will pay as much as *P* + 3, which though not best is still acceptable. In that case he surely will pay *P* + 3 and will have failed as a negotiator. He will have failed, for by concealing his top price he might have avoided paying it. And that is an integral part of his job. However, it does not necessarily follow that because concealment is inseparable from negotiation, deception also is.

Once again, a summary will help. Although concealment is inseparable from negotiation, concealment does not assure negotiation. In fact, given even implicit acceptance of the upper and lower limits of the negotiating range by the participants, it remains impossible to understand how any negotiating can proceed. The participants will merely sit on their initial offers each waiting for the other to move off his. But deception offers a way out of this dilemma. Suppose the buyer to have opened the proceedings by making a bid (which turns out to be not lower than the seller's minimum acceptable price). He is then making explicit his idea of the lowest reasonable price, the lowest price at which he thinks the seller will do business.[6] The seller, in effect, either must accept the bid (and fail in his job), or must reply by doing his best to mislead the buyer by making him believe that the price is *not* acceptable, that it is below the bottom of the range; that the seller, if the buyer will not improve his bid, can and will offer and sell his wares elsewhere at a higher level. But

this is not the truth; it is deception. What the seller has to do is to mislead the buyer into believing that the lowest selling price is higher than it really is. Even if the buyer's initial bid was, due to misreckoning, *higher* than the seller's minimum acceptable price, the seller's responsibility nevertheless remains the same—to get the highest possible price, to reach, if possible, the top of the range. Thus his reply—deception—also remains the same. Similar remarks, of course, obtain for the buyer. Note also that simple silence as a response to a bid (concealment) will not accomplish the purpose. If the seller only rejects the buyer's offer, and at the same time does not convey to the buyer the idea that this rejection was made because his offer was out of the acceptance range, he has simply retreated to a position of non-negotiation, of take-it-or-leave-it. And we have excluded this case. But if he conveys to the buyer the idea that silence is his response because the buyer's offer was unreasonable, he has conveyed something that is untrue—he has made use of deception. In the end what the negotiators finally do is to narrow the range down to that point where negotiation becomes trivial, where one or both can concede without losing anything important. This narrowing process is accomplished by deception. It is a peculiar kind of deception in which both parties are aware that each is trying to deceive the other; and of course it makes a sad mockery of protestations of trust and fidelity. It seems also that the two deceptions do not cancel each other in some sort of cheerful acceptance of the rules of the game. Instead they sum. For if I, the buyer, intending to deceive you, the seller, think that you are aware of my intent, then I must be that much more subtle, disguising my intentions that much more carefully. And I must reason that you too are following the same logic; and so I must be that much more aware of what subtleties *you* might be employing. In the end, perhaps, our *skills* cancel each other; but our mutual *intent* has never wavered—

to gain an advantage over the other by means of deception.[7]

IV

We now take a closer look at the limiting case of bilateral monopoly in order to ascertain how well it fits (or contradicts) our examination just concluded of negotiation in less general markets.

Bilateral monopoly, in which a single seller (monopolist) faces a single buyer (monopsonist) is indeterminate. Quantity will not set price; price will not set quantity. The economist assumes:

(1) The buyer knows the monopolist's costs and so also knows his marginal cost curve, and

(2) The seller knows the monopsonist's demand curve—that unit cost, which for any given quantity of input purchased, will not exceed the market value of that input's last (marginal) product.

These two curves define a range since, for any given quantity, a price out of it would be irrational for either the buyer or seller. If the price were lower than the monopolist's rising (or horizontal) marginal cost curve, it would be irrational for him to make as much as (or any of) the requested quantity. If it were higher than the monopsonist's (downward sloping) demand curve, it would not be rational for him to buy as much. The difficulty is that for any given quantity, the boundary marking rationality (not necessarily profit maximization) is different for each. Given this conclusion, the economist throws up his hands, so to speak, and declares that to find a mutual price and quantity will require bargaining "and the better bargainer will obtain the more favorable terms"[8] or "bargaining power and negotiating skill and public opinion are among the factors determining the final outcome."[9]

There are a number of similarities to our prior conclusions in this analysis. Not only

is there a range, its upper and lower boundaries are both known to both parties. (This knowledge of the other's limits also allows each to establish his own profit maximizing point which is any firm's goal.[10]) There is a difference since the range is defined explicitly rather than implicitly. But there remains the identical difficulty in understanding how any trade could be concluded. And deception still provides the same possible solution. Let the seller misrepresent his costs and the buyer the worth to himself of the seller's product, and negotiation has commenced. The very act of misrepresenting would be a negotiating step.

Now in less general markets, insofar as they are dealing with each other, almost any buyer and seller in negotiation will be acting in part as bilateral monopolists. Each is a single actor dealing with another single actor. And there is no escape into a more general market once they have begun negotiation. For their, and our, assumption is that they have decided (possibly incorrectly) that it is not worthwhile to seek a trading partner elsewhere, that the (implicit) range is reasonable, and so trading skills must determine the outcome.

Thus, both in theory and by observation, we have seen markets that demand or admit true negotiation. And if theory does not altogether fit, neither does it contradict observation. In brief, when we cannot have recourse to general markets, when there is no appeal from two traders with proper names dealing with each other, there is also no solution but bargaining.

V

We have seen that more general markets tend to preclude deception; but firms continually seek less general markets which tend to demand it. To see why, consider that the profit motive is the engine of economic competition. If profits were not the hoped-for reward of business activity, other incentives would have to supply the motives to produce, to distribute, or to provide other services. Now in perfect competition, which is the most general of markets and in which negotiation is meaningless and unknown, there are no economic profits. Therefore a firm will flee those situations that approach the conditions of perfect competition if it can find other markets that will afford it greater returns on its investment. In fact, it will strive for monopoly, that best of economic schemes for the firm and the worst for society. And even within monopoly, if it can do so, the firm will engage in price discrimination. That is, it will fragment its market in order to maximize its profit.

Most firms cannot attain monopoly. But many can differentiate their products to some degree and so dissociate themselves from the profit-stifling conditions of perfect competition—and if they can, they must. By doing so they not only reduce each single market they serve, but also tend to increase the variety of inputs they require. It is clear that the quest for profits is the irresistible force which draws firms to the less general side of the market spectrum.

These are grave matters. For they indicate that the world in which we get and spend is partially, but ineluctably, built on a structure of lies. And if we do agree that at least it is not *prima facie* implausible that our commercial world is in part so structured, it will do no good, I believe to hunt for excuses or justifications. Even if my trading partner may be clearly lying and so in sheer self-defense I must lie too, my lie remains a lie. Although by lying to me he has diminished me as a human being by making me mere means to his ends; in treating him the same way I have diminished him also. And worse, I have diminished myself. For by the very act of treating him as less than human, I have become less human.[11] Given the logic of commercial negotiation, perhaps this is an inevitable consequence. But given its human implications it is also

one of great horror. It does not seem altogether bearable that for the sake of solving the vast problems of allocation and distribution in a manner at least free of central command, men must have recourse to a self-imposed moral catastrophe.

ENDNOTES

1. There seems to be widespread acceptance of the fact that negotiation and deception go hand-in-hand. See for example Thomas L. Carson, Richard E. Wokutch, and Kent F. Murrmann, 'Bluffing in Labor Negotiations: Legal and Ethical Issues', in this book; A.Z. Carr, 'Is Business Bluffing Ethical?', *Harvard Business Review* 46 (1968), 143–153; W.M. Bulkeley, 'To Some at Harvard, Telling Lies Becomes a Matter of Course', *The Wall Street Journal*, 15 Jan. 1979, pp. 1, 37; Sissela Bok, *Lying: Moral Choice in Public and Private Life* (Pantheon Books, New York, 1978). But it is interesting how little attention Bok pays to commerce in her book.

2. Carson et al., *Bluffing in Labor Negotiations: Legal and Ethical Issues*.

3. Though we arrived at our ideas independently, they are in very close agreement. This is not surprising for upon reflection they seem almost self-evident.

4. Even if his market is monopsonistic he eventually can shift his resources into serving others which are more remunerative.

5. Excluding monopoly, of course. But even the monopolist must keep his customers in business. If he sets his prices too high he will drive them into other ventures.

6. This explicit offer does not violate the conditions of implicit boundaries. Any offer must be explicit. But the buyer and seller still have not conveyed to their opposites what the limits of the range re-

ally are. The buyer's offer is an attempt to define what only the seller has the right to define—the bottom of the range.

7. Those, like Carr, who justify commercial deception by analogies with games like poker—because both in commerce and poker everyone knows the rules—forget that in poker no one *claims* honesty, trustworthiness, and the rights of friendship. This is a vital difference.

8. See Richard A. Bilas, *Microeconomics: Theory*, 2nd ed. (McGraw-Hill, New York, 1971), p. 301.

9. See Edwin Mansfield, *Microeconomics: Theory and Applications* (Norton, New York, 1970), p. 272. 'Public opinion' refers to labor negotiation.

10. For accessible accounts of bilateral monopoly see Bilas, *op. cit.*, p. 301, and Mansfield, *op. cit.*, p. 272.

11. There is, of course, nothing original in this notion. And it is not confined to philosophers or theologians. For example, see Gene Levine, 'Authenticity,' *Bobbin*, Oct. 1981. *Bobbin* is a trade magazine serving the apparel industry.

THE ETHICS OF INSIDER TRADING

Patricia H. Werhane

Insider trading is the reverse of speculation. It is reward without risk, wealth generated—and injury done to others—by an unfair advantage in information … [T]he core principle is clear: no one should profit from exploitation of important information not available to the public.[1]

Insider trading in the stock market is characterized as the buying or selling of shares of stock on the basis of information known only to the trader or to a few persons. In discussions of insider trading it is commonly assumed that the privileged information, if known to others, would affect their actions in the market as well, although in theory this need not be the case. The present guidelines of the Securities and Exchange Commission prohibit most forms of insider trading. Yet a number of economists and philosophers of late defend this kind of activity both as a vi-

able and useful practice in a free market and as a practice that is not immoral. In response to these defenses I want to question the value of insider trading both from a moral and an economic point of view. I shall argue that insider trading both in its present illegal form and as a legalized market mechanism violates the privacy of concerned parties, destroys competition, and undermines the efficient and proper functioning of a free market, thereby bringing into question its own raison d'être. It does so and therefore is economically inefficient for the very reason that it is immoral.

That insider trading as an illegal activity interferes with the free market is pretty obvious. It is like a game where there are a number of players each of whom represents a constituency. In this sort of game there are two sets of rules—one ostensive set and another, implicit set, functioning for some of

From *Journal of Business Ethics,* 8 (1989), 841–845. © 1989 Kluwer Academic Publishers. Reprinted by permission of Kluwer Academic Publishers.

the players. In this analogy some of the implicit rules are outlawed, yet the big players manage to keep them operative and are actually often in control of the game. But not all the players know all the rules being played or at least they are ignorant of the most important ones, ones that determine the big wins and big losses. So not all the players realize what rules actually manipulate the outcome. Moreover, partly because some of the most important functioning rules are illegal, some players who do know the implicit rules and could participate do not. Thus not everyone in a position to do so plays the trading game the same way. The game, then, like the manipulated market that is the outcome, is unfair—unfair to some of the players and those they represent—unfair not only because some of the players are not privy to the most important rules, but also because these "special" rules are illegal so that they are adopted only by a few of even the privileged players.

But suppose that insider trading was decriminalized or not prohibited by SEC regulations. Then, one might argue, insider trading would not be unfair because anyone could engage in it without impunity. Although one would be trading on privileged knowledge, others, too, could trade on *their* privileged information. The market would function more efficiently since the best-informed and those most able to gain information would be allowed to exercise their fiscal capabilities. The market itself would regulate the alleged excesses of insider trading. I use the term "alleged" excesses because according to this line of reasoning, if the market is functioning properly, whatever gains or losses are created as a result of open competition are a natural outcome of that competition. They are not excuses at all, and eventually the market will adjust the so-called unfair gains of speculators.

There are several other defenses of insider trading. First, insider information, e.g., information about a merger, acquisition, new stock issue, layoffs, etc., information known only to a few, *should* be and remain private. That information is the property of those engaged in the activity in question, and they should have the right to regulate its dissemination. Second and conversely, even under ideal circumstances it is impossible either to disseminate information to all interested parties equally and fairly, or alternat[ively], to preserve absolute secrecy. For example, in issuing a new stock or deciding on a stock split, a number of parties in the transaction from brokers to printers learn about that information in advance just because of their participation in making this activity a reality. And there are always shareholders and other interested parties who claim they did not receive information of such an activity or did not receive it at the same time as other shareholders even when the information was disseminated to everyone at the same time. Thus it is, at best, difficult to stop insider trading or to judge whether a certain kind of knowledge is "inside" or privileged. This is not a good reason to defend insider trading as economically or morally desirable, but it illustrates the difficulties of defining and controlling the phenomenon.

Third, those who become privy to inside information, even if they take advantage of that information before it becomes public, are trading on probabilities, not on certainties, since they are trading before the activity actually takes place. They are taking a gamble, and if they are wrong the market itself will "punish" them. It is even argued that brokers who do not use inside information for their clients' advantage are cheating their clients.

Finally, and more importantly, economists like Henry Manne argue that insider trading is beneficial to outsiders. Whether it is more beneficial than its absence is a question Manne admits he cannot answer. But Manne defends insider trading because, he argues, it reduces the factor of chance in trading both for insiders and outsiders. When shares are traded on information or probabilities rather than on rumor or whim, the market reflects more accurately the actual economic status of that company or set of companies. Because of insider trading, stock prices go up or down according to real, factual information. Outsiders benefit from this because stock prices more closely represent the worth of their company than shares not affected by insider trading. Insider trading, then, actually improves the fairness of the market, according to this argument, by reflecting in stock prices the fiscal realities of affected corporations thereby benefitting all traders of the stocks.[2]

These arguments for insider trading are persuasive. Because outsiders are allegedly not harmed from privileged information not available to them and may indeed benefit from insider trading, and because the market punishes rash speculators, insider trading cannot be criticized as exploitation. In fact, it makes the market more efficient. Strong as these arguments are, however, there is something amiss with these claims. The error, I think, rests at least in part with the faulty view of how free markets work, a view which stems from a misinterpretation that derives from a misreading of Adam Smith and specifically a misreading of Smith's notions of self-interest and the Invisible Hand.

The misinterpretation is this. It is sometimes assumed that an unregulated free market, driven by competition and self interest, will function autonomously. The idea is that the free market works something like the law of gravity—autonomously and anonymously in what I would call a no-blooded fashion. The interrelationships created by free market activities based on self-interested competition are similar to the gravitational relationships between the planets and the sun: impersonal, automatic interactions determined by a number of factors including the distance and competitive self-interest of each of the market components. The free market functions, then, despite the selfish

peculiarities of the players just as the planets circle the sun despite their best intentions to do otherwise. Given that picture of the free market, so-called insider trading, driven by self-interest but restrained by competitive forces, that is, the Invisible Hand, is merely one gravitational mechanism—a complication but not an oddity or an aberration in the market.

This is a crude and exaggerated picture of the market, but I think it accounts for talk about the market *as if* it functioned in this independent yet forceful way, and it accounts for defenses of unrestrained self-interested actions in the market place. It allows one to defend insider trading because of the positive market fall-out from this activity, and because the market allegedly will control the excesses of self-interested economic activities.

The difficulty with this analysis is not so much with the view of insider trading as a legitimate activity but rather with the picture of economic actors in a free market. Adam Smith himself, despite his 17th century Newtonian background, did not have such a mechanical view of a laissez-faire economy. Again and again [in] the *Wealth of Nations* Smith extols the virtues of unrestrained competition as being to the advantage of the producer and the consumer.[3] A system of perfect liberty, he argues, creates a situation where "[t]he whole of the advantages and disadvantages of the different employments of labour and stock ... be either perfectly equal or continually tending to equality."[4] Yet for Smith the greatest cause of inequalities of advantage is any restrictive policy or activity that deliberately gives privileges to certain kinds of businesses, trades, or professions.[5] The point is that Smith sees perfect liberty as the necessary condition for competition, but perfect competition occurs only if both parties in the exchange are on more or less equal ground, whether it be competition for labor, jobs, consumers, or capital. This is not to imply that Smith favors equality of outcomes.

Clearly he does not. But the market is most efficient and most fair when there is competition between equally matched parties.

Moreover, Smith's thesis was that the Invisible Hand works because, and only when, people operate with restrained self-interest, self-interest restrained by reason, moral sentiments, and sympathy—in Smith's case the reason, moral sentiments and sympathies of British gentlemen. To operate otherwise, that is, with unrestrained self-interest, where that self-interest causes harm to others would "violate the laws of justice"[6] or be a "violation of fair play,"[7] according to Smith. This interferes with free competition just as government regulation would because the character of competition, and thus the direction of the Invisible Hand, depends on the manner in which actors exploit or control their own self-interests. The Invisible Hand, then, that "masterminds" the free market is not like an autonomous gravitational force. It depends on the good will, decency, self-restraint, and fair play of those parties engaging in market activities.[8] When self-interests get out of hand, Smith contends, they must be regulated by laws of justice.[9]

Similarly, the current market, albeit not Smith's ideal of laissez-faire, is affected by how people operate in the market place. It does not operate autonomously. Unrestrained activities of insider traders affect competition differently than Smithian exchanges which are more or less equal exchanges between self-interested but restrained parties. The term "insider trading" implies that some traders know more than others, that information affects their decision-making and would similarly affect the trading behavior of others should they become privy to that information. Because of this, the resulting market is different than one unaffected by insider trading. This, in itself, is not a good reason to question insider trading. Henry Manne, for example, recognizes the role of insider trading in influencing the market and finds that, on balance, this is beneficial.

Insider trading, however, is not merely a complication in the free market mechanism. Insider trading, whether it is legal or illegal, affects negatively the ideal of laissez-fair of *any* market, because it thwarts the very basis of the market: competition, just as "insider" rules affect the fairness of the trader even if that activity is not illegal and even if one could, in theory, obtain inside information oneself. This is because the same information, or equal information, is not available to everyone. So competition, which depends on the availability of equal advantage by all parties is precluded. Insider trading allows the insider to indulge in greed (even though she may not) and that, by eschewing stock prices, works against the very kind of market in which insider trading might be allowed to function.

If it is true, as Manne argues, that insider trading produces a more efficient stock market because stock prices as a result of insider trading better reflect the underlying economic conditions of those companies involved in the trade, he would also have to argue that competition does not always produce the best results in the marketplace. Conversely, if competition creates the most efficient market, insider trading cannot, because competition is "regulated" by insiders. While it is not clear whether outsiders benefit more from insider trading than without that activity, equal access to information would allow (although not determine) every trader to compete from an equal advantage. Thus pure competition, a supposed goal of the free market and an aim of most persons who defend insider trading, is more nearly obtained without insider trading.

Insider trading has other ethical problems. Insider trading does not promote the privacy of information it is supposed to protect. To illustrate, let us consider a case of a friendly merger between Company *X* and Company *Y*. Suppose this merger is in the planning stages and is not to be made public even to the shareholders for a number of months. There may be good or bad reasons for this secrecy, e.g., labor problems, price of shares of acquired company, management changes, unfriendly raiders, competition in certain markets, etc. By law, management and others privy to knowledge about the possible merger cannot trade shares of either company during the negotiating period. On the other hand, if that information is "leaked" to a trader (or if she finds out by some other means), then information that might affect the merger is now in the hands of persons not part of the negotiation. The alleged privacy of information, privacy supposedly protected by insider traders, is now in the hands of not disinterested parties. While they may keep this information a secret, they had no right to it in the first place. Moreover, their possession of the information has three possible negative effects.

First, they or their clients in fact may be interested parties to the merger, e.g., labor union leaders, stockholders in competing companies, etc., the very persons for whom the information makes a difference and therefore are the objects of Company X and Y's secrecy. Second, insider trading on privileged information gives unfair advantage to these traders. Even if outsiders benefit from insider trading, they are less likely to benefit as much or as soon as insider traders for the very reason of their lack of proximity to the activity. Insider traders can use information to their advantage in the market, an advantage neither the management of X or Y nor other traders can enjoy. Even if the use of such information in the market makes the market more efficient, this is unfair competition since those without this information will not gain as much as those who have such knowledge. Even if insider trading does contribute to market stabilization based on information, nevertheless, one has also to justify the fact that insider traders profit more on their knowledge than outsiders, when their information becomes an actual-

ity simply by being "first" in the trading of the stock. Do insider traders deserve this added profit because their trading creates a more propitious market share knowledge for outsiders? That is a difficult position to defend, because allowing insider trading also allows for the very Boeksyian greed that is damaging in any market.

Third, while trading X and Y on inside information may bring their share prices to the value most closely reflecting their real-price earnings ratio, this is not always the case. Such trading may reflect undue optimism or pessimism about the possible outcome of the merger, an event that has not yet occurred. So the prices of X and Y may be overvalued or undervalued on the basis of a probability, or, because insider traders seldom have all the facts, on guesswork. In these cases insider trading deliberately creates more risk in the market since the stock prices of X and Y are manipulated for not altogether solid reasons. So market efficiency, the end which allegedly justifies insider trading is not guaranteed.

What Henry Manne's defenses of insider trading do show is what Adam Smith well knew, that the market is neither independent nor self-regulatory. What traders do in the market and how they behave affects the direction and kind of restraint the market will exert on other traders. The character of the market is a product of those who operate within it, as Manne has demonstrated in his defense of insider trading. Restrained self-interest creates an approximation of a self-regulatory market, because it is that that allows self-interested individuals and companies to function as competitively as possible. In the long run the market will operate more efficiently too, because it precludes aberrations such as those exhibited by Ivan Boesky's and David Levine's behavior, behavior that created market conditions favorable to no one except themselves and their clients.

ENDNOTES

1. George Will, "Keep Your Eye on Guiliani," *Newsweek*, March 2, 1987, p. 84.

2. See Henry Manne, *Insider Trading and the Stock Market* (The Free Press, New York, 1966), especially Chapters X and XI.

3. Adam Smith, *The Wealth of Nations*, ed. R. A. Campbell and A. S. Skinner (Oxford University Press, Oxford, 1976), 1.x.c, II.v.8–12.

4. *Wealth of Nations*, 1.x.a.1.

5. *Wealth of Nations*, 1.x.c.

6. *Wealth of Nations*, IV.ix.51.

7. Adam Smith, *The Theory of Moral Sentiments*, ed. D. D. Raphael and A. L. Macfic (Oxford University Press, Oxford, 1976), II.ii.2.1.

8. See Andrew Skinner, *A System of Social Science* (Clarendon Press, Oxford, 1979), especially pp. 237 ff.

9. See, for example, *The Wealth of Nations*, II.ii.94, IV.v.16.

CASE 12   Hollis v. Dow Corning Corp.

In 1993, breast implants, manufactured by the defendant corporation, Dow Corning, were implanted in Susan Hollis's breasts by her surgeon, Dr. John Robert Birch. The purpose of the implants was to correct a congenital deformity of Ms. Hollis's breasts. One of the implants ruptured, required removal and further surgery. The literature accompanying the product warned of rupture during surgery, but made no mention of post-surgical rupture except from abnormal squeezing and/or trauma. Ms. Hollis brought an action for damages against Dow Corning and Dr. Birch, and won at trial against the manufacturer. The action against Dr. Birch was dismissed. Dow Corning appealed to the British Columbia Court of Appeal. The appeal was dismissed, not on the ground that Dow Corning was negligent in the manufacturing of its breast implants, but on the ground of a failure to warn of dangers inherent in its breast implants. The evidence showed that, by 1983, Dow Corning had received reports of over 50 cases of ruptures. Dow Corning's further appeal to the Supreme Court of Canada was dismissed on the ground that Dow Corning had a duty to warn the medical profession of potential dangers, including those coming to its attention after the manufacture and distribution of its implants.

What follows is a portion of the analysis provided by Supreme Court Justice La Forest (L'Heureux-Dube, Gonthier, Cory and Iacobucci JJ. concurring).

18. The sole issue raised in this appeal is whether the Court of Appeal erred in finding Dow liable to the respondent Ms. Hollis for failing adequately to warn the implanting surgeon, Dr. Birch, of the risk of a post-surgical implant rupture inside Ms. Hollis's body. The appellant Dow does not contest Bouck J.'s factual finding that Ms. Hollis's seven-year surgical ordeal caused her great physical and psychological pain, residual scarring on her breasts, and a loss of past and future income. However, Dow submits that it was not responsible for Ms. Hollis's

injuries. In support of this submission, Dow argues, first, that the warning it gave to Dr. Birch was adequate and sufficient to satisfy its duty to Ms. Hollis, and second, that even if it did breach its duty to warn Ms. Hollis, this breach was not the proximate cause of her injuries.

19. For the reasons that follow, it is my view that the Court of Appeal reached the correct conclusion and that the appeal should be dismissed ... In the first part of these reasons, I will address the question whether Dow breached its duty to warn, and the related question whether Dow can rely on the so-called "learned intermediary" rule to absolve itself of liability …

1. Dow's Duty to Warn and the "Learned Intermediary" Rule

(a) The General Principles

(i) The Duty to Warn

20. It is well established in Canadian law that a manufacturer of a product has a duty to warn consumers of dangers inherent in the use of its product of which it has knowledge or ought to have knowledge …

The duty to warn is a continuing duty, requiring manufacturers to warn not only of dangers known at the time of sale, but also dangers discovered after the product has been sold and delivered … All warnings must be reasonably communicated, and must clearly describe any specific dangers that arise from the ordinary use of the product …

21. The rationale for the manufacturer's duty to warn can be traced to the "neighbour principle," which lies at the heart of the law of negligence, and was set down in its classic form by Lord Atkin in *Donoghue v. Stevenson* [1932]. When manufacturers place products into the flow of commerce, they create a relationship of reliance with consumers, who have far less knowledge than the manufacturers concerning the dangers inherent in the use of the products, and are therefore put at risk if the product is not safe. The duty to warn serves to correct the knowledge imbalance between manufacturers and consumers by alerting customers to any dangers and allowing them to make informed decisions concerning the safe use of the product.

22. The nature and scope of the manufacturer's duty to warn varies with the level of danger entailed by the ordinary use of the product. Where significant dangers are entailed by the ordinary use of the product, it will rarely be sufficient for manufacturers to give general warnings concerning those dangers; the warnings must be sufficiently detailed to give the consumer a full indication of each of the specific dangers arising from the use of the product. This was made clear by Laskin J. in *Lambert* … where this Court imposed liability on the manufacturer of a fast-drying lacquer sealer who failed to warn of the danger of using the highly explosive product in the vicinity of a furnace pilot light. The manufacturer in *Lambert* had placed three different labels on its containers warning of the danger of inflammability. The plaintiff, and engineer, had read the warnings before he began to lacquer his basement floor and, in accordance with the warnings, had turned down the thermostat to prevent the furnace from turning on. However, he did not turn off the pilot light, which

caused the resulting fire and explosion. Laskin J. found the manufacturer liable for failing to provide an adequate warning, deciding that none of the three warnings was sufficient in that none of them warned specifically against leaving pilot lights on near the working area ...

23. In the case of medical products such as the breast implants at issue in this appeal, the standard of care to be met by manufacturers in ensuring that consumers are properly warned is necessarily high. Medical products are often designed for bodily ingestion or implantation, and the risks created by their improper use are obviously substantial. The courts in this country have long recognized that manufacturers of products that are ingested, consumed or otherwise placed in the body, and thereby have a great capacity to cause injury to consumers, are subject to a correspondingly high standard of care under the law of negligence ... Given the intimate relationship between medical products and the consumer's body, and the resulting risk created to the consumer, there will always be a heavy onus on manufacturers of medical products to provide clear, complete and current information concerning the dangers inherent in the ordinary use of their product ...

26. In light of the enormous informational advantage enjoyed by medical manufacturers over consumers, it is reasonable and just to require manufacturers, under the law of tort, to make clear, complete and current informational disclosure to consumers concerning the risks inherent in the ordinary use of their products. A high standard of disclosure protects the public health by promoting the right to bodily integrity, increasing consumer choice and facilitating a more meaningful doctor-patient relationship. At the same time, it cannot be said that

requiring manufacturers to be forthright about the risks inherent in the use of their product imposes an onerous burden on the manufacturers. As Robins J.A. explained in *Buchan* ... "drug manufacturers are in a position to escape all liability by the simple expedient of providing a clear and forthright warning of the dangers inherent in the use of their products of which they know or ought to know."

(ii) The "Learned Intermediary" Rule

27. As a general rule, the duty to warn is owed directly by the manufacturer to the ultimate consumer. However, in exceptional circumstances, a manufacturer may satisfy its informational duty to the consumer by providing a warning to what the American courts have, in recent years, termed a "learned intermediary." The "learned intermediary" rule was first elaborated in *Sterling Drug Inc. v. Cornish* ... a suit brought by [an American] patient blinded after taking the drug chloroquine phosphate. The rationale for the rule was outlined in [a later American case] against a manufacturer of oral polio vaccine, in the following terms:

> Prescription drugs are likely to be complex medications, esoteric in formula and varied in effect. As a medical expert, the prescribing physician can take into account the propensities of the drug, as well as the susceptibilities of his patient. His is the task of weighing the benefits of any medication against its potential dangers. The choice he makes is an informed one, an individualized medical judgment bottomed on a knowledge of both patient and palliative. Pharmaceutical companies, then, who must warn ultimate purchasers of dangers inherent in patent drugs sold over the counter, in selling prescription drugs

are required to warn only the prescribing physician, who act[s] as a 'learned intermediary' between manufacturer and consumer....

28. While the "learned intermediary" rule was originally intended to reflect, through an equitable distribution of tort duties, the tripartite informational relationship between drug manufacturers, physicians and patients, the rationale for the rule is clearly applicable in other contexts. Indeed, the "learned intermediary" rule is less a "rule" than a specific application of the long-established common law principles of intermediate examination and intervening cause developed in *Donoghue v. Stevenson* ... and subsequent cases... Generally, the rule is applicable either where the product is highly technical in nature and is intended to be used only under supervision of experts, or where the nature of the product is such that the consumer will not realistically receive a direct warning from the manufacturer before using the product. In such cases ... a warning to the ultimate consumer may not be necessary and the manufacturer may satisfy its duty to warn the ultimate consumer by warning the learned intermediary of the risks inherent in the use of the product.

29. However, it is important to keep in mind that the "learned intermediary" rule is merely an exception to the general manufacturer's duty to warn the consumer. The rule operates to discharge the manufacturer's duty not to the learned intermediary, but to the ultimate consumer, who has a right to full and current information about any risks inherent in the ordinary use of the product. Thus, the rule presumes that the intermediary is "learned," that is to say, fully apprised on the risks associated with the use of the product. Accordingly, the manufac-

turer can only be said to have discharged its duty to the consumer when the intermediary's knowledge approximates that of the manufacturer. To allow manufacturers to claim the benefit of the rule where they have not fully warned the physician would undermine the policy rationale for the duty to warn, which is to ensure that the consumer is fully informed of all risks. Since the manufacturer is in the best position to know the risks attendant upon the use of its product and is also in the best position to ensure that the product is safe for normal use, the primary duty to give a clear, complete, and current warning must fall on its shoulders.

(b) Application of the General Principles to the Case at Bar

30. The first question to be answered in this appeal is whether Dow owed Ms. Hollis a duty to warn her that the Silastic implant could rupture post-surgically inside her body and, if so, whether Dow satisfied that duty ... [I]t is clear that the answer to this question depends on the answers to two subsidiary questions. First, did Dow have a duty to warn Ms. Hollis directly, or could it satisfy its duty to warn her by warning a "learned intermediary," namely Dr. Birch? Second, assuming that Dow could properly discharge its duty to Ms. Hollis by warning Dr. Birch, did Dow adequately warn Dr. Birch of the risk of post-surgical rupture in light of its state of knowledge at that time?

31. Turning to the first of these questions, it is my view that the "learned intermediary" rule is applicable in this context, and that Dow was entitled to warn Dr. Birch concerning the risk of rupture without warning Ms. Hollis di-

rectly. A breast implant is distinct from most manufactured goods in that neither the implant nor its packaging are placed directly in the hands of the ultimate consumer. It is the surgeon, not the consumer, who obtains the implant from the manufacturer and who is therefore in the best position to read any warnings contained in the product packaging. In this respect, breast implants are, in my view, analogous to prescription drugs, where the patient places primary reliance for information on the judgment of the surgeon, who is a "learned intermediary," and not on the manufacturer ...

32. However, the mere fact that the "learned intermediary" rule is applicable in this context does not absolve Dow of liability. As I mentioned earlier, the "learned intermediary" rule presumes that the intermediary is fully apprised of the risks, and can only provide shelter to the manufacturer where it has taken adequate steps to ensure that the intermediary's knowledge of the risks in fact approximates that of the manufacturer. Thus, the second, and more important question to be resolved is whether Dow fulfilled its duty to Ms. Hollis by adequately warning Dr. Birch of the risk of post-surgical rupture of the implant.

33. Although Bouck J. declined to rule on this issue, a majority of the Court of Appeal found that Dow's warning to Dr. Birch was inadequate. In my view, the Court of Appeal [w]as correct in reaching this conclusion ... [T]here was sufficient evidence on the record to allow the Court of Appeal to make a full and proper re-assessment of the duty to warn issue without sending the case back to trial ...

34. Turning now to an assessment of the evidence itself, it is my view that the most compelling evidence supporting the Court of Appeal's decision can be found in the product inserts and literature which

Dow supplied to doctors shortly before and after Ms. Hollis's surgery. By 1983, when Dr. Birch advised Ms. Hollis to have implantation surgery, Dow had made available to doctors two warnings regarding the risk of rupture of the Silastic implants. The first was a brochure directed at the medical community, dated 1976, and entitled "Suggested Surgical Procedures for Silastic Mammary Prosthesis," which provided instructions regarding the use of the Silastic I breast implant ...

35. It is significant that the only reference in the 1976 and 1979 warnings to a risk of post-surgical rupture was the statement that "abnormal squeezings or trauma" might rupture the implants. There is no reference in these warnings to the possibility of rupture arising from normal squeezing or non-traumatic everyday activity. This is significant because, in 1985, Dow began warning physicians of the possibility of rupture due to normal, non-traumatic activity in the product insert for the Silastic II implant, a new breast implant developed in the early 1980s with a thicker envelope and greater durability than the earlier Silastic I model ...

36. It is clear from a comparison of the 1985 warning with the earlier warnings that the 1985 warning is far more explicit, both with respect to the potential causes of post-surgical implant rupture and the potential effects. Of particular significance, in my view, is the statement in the 1985 warning that rupture can be caused by "excessive stresses or manipulation as may be experienced during normal living experiences" such as "vigorous exercise, athletics, and intimate physical contact." There is, without question, a substantial difference between "trauma," on the one hand, and the "stresses" and "manipulation" of "everyday living experiences," on the other hand. The difference is that, while the

earlier warnings implied that rupture would occur only in extreme cases of violent impact, the 1985 warning made it clear that a patient who received an implant would have to consider altering her lifestyle to avoid rupture. The difference between the 1985 warning and the earlier warnings was significant to a woman in Ms. Hollis's position because, subsequent to her surgery, she decided to enrol in a baker's course, which involved regular and heavy upper body movements. While a baker's course may not cause "trauma" to an implant, it would certainly create a risk of "excessive stressed [sic] or manipulation." Thus, a more accurate warning could quite reasonably have affected her choice of profession and her resulting exposure to unnecessary risk.

37. This is not to say, of course, that the standard of care to which Dow must be held for its warning practices in 1983 should be measured according to its knowledge of the risks of implant rupture in 1985. In light of the significant differences between the 1985 warning and the earlier warnings, the crucial next question is whether Dow knew or should have known of the risks referred to in the 1985 warning when Ms. Hollis had her implantation surgery in 1983. In my view, there was sufficient evidence adduced at trial to establish that Dow did have such knowledge. At trial, evidence was introduced that, between 1976 and 1984, Dow had received 78 field reports from doctors of post-operative "unexplained" ruptures occurring in the Silastic implants. These ruptures were categorized as "unexplained" because they were not attributable to any known causes of rupture, such as trauma or surgical mishap ... [B]y late 1983, Dow had already received between 48 and 61 of the 78 unexplained rupture reports it received before issuing its revised 1985 warning. Counsel for

Dow conceded [t]hat the nature and quantity of the information available to Dow did not change significantly between late 1983 and early 1985. Thus, although the reports were admitted into evidence at trial for the purpose of establishing their existence and not as to the truth of their contents, the mere fact that Dow had these reports in their possession demonstrates that, in 1983, Dow had notice[d] that ruptures were occurring that were not directly attributable to abnormal squeezing or trauma. Counsel for Dow was unable to explain why it took Dow more than two years to convey the information concerning the unexplained ruptures to either the medical community or the consumers.

38. A similar time lag can be discerned with respect to Dow's warnings concerning the effects of implant ruptures on the body. The evidence indicates that, prior to 1983, and even as early as 1979, Dow was aware that implant ruptures could cause adverse reactions in the body arising from loose ge[l] ... In light of the state of Dow's knowledge in 1979, it is significant that none of the Dow warnings before 1985 made reference to adverse reactions to loose gel in the body ...

39. In my view, Dow had a duty to convey its findings concerning both the "unexplained" rupture phenomenon and the possible harm caused by loose gel inside the body to the medical community much sooner than it did. In light of the fact that implants are surgically placed inside the body, and that any defects in these products will obviously have a highly injurious effect on the user, the onus on Dow to be forthcoming with information was extremely high throughout the relevant period. Despite this fact, for over six years Dow took no action to express its concerns to the medical community. Given Dow's knowledge of the potential harm caused by loose gel in the

body, this lag time is simply unacceptable. The duty to warn is a continuing one and manufacturers of potentially hazardous products have an obligation to keep doctors abreast of developments even if they do not consider those developments to be conclusive ...

40. In its submission to this Court, Dow attempted to justify its recalcitrant warning practices by arguing that the number of "unexplained" ruptures were small over the relevant period (the rate of rupture was less that 1/10 of 1 percent) and by arguing that "unexplained" ruptures, being unexplained, are not a distinct category of risk of which they could realistically have warned. In my view, these arguments fail because both are based upon the assumption that Dow only had the obligation to warn once it had reached its own definitive conclusions with respect to the cause and effect of the "unexplained" ruptures. This assumption has no support in the law of Canada. Although the number of ruptures was statistically very small over the relevant period, and the cause of the ruptures was unknown, Dow had an obligation to take into account the seriousness of the risk posed by a potential rupture to each user of a Silastic implant. Indeed, it is precisely because the ruptures were "unexplained" that Dow should have been concerned. Certainly, it would not have been onerous for Dow to have in-

cluded an update in their product inserts to the effect that "unexplained" ruptures had been reported which were not attributable to surgical procedures, and a list of the possible side-effects of such ruptures. As Prowse, J.A. observed [in] her reasons in the Court of Appeal:

> Dow was in a much better position to advise of the incidence of rupture than was any individual doctor or even the community of plastic surgeons performing breast implantations, since Dow was the repository for complaints of rupture. This placed a significant onus on Dow to keep the medical community advised of developments with respect to its products which could have serious consequences.

Dow was not required to issue a warning each time a rupture occurred, but it would not be expecting too much to issue updated information in this regard to the medical community on a yearly basis, or sooner, if the circumstances warranted it.

41. I conclude, therefore, that the Court of Appeal made no error in ruling that Dow did not discharge its duty to Ms. Hollis by properly warning Dr. Birch concerning the risk of post-surgical implant rupture ...

Supreme Court of Canada, 129 D.L.R. 609, December 21, 1995.

CASE 13 | Lana Joan Thompson & Allen Barrie Kilner v. Boise Cascade Canada Ltd.

Per: The Honourable Mr. Justice T.A Platana

These actions arise from the termination of employment of the Plaintiffs Lana Thompson and Allen Barrie Kilner by the Defendant on January the 6th, 1992. Although there are two actions, the matters were tried together with the consent of counsel and all evidence was led at one time. The Plaintiffs both allege that the dismissals were wrongful and claim damages for breach of contract, and punitive damages. For reasons set out herein, both actions are dismissed.

The sole incident relied upon by the Defendants for the dismissal relates to the completion of expense reports filed by each of the Plaintiffs after travelling on Company business to New Orleans in November of 1990. The expense accounts were prepared jointly.

The focal point around which this case turns is the claim by the Plaintiff Lana Thompson of having incurred certain business expenses for the purpose of entertaining other Company employees. Following the filing of such claim, it was discovered by the Defendants that in fact those employees had not been entertained. Although the Plaintiff Kilner's report contained no errors or incorrect information, it is the position of the Defendant that since the parties travelled together, and essentially submitted joint expense accounts, the incorrect information in Miss Thompson's account ought also to be properly attributed to Mr. Kilner.

After being given ... an opportunity to clarify such accounts, the Plaintiffs failed to reveal the true nature of the expenditure following which the Defendant terminated both ...

In order to deal clearly with each of the matters, I propose to deal with the background of each of the Plaintiffs individually and then to deal with the facts common to both Plaintiffs which led to the termination.

The Plaintiff

Lana Thompson

This plaintiff is a Mechanical Engineer who, after previously working as a clerk and summer student for the Defendant, began her employment on a full-time basis as a mechanical engineer in the Maintenance Department in January of 1988.

She performed a number of different tasks for the Defendant and prior to January, 1992, when she was terminated, she received regular salary increases after positive performance reviews. Her latest salary increase, from approximately $40 000 to approximately $47 000, was in December of 1991 when she was promoted to Engineer Two.

Throughout the course of her employment as an engineer with Boise she had attended various training courses and upgrading programs. She had travelled on numerous occasions and had been involved in filling out expense accounts on those occasions.

She dated the Plaintiff Kilner for one summer prior to her going away to university. He then became a very positive influence and a support for her. Between the time she commenced employment in January 1988 and the summer of 1990, she dealt with him on a daily basis and he would assist her in various job functions. Their relationship between January of 1988 and November of 1990 was always job related except for minimum personal contacts. In the summer of 1990 the Plaintiffs began talking about being with each other but also talked about avoiding a scandal in the job place at the Defendant. The Plaintiff Kilner's wife also worked at the Defendant Boise. The Plaintiff Thompson was living with someone else.

The relationship between the Plaintiffs continued to the point where Thompson moved in with Kilner in April of 1991.... Prior to November of 1991 and the trip to New Orleans, the Plaintiff's evidence is that her career was going very well. She was doing larger projects and was involved much more in a hands on type situation.

The Plaintiff Barrie Kilner

The Plaintiff Kilner is currently age forty-seven and commenced employment with the Defendant Boise in October of 1977. He initially began as a Mechanical Supervisor in the garage and in 1980 or 1981 was promoted to General Services Superintendent. In 1986 he became the Mechanical Superintendent in the papermill. He indicated that he considered himself to be a true Company man in that he worked long hours and was very much a team player.

During 1986, part of his employment necessitated him becoming involved in collective agreement issues. Evidence filed at trial indicated that on at least two occasions he signed letters dismissing other employees for instances of theft. It was very clear in his mind that Company Policy was such that "theft equalled dismissal."

Throughout the period of his performance ratings, he indicated that no issues

of honesty or character were ever raised. He became a team manager and was at times responsible for performing supervisory functions after hours ... [H]e had never received anything negative with respect to his job performance and had never been the subject of any disciplinary action.

As part of his normal duties, he frequently approved expense reports for other individuals who travelled. He also indicated that he himself had travelled frequently and had filled out expense reports on each and every occasion. The policy as understood by him is that while travelling, employees "live as you normally live but don't go overboard."

The Trip to New Orleans in November 1991

... In November, 1991 both Plaintiffs attended a company-approved Seminar in New Orleans. The Plaintiffs departed Fort Frances early in order to spend the weekend in New Orleans. This had been approved in advance by the Company. They arrived in New Orleans at approximately midnight Friday evening.

Thompson described that ... she and Mr. Kilner had [each] received $500 cash advances and that she also had an American Express Card which was used for Company business only. She indicated that they took no cash of their own when they departed for New Orleans. The Plaintiff Thompson was the record keeper in the relationship. It was decided between the two of them that the Plaintiff Thompson would be the bookkeeper and would handle all the accounting of the expenses for both of them. She paid the hotel bill and the evening meals and would collect receipts. The Plaintiffs' evidence of their routine in New Orleans is that they would eat breakfast in the morning, and would sometimes eat lunch in the hotel and sometimes out.... They found the meal costs high. They attended the seminars during the day and then on occasion after the evening meal they would go for late night drinks which they indicated were charged to the Defendant. Their understanding is that those expenses were allowable. They indicated that they were not concerned with respect to the actual costs inasmuch [as] they understood the Company Policy to be to follow the same routine which they would have followed if they were at home ...

Preparation of

Expense Accounts

On return the Plaintiffs prepared their expense accounts jointly. They determined how much cash they had left over from the $1000 advance initially given to them. They then added the credit card vouchers and the hotel receipts. In addition, they had other receipts which had been filled out as to the amounts and also had some blank receipts. Their evidence was that the company policy was that it was allowable to use blank receipts, which claimants would fill in themselves, provided that the receipts were for the actual amount of monies spent. In addition to the receipts which the parties had, the Plaintiff Thompson kept track of all of their expenses in a notebook.

After they determined how much cash was spent, they decided that the Plaintiff Kilner would claim the hotel rooms and the costs of the evening meals. With respect to other items on the expense accounts, it was decided that both he and she would claim business meals.

Their understanding of meal allowances is that they were entitled to claim $75 per day with no receipts necessary up to that amount.

The plaintiffs prepared the Kilner account first. His claim was $1270.61. Reviewing all of the information which they had received they knew that they had spent more than $1270.61 and therefore used Thompson's account as the balancing account.

Her evidence is that it was fair to describe the expense reports as joint reports. She stated that after completing Kilner's report, which they knew was detailed, they had to account for approximately $811 on her account in order to have the expense reports balance with what they had actually spent. After using all of the allowable expenses which were available to them, they had a shortfall of $340. They the[n] used two of the blank receipts and the Plaintiff Thompson created two receipts in the amount of $169 and $180 to make up the balance of what was spent. Her evidence was that that was a collection of monies spent throughout the week. The receipts were prepared in different handwriting.

All allowable personal expenses had been accounted for and therefore the $340 ... had to be included as a business expense in the detailed expense items. In justifying those expenditures, it was claimed on the expense account that other individuals from the Defendant Company had been entertained in New Orleans. The Plaintiffs indicated that they had no apprehension about doing their accounts in this way since that was the past practice. Their evidence further was that they had never been specifically told how to do expense accounts and had simply prepared them on the basis of what they had been told by other employees over the period of time that they had worked for the Defendant. The Plaintiffs had filled in receipts in this fashion on earlier occasions.

Thompson's evidence is that after the expense accounts had been prepared, she then discarded the notes which she had kept in her notebook with respect to a complete accounting of all monies spent. Both Plaintiffs' evidence is that the individuals named as being entertained had in fact been at the conference in New Orleans but that the Plaintiffs had not entertained them. The only reason given for placing their names as having been entertained was to satisfy the requirements of the detailed business expense section of the expense report.

Thompson acknowledged in cross-examination that there were occasions where monies had not actually been spent on certain items in one particular day for meals but that her understanding was that the account could be balanced overall throughout the week. She indicated that although the expense report contained certain instructions with respect to how it ought to be completed, she had never read the form and didn't see any need as she had always followed the instructions of her co-workers who explained to her how to complete the reports. She understood from her co-workers that it was acceptable to complete her own receipts and that she could include inaccurate information as long as the expenses did not exceed what was actually spent. Her evidence was that everybody used the same system in the maintenance department. She did indicate that she had never previously claimed to entertain people that she had not entertained.

Following the preparation of the reports the Plaintiffs submitted them at different times ... The total of the two reports was $2651 for which the Plaintiffs had actual receipts for $1812.94 ...[1]

Disciplinary Committee Meeting—January 6

... [A] meeting was convened of the Disciplinary Committee of the Defendant. The Committee reviewed various aspects of company discipline policy and decided that the more important issue to be dealt with was one of deceit.

The evidence is that the basis of the decision to terminate made by the committee was the failure to come forward with true explanations, with an attempt to cover up, and the failure to tell the true and accurate version of the expense accounts.

[It was] acknowledged that such action was not specifically covered in the policy dealing with termination of employment. The conduct was viewed by the disciplinary committee as being "intolerable." In referring to the intolerable offenses category set forth in the disciplinary policy guidelines of the Company it indicates as one element of "Intolerable Offenses":

> Falsifying permanent or semi-permanent company records, operating reports, check sheets, storeroom issue slips, material passes, time cards, employment forms, medical records, etc.

Rule 13 goes on to indicate as an intolerable offense, "Failure to provide needed or required information or factual materials, records or history."

... [T]he committee decided that because there had been so many opportunities [for] the Plaintiffs to give the correct story that termination was the only way to proceed.

I do not propose to review the Company Policy in detail ... [S]uffice to say only that I am satisfied on the basis of all of the evidence given by this witness and others that there was no clear stated policy which said you could not claim business expenses for people entertained if they had not in fact been entertained.

Meeting of January 7

The following day, both Plaintiffs were called into [their Supervisor's] office. They were both given formal letters indicating that they were being terminated, the reasons being:

> This action is being taken as a result of an extensive investigation by Company representatives which revealed that you claimed expenses on your signed expense report for activities that did not occur, and when you were given an opportunity to correct this report and provide accurate information you failed to do so.

Position of the Plaintiffs

The Plaintiffs, in essence, put this case to be decided on the issue of credibility. Counsel places the question as being, "Was the conduct of the Plaintiffs so untrustworthy as to be no longer compatible with continued employment?"

Both Plaintiffs present themselves to the Court with excellent work histories. In Counsel's submission, the incidents involving the expense reports can only be looked at in light of the evidence that the spending policies in effect at the Defendant Boise were at best unclear. The only policy that was indicated to employees is that expenses must be reasonable and that all legitimate expenses must

be accounted for by way of receipts if they exceeded a daily maximum. Counsel indicates that at all times [the Supervisor] took no issue with the amount of monies spent by the Plaintiffs but rather with the accuracy of the accounting ... Counsel then submits that the Plaintiffs were never given a proper opportunity to explain any errors which may have existed in the accounts ...

Counsel suggests that [the meetings of January 6] were clearly not fair and impartial. He points out that the important thing is that over the course of the day the Plaintiff Thompson did in fact give an explanation. Counsel submits that any deceit in filling out the receipts by the Plaintiffs was only because they believed that they were carrying out what was common Company practice.

Counsel suggests that the discipline policy in effect in the Company was so vague and unclear that it did not cover the facts surrounding this incident in sufficient detail and that in fact the Defendants have breached their own policy in terminating in this fashion ...

Position of the Defendant

Counsel for the Defendant has submitted that the question for determination in this matter comes down to two simple questions:

1. Whether the acts of the Plaintiffs Kilner and Thompson are sufficient to be just cause for termination.

2. Was there condonation by the employer with respect to the completion of the expense reports such as would justify the actions of the employees?

Counsel acknowledges that with respect to the first question, the onus is on the employer to show just cause and submits that with respect to the second question, the onus is on the Plaintiffs.

The essential position of the Defendant is that the Plaintiffs knowingly submitted requests for payment and received reimbursement for expenses which, in the case of the Plaintiff Thompson, she misdescribed, and in the case of Mr. Kilner, knowingly permitted that misdescription. Defense counsel then submits that when the Plaintiffs were questioned about the accuracy of the reports ... they either lied or misled their employer with respect to the accuracy of those accounts. Further when they were confronted in a manner which verified the seriousness of the situation on January the 6th [at the Disciplinary Committee meeting], each of them separately lied and in the case of Mr. Kilner, he altered his story to a second lie in indicating while the two named employees had not been entertained, others were.

Counsel submits that those factors alone are sufficient to constitute just cause for termination because the actions demonstrate that the character of the Plaintiffs is not consistent with the trust that is essential for the employment relationship. Counsel submits that the Plaintiffs, by their dishonest conduct in failing to reveal to the officials of the Defendant on different occasions the true facts as they related to the expense account, repudiated the employment contract ...

Defense counsel submits that with respect to the issue of condonation there is no evidence to suggest that there has ever been any condonation of the specific act in question. There is an acknowledgement that on occasion a practice had arisen within the Defendant Company that hand-written receipts could be completed for certain expenses, however, the practice was always that the amount, the date, and the description be accurate. Counsel suggests that the evidence reveals that it was never a practice that the actual expense account could be a misdescription and certainly never the practice that employees could claim to have entertained people when such entertainment expenses were not incurred ...

The Law

The general principle of wrongful dismissal is that an employee is entitled to reasonable notice of termination of his/her contract by the employer. The exception to the general rule exists when there is just cause for dismissal. *Durand v. Quaker Oats Co. of Canada* (1990) ... states:

> [I]t is trite law that in a contract of employment there is an implied duty of faithfulness and of honesty owed by the employee to the employer. Breach of that implied duty has long been held to be cause for dismissal, the principal reason being because of a lack of confidence and trust which must exist between employer and employee, particularly if the employee is in a responsible position.

In a wrongful dismissal action, the onus is on the employer to show cause for the dismissal ... The employer must act reasonably in discharging the employee ...

The tests to determine wrongful dismissal have been stated by various courts in various ways. It is clear that there are no fixed definitions of what can constitute justifiable dismissal and that each case is totally dependent on its facts. What is clear is that for conduct to justify dismissal, it must be such that by its nature it shows that the employee is repudiating the contract or one of its essential conditions. It is also clear that employees' conduct, and the character it reveals, must be such as to undermine, or seriously impair, the essential trust and confidence the employer is entitled to place in the employee in the circumstances of their particular relationship. In essence, the conduct must be such as the employer can point to it as a good reason for having lost confidence in the employees' ability faithfully to discharge his/her duties …

While dishonesty has always been held to be a justifiable ground for dismissal, Counsel for the Plaintiffs submits that isolated acts of dishonesty may be insufficient to constitute just cause … Further, some cases have held that an employee who fails to be completely honest over relevantly insignificant items indicates a lack of judgment rather than a conscious act of dishonesty and that a lack of judgment does not constitute grounds for dismissal …

Past good conduct of the Plaintiffs must be taken into account and the degree of misconduct complained of should be more significant where a status of an employee is more elevated …

Counsel for the Plaintiff submits further that in order to dismiss for abuse of an expense account it is necessary that the guidelines for the use of such expense accounts be clear and that a warning be required …

It is submitted that in any event the behaviour complained of has been condoned by the employer. Counsel suggests in this case that there [have] been similar acts of employees completing their own expense reports and filing hand-written receipts. Counsel suggests that since the Defendant tolerated that type of conduct from other employees, the Defendant ought not to be able to rely upon that same form of conduct to terminate the Plaintiffs …

Conclusions

Both Counsel placed much emphasis on the misstatements in the expense reports. The more crucial issue in my mind rests on the conduct of the Plaintiffs subsequent to the preparation and filing of the reports. It is very clear on the evidence that there was a deliberate misstatement which was not remedied when opportunities arose to do so. For that reason, it is not necessary for my findings to decide whether the monies claimed to have been spent were legitimately spent. The issue is not solely whether the Plaintiffs lied about spending the money, but rather whether they lied about how such money, if spent, was spent, and whether the Plaintiffs were honest in reporting such expenses.

The evidence led by the Plaintiffs is that Miss Thompson is a meticulous record keeper. That being the case, there is no explanation for the discrepancies which appeared on the expense report.

I note in particular the two receipts prepared by the Plaintiff Thompson. The Plaintiffs would have me accept that they saw nothing wrong in submitting their own handwritten receipts. In view of the evidence of other witnesses who worked for the Defendant, I may have had no difficulty in accepting that. However, I note that the receipts handed in by the Plaintiff Thompson were deliberately done in different handwriting. If there was no problem in submitting receipts in the fashion described by the Plaintiffs, I have difficulty in understanding why the receipts were made out in such a fashion as to appear that they were made out by two different individuals. This appears to me to be a deliberate attempt to conceal the truth about such receipts.

... [B]oth Kilner and Thompson knew that with respect to the expense accounts, questions had been raised. Neither of them came forward to offer any explanation in response to ... questioning ... There is a particular standard of conduct that is expected [of] any employee and once such questions were raised it was in my view the responsibilities of the employees to clarify same.

It is clear that there was deceit on the part of the Plaintiffs in submitting their expense reports. When presented with an opportunity ... to explain the reports, Mr. Kilner's response ... was to reiterate that indeed those people claimed had been entertained on those dates. That was a clear opportunity for Mr. Kilner to demonstrate his truthfulness and lack of intent to deceive, by putting forth the correct explanation ...

[T]he evidence is again that when confronted a second time Kilner said that the people claimed to have been entertained had not been but that others had been. That again is a deliberate attempt to deceive. Kilner had an obligation to tell the truth and deliberately and intentionally did not do so ...

The real question to be determined is whether the actions of the Plaintiffs constituted an error in judgment or a deliberate attempt to deceive ... The actions of the Plaintiffs in falsifying the expense reports by deliberately including inaccurate information and thereafter on numerous occasions attempting to carry on that deception can only be considered to be acts of dishonesty. They were acts intended to deceive which are sufficient to constitute a total breakdown in trust in the employer/employee relationship and justified the dismissal of the Plaintiffs without notice ...

Ontario Court (General Division), Fort Frances, Ontario, June 3, 1994.

ENDNOTE

1. Editor's note: Irregularities in the expense reports were discovered by the Controller and Manager of Planning for Boise. Following several meetings between the Defendants and Supervisory staff, at which the Plaintiffs were asked to explain the irregularities, a Disciplinary Committee meeting was held on January 6, 1992.

SUGGESTED READINGS

Beach, John. "Bluffing: Its Demise as a Subject unto Itself." *Journal of Business Ethics*, Vol. 4, No. 3 (June 1985), pp. 191–196.

Blodgett, Timoty B. "Showdown on 'Business Bluffing,'" *Harvard Business Review* (May–June, 1968), pp. 162–170.

Bok, Sissela. Lying: *Moral Choice in Public and Private Life*. New York: Pantheon Books, 1978.

Bowie, Norman E. "Should Collective Bargaining and Labor Relations Be Less Adversarial?" *Journal of Business Ethics*, Vol. 4, No. 4 (August 1985), pp. 283–293.

Brown, L. "Ethics in Negotiation." *Female Executive*, Vol. 7 (January/February 1984), pp. 34–37.

Bulkeley, W.M. "To Some at Harvard, Telling Lies Becomes a Matter of Course." *Wall Street Journal* (January 15, 1979), pp. 1, 37.

Carr, A.Z. "Is Business Bluffing Ethical?" *Harvard Business Review* 46 (Jan./Feb., 1968), pp. 143–153.

Chisholm, R. and Feehan, T. "The Intent to Deceive." *Journal of Philosophy* 74 (1977), pp. 143–159.

Isenberg, A. "Conditions for Lying," in T. Beauchamp and N. Bowie (eds.), *Ethical Theory and Business*. Englewood Cliffs, N.J.: Prentice-Hall, 1979, pp. 466–468.

Kant, I. *Lectures on Ethics* (1775-1780) (Louis Infield, trans.). New York: Harper and Row, 1963.

Kant, I. (1797), "On a Supposed Right to Tell Lies from Benevolent Motives," in B. Brody (ed.), *Moral Rules and Particular Circumstances*. Englewood Cliffs, N.J.: Prentice-Hall, 1970, pp. 31–36.

Leland, H. "Insider Trading: Should It Be Prohibited?" *Journal of Political Economy*, 100, 1992, pp. 859–887.

Ma, Yulon and Huey-Lain Sun. "Where Should the Line be Drawn on Insider Trading Ethics?" *Journal of Business Ethics*, 17, 1, 1998, 67–75.

Martin, D.W. and J. H. Peterson. "Insider Trading Revisited." *Journal of Business Ethics*, 10, 1991, pp. 57–61.

Ross, D. *The Right and the Good*. Oxford: Oxford University Press, 1930.

Seigler, F. "Lying." *American Philosophical Quarterly*, 3, 1966, pp. 128–136.

Tsalikis, J. and M.S. LaTour. "Bribery and Extortion in International Business: Ethical Perceptions of Greeks Compared to Americans." *Journal of Business Ethics*, 14, 4, 1995, pp. 249–264.